Preface

Most of the English medium schools in Asian countries stop teaching English Grammar after Matriculation or equivalent level as though there is nothing left to learn thereafter.

The Matriculation syllabus covers only a part of the total grammar. What about the balance? Shouldn't students at Junior/Senior College levels continue to build up their knowledge to a higher standard?

Isn't possible that some students after schooling may change over to English medium at Junior/Senior College levels including professional colleges like Engineering, Medical and Law? Wouldn't such students, who have studied in their local language, need a solid foundation on English Grammar assuming that they would have had very little exposure to the English language during school years?

These considerations would lead us to the necessity of having a suitable book that would start from the scratch and go to the highest level in English Grammar. This book has been written with such a target in mind so that all students are on level playing ground and is recommended for adoption in Junior/Senior Colleges.

Besides touching the highest peak, this book advocates a new method known as the **'structural method'** as opposed to the **'functional grammar method'**. This is a much easier and faster method to achieve mastery over the language. Several discoveries made by the Author have been revealed in the book along with some new definitions.

In addition to the elements of grammar and essay/composition/article writing, it also covers conversation techniques in diverse situations and the etiquette to be observed with seniors, equals and juniors.

- Author

I Dedicate this Book
To my dear wife,
Chandra Jayakaran
who has been a tremendous
inspiration behind its creation.

CONTENTS

CONTENTS

CONTENTS

Part - II

COMPOSITION

CONTENTS

Part - 1

GRAMMAR

Chapter 1

PARTS OF SPEECH

Every word in the English language belongs to a particular family or group or category named "Part of speech".

There are in all **ten** "parts of speech" in the English language. This means that every English word would fall under one of these parts of speech. They are: NOUN, PRONOUN, VERB, AUXILIARY, ADJECTIVE, ADVERB, PREPOSITION, CONJUNCTION, ARTICLE and INTERJECTION.

1. Noun

Noun is a word used for person, place or thing. Every noun has *number, gender* and *kind.*

Number

There are singular nouns and plural nouns as shown below:

Singular	Plural
girl	girls
school	schools
pencil	pencils
box	boxes
watch	watches
fish	fishes
knife	knives
wife	wives
thief	thieves
city	cities
lily	lilies
victory	victories

In order to get the plural, we add the letter 's' to some nouns, letters 'es' to some, 'ves' to such nouns that end in 'f', and 'ies' to the nouns that end in 'y'.

Write the plurals for the following nouns:

Bulb, light, catch, kiss, pencil, calf, mango, brush, goose, address, circus, match, potato, radio, baby, life, leaf, shelf, story, dish, echo, desk, cow, bread-loaf, safe, roof, tax, book.

For some nouns, the plural spelling is altogether different like the following:

man	men
woman	women
foot	feet
oasis	oases

Some nouns have the same form for singular and also plural as shown below:

Sheep, deer, series, corps, swine, species, means,

Some nouns are used only in the plural even if the noun referred and used is in single quantity as shown below:

Scissors, tongs, pincers, spectacles, trousers, drawers, breeches, arrears, gallows, tidings, proceeds, bellows, clothes, contents, goods, findings, riches, nuptials, assets, obsequies, alms, funds, wages, thanks.

Some are used only in singular form though they sound like plurals in terms of the spelling. The following are the examples:

news, innings, ethics, civics, physics, athletics, economics, mathematics, measles, mumps, billiards.

We write the plurals for the compound words in a different way as shown below:

son-in-law	sons-in-law
daughter-in-law	daughters-in-law
brother-in-law	brothers-in-law
mother-in-law	mothers-in-law
man-of-war	men-of-war
passer-by	passers-by
looker-on	lookers-on
manservant	menservant
maidservant	maidservants
bookseller	booksellers
footman	footmen

Add an apostrophe and the letter 's' to get the plurals of letters, figures and symbols like shown below:

Subtract two 5's from seven 3's.

There are too many e's and i's in your spellings.

Gender

All nouns would come under one of the four **genders** as follows:

Masculine	Feminine	Common	Neuter
(Male)	(Female)	(Both M and F)	(Lifeless)
father	mother	child	book
husband	wife	person	rubber
king	queen	teacher	cycle
son	daughter	student	window
brother	sister	friend	classroom
brother-in-law	sister-in-law	relative	sweets

Kind

Nouns are of **four** kinds as follows:

Proper noun

The name of a **particular person** or **place** is called a proper noun. They are unique and we cannot use that name to any other person or place. Here are the examples:
Rajendran, Narayanan, Nirmala, Samuel.
Chennai, Mumbai, High court, Parliament house.

Common noun

A noun used for <u>any</u> person or place. Here are the examples:
Man, teacher, student, graduate, athlete, leader.
City, village, town, sea, road, church.

Collective noun

It is a noun used for a group of persons or animals or things taken together and considered as one single unit. Here are the examples:
Crowd, mob, herd, family, army, navy, fleet, jury, nation, Lok sabha, committee, cattle.

Abstract noun

It is a noun used for quality or action or a state as shown in the following examples:

Quality - honesty, wisdom, truth, bravery, goodness, sensibility, sensitivity
Action - theft, movement, hatred, sympathy.
State - youth, slavery, boyhood, girlhood, manhood.

Exercise

Pick out the **nouns** in the following sentences and state their (i) number, (ii) gender and the (iii) type:

There were too many <u>sheep</u> in the animal market.
Tell the <u>truth</u> always.
<u>Ramanujam</u> was a great Indian mathematician.
God ordained great <u>wisdom</u> to king Solomon.
We spotted a <u>fleet</u> of ships in the center of Bay of Bengal from our plane.
Cleanliness is next to Godliness.
Several soldiers received <u>bravery</u> awards for their action in Kargil operation.
The <u>judge</u> did not accept the accused's innocence in the case.
<u>Sincerity</u> was his strength.
The <u>jury</u> gave an unanimous verdict on the case.
The <u>tigers</u> and <u>lions</u> sat together during the circus show.

The jokers made us all laugh.

The laughter was so loud that one could not hear the music in the circus show.

The crowd dispersed very quietly after the show.

The spectators applauded and hailed the school girls' performance.

Krishnan and his sister Malathi live in Chindadripet.

The Principal and his staffs would come to the auditorium shortly.

Esther and her brother had gone to New Delhi.

Would Janaki join my drama group?

Madurai is not too far from Trichinopoly.

Pronoun

Pronoun is a word used in place of a noun. Instead of repeating the same noun a second time, we can use a pronoun in its place There are over 40 pronouns in the English language. We shall cover some in this Chapter and some later.

The most important ones are, **Personal pronouns**. They are shown under three columns below:

Person	Subjective	Objective	Possessive
First person	I	ME	MY, MINE
	WE	US	OUR, OURS
Second person	YOU	YOU	YOUR, YOURS
Third person	HE	HIM	HIS
	SHE	HER	HER, HERS
	IT	IT	ITS
	THEY	THEM	THEIR, THEIRS

Subjective pronouns are used only in the Subject part of a sentence and the Objective in the Object part. The possessive pronouns can appear in the subject or object but always followed by a noun. A possessive pronoun can never appear alone.

The pronouns HE, SHE, IT and THEY represent every noun in the world. HE is for all males including animals, birds, insects etc; SHE for all females; IT for all lifeless singular thing like table, chair, village, building etc. THEY for plurals of all males, females and things of above.

I, WE and YOU do not represent any noun. We use them as they are. Therefore, we call them "pure pronouns" because there are no corresponding nouns for them.

3 & 4 Verb and Auxiliary

Verb is a word of 'action'. We can see action, in a broad sense, when there is a movement of any part(s) of the body of a living being, be it a human being or animal or bird or fish etc. We cannot use a verb in a sentence without supporting it with a word called **auxiliary**. The auxiliary will usually be to the left of a verb. In some cases we may use more than one auxiliary to help a verb. We call such a group of auxiliaries as "auxiliary set". All the auxiliaries that go to form a set will also be out of the same list of 32. Thus, a verb and an auxiliary (or, auxiliary set) would form an inseparable pair. We can never use an auxiliary or a verb singly at all but always as pairs.

Every verb has three forms, namely, PRESENT, PAST and PAST PARTICIPLE forms.

There are in all only 32 auxiliaries in the English language. The job of an auxiliary is to help a verb. It has no other function. There are two types of auxiliaries: **pure auxiliaries** (21) (whose sole job is only to help a verb in any of its 3 forms in a sentence) and **auxiliary cum verbs** (11). We can use these 11 words either as auxiliaries or as verbs. When used as verbs, they help themselves; they become then self-supporting verbs; we may also call them as 2-in-1 words. We use the symbol A.V for them and pronounce it as A dot V.

The pure auxiliaries are (Also known as "Universal auxiliaries" because we use them for more than one Tense and for All Persons): WILL, SHALL, CAN, MAY, WOULD, SHOULD, COULD, MIGHT, MUST, NEVER, BEEN, NEED, DARE, BE, BEING, KEEP, KEPT, BETTER, OUGHT TO, USED TO and GOING TO. (21)

Although three auxiliaries are of two words - 'used to', 'ought to' and 'going to', we consider them as 'one' for the counting.

The A.Vs are: AM, IS, ARE, HAS, HAVE, DO, DOES, WAS, WERE, DID, HAD (11). Except for DO, DOES, and DID, one cannot see 'action' in the remaining 8. Sentences that use these 8 words as verbs will be actionless ones as we will see later.

Auxiliaries do not have a precise meaning like other English words. Every auxiliary is used for a particular situation(s). You need to know that before you could select an auxiliary to use in a sentence.

Auxiliaries enable us to frame negative answers. There are only two categories of answers, as we saw a little earlier - Positive and Negative. We write or speak a Negative sentence by making the auxiliary negative i.e. by putting the adverb NOT after the auxiliary.

5. Adjective

Adjective is a word that describes a noun and is written to the immediate left side of a noun. If there is no noun after an adjective, it will not be an adjective at all. Many parts of speech such as verbs, nouns, pronouns could be doing the job of adjectives. Thus, there is no stamp mark for adjectives. So long as a word is placed to the left of a noun and if it describes that noun, we may call such words, adjectives.

Exercise

Pick out the adjectives in the following passage:

Martin is a fine boy. He is studying in an Engineering college in the first year. That college is a famous one in Chennai. Most of the students living near the college join it. It has several beautiful buildings. Each building has 10 class rooms. The final year students have their class rooms in the ground floor.

6. Adverbs

Adverb is a word that amplifies the action of a verb or it gives more information about the verb's action. We cannot identify an adverb just by looking at it as in the case of an adjective. The adverb can be at any place in a sentence. It can be a single word or a group of words. We could recognise an adverb or adverb-phrase only by applying a test called, "Complement or Adverb test". For this purpose, we use the test questions HOW, WHEN or WHERE as shown below:

Natesan ran very fast. (Natesan ran HOW? Ans: **fast.** So, 'fast' is an adverb)
Children must eat their food slowly. (TQ:......eat HOW? Ans: **slowly**)
Do you sleep here? (...sleep WHERE?)
Shall I meet you in the evening? (.... meet WHEN? Ans: "in the evening". This is a group of words or adverb phrase)

I will appear for the interview tomorrow. (TQ: WHEN? Ans: "tomorrow")

Adverbs are of many types such as, MANNER, QUALITY, FREQUENCY, VALUE (TQ: HOW - How much, How often, How far, How long), TIME (TQ: WHEN?) and PLACE (TQ: WHERE?)

Take the word "tomorrow". We know "tomorrow" is a noun but we have used it as "adverb of time" here. Thus many nouns could be doing the job of adverbs. Except for the test question method, you may mistake them for words of some other parts of speech.

If the answer to the test question is a single word, we call it "Adverb". If the answer contains a group of words, we call it "Complement". The main word in a Complement will be an adverb, which may be supported by words of other parts of speech.

7. Preposition

Preposition is a word that shows the relationship between any two words in a sentence. The two words may be,

a noun/pronoun	and	a noun/pronoun.
	or	
a verb	and	a noun/pronoun
	or	
an adjective/adverb and		a noun/pronoun

Study the following examples:

(a) We saw a dog <u>inside</u> that house. (Relationship between a noun and a noun)
(b) Will you come <u>to</u> my house this evening? (between a verb and a noun)
(c) My father is angry <u>with</u> me. (between an adverb and a pronoun)
(d) I am travelling <u>in</u> a car. (between a verb and a noun)
(e) My brother is <u>behind</u> me always. (between an aux.verb and a pronoun)

The words underlined are prepositions and show the true relationship between the word to its left and right. If you remove the preposition, you will not get the correct meaning out of the sentence or you may get several possible meanings. Thus if you want to know the accurate meaning of sentence, you must use the correct preposition.

Simple prepositions are recognisable words. Some of them are : AT, BY, FOR, FROM, IN, OF, TO, DOWN, ON, OUT, THROUGH, TILL, WITH, WITHOUT, ABOUT, UNDER, ACROSS, ALONG, AMONG, AROUND, BEFORE, AFTER BEHIND, BETWEEN, BEYOND, INSIDE, OUTSIDE.

In addition, there are Preposition-phrases which we use in our sentences. We shall cover these in later years.

8. Conjunction

Conjunction is a word that joins two or more **Simple sentences.** "And" is the only conjunction which in addition can connect any two words also, except two verbs.

Conjunctions are used in Complex sentences. A Complex sentence will consist of two **Simple** sentences connected by one conjunction.

Conjunctions are also recognisable words. Some of the single word conjunctions are: AND, SINCE, BECAUSE, IF, THAT, UNLESS, BUT, STILL, YET, UNTIL, AS, THOUGH, AFTER, BEFORE.

In addition, there are conjunction-phrases and conjunction-pairs. We shall cover these in later years.

Whether a single word or phrases or pairs, the job of a conjunction is to join two Simple sentences.

9. Article

Article is a word we use to refer to the 'number' of a noun. For a singular noun we use the article A or AN. AN is used for a noun that starts with a vowel or vowel sound. Examples are,

an umbrella, **an** egg, **an** elephant.

For all other single nouns, use A. A and AN are also known as indefinite article because it will refer to **any** single noun like, a doctor, a book, a pencil, an instructor, an engineer and so on.

We also use A and AN before an adjective if that adjective describes a single noun. Here are the examples:

An *intelligent* student never has any doubts.
A *good* boy will always obey his parents.
Ronald is an *excellent* football player.
No one could find an *immediate* solution to the problem.
Samuel was a *great* prophet.

Use A or AN for every common noun if it appears in the middle of a sentence as shown below:

It was **an** earthquake.

Won't she be **a** good dancer for our entertainment programme?

Use A or AN as applicable, in expressing quantity or certain numbers as shown in the examples given below:

a lot of, a dozen, a couple of runs, an occasional cup of coffee, a hundred, a thousand, a million.

Use A or AN before "half" when it follows a whole number like this,

1 ½ kilo = one and **a** half kilo. (But, don't use 'a' if only ½ is to be pronounced,

½ k = half kilo. " Half a kilo" is wrong English)

Whereas, with other numbers, "a" must be used as shown below:

a third, a quarter, a fifth

When we want to refer to a particular doctor or a book or an instructor, we use the **definite article** THE. Study the following sentences:

The doctor examined Susan. ('the' here refers to a particular doctor, possibly the family doctor)

The class teacher is sick today.

We use THE also to refer to any large numbers or plural nouns. Here are the examples:

the boys, the students, the colleges, the people and so on.

The overall meaning of the sentence will make it clear whether the definite article THE refers to a particular noun or any plural nouns.

We saw that for a single number we use A or AN and for a large number, THE.

What then about the intermediate numbers, say 2, 3 .. 8..10 11 or so? For such small numbers, we use the articles SOME, ANY, A FEW, A LITTLE, MANY, ALL and SUCH. Study the following sentences:

Some boys were at the football ground. (A small number of boys, say 7 or 8)

Did **any** students fail in English?

A few persons only accepted our invitation.

Please give me **a little** sugar. (Here "a little sugar" would mean a couple of spoons of sugar)

Many students failed in mathematics.

All the winners were present at the prize awarding ceremony.

There are many bad boys in your school; don't go near **such** boys.

If the words in **bold** describe the noun, we may treat them as adjectives. But if they refer to the 'number' of the noun concerned, then we treat them as articles. In all the examples given above, the words in bold refer to the 'number' of the noun, hence they are articles.

10. Interjection

Interjection is a symbol that we use to show a sudden feeling of joy, surprise or shock. We will show such feelings in spoken English through body movements or signs or by aural sounds. But in written English we use the symbol after a word or after a full sentence, to create the same feelings, as shown below:

Oh! I didn't know it.
Alas! The woman is dead.
Don't believe her. All her statements are lies!
He ran 100 meters in 5 seconds!

Exercise

1. How many parts of speech are there in English? List them out. 10 speech
2. How do we get the plurals of common nouns? Give examples. by adding c, es ies
3. Explain 'Abstract noun' used for quality, action, state. Yes at the end.
4. Give the plurals of the following compound nouns:
   Daughter-in-law, Brother-in-law, Father-in-law, Woman-servant
   Passer-by, Looker-on, Foot soldier.
5. Give a few examples of collective noun. family, navy, crowd, herd.
6. What do you understand by 'subjective pronouns'?
7. What do you understand by 'pure pronouns'?
8. How many pronouns represent every singular common noun in the world?
9. How many forms are there for every verb?
10. Can we use a present or past form verb in a sentence by itself?
11. What do you understand by "auxiliary cum verbs"?
12. What is the primary job of a pure auxiliary?
13. Can an A.V help a verb?

14. How many A.Vs are there in the English language?
15. List out all the "actionless verbs".
16. How will you identify an adjective?
17. Can a noun do the job of an adjective? Give two examples.
18. How will you identify an adverb in a sentence?
19. Can some nouns do the job of adverbs in a sentence?
20. What is the test to pick out a preposition in a sentence?
21. What is the job of a conjunction?
22. "And" is a peculiar conjunction; it can connect two words also. Can it join any two words or is there some exception?
23. Which articles will you use to represent some small numbers of a common noun?
24. When do we use the article THE?
25. What do you understand by Objective pronouns?
26. Can we use a Subjective pronoun in the object part of a sentence?
27. Can we use a possessive pronoun in the Subject and Object?
28. When will an adjective become an adverb?
29. What do you understand by neuter gender?
30. A verb is like a lame man. Justify.

Chapter 2

SENTENCE STRUCTURE

General

The English language uses only three types of sentences – SIMPLE, COMPLEX and COMPOUND. The **Complex** and **Compound** sentences also use Simple sentences only. For instance, a Complex sentences will have two Simple sentences connected by a conjunction; a Compound sentence, three or more Simple sentences, connected by two or more conjunctions. A Compound may also contain clauses in the form of Simple sentences.

Thus, the common factor is a SIMPLE sentence. Once you understand the structure of a Simple sentence, writing Complex and Compound sentences will be an easy matter.

Structure of a Simple sentence

We may divide every Simple sentence into two distinct parts - the GRAMMAR part and MEANING part. One makes mistakes only in the grammar part and seldom in the meaning part; or, one cannot make any serious mistakes in the meaning part at all. The meaning part has nothing to do with the grammar part. We can take the grammar part of one sentence and attach it to the meaning part of another sentence and *vice versa*. Here are the examples:

(a) Mani could have beaten up / this poor street dog.
    Grammar part   *meaning part*
(b) Isaac loves / the small children in his colony.

We can swop the meaning part like this,

(aa) Mani could have beaten up / the small children in his colony.
(bb) Isaac loves / this poor street dog.

The new sentences sound meaningful all right.

The grammar part is different for each **tense**. And the English language uses in all 18 tenses. Each of these tenses has its own 'grammar rules'. Once you master these grammar rules, you could never make any mistake in composing an English sentence.

The grammar rules themselves are very simple indeed and very simple to remember too. The grammar part is divided into three **sections** - SUBJECT, AUXILIARY and VERB. In short, **S - A - V.**

The meaning part consists of OBJECT or COMPLEMENT or both in any combination. We will indicate this part henceforth as, **O/C.**

Thus, the formula for a Simple sentence will be like this,

$$\textbf{S - A - V - O/C}$$

(Note: This is not the final formula for a Simple sentence; two more sections will get added to the O/C part as we go along)

There are seven categories of Simple sentences: five in question forms and two in answer forms, as follows:

Question forms

1. General question.   (Gen Q)
2. Specific question.   (Sp. Q)
3. Negative question.   (Neg. Q)
4. Emphatic question - 1 (EQ 1)
5. Emphatic question - 2 (EQ 2)

Answer forms

6. Positive or Affirmative answer. (a1)
7. Negative answer.   (a2)

Formulae for all the above are:

Gen Q : **Interrogative-Auxiliary-Subject-Verb-Object/Complement.**
(I - A-S - V -O/C)

Sp. Q : **Auxiliary - Subject - Verb - Object/Complement**
(A - S- V- O/C)

Neg.Q : **Neg. Auxiliary - Subject - Verb - Object/Complement**
(Neg. A - S - V - O/C)

a1   : **Subject - Auxiliary - Verb - Object/Complement**
(S - A - V - O /C)

a2   : **Subject - Neg. Auxiliary - Verb - Object/Complement**
(S - Neg A - V- O/C)

EQ 1 : a1, Auxiliary, Subjective pronoun
EQ 2 : a2, Neg. Auxiliary, Subjective pronoun

The difference between a1 and a2 lies in the auxiliary used. While a1 has a positive auxiliary, a2 will have a negative auxiliary. We make an auxiliary negative by adding the adverb NOT after it.

We frame EQ1 or EQ2 by making use of a1 or a2 followed by the auxiliary used for the tense concerned and the subjective pronoun of the subject, which will be always, I, WE, YOU, HE, SHE, IT or THEY and no other words. You will recall that all these words are "subjective pronouns".

The above 7 formulae hold good for any tense. Only the S-A-V sections will differ from tense to tense. Every tense has its own A-V combination and this combination has a definite relationship with the Subject.

Contents of the individual part in the sentence formula

Interrogative : This part will contain one of the 9 interrogatives, viz, WHO, WHICH, WHAT, WHOSE, WHOM (Also known as "interrogative pronouns".) WHEN, WHERE, WHY, HOW -How much, how many, how long, how far, how often: (Also known as "interrogative adverbs")

Subject : The main word in this part will be a noun which may be supported by words of all parts of speech <u>except Auxiliary and Verb.</u> It may also contain a "subjective pronoun", in which case, the subject will have a single word out of I, WE, YOU, HE, SHE, IT or THEY. A subjective pronoun will not have any supporting word.

Auxiliary : This part will contain one of the 32 auxiliaries we have listed in Chapter 1. Sometimes, the auxiliary part may contain more than one word ,but drawn out of the list of 32 only, in which case we call it an 'auxiliary set'. An auxiliary or auxiliary set will always partner a Verb and will be usually to its left side and nowhere else.

Verb : This part will have the verb in one of its three forms- PRESENT form, PAST form or PAST PARTICIPLE form. You will also see in all the continuous tenses, a 'continuous present verb' i.e. the present form verb ending in the letters - ING.

(<u>Note</u>: The auxiliary and verb will always appear as a pair. We cannot separate the auxiliary from the verb and *vice versa*)

Object : The main word in the object will be a noun which may be supported by words of all parts of speech <u>except auxiliary and verb</u>. Instead of a noun, this part may also contain an objective pronoun out of ME, US, YOU, HIM, HER, IT or THEM. Sometimes, the objective pronoun may be preceded by a preposition. e.g. FOR **me**, TO **them**, AGAINST **her.**

A sentence may have more than one object.

Complement : The main word in a complement will be an ADVERB which may be supported by words of all parts of speech <u>except auxiliary and verb</u>.

O or C : While we may get some meaning from the S - A - V sections, we will get the full meaning of a sentence only from the object or complement or through both.

A Simple sentence must be self contained in meaning. In other words, it must have the O/C part. Some sentences may have only S-A-V. Although this is an English sentence, we cannot call it a Simple sentence until O/C is included in it. And do remember that an **English sentence must have S-A-V.** It may have **S - A.V** instead of **S -A-V.**

Though both the O and C parts will provide the meaning, it would be useful to know which part is O and which C.

Object test   :   We pick out the **object** by putting a test question using any of the "interrogative pronouns" viz, WHO, WHAT, WHICH, WHOSE or WHOM after the S - A - V. If the word or group of words concerned become the answer, it/they will constitute the object(s). Here is an example:

"We   do   eat   breakfast   at 7.30 a.m.

      S   A   V   ?   ?

TQ: We do eat WHAT? Ans: breakfast. Hence the object is "breakfast" because it answers the 'object test' question.

"We do eat a quick breakfast at 7.30 a.m."

In this sentence, the object is "a quick breakfast".

'a quick' are additional words supporting the main noun 'breakfast' a = article, quick = adjective (Do remember, that the main word in an object will be a noun which may be supported by words of all parts of speech except A and V).

Complement test :   For spotting out the complement, we put a test question using any of the "interrogative adverbs" i.e. WHEN, WHERE, WHY or HOW.

We do eat a quick breakfast WHEN?

Ans: at 7.30 a.m.

"at 7.30 a.m." is the complement. We know that '7.30 a.m' is a noun but we have used it as 'adverb of time' here. 'At' is a preposition supporting the main adverb of time. Adverb of time (TQ: WHEN) and adverb of place (TQ: WHERE) will be always a noun. Just because you see a noun in the O/C part, don't jump to the conclusion that it is an object/objects. Only the test question will make it clear whether it is an object or adverb of quality/quantity/time/place.

(ADVERBS are of various types. Many parts of speech may be doing the job of an adverb. Always apply the test to identify it.)

Sentence analysis

Breaking (or splitting) a sentence into its component parts/sections is called "sentence analysis". Having split a sentence, you must identify every word in each part. The identification problem will arise only in the **subject** and **object/complement** parts.

'V' will always be a single word and 'A' will have a maximum of 4 words (4 auxiliaries) but all drawn out of the list of 32.

Exercise

1. Analyse the following sentence:

    a2. "A small dog cannot chase a big cat."

Method

If you try to locate the Subject part initially, you may run into difficulties. So, go in for the V first because it will be in most cases a single word in one of its 3 forms. Here, the Verb is "chase". To its left will be the auxiliary - here it is, CANNOT (Negative form of CAN is CANNOT)

Now, all the words to the left of the 'auxiliary' will be the SUBJECT (in most cases) and right of the verb the OBJECT or COMPLEMENT. We can split O or C into two parts and put one in any place in a sentence where it will give a clearer meaning. Usually one of the parts of O or C would be at the beginning. The Object or Complement test alone will distinguish it from the Subject. A Subject will always contain the "doer" of the action.

So, the analysis is,

A small dog	cannot	chase	a big cat
S	Neg. A	V	O/C

What is "a big cat"? To find out, apply the 'object test' or 'complement test'. We see that 'a big cat' answer the test question, "A small dog cannot chase - WHO" Therefore, this group of words becomes the object of the sentence.

Identification of the words in the SUBJECT and OBJECT parts:

Subject - a (article), small (adjective), dog (noun, the real subject)
Object - a (article), big (adjective), cat (noun, the real object)

2. Analyse,

Gen Q: What will you bring for me from the supermarket?

Ans :	What	will	you	bring	for me	from the supermarket
	I	A	S	V	O	C

"me" is an objective pronoun and "for" (preposition) is a supporting word.

"super market" is the answer to the TQ: WHERE. It is thus an adverb of place. "From" (prep) and "the" (article) are the supporting words.

3. Analyse,

EQ1: Esther and John are going to the circus, aren't they?

Ans:	Esther and John	are	going	to the circus,	aren't	they?
	S	A	V	C	Neg.A	S.pro

(Note: "aren't they" is known as the "Question tag". Thus we may write the formula for EQ1 as: a1, Q tag.)

4. Analyse,

a1   :   By now, my brother would have left for New Delhi by aeroplane.

Ans :   By now, my brother would have left for New Delhi   by aeroplane
           C   S   A set   V   C   O

(Here, "By now" is a complement and it is at the beginning of the sentence) and answers the TQ: WHEN?)

5. Analyse,

a2   : On account of headache, my sister didn't attend class today.

Ans : On account of headache, my sister didn't attend class today.
                 O   S   Neg.A V   O Adv

(Note: "Complement" is a group of words wherein the main word will be an adverb and may be supported by words of all parts of speech except A and V. When the word in a Complement is a single word, we show it as "adverb" in the sentence analysis)

Here are some mixed sentences:

6. Analyse,

Gen Q: Where was the football match?

Ans   : Where   was   the football match?
           I   A.V   S

Note:

Some sentences may have S - A.V instead of A and V being separate.

7. Analyse this Complex sentence:

Madhavan is a clever person because he had studied in a good college.

Ans: Madhavan is a nice person because he had studied in a good college.
        S   A.V   O   Conjn S A   V   C

8. Analyse this Compound sentence:

Pushpa has some good habits and her mother knows it but her friends have not discovered them.

Ans: Pushpa has some good habits   and   her mother does not
        S   A.V   O   Conjn   S   Neg A

know it but   her friends have noticed them   long back.
  V O Conjn   S   A   V   O   C

Note:

You should identify 2 Nos S-A-V (or 1 S-A-V and 1 S - A.V)in a Complex sentence along with one conjunction and 3 Nos S-A-V with 2 conjunctions in a Compound sentence.

Don't forget, the grammar part may have S - A - V or S - A.V

9. Where have you gone the whole day?
10. Is Nandakumar your close friend?
11. Many weak children did not get the promotion at all.
12. College boys shouldn't fight with anyone.
13. How will you return from the cinema house after the show?
14. Sachdeva was a bright student in Plus one class.
15. Why didn't you bring your drawing instruments to the class?
16. You should always carry an umbrella with you during the rainy season.
17. Could you have crossed the river without a boat?
18. Do you know swimming? ('swimming' is a noun)
19. Where is your house?
20. You take this book or you take nothing. (Complex sentence)
21. Can't you keep more costly things in your shop?
22. Gold is a very precious metal.
23. USA is a very large country, isn't it?
24. John was the best football player in our college last year, wasn't he?
25. What did you do when you saw the snake on your path? (Complex sentence)
26. Whose cycle is this?
27. Jesus did ask, "Whom do you seek?"
28. No spectator ought to go beyond this line because it is dangerous and it may cause you harm. (Compound sentence)
29. You ought not to have violated the hostel rules.
30. A farmer from your village has come to our house, hasn't he?
31. A farmer, his son and daughter could not trace my address in our city.
32. When Vijayan was playing tennis he had got wet because it was raining for some ten minutes. (Compound sentence)
33. In whose house are we meeting for the drama rehearsal?
34. Weren't all the award winners present during the ceremony?
35. Wherever you had turned you could see only water and water. (Complex sentence)
36. How many children had not travelled in a train in this class?
37. How often were Lily and Saroja visiting the Marina beach last month?
38. Do you know where Lodhi garden is in New Delhi?
39. How long were you weeping after the examination?
40. So many children cannot sit in this small car, can they?
41. Mahadevan doesn't fail in any test even once in a while, does he?

42. Shall we report this matter to our class teacher?

43. Ravindran couldn't be sitting in the auditorium for so many hours.

44. Such high marks could not have been scored by some of you without those extra classes.

45. This picture had been drawn by my small sister.

46. This bridge is being constructed by my uncle.

Sentence construction

Learn the 7 formulae by heart so that you are able to frame your sentences correctly. If ONE sentence is given to you, you could frame the remaining 6 out of it. Take the following sentence:

a2   :   "We could not reach the station on time."

This is a2 type following the formula : S -.Neg A - V- C

And

a1 is: We could reach   the station on time.
      S   A   V   C

Gen Q : Where could you reach on time?
           I   A   S   V   C

Sp Q   : Could you reach the station on time?
           A   S   V   C

Neg Q : Couldn't you reach the station on time?
         Neg A   S   V   C

EQ1   : You could reach the station on time, couldn't   you?
                                        Neg A   Subj pro

EQ2   : You could not reach the station on time, could   you?
            S   Neg A   V   C   A   Subj pro

So, when we study the various tenses, all you need is 'one' sentence out of the 7 categories and you should be in a position to expand that 'one' sentence into 6 for that particular tense.

Conclusion

Do note that an English sentence must have S - A - V or S - A.V. It need not have O/ C at all. But, without O/C, you may get only a small meaning out of S-A-V. It is the O/C parts that give the full meaning of a sentence. A Simple sentence is one that **is self contained in meaning**. In other words, there must be the O/C parts in the sentence.

Exercise

Write the remaining 6 categories of sentences for the following statements:

1. This ship did not call at Madras port last month.
2. The sales girl greeted me heartily.
3. Won't you get used to this new house within a week? ("used to" is the auxiliary and the verb is 'get'. This is a peculiar situation where the verb is to the left side of the auxiliary. We shall see the reason in a later lesson.)
4. You should not keep visiting your ward every day in this hostel.
5. You shouldn't have copied this assignment from your friend.

Make EQs out of the following statements:

6. We must not disobey the government orders.
7. One cannot master every thing in life.
8. You ought not to feel happy at other people's failures.
9. We didn't see you at the cinema theatre last night.
10. Ramu does like lemon juice and pepsi cola.
11. We aren't used to ragging in this college.
12. You should report at the office at 10 a.m
13. Some people are bad.
14. We have a big house.
15. You had a headache last night.

Chapter 3

PRESENT TENSE (1)

General

Now that we have studied everything about sentence structure, we are ready to deal with sentence-construction methods in various TENSES.

As already pointed out, the English language uses 18 tenses in all. These fall under three main families - PRESENT, PAST and FUTURE. Each family has a number of tenses under it.

We may look at a SIMPLE sentence from another angle also. Out of the 18, you will notice **actions** in 16 tenses. You can say that **actions** constitute the 'meaning part'. Every action will have some 'timing'. The 'time' part will be the grammar, in other words S -A -V. So, when you look at a sentence, ask yourself, "What is the activity in the sentence?" and "what is the 'time element' of that activity?"

"Time" is nothing but TENSE. Tense means 'time.'

But, there are some sentences in which you cannot see any "action". They are **actionless** sentences. Yet, they will have the time element in them. There are only <u>two</u> tenses that belong to the 'actionless' category. These two tenses use "auxiliary cum verbs" (A.V) in the A-V sections. You will recall, there are 11 words which are the 2-in-1 types, i.e, we could use them as "auxiliaries" or as "verbs".

The PRESENT tense and PAST TENSE alone use auxiliary cum verbs (A.Vs) and the remaining 16 tenses use the auxiliary separately and verb separately.

PRESENT TENSE

When to use

We use

(a)   it to denote the existence of or give information about yourself, another person or thing that we see before our eyes or hear about, in present time.

(b)   it to convey information about the things and qualities we and the Third persons possess in present time.

(This is an important tense because most of what we say about people, things or about ourselves will always be in the PRESENT TENSE)

S - A - V rules

Subject	Auxiliary	Verb form
I	AM	AM
HE, SHE, IT	IS	IS
WE, YOU, THEY	ARE	ARE

Possessive case

I, WE, YOU, THEY	HAVE	HAVE
HE, SHE, IT	HAS	HAS

Universal auxiliary

All persons	am/is/are USED TO	Am/is/are act as Verbs and will be to the left of the auxiliary.

Since we use the auxiliary cum verbs (A.Vs) in this tense, the sentence formulae will stand modified like this,

Gen Q : I — A.V — S — O/C
Sp Q : A.V - S - O/C
Neg Q : Neg A.V - S - O/C
EQ1 : a1, NegA.V, Subj pro
EQ2 : a2, A.V, Subj; pro
a1 : S — A.V — O/C
a2 : S — Neg A.V — O/C

In the subject section we may use the subjective pronouns or their corresponding nouns.

Now, we put the words of different parts of speech in the sentence formula like this,

Gen Q : What   is   your name?
         I   A.V   S

a1 : My name   is   P.Ramanathan.
       S   A.V   O

a2 : My name   is not   W.Shakespeare.
       S   Neg A.V   O

(The short form for "is not" is "isn't" and we pronounce it as written)

Sp Q : Is   your Maths lecturer very strict with you?
        A.V   S   C   O

a1 : He   is   very strict with us sometimes.
      S   A.V   C   O   C

a2 : He   isn't   very strict at all with us.
      S   Neg A.V   C   O

Neg Q : Aren't   you all from the local college?
         Neg A.V   S   C

a1 : We   are   from the local college.
      S   A.V   C

```
a2    :   We      are not    from  the Municipal college.
          S     Neg A.V                   C
```

A negative question is more powerful than a specific question. The short form of "are not" is "aren't" and we pronounce it in the same way as written. Use always the short form of the auxiliary in Negative questions. If you use the long form, the power will seem reduced. Whether the question is a specific one or a negative one, the answer (a1 or a2) given will be the same.

```
EQ 1  :  You    are  in St Paul's college,  aren't you?
              S    A.V       C                Q tag
a1      :  I    am    in  St Paul's college.
              S   A.V            C
a2      :  I    am not   in  any Tutorial college.
              S   Neg A.V            C
```

When a question is asked in Second person, the answer must be given in the First person and *vice versa*. The short form of "am not" is "amn't" and is pronounced in the same way as written. Even when the question is in the emphatic form, the answer given is the same.

```
EQ 2  :  You   aren't    a  vegetarian,  are you?
              S   Neg A.V        O         Q tag
a1      :  I   am    a  vegetarian  indeed.
              S  A.V       O          C
a2      :  I   amn't    a  non-vegetarian.
              S  Neg A.V       O
```

EQ1 and EQ2 are more powerful than negative questions.

Here are more sentences of daily use; analyse them all as you read them. Become an expert in analysis. It would be possible to analyse any sentence within 5 seconds. You must reach that speed.

```
Q     :  How is your mother today in the hospital?
a2    :  She is not well enough still.

Q     :  Isn't Nagaraj older to you?
a1    :  He is older to me by 2 years.

Q     :  Aren't Soundari, Sudha and Mala intimate friends in their class ?
a1    :  They are intimate friends.

EQ1  :  Soundari, Sudha and I aren't your friends, are we?
a2    :  We are not your friends.
a1    :  We are your friends.

EQ2  :  Kritika is not your mother's sister, is she?
a1    :  Kritika is her sister.
```

"Mother's" is a possessive noun. This is = her friend ('her' is a possessive pronoun)

Q   : Whose seat is   this?
          I   S A.V   O

a1 . : This is P.N.Chandran's seat. He is absent today.

(P.N.Chandran's seat = his seat. "This" is a demonstrative pronoun.

We shall learn about such pronouns in a later chapter).

EQ 1 : <u>My brother and your younger brother</u> are classmates, aren't they?
                            S

a1   : They are classmates.
Q   : How much money is in your pocket?
a1   : There is some money.
a2   : There isn't any money in my purse.

Analyse a1 and a2. Shall we find out what exactly the word "there" is?

There   is   some money
  ?   A.V   S

This   sentence has S - A.V all right. But then, what is "there"? It is called the 'temporary subject'. This also means that the real subject will come later. The real subject here is "some money".

We start many sentences with THERE as the temporary subject. For example,

There is   a cat inside my bathroom. (We never say, "A cat is in my bathroom?)
TyS A.V   S   C

Is there any food inside the refrigerator? ('there' is a temporary subject and we may look at it as "the introducer of the real subject" which will follow a couple of words later)

There is some food in the refrigerator.
Is there anyone at the reception counter?
There are several mistakes in your essay.
There is   no doubt   about it   at all.
Ty S A.V   O1   O2   C

But, THERE is a natural adverb (adverb of place; answer to the TQ: WHERE?) and will pass the 'complement/adverb test'. When used as an adverb it will have its place in the complement part of the sentence. Study the following examples and carry out the complement test:

Many children   are over <u>there</u> in the corner.
     S   A.V   C

I will be at the football ground for an hour. Don't come <u>there</u>.

ANY and SOME are articles. We normally use ANY in the Q or in a2 and SOME in a1. You can notice that in the above examples.

Here are more examples of Present tense with AM, IS, ARE.

Q : Isn't this a very big building?
   NegA.V S O

a1 : It is a very big building.

Q : Are all your teachers Nuns and Sisters?

a1 : Most of our teachers are Nuns. There are some civilian ladies also along
   with them.

Q : There are some naughty students among you, aren't there?
   (There is no corresponding subjective pronoun for the temporary subject
    THERE. So, we use 'there' in the Q tag)

Q : How many nurses are on night duty today?

a1 : Very few are on duty today.

Q : Who am I ?
   I A.V S

a1 : You are our English lecturer.

Q : Am I your Maths lecturer?

a2 : You are not our Maths lecturer.

Gen Q : Who is your teacher?
    I A.V S

Here are more sentences that we use in our daily life:

My mother is very busy now in the kitchen.
My sisters aren't in the house just now.
Which is your room?
My room is on the first floor.
How many floors are there in this building?
This staircase is very steep, isn't it?
How high is your church building?
It is 150 feet high.
Are you a bright student ?
I amn't a bright student. Raju, is the best student in my class.
Why are your shoes dirty?
My shoes are dirty due to heavy dust on the street.
Isn't your house at the far end of this street?
It is indeed at the far end.
Whose books are these?
They are my friend's books. They are not my books.
Is that a friendly dog? ('that' is a demonstrative pronoun)
A.V S O

It   isn't   a very friendly dog. It is a ferocious dog actually.
S   Neg.A.V   O

My cat is a nice pet.

Possessive case

Model sentences:

GenQ :   What have you   in your hand.
          I A.V S   C

a1   :   I have   two pens   in my hand
        S. A.V   O   C

a2   :   I haven't anything in my hand.
        S Neg AV   O   C

("Haven't" is the short form of "have not" and we pronounce it in the same way as written)

Gen Q : How many sisters have   you?
          I   O   A.V   S

a1   :   I have   two small sisters.
        S A.V   O

a2   :   I have no sisters at all.

a2   :   I haven't any sisters at all.

Sp Q :   Have you any T-shirts in your shop?

a1   :   We have several varieties of T-shirts in our shop.

a2   :   We have no T-shirts at all.

a2   :   We haven't any T- shirts of your choice, Sir.

Neg Q : Haven't you any heavy silk sarees on the shelves?
        (Alternate construction: Have you no heavy silk sarees on the shelves?)

a1   :   We have plenty of heavy silk sarees on the ground floor.

a2   :   We have no stock of silk sarees at present, Madam.

a2   :   We haven't any stock of silk sarees at present, Madam.

Neg Q : Haven't you any fear of darkness?

a1   :   I am scared of darkness actually. ("scared" is an adverb here)
        S A.V Adv   O   Adv

a2   :   I have no fear of darkness at all.

a2   :   I am not scared of darkness.

EQ1   :   Luther and his sister have two pet dogs, haven't they?

a1   :   They have two pet dogs.

a2   :   They have no pet dogs at all.

a2   :   They haven't any pet dogs at all.

EQ2   : Your friends haven't many kinds of sports-wear, have they?

a1   : They have many kinds indeed.

a2   : They haven't many kinds as such. They have a few only.

EQ1   : All my classmates have a bicycle each, haven't they?

a1   : They have a bicycle each.

a2   : Many of your classmates haven't any cycle.

a2   : Many of your classmates have no cycle at all.

Gen Q : What   has   Neela   in her   bag?
           I   A.V   S   C

a1   : She   has   all her books and   lunch box   in her bag.
            S   A.V   O   C

a2   : She   hasn't   anything except her books.
             S   NegAV   O

("Hasn't" is the short form of "has not")

a2   : She   has   nothing except her school books in her bag.
            S   A.V   O   C

(An alternate a2)

Sp Q   : Has   your mother any cousin sisters?

a1   : She has some cousin sisters.

a2   : She hasn't any cousin sister.

a2   : She has no cousin sister.

Neg Q : Hasn't Chandra Leela a very large house?

a1   : She has a large house

a2   : She hasn't a large house at all.

EQ1   : Mr. Nambiar has a pair of big ears, hasn't he?

a1   : He has a pair of big ears.

a2   : He hasn't any big ears at all.

a2   : His ears are not big at all.

EQ2   : My sister hasn't any sense of humour, has she?

a1   : She has a good sense of humour.

a2   : She has no sense of humour at all.

The sentence structure and analysis with the "Universal auxiliary" :

Here, we use the auxiliary separately and verb separately. Study the sentence analysis carefully:

a1   : Many students in our class   are   used to   regular homeworks.
                       S   A.V   A   O

a2   : All the young residents in my colony   are   not used to   ragging .
                                 S   A.V   Neg A   O

Gen Q : Why   are   you   used to   white canvas shoes?
               I   A.V   S   A   O

Sp Q   : Is   Ramanujam used to a city life?
            V   S   A   O

Neg Q : Aren't   your elder brothers used to big class rooms?
           NegA.V   S   A   O

EQ1   : I   am not used to a strict tuition-teacher, am I?
           S   Neg A.V   A   O   Q tag

EQ2   : Your friends aren't used to coffee, are they?
           S   NegA.V   A   O   Q tag

USED TO -   Universal auxiliaries have no meaning. We use them for particular situations. And they don't belong to any particular tense either. Here, we use this auxiliary to show a habit which becomes part of our routine activities.

Have you noticed that although the words AM, IS, ARE are A.Vs, we have used them in the place of Verbs; actually as regular verbs? And the **verb** so used is to the left of the auxiliary? Next, we use these **verbs** in the Q tag as well instead of an auxiliary? These are the peculiarities of USED TO and exceptional cases as well.

In this tense, USED TO must be followed **always** by a noun (or OBJECT) and never a complement.

Expansion

Given one sentence, you could expand it into the remaining six categories. Here are some examples:

Sp Q : **Isn't your elder brother the captain of the hockey team?**

Out of this single sentence, the remaining 6 derived ones are:

a1   : My elder brother is the captain of the hockey team.
a2   : My elder brother isn't the captain.
Gen Q : Who is the captain of the hockey team?
Neg Q : Isn't your elder brother the captain of the hockey team?
EQ1   : Your elder brother is the captain of the hockey team, isn't he?
EQ2   : Your elder brother isn't the captain of the hockey team, is he?

EQ1   : **Mahesh's uncle has two Siamese kittens, hasn't he?**

The remaining six categories are:

a1   : Mahesh's Uncle has two Siamese kittens.
a2   : He hasn't any kittens at all.
Gen Q : What types of kittens has Mahesh's uncle?
Sp Q : Has Mahesh's uncle two Siamese kittens?
Neg Q : Hasn't Mahesh's uncle two Siamese kittens?
EQ 2 : Mahesh's uncle hasn't any Siamese kittens, has he?

Sp Q : **Is Peter Samuel used to Marie biscuits?**

The remaining 6 categories are:

Gen Q : What is Peter Samuel used to?
a1   : He is used to Marie biscuits.
a2   : He is not used to Britannia biscuits.
Neg Q : Isn't Peter Samuel used to Marie biscuits?
EQ1   : Peter Samuel is used to Marie biscuits, isn't he?
EQ2   : Peter Samuel is not used to Britannia biscuits, is he?

Exercise

Fill up the blank with a suitable aux.verb:

1. .Am... I your brother's friend?
2. Can.. we good neighbours?
3. We have no friends in this area. We have a lot of friends in our own colony.
4. These street children .... any decent dress at all.
5. Your college ..is.. very big.
6. How many neighbours have you in your street?
7. Where is your shoulder bag?
8. Where are . your friends' shoulder bags?
9. Thangaraj .is. a very happy student, isn't he?
10. Thangaraj, Soman and Susheela .are. very intelligent in your class.
11. Has... you any bread for sale now?
12. My friend is. not all that clever.
13. How many night dresses are. there in the cupboard?
14. Where are all the football players? Why .are. they present at the stadium?
15. We are not used to heavy rains in our city during Summer months.

Write suitable Questions for the following a1 and a2 answers.

16. I have all the spare parts for your Moped.
17. There is nothing like double-barrel hockey stick, Sir.
18. Certainly, I am not very happy with your performance in the last exams.
19. Mohana is not at all a hardworking student.
20. Vandana is not used to this club.
21. I have some spare pencils, Sir.
22. Hanuman hasn't any dividers in his instrument box.
23. You are not a clever engineering student either.
24. I am a brave young man, Sir.
25. We have two T.V. sets in our house.

Correct the mistake(s) in the following statements:

26. This girl aren't in her room now.

27. Susan have only two sisters.
28. Very few students are unhealthy, isn't he?
29. Women and children is not welcome in this meeting.
30. Amn't I a good swimmer, am I?
31. Has you some spare chairs in your house?
32. My mother and I has no fear of ghosts.
33. Where is all your classmates?
34. Ramanathan are a good man according to his own opinion.
35. They aren't a good volley ball players.

Use the correct A.V in the following sentences:

36. What have. these students anyway?
37. Everyone in their group have good manners.
38. Where are the remaining students?
39. How are your friends today after a hectic week-end?
40. When is.. your birthday?
41. What are these men?
42. Who has a ballpoint pen in his pocket?
43. What is this?
44. Why is your uniform dirty today?
45. Whose socks ...is these?

Write the remaining six categories of sentences for each of the following statements:

46. We have a big house in Rajinder colony.
47. Some students are weak in Differential calculus, aren't they?
48. My sister and brother are very clever in their class.
49. Isn't Madhuri's acting good in all the films?
50. What are you used to for breakfast?

Analyse the following sentences: (i.e. Break them into parts and state the part of speech of every word in each part)

51. We are good students from Tarapore tower colony.
52. Susheela and Mona haven't any brothers at all.
53. You are used to a big house for living, aren't you?
54. Juneja is a bright student in the Third Semester, isn't he?
55. We are not at all used to too much of lazing about during holidays.

Chapter 4

PRESENT CONTINUOUS TENSE (2)

When to use

We use this tense to describe an action actually in progress or going on at the time of talking. The person performing the action may be yourself or a Second or Third person.

Rules

Subject	Auxiliary	Verb form
I	AM	Present ending in - ING
HE, SHE, IT	IS	- do -
WE, YOU, THEY	ARE	- do -

<u>Universal auxiliaries</u>

All persons		
	CAN BE	Present verb ending in ING)
	MAY BE	"
	COULD BE	"
	WOULD BE	"
	SHOULD BE	"
	MUST BE	"
	SHALL BE	"
	WILL BE	"
	NEED BE	
	OUGHT TO BE	"
am/ is/ are	GOING TO BE	"

am/is/are/can be/may be/could be/ |
would be/should be/must be/ |
shall be/ will be/ought to be | USED TO   Use only **Getting** and
GETTING/BECOMING | **Becoming** and no other verb.

(15 auxiliaries)

Sentence structure

This tense uses the auxiliary separately and verb separately, hence the sentence formulae will be like this,

```
Gen Q : I - A - S - V - O/C
Sp Q  : A -S -V - O/C
Neg Q : Neg A - S - V - O/C
a1    : S - A - V - O/C
a2    : S - Neg A - V - O/C
```

EQ1   : a1, Aux. Subj pronoun (Use the auxiliary always in its short form)
EQ2   : a2, Neg Aux, Subj pronoun ("   "   )

Sample sentences

Q   : Where   are   your parents   living   in the city?
          I   A   S   V   C

a1   : They   are   living   in Ashok tower   area.
          S   A   V   C

a2   : They   are not   living   in Defence colony.
          S   Neg A   V   C

Sp Q : Is   the English lecturer   giving   tuition   for you   daily?
          A   S   V   O1   O2   C

a1   : He   is   giving   me   tuition   daily in the evening time.
          S   A   V   O1   O2   C1   C2

a2   : He   isn't   giving   tuition   to anyone   nowadays.
          S   Neg A   V   O1   O2   C

Neg Q : Aren't   you and your sister   learning   English   in Raman Institute?
          Neg A   S   V   O   C

a1   : We   are   learning   English   there.
          S   A   V   O   C

a2   : Only   I   am   learning   in Raman Institute.
          C1   S   A   V   C2

(Note: A sentence may also start with O or C. Carry out the O/C test if you find some odd words at the beginning of a sentence and they will not look to be the Subject. Subject will always be the "doer of the action".)

EQ1   : You   are   going   to the supermarket   now,   aren't you?
          S   A   V   C1   C2   Q tag

a1   : I   am   going   over there   now.
          S   A   V   C1   C2

a2   : I   amn't   going   to the supermarket now.
          S   Neg A   V   C2

EQ2   : You and I   aren't   enjoying   this T.V. serial   very much,   are we?
          S   Neg A   V   O1   C   Q tag

a1   : We   are   enjoying   it   once in a while.
          S   A   V   O   C

a2   : We   aren't   enjoying   every episode   in the serial.
          S   Neg A   V   O1   O2

Sentences with Universal auxiliaries:

We use the universal auxiliaries for the same purpose i.e. to describe an action in progress at the time of talking. Here is one sample sentence for each of the "12 universal auxiliaries" assigned for this tense. Expand each into the remaining 6 categories:

Gen Q : How can a small boy be swimming in the pool for 2 hours?
       I   A   S   A   V   C1   C2

Note:

When the auxiliary is of 2 or more words, we put the Subject after the first auxiliary in the Q form. In the answer forms, they will be together. In the Q tag, we use only the first auxiliary.

a2   : Some students may not be coming with us for the picnic.

Sp Q : Could your brother be working on this problem as of now?

a1   : We should be moving out within the next five minutes.

Gen Q : When would the football match be starting?

Neg Q : Mustn't you be helping your mother in the kitchen on a holiday?
         (While pronouncing this negative auxiliary, we silence the first "t" and say 'musn't')

a2   : Hostel students ought not to be loitering about even during holidays.

Neg Q : Won't you be helping me in my studies?
         ("Won't " is the short form of "will not". While writing it, do use an apostrophe between **n** and **t**)

Neg Q : Shan't we be seeing the Principal this afternoon about extra classes?
         ("Shan't" is the short form of "shall not")

EQ 1 : Some students could be watching the T.V programme, couldn't they?

Sp Q : Are you going to be writing a letter to your mother?

Neg Q : Aren't you becoming/getting used to coffee?

a1   : We could be getting used to the hard work necessary in this college.

a2   : We won't be getting used to the new Maths lecturer for a long time.

Sp Q : Why must you be getting used to a wrong method in your practicals?

EQ 1 : We shall be getting used to him shortly, shan't we?

Note: We don't use any other continuous verb with the auxiliary USED TO. Use only "getting" and "becoming".

USED TO is such an auxiliary that would need one or more auxiliaries to help it. Here we use any of the 13 auxiliaries to help it.

In the Present case, we used AM, IS, ARE along with USED TO. There these words were doing the job of verbs. In this tense we find that AM, IS, ARE are acting as supporting auxiliaries and the verbs are GETTING and BECOMING.

Situations for the use of the Universal auxiliaries

As already pointed out, universal auxiliaries have no meaning like a normal English word. They are to be used for some particular situation in the tense concerned as explained herein:

CAN   - Use it when some skill is required to do a job.

MAY	- Used to express possibility; to ask for permission; grant permission for some action.
COULD	- To show ability to do a certain work; to make a polite request
SHOULD	- To express one's duty/obligation
WOULD	- To show stronger form of determination to carry out a certain action.
MIGHT	- To show a distant possibility
MUST	- To show duty/obligation and is stronger in tone than "should".
OUGHT TO	- To show duty/obligation and is stronger than "must"
WILL	- Used to show a desire to carry out a certain action
SHALL	- Stronger than "will" in tone and to be used for First person in Q form.
GOING TO	- To show a desire to do an action.

(Note: We have already seen that the auxiliary USED TO, would need one or more auxiliaries to help it. GOING TO, KEEP and KEPT (will be covered later) are the other auxiliaries that would need one or two more helping auxiliaries, from the list of auxiliaries, before they could help a verb in a sentence. You may say that these 4 auxiliaries need a helper(s) themselves before they could help a verb !!)

Sentences of daily use

Here are more sentences that we would be using daily. Analyse everyone of them quickly in your mind until the grammar portion is fully firmed up in your mind. Do not speak out the sentences mechanically but always with full understanding of the grammar part.

Q   : What are you eating?
a1 : I am eating some grapes.
a2 : I am not eating anything now.

Q   : Aren't you showing much disrespect to some of your friends?
a1 : At times, I am showing disrespect.
a2 : I am not showing any disrespect to any of my friends.

Q   : Mohini, are   you   awake?
         O   A.V   S   C1
a1 : I am quite awake, Sulochana.
a2 : I am not sleeping, Sulochana. I am very much awake.

Q   : In which college are you studying nowadays?
           C1   A   S   V   C2
a1 : I am studying in St Peter's college.
a2 : I am not studying in any Govt college.
a2 : I amn't studying in any Govt college.

Q   : Isn't your elder brother working in a computer shop?
a1 : Yes. He is a salesman there.

Q   : What exactly are you doing now?

a1   : I am petting my little dog. It is very sick.

Q   : Aren't you walking a little too fast?

a1   : I am indeed walking a little fast. You are rather slow, aren't you?

Mustn't you be revising your lessons today for tomorrow's exam?

We could be going to the Exhibition this evening.

We ought to be submitting our assignment work regularly.

Small children may be watching the cartoon channel on the T.V.

Will you be coming with us to the Children's park?

You can't be sleeping the whole afternoon.

I may be working late tonight.

Would you be watching a movie the whole night?

We shouldn't be spending so much time in the library.

Aren't you going to say 'sorry' to your brother?

All of us shall be leaving for Mumbai in a short while from now.

Aren't you getting used to this friend rather too much?

We ought not to be getting used to this servant so much.

Exercise

Correct the mistake(s) if any, in the following sentences. The sentences are a mix of Present tense and Present continuous tense.

1.   Aren't you hold the tennis racket in the wrong hand? You is a left-hander, aren't you?
2.   Ahmed isn't doing well in his class, isn't he?
3.   How is the children progressing in their studies?
4.   Clever children, not necessarily, has clever parents.
5.   When are your friend coming to my house?
6.   You are using your cycle yesterday, aren't you?
7.   I am not revise my lessons now.
8.   We are always proceed to the college by foot, aren't we?
9.   I am feel like a little frog from this morning.
10. The teachers is always nice to us during class hours.
11. Where is your mother? Is she work or resting?
12. Mohanrao isn't a good monitor, are he?
13. I am sitting here till the Professor's arrival. Is you satisfied?
14. You are not going for the picnic without me. Is it clear to you?
15. Why is you running round the football ground every morning?

Fill up the blank with a suitable word:

16. ……. all college students above the age of 17?
17. Suresh Koshi …… attending hockey coaching class these days.
18. Pratap's sister …. quite tall, isn't she?

19. ..... not the carpenter repairing the chairs now?
20. What ..... you purchasing from this shop?

Write emphatic questions for the following a1/a2 sentences:

21. Mangalore mail may be running late by 1 hour. (There is no short form for
   'may not'. Use it as it is in the Q tag.)
22. The watchman is walking up and down at the front gate. *isn't he*
23. Chetan would not be coming for work today. *wouldn't he*
24. Everyone should be sleeping in the dormitory now. *shouldn't they.*
25. Alexander could be worrying about his younger sister's health. *could he*
26. The labourers would not be striking today. *wouldn't they.*
27. We are looking for a good servant maid. *are we*
28. You are not the right person for this job. *aren't I*
29. No one is suitable among you for the vice captain's place.
30. We are playing the final match at the moment. *are we.*

Answer the following questions in a1 and a2 form in Present tense or Present
continuous tense whichever is suitable:

31. Is your mother making paper dolls now?
32. Are you a well-mannered person?
33. Is George wearing his slippers?
34. When is your birthday party?
35. Aren't you a cricket player?
36. Where is your classmate taking tuition from ?
37. Who are sitting next to you during your chess game?
38. Which class teacher of your school is living in your colony?
39. Hasn't Mahadevan's father much money in his bank account?
40. Meena and Roja are good actresses, aren't they?

Analyse the following sentences and identify the part of speech of every word in each
part:

41. Most of the time, this child would be spending his day inside my house.
42. Flies ought to be crowding around in every heap of filth.
43. Whom are you looking for in this big crowd?
44. Isn't the Principal of our college present in every function?
45. Nowadays, Computer is a household item in many homes.
46. We are used to at least 15 minutes' break between the two halves of any match.
47. Aren't you going to greet your teaching staff a happy new year?
48. Wouldn't you be coming across some mischievous students during this course?
49. We should not be obeying any illegal orders from anyone.
50. The stragglers ought to be catching up with us anytime now.

Expand the following statements into their remaining six categories:

51. Might our History lecturer be sitting in the Rest room?
52. We shan't be returning before next Sunday.
53. The HOD could be correcting our answer papers now.
54. All students may not be attending today's match.
55. You will be coming to my house this evening , won't you?
56. Isn't Madhavi thinking too high of herself?
57. We are not going to give our support to this student-leader, are we?.
58. Aren't we overreacting over a simple lapse on the part of our seniors?
59. Amn't I supporting you in every one of your quarrels with others?
60. Of course, I am going to give you some financial help.
61. You should not be getting used to this variety of T shirts.
62. Is your brother becoming used to Cadbury chocolates?

Chapter 5

Part I

SIMPLE PRESENT TENSE (3)

Use

We use the Simple present tense,

(a)   to talk about the activities we do as a routine - daily or weekly or monthly or at some periodicity.

(b)   to give an order/command.

(c)   to make a suggestion in Question form.

(d)   to acknowledge an order/command or a suggestion.

Rules

Subject	Auxiliary	Verb form
I, WE, YOU, THEY	DO	Present form
HE, SHE, IT	DOES	Present form

<u>Universal auxiliaries</u>

All persons		
	CAN	Present form
	MAY	"
	COULD	"
	SHOULD	"
	WOULD	"
	MUST	"
	OUGHT TO	"
	WILL	"
	SHALL	"
	DARE	"
	NEED	"

Can/may/would/should/must/ought to/ will/shall GET/BECOME/BE USED TO	use only **get, become** or **be** and no other verb
Do/does/can/may/would/should/must/ ought to/will/shall KEEP	Continuous verb

The Simple present tense also uses 15 auxiliaries.

This tense uses the auxiliary separately and verb separately. Apply the S-A-V rules in the Simple sentence formulae. Here are some model sentences using the auxiliary DO:

```
Gen Q :  When   do   you   start    for your college ?
               I    A    S     V          C
Ea1   : I    do  start  for my college  at 10 a.m.
            S    A    V        C1            C2
a1    : I    start   for my college   at 10 a.m.
            S   (A)V         C1              C2
a2    : I    do not  start  for college   before 10 a.m.
            S   Neg A   V        C1             C2
```

(The short form for "do not" is "don't")

```
Sp Q  :  Do  all the hostel students   rise   from bed   at 6 a.m?
              A            S              V        C1          C2
Ea1   : They   do  rise   from bed      at 6 a.m..
             S    A   V       C1             C2
a1    : They   rise    from bed    at 6 a.m.
             S   (A)V       C1          C2
a2    : They  don't   rise   from  bed    before 6 a.m.
             S   Neg A   V        C1             C2
```

Neg Q : Don't all the children play games in the evenings?
Ea1   : They do play games in the evenings.
a1   : They play games in the evenings.
a2   : They don't play games every evening.

EQ 1 : The Principal and the staffs attend the daily prayer, don't they?
Ea1   : They do attend the daily prayer without fail.
a1   : They attend the daily prayer without fail.
a2   : They don't attend the daily prayer on Fridays.

EQ 2 : Manohar and Tony don't write good English, do they?
Ea1   : They do write good English.
a1   : They write good English.
a2   : Manohar and Tony don't write good English.

A small modification is necessary in the a1 formula for this tense. In the first case "do start .." is an emphatic answer(Ea1). We don't give an emphatic answer for every question. Often we give a normal answer without any stress in it. For normal answer(a1) therefore, we simply omit the auxiliary 'do' and give the answer like this: I start for college at 8 a.m. We have only silenced the auxiliary (do); it is very much present. To remind ourselves that Simple present auxiliary DO is present there, we show it inside

brackets(A) to the left of the verb. Do remember that there is no English sentence without
S - A -V.

Here are more examples with auxiliary DO:

Gen Q : When do we go for our field event practice?
Ea1   : We do go at 6 a.m. every day except Sundays.
a1   : We go at 6 a.m. every day except Sundays.
a2   : We don't go for it until next week.

Gen Q : How do you travel to Arakonam from Chennai?
Ea1   : I do travel by the local train.
a1   : I travel by the local train.
a2   : I don't go by bus to Arakonam.

Sp Q   : Don't Sheila and Premila go to temple on every Tuesday?
Ea1   : They do go to temple on every Tuesday.
a1   : They go to temple on every Tuesday.
a2   : They don't go to any temple on Mondays.

Neg Q : Don't you watch some T.V serial every Saturday?
Ea1   : I do watch some T.V serial every Saturday.
a1   : I watch some T.V serial every Saturday.
a2   : I don't watch any T.V serial at all.

EQ1   : Our friends play Scrabble with us every day, don't they?
Ea1   : They do play Scrabble with us every day.
a1   : They play Scrabble with us every day.
a2   : They don't play Scrabble with us on holidays.

EQ2   : Ram Mohan and I don't drink coffee, do we?
Ea1   : We do drink coffee at times.
a1   : We drink coffee at times.
a2 .   : We don't drink tea ever.

Analyse the following sentence and locate the verb:

Q   : When   do you   do   your yoga exercises?
              I   A   S   ?   O
a1   : I   do   my yoga exercise   at 5.30 a.m. ("do" used as A.V):
        S   A.V   O   C

What part does the second 'do' play in the Q? It is doing the job of a verb, isn't it?
But, we know that DO is an aux.verb. From this example we come to the conclusion that
DO can be a normal verb also. When DO is used as a normal verb in a sentence it too
would need a helper auxiliary. Thus, the first DO is doing the job of an auxiliary and the
second DO, a regular verb. When used as a verb its other two forms are - DID, DONE.

DO is in fact a 3-in-1 word. We use it as (i) auxiliary (in Simple present tense) (ii) as auxiliary cum verb in Simple present (see a1 above) and (iii) as normal present form verb.

Here are some examples with the auxiliary DOES:

```
Gen Q :  Where does Thangaraj work?
              I     A      S      V
Ea1    :  He  does work  in a  cycle mechanic's shop.
              S    A    V         C
a1     :  He works  in a cycle mechanic's shop.
          S   (A)V            C
a2     :  Thangaraj  doesn't  work  anywhere at present.
              S       Neg A     V          C
```

Sp Q : Does the office peon sit in front of the HOD's office always?
Ea1   : He does sit in front of the HOD's office always.
a1   : He sits in front of the HOD's office always.
a2   : He doesn't sit there always.

Neg Q : Doesn't this old woman look after the creche?
Ea1   : She does look after the creche sometimes.
a1   : She looks after the creche sometimes.
a2   : She doesn't look after the creche regularly at all.

EQ1   : Mona spends her week-ends in my house doesn't she?
Ea1   : She does spend her week-ends in my house.
a1   : She spends her week-ends in my house.
a2   : She doesn't spend every week-end in my house.

EQ2   : Leela doesn't attend the English tuition class every day, does she?
Ea1   : She does attend the tuition class every day.
a1   : She attends the tuition class every day.
a2   : Leela doesn't attend the tuition class on Sundays.

```
Sp Q  :  Does  Vijayan   eat   his breakfast   at 7.30 a.m.?
                A      S     V      O               C
Ea1    :  Vijayan   does  eat  his breakfast    at 7.30 a.m.
              S       A    V      O               C
a1     :  He    eats   his breakfast   at 7.30 a.m.
          S    (A)V        O               C
a2     :  He   does not   eat   his breakfast   before 7.30 a.m.
          S    Neg A      V       O                C
```

(The short form for "does not" is "doesn't")

"Vijayan does eat his breakfast at 7.30 a.m." is an emphatic answer (Ea1). For normal answer (a1), all we do is, remove the auxiliary DOES and give an 's' sound to the verb. We get the 's' sound in the present form verb by adding the letter 's' in certain cases, letters 'es' in some and letters "ies" in some verbs. The rule to follow here is like this:

does + eat	=	eats
does + write	=	writes
does + catch	=	catches
does + brush	=	brushes
does + fly	=	flies
does + cry	=	cries

Although we have removed the auxiliary DOES and given an 's' sound in its place, it continues to be present in the sentence. To remind ourselves that the Simple present auxiliary DOES is very much there, we show it inside brackets (A) to the left of the verb. We give the 's' sound only when we use the auxiliary DOES. (When we use the universal auxiliaries in the Simple present, we don't give any 's' sound even when the subject has HE, SHE or IT.)

Here are some more examples with DOES:

Q : Doesn't Monica visit her grandparents every week end?
Ea1 : She does visit her grandparents every week end.
a1 : She visits her grandparents every week end.
a2 : Monica doesn't visit them during holidays.

Gen Q : Where does our Administrative officer live?
a1 : He lives in Gomathi colony
a2 : He doesn't live in our colony.

Q : Doesn't Manohar kill too many birds with his catapult as a hobby?
a1 : He kills far too many birds with his catapult.
a2 : He doesn't kill all birds with his catapult. He kills only some specials like sparrows.

EQ1 : Rohit recites English poems beautifully, doesn't he?
Ea1 : He does recite them beautifully.

EQ1 : Johnson does write excellent essays in English, doesn't he?
(This is a double emphatic or a double powerful question!)
Ea1 : He does write excellent essays.
a1 : He writes excellent essays.

Note:

We cannot write EQ2 in such double emphatic forms.

Analyse the following sentence :

Ea1 :Manju   does   do   all the homework by herself   only.
       S   A   V   O   C

a1   : Manju   does   all the homework by herself   only.
       S   A.V   O   C

In the first case (Ea1), we have used DOES as an Auxiliary and in this capacity it supports the present form verb DO. DOES is a 2-in-1 word. In a1, we have used it as A.V.

Here are more examples of daily use with DOES:

What does Saroja do on Sunday mornings?
She usually spends her time reading some English magazines.
Doesn't your father go for a constitutional walk every morning?
Yes, he does go for it every morning without fail.
When does our English lecturer prepare his lectures?
He does it during the previous night. ('does' used as A.V)
Doesn't every mother bring the nursery class kids all by herself?
Every mother does bring her kid all by herself usually.
How does one find out about the life styles of the domestic servants?
At what times does the public library open on holidays?
Everyone washes their hands before ever meal, doesn't one?

Note: All the examples discussed above belong to the 'routine' actions we do.

Use of HAVE as verb

We used HAVE as an auxiliary cum verb in Present tense (See Chapter 3) . We can use it as a normal present form verb also (Its other two forms then are - HAD, HAD). This is also a 3-in-1 word.

Analyse the following sentences where HAVE is a present form verb:

1.   What   do   you   have   in your bag?
       I   A   S   V   C

2.   I   do   have   some toilet items in it.
     S   A   V   O

In 2, HAVE is a normal present form verb supported by the auxiliary DO. But see 3 below:

3.   I   have   all my books   in my bag
    S   A.V   O   C

Here, HAVE is an A.V. But we may also view it as a normal verb with the auxiliary DO made silent. (Simple present case)

Here is another peculiar case:

Q   :   What does Peter have in his pocket?
        I   A   S   V   C

Ea1 :   Peter does have some money in his pocket
        S   A   V   O   C

a1   :   Peter has some money in his pocket.
        S   A.V   O   C

For the normal answer (a1), we switch over to the auxiliary cum verb HAS. Thus it would appear that,

Does + have = has

We cannot give an 's' sound to the present form verb HAVE. If we do, the word HAVES would become a noun. This is an exceptional case. In the entire English language, HAVE is the only verb that cannot accept the 's' sound for its present form.

Order/command/suggestion type sentences

The second use of the Simple present tense lies in giving an order or command or making a suggestion in the present time. Such orders/commands/suggestions are always directed at a second person or second persons. Here are a few examples:

Sit down. Come here. Stand up on the bench. Make two cups of tea. Copy this lesson. Write this sentence 50 times. Stop writing. Stop gambling.

Don't come to me. Don't play in the morning time. Don't sleep in the afternoon.

Be careful
Be silent during the prayer
Don't be silly.
Don't be rude to your elders.
Don't be proud.

Are all the above examples English sentences? If so, where are the Subject and Auxiliary? (We know that every English sentence must have S-A-V). We have silenced the S and A, that's all. So, the true construction will be as follows:

(You do) sit down.
   S   A V Adv
(You do) come here.
(You do) write this sentence 50 times.
(You do) stop writing. ('writing' here is a noun)

But, for the negative commands, we bring in the A like this,

(You) don't come to me.
   S   Neg A   V   O

(You) don't play in the morning time.

Analyse the next lot of orders:

(You do) be careful
  S   A   ?   C

(You do) be   silent during the prayer.
  S   A   ?   C

(You) don't   be silly
  S   Neg A ?   C

(You) don't be proud.
  S   Neg A ?   C

So, what is BE in the above sentences? BE is doing the job of the 'verb', isn't it? It also happens to be a 3-in-1 word. BE is equal to AM, IS, ARE. We used AM, IS, ARE in the Present tense. Thus, we use BE indirectly as A.V in Present tense.

But, in the Simple present case, we have used BE as a present form verb. (Its other two forms are - WAS/WERE and BEEN). We shall see its third use as Auxiliary a little later.

More examples of order/command/suggestion type sentences:

Do you see a big building over there? (Suggestion)
Yes, I do see a big building. (Acknowledgement)
Don't come into my office without permission. (Command)
Where do we sit for our usual chit chat? (Suggestion)
Don't you eat plenty of mangoes in the summer months? (Suggestion)
I prefer banana to mangoes actually. (Acknowledgement)
Why don't you come to me in case of doubts? (Suggestion)
Do I mark the late-comers absent? (Order/command)
Yes, mark them absent. (Command)
Today, please take charge of the Arts group in addition to your normal work. (order)
See me after the college hours. (Command)
Why do you make so many mistakes in your sentence-construction? (Suggestion)
Please accompany the students on their excursion to Ooty. (Order)
Be a good boy in the party. (Suggestion)
Don't be afraid of that young man. (Suggestion)
Be cautious during your night journey. (Suggestion)
Don't go too near the wild animal cages. (Command)
Stop all your tantrums. (Order)

Here is something special. Analyse the following question:

(a) Who   goes to the market?
     I   (A)V   C

(b) Who   go   to the market?
       I   (A)V   C

(c) Who don't go to the market?
      I   Neg A V   C

Where is the 'Subject' in the above examples? An English sentence must have a Subject. WHO is doing two jobs - that of an Interrogative and also Subject. So, the true analysis will be like this,

Who   goes to the market?
I/S   (A)V   C
Who   go to the market?
I/S   (A)V   C

Since WHO is also the subject, what about its number? Is it a singular or plural noun? This we will know by looking at the verb. If WHO is to be singular, use a singular verb (GOES) and if plural, a plural verb (GO). But in a2 type order/command/suggestion, the Auxiliary section has to be present.

Who does not eat mutton in this group?
Who doesn't speak Tamil fluently in this class?

Who write letters regularly to their parents?
Who don't sleep well at night?

Sentences with Universal auxiliaries

Sp Q : Can you lift this heavy box all by yourself? (Suggestion and ability)
a1   : Surely I · can lift it, Madam.
          Adv S   A   V   O   O
Neg Q: Mustn't you be more punctual for all meetings? (Suggestion)
          Neg A S V   C   O
Gen Q: What could you do for your country?   ("   ")
Sp Q : Need you go to your sister's house of all days today?
          A S   V   C

(See how polite and diplomatic this order/suggestion is when NEED is used as the auxiliary. Use NEED only in Q and a2 form. In a1 form, the sentence may not sound well.)

You dare not touch a live electric wire. (Suggestion)
How dare you insult me like this?   "

(DARE is used only in Q and a2 form. In Gen Q, we can use only HOW and no other interrogative)

We ought not to disobey our elders. (Suggestion - acknowledgement)

Some students would not   get used to   strict discipline (Ack)
    S   Neg A   V   A   O

Won't you get used to the new set of students very fast? (Suggestion)

Certainly, we could complete this job within an hour. (Ack)
Would you disobey my order? (Order)
We must attend office punctually at 10 a.m. (Ack)
May we proceed to the football ground now, Sir? (Suggestion)
Shall we now march towards the Principal's office?   "
Can you keep meeting me every day at this place? (Routine action)
  A   S   A   V   O   C

He does keep seeing me every morning. (Routine action)
  S   A   A   V

("He keeps seeing me every morning" is wrong because we cannot give an 's' sound to an auxiliary; we do that only for a present form verb with the auxiliary DOES.)

This student would see me every morning before college time. (Routine action)
Could you come to my office at 10 a.m? (Order)
Would you please send a quick reply?   "

Uses of Universal auxiliaries in Simple present

We use the Universal auxiliaries for the same situations as for DO and DOES. Most of them, of course, would be for, 'suggestions/acknowledgements and orders'. We don't have to give any 's' sound to the present form verb when an Universal auxiliary has been used in a sentence.

For routine activities, we use DO and DOES, "would" and "… keep" only out of the universal auxiliaries list, as shown in the examples given below:

   (i) This peon would open my office room sharp at 8 a.m. daily.
   (ii) You could keep submitting the 'absentee report' to the Principal's office daily.

The orders/suggestions given with the Universal auxiliaries would sound somewhat more polite as against with DO. For example,

   (a)   Could you come to my office now?
   (b)   Would you send a reply to this letter immediately?
   (c)   You should not wait here unnecessarily.
   (d)   You must vacate your hostel seat by this evening.
   (e)   You dare not challenge my authority.
   (f)   You need not come to my house any more. (Compare this with, "Don't come to my house anymore". This is blunt while with NEED the order is more polite and yet firm).

(g)   You ought not to question the office staff about over-billing.

(h)   You shall not chew *pawn* during class time.

(i)   Will you see me sharp at 1 p.m.?

(j)   You are not going to see me ever again.

(k)   Can't you get used to the hostel life within a couple of days?

(l)   You would get used to my American pronunciation soon, wouldn't you? (suggestion type)

(m)   You ought to be more careful henceforth (suggestion)
          A   V

Analyse the sentences that employ USED TO and note the peculiarities:

1.   All of us   should **get** used to   the culture of a new college.
      S   A   V   A   O

Unlike in other cases, here the verb is placed in between the auxiliaries.

2.   You   shall   **become** used to the idiosyncrasies of the HOD of English
                 V

department in course of time."

3.   Won't we **be** used to the hostel life by next month?
            V

4.   You could get used to my peculiar accent, couldn't you?

(In the Q tag, we use the 'supporting auxiliary' and not USED TO)

Situations for which the Universal auxiliaries are to be used

DARE   - Use it where some courage or even defiance is called for.

NEED   - To be used where some absolute necessity is required.

KEEP   - Used for a continuing action or an action that does not come to an end or we never think of the end of certain actions.

(Others have been covered in Chapter 4)

Exercise

Answer the following questions in the affirmative:

1.   In which college ground, do we play the semi final match this evening?

2.   Do all your teachers sit in the library hall during the lunch recess?

3.   How does Ramanujam know my brother?

4.   When does your servant maid buy the vegetables from the market?

5.   Chandran always takes help from me in Mathematics, doesn't he?

6.   Who live in the coastal area?

7.   Who lives next to you in your colony?

8.   How do the foreign students convey their demand to a shop keeper ?

9. Don't the students from Nepal talk in sign language often with a shop keeper in Chennai?
10. Whom do you like most in your college?

Answer in the negative. Your answer may be in any suitable tense out of the Present family:

11. Does Preeti sleep on the first floor?
12. Why do some lady students do badly in the Tamil language paper?
13. Don't these books belong to the II year students?
14. Does your cousin know cooking?
15. Shouldn't you visit the Thiruverkadu temple some time?
16. Don't you hear some strange noise through that window?
17. Do my father and your uncle ever talk with your parents?
18. Why wouldn't this child cry now?
19. Isn't your final examination in March"
20. Do you have your final examination in March or April?

Give affirmative and negative answers:

21. Would you help your mother in the housework?
22. Must some of your friends always disobey the college rules?
23. Wouldn't our small son get used to the new ayah within a week?
24. Who could sing well in this class?
25. Who are the good singers in your class?
26. Need all hostel children get a locker each?

Locate the mistake if any in the following sentences and rewrite the concerned sentence where necessary:

27. Mohana do not talk to you.
28. Subramaniam does not entertain anyone, doesn't he?
29. The Sun do rise in the East.
30. Where does you buy your shoes from?
31. My history lecturer does comes to my house once in a while.
32. Don't you has two sisters?
33. Ramudu and Selvam owns this house.
34. Don't careless during your examination?
35. Do you have some spare pencil with you now?
36. I do has three pencil.
37. There is some pencils in my bag.
38. Sudhir isn't use his own cycle to college.
39. When is your mother take rest?
40. Meena and Mumtaz does love us very much.
41. Who do not know the National anthem?
42. Who does not know this person on the dais?

Analyse the following sentences and identify every word in each part of the sentence:

43. Some children are fond of stories.
44. Surely, many children would not like sandwiches for lunch, would they?
45. Aren't we all getting used to pure vegetarian food?
46. Besides these friends, you have two more in the other section, don't you?
47. One man, his son and his school friend must be waiting outside our house now.
48. He must be a man of great fame and name.
49. When evening comes, all birds would go to their nest.
50. Don't keep coming to my house in the morning time.
51. Madanlal and his friend Joseph are always after the I year lady students during the lunch recess.
52. Do you dare go out in the dark all by yourself?
53. Your girl friend could get used to friendship with other men students also.
54. Doesn't Soundarya keep meeting you in the afternoons?
55. Will you get used to my words of command during the drill period?

State which sentences belong to the routine actions and which to orders/suggestions/acknowledgement?

56. We play cricket only on Sunday mornings.
57. Don't you ever play cricket during holidays?
58. Why don't you talk nicely with your classmates?
59. You shouldn't tell lies.
60. You may leave my office now.
61. My intimate friend doesn't believe my statements.
62. Are you going to the library?
63. Is it raining outside?
64. You do keep taking drugs once in a while, don't you?
65. You see a tall man over there, don't you?
66. We don't belong to the SC community.
67. Need I advise you any more?
68. You ought to work harder in this office.
69. Shouldn't you be more gentle with this puppy dog?
70. Can you collect some firewood from the nearby forest?
71. You may not like everybody in this house.
72. Must you keep troubling me for help every now and then?
73. Wouldn't you accompany me in my morning jogging?
74. Could you keep walking behind me during my morning constitutional?
75. You ought not to be used to bad company in this college.

Give emphatic affirmative answers:

76. Do you all know some yoga exercises?
77. What does this new coach teach you all ?

78. Does Padmanabiah criticise your work?
79. When do you revise all your lessons?
80. Where does the English professor live in this colony?
81. Doesn't Nisha throw stones frequently at stray dogs?

Write the remaining 6 categories of sentences for the following statements:

82   Mustn't you get used to your new Head of Department pretty fast?
83   You dare not keep visiting me every day, dare you?
84   We could meet your friend in the hospital this evening.
85   You should not violate the college rules and conventions.

Chapter 6

MORE ABOUT PRONOUNS

Objective pronouns

The pure objective pronouns are - ME, US, YOU, HIM, HER, THEM. We use these only in the Object part of a Simple sentence. But, we can use US, and THEM in the Subject part, in which case we must precede these objective pronouns with any of the phrases shown below:

All of / Any of / Some of / Many of/ Most of / One of / None of.... US.
All of / Any of / Some of /Many of / Most of / One of ./ None of .... THEM

Here are some examples:

a1. One of **us** visits some patients in the local hospital. (Subject is singular)

a1. Most of **us** cannot converse in Telugu in this class.

a2. None of **them** fights back

Q . Does any of **us / them** recognise this old man?

When we use an *objective pronoun* in the object part, it can be preceded by a preposition as shown below:

a1. Many students in this class   work   **against (or, without)** me.
         S   (A)V   O

a2. Some members of your group   actually   belong   **to** me.
         S   Adv   (A)V   O

The same rule does not hold good when we use a subjective pronoun in the subject part. It will then be a single word only.

Demonstrative pronouns

When we want to point at something, we invariably have to use our index finger to show the item. In other words we have to *demonstrate* with a finger or the hand. Hence the name "Demonstrative pronouns". They are,

THIS, THAT   - for singular nouns.

THESE, THOSE - for plural nouns.

SUCH   -   For singular or plural nouns.

You can place the **Demonstrative pronouns** in the Subject part or Object part as shown in the examples given below:

This is my pen.
This would not be sufficient for so many of us.
I love **those**.

You shouldn't keep **these** on the balcony.
Those could be the braver boys in our school.
Such would be my fate.
Boys **such** as you, should not volunteer for any tough work.
Don't you know **that**?
What is **this**?
Whose book is **this**?

Since these are pronouns we must refer to them by the sign language. But, don't use them before a noun. In which case, they will become adjectives. Here are the examples

This boy   is   very clever.
    S   A.V   C

In this sentence, the real subjective noun is "boy". The word "this" describes the noun.

Those children live near my house.
      S   (A)V   C
You mustn't condemn such children at all.
 S   Neg A   V   O   C
Don't keep company with   these children.
Neg A   V   O   O

Use of possessive pronouns

The possessive pronouns are - MY, OUR, YOUR, HIS, HER, ITS, THEIR. We use them in association with a Common noun. We cannot use a possessive pronoun by itself in a sentence. It is not an independent word. It must be always to the left side of any common noun as shown below:

MY book, YOUR mother, HIS cycle, HER son, THEIR children.

There can be an adjective also before the noun like this,

MY precious child, YOUR naughty son, THEIR private property.

Once a possessive pronoun is coupled with a common noun (with or without an adjective) we may use the combination in the Subject part or Object part of a sentence. Study the following sentences:

OUR students would not quarrel with YOUR students.
      S   Neg A   V   O
HIS sister is   very friendly with   OUR daughter.
    S   A.V   C   O
THEIR bright idea cannot   succeed   with MY average students.
       S   Neg A   V   O

Possessive nouns

All possessive pronouns have corresponding nouns for the simple reason that they are not independent words; they must be coupled to any common noun. We can convert a possessive pronoun into its corresponding "possessive noun form." The peculiar thing here is that the noun used can be a Common noun or Proper noun. Here are the examples:

Proper noun case

This is his book = This is **Krishnamurthy's** book. (For a possessive noun, we use an "apostrophe sign and the letter 's' to the noun". The symbol is pronounced as "apostrophe s"- Krishnamurthy, apostrophe s.

Raman's watch is always slow. (His watch is always slow)
Leela's sister is a pretty little girl.

When a Proper Noun is in plural form or ends in letter 's', we use the apostrophe after the 's' like this,

The Daniels' house is over there (See Chapter 1 - Articles).
The Krishnans' daughter is a clever girl.
Ramdoss' brother is ill.
Moses' house is a fine one.

Common noun case

This is a **girl's** book.
The **town's** population is very small.

When the common noun concerned is in plural form, the apostrophe s is placed after the plural **s** or **es** or **ies.** If the noun is a collective noun, no change is required in using the apostrophe s. Here are the examples:

The boys' book
The students' performance.
The boxes' size is very big.
The watches' hands are small.
The thieves' accomplices are missing.
The cities' fathers are generous persons.

The children's mother is here now.
The audience's behaviour was reprehensible.

Indefinite pronouns

The next type is **indefinite pronouns.** When we refer to persons or things in a general way and not directed at any particular person or thing, we use the indefinite pronouns which are - ONE, THEY, ALL, A FEW, FEW, OTHERS and MANY.

We use them in the following manner:

One cannot be a master of all trades. (ONE refers to any person)

They may say all sorts of things about you. (THEY refer to plural persons in general and not to any particular group)

All attended the closing ceremony.

Be kind to **all**.

A few tickets only are available. (A FEW means, a very small number)

The animals we saw were only **a few.**

Few take interest in politics these days. (FEW means, nearly none)

Always do good to **others**.

Many speak good English in India.

I do not know **many** in this group.

O

Except for THEY and FEW, we can use the rest as Subject or Object. THEY and FEW are fit only for the subject part. Do note that they are independent pronouns and do not point to any noun used before.

Exercise

1. Can you use objective pronouns in the subject part? If yes, give examples.
2. Which objective pronouns we cannot use in the subject part?
3. Write sentences using the indefinite pronouns ONE, FEW and MANY as Subject.
4. Can you use the following indefinite pronouns in the object part: THEY, FEW.
5. When will a demonstrative pronoun become an adjective? Give examples.
6. Can you use a possessive pronoun in the Subject and Object part? Give examples.

Use suitable possessive nouns in the following sentences.

7. The boy's sister is too young.
8. The teacher's mood could be bad today.
9. My mother's left hand is in plaster now.
10. Your parents' names don't appear in the invitation list.
11. Our cat's tail is very bushy. (Name of the cat is, BROWNIE)

Locate the mistake if any and rewrite the wrong sentences:

12. We and them do not buy vegetables from this shop.
13. Are all of they our school boys?
14. Isn't that your book?
15. Surely this book is his, doesn't it?
16. Our teacher scolds they very strongly.
17. My elder sister is looking after mine small sister today.
18. This boy's car driver are rough with the car.
19. Madans marks are low in History.
20. My wishes are for all.

Distributive pronouns

The next type is **Distributive pronouns.** They are, EACH, EITHER and NEITHER. These pronouns refer to persons or things taken one at a time from a group. EACH refers to everyone in a group but taken singly. EITHER means, the one or the other of two persons or two things. NEITHER mean, not the one and not the other of two. Here are the examples:

Each of these boxes costs Rs 250.00
Either of you only may come with me to the meeting. (Only one of the 2 persons)
Neither of the reports is true. The match is a draw.

When we use EITHER or NEITHER, the verb should always be singular.

Reciprocal pronouns

Reciprocal pronouns are also called **Compound pronouns.** They are EACH OTHER and ONE ANOTHER. Here are the examples on how to use them:

The two cousin brothers might hate **each other**.
The thieves could cheat **one another**.

The two sentences shown above are grammatically wrong because EACH or ONE is to be used only in the Subject part and OTHER or ANOTHER in the object part. Therefore we should write the above sentences like this,

Each cousin hates the **other.**
Each sister quarrels with the **others**.
One thief cheats **another**.

But in practice, people use these compound pronouns together as shown in the first examples. And the English world seems to have accepted such aberrations.

Use of the second possessive pronouns

The table of PRONOUNS in Chapter 1, shows a second set of **possessive pronouns.** They are - MINE, OURS, YOURS, HERS, THEIRS. This is the way we use these:

1. (a) This is **my** book.
    (b) This book is **mine**.

2. (a) Those are **our** soaps?
    (b) Those soaps are **ours**?

3. (a) Isn't this **your** pencil?
    (b) Isn't this pencil **yours**?

4. (a) This was **her** house till last year.
    (b) This house was **hers** till last year.

5. (a) Those weren't **their** achievements at all.
    (b) Those achievements weren't **theirs** at all.

6. (a) Your friend will be **my** friend too.
    (b) Your friend will be **mine** too.

7. (a) Your parents could be **their** parents too.
    (b) Your parents could be **theirs/ours/hers** too.

8. (a) Our house would have been his house.
    (b) **Ours** would have been his house.

9. **Yours** cannot be as big as my house.

10. **Hers** must not be your policy as well.

Shall we analyse some sentences and see what rules have been followed here?

Those soaps   are   ours.
  S   A.V   O

(OURS here passes the 'object test' - Those soaps are WHOSE?)

This house was   hers · till last year.
  S   A.V   O   C

Ours has not become an abandoned house.
S Neg. A   V   O

Hers should not be as big a house as theirs.
 S   NegA   V   O

After a thorough scrutiny the following points will be noticeable:

(i)   The statements with the second set of possessive pronouns sound very emphatic indeed. So, we may name them "emphatic possessive pronouns."

(ii)   We could make such emphatic statements in any tense but with BE as the verb or as A.V in it.

(iii) While the normal possessives attached to a noun can be in the Subject or Object parts, an emphatic possessive is on its own i.e. without attaching itself to any noun.

(iv)   When so used, the emphatic possessives become OBJECT in the sentence. All of them pass the 'object test'. As Object, they become 'objective pronouns', don't they? So then, do they have a dual personality? That is, they could be possessive pronouns and also objective pronouns? This inter -pretation is correct. You take them as either in your sentence analysis.

(v)   Similarly we can use these pronouns as 'subject' also. In which case, we could call it "subjective pronoun" as well.

(vi)   It is essential that a sentence has an object. Without an object, the sentence cannot be rewritten in the emphatic possessive form.

(vi)   The second possessive pronouns (MINE, OURS, YOURS, HIS, HERS and THEIRS are interesting pronouns. They are not only possessive pronouns but we can use them also as "Objective and Subjective pronouns" also.

Reflexive pronouns

We can give emphatic statements in another way as well. If you add the words -**self** to the normal possessive pronouns MY, YOUR, HIM, HER, IT and the words - **selves** to OUR, YOUR and THEM they become known as **Reflexive pronouns.**

By adding **self** or **selves** to some of the possessive pronouns, the action done by the Subject reflects back upon the subject and turns emphatic. Study the following examples:

I saw it **myself**.

You will ruin **yourself**.

This boy completed the work **himself**.

My mother stitched this skirt **herself**.

The parrot hurt **itself** inside the cage.

We witnessed the incident **ourselves**.

The children shall go to school by **themselves**.

One day you will regret this decision **yourselves**.

We **ourselves** went to the site of the accident.

I **myself** am a busy person.

Analyse some sentences:

You   will   ruin   **yourself**.
S   A   V   O

The parrot   hurt   **itself**   inside the cage.
      S   (A)V   O   C

I   **myself**   am   a busy person.
S   O1   A.V   O2

No matter where you position the reflexive pronoun, it becomes the object in a Simple sentence. As object, we can call it an 'objective pronoun' as well, can't we? Thus, we cannot use any reflexive pronoun in the subject part at all as if it were a 'subjective pronoun'. Yet, you will hear some people use sentence such as, "Myself and Somu went to a cinema theatre." This is bad English.

Exercise

Correct the mistake(s) if any in the following sentences and rewrite them:

1.   Could we be our own enemies at times?

2. You and me must sit together on the same bench in the class.
3. Yourself and Banerjee are not very helpful students, are you?
4. We don't interfere in other people affairs.
5. Surendran is mine class monitor.
6. Won't ours be at least the second best drama in the final competition?
7. Do your best and the prize would certainly be your.
8. Didn't you reserve our seat on this train ourselves?
9. Should every good praise go to hers only?
10. If the first prize is not their, it should be yours.
11. Sumitra and me are going for a movie just now.
12. Ram keeps talking during every lecture doesn't he?
13. Many of we do not express ourselves well in good English.
14. His books cannot be your.
15. Sometimes, some of we, are not ourselves in a difficult situation.

Analyse the following sentences:

16. Kolkata itself is not equal to New Delhi in all respects.
17. Our HOD and your English Lecturer have their home in Geetha colony, haven't they?
18. Yours is not a big house like ours is.
19. One ought not to feel jealous of others.
20. Many would take part in the Entrance examination but only a few could through.

Convert the following into emphatic sentences in Simple present:

(Tip: Universal auxiliaries could be emphatic too besides EQs)

21. Do this job.
22. Don't come to my house.
23. Do you write poetry?
24. Swim in the sea.
25. All of you go to the library.
26. This is my school tie. Don't touch it.
27. Surely, this is not Swarna's house?
28. This is our cycle.
29. Isn't this your pen?
30. All our friends are not your friends.

Analyse the following sentences:

31. We ourselves would witness your performance from our flat.
32. These books couldn't be yours.
33. Some of us wouldn't be attending your extra classes, Sir.
34. Mine is the best painting in this exhibition.
35. You do keep some pets in your house, don't you?

36. One must be very punctilious about their dress.
37. They say many bad things about you.
38. He and I are partners in this venture.
39. You ought not to be everyone's advisor.
40. The Davids' house is over there.

Chapter 7

ADJECTIVES

General

In Chapter 2, we learnt how to analyse a Simple sentence i.e, breaking a sentence into its component parts. We also learnt that the Subject and Object/Complement parts of a sentence may contain words of all parts of speech except auxiliary and verb. Therefore, you must acquire a high level of competence in identifying every word in terms of its parts of speech in S and O/C. Unless you are thorough in it, you wouldn't know why a particular word has been used and for what purpose. In this Chapter we shall learn how to identify the **adjectives**.

In Chapter 1 we learnt that adjective is a word that (i) describes a noun in some way and (ii) is always placed to the immediate left of a noun. We recognise an adjective by the above two conditions. Incidentally, adjectives add colour to the nouns! If you write a noun in a sentence without adjectives, it may sound insipid.

Adjectives do not have any stamp mark as adjectives. Some are natural adjectives like, LONG, SMALL, BEAUTIFUL, BRIGHT, DULL, BIG, LARGE, SHORT, NICE, TALL and so on. Further, we can use words of other parts of speech also as adjectives.

Use of other parts of speech as adjectives

In terms of the conditions, could we say that any word found to the left of a noun will be an adjective? The answer is 'yes'. Incidentally, only three types of words will be to the left side of a noun. They are, an article, a possessive pronoun or an adjective. If you can isolate the article and possessive pronoun (It is easy to pick out an article and a possessive pronoun too) the word remaining will indeed be an adjective.

Exercise

Identify the adjectives in the following sentences:

1. Ramanujam is not my brother.
2. Isn't Vandana your neighbour?
3. We have some oranges in our bag.
4. Do you have any objection for this person?
5. Leela is a nice girl.
6. Smart boys are easily traceable anywhere.
7. A child more often than not is always a mischievous being.
8. The winners are over there.
9. Our friends are not your friends.
10. There are some maidens in our college in every group.

Apart from the natural adjectives, we could use many words to do the job of adjectives. The condition is that it should be to the left of a noun and should not be an article or possessive pronoun.

Demonstrative pronouns as adjectives

Study the following examples:

(a) **This** boy acts like a grown up adult.
(b) **These** grapes are very sweet.
(c) **That** teacher is ours.
(d) Do not touch **those** books.
(e) **These** elders are honest people. We cannot find **such** people everywhere.
(f) Bring **that** gent to my office immediately.

All the words in **bold** are Demonstrative pronouns but they are doing the job of adjectives because they are describing a noun in some way.

Interrogatives as adjectives

The following examples show that we can use some of the interrogative pronouns also as adjectives:

(a) **What** time is it now?
(b) **Which** lady student stood first in your class?
(c) **Whose** house is this?

Nouns as adjectives

We can use some nouns also as adjectives like this:

(a) Aren't they the **seventh standard** students?
(b) The **Tamil Nadu** express is running late by one hour.
(c) Isn't there a famous **tailor** shop in this lane?
(d) **Ten** students from our colony do not return home from college before 5 p.m.
(e) **College** boys are quite clever.

Verbs as adjectives

We may use quite a few PP verbs and continuous verbs also as adjectives as shown in the following examples:

(a) Do you see a **hanging** garden over there?
(b) My aunt is a **loving** mother.
(c) The **waiting** passengers do not have any hope of travelling today.
(d) Isn't your elder sister a **married** woman now?
(e) These **reserved** seats are for the VIPs.
(f) A **barking** puppy seldom bites anyone.
(g) The **running** train came to a stop after a long time.
(h) Aren't you a **blessed** person in your community?
(i) Kannan is a **daring** fighter. ·
(j) Is this your own book or a **borrowed** book?
(k) I don't read **uninteresting** news items in the daily newspaper.

Articles as adjectives

We know that SOME, ANY, MANY and ALL are articles which we use for small *numbers*. These also can be adjectives if we use them to describe a noun. Study the following examples:

(a)   Our class monitor is eating **some** mangoes in that corner.

(b)   **Many** Indians do not worship in any temple.

(d)   Does **any** student understand Urdu in this class?

(e)   Don't summon **all** candidates but only the selected candidates.

Analysing a long sentence

My village headman, his young charming daughter and   his tall son   are

                   S   A

staying   in   that little house   along with all their   loving friends.

    V   C   O

Now, identify all the adjectives in the S, O and C parts:

Subject	- village, young, charming, tall
Object	- all, loving
Complement	- that, little

It is permissible to use two adjectives together with or without "and" between them. You could see such an example in the above long sentence - "young, charming." We could also write them as, "young and charming".

To summarise,

Though some words have a natural identity as **adjectives,** we could make use of words of other parts of speech also to do the job of adjectives. Accordingly, if you find a word to the left of a noun and it is not an article or possessive pronoun, you must look at it as a word doing the job of an adjective.

But, if there is NO noun to the right side of an ADJECTIVE and the word itself looks like a natural adjective, don't think it is an adjective. It may be doing the job of an adverb! So, before calling a word an adjective make sure that it fulfils the two conditions discussed in this Chapter.

We use adjectives only in the Subject or Object/Complement parts of a Simple sentence.

Exercise

Fill up each blank with a suitable adjective:

1. This is not a big matter at all.
2. Has Shanmugam any logical reason for scoring such low marks in English?

3. Isn't Paul a person of *great* ambition?
4. Aren't all the girls of St Paul's school wearing *beautiful* ....sarees today?
5. Today is a *bright* day, isn't it?
6. This mother has a ......story about her life. *intresting*
7. Mohini is a *great* Bharatanatyam dancer, isn't she?
8. Take Ajay in your Chess team. He is a *best* player in Chess.
9. Don't you ever find yourself in any *complicated* situations?
10. How many students read Dennis the <u>Menace</u> comics? Only *some* ..... boys do, Sir.

Identify the adjective(s) in the following sentences:

11. Soundarya is a <u>clever and modest</u> student in my class.
12. Doesn't your cousin brother <u>resemble</u> you very much?
13. Before any general strike, stock yourself with <u>adequate</u> kitchen materials.
14. Do you call this person an <u>angry young</u> man?
15. You do find <u>many good</u> teachers in English these days, don't you?
16. These are <u>faded</u> shirts; change them at once.
17. Johnson is not a <u>ferocious</u> fighter.
18. The competing teams are <u>meeting</u> in the National- stadium today.
19. We want two <u>suitable</u> players in our B team.
20. Don't buy <u>this</u> hockey stick but take that one.
21. Aren't there <u>many</u> candidates this morning for one lone post?
22. Those <u>green-looking</u> oranges are sour but they are nice-looking ones, aren't they?
23. Don't discard them as such; <u>such</u> persons would be useful to you <u>some</u> day.
24. We do experience <u>some</u> April showers in Chennai.
25. Five boys and six girls live on this road near our <u>big</u> hostel.

Use a suitable adjective in the blank other than the conventional adjectives:

26. Is your aunt a *old* .... lady?
27. Narendran is a *famous* politician, isn't he?
28. The *all* .....employees want a meeting with you immediately, Sir.
29. These *reserved* seats are for the VIPs.
30. Maragatham is .... baby-sitter. *easy going*
31. They don't allow *small* children in a college function.
32. Admission for the *nursery* class in this nursery school closes today.
33. Of the 10 women in this class, *some* students secured distinction in English.
34. *Those* ... dogs run away if you throw a stone at them.
35. A *sons* father is at the gate looking for his son, Sir.

Fill up the blank with a suitable 'demonstrative' or 'article' adjective:

36. *Which* pen do you like in this lot?
36. I invite her *several* times in a year but she never turns up.
37. You take *all* item or nothing.
38. In *this* ... house are you residing nowadays?

39. This foolish person loses . ⌐⌐ wealth of his in every horse racing season.
40. ..These. students usually fail in any entrance examination.

Degrees of Adjectives

All the adjectives found in the examples given above are said to be in POSITIVE degree.

We can use every natural adjective in two more degrees - COMPARATIVE and SUPERLATIVE.

Comparative degree

Adjectives deal with 'quality'. The quality of two adjectives may not be exactly equal; there would be some difference between them. To highlight that difference only, we use the comparative degree like this,

(a) Mahesh is a **cleverer** student than Saravanan is.
(b) Manjula was a **smarter** woman last year than Sangeetha was.
(c) This boy is a **shorter** person than Lakshman is.
(d) Isn't this little girl wearing a **costlier** dress than the other one over there is wearing?

Examine the four sentences given above. You will notice the following points:

(i) we have used the letters **er** or **ier** to the positive degree adjectives to convert them into comparative degree.

(ii) every comparative degree adjective is followed by a noun. (If there is no noun, the word will not be an adjective. Recall the conditions for identifying and adjective)

(iii) all sentences are 'Complex sentences' with **than** acting as conjunction. (You would also locate 2 sets of S-A-V's in each sentence. We shall learn Complex sentence in greater detail in a later lesson.)

If a comparative degree sentence is written in the way shown below, it will be a wrong sentence. Why?

"Manjula was smarter than Sangeetha was."

Because the word 'smarter' is not describing any noun. 'Smarter' is not doing the job of an adjective at all. Therefore make sure that a noun is always present after the adjective, whether it is in the Positive degree or Comparative degree.

So long as you remember that a comparative degree sentence is a Complex sentence, you may silence the 'V' in the second sentence and write them like this,

"Mahesh is a cleverer student that Saravanan"
"Manjula is a smarter woman than Sangeetha"

In the second sentence, if you have to use a pronoun, it must be a "Subjective pronoun" and never an objective pronoun.

"This boy is a shorter person than <u>he</u>."

"Isn't this girl wearing a costlier dress than <u>she</u> over there"

We add the letters **er** or **ier** only to the single syllabled positive adjectives. For the multi-syllable words we use MORE or LESS before it, like this,

Positive	*Comparative*
Sweet	Sweeter
Happy	Happier
Brave	Braver
Sad	Sadder
Bright	Brighter
Abnormal	More abnormal
Cheerful	More cheerful
Favourable	More favourable
Troublesome	More troublesome
Useful	More useful
Beautiful	Less beautiful
Handsome	Less handsome
Expensive	Less expensive

(e) In this factory, Kumaran is a **more productive** worker than the others.

(f) At the reception counter, you need to be a **more courteous** person than others.

(g) Wouldn't this condition be a **more favourable** one for us than those.

(h) Surely, this shirt is a **less expensive** one than the other, isn't it?

(i) Krishnan is a **less aggressive** player than Lakshmanan.

<u>Note</u>: The method of arriving at the comparative degree by adding letters **er, ier, more,** and **less** is applicable only for the natural positive adjectives. We cannot adopt this method for the *derived* adjectives out of NOUN, VERBS, PRONOUNS, INTERROGATIVES.

Superlative degree

When we look for quality in a group of persons or things, one of them will turn out to be the topmost; far superior to others. We use the superlative degree for such person or thing. Study the following examples:

(a) Sudarshan is **the best** student in my class.

(b) This restaurant in this area serves **the best** coffee.

(c) Is Sarojini **the most beautiful** lady student in your college?

(d) Mohammed scored **the least** marks in Mathematics.

(e) Ranganathan is **the most extravagant** money spender in our group.

(f)   Murugan is **the least known** peon in our school.

(g)   Sunitha is **the sweetest** child in the baby class.

(h)   Here comes **the bravest** student of the Fourth semester.

What have we done? We have added the letters **est** to the positive adjectives, **the most** or **the least** to the multi-syllable type positives to derive the superlative degree. We must use the definite article **the** before a superlative adjective.

The following sentences are wrong. State why?

1.   Ramachandran is the cleverest in my class.
2.   He is running the fastest in the track events.
3.   Chandran is fattest boy in the plus 2 class.

The errors are : the superlative does not describe any noun or a noun is absent after the superlative in 1 and 2. In sentence 3, the article **the** is missing before the superlative.

In our effort to spot out the topmost, we may find more than one person or thing come into the topmost slot. In other words, say five or more persons score the same marks in the quality test. How do we describe such a situation. We do it in the following manner:

(j)   Shakuntala is **one of the cleverest** students in my class.

(k)   Mukundan is **one of the fastest** runners among all the schools in the city.

(l)   Isn't Rabindranath Tagore **one of the greatest** poets of the 20th century?

(m)   Tokyo is **one of the most crowded** cities in the world.

(n)   **One of the best** play back singers of Tamil films is present at our school function today.

(o)   Isn't Adityan **one of the most** wanted hockey players in our city?

(p)   There goes **one of the best** demonstrators of this college.

In the above examples, we have followed one additional rule in composing the superlatives. What is it?

"One of the ...." is a singular subject. Therefore, we must use a singular verb. The noun used after "one of the ...." must be always in plural. To say, "One of the greatest poet" will be wrong.

Exceptions

We derive the comparative degree by adding some extra letters or words to the original positive adjective. This is not the case with all adjectives. For certain adjectives, the comparative and superlative are totally new words without any relationship with the original positive adjective. Such however, are only a few. They are as follows:

Positive	*Comparative*	*Superlative*
Good	Better	Best
Bad, Evil, Ill	Worse	Worst

Positive	Comparative	Superlative
Little	Less, Lesser	Least
Far	Farther	Farthest
Much	More	Most
Many	More	Most
Less	Lesser	Least

LESS is a peculiar word. We can use it as a comparative and also a positive. For example, "We have less money than he." Here, LESS is a comparative degree.

"We have less number of supporters." Here, LESS is a positive degree adjective.

To summarise

We can write every adjective under three categories. For the natural adjectives, we add the letters **er** or **ier** (to derive the comparative degree) and letters **est** (to derive the superlative) and for the multi syllable variety, we put before the positive **more** and **most** or **less** and **least**. We can use the *derived adjectives* in the positive degree only.

Exercise

Locate the mistake if any and rewrite the sentence:

1. Have you any more cheap shirts in your shop?
2. Your daughter has certainly done worse in this year's examinations.
3. Between you and Susheela who ran farthest distance?
4. Isn't Rekha a more prettier maiden than Shankari?
5. Your daughter has been more affectionate than him.
6. One of the basic rule in football is, "Kick the ball and not the player."
7. Matthew is best boxer in the Plus 2 sections.
8. Are you most senior student in this school?
9. Didn't Maniram do worst thing during today's match?
10. You are surely cleverer than your sister, aren't you?

Write the opposite with reference to the Adjectives:

11. Isn't this restaurant a more costly one than the others on this road?
12. Who is the worst dressed female in your class?
13. This is the least popular item in today's entertainment programme.
14. Venkataraghavan is one of the most popular umpires in the cricket world.
15. We don't have much money with us today.
16. These are the most genuine pearls in our shop.
17. This is not the longest river in the South.
18. We won't go to the nearby market today.
19. Good students seldom fail in any test.
20. Many children do not know swimming.

Convert the following positive degree sentences into comparative and superlative ones. You may make any assumptions in composing your sentences:

21.   They are not sweet mangoes at all.
22.   Sudhakaran is an intelligent student.
23.   Madhavi scored less marks this time.
24.   We won't spend much money on soft drinks today.
25.   He is a troublesome boy in this group, isn't he?

Use suitable verbal or noun type adjective in the blank:

26.   Is that person over there a ~~troublesome~~ man?
27.   Sundaram is a ~~famous~~ politician, isn't he?
28.   Of the 40 students in my class ~~the least~~ students got distinction in Mathematics.
29.   These are for the V.I.P. guests.
30.   The poor father lodged a complaint with the police about his missing son.

Fill up the blank with demonstrative adjectives (WHICH, WHOSE, NEXT, THIS, THAT, THESE, THOSE, OWN, VERY) or adjectives of quantity (MOST, SOME, ANY, MUCH , ALL , NO, ENOUGH, WHOLE, CERTAIN, SEVERAL, MANY) or, ordinary adjectives (SAME, SUCH, LESS):

31.   Which pen do you want out of this lot?
32.   Does your grandmother live in the Those house?
33.   NO students shall fail in any test.
34.   Whose house had burnt in the fire.
35.   That wonderful man had lost own wealth on silly business ventures.
36.   All are lucky in life.
37.   I have invited Shalini Several times but she declined it every time.
38.   People must mind their own business.
39.   Our tuition master stands …. nonsense from us.
40.   Don't praise her much; she hates such praises.
41.   Do you have any suggestions on this issue?
42.   There is too much sugar in my tea.
43.   Is this your own house or someone else's?
44.   Same route do you take for your office?
45.   In which house are you staying nowadays?

Chapter 8

ADVERBS

General

Unlike the adjectives, we will find ADVERBS mostly only in the Complement part of a Simple sentence. The Subject part may carry an adverb only if there is a *clause* in it. We shall learn about *clauses* in a later lesson.

We can use all the natural adjectives as adverbs. How then do we distinguish an adverb from an adjective? Although adverbs are supposed to amplify the meaning of a verb, the sure method of identifying it is only through the 'Complement or Adverb test' questions using the "Interrogative adverbs." (See Chapter 1). Do remember that an adverb or complement may appear anywhere in a sentence and not necessarily after the Verb. Except for the test questions, you may mistake an adverb for something else.

Complement /Adverb test

Study the following sentence and analyse it:

"These school children   are   great"
   S   A.V   ?

What is "great" here? It certainly is not an adjective because there is no NOUN to its right. But the word is the answer to the test question: "These school children are, HOW?" Therefore, 'great' is an adverb. (Frame the test questions always along with the S-A.V or S-A-V.)

Analyse the next sentence:

"Some children talk   big and stylishly"
    S   (A)V   ?

In this sentence, the group of words "big and stylishly" answer the test question HOW? Some children talk HOW? Since this is a group of words, we call it COMPLEMENT. The main word in a complement will be an adverb and words of all parts of speech may be supporting it, except Auxiliary and Verb.

The test question HOW will show adverbs of various types such as, Adverb of manner/quality, adverb of frequency (HOW often), adverb of degree (HOW much?), adverb of number (HOW many?), adverb of time (HOW long?) and adverb of distance (HOW far?) Do you see that the answers for the test questions HOW many, HOW long, HOW far, HOW often will be always **nouns?** For example,

5 girls   - HOW many?
2 days   - HOW long?
3 KM   - HOW far?
Twice   - HOW often?

So, it would appear that nouns could also turn out to be adverbs. Therefore, don't jump to the conclusion that every noun found in the O/C parts will be an object. Only the test question will show the true identity of any word.

Let us take the other two interrogative adverbs - WHEN and WHERE? Answers for these two test questions will always be **nouns,**

WHEN   -   morning, daytime, 8 a.m., now, afterwards, later

WHERE -   (any place) there, here, market, church, school, London, Chennai.

In fact no word other than a noun will answer the test question WHEN and WHERE? Thus, it would appear that more nouns would be doing the job of **adverbs** than words of *manner* and *quality* (TQ: HOW?)

Examine some typical sentences whose complement will contain various types of adverbs:

(a)   We don't go home   straight   after college hours.
               (place)   (manner)   (time)

(b)   The lady comes late   towards the evening.
               (time)   (time)

(c)   I visit Tajmahal at least   twice a month.
               (manner) (freq)   (time)

(d)   We get good mineral water only at a place deep in the Himalayan range.
                                  (Adverbs of manner and place)

(e)   The attendance at the rally is usually large and pompous.
                        (Adverbs of freq and quality)

(d)   I meet my friends   near the market.
               (Adv of place)

Exercise

Pick out the adverb(s) from the following sentences and state what type each is:

Don't ask him too many questions on his return home.

We are very grateful to you, Sir.

Isn't the price of this shirt a little too much?

Kannan works hard on every day of the week.

Our old uncle lives carefully and frugally.

Aren't these sums too difficult?

Every soldier does his duty obediently and sincerely according to his officer's orders.

Often we see a snake near the rose plants in the garden.

Many times, people make me feel bad and low.

Do this job well and properly.

Analyse the following sentences and underline the complement/adverb:

Quite a few hours are there <u>before twilight</u>.
Your timing of the shots is <u>always</u> perfect.
Everything happens all <u>at once</u>.
Suddenly he applies the brakes and <u>several times as well</u>.
Life is valuable <u>every day of the year</u>.
Davidson always scores the goals with <u>great accuracy</u>.
Victor is very <u>intelligent</u>.
In spite of some 50 years of independent life, India is still <u>developing</u>.
One must remain unmarried till the age of <u>21</u>.

Degrees in adverbs

Like the adjectives, we use the adverbs also in three degrees - POSITIVE, COMPARATIVE and SUPERLATIVE.

Positive degree

(a)   Susan sings **very well**. (Sings HOW?)
(b)   Isn't this little girl **very pretty**?
(c)   She gave this present to me **happily**.

Comparative degree

We frame the **adverb comparative** in exactly the same way as the adjective model but with some differences. We saw already that we can use all the natural adjectives as adverbs. An adjective becomes an adverb if there is no noun to its right. Study the following adverb comparatives:

(a)   Randhawa is **stronger** than Sandhu.
(b)   This boy does **better** in sports than that boy.
(c)   Sujatha surely is **prettier** than Jane.
(d)   Sujatha surely is **prettier** than her.
(e)   Aren't Radha's paintings **more attractive** than yours?
(f)   Mona is **more beautiful** than Archana, isn't she?

What are the differences between adverb comparatives and adjective comparatives? They are,

(i)   There is no noun after the comparative.
(ii) An adverb comparative is a Simple sentence. (The pronoun used at the end after **than** must be an objective pronoun and not subjective. See (d))

Thus we can rewrite all the adjective comparatives in the adverb comparative form incorporating the two differences. Here are some examples:

(g)	Madan has a softer voice than my brother (he)	- Adjective case
(gg)	Madan's voice is softer than my brother's (his)	- Adverb case
(h)	This boy eats more laddus than Robert (he)	- Adjective
(hh)	The laddus this boy eats are more than his.	- Adverb
(i)	Pandian is a cleverer student than I (am).	- Adjective case
(ii)	Pandian is cleverer than me.	- Adverb case
(j)	Chandran is a more obedient boy than Sundar (he)	- Adjective case
(jj)	Chandran is more obedient than Sundar (him)	- Adverb case

Equal quality

We have used adverb comparatives to bring out <u>the difference in quality between two nouns</u>. What if there is no difference in the quality between the two qualities? How do we express the exactness of quality between two nouns? This is done through the adverb phrase **as ... as** and in the Simple sentence form like this,

(a) Shakuntala sings as good as Madhuri.
(b) Manimaran is as poor as Sanjay. (him)
(c) Peter ran as fast as Carl Lewis in the 100 meters race.
(d) Doesn't Seema dance as nicely as her?
(e) Dharmaraj plays golf as delightfully as my brother.

What rules have we followed here?

(i) All are Simple sentences.
(ii) We have used the phrase, **"as ... as"** with an **adjective** or **adverb** in the middle.
(iii) All are a1 sentences. (There is no question of bringing out equality in a2 type sentences)

It is possible to use this phrase for non-equality type cases also. In which case the phrase will look more like a preposition phrase than adverb phrase. Examine the following sentences:

(f) Meet me in my office **as soon as** possible.
(g) He stood on the dais **as near as** possible with the chief guest.
(h) You may contact me as fast as necessary.

The phrase **as well as** is an exception and is to be used only as a parenthetical phrase as discussed later.

Note: Use the "as .. as" phrase only in Simple sentences. Accordingly, never use a subjective pronoun after "as ... as". In which case, the sentence will become a Complex sentence, the phrase **as ... as** turning into a conjunction.

Superlative degree

Superlative-adverb is a peculiar type. In some respects, we adopt the same rules as for superlative-adjectives and in some we introduce some modifications.

When we use a single syllable or simple adverb in superlative form, we follow the adjective pattern (but without describing or using any noun after the adverb) as shown below:

(a) This shop is **the best** in this area.
(b) Samuel is **the cleverest** in our college.
(c) The sweets available in this shop are **the worst**.
(d) Didn't we work **the hardest** for this final match?
(e) Ramesh's shopping list is **the smallest.**
(f) Our team turned out to be **the poorest.**

But, when we use a multi syllable-adverb along with MOST, the pattern is slightly different like this,

(g) Mohammed played **most admirably**.
(h) Savita was **least successful** in all her attempts.
(i) Yesterday's drama was **most enjoyable.**
(j) Our small sister behaved **most gracefully** in the birthday party.
(k) They were **most apologetic** towards me.
(l) This news item is **most revealing** indeed.

What is the difference? We don't use the article **the** before the adverb.

But, when we refer to more than one number of superlatives, we revert to the adjective-superlative pattern and yet with one small difference:

(m) This child is **one of the sweetest** in our creche. child care.
(n) Today is one of **the most memorable** in our life.
(o) This painting is **one of the best** seen by us this year.
(p) Rather strange that this song has turned out to be **one of the most popular**.

Have you spotted that small difference? In the adjective case, we use a plural noun in the phrase, "one of the greatest poets; one of the best cities" etc. But here, there is no 's' to indicate a plural noun. Again why? We add 's' to indicate plural number for NOUNS and not for plural ADVERBS!!

Use of MOST, MORE, MUCH, LESS, LEAST

We have been using the above words in the comparative degree form and superlative degree form. They are also independent words. We can use them as adjectives or adverbs in our day to day sentences like this,

(a) Who makes **most** mistakes in English spellings? (Adjective)

(b) **Most** intellectuals in India shun politics. (Adjective)

(c) Nowadays **most** of our time is spent on T.V. watching. (Adjective)

(d) Who is troubling you **most** in this school? (Adverb)

(e) Isn't this medicine **mostly** sugar and salt? (Adverb)

(f) We need **more** members in our club. (Adjective)

(g) Do you need **more** money? (Adjective)

(h) Don't you always ask for **more** and **more**? (Adverb)

(i) Where there is **more, more** claimants there will be. (The first one is an adverb and the second an adjective)

(j) Have you **much** money? (Adjective)

(k) I need so **much.** (Adverb)

(l) Doesn't Peter love that girl too **much**? (Adverb)

(m) You need **less** friends in this colony. (Adjective)

(n) The **less** you have, the happier you will be. (Adverb)

(o) Work more and talk **less.** (Adverb)

(p) This is the **least** you could do for us. (Adverb)

(q) You give the **least** donation for our cause. (Adjective)

Use of AS WELL AS

We cannot use this phrase to bring out total equality nor will it sound like a preposition phrase when used in a sentence. Study the following examples:

(a) He is intelligent **as well as** honest in all his dealings with the public.

(b) Radha, her friend **as well as** a few girls from our colony visited the stadium today.

Does the adverb phrase show any equality of qualities or does it act as a preposition? Neither. It stands for a meaning "also". So, why not use "also" instead of **as well as**?

As well as is a parenthetical clause (supposedly placed inside brackets); and is to be used only in the Subject part of a sentence as shown below:

(c) The Minister, as well as his staffs, is addressing a mammoth meeting now.

The real subject in the sentence above is, "The Minister" which is a singular noun. The parenthetical clause - as well his staffs - has no influence on the selection of the verb. The verb to be chosen would depend entirely on the number of the real subject only.

The Prime Minister, as well as his cabinet colleagues, *arrives* in the city today.

The departmental head, as well as the Principal, *is* present here.

Exercise

Identify the objects and adverbs/complements in the following sentences:

1. I myself leave him at the railway station daily.
2. He expresses himself very clearly.
3. Somebody had stolen my watch yesterday.
4. My old class friend came to my house yesterday.
5. Don't talk like a saint from the Himalayas.
6. Are you wiser than King Solomon?
7. I am always correct in my judgement of other people.
8. This task is very simple indeed.
9. You must never repeat such mistakes ever.
10. Isn't this too little?

Adjectives are shown in italics in the following sentences. Modify the sentences using them as adverbs:

11. Ramola is a *mentally retarded* child.
12. Have you seen a *better* photograph than this one?
13. Wasn't Leela the *most cheerful* performer in yesterday's play?
14. Madubala is a *passionate* lover of dogs.
15. Didn't we get a *warm* welcome in the nearby college?

Correct the mistake(s) if any in the following adverb-comparatives and adverb-superlatives:

16. Our class students are smarter young men than them.
17. You are a more courageous player than him.
18. This young lady is the cleverest student in Mechanical engineering, third semester.
19. Your house mangoes are more sweeter than they.
20. In yesterday's social, Jemima was the most attractive.
21. He gave me the lesser money than he.
22. This exhibition has been one of the greatests.
23. Isn't this book the least expensive one in this stall?
24. Yours is a prettier child than hers.
25. The smarter people will get along well in life.
26. Isn't Gopaldoss one of the eminent person in this State?
27. This book isn't as good as the other one is.
28. As an Arts college, we are more progressive than the other colleges are.
29. This is the best essay so far.
30. You will get more marks if you make less mistakes.

Rewrite the following low level sentences with appropriate adverb phrases:

31. Ragini and Soundarrajan scored equal marks in the English II paper.

as well as.

32.   The singing standard of Vijji and Soundarya is exactly the same.
33.   I can run at the same speed as you. *well as.*
34.   Both of you were equally graceful in the party last evening. *as well as*
35.   You and Shakuntala are both pretty girls.

Rewrite the following adjective-superlatives as adverb-superlatives:

36.   We have produced in our college the best orators.
37.   The ice cream you get from this vendor is one of the worst ice creams in town.
38.   Monica is the sweetest child any mother has produced.
39.   English is my most favourite subject during this year.
40.   Tell me the shortest way to the station from here.
41.   The other day I walked the farthest distance.
42.   Kandaswamy is the senior most student in our class.
43.   Edward is one of the most hardworking students in our class.
44.   The nearest place to my house is a tailor's shop.
45.   This box contains the least mangoes.

Analyse the following sentences:

46.   Radha's sisters, as well as my elder sister, have arrived at the airport now.
47.   A mere remark from the Professor would not make you academically dull.

Write the remaining 6 categories of sentences for the following statements:

48.   Doesn't Samuel score as high marks as Jennifer?
49.   Rachel is most beautiful in the Fourth semester.
50.   Soundari is one of the poorest in our college, isn't she?

Chapter 9

PREPOSITION

General

Preposition is another word you will find in the Subject and/or Object part of a Simple sentence.

We may define **Preposition** as a word that shows the true relationship between any two words. Put in another way, but for prepositions we may not know the correct relationship between any two words or there may be several possible relationships between those two words.

Take the following sentence:

A cat is ...... the wall.

What is the relationship (or connection) between CAT and WALL. Does the sentence tell us precisely what it is? If we put some words in the blank, we may get several possible meanings like this,

(a)   A cat is **near** the wall.
(b)   A cat is **above** the wall.
(c)   A cat is **under** the wall.
(d)   A cat is **over** the wall.
(e)   A cat is **behind** the wall.
(f)   A cat is **on** the wall.
(g)   A cat is **at** the wall.
(h)   A cat is **inside** the wall.
(i)   A cat is **outside** the wall.
(j)   A cat is **below** the wall.
(k)   A cat is **after** the wall.
(l)   A cat is **before** the wall.

Every word in **bold** gives a different picture of the cat and the wall. All the sentences appear to be meaningful too. So, the conclusion is that in order to get the correct relationship (connection or link) between any two words, we must use a proper connecting word. That connecting word is called **Preposition.** And the two words could be,

The relationship between   a noun and a noun
a pronoun and a pronoun
a noun and a pronoun
a verb and a noun/pronoun
an adjective/adverb and a noun/pronoun

The examples given above refer to two nouns (cat and wall). Here are some examples between a verb and noun/pronoun :

(m) I go **to** your house.

(n) I come **from** your house.

(o) I don't come **near** your house.

(p) I am coming **into** it.

(q) He is coming **through** it.

The next case is the use of prepositions between an adjective/adverb and a noun:

(r) Manuel is happy **with** me.

(s) She is unhappy **without** me.

(t) We are helpful **because** of you.

(u) She is wild **on** me.

(v) My Professor is always nice **to** me.

So, could we then say that without a preposition, the Subject part or Object part of a sentence may not convey any meaning? Or, if the correct preposition is not used, a sentence may convey a wrong meaning? Both statements are true.

Because of the above definitions, don't think that every sentence will have one or two prepositions in the S or O/C parts. Not necessarily at all. There are many sentences which do not use any preposition at all. Yet, such sentences will convey the accurate meaning all right. Study the following examples:

1. There is chaos here every morning.
2. I have not eaten anything today.
3. I am joining the new class this morning.
4. Are you happy now?
5. My friends have always been often un-cooperative.

How do we identify a preposition in a sentence? What is the test?

Remove the 'word concerned' and see if the sentence conveys any meaning. Study the following examples:

(i)   Parthiban is a man <u>of</u> great honour.

(ii) Is anyone <u>among</u> you a singer?

(iii) If you go <u>around</u> that tree, you will see a rose plant.

Assume you do not know what job the words underlined are doing. Remove them from the sentence and see if you get any meaning?

"Parthiban is a man great honour." What is the precise meaning of such a sentence? Nothing at all until we introduce the word 'of'. So, 'of' is a preposition because it shows the correct relationship between a noun and an adjective/noun.

Similarly,

"Is anyone you a singer?" The sentence conveys no accurate meaning whatever until we introduce that little word 'among'. So, 'among' is a preposition.

Simple prepositions are recognisable words. We identified them in Chapter 1 itself. They are: AT, BY, FOR, FROM, IN, OF, TO, DOWN, ON, OUT, THROUGH, TILL, WITH, WITHOUT, ABOUT, UNDER, ACROSS, ALONG, AMONG, AROUND, BEFORE, AFTER, BEHIND, BETWEEN, BEYOND, INSIDE, OUTSIDE.

Sometimes you may not recognise a preposition because there are some multi purpose words in the English language i.e, the same word used in different parts of speech. It is in such situations that the identification method will come to your rescue.

We know that UNTIL and AS are conjunctions. (See Chapter 1). Are these two words in the following sentences doing the job of a conjunction? Apply the identification formula and verify:

1   (a) Don't come into my room <u>until</u> 6 p.m. (Preposition)
     (b) <u>Until</u> it is 6 p.m., don't walk into my house. (Conjunction in a Complex sentence)
2   (a) You are acting <u>as</u> an enemy. (Preposition)
     (b) <u>As</u> you are in the other side, I am not talking with you. (Conjunction)

Exercise

Underline the preposition in the following sentences:

1. We have not seen him <u>since</u> Monday.
2. Doesn't it snow in Srinagar <u>during</u> December?
3. I am present here along with my brother today because <u>of</u> your father.
4. I write this application in my own hand <u>for</u> your personal benefit.
5. Many people in my area walk into trouble <u>without</u> their knowledge.
6. You always come late <u>for</u> class, don't you?
7. A friend <u>of</u> mine, could converse well in French.
8. During games period, none should sit idle.
9. When I am busy <u>in</u> my work, you ought not to talk to me.
10. Aren't you talking like a saint?

Use suitable prepositions in the following sentences so as to convey an accurate meaning

11. Couldn't you see a doctor your illness?
12. My mother usually would take me a doctor.
13. Don't draw anything this black board.
14. I do all my homework early evening.
15. I don't like History too many dates.
16. I am scared Mathematics.
17. Today the Principal may not be a good mood.
18. The Electrical machines laboratory our college is observing a holiday today.
19. There are far too many Film magazines Chennai.
20. Tamil Nadu produces a large number Tamil films every year.

21.   The thief jumped ^(through) our compound wall.
22.   My friend Ramu is afraid ^(of) my Alsatian dog.
23.   These young men go ^(to) church all Sundays. ^(on)
24.   This man from Andhra Pradesh speaks ^(to) me ^(,) Telugu.
25.   This is a matter ^(of) great importance to all students.
26.   Aren't you ever tired ^(of) running?
27.   God is good ^(to) everyone.
28.   Do not cry ^(for) spilt milk.
29.   We do not leave our house ^(at) 9 a.m. ^(to) college.
30.   Come and sit ^(by) me.
31.   I must start ^(at) six a.m. ^(to) the railway station.
32.   While I am ^(in) Trichy I may meet my friend daily.
33.   I pour a lot ^(of) sambar ^(in) my rice.
34.   Nobody here is familiar ^(with) all trigonometrical formulae.
35.   The TN Express leaves Chennai 8.15 p.m. New Delhi.
      ^(from)   ^(at)   ^(for)

Write sentences of your own in Present, Present continuous and Simple present tenses using the following simple prepositions:

BY, FROM, OFF, OUT, UP, ABOUT, WITHOUT

By → Where is your house by the way?
      S A V
      Where are you going by the way?
      When do you start your joday the way?

FROM → Where you come from?
        Where are you coming from?
        I do come from college just now.

OFF → You will get day off tomorrow?
       You are going to get day off?
       When do you want day off.

Chapter 10

PAST TENSE (4)

General

This is the second and final tense that uses Auxiliary cum verbs (A.Vs)

Use

We use the **Past tense,**

(a) to denote the existence of or give information about yourself, another person or what we saw before eyes in the past time.

(b) to give information about the things/qualities a person(s) possessed in the past time. (Possessive case)

Rules

Subject	Auxiliary	Verb form
I, HE, SHE, IT	WAS	WAS
WE, YOU, THEY	WERE	WERE
Possessive case		
All persons	HAD	HAD
Universal auxiliary		
All persons	was/were USED TO	was / were take the place of verbs (A noun must follow USED TO)

Sentence structure

Since we use the auxiliary cum verbs (A.V) in this tense, the sentence formulae will be like this,

Gen Q : I - A.V - S - O/C
Sp Q : A.V - S - O/C
Neg Q : Neg A.V - S - O/C
EQ 1 : a1, Neg A, Subj pro
EQ 2 : a2, A.V, Subj pro
a1 : S - A.V - O/C
a2 : S - Neg A.V - O/C

Sample sentences

Gen Q : Where were you yesterday morning?
          I   A.V   S   C

a1   : I   was at my aunt's house.
         S   A.V   C

a2   : I   was not   in my new house   yesterday morning.
         S Neg A.V   C1   C2

(The short form for "was not" is "wasn't" and we pronounce it as written)

Sp Q : Was   Robert   present at the football ground   during games period?
          A.V   S   C1   C2   C3

a1   : He   was   present,   Sir.
         S   A.V   C   O

a2   : He was not   present,   Sir.
         S Neg A.V   C   O

a2   : Sir, he   was   absent.
         O   S   A.V   C

Neg Q : Weren't the III year students keen on a visit   to the zoo?
         Neg A.V   S   C1   O   C2

a1   : They were   very keen, Madam.
         S   A.V   C   O

a2   : The Civil engineering students were not keen at all, Madam.
                 S   Neg A.V   C   O

(The short form for "were not" is "weren't" and we pronounce it as written.

All Negative questions must start with the abbreviated negative A.V form)

EQ 1 : We were at the tracks till 7 a.m. this morning, weren't we?
         S   A.V   C1   C2   C3   Q tag

a1   : You were   there.
         S   A.V   C

a2   : Some of us weren't   there till 7 a.m.
            S   Neg A.V C1   C2

EQ 2 : All the Lecturers   weren't in the class room during the lunch break.
             S   Neg A.V   C1   C2

        were they?
        Q tag

a1   : They were in the staff room during the lunch break.
         S   A.V   C1   C2

a2   : They   weren't in the class room.
         S   Neg A.V   C

Here are more sentences we use in our day to day life with WAS and WERE:

Q   : Who were your wonderful classmates in the First year?
a1   : All these Men and Lady students were my nice classmates in First year.
a2   : Some of these students weren't my classmates last year.

Q	:	How long were you and Sriram at the National park yesterday?
a1	:	We were there for some 3 hours.
a2	:	We weren't there for more than 3 hours.

Sp Q	:	Weren't you the Prefect of your class last year?
a 1	:	I was the Prefect, Sir.
a2	:	I wasn't the Prefect for the whole year.

Neg Q	:	Wasn't your sister with you at the railway station last evening?
a1	:	She indeed was with me.
		(Adv)
a2	:	She wasn't at the railway station the whole evening.

EQ 1	:	Sweet and cheerful Sheila was in the hospital for a week, wasn't she?
a1	:	She was in the hospital for a week.
a2	:	She wasn't in the hospital for more than 2 days.

EQ2	:	The hockey match wasn't at 3 p.m., was it?
a1	:	It was at 4 p.m.
a2	:	It wasn't at 3 p.m.

Use of HAD in possessive cases

Neg Q	:	Hadn't you a bicycle last year?
a1	:	Yes, I had one last year.
a2	:	I hadn't any bicycle last year.

(The short form for "had not" is "hadn't" and we pronounce it as written)

EQ1	:	Many children had a severe headache after the heavy rain this afternoon, hadn't they?
a1	:	Indeed all of them had a severe headache.
a2	:	They had no headache this afternoon. They were OK even after the rain.
a2	:	They hadn't any headache this afternoon.
a2	:	They never had any headache this afternoon.

Note

Note the alternate forms of giving a2. "Never" is stronger than "not". We use it in a2.

a1	:	My young sister and I had a social party in my house yesterday evening.
a1	:	We had a nice picnic last week.
a1	:	Many of my friends and I had a nice holiday in Kodaikanal during summer.
a2	:	The school had no PT master till this year.
a2	:	My energetic father had no job for 2 days last week.
a2	:	Somu had no friends in the next colony till last month.
EQ 1	:	You had a pet dog last year, hadn't you?
EQ 1	:	I had a moped last year, hadn't I?

a1   : We had a very affectionate maid servant some 2 years back.

a2   : We hadn't any music class yesterday.

a2   : We had no music class yesterday.

Note:

We use the auxiliary cum verb HAD mostly in a1 or a2 and seldom in Q. While the answer can be with HAD, the corresponding questions would normally be in Simple past tense. EQ1 would sound all right with HAD, but not EQ2.

Sentences with Universal auxiliary

a1   : We were used to this college till last year.
         S   V   A   O   C

Neg Q : Wasn't this child used to this ayah for quite a few months?

EQ1   : Pankaj was used to this servant very well, wasn't he?
        (We follow the same method as for Present tense as regards Q tag)

EQ2   : Our children were never used to powder milk during their childhood.

a2   : Some of us weren't used to harassment inside the class room.

Note:

USED TO must be followed always by a Noun (object)

Sample conversation using the Past and Present Tenses

Q   : Why were you late for the prayer this morning?

a1   : I was late because of a puncture in my cycle.

Q   : Were you away from your house last evening at 7 p.m.?

a1   : I was out with a friend for about an hour.

Q   : Your parents were very pleasant and sweet to my parents. Are they always kind to strangers?

a1   : They are nice to everyone. They are never rude to anyone.

Q   : What was your elder brother last year?

a1   : He was an Assistant Sales Manager in Johnson & Johnson till last year. Now he is a Sales Manager in a multinational company.

Q   : There was a huge crowd in the Connemara library compound yesterday evening, wasn't there?

Note   : There is no equivalent pronoun for 'There'. Hence use it as it is in the Q tag.

a1   : Indeed there was. Were you one of the spectators there?

a2   : No. But, my brother was there. There was an exhibition of some kind on computers. My brother is very keen on computers.

Q   : Who all were with you at the Spencer plaza last evening?

a1   : Sukumar, Tandon and Pratap were with me there.

Q   : What is your father? (= what is your father's job)

a1   : He was an office superintendent in a private organisation till last year. Now, he is a businessman.

Q   : When was your parents' wedding anniversary?

a1   : It was on 14 February this year.

Q   : Were your grandparents present at their anniversary celebration?

a2   : I'm afraid, no. ("I am afraid" is a connector phrase which means, "I am sorry / no" etc. This is a polite negative form which usually precedes any negative answer. Learn how to use this phrase in your conversation)

Q   : Are you a 100 meters sprinter?

a2   : I'm afraid, no.

Q   : Were you one in your younger days?

a1   : I was a sort of runner all right. I was not a famous fellow as such.

Q   : The pudding after the lunch wasn't good at all, was it?

a2   : It wasn't nice at all. It was sort of insipid.

Q   : Were you ever used to flashy dresses?

a2   : I was never used to flashy dresses at all. I am always used to sober clothes only.

Q   : Some people were uncontrollable in the meeting yesterday, weren't they?

a1   : They were indeed rowdy and uncontrollable even by the police.

Exercise

Give affirmative answers for the following questions:

1. Whose mistake was this one?
2. Where was this bag? Whose school bag was this?
3. Wasn't this calculator inside your brief case?
4. You were wrong in your judgement, weren't you?
5. Why weren't you present in the football field at 7 this morning?
6. Weren't you at the sports stadium till late evening?
7. You had two good friends in your previous class, hadn't you?
8. It was a beautiful flower-show, wasn't it?

Give negative answers:

9. Who was responsible for this goof-up in yesterday's stage show?
10. Your small sister was very rude towards me, wasn't she?
11. You had an interesting lesson this morning, hadn't you?
12. Was the magic show interesting or not?
13. Our week end in your house was enjoyable, wasn't it?
14. Weren't the Govt hospital nurses very impolite with us students?
15. How long were you in the hospital?
16. It was a very easy paper, wasn't it?

17. Was our HOD present during the final match?
18. I was fully prepared for the competition, wasn't I?

(Adv)

Locate the mistake(s) if any and rewrite the sentences:

19. The hostel girls wasn't ready for the college function till 5 p.m.
20. The college function were at 4 .30 p.m. sharp.
21. Weren't I nice with your pet dog?
22. Wasn't Roja and Meena good dancers?
23. Madam was absent at the rehearsal, weren't she?
24. Who were the bridesmaid at the church wedding?
25. The groom's best man were Surinder, wasn't he?
26. There was too many stones in the rice in today's lunch.
27. How were the breakfast?
28. Why was you so unpleasant with my parents?
29. Had you any complaints about the food?
30. Where was your friends when you were at the cinema hall?
31. All of us were not used to bad language at all.
32. When were your birthday?
33. Whose bicycle were this?
34. When was you 10 years old?
34. Johnny and I was good friends.

Convert he following Present tense sentences into equivalent Past tense sentences:

35. Isn't Dolly used to this nursery school?
36. My younger brother has too many friends in the next colony.
37. The bus conductors sometimes are not nice with students.
38. Haven't you any money in your purse?
39. Aren't all your relatives in Chennai at present?
40. I am a very helpful person, amn't I?

Analyse the following sentences:

41. Weren't many of them among the successful candidates?
42. We had no problem with this Physics demonstrator.
43. I was bright in the first year, wasn't I?
44. Who were all used to this tiny canteen?
45. Wasn't Madanlal used to a grass court till last year?

Write the remaining 6 categories based on the following sentences:

46. We were never used to mineral water till last month.
47. Wasn't your English teacher from St Paul's college, Kolkata
48. Ram was never a dull student, was he?
49. We were practising yoga till 7 a.m.
50. Weren't your friends used to this city some 10 years back?

Chapter 11

PAST CONTINUOUS TENSE (5)

Use

We use the Past continuous tense,

(a) to talk about an action or activities going on for a certain duration of time in the past and also finished in the past time.

(b) to refer to a point of time in that duration. This use will be only in Complex sentences.

Since this tense deals with a "completed activity," it is interchangeable with Simple past. But, if we want to give *importance* for the duration of the action, we opt for the Past continuous tense.

Rules

Subject	Auxiliary	Verb form
I, HE, SHE, IT	WAS	Present form ending in ING
WE, YOU, THEY	WERE	" "

Universal auxiliary

All persons	did KEEP was/were **getting /** **becoming** USED TO	Continuous present verb Use only **getting /** **becoming** and no other verb

Sentence structure formulae:

Gen Q : I - A - S - V - O/C
Sp Q : A - S - V - O/C
Neg Q : Neg A - S - V - O/C
EQ1   : a1, Neg A, Q tag.
EQ2   : a2, Aux, Q tag.
a1   : S - A - V - O/C
a2   : S - Neg A - V - O/C

Sample sentences

Gen Q : Who was talking so loudly inside the auditorium?
       I A V   C1   C2
a1   : Shobana was talking very loudly, Madam.
        S   A   V   C1   O
a2   : I wasn't talking loudly, Madam.
     S Neg A V   Adv   O

Sp Q : Weren't some children of your colony rehearsing the National anthem?

a1 : They were rehearsing the National anthem, Sir.

a2 : They weren't rehearsing the National anthem Sir; they were rehearsing the theme song of today's drama.

Neg Q : Wasn't one of your class students standing in the Sun for an hour?

a1 : Thangaraj was standing in the Sun for an hour.

a2 : Nobody was standing in the Sun from our class.

EQ1 : The selected players were practising basket ball today, weren't they?

a 1 : They were practising basketball very seriously.

a2 : They were simply wasting time in the basketball ground.

(Although there is no negative auxiliary here, the tone of the sentence is negative, hence it is equivalent to an a2 type sentence)

EQ1 : Some of you were becoming used to copying others' answers, weren't you?

Reference to a point of time

a1 : When I walked into my father's office, he was reading the Bible.

a2 : Sekar wasn't doing anything when I rang him up.

Q : Didn't the final whistle go off when you were attempting a goal?

Q : What were you doing when I called at your house?

EQ : You were eating breakfast when your father called you, weren't you?

EQ : You weren't standing idle when I passed by you, were you?

In the case of the above 6 sentences, you could notice that the 'action was not finished'; action was going on when a second action took place simultaneously. Thus, we use the past continuous tense also to refer to a particular point of time in the duration of that action. We do so only in Complex sentences. In a Simple sentence, it would imply that the action concerned had finished. The sentence, "I was playing volley ball" would imply that your action of 'playing volley ball' had finished for the simple reason that you wouldn't be in the volley ball ground for *ever!* Past continuous tense is not to be used for a "continuing action".

We use the auxiliary "did KEEP" for such actions that never come to an end or we never think of such actions ending. We shall study some examples later.

As a general rule, except for "did KEEP", we use all the Past family sentences only for such actions that started in the past time and finished in the past time too. "The finishing part" is inbuilt in these including the Past continuous tense.

More model sentences

Q : What were you teaching your class during the second period?

a1 : I was teaching them geography.

Q : Who was visiting you last evening?

a2 :Nobody was visiting me at all.

Q :In whose house was the young maiden from Mumbai staying?

a1 :The young maiden was staying in her cousin's house.

a2 :She wasn't staying with me.

Q :With whom were you talking for such a long time just in front of your house?

a1 :I was talking with a beggar. He is a regular visitor to my house at 9 p.m.

Q :Wasn't your house maid working in the Professor's house earlier?

a1 :She was working there, I think. (Complex sentence)

Q :Were two of your close friends using someone else's motor cycle?

a1 :They were using my uncle's motor cycle for one day.

a2 :They weren't using it for more than a day.

Q :Weren't the First year students teasing the monkeys during our visit to the Zoo?

a1 : Some of them were teasing the monkeys.

a2 : All of them were not teasing the monkeys.

EQ : The juniors were enjoying our dance drama immensely, weren't they?
         extremely.

a1 : They were indeed enjoying it.

Q : What were you doing when the master was solving this equation on the blackboard?

a2 : I wasn't very attentive at that time.
                    (Adv)

EQ : This child was nearly drowning when the beach-guard was swimming towards her, wasn't it?

a1 : Truly she was drowning and panting.

EQ : We were reading a couple of magazines when the teacher walked into the class, weren't we?

a1 : Of course, we were reading some magazines when the teacher walked in.

Sentence construction with the Universal auxiliary

Neg Q : **Didn't** you **keep** writing to your parents during your stay abroad?

a1 : I **did keep** writing to them every week.
        ("I kept writing…." will be wrong)
        (We normally don't use a2 and EQ2 with this auxiliary set)

EQ1 : You did keep worrying your parents for more and more pocket money during your college life, didn't you?

a2 : We **weren't** getting **used to** this hotel food at all.

a1 : My friend **was** getting **used to** the hostel life very slowly.

Note:

We use "did keep" only for an action whose end is not known. This is the basic difference between this auxiliary set and "was/were".

Dialogue using all tenses covered so far: (Analyse every sentence and note down some of the important aspects and talking styles in a conversation).

PINKY : Where are you going, Radha?

RADHA : I am going to the Club library. Are you coming with me?

PINKY : (You do) Wait for me for five minutes, please?

RADHA : OK. Come fast. (You do come fast)

PINKY : Here I am. Come along (You do come along)

RADHA : Are we going by bus or by walk? (Complex sentence)

PINKY : By walk, surely. (we are going by walk, surely) Are you lazy or what? ("or what?" is an end phrase. This means nothing. We just end a sentence this way in conversation, that's all.)

RADHA : I am equally energetic, Pinky. I am ready for a run too.

PINKY : Don't show-off. You are always showing-off. Be modest always.

RADHA : OK. OK. Grandma!

(At the library)

PINKY : To which section, are you going here?

RADHA : I am happy at the magazine desk. And you? ("And you" here is a shortcut for "To which section, are you going?")

PINKY : I am fond of the History section, you see? ("You see" is an end phrase. You could view this sentence as a Complex sentence as well)

RADHA : Are you writing a thesis of sorts or what?

PINKY : Actually speaking, I am. It is really an article on the Chola period.

RADHA : My, my. You are a wizard, aren't you? ("My, My" is a colloquial expression used mostly by students. It means, 'well done, great, you are great, keep it up etc.)

PINKY : Thank you, Radha. (I do thank you, Radha)

(On their way home)

RADHA : Was the visit to the library useful?

PINKY : Of course, it was. Do you visit this place regularly, Radha?

RADHA : Actually, I was visiting it almost daily till last year. I am visiting it these days only during week ends.

PINKY : Which ones are you very fond of?

RADHA : I am very much used to Woman's Era, India today, Alive, Times and so on.

PINKY : All of them are Indian magazines, aren't they? Do you read any foreign ones?

RADHA : Yes. "Times" is an American magazine. Incidentally, how is your younger brother faring in studies?

PINKY : OK, I suppose.
          Adv S (A) V

RADHA : He is in +1 class, isn't he?

PINKY : He is. ("He is" is a shortcut answer for "He is in +1 class").

RADHA : Wasn't he in St Peter's school earlier?

PINKY : Yes, he was doing his Matric there. St Peter's has no +2 course, you see?
PINKY : Your father is in Leather exports, isn't he?
RADHA : He was working in that company only till last year. Now he is in Martin & Co.
PINKY : Good.

   (They reach home)

RADHA : Thank you Radha. It was very nice of you.
PINKY : You are welcome, Pinky. ("You are welcome" is the correct response to "(I do) Thank you.")
RADHA : When is your next visit to the club?
PINKY : Next Saturday, I think
RADHA : Why? (Shortcut for, "Why do you ask?")
PINKY : Take me also with you. OK?
RADHA : Sure. (Shortcut for, "I will surely take you." Do remember that WILL is also a Simple present auxiliary.)

Exercise

Answer the following general questions in affirmative or negative form whichever sounds appropriate. But, use only the past continuous tense:

1. How is your brother doing in XII Standard?
2. Where were you learning cricket?
3. In your XII Standard, who was teaching you English?
4. Whose cycle were you riding for school this morning?
5. Weren't you weeping after the last examination?
6. Who was accompanying you to the Principal's office?
7. Were you busy when your mother returned home from shopping?
8. What were you doing in the library? Which books or magazines were you reading?
9. You were standing at the college gate for over 15 minutes, weren't you?
10. You were waiting for someone, weren't you?

Correct the mistake in the following sentences and rewrite the faulty ones:

11. The Football coach was explain the tactics very well.
12. Norton kept knocking on your door for a long time, didn't he?
13. Yesterday, some hostel boys playing cards till midnight, weren't they?
14. Wasn't it rain very heavily last night?
15. Wasn't you copying my notes quietly without my permission?
16. Some students don't doing well in their final exams.
17. Our little brother always twisting the cat's tail when cat sleeping.
18. How often are Surinder and Shyamala visit the beach during holidays?
19. Was we responsible for this mistake?
20. Was you not sure about your stand on this issue?
21. We were overtaking the girls at that bend over there, wasn't we?

22. Whenever I see your grandfather he ~~always~~ *was* reading a newspaper.
23. Why weren't you get used to the tin-milk in your hostel?
24. Our master did keep losing hair on his head after the age of 40.
25. Meera were becoming used to much praises about her beauty.

Fill up the blank with the correct word.

26. Meenakshi and Kalyani *were* fighting for 10 minutes yesterday.
27. *Were* you the right person? ..*Or*.. we look for another?
28. I *was* a very simple person. I *won't* show off like you.
29. I *was* concentrating on something.
30. Anandan *were* preparing for his term tests.
31. Is Past continuous interchangeable with Present continuous. Why or why not?

Analyse the following sentences:

32. Weren't we waiting for the train on the platform for more than an hour?
33. Was one of us a guilty person by any chance?
34. One of them did keep standing at the gate for someone.

Write the remaining 6 categories of sentences:

35. Our parents did keep worrying about us due to our extended stay at the excursion, didn't they.
36. The college staffs weren't worried unduly over the poor result.
37. We were not walking to your house during your play time.
38. You were used to a better life in your previous posting, weren't you?
39. Your friend, Neelam was used to loud reading.
40. I was never wrong in my assessment of other people.

Chapter 12

SIMPLE PAST TENSE (6)

Use

We use the **Simple past tense** to talk about the action/activities that started in the past time and also finished in the past time.

If you look back, we gave the same definition for the Past continuous tense also.

So, this tense is interchangeable with Past continuous since both deal with a completed activity. But, when we want to give importance for the duration of the action, we opt for the continuous tense.

Rule

Subject	*Auxiliary*	*Verb form*
All persons	DID	Present form
Universal auxiliaries		
All persons	COULD	"
"	WOULD	"
"	did USE TO	"

Sample sentences (with auxiliary DID)

Gen Q : When   did Sheila leave college   for home?
        I   A   S   V   O   C

Ea1   : She did leave college   at 4 p.m.
        S   A   V   O   C

a1   : She left college at 4 p.m.
        S (A)V   O   C

a2   : She did not leave college before 4 p.m.
        S Neg A   V   O   C

The short form for "did not" is "didn't" and we pronounce it as written.

In the above sentence, the word "college" would answer the test question WHAT and also WHERE. So it could be a Complement or Object. Take it as either.

Sp Q : Did Anwar Hussain really   dropout of college?
        A   S   Adv   V   O

Ea1   : He did drop out of our college   in April last year.
        S A   V   O   C

a1   : He dropped out   of our college in April last year.
        S   (A) V   O   C

a2   : He did not dropout. He did take leave for six months.
          S Neg A   V   S A V   O   C

Neg Q : Didn't some smart students pose   some tricky questions to the
        Neg A   S   V   O1
        new Lady Lecturer?
            O2

Ea1   : They did pose some difficult questions.
           S   A   V   O1

a1   : They posed some difficult questions.
          S   (A)V   O2

a2   : The smart students didn't pose many questions.
          S   Neg A V   O

EQ1   : My children went to college on time, didn't they?
            S   (A)V   C1   C2   Q tag

Ea1   : They did go to college on time.
           S   A   V   C1   C2

a1   : They went to college on time.
          S   (A)V   C1   C2

a2   : They didn't   go to college late.
         S Neg A V   C1   Adv

EQ2   : Your baby cried nearly all night, didn't it?
            S   (A)V   C   Q tag

Ea1   : It did cry nearly all night.
           S A V   C

a1   : It cried nearly all night.
         S (A)V   C

a2   : It didn't cry   all night at all.
        S Neg A V   C

Ea1 stands for emphatic answer. Like in the case of the Simple present, here too we make some modification to derive the <u>normal answer</u> (a1). We silence the auxiliary and at the same time, change the present form verb into its past form. We may look at the modification rule like this,

did + Present form verb = Past form verb.

Thus,

did + ask   = asked
did + play   = played
did + go   = went
did + speak = spoke

Past form of verbs

We saw in Chapter 1 that every verb has a **present form** and **past form**. Here is a list of some commonly used verbs that shows their present and past forms:

Present form	*Past form*
learn	learnt, learned
talk	talked
rest	rested
wash	washed
punish	punished
lock	locked
improve	improved
land	landed
dry	dried
carry	carried
study	studied
cry	cried
bury	buried
worry	worried
go	went
write	wrote
sleep	slept
leave	left
shake	shook
swim	swam
throw	threw
ride	rode
take	took
fly	flew
sit	sat
run	ran
put	put
cut	cut
hurt	hurt
read	read (pronounced as 'red')
am ⎫	was
is ⎬ =	were
are ⎭	
has	had
have	had
do	did
does	did

There is no shortcut to find the past form for every present form verb. Different rules are followed: in some cases, we add the letters - **ed** , to some - **ied** to derive the past form. Some past forms have entirely different spelling and yet in a few cases both forms are the same with the same pronunciation too i.e put, cut. In a special case, though the spelling is the same, the pronunciation is different i.e. read, read (red).

So, when you come across a new verb or learn new ones, find out their past form as well. A good dictionary will give both the forms for all the verbs.

Examples of sentences of daily use.

Analyse each as you read them:

Where did you spend your summer vacation last year?
I spent my summer vacation in Yelagiri hills.
Did all of you go to the exhibition yesterday?
All of us did go the exhibition.
Didn't you meet Saraswati at the football ground during the lunch break?
I did meet my Maths Professor for some clarification on integral calculus.
Did the Registrar call you today for a good dressing-down?
He did call many students from three classes for a good rebuke.
At what time did the drama rehearsals give-over yesterday?
Did you spend your week end usefully?
Yes Madam, we did. (Yes Madam, we did spend our week end usefully)
In whose house did you stay during your visit to Bangalore?
How much money did you spend on this book?
How much did you pay for this book?
Didn't someone knock on your door around 10 p.m. last night?
How many students did not take part in the debate competition?

Sentences with WOULD and COULD

Gen Q : Why didn't you attend the net practice yesterday?
a 2   : I couldn't attend due to acute pain in my right leg.
         S Neg A V   O   C

Sp Q : Are you meeting your class friend today?
a2   : How could I meet him? He wouldn't look in my direction at all.
Sp Q : Could you get your bicycle repaired yesterday?
                                                    Adv
a2   : I could not get it back from the cycle mechanic yesterday.

Sp Q : Did you hear any noise yesterday from the dining hall?
a1   : I could hear some noise all right. It was very faint.
Neg Q : Couldn't you return this book to the owner?
a2   : I couldn't do so yesterday for some reasons.

EQ1   : Your parents wouldn't agree with our picnic programme, would they?

EQ2   : My small brother would have his own way always, wouldn't he?
        (This sentence covers all the three time periods)

Note:

We used COULD and WOULD in Simple present and Present continuous tenses also. So, how do we distinguish the tenses? It is only by looking at the overall timing of the activity. So, it may not be possible to form all the categories of sentences with these two auxiliaries.

However, take the sentence, "I could not attend college yesterday". We cannot express this idea (of inability) with any other auxiliary when the past time period is involved.

We can use WOULD for a regular habit of the past, present and future. For example, "This little fellow would spend all his evening hours in my house" would cover the past period, present period and also the future period.

Hence, we must consider COULD and WOULD as special auxiliaries with limited usefulness in the Simple past tense.

Sentences with "Did USE"

Gen Q : When did you use to live in London?
         I   A   S   A   V   C

a1   : I did use to live   there till last year. (Consider this as Ea1 also)
          S A   A   V   C
          ("I used to live there till last year" is also correct. We shall see the reasons later)

Sp Q   : Did you use to lend your class-notes to Krishnan regularly?

    a1 : I used to lend it to him almost every week end.

Neg Q : Didn't you use to visit a Temple every Friday.

a2   : I didn't use to visit every Friday.

EQ1   : You used to seek my help for every subject last year, didn't you?

EQ2   : You didn't use to go home during every Govt holiday, did you?

There is something special about this auxiliary. We use it "for a regular habit of the past but given up sometime in the past; and, the habit is not continuing in the present time."

Although it is an auxiliary, we treat it as if it is a present form verb. One could say, this auxiliary is also an "imperfect verb" because it has only a past form and no PP form. Thus, to use the auxiliary as a past form of verb is legitimate although we cannot explain the logic behind it.

Viewed from this angle the sentence, "I used to visit my brother" is correct.

<u>Note:</u>

There is no Ea1 form with the universal auxiliaries.

Imaginary dialogue between two students using the Present and Past family tenses:

Sastry   : Natarajan, did you see the latest movie of Maniratnam's?

Natarajan : Who is Maniratnam?

Sastry   : He is a famous cinema director. He could produce Box office hits just like that.

Natarajan : Really? You know, I don't see movies at all. My parents don't allow me.

Sastry   : Good. But, still you must have some general knowledge about the film world, you know?

Natarajan : Why? (short form for: Why should I know anything about the film world.)

Sastry   : You are a sad case, *yaar*. How do you spend your spare time anyway?

Natarajan : I usually sit with my text books. Sometimes I used to read some magazines.

Sastry   : So, you are a book-worm, aren't you? You are used to books!

Natarajan : Indeed, I am used to books. Incidentally, do you play cricket?

Sastry   : No. I only play football. Isn't cricket a rich man's game?

Natarajan : It is in a way. But, if you are a member of a cricket club, they provide all the materials.

Sastry   : Is it so? Which club are you member of?

Natarajan : Actually my father is the real member. So I take advantage of his membership?

Sastry   : How many times in a week do you go to the cricket club?

Natarajan : I go only on Sundays and I play for about two hours. (Complex sentence)

Sastry   : Did you use to play cricket on all Saturdays? Yesterday was Saturday, wasn't it?

Natarajan : Of course. As usual I did play from 4-6 p.m. I am a batsman, you see?

Sastry   : You don't bowl?

Natarajan : I used to. I couldn't specialise in it. So, I took to batting. I prefer batting to bowling now.

Sastry   : You know anything about football? (The long form is: "Do you know ....)

Natarajan : Are you joking? Amn't I the Captain of the college 'B' team?

Sastry   : Sorry, sorry. (Long form: I am sorry, I am sorry) Clean forgot, you know? (Subject I and the auxiliary DO are silent)

Natarajan : If you take some interest, you too can become a cricketer.

Sastry   : Well, why couldn't you take me with you to your club next Sunday?

Natarajan : Sure. (Short form for: I shall surely take you. "Shall" is also a Future tense auxiliary. We shall cover its use in the next Chapter.

Use of interrogative WHO

In the Simple present case we learnt that the auxiliary is omitted when a Positive question starts with the interrogative WHO. We follow the same rule in Simple past also. Here are some examples:

Who sang the National anthem out of tune in the auditorium yesterday?

Who returned to the hostel late from summer vacation?

Who scored the lowest marks in English?

In the Simple past, there is no question of singular subject verb and plural subject verb since the auxiliary DID is used for all singular and plurals persons. This sub rule applies only to DID. When we use the universal auxiliaries with WHO, we have to use the auxiliary. But, do note that we omit the auxiliary only in the Positive questions and it is introduced into the sentence for Negative questions.

Who could not attend the progress test yesterday?

Who could play in today's match?

Exercise

Answer the following questions in the affirmative. You may make any assumptions you like:

1.   When did you finish the extra class yesterday evening?
2.   Did your alsatian dog kill a stray cat last week?
3.   What rumour did these students spread about my performance in yesterday's match?
4.   How did you travel to Ooty last month?
5.   You didn't talk to the lady students about the painting class, did you?
6.   Did any of you send this unsigned letter to the Vice Chancellor?
7.   Who copied whose homework in yesterday's assignment?
8.   Did you fail wantonly in Mathematics?
9.   Who borrowed Raman's calculator?
10. Our Chemistry lecturer drew a beautiful picture on the board today, didn't he?

Answer in the negative:

11. Could you polish these vessels with silvo?
    I could not polish these vessels with silvo
12. Who did not wear canvas shoes for today's badminton match?
13. When you were sick, did the doctor come to your house during your sickness days?
14. Who prescribed this medicine for your pet dog?
15. Why couldn't you come at the starting point on time?

Give emphatic affirmative answers (Ea1) for the following questions:

16. Did your brother like my gift?
17. Who put this cross mark on my T shirt?
18. Didn't you take away the cycle from my portico during my short absence?
19. You whispered something into Sudarshan's ear, didn't you?
20. Out of these three, which young man did you kick?

Write emphatic questions for the following statements:

21. I did not want my shirt stitched in this style.
22. I flew that kite myself.
23. My small sister used to play in the park till 6 p.m.
24. Rupika rested for half an hour after a serious game of table tennis.
25. Mohini did not improve her English at all.

Convert the following Past continuous sentences into Simple past without significantly changing the meaning:

26. You were purchasing some sweets in that shop, weren't you?
27. I was mopping my room floor early morning.
28. That boy was playing hockey till 6 p.m.
29. We were working on an Article for the college magazine together last night.
30. Some students were protesting unnecessarily against the new timings, weren't they?

Locate the mistake(s) and rewrite the sentences without error:

31. Some students in my class would came well prepared for the English test.
32. Madhu learns music from my institution, didn't she?
33. When did your small brother joined this school?
34. Mahesh Gupta really did not meant any harm to us, did he?
35. When did you travelled by this new bus?
36. Some always fail in every examination, did they?
37. Where did the police caught up with the fleeing thieves?
38. You forget his name, didn't you?

Analyse the following sentences and identify the part of speech of every word:

39. Never sir, never did I hit this tiny boy with any stick.
40. All the king's men and all the king's horses did not put humpty-dumpty together again.
41. Who gave you approval for this kind of work?
42. Some of us could not submit our application for a scholarship on time.
43. A man with a big moustache and short sleeved shirt threatened me with a knife.
44. Wasn't my dress perfect?
45. I wasn't used to T shirts, was I?
46. I used to make my purchases in this shop for several years.
47. Did you use this pen?
48. Could you solve all these equations?
49. This particular Lecturer would always give me low marks.
50. We never used to visit this hotel, did we?

Write the remaining 6 categories of sentences wherever possible:

51. I could not complete my revision even by 2 a.m. last night. (Simple past)
52. When did you speak with my sister?
53. This little stray dog came to my house every evening.
54. We used to enjoy this Producer's T.V serials.
55. A few of us did not call on the new Lecturer for several days.

Chapter 13

FUTURE TENSE (7)

Use

In Chapter 3, we saw that one way of looking at a sentence is, "What is the activity and what is its timing?" We also saw that Present tense and Past tense sentences are "actionless type sentences" because we use A.Vs in them. Wouldn't this mean that there ought to be **action** in such sentences that use auxiliary separately and verb separately? This is true indeed. And, we do see action in the remaining four tenses covered in the Present and Past families, don't we?

There is however, an exception to this interpretation, in the Future tense.

We use the **Future tense** to talk about an action we propose to do in some future time. The 'action' is only in your mind as an intention. This action will take shape only at a later time. Thus, in a Future tense sentence, we cannot see any action whatever though it uses auxiliaries and verbs separately.

We make a Future tense statement only in Present time.

Rules

Subject	Auxiliary	Verb form
All persons	WILL, SHALL	Present form
Universal auxiliaries		
All persons	COULD	Present form
"	WOULD	"
"	MIGHT	"
"	will/shall/might/would/could GET/BECOME/BE USED TO	use only **get/become/be** as verbs
I	am GOING TO	Present form
WE, YOU, THEY	are GOING TO	"
HE, SHE, IT	is GOING TO	"

7 Auxiliaries/auxiliary sets are used in this tense.

Sample sentences (With WILL and SHALL)

Gen Q : How will you go to college tomorrow?
             I   A   S   V   C
a1   : I will go by walk to college tomorrow.
           S   A   V   C1   C2

a2   : I will not   go by cycle tomorrow to college.
          S   Neg A   V   O   C1   C2

a2   : I won't go by cycle tomorrow to college.

(The short form for "will not" is "won't" and we pronounce it as written. Never fail to put an apostrophe between the letters n and t.)

Sp Q : Will   you   stay at home   tomorrow?
            A   S   V   C1   C2

a1   : I   shall   stay   at home.
          S   A   V   C

a2   : I shan't be at my home   tomorrow. ("be" is present form verb here)
          S Neg A V   C1   C2

(The short form for "shall not" is "shan't" and we pronounce it as written.)

Neg Q : Won't Raphel come   with me to the play ground?
          Neg A S   V   O   C

a1   : He shall go with you to the play ground.
           S   A   V   O   C

a2   : Raphel shan't go with you   to the play ground.
          S   Neg A V   O   C

EQ 1 : Sheila will   spend the next week-end in your house, won't she?
            S   A   V   O   C   Q tag

a1   : She will   spend the next week-end in my house.
           S   A   V   O   C

a2   : Sheila shan't   spend the next week-end in my house.
          S   Neg A V   O   C

EQ 2 : Most of the students of my class shall   surely pass, shan't they?
                    S   A   Adv   V   Q tag

a1   : They shall surely pass.
          S   A   Adv   V

a2   : They surely shall not   fail.
          S   Adv   Neg A   V

Use of SHALL

SHALL is stronger in meaning than WILL. When we want to show some determination in completing a job we use SHALL. "We will complete this job by tomorrow morning" is a normal future tense sentence. But if we say, "We shall complete this job by tomorrow", the sentence shows some determination/certainty.

We may use SHALL with all persons. But with I and WE in the Question form, we normally use SHALL and not WILL. "Will we see the principal today?" is not good English. "Shall we see the principal today?" is the correct form.

Sentences with the universal auxiliaries assigned for this tense:

Gen Q :   When could you meet me in my house?
         I   A   S   V   O   C

a1   :   I could meet you any time before your dinner time, Sir.

a2   :   I can't come to your house today, Sir.
            (Here, we have switched over to the auxiliary CAN. The statement is made in present time, hence a Simple present auxiliary would be more suitable than COULDN'T)

Neg Q :   Couldn't you come to the class on time?

a1   :   I could come on time, Sir.

Gen Q :   What might   be   the reason   for your late arrival here?
         I   A   V   O   C

a2   :   I have no valid reason at all, Sir
            (Use of MIGHT in a2 would sound bad, hence we have gone over to the A.V, HAVE)

Sp Q :   Will   you   get used to   tea   shortly in our hostel?
         A   S   V   A   O   C

a1   :   I shall be used to tea very shortly.
                     V   A

a1   :   I shall get used to tea very shortly.
                     V   A

a1   :   I shall become used to tea very shortly.
                     V   A

Gen Q :   When could you become used to this type of food?
a2   :   I might never get used to a lunch with beef.

Gen Q :   When are you going to submit your essay?
         I   A   S   A   V   O

a1   :   I shall submit it next Monday morning, Sir.

Neg Q :   Isn't your uncle going to see me this afternoon?
a2   :   He shall not see you before next Monday, Sir.

Examples of sentences of daily use. Analyse each as you read them:

Will you please explain this equation?
I shall explain it nicely.
Will all of you visit Shakuntala in the hospital this evening?
Our Lecturer would come into the class shortly.
Won't you lend me your notes for a day?
When could you play your badminton match with me?
I shall play it this evening at 4 p.m.
When will this movie start?
It will start at 6.30 p.m. sharp.

When will you cook my breakfast?

I won't cook it before 7 a.m.

We might not return home before 9 p.m.

Would all of you be at your seat by 8.30? ("be" is present form verb)

We shall surely be at our seat by that time, Madam.

Won't two of you be enough for this job.

Two will be enough, Sir.

You shall not see me again ever, shall you?

You shall not mix with that student ever again.

You could get used to this new room, couldn't you?

We might not get used to the South Indian food for a long time.

Aren't you going to coach me in Mathematics?

Use of WILL in Simple Present also

We saw that WILL is also a Simple Present auxiliary for issuing a command, an order or a direction or a suggestion <u>in present time</u>. Do you remember we used DO also for such a purpose? See Chapter 5. WILL is also used for acknowledging such commands, orders and suggestions.

Here are some examples:

Will you please type out this letter immediately?

I will/shall, Sir.

When will you commence your repair work on my cycle? (You may consider this
    sentence also as a future tense type or as a command in present time.)

I shall do so after 10 minutes. (acknowledgement)

You will cook my breakfast, won't you? (suggestion)

You will not repeat such mistakes ever again, will you? (suggestion)

Will you please see me in my office before 1 p.m.? (order/command)

Shall we accept his proposal? (suggestion)

We could frame all the above in Simple present also with the auxiliary DO. So, for giving an order/command/suggestion, use the auxiliary DO or WILL/SHALL.

Imaginary dialogue between two girls using all the 7 tenses covered so far.

(Do note that during a conversation we will use around three tenses. Sometimes, you may give an answer in a different tense also and not necessarily in the same tense as the question.)

Dolly   : Arti, is your sister all right today?

Arti   : She is fine. She would go to school from tomorrow.

Dolly   : Good. Send her in an auto and not by foot.

Arti   : Why?

Dolly   : Until she becomes physically strong, don't send her by foot. OK?

Arti	: All right. Thank you for the advice anyway.
Dolly	: When will you do your homework?
Arti	: Tonight, around 7 p.m. Why?
Dolly	: I am thinking of joining you. Are you agreeable? I am not good at Maths, you see? That's why. (Short form for, "That is why I shall come to you.")
Arti	: You are always welcome, Dolly. Don't feel bad in future also.
Dolly	: Mohan is meeting you frequently, isn't he?
Arti	: Oh yes. He is my next door neighbour too. He is a very nice young man, you know?
Dolly	: I know. He stands first always in every test, doesn't he?
Arti	: He used to stand first till a few months back. But, he is a little erratic now. Yet, he does help weak students also?
Dolly	: Would he help me? I am only an average student.
Arti	: I think he will. But then, couldn't you ask him directly? He is very cooperative too.
Arti	: When could we see him then?
Dolly	: Why not tomorrow evening?
Arti	: Yes, OK by me. (= It is OK for me)
Dolly	: Aren't both of us going to meet Mohan tomorrow?
Arti	: Of course, both of us are going to meet Mohan.

Exercise

Answer in the affirmative:

1. Will the Physics Lecturer punish us for our absence from the Practicals?
2. Won't the top colleges meet in the finals today?
3. When will our inter-college sports-meet start?
4. How will all of us reach the play ground in St Michael's college?
5. When will you post this letter?
6. You shall not mislead weak students anymore, shall you?
7. You shall always be on time for college, shan't you?
8. Won't you get me a cup of ice cream?
9. Where shall we sit in the park for a game of cards?
10. Will you come with me now to that shop?

Answer in the negative:

11. Padmini will come to my house on time, won't she?
12. Which saree will your mother wear today for the college function?
13. Won't this rag burn out in the hot sun?
14. Shall we remove this table from this room to the next?
15. Will your small brother and sister also come with us to the snake park?

Write emphatic questions for the following a1/a2:

16. I shall not sign this letter today.
17. My teacher will certainly accept your birthday gift.
18. Manisha will not talk to me on this point.
19. All our friends shall assemble in my house without fail.
20. Ten chairs will not be enough in this room for all the guests. (Remember, "be" is present form verb)

Correct the mistake(s) and rewrite the sentence concerned:

21. Will this guest stay late, will she? *won't he*
22. All my classmates will never oppose this idea, won't he? *they*
23. Where will Maniben wrote the final exam? *write*
24. Won't Madhubala writing a reply to me within a week? *write* *Will*
25. When will your sister playing tennis?
26. Why shall we accept this girls in our team?
27. Shan't they see me during my hospitalisation? *shan't*
28. Will you go to the toilet straightway? *will*
29. There won't sufficient seats for all of us in the theatre.
30. Be still, will you? *Will you be still?*
31. Won't you not write your exam?

Change the following orders of Simple present with WILL / SHALL:

31. Don't come to me until next week. *You shall*
32. You see a small building over there, don't you?
33. You write letters to your friends regularly, don't you?
34. Do these small jokes humour you a lot?
35. Don't I take you with me during my morning constitutionals?

Change the following orders/commands with the auxiliary COULD/WOULD:

36. Stop writing.
37. Stand up.
38. Do not smoke here.
39. You eat chocolates daily, don't you?
40. When will you finish your allotted work?

Write the balance 6 categories of sentences:

41. He would not listen to me at all.
42. Shan't we stop at the tree over there for some rest?
43. You might not like the taste of this sweet.
44. Couldn't you do this favour for me?
45. Won't you become highly used to our style of life?
46. Is your small sister getting used to the Perambulator?

47. How are you going to travel to your aunt's house?
48. Some of them could be used to rich food.
49. We might not join your chess group.
50. I am not going to talk against any of our staffs.

Analyse the following sentences:

51. Shan't we all go as a party to the railway station tomorrow morning?
52. Only a few of us are going to meet the new Master of Std. XII
53. If you could get used to a new member in your team, so could I? (Complex sentence)
54. You would always complain about something or the other.
55. When you get used to apples, see me. (Complex)

Chapter 14

FUTURE CONTINUOUS TENSE (8)

Use

We use this for an action we propose to do sometime in the future. This definition is the same as for the 'Future tense'. Thus, the continuous tense is interchangeable with the Future tense. But when we want to give importance for the duration of the intended action we choose the continuous tense in preference to the Future tense.

Rules

Subject	Auxiliary	Verb form
All persons	WILL BE	Present form in -ING
	SHALL BE	"
Universal auxiliaries		
All persons	COULD BE	Present in -ING
"	WOULD BE	" "
"	MIGHT BE	" "
"	shall/will/could/would/ might KEEP	" "
"	will be/shall be/could be/ would be/might be getting/ becoming USED TO	use only the verbs **getting** and **becoming**

This tense uses 7 auxiliary sets.

Be is an auxiliary here. Do recall that BE is a 3-in-1 word. We have used it as a verb already.

Sample sentences (with WILL BE / SHALL BE):

Gen Q : When will Shobana be seeing me?
         I   A   S   A   V   O

a1 : She will be seeing you at 3 p.m.
       S   A   V   O   C

a2 : She won't be seeing you before 3 p.m.
       S   Neg A   V   O   C

Sp Q : Shall we be meeting our parents this Saturday?
        A   S   A   V   O   C

a1   : We shall be meeting them   certainly this Saturday.
           S   A   V   O   C

a2   : We shan't be meeting them   on Friday.
           S   Neg A   V   O   C

Neg Q : Won't we be touching Madras on our train route?
          Neg A   S   A   V   C   C

a1   : We shall be touching Madras en route to Bangalore.
           S   A   V   C   C

a2   : We shan't be touching that place.
           S   Neg A   V   O

EQ 1 : You will be changing train at Delhi, won't you?
           S   A   V   O   C   Q tag

a1   : I will be changing train at Delhi for Kalka.
          S   A   V   O   C

a2   : I won't be changing train at Nizamuddin for Kalka.
          S   Neg A   V   O   C

EQ 2 : The tenants shan't be vacating the house before Monday, shall they?
              S   Neg A   V   O   C   Q tag

a1   : They shall be vacating the house on Monday.
             S   A   V   O   C

a2   : They shan't be vacating the house   before Monday next.
             S   Neg A   V   O   C

Sample sentences with universal auxiliaries:

Gen Q : When might you be taking leave for your sister's wedding?
           I   A   S   A   V   O

a1   : I might be taking it on 15 and 16th of next month.

a2   : I might not be taking it before 15th of next moth.

Sp Q : Wouldn't you be taking part in the sports competition next month?

a1   : I could be taking part in it.

Neg Q : Couldn't you keep practising your running till then?

EQ1   : You could be getting used to a new coach, couldn't you?

a2   : I couldn't be getting used to a new foreign coach at all.

EQ2   : You won't be becoming used to modern dancing, will you?

a2   : Surely I shall not. I would keep performing classical dances only.

Examples of sentences of daily use.

When would you be changing into your nightie?
I shall be changing into my nightie usually after dinner.
Will you be going with your father to church?
Who all could be accompanying your father to church?

All of us will be accompanying our father to church.

How will you be proceeding to your Institute tomorrow morning?

I will be proceeding to hockey ground on my bicycle.

Can't you keep riding your moped for college up and down daily?

I won't be using it because I can't afford that much of petrol. (Complex)

Who all will you be inviting for your birthday party?

Wouldn't you be getting used to swimming in the pool within a week?

I shall keep using the pool until I get used to it. (Complex)

When will you be applying for a seat in the Arts college?

I might be eating my lunch around 12 noon today.

We will be playing volley ball towards evening, won't we?

We shall be revising our history lesson tonight, shan't we?

Mother could be joining us shortly.

Won't your mother be getting angry with you?

I will be buying my notebooks this evening.

My sister and I will be going to a movie this evening.

We won't be mixing with you all from now onwards.

Implied future tense

We often use the 'Simple present or Present continuous tenses' for future actions instead of the conventional Future and Future continuous tenses. In order that the sentence is not misunderstood we must indicate that the timing of the action will be in some future time when we use the Simple present and Present continuous for future actions.

Study the following examples:

(a)   I am going to Bangalore tomorrow. (This sentence is equal to, "I will be going to Bangalore tomorrow")

(b)   We write our final examination next Monday. (Here the timing of the action is in the future)

(c)   The PM of England visits Chennai next week.

(d)   We go to New Delhi this evening.

(e)   We are not meeting my Aunt in her house till next Friday.

Q.   When do you take up your new job?

a2.   I don't take up the new job till next month.

Q.   Is your father coming to the hostel this week-end?

a1.   He is coming here next week-end.

Q.   Won't the coach be teaching us hockey next Saturday morning?

a1.   He is teaching us hockey definitely next Saturday morning.

The newspapers and journalists will never use the conventional Future and Future continuous auxiliaries for future events/actions. They will always use the Simple present or Present continuous for them. Look for such expressions in the papers or when you hear the news broadcasts/telecasts.

But, if we do not indicate the timing of the proposed action, the sentence indeed will refer to actions of genuine Simple present or Present continuous.

Imaginary conversation between three friends using all the 8 tenses learnt so far.

Sugirtha	:	Venu and Jeevitha, aren't we visiting the zoo tomorrow?
Venu	:	Of course we are visiting. Wouldn't you be coming Jeevitha?
Jeevitha	:	Well, I am not very sure, you know? My mother is arriving from Trichy tomorrow.
Sugirtha	:	At what time is she arriving?
Jeevitha	:	At 7 a.m., I think. (Complex sentence)
Venu	:	But, we are leaving only at 9 a.m. aren't we?
Sugirtha	:	So, you are coming with us to the zoo. Don't make any excuses.
Venu	:	Did you invite anyone else, Sugirtha?
Sugirtha	:	I did invite Pandian from our colony but he was not very keen.
Venu	:	I know Pandian well. He is very much used to outright lazyness. Would never take part in any activity. He would keep mixing with his own immediate relatives only.
Jeevitha	:	That is very selfish, don't you think?
Venu	:	It is a selfish attitude, I agree. (Complex sentence) He could be getting used to some new persons if we advise him.
Jeevitha	:	How does he spend his holidays?
Venu	:	He would be usually spending it at home. Never combines with any of his classmates.
Sugirtha	:	He doesn't perhaps get bored with the same persons. Anyway, why are you wasting time on his conduct? (This is a conventional Present Cont. statement)
Jeevitha	:	Quite right. Forget about Pandian. Think about our visit to the zoo.
Venu	:	How are we going to Vandaloor?
Sugirtha	:	We take the Vandaloor bus from Parry's corner at 10 a.m.
Jeevitha	:	Surely we are taking pack lunch with us, aren't we?
Venu	:	Yes, we are. Bring some nice things with you. OK?
Sugirtha	:	I bet she will. Jeevitha's aunt is a good cook.
Jeevitha	:	Don't tell me your mother is not?
Sugirtha	:	My mother too is a good cook. Listen, no mother will ever send her children on a picnic without a heavy bag of meal.
Venu and Jeevitha	:	Agreed. Don't argue about it unnecessarily. OK?

Exercise

Give affirmative answer:

1. Will all the invitees be staying back here even after dinner?
2. What will your father be doing tomorrow morning?

3. How shall the mechanic repair this TV set? It is a foreign make.
4. Which Chapter will we be revising next week?
5. Aren't you leaving for Kolkata by tomorrow's Coromondal express?
6. Won't you be watching your favourite programme on TV tonight?
7. When will the duty doctor be visiting you next?
8. The librarian will not be loaning me any book, will he?
9. Aren't your elder sister and her husband returning to India next month?
10. Surely, you won't let me down, will you?

Give negative answer in the continuous tense or in implied future tense:

11. Where will you keep this table inside your house?
12. Are you going with your mother to temple this evening?
13. Isn't the Education minister visiting our college today along with the D.T.E.?
14. Some foreign tourists will be visiting our school today, won't they?
15. Who is looking after you when your parents go on a short leave?

Point out the mistake(s) in the following sentences and rewrite them:

16. They shan't travelling together on the same train.
17. We are indeed doing to the supermarket early morning today.
18. How will be Madhavi reaching the school in this heavy rain?
19. I shan't walking on the sand.
20. We could going to the beach all by ourselves.
21. We also coming with you to the hotel.
22. My brother and sister are joining this library from last month.
23. Will India supporting the Tamils' cause in Sri Lanka?
24. India always supporting her neighbours against any kind of injustice.
25. Who acting in tomorrow's school drama?

Give answers in a suitable Future tense and Implied future tense for every question:

26. Are you joining the protest march or not?
27. Would you be watching the Euro 2000 football match on the T.V later today?
28. Couldn't you be taking part in the elocution competition?
29. The History Professor will scold you for your negligence in the last exam, won't he?
30. Shan't the juniors be singing the National anthem after the function?

Write the remaining 6 categories of sentences:

31. We might meet a stronger team in tomorrow's match, mightn't we?
32. How long could we keep helping this poor boy?
33. Some of us could be getting used to early sleep.
34. Our friends might still be waiting at the bus stand for us.
35. Isn't Moses coming with us for the week-end trek?

Analyse the following sentences. i.e. state the tense, divide it into parts and identify the part of speech of every word:

36. We couldn't be becoming used to this style of playing hockey.
37. Three males and 2 females along with their parents would keep visiting you in the hostel every Saturday.
38. One of the students from II year could be taking our class today.
39 When could some of us meet the Principal about some extra classes in English?
40. Mukherjee cannot explain any rules to us clearly.

Chapter 15

RECAPITULATION

So far we have learnt 8 tenses, which fall under three distinct families as shown below:

Present family	-	Present tense
		Present continuous tenses
		Simple present tense
Past family	-	Past tense
		Past continuous tense
		Simple past
Future family	-	Future tense
		Future continuous tense

You can see that there is an option in each family. If a question is asked in the Past tense, you may answer it in any of the three tenses belonging to that family, whichever you consider most suitable. And similarly in the future family. Besides the conventional Future and Future continuous, you may also use the Implied future tense. But this flexibility is not available in the Present family because the use is different for each.

Tenses and their auxiliaries

We use many auxiliaries for every tense. You would recall that auxiliaries don't have a meaning. We use each for certain situation(s). You need to be clear about them before you pick out a suitable auxiliary for the tense concerned.

Now, list out the auxiliaries for the above 8 tenses:

Present family

1. *Present tense* - AM, IS, ARE, HAS, HAVE, am/is/are USED TO. (6)

2. *Present continuous* - AM, IS, ARE, CAN BE, MAY BE, WOULD BE, COULD BE, SHOULD BE, MUST BE, NEED BE, OUGHT TO BE, WILL BE, SHALL BE, am/is/are GOING TO, am/is/are/can be/may be/would be/could be/should be, must be/need be/will be/shall be **getting/becoming** USED TO (15)

3. *Simple present* - DO, DOES, CAN, MAY, WOULD, COULD, SHOULD, MUST, DARE, NEED, OUGHT TO, WILL SHALL, can/may/would/could/should/must/ought to/will/shall **get/become/be** USED TO. do/does/can/may/would/could/should/must/dare/need/ought to KEEP (15)

Past family

1. *Past tense*	-	WAS, WERE, HAD, was/were USED TO (4)
2. *Past continuous*	-	WAS, WERE, did KEEP, was/were **getting/becoming** USED TO (4)
3. *Simple past*	-	DID, COULD, WOULD, did … USE TO (4)

Future family

| 1. *Future* | - | WILL, SHALL, COULD, WOULD, MIGHT, am/is/are GOING TO, will/shall/could/would/might **get/become/ be** USED TO (7) |
| 2. *Future continuous* | - | WILL BE, SHALL BE, COULD BE, WOULD BE, MIGHT BE, shall/will/could/would/might KEEP, will be/shall be/could be/would be/might be **getting becom- ing** USED TO (7) |

Summary

USED TO appears in all the 8 tenses.

WOULD and COULD appear in all families but in 6 tenses only (i.e. except Present and Past tenses)

Exercise

Answer in the affirmative in more than one tense:

1. Weren't you revising Lord Tennyson's poem last night?
2. What were your tutor's comments on your yesterday's essay?
3. When will we go to the computer center?
4. Hasn't Mano returned your class notes notebook till now?
5. What job is your elder brother doing nowadays?
6. Don't the hostel students come to class often with dirty shoes?
7. Mrinalini doesn't wear a saree these days for college, does she?
8. Who is your partner in the Physics lab?
9. How many dogs have you in your home?
10. Why are you always borrowing money from Mohan?
11. Are you the leader of your class?
12. Do you teach History to your small brother without reference to any book?
13. Doesn't Rajan have a good memory for History dates?
14. Have you any marbles inside your pocket?

Answer in the negative in any suitable two tenses:

15. Doesn't Saroja stand first in most of the subjects?
16. The lazy boys don't study hard for any exam, do they?
17. Would you be in the library today after college hours?

18. Shouldn't you report to the warden about the theft of your bath-towel?
19. Did you keep beating the snake until its death?
20. This point surely wasn't in the agenda, was it?
21. Didn't your cousin brother take the AFMS entrance examination?
22. Who is representing your class in the Students' meeting?
23. Is there something wrong in your house?
24. Why must I give-up the practice of eating chocolates?
25. Don't buy cheap magazines.
26. Somasundaram never fails in any subject, does he?
27. Is New Delhi a city of sky scrapers?
28. How far is Coimbatore from Chennai?
29. Who will be addressing the football team today?

Analyse the following sentences which have long Subject and long O/C:

30. All the students of B.Sc II year and B.A. I year will line up in front of the Principal's office this afternoon.
31. Nanavathy wasn't in a good physical condition during today's football match, was he?
32. You did show your water colour painting along with a canvas work to your drawing teacher, didn't you?
33. The Chief Minister and his 6 Cabinet Ministers are visiting our village school at 4 p.m.
34. Some people from our city don't observe prohibition at all.
35. Is Present continuous tense interchangeable with Simple present? Why or why not?
36. Past continuous is interchangeable with Simple past. Justify your answer.
37. Is Future continuous interchangeable with Present continuous? If yes, give three examples.
38. In which respect(s) does the Future tense differ from the Simple past and Simple present?
39. What are the two different methods of viewing an English sentence?
40. What is the common factor between Object and Complement in a sentence?

Chapter 16

PERFECT TENSES
PRESENT PERFECT TENSE (9)

General

All the 8 tenses we learnt so far come under one particular time period only.

In the PAST time period, there are three tenses - Past, Past continuous and Simple past. All the activities in these three tenses will be confined to the PAST time period only.

In the PRESENT time period, there are three tenses - Present, Present continuous and Simple present. The activities in these tenses will be confined to the PRESENT time period only.

As regards the two Future tenses, there are no activities in these at all. We only talk about an activity that will take place in some future time and we make such pronouncements in the PRESENT period.

What about an activity that starts in one time period and goes into the next? Say, an activity that started in the past entered into the present time and continues till the time of talking? What tense do we assign for such an activity? Similarly, an activity that starts in the present time and goes into the future time and ends at a certain point of time in the future time period. What tense do we use for that? Take the next case, an activity that starts in the past and ends at a particular point of time in the future; this activity will obviously cover all the three time periods. What tense do we use for that? This is where the PERFECT TENSES come to our aid. We can say that PERFECT TENSES deal with inter-time periods or 'between the three time periods'.

PRESENT PERFECT TENSE

Use

Present perfect tense belongs mostly to the Past period and partly to the Present time Period. We use it for four different activities as described below:

(a)   To indicate a completed activity in the immediate past, say a short while back.

(b)   To talk about an action that began sometime in the past and is continuing at the time of talking into the present time period.

(c)   To talk about past completed activity whose time is not known. (The action probably finished some years back!)

(d)   To describe a completed activity in the past period when we think more about the <u>effect of the activity</u> at the time of talking (present time) than about the action itself.

Rules

Subject	*Auxiliary*	*Verb form*
I, WE, YOU, THEY	HAVE	PP form
HE, SHE, IT	HAS	"

<u>Universal auxiliaries</u>

All persons	MAY HAVE	PP form
"	Has/have/may have **got/**	Use only the
PP verbs	**become/been**	USED TO

shown in bold.

We know that HAVE is a 3-in-1 word. We have used it as A.V in Chapter 3 and as normal verb in Chapter 5. Here, in the Present perfect tense we use it as 'auxiliary'. Further, in this tense we use the third form of verb - Past participle. The PP forms of all the verbs we listed out in Chapter 12 (Simple past) are shown below:

Present form	*Past form*	*Past participle*
learn	learned	learnt
talk	talked	talked
rest	rested	rested
wash	washed	washed
punish	punished	punished
lock	locked	locked
improve	improved	improved
land	landed	landed
dry	dried	dried
carry	carried	carried
study	studied	studied
cry	cried	cried
bury	buried	buried
worry	worried	worried
go	went	gone
write	wrote	written
sleep	slept	slept
leave	left	left
shake	shook	shaken
swim	swam	swum
throw	threw	thrown
ride	rode	ridden
take	took	taken
fly	flew	flown
sit	sat	sat

Present form	Past form	Past participle
run	ran	run
put	put	put
cut	cut	cut
hurt	hurt	hurt
read	read (red)	read (red)
am |		
is | =	was	been
are |	were	been
has	had	had
have	had	had
do	did	done
does	did	done

Like before, there is no shortcut to knowing the PP form of every verb. Different rules are followed. In most cases, the past forms and PP forms are the same. In some specific cases, the PP form seems to bear no relation to the Present or Past form; they are entirely new words.

It would be news to you that we use a number of PP form verbs as *adverbs*, in which case they would pass the adverb/complement test. If a PP verb appears in a sentence unaccompanied by an auxiliary, you may consider that word is doing the job of an adverb.

Sample sentences (with HAVE)

Gen Q : Where have you worked before?
          I   A   S   V   Adv

a1   : I have worked in a number of shops on part time basis.
          S   A   V   C1   C2

a2   : I haven't worked anywhere before.
        S Neg A   V   C

Sp Q : Have your students written any essays before?
           A   S   V   O   Adv

a1   : They have written one or two essays only.
          S   A   V   O   Adv

a2   : They haven't written more than two essays before.
          S Neg A   V   O   Adv

Neg A : Haven't we read this story already?
         Neg A S   V   O   Adv

a1   : We indeed have read this story already.
          S Adv   A   V   O   Adv

a2   : We have never read this story before.
          S   Neg A   V   O   Adv

EQ 1 : I   have   met   you already, haven't I?
        S   A   V   O   Adv   Q tag

EQ 2 : They haven't been here before, have they?
        S Neg A   V   C   Q tag

Sample sentences (with HAS)

Gen Q : How has this boy come here?
        I   A   S   V   Adv

a1   : He has come here by foot.
          S   A   V   C

a2   : He hasn't come here by any vehicle.
          S Neg A V   C

Sp Q : Has he noted down our house number?
       A   S   V   O

a1   : He has noted down our house number.
          S   A   V   O

a2   : He hasn't noted down anything at all.
          S Neg A V   O   C

Neg A : Hasn't this cat cried for a long time?
       Neg A   S   V   C

a1   : It has cried for a long time.
          S   A   V   C

a2   : It hasn't cried for more than two minutes.
          S Neg A V   C

EQ 1 : Kumudhini has sung well this time, hasn't she?
         S   A V   C   Q tag

EQ 2 : The new candidate hasn't done well at all, has he?
            S   Neg A V   C   Q tag

Sample sentences with the Universal auxiliaries

a1   : We may have contacted malaria during our overnight stay in the forest.

EQ1 : You may have committed a big mistake, may you not?

(<u>Note</u>: There is no abbreviated form for 'may not'. Next, we don't use normally MAY HAVE in General Q and Negative Q)

Sp Q : Have you got used to these hostel mates?
          A   S   V   A   O

a2   : (You) Don't ever get used to drugs during your college life, OK?
          S Neg A Adv V   A   O   C   Adv

Sp Q : Have you been used to late nights during your school days?
          A   V   A

EQ2 : Jonathan has got used to bad language, hasn't he?
              A   V   A

Sample sentences in various situations

Completed activity in the immediate past

Q   : Where is your brother?

a   : My brother has left for school (In other words, "He left for school just a few minutes back." If he left a long time back, the answer will be in the Simple past such as, "He left long back")

a   : My brother has gone out just a while ago.

a   : My brother may have left for school already.

Q   : What has the thief done to this lady?

a   : He hasn't done any physical harm to her; he has shaken her a bit.

Q   : Hasn't Robert got used to the Chemistry experiments?

Action that began in the past and is still continuing

a   : My father has functioned as a Govt officer for over 15 years. (This also means, that he is still functioning)

a   : We have stayed in this house for 3 years. (We are still staying here till now)

a   : Sanjay has been sick since Monday. (He is sick even now)

a   : Have you met this person before?

Past action whose time is not known

Q   : How long have you known this man?

a   : I have known him for a number of years.

Q   : How many times have you visited this supermarket?

a   : I have visited it dozens of times.

Q   : How many times has your father visited New Delhi?

a   : He has visited New Delhi at least a hundred times.

Effect of a completed activity than the activity itself

a   : I have finished all my assignments. (I am free now)

b   : The little child has cut its finger. (The finger is bleeding now)

c   : I have seen that T.V. serial. (Shall we talk about that serial?)

d   : We have examined the patient. (Compare this with, "We examined the patient." The former statement implies, 'shall we talk about the effect of the examination' while the latter is a closed file case.)

Q   : Have you been to London?

a   : I have been to London a couple of times during 1980's.

Examples of sentences of daily use

My pen is missing. Have you seen it?

I haven't seen your father for a long time. Has he gone somewhere?

I have marked you absent today. Why were you late?

Who has done this mischief?

Surely, you haven't done it, have you? Or, have you become used to trickeries?

We have searched for him all over the town but he hasn't shown up at all.

Haven't you borrowed my class work note book?

Haven't we played a match with this team some time back?

All of us have lied some time or the other, haven't we?

Father has left the office a little while back. He will be here shortly.

Why haven't you told your mother about the college excursion?

My sister hasn't told me anything about this plan at all.

Have you understood today's lesson well?

I haven't understood a thing about specific gravity.

We may not have noticed the Lecturer's presence inside the auditorium.

Imaginary conversation between three friends who use several tenses

Samuel	:	I am going to the public swimming pool now; are you coming with me?
Andrew	:	Sorry, Samuel. (I am sorry, Samuel) I am a little busy now. Shall I join you after half an hour?
Balaji	:	Hey! I am game. Wait a minute. Shall inform Mummy and come.
Samuel	:	Come along Balaji. By the way, have you taken your swimming costume?
Balaji	:	Yes, I have. Andrew also has got one, hasn't he?
Samuel	:	Andrew may have borrowed one from some one. He will be joining us a little later. Haven't you told him about our plan?
Balaji	:	I did. He said, he has some urgent work. (Complex sentence)

<u>Sam and Balaji are on their way to the pool.</u>

Samuel	:	Are you used to this public swimming pool?
Balaji	:	I haven't visited the public pool before. I always go to the club for a swim.
Samuel	:	Is your father a member there? Is it a big one or a small one?
Balaji	:	Not a big one. I think it is a 50 meter pool.
Samuel	:	The public pool is 100 meters long, you see?
Balaji	:	How long back have they built it?
Samuel	:	They may have built it about two years back.
Balaji	:	From where have you learnt swimming, Sam?
Samuel	:	Frankly, in a pond next to my house.
Balaji	:	Is it very deep?
Samuel	:	Not quite deep. About waist high.

<u>At the pool</u>

Samuel	:	Come fast. Haven't you removed your clothes?
Balaji	:	Wait, I see Andrew over there.
Samuel	:	He has come after all?
Balaji	:	Yes, he has. OK, jump. Andy boy, you may join us after you have got into your swimming costume, OK?
Andy	:	I say, the water is a little hot, isn't it? ("I say" is a starting phrase. You could view this sentence as a Complex sentence as well)

Samuel   : The outside temperature now is 37 degrees C. So, the water will be somewhat warm, won't it?

Balaji   : I am feeling nice, actually.

Samuel   : Have you taken part in any swimming competition, Andy?

Andy   : No, I haven't. I am not an expert as yet in swimming. Balaji swims well, doesn't he?

Balaji   : Thank you, Andy. I have learnt swimming from a good coach, you know? Lately I have become used to the sea-swimming as well.

    Adv   S   A   V   A   O   C

Samuel   : That makes all the difference, doesn't it? Learn anything from an expert and you will become an expert as well.

Balaji   : Quite a number of my friends too have learnt it from the same coach.

Samuel   : I am sure, Balaji has participated in some competition, hasn't he?

Andy   : Perhaps, he has.

Samuel   : Has Balaji arranged some competition for anyone?

Andy   : Have you Balaji?

Balaji   : I am afraid, no. I shall enquire about it with my father.

Andy   : Incidentally, have you won any prizes, Balaji?

Balaji   : I have participated in one or two competition all right. But I have not won any prizes at all.

- - - -

Exercise

Fill up the blank with the correct auxiliary of Present perfect tense and PP verb. The verb to be used is shown in bracket in present form.

1. Radhika have   read   4 books of James Harriet during her summer vacation. (read)

2. Some children from my colony have participated in the school drama during the final term. (participate)

3. My grandfather have arrived from Coimbatore. (arrive)

4. What have Surendran got in his hand (get)

5. Where have you been all morning? (are)

6. Many students have failed in the surprise quiz test yesterday, haven't they? (fail)

7. The Sports coach have already reported at the stadium. (report)

8. My good old friend have bought a brand new bicycle. (buy)

9. How much work have these boys done since morning? (do)

10. Have anyone brought a calculator (bring)

Answer the following in a1 or a2 form of Present perfect tense, as necessary:

11. From when did you start riding?

12. Are you doing well in your studies?

13. Do you know this man well?
14. Wasn't Rajan a clever student in B.A final year?
15. The University examiners were very considerate towards us, weren't they?

Locate the mistake(s) and rewrite the wrong sentence concerned:

16. Where has Ramanand ~~went~~? *gone*
17. How much time ~~have~~ *has* this student spent on this lesson?
18. Haven't everyone sat down in their seat?
19. When has Madhuri ~~wrote~~ *written* down her notes?
20. Has Malati counted all the children?
21. How ~~has~~ *have* they ~~come~~ *came* to church?
22. A man from a nearby village and his son has ~~come~~ *came* to our house.
23. We all ~~has~~ *have* some health problems in us.
24. We have secured admission in a new college, ~~have we~~? *haven't we?*
25. You and I haven't done badly in today's exam at all, have ~~you~~? *we?*

Write the following sentences in their equivalent Present perfect tense:

26. The HOD ~~did not come~~ *haven't came* to the class this morning.
27. The Asst. Professor *have* left the office at 3 p.m.
28. Except three students, all the others *have* understood the method well.
29. The lady students ~~did not go~~ *haven't gone* home till 4 p.m.
30. When ~~did~~ *have spoken* you speak to the HOD about me?
31. Today the Maths lecturer *have* taught us a new formula for partial differentiation.
32. ~~Didn't~~ *Haven't* my friends act very well in yesterday's stage play?
33. Miss.Hilda ~~was~~ *have been* very kind to us last year, ~~wasn't she~~? *hasn't she,*
34. These students ~~are~~ *have been* weak in English.
35. My elder sister ~~did not cook~~ *have been cooked* the meal well at all.
36. One day, my mother *has spoiled* spoilt all the dishes.
37. Ravindran *has run* runs the one hundred meters race quite fast.
38. My sister isn't failing in any test at all.
39. Your sister ~~sang~~ *has sang* well in the singing competition. *hasn't failed*
40. We ~~did not fight~~ *haven't fought* at all.

Analyse the following sentences:

41. Haven't we been used to late breakfast on Sundays?
42. You may not have met my brother.
43. You have never seen me in a swimming costume before, have you?

Write the remaining 6 categories of the following sentences:

44. Samson has never seen a video movie.
45. Hasn't he got used to too many cinemas?

Chapter 17

PRESENT PERFECT CONTINUOUS TENSE (10)

Use

We use the **Present perfect continuous tense** for three out of the four situations as applicable to the Present perfect tense. They are,

(a) For an activity that started in some past time period and is continuing into the present till the time of talking.

(b) For an activity completed in the immediate past time (same as in the Present perfect case) but we want to give importance for the duration of that action than the time of its completion.

(c) For an activity already completed but as a statement of explanation of that action at the time of talking.

Thus, this tense is interchangeable with the Present perfect tense.

Rules

Subject	Auxiliary	Verb form
I, WE, YOU, THEY	HAVE BEEN	Present in -ING
HE, SHE, IT	HAS BEEN	"
Universal auxiliaries All persons	MAY HAVE BEEN	"
"	HAS/HAVE KEPT	"
"	Has been/Have been **getting/ becoming** USED TO	Use the verbs getting/becoming only

Sample sentences (With have / has BEEN)

Gen Q : What have your friends been doing all these days?
         I   A   S   A   V   C

a1   : They have been learning several subjects including English.
         S   A   V   O

a2   : They haven't been learning Hindi or Sanskrit.
         S Neg A   V   O

Sp Q : Has Pushpa been mending these old clothes?
         A   S   A   V   O

a1   : She has been mending all these old clothes of hers.
         S   A   V   O

a2   : Pushpa hasn't been mending too many clothes.
         S Neg A   V   O

Neg Q: Hasn't Manjula been playing   too much of table tennis nowadays?
       Neg A   S   A   V   O   C

a1   : She has been playing too much of table tennis   lately.
           S   A   V   O   Adv

a2   : Manjula hasn't been playing much of table tennis   at all.
          S   Neg A   V   O   C

EQ1 : Most of the students have been conducting themselves very well
                S   A   V   O   C
        during the class hours, haven't they?
             C   Q tag

EQ2 : Some of you haven't been picking up grammar well at all, have you?
         S   Neg A   V   O   C   Q tag

Action started in the past and is continuing at the time of talking

My uncle has been playing cricket for the last 5 years. (Even now he is playing)

Hasn't your baby been sleeping for over two hours?

Our engineers have been constructing this multi storey building for over 2 years.
                               (The work is still going on)

My father has been working on his thesis from last year.

My sister has been studying in this school for over 7 years.

Note:

For an action that started in the past and is continuing till the time of talking, always use the Present perfect continuous tense and not the Present perfect. The reason is that the latter could be misunderstood for a "closed case but reopened."

Importance for the duration of the action though completed in the immediate past:

Q   : Where was your brother all these years?

a1   : He has been doing his engineering course for 4 years. (A completed activity)

Q   : Haven't all of you been living in this house till last year?

a1   : All of us have been living in this house till last year.

Q   : Haven't we been playing football for too long?

EQ1 : We have been eating too many mangoes during this season, haven't we?

a2   : We haven't been reading the Bible regularly at all in recent times.

You can see that the action is over in the above sentences. But since we want to give importance for the duration of the completed activity, we have gone in for the Present perfect continuous tense instead of the conventional Present perfect. "We have lived in this house till last year" would also be correct because this then would be a "re-opened case" model.

As statement of explanation for a completed activity

Q   : Where have you been the whole day?

a1   : I have been revising my English lessons in my friend's house. ("Action completed" case)

a 2   : I haven't been wasting my time at all.

Sentences with Universal auxiliaries

Use: For an action that started in the past and is continuing till the present time of talking. (This is the only use of the auxiliaries...KEPT and .... USED TO)

Sp Q : Hasn't your younger daughter kept pestering you for more and more sarees?

a1   : Indeed she has kept worrying me for more sarees.

a1   : Many students from the final semester have kept asking for more study leave.

(We don't normally use a2 with the auxiliary KEPT as the sentences would not sound well. A Simple past sentence would be more suitable)

a1   : Some of us have been getting used to the new canteen contractor's food for our lunch, haven't we?

Gen Q : Since when have you all been getting used to tea and coffee during lunch hour?

EQ1   : You haven't been getting used to late nights, have you?

We don't use these 2 universal auxiliaries for the remaining situations.

For a completed activity in the immediate past:

Neg Q : Hasn't Usha been going home for all her short holidays?

a1   : She may have been going, but I am not sure.

Gen Q : When did Mahima learn shuttle-cock badminton?

a1   : She may have been learning it during her summer vacation.

Exercise

Rewrite the following sentences in Present perfect continuous tense:

1. Is your sister preparing breakfast for the family?
2. We were learning French during the previous term.
3. It is raining heavily outside, isn't it?
4. My small brother often tells lies just for fun.
5. Vishal and Meenakshi are playing Chess inside the living room.
6. Wasn't Malathi painting a view of the lake-side?
7. Some of you have played in the rain, haven't you?
8. Our elder sister is protecting us from punishment.
9. We have study time between 7 and 8 p.m.
10. Sudhir hasn't any sense of humour at all.

Give your answer in the Present perfect or Present perfect continuous tense whichever appears more suitable:

11. Madhuri ~~went~~ to Shimla for summer vacation, ~~didn't she?~~
12. ~~Didn't~~ you ~~break~~ that window-pane?
13. ~~Did~~ all your friends return home on time after the match?
14. All the girls of our class ~~walked~~ to the library, ~~didn't they?~~
15. They ~~hid~~ themselves under a tree when it rained heavily, ~~didn't they?~~

Answer the following questions in the affirmative in Present perfect continuous tense:

16. How much work have the sweepers done since 8 a.m.?
17. The orphanage inmates have locked up the dormitory from inside, haven't they?
18. Hasn't this beggar kept sitting near our gate the whole afternoon?
19. Where has your father been taking treatment for his Asthma?
20. You haven't told me the real truth at all.

Correct the mistake(s) and rewrite the wrong sentence concerned:

21. Hasn't Mahesh wrote this unsigned letter?
22. Some children has not slept in the afternoon.
23. Surely the bright students haven't doing badly in any test.
24. How much time you have spend on this problem?
25. Some parents haven't visited their ward for many days, did they?
26. Two of my friends have getting used to a few card games.
27. Have they regret their mistake?
28. How have the villagers used to the cricket game?
29. All of you have indeed worked hard for your finals, hasn't you?
30. Have you ever score the lowest mark in any of your tests?

Convert the following sentences into equivalent Present perfect tense:

31. How are you?
32. I am doing well, thank you very much.
33. Am I your enemy?
34. I have a nice brief case, haven't?
35. We are not fools.

Write the remaining 6 categories of sentences:

36. Our HOD may have been contributing some articles to the city Newspapers.
37. Hasn't our Associate lecturer kept postponing her marriage for more than 2 years?
38. Mahadevan from Mechanical engineering dept has been getting used to electronic gadgets, hasn't he?

Analyse the following sentences:

39. We may not have been protecting you very seriously all these days.
40. Sharda has been becoming used to dozens of bananas daily.

Chapter 18

PAST PERFECT TENSE (11)

Use

We use the **Past perfect tense,**

(a)   For an action that started and finished in the past period. (Thus, this tense is interchangeable with the Simple past)

(b)   If two actions took place in the past, we use the Past perfect for the first action and Simple past for the second.

(Such use is applicable in Complex sentences which we shall learn later).

(c)   When we refer to an action of the past as a follow up matter.

(d)   In reported speeches. i.e. When we describe what someone had said sometime in the past. (This use also comes in Complex sentence)

Rule

Subject	Auxiliary	Verb form
ALL PERSONS	HAD	PP form
Universal auxiliary		
"	Had **become/got/been**	Use only the PP
	USED TO	verbs shown in **bold**.

Sample sentences (with HAD)

For a completed activity in the past. (The first situation)

Gen Q : When had Sasikaran obtained his Science degree?
          I   A   S   V   O

a1   : He had obtained it in 1999.
         S   A   V   O   C

a2   : He hadn't obtained it in 1998.
         S Neg A   V   O   C

Sp Q : Had Reshmi continued her studies for 2 more years?
         A   S   V   O   C

a1   : She had continued her studies for 2 more years.
         S   A   V   O   C

a2   : She hadn't continued her studies after two years.
         S Neg A   V   O   C

Neg Q : Hadn't you met my maternal uncle before?
         Neg A S   V   O   Adv

```
a1    : I   had   met   him   once before.
        S    A    V     O        C
a2    : I   had never   met   him   before.
        S   Neg A    V     O    Adv
EQ1   : You  had  already  abandoned  this idea, hadn't you?
         S    A    Adv       V         O      Q tag
EQ2   : You  hadn't  done  anything  seriously wrong in class today, had you?
         S   Neg A   V     O             C                          Q tag
```

We can write all these sentences in Simple past as well. So, how do we choose one in preference to the other? We use the Simple past only for the 'closed cases'; in other words we can never open that file again. But, if we have to or talk about that past event, we prefer the Past perfect. For instance, if we say, "This student withdrew from our college" it is such a case we don't want to talk about any further. But, if we want to talk some follow up matter, we frame the sentence as, "She had gone away from our college, but she might return next year."

In certain respects, we use the Past perfect for distant past cases and Simple past for recent past cases.

For the other 3 situations, we normally use this auxiliary in Complex sentences. When we study Complex sentences in detail, we shall come back to the Past perfect tense.

Sample sentences (with …. USED TO)

Neg Q : Hadn't your children got used to your new house?

a1   : My classmates had been used to this location already as a picnic site.

Gen Q : When had you become used to your new motorbike?

a1   : I had become used to it within a week.

a2   : I hadn't been used to it as yet.

Note:

More auxiliaries would get added to "Past perfect tense". We shall revert to this tense after we cover 'Future in the past' tense. (Chapter 22)

Exercise

Rewrite the following Simple past sentences in Past perfect tense:

1. My sister decorated this birthday cake.
2. Did your tuition master revise 'The Ancient mariner' today?
3. The door-to-door sales girl brought several samples with her.
4. All of you witnessed the demonstration on coffee making, didn't you?
5. Some students didn't make the grade in the entrance test, did they?

Answer the following questions in Past perfect affirmative:

6. How many of you were eligible for voting in the recent Elections?
7. When were you eighteen years of age?
8. Where all have you studied before?
9. Didn't the Physics demonstrator scold you for your poor performance?
10. Suguna has told a lie, hasn't she?
11. Some of us walked to the station in the rain, didn't we?
12. Didn't you send my telegram?

Locate the mistake if any and rewrite the wrong sentence concerned:

13. i written some letters to my friends last year.
14. The train had stop just before the signal post.
15. Hadn't all the passengers ran out of the bus immediately after the accident?
16. The flash floods did caused serious damage to many thatched houses.
17. Karuna never told me about your brother's selection as captain.
18. You had spoke to my class teacher, hadn't you?
19. We had have a surprise test today on two English poems.
20. Ramachandran had cut classes today, hasn't he?
21. Some Staffs had used to the mischievous students.
22. We hadn't saw any such cases of theft in our school.

Try rewriting the following sentences in Past perfect tense:

23. Wasn't Mr. Sebastian a good English tutor?
24. We have played against the 'A' team several times.
25. Where was your father when the fire broke out? (Complex sentence)
26. There were far too many mistakes in your essay.
27. Weren't you the top sportsman in the Post graduate section last year?
28. I was your prefect till last month, wasn't I?
29. My parents were spending their holiday in the next village for 3 days.
30. We had an ideal holiday for a change.
31. Haven't you been an angry young man?
32. My sister hasn't failed in any subject last year.
33. I don't have any money with me now.
34. You are not a perfect lady, are you?
35. No college student ever shied away from responsibility.

Bring out the differences between the pairs of sentences given below:

36. (a) He has worked in my house. (b) He had worked in my house.
37. (a) This student has been too poor. (b) He is too poor.
38. (a) He had voted against this political party. (b) He has been voting against this political party every time.
39. (a) Some students did run away at the sight of a heavy bull. (b) They had run away.
40. (a) Chennai is a big city. (b) Chennai had been a big city.

Write the remaining 6 categories for the following sentences:

41. My aged uncle hadn't had a bad headache for several weeks.
42. Your District hadn't been used to severe drought lately, had it?
43. We had become immune to criticism in recent days.
44. Hadn't you been getting used to cornflakes for breakfast?
45. When had you started your horse riding practice?

Analyse the following sentences:

46. Where all had you gone today?
47. On every attempt, you had seen only water and water.
48. You hadn't got used to the Nun so easily, had you?
49. We have had a bad time today.
50. Some of us had not forgotten till this day the good tips from our football coach.

Chapter 19

PAST PERFECT CONTINUOUS TENSE (12)

Use

We use **the Past perfect continuous tense** for the same 4 situations as given for the Past perfect tense. When we want to give importance for the duration of the action concerned we choose the continuous tense. Thus, the continuous tense is interchangeable with the Past perfect tense.

Rule

Subject	Auxiliary	Verb form
ALL PERSONS	HAD BEEN	Present in -ING
Universal auxiliaries		
"	HAD KEPT	"
"	had been **getting/becoming** USED TO	Use only the verbs shown in **bold**.

Sample sentences

For a completed activity. (The first situation)

Gen Q : What had our Principal been planning about the sports programme?
             I   A   S   A   V   O

a1   : He had been planning it on a grand scale.
           S   A   V   O   C

a2   : He hadn't been planning anything as yet.
           S   Neg A   V   O   C

Sp Q : Had our peon been distributing these notices to all students?
           A   S   A   V   O1   O2

a 1 : He had been distributing these notices to all students.
           S   A   V   O

a2   : He hadn't been distributing them to outsiders.
           S   Neg A   V   O

Neg Q : Hadn't the children been driving the parents mad during the long
        Neg A   S   A   V   O1   C
        summer vacation?
             C

a1   : The children had been driving the parents crazy actually.
              S   A   V   O1   C

a2   : They hadn't been pestering the parents so much as all that.
           S   NegA   V   O   O

EQ1 : Only   some of you   had been   preparing   yourselves   well
        Adv   S   A   V   O   Adv

for the finals, hadn't you?
    O   Q tag

EQ2 : The class IV staffs hadn't been doing their work properly, had they?
          S   NegA   V   O1   Adv   Q tag

With universal auxiliaries

EQ1 : Your wards had kept guessing about their future, hadn't they?

a1 : They had kept driving you mad surely during holidays.

Sp Q : Had you been getting used to the rowdy students in this school?

a2 : Some of us hadn't been becoming used to their hostile attitude.

Note:

We shall revert to the remaining 3 situations when we learn in detail about Complex sentences.

Exercise

Rewrite the following sentences in Past perfect continuous tense:

1. Two peons had come again with their leave application.
2. Mary was continuing in the same class for another year.
3. Suresh had played in the cricket team for over 3 years, hadn't he?
4. When had you seen this person in our compound?
5. Who was walking with you last evening?
6. That person over there had told me a big lie.
7. Have you been practising your football?
8. Where were you taking tuition in English last year?
9. Why hadn't you told me about the illicit liquor brewing?
10. Weren't you staying in your aunt's house for 3 full days?
11. Who were your close friends in the previous colony?
12. Was this young lady your classmate last year?
13. Didn't you write an article of sorts on 'Camels' last week?
14. Sudhir ran faster than you in the 100 meters race, didn't he?
15. Manohar warned you about heavy rains tomorrow, hasn't he?

Correct the mistake(s) if any in the following sentences and rewrite the concerned one:

16. Shobana had suffering from fever since yesterday.
17. Hadn't Raghavan been forgotten his responsibilities lately?
18. Varadhan been taking part in classical music classes quietly.
19. Ravichandran hadn't scoring high marks these days in every test.
20. Many people were been taking away their children from the new school.
21. Geography never been his strong subject at all.

22. Mettur dam reservoir never gone dry in the last 50 years.
23. Rabindranath Tagore had been my favourite poet.
24. Why hadn't Srinivasan met me during the games period yesterday?
25. Were you ever rash in your life?

Rewrite the following sentences in any of their equivalent past family tense without significantly changing the meaning:

26. We had been here before.
27. All of you some time or the other had behaved childishly, hadn't you?
28. They had been waiting for the train for over 2 hours.
29. All of us had kept quiet during their fight.
30. You hadn't a good training in boxing at all.
31. We were keen students, weren't we?
32. We haven't studied well at all for every test.
33. Were you meeting this boy for the first time?
34. Weren't you sick at home for 4 full days?
35. My parents weren't at home last evening at 7 p.m.

Answer in the affirmative:

36. Hadn't the HOD kept you waiting outside his office for more than an hour?
37. You had been getting used to staying with your elder brother, hadn't you?

Analyse the following sentences:

38. Some of us had got used to low level English.
39. You have kept using my class notes, haven't you?
40. You might have hidden some of my things in your room.
41. You must have been getting used to a few bad habits.
42. He ought not to have been copying the bright students' answers.

Write the remaining 6 categories of sentences:

43. Lately, we hadn't been doing well in our class tests.
44. We had kept absenting ourselves for so many days.
45. When had we been getting used to late-rising?

Chapter 20

FUTURE PERFECT TENSE (13)

Use

We use the **Future perfect tense** to indicate the completion/termination of an activity by a specified time in the future time period. (What about the action itself? It could be in progress at the time of talking and positively continuing into the future period or the activity could start at some time in the future period but well before the completion time. Thus, this tense could link up all the three time periods.)

If the time of termination of the activity is not shown, it will not be a Future perfect tense at all but some other.

Rules

Subject	Auxiliary	Verb form
ALL PERSONS	WILL HAVE	PP form
	SHALL HAVE	"

Universal auxiliary

ALL PERSONS	will/shall have **got/ become/ been** USED TO	Use only the PP verbs shown in bold.

Sample sentences (with WILL/SHALL HAVE)

Gen Q : When will you have obtained your Science degree?
        I   A   S   A   V   O

a1   : I will have obtained my degree in the year 2005.
        S   A   V   O   C

a2   : I won't have obtained my degree before 2005.
        S   Neg A   V   O   C

Sp Q : Shall we have reached Frankfurt by this evening?
        A   S   A   V   C

a1   : We shall have reached Frankfurt positively by 6 p.m. local time.
        S   A   V   C

a2   : We shan't have reached before 6 p.m. at all.
        S   Neg A   V   C

Neg Q : Won't your elder son have obtained his engineering degree
        Neg A   S   A   V   O
        by May next year?
             C

a1   : He will have obtained it by May next year.
        S   A   V   O   C

a2   : He   will not have obtained   it   before May next year.
        S   Neg A   V   O   C

EQ1 : All students will have paid   their term fees by next week, won't they?
           S   A   V   O   C   Q tag

EQ2 : All staffs shan't have received   their salary before 2nd of next
          S   Neg A   V   O   C
       month, shall they?
          C   Q tag

<u>Note</u>

If we frame a question in the conventional Future tense such as "When will you reach your house?", it will merely show an *intention*. But when we want to know the exact time of reaching the house, we have to use the Future perfect tense.

In response if a person replies "I shall reach my house by 6 p.m." it will merely show an *intention*. Nor will it show that the action is already in progress or that the action will surely start well before the 'reaching time'. Thus, the conventional Future tense will not be an accurate answer to indicate the exact time of completion of an activity.

Sample sentences (with …. USED TO)

Gen Q : How will you have become used to a new country within 2 days?
          I   A   S   A   V   A   O   C

a1   : We shall surely have become used to a new country within 2 days with the help of some of our relatives.

a2   : We shan't have become used to a new country within 2 days without someone's help.

SpQ   : Will you have got used to your lady lecturer by next week?

Neg Q : Won't your baby have got used to a new ayah by tomorrow?

EQ1   : My friend will have been used to your strict routine by next week, won't he?

EQ2   : Your mother shan't have got used to a new servant maid even after a week, shall she?

Exercise

Rewrite the following sentences in Future perfect tense:

1. I shall return your loan next month.
2. Will you inform the doctor?
3. Someone will fetch a chair for you before the Chief guest's arrival.
4. My baby sometimes will cry continuously for some 10 minutes before I fetch the milk for her. (A Complex sentence)
5. When will you invite me for a game of Bridge in your house?
6. Surely we shall get used to your method of teaching Mathematics.

Answer the following questions in the negative in Future perfect tense:

7. Isn't Thambidurai meeting you this evening?
8. Your friends are leaving Mumbai for Chennai tomorrow morning, aren't they?
9. Won't you spend another hour in my house?
10. Shan't we know the lottery result by tomorrow morning?
11. When does your cousin brother leave for school?
12. Will all your friends get used to this new play ground?

Locate the mistake(s) and rewrite in proper Future perfect tense:

13. My senior brother shall have discuss the issue with my teacher by next Saturday.
14. When will the Inspector of schools visited our school?
15. My maternal uncle didn't have like your food preparation at all.
16. Meeran will have ran 2 KM by 5 p.m. this evening.
17. Won't Pandian has won the match tomorrow?
18. We won't agreed to this proposal even on your insistence.
19. All the guardians will attend the function without exception.
20. My mother will finished her cooking by 12 noon.
21. Kumar will boarded the train by 7 p.m. this evening.
22. Surendran completed this job sharp at 4 p.m. The time now is 1 p.m.

Rewrite the following sentences to have 'activities' in them:

23. We ought to complete this essay by 6 p.m. tomorrow.
24. Your friends and I will be going out on an excursion to Mamallapuram tomorrow.
25. Our teacher will teach us a new subject tomorrow.
26. We shall play a friendly football match tomorrow, shan't we?
27. They will not visit my house even by next week.

State if there is any activity in the following sentences. Justify your answer:

28. All the voters will cast their votes by tomorrow evening.
29. Will you coach me in tennis?
30. Will you have come out of the hospital by tomorrow forenoon?
31. Not all of them shall have finished their education by next year, will they?
32. The doctors won't have completed the operation even by 2 p.m. tomorrow.
33. We shall look into your personal problem next week.
34. My uncle will have seen his daughter in the hostel by the following evening.
35. All the players of our hockey team will not drink more than one cup of tea.
36. Some children will not spend their vacation in a profitable way at all.
37. Some of us shall have finished reading at least a dozen books before our summer vacation ends.

Fill up the blank with the correct auxiliary according to the intended meaning of the sentences:

38. Our guests .... arrived by 10 p.m. tonight.
39. Some of my classmates .... going for a long car drive next week.
40. Will your father .... met my teacher by this evening?
41. Naughty children .... have escaped the teacher's punishment.
42. Two and Five .... make Eight.

Write the remaining 6 categories of sentences:

43. Won't you have completed your college studies by March next year?
44. You shall have met your cousin sister tomorrow by this time, shan't you?
45. The low income group people won't become used to begging even during hard days.

Chapter 21

FUTURE PERFECT CONTINUOUS TENSE (14)

Use

We use the **Future perfect continuous tense** to indicate an activity as being in progress over a period of time and will end by a particular time in the future time period.

Thus, for the concerned situation we may use either the Future perfect or Future perfect continuous tense but the latter will give prominence for the *duration* of the activity.

Rules

Subject	*Auxiliary*	*Verb form*
ALL PERSONS	WILL HAVE BEEN	Present in - ING
	SHALL HAVE BEEN	"

Universal auxiliaries

"	will/shall have KEPT	"
"	will/shall have been **getting/ becoming** USED TO	Use only the verbs shown in **bold**

Sample sentences

Gen Q : When will our Professor have been living in the official house for 4
        I   A   S   A   V   C
years by next March?
       C

a1   : He will have been living in the official residence for 4 years.
          S   A   V   C

a2   : He won't have been living in the official house for less than 4 years.
        S   Neg A   V   C
in the official residence.
       C

Sp Q : Will these three sisters have been fighting their property case
        A   S   A   V   O
for 3 years by next February?
       C

a1   : They will have been fighting their property case for 3 years.
         S   A   V   O   C

a2   : They shan't have been fighting the property case for less than
         S   Neg A   V   O   C
3 years by next February.
       C

Neg Q: Won't your elder brother have been staying as paying guest for 2
     Neg A   S   A   V   O
     years by next April?
         C

a1   :   He will have been staying as paying guest for 2 years by next April?
         S   A   V   O   C

a2   :   My elder brother won't have been staying as paying guest for less
                  S   A   V   O
     than 2 years by next April.
         C

EQ1 : Peter will have been changing room three times by next year, won't he?
        S   A   V   O   C   Q tag

EQ2 : Miss. Ratna won't have been teaching for more than 15 years in this
        S   Neg A   V   C
     college by next decade, will she?
         C   Q tag

Sample sentences (with the Universal auxiliaries)

a1   :   We shall have kept visiting him till the end of his college studies.
a1   :   You shall have been getting used to this tennis court by end of next month.
a2   :   We won't have been getting used to this tennis court even by end of next year!
Sp Q : Will you have been becoming used to your new Moped by next week?

Note:

We can write all the above examples in Future perfect tense also with equal effect. In fact, that's what we normally do. We seldom use the Future perfect continuous tense either in spoken form or written form. Thus, this continuous tense is of academic interest only but yet, you must know the rule how to use the continuous tense.

Exercise

Rewrite the following sentences in Future perfect and Future perfect continuous tenses:

1. Martha shall attend the tuition class till next March.
2. Our present History teacher will not be teaching in our school next year.
3. You will hand over your assignment positively by tomorrow morning, won't you?
4. Mrs.Radha will not be handling the II year class anymore, will she?
5. Won't the hostel matron feel offended if we disregard her? (Complex sentence)
6. How will we go for our weekly outing tomorrow?.
7. Aren't we coming for the extra class tomorrow?
8. Which position will you accept in the football team?

9. What shall your parents be doing next Sunday morning?
10. Why shall we protest against the new time table?

Convert the following sentences in Future perfect continuous tense:

11. They shall have completed the project assignment by tomorrow evening.
12. We shall have covered at least 8 KM by 2 p.m. this afternoon.
13. All of us shall have completed our degree by next April.
14. Krishna water will have reached Chennai reservoirs by the first week of next month.
15. My parents will have stepped out of this train by tomorrow morning.

Convert the following continuous tense sentences into Future perfect continuous tense and verify whether the meaning is the same or has changed:

16. I was proceeding to the restaurant at 7 a.m.
17. We had been studying till 1 a.m.
18. Weren't we feeling sorry for all our misdeeds in the library?
19. That boy over there had not been playing the game in the right spirit at all.
20. One of my students had been failing in all progress tests.

Note:

You have mechanically converted the S-A-V parts into another tense.

All sentences are grammatically correct. But when we view them from the angle of the "timing of the activity" the sentences convey no proper meaning at all.

State the reasons why. What lesson do we draw out of the questions 16 - 20?

Lesson:

The time element of the activity/activities in the O/C parts of a sentence must match with the timing (tense = time) in the S-A-V parts.

Answer in the negative using Future perfect continuous tense:

21. Where shall you have kept waiting for me?
22. Will you have been getting used to any gardener in your large house?
23. How will you have managed your affairs without sufficient financial help?

Write the remaining 6 categories of sentences:

24. From when have you been getting used to this small room?
25. Some of you will have kept worrying about your final result, won't you?

Chapter 22

FUTURE IN THE PAST TENSE (15)
and
FUTURE IN THE PAST CONTINUOUS TENSE (16)

Definition

In a "Future tense" sentence, there is no action at all. The proposed action is only in your mind as an intention. The action itself will commence only at a specified time in the future time period. Once that action starts, it won't remain a future tense sentence any longer but a 'Simple present' or 'Present continuous tense' kind sentence. The most important point is that we make a "Future tense" sentence/statement in Present time only. It would be more correct to say that any future tense statement is a <u>Future looking</u> one. There will be no action in it at all.

Supposing we pronounce a "Future tense" sentence/statement from a past time point? In other words, we take our mind to some past time period and make the Future looking statement ('Future tense' statement) from there? Won't then two time periods be involved in it? Of course, there will be no action in this case either. Action, like before, will be only in your mind. We can represent such a situation diagrammatically like this -

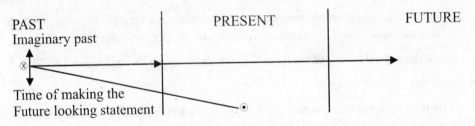

We may call such a tense as, **Future in the past tense (FIP tense)** because two time periods are invoived in the statement.

When to use

We use the FiP tense or FIP continuous tense to talk about an action we **wanted to do** in some past time and the action itself did not take place.

Rules (for FIP and FIP continuous tenses)

Tense	Auxiliary	Verb form
(a)Future in the past	MIGHT HAVE	PP verb
	WOULD HAVE	"
	COULD HAVE	"
	SHOULD HAVE	"
	MUST HAVE	"

Tense	Auxiliary	Verb form
	NEED HAVE	PP verb
	OUGHT TO HAVE	"
	might/would/could/should/ must/need/ought to have/ **got/become/been** USED TO	use only the verbs shown in **bold**
	was/were GOING TO (9 auxiliary sets)	Present form
(b) FIP continuous	MIGHT HAVE BEEN	Present in - ING
	WOULD HAVE BEEN	"
	COULD HAVE BEEN	"
	SHOULD HAVE BEEN	"
	MUST HAVE BEEN	"
	NEED HAVE BEEN	"
	OUGHT TO HAVE BEEN	"
	might/would/could/should/ must/need/ought to have been **getting/becoming** USED TO	use only the verbs shown in **bold**.
	might/would/could/should/ must/need/ought to HAVE KEPT (9 auxiliary sets)	Present in - ING

Sample sentences (FIP tense)

Gen Q : What would you have done in my place?
         I   A   S   A   V   C

a1   : I certainly would have ticked him off nice and proper.
          S Adv   A   V   O   C

a2   : I could not have done much at all.
          S   Neg A   V   O

Sp Q : Could you have painted this piece better?
         A   S   A   V   O   Adv

a1   : I would surely have painted it far better.
         S   A Adv A   V   O   C

a2   : I couldn't have done a better job of it at all.
       S Neg A   A   V   O   C

Neg Q : Mustn't you have reported   this case to the Principal earlier?
         Neg A   S   A   V   O

a1   : We were going to report but something stopped us.
           S   A   V

a2   : We ought not to have reported it to the Principal.
        S   Neg A   V O   O

EQ1 : We should have stopped near the accident site, shouldn't we?
$\quad\quad$ S $\quad\quad$ A $\quad\quad$ V $\quad\quad\quad\quad$ C $\quad\quad\quad$ Q tag

EQ2 : All our staffs need have attended the children's variety show, needn't they?
$\quad\quad\quad$ S $\quad\quad$ A $\quad\quad$ V $\quad\quad\quad\quad\quad$ O $\quad\quad$ Q tag

Here are more sentences with the remaining auxiliaries. One category only has been given. Write the remaining 6 by yourselves:

a2 $\quad$: We might not have met our uncle before departure because of our late arrival at the airport.

a1 $\quad$: You should have got used to the new college within a month.

a1 $\quad$: Some of us ought to have been used to the habit of avoiding the company of mischievous students.

Neg Q : Wouldn't you have become used to ginger coffee of our college canteen sooner or later?

Gen Q : Who was going to change their group from the first to the third?

EQ1 $\quad$: You ought to have apologised to the Vice principal immediately after the convocation, oughtn't you?

EQ2 $\quad$: You wouldn't have been getting used to a new work-bench in the Lab so easily, could you?

EQ1 $\quad$: You must have thought of a better excuse, mustn't you?

Sample sentences (FIP cont. tense). In each case, write the remaining categories of sentences:

Gen Q : Who might have been thinking of a new syllabus for English for us?

a1 $\quad$: Some enthusiastic new lecturers might have been thinking about it.

a2 $\quad$: No one might have been thinking about such a plan at all.

Sp Q $\quad$: Could all the small children in the nearby orphanage have been sleeping when you visited the orphanage?

a1 $\quad$: Most of the small children in the nearby orphanage could have been sleeping when you called at the orphanage.

a2 $\quad$: All the children could not have been sleeping at the orphanage.

Neg Q : Shouldn't the contract workers have been staying at the building site itself?

a1 $\quad$: They should have been normally staying at the site.

a2 $\quad$: They need not have been staying at the construction site.

EQ 1 : Your class students ought to have been doing better in their studies, oughtn't they?

EQ 2 : The circus animals couldn't have been wandering all around the circus arena, could they?

EQ2 $\quad$: You need not have been getting used to the anti staff-agitations in the college campus, need you?

a1 $\quad$: You must have kept going with the Professor on all his tours.

a1 $\quad$: You could have kept helping the weak students for some more time.

Note:

We normally don't use the FIP continuous tense unless we want to highlight the duration of an intended action.

Examples of sentences of daily use:

a1. Some of you should have gone to the zoo along with your teachers.

a1. You should have been more careful with your personal belongings.

a1. Your ward should have approached me immediately after the results.

Q. Couldn't you have described the way to your house more clearly?

a1. We could have gone to a Tamil movie instead of this stupid English film.

a1. All of us must have become used to a lot of hard work during the first semester itself.

Q. Shouldn't you have attempted all the compulsory questions?

Q. Would you have loaned me any money if I had requested you. (Complex)

a1. Of course I would have given you some money happily if you had asked me for it.

a1. Many more passengers could have died in the accident.

a1. I surely would have gone with you to the library.

Q. Would your parents have permitted you on our trek programme?

a1. You ought to have expressed your liking for this person much much earlier.

a1. The nurses in the Govt hospital ought to have looked after the helpless patients with greater devotion, don't you think? (Complex)

a1. Your younger sister ought to have got used to all the Nuns in St.Patrick school.

a1. I certainly would have helped you in Maths.

a1. I might have erred in my judgement of this boy if the class teacher had not put me wise about him.

EQ. We need not have gone out of our way for a humanitarian work such as that, need we?

a1. We could have practised a little more for our Software test.

a1. We are late. The train could have left the platform by now.

EQ1. We must have left our servant girl behind, mustn't we?

EQ1. You should have pointed out my grammar mistakes much earlier, shouldn't you?

a1. We could have got used to the new auditorium pretty fast.

Action completed cases

Examine all the FIP sentences given above more carefully. Has action taken place in any of them? No. An FIP statement is only "future looking". What if action has taken place? Truly it would be so in a2 type sentences.

Examine the following sentences which use the FIP auxiliaries:

(a)   We shouldn't have halted here at all. (This means that they have halted)

(b)   The candidates need not have met the Registrar at all.

(c)   The soldiers would not have got used to the snow except for the Commanding officer's insistence.

(d)   Sudhir wouldn't have scored such low marks in Physics if he had studied a little harder. (Complex sentence)

(e)   Would you have got used to the tantrum of my small brother if I hadn't compelled you on baby-sitting?

(f)   Your cousin sister might not have attended the birthday party if you had not sent a vehicle for her.

Though we have used the FIP auxiliaries, you could notice that action had truly taken place. They happen to be a2 sentences as well. Hence, are they still FIP sentences or something else? What tense do we use for completed activities? Simple past or Past perfect tenses, don't we?

Don't get away with the impression that all a2's with the FIP auxiliaries will indicate completed activities. Not necessarily at all. Examine the following a1 types, wherein you could see completion of action:

(g)   Must you have agreed to every proposal without any kind of reservation?

(h)   Need all of you have gone to a movie on a holy day like today?

So, it would appear that the FIP auxiliaries turn into "Past perfect" auxiliaries if action had taken place. This inference is true indeed. You could make a mistake here. Always look for the "Activity" and its "timing" before you decide whether the sentence concerned belongs to the FIP or Past perfect tense case.

Accordingly, we could include all the FIP auxiliaries except "was/were GOING TO" against the "Past perfect tense" also.

Past perfect tense auxiliaries (Updated)

The S-A-V rules for the Past perfect tense (Chapter 18) stand updated as follows:

Person	Auxiliary	Verb form
All persons	HAD	PP verb
"	Had **got/become/been** USED TO	Use only the verbs shown in **bold**
"	COULD HAVE	PP
"	WOULD HAVE	"
"	MIGHT HAVE	"
"	MUST HAVE	"
"	NEED HAVE	"
"	SHOULD HAVE	"

Person	Auxiliary	Verb form
All persons	OUGHT TO HAVE	PP
"	could/would/might/must/need/ should/ought to have **got/ become/ been** USED TO	Use only the PP verbs **got/become/been**

(HAD + 9 auxiliary sets = 10 auxiliaries)

Exercise

Rewrite the following sentences in the FIP tense using the most appropriate auxiliary set: (Do make sure that 'action' does not take place)

1. I shall accompany you upto the post office.
2. Can you translate this letter into Hindi?
3. Shan't we revise our Shakespeare's plays today?
4. My brother will marry Shivani if she waits for one year. (Complex)
5. We are flying off to Kolkata.
6. Our house maid will not clean your verandah.
7. Martha does not feed the chickens in her poultry farm.
8. He would eat this fruit if you gave him.
9. We must not play the match.
10. We could not reach your house on time.

Locate the mistake(s) if any and rewrite the following sentences:

11. We could corrected the Juniors' class notes.
12. My uncle shall not have misled you as regards the rules of the game.
13. Do you need changed the positions of the players?
14. You ought not helped this student because he is an outright malingerer.
15. Shouldn't you keep quiet in yesterday's meeting?
16. I would have told you the truth.
17. All of you must have brought your drawing instruments for the test.
18. She cannot have rowed the boat all by herself.
19. These tablets may have healed your cough within two days.
20. Small children oughtn't have read Adults magazines.

Write each of the following sentences in three different ways using any Universal auxiliaries without significantly changing the meaning:

21. Lakshmi will write her final exam in March next year.
22. Manmohan is acting in tomorrow's play.
23. Muthu will thrash Benjamin nicely.
24. Thomas speaks good English.
25. The New Delhi express arrives in an hour's time.

Answer the following questions in the FIP or FIP continuous tense:

26. Were you visiting the stadium yesterday?
27. Did you run fast in yesterday's 100 meters race?

28. Weren't you standing helplessly there during the street quarrel?
29. Why didn't you buy more useful toys?
30. Could we ruin his chances of the first position?

Analyse the following sentences:

31. We were all going to see this movie before the Independence day.
32. Shouldn't you have been used to this new approach in English grammar some days back?
33. Could you have completed this assignment without outside help?
34. All the elderly persons in my house had got used to sugar-free eatables within a month, hadn't they?
35. You would have been getting used to rich food in my house, wouldn't you?

Rewrite the following FIP sentences into Past perfect sentences yet using the FIP auxiliaries:

36. We should have selected more greener area for our picnic site.
37. The freshers would have complained to the Principal about our silent ragging if we had been rough with them.
38. All of you should have been present in the hall well before time.
39. We would have got used to the new routines if you had advised us previously.
40. I certainly would have given you special coaching if you had requested me.

Write the remaining 6 categories of sentences:

41. Wouldn't the audience have kept the ushers running for more seats?
42. The speaker was going to start his speech in the next minute, wasn't he?
43. You could have been getting used to Pizzas if you had been Peter's friend.
44. The VC's office peon would have kept you waiting in the verandah.
45. Your friend wouldn't have got used to smoking if you had warned him about its ill-effects.

State the tense of the following sentences:

46. Surendran was going to finish the race in the first place but didn't.
47. You ought to have stopped these children from crossing the zebra lines.
48. You must not have done a stupid thing like that?
49. Couldn't you have got used to the new English grammar much earlier?
50. The police should have checked all your vehicle documents before booking you.
51. You need not have come to my house at all.
52. The ticket collector wouldn't have penalised you if you had hidden yourself inside the toilet.
53. I couldn't have finished copying these notes even by day after tomorrow.
54. He was going to see me yesterday.
55. The surgeon might not have operated upon you if he had known about your high blood sugar.

Chapter 23

WRITING ALTERNATE or SIMILAR SENTENCES

General

Now that we have studied sentence-construction in all the 16 tenses, it would be useful to go through them with a different eye.

Which are the auxiliaries that we can use in maximum number of tenses?

They are 4, viz, **WOULD, COULD, KEEP/KEPT** and **USED TO.**

We use WOULD and COULD in all the three tense families; KEEP/KEPT in all the 7 continuous tenses plus Simple present (for routine activities); USED TO is such a versatile auxiliary that we can use it in all the 16 tenses.

If this be so, how do we pinpoint the tense of the sentence if any of these 4 auxiliaries appear in it? It is only by "studying the activity and its timing." The "timing" angle will tell you, to which of the 3 time families it belongs. Once the family is known, then it is not difficult to identify the exact tense.

There are many tenses in each family and each tense uses several auxiliaries. So, we can express a sentence idea in different ways in the same family. We use the maximum number of auxiliaries (15) for the Present continuous tense and Simple present tense. Doesn't it mean that we can express the same sentence idea in 15 different ways using different auxiliaries? It is true that the sentence meaning will not be exactly the same but will be similar in meaning or nearly the same in meaning.

Writing similar sentences

Present family

Let's take a humble sentence like, "My friend lives in Salt Lake." This is a Simple present sentence. In how many ways can we express the same idea using different tenses/ auxiliaries of the Present family but without radically changing the original meaning? They would be as follows:

(b) My friend does keep living in Salt Lake.

We cannot use any other Simple present auxiliaries because the meaning then becomes far removed from the original. But, we can use the Present continuous auxiliaries to maintain the original meaning. They would be like these:

(c) My friend is living in Salt Lake.
(d) My friend will/shall be living in Salt Lake.
(e) My friend ought to be living in Salt Lake.
(f) My friend will be getting used to living in Salt Lake. ("living" here is a gerund)
(g) My friend would keep living in Salt Lake.

Let us now try other tenses also from the Present family:

(h)   My friend has got used to living in Salt Lake. (Present perfect)
(i)   My friend has been living in Salt Lake. (Present perfect cont.)
(j)   My friend has kept living in Salt Lake. (Present perfect cont.)
(k)   My friend has been getting used to living in Salt lake. (Present perfect cont.)

Do you see we have expressed the same sentence idea in 10 different ways by using auxiliaries belonging to the same family?

In certain cases we may be able to write upto 15 or more varieties. Take an a2 type sentence and see in how many ways could one write the same:

(a)   Shanta cannot converse in Hindi.
(b)   Shanta does not converse in Hindi.
(c)   Shanta would not converse in Hindi.
(d)   Shanta could not converse in Hindi.
(e)   Shanta might not converse in Hindi.
(f)   Shanta doesn't keep conversing in Hindi.
(g)   Shanta is not used to conversing in Hindi.
(h)   Shanta could not have been conversing in Hindi.
(i)   Shanta would not have been conversing in Hindi.
(j)   Shanta might not have been conversing in Hindi.
(k)   Shanta has not been conversing in Hindi.
(l)   Shanta has not been used to conversing in Hindi.
(m)   Shanta is not conversing in Hindi.
(n)   Shanta would not be used to conversing in Hindi.
(o)   Shanta has not kept conversing in Hindi.
(p)   Shanta will/shall not converse in Hindi.
(q)   Shanta will/shall not be conversing in Hindi.

Past family

Shall we take next a Past family sentence and see in how many different ways we could express the same idea? The sentence is: "This student didn't come to my house yesterday."

The alternate sentences are:

(a)   This student hadn't come to my house yesterday.
(b)   This student hadn't been to my house yesterday.
(c)   This student hadn't been coming to my house.
(d)   This student need have come to my house yesterday.
(e)   This student should have come to my house.
(f)   This student ought to have come to my house.
(g)   This student must have come to my house.
(h)   This student hadn't kept coming to my house.

(i) This student should have been coming to my house.
(j) This student could have been coming to my house.
(k) This student must have been coming to my house.
(l) This student ought to have been to my house.

Future family

Here are some examples on Future family:

(a) When will you finish your studies in this college?
(b) When are you finishing your studies in this college? (implied future)
(c) When will you have finished your studies in this college?
(d) When shall you be finishing your studies in this college?
(e) When would you finish your studies in this college?
(f) When would you be finishing your studies in this college?
(g) When might you finish your studies in this college?
(h) When might you be finishing your studies in this college?
(i) When will you have finished your studies in this college?
(j) When could you have finished your studies in this college?
(k) When will/shall you have been finishing your studies in this college?
(l) When would you have been finishing your studies in this college?
(m) When need you have been finishing your studies in this college?
(n) When ought you to have been finishing your studies in this college?
(o) When must you have been finishing your studies in this college?
(p) When are you going to finish your studies in this college?

Such expansion is possible even with Present and Past tense sentences and also Future in the past tense albeit not to the same extent. Here are the examples:

Present tense

(a) Mrs. Shobana Raj is a good Lecturer.
(b) Mrs. Shobana has been a good Lecturer.
(c) Mrs. Shobana must be a good Lecturer.
(d) Mrs. Shobana ought to be a good Lecturer.
(e) Mrs. Shobana happens to be a good Lecturer.

Past tense

(a) Ranjan was never my enemy.
(b) Ranjan had never been my enemy.
(c) Ranjan never used to be my enemy.
(d) Ranjan could never have been my enemy.
(e) Ranjan never need have been my enemy.
(f) Ranjan and I were used to be good friends.
(g) Ranjan and I had been used to good friendship.
(h) Ranjan and I had always been good friends.

Future in the past tense

(a)   Menon would have got admission in the M.Phil course by now.

(b)   Menon should have got admission in the M.Phil course by now.

(c)   Menon ought to have got admission in the M.Phil course by now.

(d)   Menon must have got admission in the M.Phil course by now.

(e)   Menon shall have been admitted in the M.Phil course by now.

What is the purpose behind this exercise, you might wonder?

When we learn "para writing" in a later lesson, this method would be useful in matching one sentence with another in a paragraph.

Next, your English standard would sound high and sophisticated if you use the universal auxiliaries liberally. At +2 and college level, you must desist from using the basic auxiliaries; that's the only way you could show your superiority over the school boys. After all, at school level also they learn the same tenses. Therefore, master the use of universal auxiliaries in all tenses if you want your English style to fly high!

Exercise

Write the following sentences in as many ways as you can without changing the original meaning significantly:

1.   Sundaresan has been whiling away his time after obtaining his Science degree.
2.   Sujatha should be studying in B.A. first year now.
3.   Aren't you getting used to this colleague of yours a little too much?
4.   You may have been an excellent student in your previous year.
5.   I was never used to this method of writing an Essay during my Plus 2 course.
6.   You ought not to have got used to drugs.
7.   We could keep learning music even after our college studies.
8.   Won't Shalini have achieved her goal by July next year?
9.   Couldn't she have secured First division in her finals?
10.   We shall attend your birthday party without fail.

Chapter 24

INFINITIVE

We saw that a Simple sentence will have only one verb. We can interpret this rule in another way too. One auxiliary or one auxiliary set can support only one verb.

There is no question of one auxiliary/auxiliary set supporting two or more consecutive verbs. The formula also says that there could be only verb in a Simple sentence. What if we feel compelled to use a second verb?

In this Chapter we shall learn that a Simple sentence can have more than one verb but that verb must be in a modified form called, INFINITIVE.

What is an INFINITIVE?

If we use the preposition "to" before any present form verb, the combination is known as **infinitive**. We may say therefore that in the English language there will be as many infinitives as the number of present form verbs.

We may use an infinitive as a *verb* or as a *noun* in a Simple sentence.

Use of INFINITIVE AS VERB

If we use an infinitive as a verb, it must be the second verb in a sentence. Examine the following sentence and analyse it:

We could not come on time to witness the opening ceremony.
S   Neg A   V   C   INFIN   O

"to witness" is an infinitive and it is doing the job of a verb. (Do recall that a VERB is a word of action). Further, "to witness" is a second verb in the above sentence. Thus any infinitive verb will always be only a second verb in a sentence. We can *never write* a sentence such as,

S - A - Infin.verb - O/C

But, once we have written the S-A-V, we are free to use an infinitive-verb. See the following examples:

We hadn't come to give you any kind of advice.
S   Neg A   V   INFIN   O   O

Would you like to meet your patient now?
 A   S   V   INFIN   O   Adv

(You do) Never hesitate to say 'sorry'.
          Neg A   V   INFIN Adv

Further, we can write two infinitive verbs one after the other like this,

S - A - V - O/C - Infin.verb - Infin.verb - O/C

Here are two sentences that use two infinitive verbs:

(a) Ahmed stays in my house during week-ends **to help, to guide** me in my studies.

(b)   Ahmed stays in my house during week-ends **to help** and **to guide** me in my studies.

Thus, the Simple sentence formula now stands as,

S - A - V - O/C - INFIN (verb) - O/C

Is there a relationship-rule between the infinitive part and S-A-V part? No, none whatsoever. The infinitive part along with O/C (or without O/C) of one sentence can attach itself to the S-A-V part of another sentence. Take the following examples:

(c)   We did not run in the race to win   any prize.
     S   Neg A V   O   INFIN   O

(d)   The children could have done something to please their elders.
           S   A   V   O   INFIN   O

(e)   Did you happen to see   my brother at the college this afternoon?
     A   S   V   INFIN   O   C

We may exchange the infinitive parts like this,

We did not run in the race to please the elders.

The children could have done something to win any prize.

Did you happen to win any prize?

The children could have done something to see my brother at the college.

So, the S-A-V part has no relationship with the infinitive part at all. The S-A-V part can be in any of the 16 tenses we have covered so far. Here are some sentences. Study them carefully:

Infinitive-based sentences:

Present family

1. I am here to teach you English grammar.
2. We aren't the students to agree with everyone of your statements.
3. My sister is going to meet you this evening.
4. We could guarantee to stop you from copying.
5. We ought to report early in order to catch a glimpse of the visitor.
6. You may have been waiting here to see Fr. Rector.
7. You have been nice to talk with, haven't you?
8. Haven't we kept you here to send you off to another Seminary?
9. The senior student does keep flourishing his hand just to frighten us.
10. We came to meet the HOD of History department.

Past family

11. You were late to enter into the hall.
12. Did you keep writing to me just to get my attention on you?
13. He was not taking part in the competition to win any prize.

14. We walked all the way to save our bus fare.
15. We couldn't do well in the entrance examination to get admission in this college.
16. You had reached the station too late to see off your friend.
17. Your friends need not have come all the way here just to say 'good bye'.
18. You had always kept promising to help the poor boys.
19. You would have been resting for hours to catch up with your sleep.
20. We had some letters to deposit in the office.

Future family

21. We might go to Marina to listen to the speech of our Prime Minister.
22. We shan't be staying here for long to help your guest.
23. Shall we keep singing to stop the audience from protesting?
24. We will have spent 2 months waiting to collect our degree.
25. Shan't you have kept practising high jump to clear greater and greater height?
26. You could have met the Principal to represent your case.
27. You must have been working very hard to complete all your homework.
28. You will have been ready to meet the visitor, won't you?
29. You needn't have come here just to congratulate me.
30. We shall have reached the grounds by 4 p.m. to witness the final football match.

Continuous infinitive-verb

Except for the Simple present tense and Present continuous tense, all other continuous tenses are interchangeable with their parent tense for the same action. We choose the continuous tense when we want to give importance for the duration of the action. The meaning however, will remain the same.

In infinitives too we have a continuous form and this is interchangeable with the parent or normal form.

Normal form	Continuous form
To see	to be seeing
To go	to be going
To sit	to be sitting

Here are some examples:

My parents have asked me **to be waiting** here for them.
Our parents told us **not to be fighting** with each other during their absence.
I have **to be doing** my homework till my tuition master's arrival.

By rule, we can use two infinitive verbs one after the other. But in such cases, it is better to use one in the normal form and the other in the continuous form like this,

We won't have **to be practising** for hours **to catch** the Principal's eye.

Did you join this college only **to be wasting** time and **to get** a transfer certificate?

Emphatics

Earlier we saw that we can give *emphatic positive answers* (Ea1) in only two tenses, viz, Simple Present and Simple past. What about emphatic negative answers (Ea2) in these two tenses? Again what about Ea1 and Ea2 in the remaining tenses?

It is possible to give Ea1 and Ea2 in any tense through the infinitive method. Study the following sentences:

Present family (with A.V)

(a)   I **am** to see my Professor before the lunch interval.
(aa)   I **am not** to see you ever again.

(b)   My friend Pyara Singh **is** to reach my home at 6 p.m.
(bb)   My friend **isn't** to mix with you.

(c)   **Are** your friends to attend a religious meeting this evening?
(cc)   We **aren't** to go to the market today.

(d)   Satish **has** to meet me at 5 p.m.
(dd)   Satish **hasn't** to play basketball today.

(e)   **Have** we to play a volley ball match today with the seniors?
(ee)   We **haven't** to play any match today with the seniors, have we?

Past family (with A.V)

(f)   Abraham **was** to read the Bible lesson in the church this morning.
(ff)   **Wasn't** Stella to take part in the Quiz programme today?

(g)   **Were** you to take this medicine twice daily as per the doctor's advice?
(gg)   **Weren't** you to appear for an interview yesterday?

(h)   All of us **had** to apologise to the HOD for our absence.
(hh)   Some of us **hadn't** to write the imposition, had we?

Simple present (with **have as verb**)

(i)   We **do have** to attend the Professor's birthday party.
(ii)   We **don't have** to go to church this morning, have we?

(j)   **Does** Ram **have** to be present here today? (= Has Ram to be present today?)
(jj)   Ram **doesn't have** to be present here.

Simple past (with **have as verb**)

(k)   **Did** you **have** to post that letter yesterday itself?
(kk)   You **didn't have** to say 'sorry' at all.

Future (with **have**)

(l)   You **will/shall have** to come with me to the Reader's office.
(ll)   You **won't/shan't have** to come with me.

The above statements in Q and A forms do sound powerful, don't they? We call these EMPHATICS. So, we can write emphatic questions and give emphatic answers, in any tense family. For the **Emphatics,** we make use of all the A.Vs.

In addition to the Ea1 in Simple present and Simple past, we can also use their auxiliaries DO, DOES and DID along with the auxiliary HAVE, to give a different kind of Ea1 and Ea2 in these two tenses as shown in (i) - (k) above.

We follow the same method for Ea1 and Ea2 in the Future tense as shown in (ll).

Use of interrogatives with infinitive-verb

When the first verb (in the S-A-V Part) is ASK, DECIDE, DISCOVER, FORGET, KNOW, LEARN, REMEMBER or FIND OUT, in any of its form, we have to, most of the time, use one of the interrogatives out of HOW, WHAT, WHEN, WHERE or WHICH followed by an infinitive-verb, as shown below:

(a)   A commuter **asked** me HOW to reach the bus terminus in my city.
(b)   My mother **decided** herself WHERE to send us for the holiday.
(c)   The nursery kids soon **discovered** WHEN to ask for sweets.
(d)   Did you **forget** WHERE to go for the meeting?
(e)   Don't you **know** WHAT to do in a situation like that?
(f)   We have **learnt** already HOW to solve Differential equations.
(g)   Will you please **remember** WHICH button to switch on.
(h)   Please **find out** HOW to get high marks in Mathematics.

Omission of "to" in some infinitive-verbs

There is a rule, "Omit the preposition 'to' in the infinitive part when the normal verb in the S-A-V part happens to be, LET, MAKE, HEAR, FEEL, SEE, BID, WATCH, DARE or HAVE, in any of their form." Here are the examples:

(a)   Will you please **let** our daughter **stay** in your house for a week?
         ("to stay" in the infinitive part will be wrong).
(b)   The police constable **made** me **do** 25 sit-up's for my traffic offence.
(c)   Will you please **hear** me **give out** my story.
(d)   We have **heard** her **sing** some good melodies.
(e)   We **felt** the car **break** into two halves.
(f)   We **watched** him **run** away into the jungle.
(g)   Did you **see** me **steal** this watch?
(h)   The Chairman of the selection board **bid** me **come** in.
(i)   Don't you ever **dare say** such things against me.
(j)   I shall **have** you **do** this job.

Help and **Enable** are exclusive verbs. We may or may not omit the preposition. Both will be correct. **Dare** too falls in this category. You may come across quite a few sentences with an absent "to" when **dare** is the main verb.

   (k)   The onlookers **helped** us **push** the car.

         The onlookers **helped** us **to push** the car.

   (l)   They **enabled** us **solve** this equation.

         They **enabled** us **to solve** this equation.

   (m) Nobody did **dare ask** the Professor for an explanation.

         Nobody did **dare to ask** the Professor for an explanation.

Non-omission of "to"

Have you noticed that all the sentences above are of the pattern,

$$S - A - V - O - INFIN - O/C$$

But if the pattern is, S - A - V - C or S - A - V - O - C, then the preposition "to" is **not to be omitted** in the infinitive even when the special verbs are present in the S-A-V part. Here are the examples:

   (a)   They have been *watching* **carefully** to catch the mischief makers.

           (S - A - V - C pattern)

   (b)   Please *make* me **prayerful** to worship thee more regularly.

           (S - A- V- O - C pattern)

   (c)   We couldn't *see* the movie **the whole time** to spot out the drawbacks.

           (S - A - V- O- C pattern)

   (d)   We won't *let* you **free** to wander everywhere.

   (e)   Do you *feel* **nice** to witness a boxing match?

   (f)   Did you *hear* every word **well** to criticise the speech?

   (g)   I will *have* you anytime **here** to complete your imposition.

   (h)   The interview board will not *bid* me **now** to walk into the hall.

So long as there is a complement (with or without an object) in the sentence, don't omit the preposition "to" in the infinitive part. The adverb present in the complement could be of any type.

INFINITIVE NOUNS

We can use all the infinitives as **nouns** as well. As nouns, we may use them either in the Subject section or Object section. Here are the examples:

Infinitive-noun as object

   (a)   Krishnaswamy went to the library **to read.**

         S   (A)V   C   O

   (b)   Did you come all the way **to fight**?

                         O

   (c)   Where shall we sit down **to discuss**?

   (d)   The brave king went to the battle **not to die** but **to win.**

In the above examples we have used the infinitive noun as object. The infinitive noun does pass the 'object test'. But, do make sure that there are no other words after the infinitive-noun. What will happen if we have some words? Analyse the following sentence and see:

Did you come all the way to fight with us?
A   S   V   C   infin V   O

Do you see that the infinitive noun has now turned into an infinitive verb? Hence, make sure that the infinitive noun is the last word in the sentence.

Infinitive noun as subject

(e) **To read** is a good habit.
     S

(f) **To err** is human.
     S

(g) **To be** or **not to be** is the question.

In the above cases, the infinitive-noun gives an understandable meaning; they are self explanatory infinitive nouns. What if the meaning is vague or with several possible meanings? Take the following case:

(h) **To ride** is dangerous.

Here a question will arise, "To ride what?" One could ride a cycle, a moped or a horse or a donkey etc. The infinitive noun has no definite meaning at all. Hence, to convey the correct meaning, we may use additional/explanatory/amplifying words after the infinitive-noun. The additional words along with the infinitive-noun will then constitute the subject.

(i) **To ride** *a race horse* could be dangerous.
     S   A   V   Adv

(j) **To read** *good books* is a fine habit.

(k) **To kick** *a dog* is a cruel act.

(l) **To tell** *lies* is ungodly.

But, you cannot make use of this privilege when an infinitive is acting as the object in a sentence.

We may use infinitive nouns as subject and object in the same sentence too:

(m) **To work** is **to pray**.

(n) **To work** is **to worship**.

(o) **To give** is better than **to receive.**

Use of infinitives as connectors

We may use infinitive verbs as connectors to connect two Simple sentences. When so done, it will appear that a miracle has taken place!. Two sets of S-A-V have reduced to one set. It is indeed a miracle, isn't it? Examine the following pairs of sentences:

(a)   Every cricket team has a captain. (b) A captain directs his players.
"Every cricket team has a captain **to direct** his players."

(b)   The intruder showed a dagger. (d) He threatened the housewife with it.
"The intruder showed a dagger **to threaten** the housewife."

(c)   Our baby brother will do anything according to his wishes. (d) We allow him.
"We allow our baby brother **to do** anything according to his wishes."

But, such connection will be possible only if there is a 'common verb of action' between the two sentences. We may pick out such a verb either from one of the sentences or even from outside provided the original meaning remains unaffected. If we cannot find such a common verb, we cannot connect those sentences by the infinitive method. Some sentences will be such that no common verb could be possible between them. For instance,

(d)   We came to this spot for a purpose. (e) The man concerned did not turn up.

(f)   Mahima was a good singer. (g) She could not participate in the function today.

Writing the remaining 6 categories of sentences

Given, a2 : To tell lies is not godly.

a1   : To tell lies is ungodly.
Gen Q   : What is ungodly?
Sp Q   : Is 'to tell lies' ungodly?
Neg Q   : Isn't 'to tell lies' ungodly?
EQ1   : To tell lies is ungodly, isn't it?
EQ2   : To tell lies is not godly, is it?

Given EQ1: We allow our small brother to do as he pleases, don't we?

EQ2   : We don't allow our small brother to do as he pleases, do we?
Gen Q   : What do we allow our small brother to do?
Sp Q   : Do we allow our small brother to do as he pleases?
Neg Q   : Don't we allow our small brother to do as he pleases?
a1   : We do allow our small brother to do as he pleases.
a2   : We don't allow our small brother to do as he pleases (always)?

Exercise

Fill up the blank with a suitable infinitive verb or infinitive noun:

1. Samson was too keen to join the coaching class for the TNPCEE exam.
2. My aunt gave me Rs 50 to buy a toy for my little brother for his birthday.
3. The servant maid has forgotten to give you the house keys.
4. Maragatham does not eat to lose weight.
5. ………. is to enjoy life.
6. Are these fruits ripe enough to eat?

7. The patient has ~~to take~~ this medicine thrice daily for 5 days.
8. Children ~~decided~~ to spend their summer vacation with the parents.
9. ………. easily and readily is a good Christian virtue.
10. Leela is a nice girl. She is ever so ready to help everyone.

Give emphatic affirmative answer.

11. Are you attending today's memorial service at the church?
12. Is Valentina writing her admission test today?
13. Does our gardener visit the nearby nursery every day?
14. Isn't he the person who sits in front of the Administrator's office?
15. Are you taking this medicine daily?
16. Did Meenakshi ultimately submit her assignment or not?
17. Don't you rise up from bed late on Sundays?
18. He took the credit all for himself, didn't he?
19. Who was responsible to lead the prayer this morning?
20. The children will not go to college today, will they?

Give emphatic negative answer:

21. Is it necessary for me to call you to the dining hall for every meal?
22. You should have turned them out of the examination hall, shouldn't you?
23. One day she must call me 'sister-in-law', mustn't she?
24. Aren't both of you to call on my parents this evening?
25. My friend and I were to be present at the auditorium, weren't we?

Locate the mistake, if any, and rewrite the sentence concerned:

26. Don't let me to catch you again for the same kind of grammatical mistake.
27. The senior sister ~~has~~ made me to sit in this place.
28. Should you have to punishing me for such small lapses.
29. Will you please hear me ~~to talk~~ about it.
30. The Junior Lecturer could not decide to report this matter to the HOD.
31. Some of ~~us learnt on our own~~ to solve simple trigonometrical equations. on their own
32. Did you dare to remove ~~this~~ box from this room?
33. Have you seen my small sister to run along this road?.
34. In total helplessness we were watching the little puppy dog to be drowning itself in the lake.
35. Bid the next candidate to walk in, please.
36. Don't make the questions easy pass everyone in the exam.
37. Haven't you watched this scene carefully pin point the mistakes?
38. We saw the movie minutely all right pick out the Director's mistakes.
39. He let me off attend the match.
40. We heard every dialogue clearly appreciate it.
41. Have you decided on your own not to donate any money to ~~this~~ orphanage?
42. Don't you remember to give corrections?

43. Find out at once to reach the next petrol pump.
44. All of them ~~do~~ know to get the work done by these gardeners.
45. We learnt to use the calculator in Std X itself.

Convert the following pairs of sentences into a single Simple sentence by using suitable "Infinitive connectors" :

46. This student from a village didn't have even ten paise with him. He could not buy anything.
47. This social worker visits the sick people in General hospital frequently. She shows her love for them.
48. This old man repairs wrist watches. He is very keen on it.
49. My sister and I don't take bath in the morning time. We hate it.
50. My uncle wants admission for his son in a famous school. He is trying hard for it.
51. I could walk in a cemetery alone at night. I am not afraid of it at all.
52. I visited the boarding school. I met my sister there.
53. The chief guest stood up. He delivered an excellent speech.
54. Our servant maid has two cousins. She looks after them.
55. Shilpa is a stubborn girl. She does not forgive others easily.

Use the following infinitives as nouns in the subject part and also the object part in your own sentences:

56. to drink
57. to condemn
58. to proceed
59. to modify
60. to kick
61. to make
62. to watch
63. to let
64. to hear

65. Write short notes on "omitting and not omitting the preposition 'to' in the infinitive part of a sentence." Also give suitable examples.

Write the remaining 6 categories of sentences:

66. Given, Sp Q   : Did we want to hear the recitation once again?
67. Given, a1   : The General went to the forward area to observe.
68. Given a2   : Not To submit the homework on time is an offence.
69. Given EQ1   : To do any work willingly is a good rule, isn't it?
70. Given Neg Q1: Hasn't your daughter to appear for the selection test?

Chapter 25

RECAP OF ALL TENSES

You have learnt till now how to frame Q, a1 and a2 in 16 tenses. These tenses fall under three Tense families, viz, PRESENT, PAST and FUTURE.

We have also covered 30 auxiliaries (including all the 11 A.Vs) out of the list of 32. Can you list out the 30 auxiliaries? Try it out by yourself before reading any further. Identify the balance 2 auxiliaries.

Present family

1. *Present.* (AM, IS, ARE, HAS, HAVE, am/is/are USED TO) (6)

2. *Simple present.* (DO, DOES, CAN, MAY, WOULD, COULD, SHOULD, MUST, DARE, NEED, OUGHT TO, WILL, SHALL, can/may/would/could/should/ must/ought to, will/shall **get/become/be** USED TO, do/does/can/may/would/ could/should/must/dare/need/ought to KEEP. (15)

3. *Present continuous.* (AM, IS, ARE, CAN BE, MAY BE, WOULD BE, COULD BE, SHOULD BE, MUST BE, NEED BE, OUGHT TO BE, WILL BE, SHALL BE, am/is/are GOING TO BE, am/is/are/can be/ may be/would be/could be/should be/must be/need be/will be/shall be **getting/ becoming** USED TO.(15)

4. *Present perfect.* (HAS, HAVE, MAY HAVE, has/have **got/become/been** USED TO) (4)

5. *Present perfect continuous.* (HAS BEEN, HAVE BEEN, MAY HAVE BEEN, has/have/may have KEPT, has been/have been/may have been **getting/becoming** USED TO. (5)

6. *Present emphatics.* (AM, IS, ARE, HAS, HAVE, DO HAVE, DOES HAVE)

Here is one sample sentence in one category only for each of the above auxiliaries serial number-wise. (You know how to write the remaining 6 categories):

1.   (a) Am I your English Lecturer?
   (b) Peter is a very good student in my class.
   (c) We are your close friends, aren't we?
   (d) Sujatha's parents have a big car.
   (e) Sujatha's small brother has only a bicycle.
   (f) We are not used to sugar cane juice.

2.   (a) You don't have any patience at all.
   (b) My elder sister doesn't make good coffee.
   (c) Can you run with me along this rocky road?
   (d) We may not reach our college on time at this speed of walking.

(e) Would you please come with me now?

(f) You surely could jump this length, couldn't you?

(g) We should be punctual for any function.

(h) They might not come to our party this evening.

(i) Must you dance to their tune always?

(j) We dare not sit on this chair.

(k) They need not say 'sorry' at all.

(l) We will definitely accompany you to the Principal's office.

(m) Shall we kick off?

(n) All of us can/may/would ....will/shall **get** used to our new maid servant in a day or two.

(o) James does keep visiting me every Sunday after the morning worship service.

(p) Don't you keep giving some alms to this beggar daily?

(q) Rajnath ought to keep writing regularly to his sister.

3. (a) I am doing yoga exercises nowadays.

(b) Rattan is playing table tennis, isn't he?

(c) The clerks are typing out all the replies.

(d) Can you be observing all the passersby a little more carefully?

(e) Our friends may be coming here by 4 p.m.

(f) You could be helping your mother a little more seriously, couldn't you?.

(g) None of us should be wasting our valuable time on working days.

(h) The doctor would be arriving here any moment.

(i) Some of our college staffs might be leaving for New Delhi next week.

(j) All of you must be marching out of the campus immediately.

(k) The Juniors need not be sitting around here any longer.

(l) Oughtn't he to be writing his entrance exam today?

(m) We will be meeting your parents this afternoon.

(n) We shan't be presenting any paper in tomorrow's meeting.

(o) I am **becoming** used to football slowly.

(p) We are/can be/ .... ought to be **getting** used to the substandard drinking water in the hostel.

(q) They must keep repeating this exercise every month.

4. (a) Ramesh has got a promotion.

(b) The football players have obtained a good recognition for themselves.

(c) We may have seen this small boy before.

(d) Hasn't he got used to this small puppy?

(e) Some of us have got used to cold milk in the morning.

(f) Haven't all of you been used to ordinary yellow banana fruit?

5. (a) My desk-mate has been copying all my answers in most of the tests.

(b) The cadets have been progressing very well in drill.

(c) He has kept knocking at my door daily.

(d) We have kept repeating our request regularly.

(e) Krishnan has been getting used to mango juice lately.

(f) Several students have been/may have been becoming used to headaches during summer afternoons.

6. (a) I am to proceed with my project assignment without delay.

(b) Are you to join my painting class from next week?

(c) Isn't Manohar to help you in Mathematics?

(d) Has Miss. Promilla to teach you English grammar?

(e) We have to reach the station before 5 p.m.

(f) All of us do have to sing the National anthem in today's convocation ceremony.

(g) Muktiar Singh does have to copy these notes by this evening.

Past family

1. *Past.* (WAS, WERE, HAD, was/were USED TO) (4)

2. *Simple past.* (DID, COULD, WOULD, did ... USE TO) (4)

3. *Past continuous.* (WAS, WERE, did KEEP, was/were **getting/becoming** USED TO) (4)

4. *Past perfect.* (HAD, had **got/become/been** USED TO, WOULD HAVE, COULD HAVE, SHOULD HAVE, MIGHT HAVE, MUST HAVE, NEED HAVE, OUGHT TO HAVE, would have/ could have/ should have/might have/ must have/need have/ought to have **got/become/been** USED TO. (10)

5. *Past perfect continuous.* (HAD BEEN, had KEPT, WOULD HAVE BEEN, WOULD HAVE BEEN, SHOULD HAVE BEEN, MIGHT HAVE BEEN, MUST HAVE BEEN, NEED HAVE BEEN, OUGHT TO HAVE BEEN, had/would/ could/should/ might/must/need/ought to have been **getting/becoming** USED TO) (10)

6. *Past emphatics.* (WAS, WERE, HAD, DID HAVE) (4)

Here is a sample sentence of one category for each auxiliary:

1. (a) Sophia was an average student in B.Sc final year, wasn't she?

(b) All the dancers were in colourful costumes.

(c) I had a severe head last night.

(d) We were used to a lot of ragging during first year in college.

(e) Our HOD wasn't used to any kind of humour at all.

2. (a) We did not write any anonymous letter to anyone.

(b) I could not attend last year's convocation.

(c) Some spoilt brats would always have their own way.

(d) Did you use to love poetry during First year?

(e) I did use (used to) love English during my first year.

3. (a) Krishnan was running very fast in the race today, wasn't he?
    (b) We were playing basketball when you came inside our colony compound.
    (c) We did keep asking for more and more model test papers.
    (d) My small sister was getting used to too much of milk chocolates.
    (e) Some of them were becoming used to much of sugar in their coffee.

4. (a) Most of us had written our exam papers well.
    (b) Rajan and Moorthy had got used to butter-milk during the first year.
    (c) You couldn't have cleared your first year without my help, could you?
    (d) We would/might/must/need/should/ought to have done far better in our finals.
    (e) They would/might/must/need/should/ought to have **got/become/been** used to strictures from the HOD.

5. (a) Our sons had been studying in the Municipal college till last year.
    (b) My uncle had kept insisting on high marks from all of us.
    (c) They ought to have been taking part in all competitions during college days.
    (d) Anyone would/could/might/must/need/should have been doing well in English.
    (e) Some of my relatives had been getting used to village life in a big way.
    (f) Many Plus 2 students could/would/might/should/must/need/ought to have been becoming used to rejection at the admission counter.

6. (a) Nandini was to give a dance performance this evening.
    (b) All the guests were to arrive by last evening.
    (c) The prospective candidates had to submit their full bio-data.
    (d) The kids did have to stay in the dormitory after 6 p.m.

Future family

1. *Future.* (WILL, SHALL, COULD, WOULD, MIGHT, will/shall/could/would/might **get/become/be** USED TO, am/is/are GOING TO (7)

2. *Future continuous.* (WILL BE, SHALL BE, COULD BE, WOULD BE, MIGHT BE, shall/will/could/would/might KEEP, will be/shall be/could be/would be/might be **getting/becoming** USED TO (7)

3. *Future perfect.* (WILL HAVE, SHALL HAVE, will/shall HAVE **got/become/been** USED TO) (3)

4. *Future perfect continuous.* (WILL HAVE BEEN, SHALL HAVE BEEN, will/shall HAVE KEPT, will/shall HAVE BEEN **getting/becoming** USED TO. (4)

5. *Future in the past.* (COULD HAVE, WOULD HAVE, SHOULD HAVE, MIGHT HAVE, MUST HAVE, NEED HAVE, OUGHT TO HAVE, could/would/should/might/must/need/ought to HAVE **got/become/been** USED TO, was/were GOING TO) (9)

6. *Future in the past continuous.* (COULD HAVE BEEN, WOULD HAVE BEEN, SHOULD HAVE BEEN, MIGHT HAVE BEEN, MUST HAVE BEEN, NEED HAVE BEEN, OUGHT TO HAVE BEEN, could/would/should/might/must/need/ ought to HAVE KEPT, could/would/should/might/must/need/ought to HAVE BEEN **getting/becoming** USED TO (9)

7. *Future emphatics.* (WILL / SHALL HAVE)

Here is one sample sentence in one category for each auxiliary:

1. (a) We will/shall proceed to Kharagpur tomorrow.
   (b) Could you please send off this letter by tomorrow?
   (c) I would talk to your Professor tomorrow itself.
   (d) We might not go for your cousin's wedding next week.
   (e) Could we become used to your style of living so fast as all that?
   (f) We won't/shan't get used to late nights ever.
   (g) They would/might be used to jogging in this college.

2. (a) Some students will be taking part in a few field events in today's Sports meet.
   (b) My sister and I shall be shopping in the Spencer complex tomorrow.
   (c) Wouldn't/couldn't/mightn't the three of us be rehearsing our parts in the college drama this evening?
   (d) Shall we keep reminding our parents so many times about our excursion programme?
   (e) We could be/would be/shall be/will be **getting** used to the new time table within a week.

3. (a) We will/shall have prepared ourselves fully by next week for the third semester exam.
   (b) All the students of XI standard will not have **got** used to the new grammar book even by the next term.

4. (a) They shall/will have been taking this medicine even till next month.
   (b) My students will/shall have kept working on this assignment until completion.
   (c) A few of us shall have been getting used to all the historical dates before the University exam.

5. (a) The adventurous students could/would/should/might/must/need ought to have swum across to the other side of the lake by 2 p.m. today.
   (b) The charming lady students of this engineering college would/could/should/ might/must/need/ought to have **become** used to oblique praises from the men students.
   (c) Our Asst. Lecturer was going to complain to the Principal about our casualness towards his subject.

6. (a) I would/could/should/might/must/need /ought to have been working for a solution to this dilemma if you had requested me. (Complex sentence)

    (b) Many patients could/would/should/might/must/need/ought to have been getting used to the callous attitude of Government doctors.

    (c) The final semester students would/could/should/ might/must/need/ought to have kept demanding for more study leave before the exam.

7. (a) All the latecomers will have to wait here till the Principal's arrival.

    (b) Some of us shall have to rewrite our entrance examination.

Summary

USED TO	- appears in all 16 tenses
KEEP/KEPT	- appear in all 7 continuous tenses plus Simple present (for routine actions) (8 tenses)
WOULD, COULD	- used in all 3 families, but not in all tenses.

Auxiliaries yet to be used: BEING and BETTER

Sentence analysis

Analysis of sentences that contain the auxiliary USED TO would appear difficult. Here you will notice violation of the S-A-V rules, in that, we put the verb in between the auxiliaries instead of to the left. Also recall to your memory that an English sentence must have S - A - V or S -A.V. Study the following analyses carefully:

a2   : Our hostel friends *are* **used to** vegetarian food for all their meals.
      S   A.V   A   O   O

EQ1   : We **must** *get* **used to** the college examination rules quite fast, mustn't we?
      S A V A   O   C Q tag

Neg Q : **Shouldn't** the foreign students be *getting* **used to** our English accents?
      Neg A   S   A V   A

Gen Q : What **have** we *become* **used to** mostly in this class?
      I A S V A Adv C

a1   : Stella **may have been** *getting* **used to** some bad habits lately.
      S   A   V   A   O Adv

EQ2   : We *were* **used to** failing in one or two subjects, weren't we?
      S A.V A   O   Q tag

SpQ   : **Did** we **use to** *go* to our Lecturer's house often?
      A S A V   C

Neg Q : **Haven't** we *been* **used to** Tetanus injections earlier?
      Neg a S V A   O Adv

a1   : You **might** *be* **used to** insults but we *aren't* **used to** them.
      S A V A O Conjn S NegA.V A O

EQ1 :   Some of us **shall have been** *getting* **used to** hard stares from ladies,
          S   A   V   A   O

     shan't we?
        Q tag

a2   :   We **need not have been** *getting* **used to** T shirts in college.
          S   Neg A   V   A   O

Exercise

Write sentences in as many ways as possible out of the following statements without significantly changing the original meaning:

1. We cannot re-form a broken glass, can we?
2. Hasn't walking early in the morning been your regular habit?
3. My friend could meet you at the bus stop at 7 a.m. tomorrow.
4. You dare not decline an invitation from your HOD.
5. You would be feeling sad at the death of your pet dog, wouldn't you?
6. Aren't you getting used to this cycle rather willingly?
7. You may have become used to mischievous children in your large family.
8. When did you use to write all these essays?
9. Your friend ought not to have promised such a heavy donation for this orphanage.
10. Weren't you getting used to too much of ice cream?
11. You need not have been visiting this old lady so many times.
12. My friend could discuss this issue with you anywhere, anytime.
13. Won't you have secured your admission for MA next month by this time?
14. You should have reported this matter to the English department without delay.
15. You could have easily got used to this technique in no time.
16. Weren't you going to talk to me about your brother's job confirmation?
17. I am going to tell your father about your poor behaviour in the college campus.
18. I cannot keep giving you warning day in and day out.
19. May we go home now, Sir?
20. You could have seen me yesterday about your doubts.
21. Am I to invite you to every function in my house?
22. We are not to scold you for any kind of lapse.
23. Has Rawat to teach you the Squash game?
24. Does Neena have to remind you about every engagement of yours?
25. Won't you have to abide by all these rules?

Write the remaining 6 categories of sentences for the following statements:

26. Aren't you used to *iddlis* for morning breakfast?
27. We ought not to keep reminding him of our loan to him.
28. Couldn't he have been used to good moral habits?
29. All of you ought to have become members of our college Chess club.
30. A few of you should have been getting used to fast walking in the mornings.

Analyse the following sentences:

31. I could have been a stern teacher during the first year.
32. All of them could have been getting used to the presence of ladies in their midst.
33. Isn't Ranjan used to hard work?
34. Many doctors would have been becoming used to frequent night calls.
35. I was used to criticism even during my second semester in this college, wasn't I?
36. To keep a sick child in bed will turn out to be a difficult task.
37. We shall not go to the station today to see off our classmates.
38. Did you go all the way to London to earn?
39. Some of us have been getting used to smoking.
40. One of you is a devil and will betray me.

Chapter 26

GERUND

What is a **gerund**?

In the English language, we can make a noun out of every present form verb by adding the letters ING to it. Such a noun is called a **Gerund**. We may look at a gerund also as a *verbal noun* because it is made out of a verb.

Unlike the other nouns, a gerund is a noun of action because we form it out of a verb which is a word of action. We form gerunds like this,

Present form verb	*Gerund*
Play	Play**ing**
Swim	Swimm**ing**
Steal	Steal**ing**
Ride	Rid**ing**
Read	Read**ing**
Write	Writ**ing**

Thus, we can form a gerund out of any present form verb.

Use

Being a noun, we can use a gerund in the Subject section or Object section of a sentence. Study the following examples:

As subject

(a) **Jogging** is a good exercise.
    S

(b) **Fishing** is many people's hobby nowadays.

(c) **Reading** makes a person more knowledgeable.

(d) **Swimming** in a swimming pool is a good pastime during summer days.
        S   A.V   O   C

(e) **Bathing** in the sea could be quite adventurous.
        S   A   V   C

(f) **Intruding** into a Queue, is an uncivil act.

(g) **Walking** in the middle of a busy road, could be dangerous.
        S   A V Adv

If the meaning of the gerund is vague, we may use additional or explanatory or amplifying words to make the meaning clear, as in (d) - (g), in which case these additional words will also become part of the Subject.

As object

(a) My friend doesn't like **smoking**.

(b) Please stop **writing** .

(c) We could not enjoy **swimming** in the sea.
   S Neg A   V   O

(d)   Don't   go   for **playing** after sunset.
      NegA   V   O

(e)   Isn't this **bragging** about oneself?

(f)   We are <u>fighting</u>   (g) Norton is <u>flying</u>   (h) I am <u>eating</u>.

Like we did in the case of Subject, in the Object also we can use additional words to make the meaning clear. In (c), the words "in the sea" are amplifying words and not Complement, hence all the words constitute the Object here. Similarly in (d), "after sunset" are explanatory words and constitute the Object.

You must be careful when you use A.Vs. The word could become a continuous verb. See (f) – (h). But in (e), **bragging** is a gerund-noun because the Subject has a demonstrative pronoun. With any other noun or pronoun as Subject, the word would not be a gerund at all. Therefore, if you have to use A.Vs, write only sentences of the pattern shown in (e).

Sometime you may spot a word ending in ING in the middle of a sentence also. Don't conclude that they are gerunds. They need not be. Carry out the 'noun test' (object test) to be sure. If the word is truly a gerund, it will come immediately after V and also pass the object test.

If there is O or C after V and a verb ending in ING follows, it will be a participle and not a gerund. Examine the sentence given below:

(i)   My mother detests   me **hugging**   every visitor.
      S   (A)V   O   ?   O

In example (i), **hugging** is not a gerund-noun because it comes after O. It is a participle. More about it in Chapter 36.

Possessive pronoun before a GERUND

You already know that we can place only one of the three words at the left side of a noun. They are, an article or an adjective or a pronoun. (This pronoun must be either a 'demonstrative' pronoun or a 'possessive pronoun' only.) But, when the noun happens to be a gerund-noun, use only a possessive pronoun and no other pronoun and no article either. (We use an article only before a common noun; Gerund is not a 'common noun' to accept an article!) Occasionally, an adjective may be suitable. (See (e) below). Study the following examples:

(a)   Mother doesn't like *your* **bringing** that girl   into our house.
      S   Neg A   V   gerund- O   O   C

(b)   We don't like *her* **marrying** our Maths lecturer.

(c)   *Your* **reading** was excellent.

(d)   Please pardon *our* **leaving**   early.
                     gerund -O   Adv

(e)   Aren't you getting used to *heavy* **smoking**?
                                  Adj

Instead of a possessive pronoun, you may use a possessive noun like this,

(f)   The mother heard *the child's* **crying** from the kitchen.

(g)   *This woman's* **caring** healed my daughter within 2 days.

But, the modern writers tend to forget this rule and use objective pronouns before a gerund like this,

(h)   Julia did not like *me* **accompanying** her to the school.

(i)   Our teacher could not see *us* **standing** behind the dais.

From grammar angle, (h) and (i) are wrong if the verb ending in ING is intended to be a gerund noun. Further, the word in bold has become a participle because it happens to come after O.

Use of Gerund with the force of a verb

Though we use these words as gerund, we cannot forget the fact that we derived each from a present form verb. That's why we called it a 'verbal noun' as well. Therefore, can't we consider a gerund also as an action-oriented verb and use it in a sentence with the force of a verb? But in order to distinguish it from a gerund-noun, we have to use a suitable preposition such as, **to, of, at, for, with, without, in, after, on, against** or any other to its left. Here are some examples:

(a)   The visitor insisted   *on* **seeing**   her son immediately.
           S   (A)V   gerund-verb   O   Adv

(b)   Isn't this student good *at* **escaping** the assembly time?

(c)   That naughty girl in the last row is crazy *about* **playing** tricks on others.

(d)   We have no objection *to* your **seeing** our eldest daughter.

(e)   We might go *for* **witnessing** the semi final match.
        S   A   V gerund-verb   O

(f)   All of us felt tired *after* **reaching** the mountain top.

(g)   A knife is an instrument *for* **cutting** vegetables and other kitchen things.

(h)   The police charged this man *with* **rioting**.

(i)   Can you touch your toes *without* **bending** your back?
        A   S   V   O   Prepn   gerund-V   O

(j)   Do you feel happy   *at* **ridiculing** the poor people?
        A   S   V   Adv   P   gerund -V   O

In all the sentences above, don't the gerunds look like a second verb or having the power of a verb? Further, isn't it extraordinary that we could make a NOUN do the job of a VERB through the gerund method? Do note that a gerund-noun turns into a gerund-verb <u>only when we place a preposition to its left</u>. Also note that the sentence may or may not have O/C after the Verb. All the examples from (a) to (j) follow either of the two sentence formulae shown below:

S – A –V – **Prepn-gerund** – O/C
gerund-verb

S – A – V - O or C – **Prepn – gerund** – O/C
gerund-verb

Next, if you have to replace an infinitive-verb in a sentence, do so only with a gerund-verb and not a gerund-noun. Here are some examples:

(k)   Couldn't you have reached here earlier **to take** part in the function?
(kk)   Couldn't you have reached here earlier **for taking** part in the function?
(l)   My aunt was very happy **to meet** you, Sir.
(ll)   My aunt was very happy **at meeting** you, Sir.
(m)   I will go to the hospital this evening **to see** my brother.
(mm)   I will go to the hospital **for seeing** my brother in the hospital.
(n)   All parents advise their children **not to fight** with each other.
(nn)   All parents advise their children **against fighting** with each other.
(o)   Mary is slow **to catch** the local train.
(oo)   Mary is slow **at catching** the local train.
(p)   Surinder would try **to win** the first prize
(pp)   Surinder would try **at winning** the first prize.
(q)   Manickam could not be quick **to see** the point.
(qq)   Manickam could not be quick **at seeing** the point.
(r)   Are you confident enough **to count** the number of people present here?
(rr)   Are you confident enough **in counting** the number of people present here?

However, it may not be possible to replace every infinitive-verb by a gerund-verb. In certain cases the conversion may look odd and may not convey the accurate meaning as well. Examine the following sentences:

(s)   I like **to go** for higher studies.
(ss)   I like **at going** (for going) for higher studies.
(t)   The peon wants **to work** in this department, Sir.
(tt)   The peon wants **at working** (in working) this department, Sir.

Don't the sentences at (ss) and (tt) sound very funny? But, instead of converting an infinitive-verb, we can write direct sentences using gerund-verbs like this,

(a)   I went near the fence **on noticing** some movements near there.
(b)   Ram reported for duty immediately **after receiving** the appointment letter.
(c)   We had to shoulder greater responsibility **at accepting** the honour from the University.
(d)   We bought our entrance tickets at black market rate **for witnessing** the finals.

The greatest plus point of the gerund-verb is, that we can start a sentence with it like this,

(aa)   **On noticing** some movements near the fence, I went near there.
(bb)   **After receiving** the appointment letter, Ram reported for duty immediately.
(cc)   **At accepting** the honour from the University, we had to shoulder greater responsibility.
(dd)   **For witnessing** the finals, we bought our entrance tickets at black market rate.

Your sentences would look stylish if you start some with the gerund-verb. When you are writing a paragraph of say 10 sentences, it will make an annoying reading if you start every sentence in the pattern of S-A-V –O/C-Infin- O/C. You could start a sentence with O or C as well. This, to provide some variety and to remove the annoyance element. So, one of the methods is to start some sentences with the gerund-verb which will form part of O or C.

Infinitive or Gerund

Infinitive and Gerund have a close relationship like they are cousin brothers. In several cases, we can replace a gerund–noun with an infinitive-noun and vice versa as shown in the examples given below:

(a)   Esther doesn't like **copying.**
(aa) Esther doesn't like **to copy**.
(b)   Do you like **forgiving?**
(bb) Do you like **to forgive?**.
(c)   <u>Toiling</u> is man's duty in life. hard and tiring work .
(cc) **To toil** is man's duty in life.

But, don't <u>harbour</u> have in mind an impression that we can replace every infinitive by a gerund and vice versa. Not at all. Certain verbs in the S-A-V part would accept only infinitives and certain only gerunds.

We must use only **gerund-nouns** when the verb in the S-A-V part is, APPRECIATE, CONSIDER, DENY, DISLIKE, ENJOY, EXCUSE, FANCY, FORGIVE, IMAGINE, KEEP, MIND, PARDON, REMEMBER, RISK or UNDERSTAND. Some of the phrasal verbs that would accept only gerund-nouns are, GIVE UP, LOOK FORWARD TO and PUT OFF (and also their synonyms). Here are the examples:

(a)   We APPRECIATE *your* **loaning** us some money.
(b)   Are you CONSIDERING **joining** our club?
(c)   Could you DENY **seeing** me at the beach?
(d)   Monica DISLIKES **shaking** hands with anyone.
(e)   IMAGINE *my* **participating** in dance competitions?
(f)   We cannot RISK **taking** this road to the exhibition grounds.
(g)   We UNDERSTAND *your* **waiting** here, but will your friend come?
(h)   We cannot GIVE UP *our* **hunting**.
(i)   The Police LOOKED FORWARD TO **arresting** a number of criminals.
(j)   We PUT OFF **meeting** our business partner till next week.

All the sentences adhere to the formula,

S – A –V — gerund noun – O/C

(Because of the presence of the special verbs in the S-A-V part, you cannot change the gerund-noun into infinitive-noun.)

In the same way, use only **infinitive-verbs** when the first verb (S-A-V) is, WANT, WISH, HOPE, TRY, AGREE, ATTEMPT DEMAND, EXPECT, LEARN, MANAGE, PROMISE, NEED, REFUSE or SEEM (and also some of their synonyms):

(a) Do you WANT **to see** the Principal now?
("Do you want seeing the Headmaster now" will be wrong)
(b) The peon WISHES **to meet** you, Sir.
(c) The policeman DEMANDED **to know** my name.
(d) Do you AGREE **to do** a piece of work for Rs 50?
(e) Sangeeta HOPES **to replace** Nancy as the Captain of the Badminton team.
(f) We EXPECT Shirly **to return** the library books within a week.
(g) Isn't Mickey LEARNING how **to ride** a horse?
(h) Do we NEED some kind of approval **to consult** anyone on this point?
(i) The B section MANAGED **to complete** the assignment just on time.
(j) The Principal has PROMISED **to give** a seat to your daughter.
(k) Narayan doesn't SEEM **to care** for your advice at all.

(Because of the presence of the special verbs, you cannot replace the infinitive-verb by gerund-verb)

We may use either an **infinitive** or a **gerund** with the following first verbs: BEGIN, CONTINUE, HATE, LIKE, LOVE, PREFER, START, INTEND.

Replacement of infinitive-noun object by gerund-noun

Replace the infinitive-noun by gerund noun in the following sentences:

(a) We moved over to the library **to read**.
(b) Couldn't you come with us to the ground **to play?**
(c) This person had kept showing all tricks to us **to impress**.
(d) James is here **to pray**.

The strange thing is, in order to retain the original meaning we have to use a preposition before the gerund-noun when we convert the infinitive-noun object. As otherwise the meaning will not be clear at all. Here are the converted sentences:

(aa) We moved over to the library **for reading**.
(bb) Couldn't you have come with us to the ground **for playing?**
(cc) This person had kept showing all his tricks to us **for impressing**.
(dd) James is here **for praying**.

You should not view the above gerunds as gerund-verbs all because there is a preposition before it. They are very much gerund-noun and acting as Object and also pass the Noun test.

You will face no such problem when you have to convert an infinitive-noun Subject into a gerund-noun Subject.

Gerund after "used to"

If you go through the infinitive examples 1 – 30 in the three tense families in Chapter 24, you would notice the absence of any sentence with the auxiliary "used to" in any tense. (You also know that "used to" is a versatile auxiliary which we can use in all the 16 tenses). It is normal to use a gerund- noun after "used to" than any other noun of action. Here are the examples:

(a) I am used to **reading** the newspaper early every morning.

              Gerund   amplifying words

(b) Some of us could get used to **eating** non-vegetarian food.

(c) At least one of us should be getting used to **learning** the local language.

(d) You may have been used to **watching** late night serials on T.V but we are used to **going** to bed early.

(e) You have been getting used to **smoking**, haven't you?

(f) He was used to **standing** first in class till last year, wasn't he?

(g) By now you should have got used to **living** alone in this village.

(h) You would become used to **running** all by yourself during your morning runs.

(i) They ought to have been used to **singing** in the choir by now.

The only exception is, with regard to "did USE TO", in Simple past. This auxiliary set is usually followed by a verb, as shown in the examples below:

(j) Did you use to **lend** your notes to this student?

(k) Yes, I used to **lend** my notes to him during week ends.

Exercise

Fill up the blank with a suitable gerund-noun:

1. My aunt uses the sewing machine frequently. She is very fond of *stiching*.
2. Constant ..... will make you wise. *thinking*
3. Did you like that star's .... in the film, Small Nawab? *performing*
4. *Sleeping* in the afternoon is not a good habit for students.
5. Ramanathan loves ..... He has many tall stories to tell about. *reading story.*
6. Don't go for *walk* during late evenings.
7. Avoid *to wear* flashy clothes on Sundays.
8. *Clean* your own shoes, is a good policy.

Replace the gerunds with suitable infinitives to maintain the original meaning:

9. Reading has been my hobby for a long time.
10. Do you want fighting with me?
11. I cannot agree doing this work for Rs 10.
12. We needed taking a loan for our trekking programme.
13. I thought you loved watching T.V serials on Saturday evenings.
14. I have requested seeing him immediately.
15. Acquiring wealth by wrong means is bad.
16. Do you like giving some kind of excuses for all your failures?

Replace the infinitive-verbs with gerund-verbs wherever appropriate in the following sentences. (Don't forget, by placing a special preposition to the left of a gerund we will turn it into a gerund-verb)

17. A thermometer is an instrument to take the body temperature.
18. The coach has no objections to listen to your suggestion.
19. The hungry prisoner refused firmly to eat any meal.
20. Couldn't you have advised me not to include Thambidurai in our hockey team?

21. I had to make a lot of effort to park my cycle at the cycle stand.
22. We should have persuaded Maran to accept Philip's apology readily.
23. Any studious person would come here to collect more information on any subject.
24. James accepted willingly to apologise to Ramanan.

Locate the mistake(s) as far as gerunds are concerned and rewrite the sentences:
25. Dad doesn't like you coming home late every night.
26. Our driver didn't reach on time to pick up the college students.
27. Did I ever neglect to seeing you?
28. I don't wish meeting you till tomorrow.
29. Pardon him correcting your mistakes so often.
30. I cannot stand him grumbling to you over every small thing.
31. Haven't I come to this place for meeting my ward?
32. I must insist to seeing my answer paper once again.

Form gerund or infinitive out of the following present form verbs and use in the blank as considered necessary:
   Sing, shine, praise, shave, fish, ply, study, ski, sell, whip, buy, touch
33. Vineeta is not at all a bright student. She prefers .... to ......
34. Singing is her pastime because she is fond of music.
35. To touch the feet of an elder is an act of praise.
36. Boys should not try to shave until their beard shows up.
37. We like to buy our own shoes.
38. Skiing happens to be a winter sport in Kashmir.
39. Selling anything door to door is not my hobby.
40. Have you ever tried to whip a horse?

Analyse the following sentences:
41. Identifying the true God is every human being's personal responsibility.
42. Are you used to bathing in hot water every morning?
43. You had got used to this new lecturer, hadn't you?
44. Examining and criticising every exhibit in the hall is not my cup of tea.
45. You are very fond of meeting every visitor personally, aren't you?

Write the remaining 6 categories of sentences:
46. Do you want to meet our HOD today or later?
47. Aren't you tired of playing cards every evening?
48. Jeremiah is used to playing football in the rain.

Replace the infinitive by gerund in the following sentences. Make sure that the original meaning is maintained:
49. We could have gone to the stadium to practise.
50. Mustn't you have acted to set an example?
51. You may not be the right role model to emulate.
52. He isn't my look-alike to represent me everywhere.
53. Are all the new students ready to join our club?

Chapter 27

COMPLEX SENTENCE

Definition

What is a **Complex sentence**? It is a single sentence that contains two Simple sentences connected by a conjunction. A Simple sentence must have S-A-V- O/C and must be self contained in meaning.

In our earlier Chapters and Exercises, we have been using / writing Complex sentences observing the simple rule that it must contain two Simple sentences. In this Chapter we shall deal with it in greater details.

Could we call a sentence a **Complex sentence** if the first has only S-A-V and the second S-A-V-O/C? Strictly speaking NO, because the part that contains only S-A-V does not fulfil the condition of a Simple sentence. (We could call sentences of the pattern, S-A-V- Conjn - S-A-V-O/C as "Sentence with a clause". More about this in Chapter 42.)

Thus far, we have learnt 16 tenses and you have become quite confident of constructing Simple sentences in all these. Even in a Complex sentence we have to use the same S-A-V formula but twice, like this:

a1: S - A - V - O/C - Conjunction - S-A-V- O/C

A full-fledged Complex sentence will have 2 Simple sentences, connected by a **conjunction** and we can extract out the two Simples from it. The conjunction only helps in providing **a joint meaning**. Remove the conjunction, you would get two meaningful Simple sentences.

Conjunctions are of two types - Simple (with only single words) and Phrases/pairs. *And* is a peculiar conjunction, in that, in addition to connecting two Simple sentences into a Complex sentence, it can also connect any two words except two verbs. In this Chapter we shall learn and use only the Simple conjunctions which are,

AND, BUT, OR, BECAUSE, AFTER, THAT, TILL, IF, SINCE, THOUGH, UNLESS, WHEN, WHILE, UNTIL, AS, BEFORE, WHETHER, HENCE, SO.

It is not necessary that the conjunction must be in between the two Simple sentences. We can start a Complex sentence with a conjunction like this,

a2:   Conjn - S - Neg A - V - O/C - S-Neg A - V - O/C

Sample sentences

a1 : I could say something about this man only if I see him personally.
        S A V   O   Adv conjn S (A)V O   Adv

a2 : We did not stop . him because he looked determined and imposing.
       S Neg A V O conjn   S (A)V   C   *noticiable because*

of large size
apperance or importance

Q   :   Could   I   enter   the exam hall   since   I   have   a   hall ticket?
       A   S   (A)V   C   conjn   S A.V   O

Here are more examples of Complex sentences. Study them carefully and note down the tense of the two Simples:

1. I am sure that you have made a mistake.
2. My father is happy that I stood first in my class.
3. Can you prove to me that the Earth is round?
4. Haven't you found the book which I had hidden?
5. He is staying at home but (you) don't disturb him now.
6. If you don't walk fast, you will miss the train.
7. Mustn't we do our work well or our HOD shall be angry with us.
8. When you listen carefully, you should understand everything.
9. I am used to this chair and it is very comfortable.
10. This beggar comes to my house daily because my mother gives him some food without fail.
    (The first sentence belongs to PRESENT FAMILY in the Present auxiliaries)
11. I wished him success yet he had declined it.
12. The master informed the students that he <u>would</u> give them a retest.
13. The Rector gave a reply that he <u>could</u> review his orders.
14. The coach advised us that we <u>should</u> always play as a team.
15. The doctor confirmed his statement that the patient <u>might</u> get cured after a long treatment.
16. The mother's opinion was that the servant reported for work on time.
17. The ward supervisor shouted loudly that the mentally ill patient was running away.
18. We had told him that he should earn his own money.
19. Galileo revealed his discovery that the Earth goes round the Sun once a year.
20. The policemen announced confidently that the accident victim is breathing.
    (The first sentence belongs to PAST FAMILY in the Past auxiliaries)
21. Rattan won't join your company until you promise Rs 5000 per month.
22. All Fathers will be nice to you when you show good results in all subjects.
23. He would not move from here since we haven't received any orders.
24. Our English professor will take us to task unless we show better performance.
25. The surgeon shall not commence this operation before the pathologist has submitted his report.
26. James will keep complaining about the food till he is satisfied with it.
27. All of them will get used to this well water though we may not enjoy its taste.
28. Our class senior student will report to the Principal if we are making noise during the Lecturer's absence.
29. Shall we return home as we have not made any progress on treasure hunt?
30. We could be late for prayer if we don't hurry.
    (The first sentence belongs to the FUTURE FAMILY in the Future auxiliaries)

Tense rules

All the examples given above are full fledged Complex sentences. What rules have we followed in selecting the tense of the second sentence? They are as follows:

First sentence	Second sentence
Present family	Any tense according the timing and to give the proper meaning.
Past family	(a) Past family, or
	(b) With past equivalent auxiliaries, i.e. WOULD, SHOULD, COULD, MIGHT
	or
	(c) Simple present in case of any universal truths.
Future family	Present family

The above is called, "The Complex sentence tense rules". You need to observe these while framing any Complex sentence.

Universal truth

What is an universal truth? This is an information that no one could challenge or oppose or disagree with? Could anyone refute the truth that the Earth is going round the Sun once a year? Similarly, would anyone have a second opinion about a person who breathes?

Study sentences 19 and 20 carefully.

The second sentence in these two serials deal with universal truth. Therefore, the second sentences here must be in Present family only even when the first sentence is in Past.

First/Second sentence

There is no stipulation about which sentence should be known as the 'first' and which the 'second'. The sentence you wish to write first is the 'First sentence' and observe the tense rules with respect to that.

The simple conjunctions used are:

AND, BUT, OR, BECAUSE, AFTER, THAT, TILL, IF, SINCE, THOUGH, UNLESS (=IF NOT), WHEN, WHILE, UNTIL, AS, BEFORE, WHETHER, HENCE, SO.

Here are more sentences:

31. Sushila and her friend will eat their lunch **after** the Staff leaves the class room.

32. **When** the clock strikes six, (you do) wake me up. (WHEN is the conjn here)
33. **If** you accompany me, I shall go to the school.
34. Won't you come to my house **until** I invite you?
35. **After** all the sportsmen leave the field, the groundsmen will redraw the tracks.
36. **Before** the drill master comes, shall we wear our sports shirt?
37. I shall verify the information **whether** it is the same person.
38. We are used to this place **since** we had lived here for 2 years.
39. **As** I know him well, I shall be helping him always.
40. This baby is a nice kid only **if** you give her sweets every now and then.
41. Mohini and Sarsu were enemies **before** they were promoted to Std XI.
42. Go to a doctor **as** your temperature is above 99 degrees.
43. **When** you come home, (You do) bring with you a loaf of bread.
44. Could I go now **or** should I stay on?
45. You can win friends **but** you must show a kind face to all.
46. Be nice to all **and** they would love you.
47. Don't tell me **that** you never learnt the multiplication tables at all.
48. Mathematics is not a difficult subject **if** you remember all the rules.
49. Do you know **why** I joined this college? (WHY is a conjunction)
50. Have you told your father **why** I didn't go for classes today?
51. Shouldn't you have completed this job **since** I had given you sufficient time for it?
52. I would have completed it **if** you had needed the result so urgently.
53. The ayah shouted from inside the burning room **that** the child is alive.
54. Galileo asserted **that** the Earth is spherical like a ball.
55. The KG children yelled in one voice **that** 2 and 2 make 4.

In all the sentences given above, you could pick out two Nos. S-A-V-O/C in Q form or 'a' form. Sentences at 32, 33, 35, 36, 39 and 43 start with a conjunction.

Some of the words look like Prepositions - but, since, after, before, until. But, we have used them as conjunctions. Similarly, we have also used some interrogatives as conjunctions - **why, who**. To know their true function in the sentence, check if there is S-A-V-O/C after the word. If S-A-V-O/C is present, then that word is doing the job of a conjunction. We will come across very many sentences of this type.

You will develop a doubt about the EQs; which auxiliary to use in the Q tag? There is no hard and fast rule; use whichever sounds nice/appropriate out of the two A's. Here are some examples:

56. EQ : You will join our group if we invite you, won't you?
57. EQ : James cannot remember many formulae yet he scores high marks, doesn't he?
58. EQ : We would go for a swim if the weather is nice, wouldn't we?
59 EQ : You were used to smoking when we last visited you, weren't you?

60. EQ : You should have taken the umbrella with you when it was raining, shouldn't you?

Use of HAD (Past perfect tense)

Of the 4 uses of the auxiliary HAD, we covered only the first one in Chapter 18. The remaining 3 uses find their place in Complex sentence.

Two action rule

If two actions took place in the past period, we use the Past perfect tense (HAD) for the first action and Simple past for the second action. Here are the examples:

61. I went out of my house after my father had stepped in.
62. The Professor had distributed the answer papers before she announced the marks.
63. Pratap declared his innocence when he had stood before the judge.

As a follow up matter

Action is over and we refer to that action for a follow-up discussion.

64. I had applied for admission in St Peter's college but they would never reply.
65. We had been to Trichy several times yet we never visited the Fort temple.
66. My cousin had asked for money in several letters but I ignored his request.

Reported speech

We describe in this what someone had said in the past. You can see such sentences in newspapers. This is a journalist's language. In such cases, the first part will have only S-A-V. (Technically, they are not Complex sentences but sentences with a clause)

67. The CM said that he had issued fresh orders for new recruitment.
68. The Administrator replied that he had already dismissed the erring sweepers.

Do you notice that the examples at 67 and 68 also come under the 'two action' rule? Similarly 64-66? Therefore, while writing Complex sentences involving past actions, follow the 2 action rule and all your sentences then would turn out to be correct.

Here are more examples of Complex sentences/Sentences with a clause that we use daily in our life:

69. Mother says that she will not give us more pocket money for this month.
70. Your friend thinks that I am an excellent writer in English.
71. Are you sure, you don't want this book? (Conjunction is silent here)
72. Daddy asks if you can do him a favour.
73. When I ask a question, my sister will turn her ears off!
74. The Lecturer replied that he would dictate the notes on the following day.
75. Sharda enquired whether you would be accompanying her to the church.
76. The Coach says, he will be present at the cricket ground today.

77. All of us must admit that we are dishonest at times.
78. I replied that I might join the picnic group.
79. I asked Shivani, where she was going.
80. She replied, she was going to a movie.

Usefulness of a Complex sentence

We know that a Complex sentence is a 'single' sentence but it will have in it two 'Simple' sentences. (2 Nos. S-A-V- O/C). We can make use of this fact to combine any two Simple sentences into one. Such combining would be possible even if both the Simples are remotely connected or totally unconnected, into a **meaningful** single sentence if we use the appropriate conjunction. Each Simple must be meaningful (i.e it must have S-A-V-O/ C) by itself. Study the following pairs of sentences:

(a)   I went to college that morning with an empty bag. (b) The market did not have mangoes that day.

You will notice that there is no connection whatever between the two Simple sentences given above; they are in two different directions. Yet we can make a meaningful single sentence out of them by using the conjunction 'since' like this,

1. **Since** the market did not have mangoes that day, I went to college that morning with en empty bag.

Here are more examples. But, make sure you observe the tense rules when you combine any two Simple sentences:

(c) We had skipped the games period that afternoon. (d) My mother gave biscuits for our afternoon tea.

2. My mother gave biscuits for our afternoon tea **because** we had skipped the games period that afternoon.

(e) I shall go straight home after college. (f) Mala is absent today.

3. **If** Mala is absent today I shall go straight home after college.

(g) Finish breakfast. (h) Shall we watch a video movie?

4. Shall we watch a video movie **after** you finish breakfast?

Such combining **would not** be possible if one of the sentences has only S- A- V. Both must be full fledged Simple sentences.

The reverse would also be true. That is, given a Complex sentence, you could split it into two meaningful Simple sentences. At this stage, the conjunction will play no part; it should not play any part actually. If the conjunction concerned does play any part in providing the meaning of one of the sentences or one Simple depends on the other for its actual meaning, then it will not be a Complex sentence even though you may identify 2 Nos S-A-V or S-A-V-O/C. More about this when you learn Compound sentence in Chapter 42.

Now, we come to a strange question. If we could extract out the two Simple sentences from a Complex sentence, what part does the conjunction actually play?

Think.

A conjunction helps in providing a 'joint' meaning of the entire Complex sentence. Combine the following sentences:

(a)   This child behaves well.   (b)   The mother has a headache..

This child behaves well **when** the mother has a headache.
If the mother has a headache, this child behaves well.

Do you see that we get the full meaning and a sensible meaning of the Complex sentence only because of the conjunction?

Do remember that we cannot extract out two meaningful sentences if one has only S-A-V.

Infinitive connectors

While we can connect any two Simples through the Complex sentence method, it may not be possible to connect every pair of sentences through the Infinitive connector method.

Writing all the categories of sentences

Writing the remaining 6 categories in Complex format may not be always possible since there will be two Simple sentences conforming to the tense rules. But, it may be possible with certain categories. However, if you do have to write them, keep intact the original meaning of the Complex sentence by suitably modifying some appropriate word(s) in any of the Simple sentences.

Length of a Complex sentence

The modern practice is to write short sentences with a length of 16 words. So, a Complex sentence should not as a rule exceed 16 words or thereabouts.

Exercise

Use the correct auxiliary and verb form in the blank. The verb to be used is shown in its present form in brackets:

1.   Didn't Samuel say that he ....wrote....to me regularly? (write)
2.   Shan't we rest here until the second group ...reached...here. (reach)
3.   Won't the next door aunty think that our mother ..will.. still ...be... in the bed room? (be)
4.   The shopkeeper told us that we ...were... wrong. (are/were)
5.   Raymond said that he ....was....sick. (is/was)

6. Nandini would be going where Sarojini ...~~go~~... (go)
7. Our senior student says that we ..see.. the Principal this afternoon. (see)
8. This gentleman asked me where the post office ..was.. (is/was)
9. He also asked me where I ..was..going. (am/was)
10. Maninder would write this essay if he ..had.. the time. (has/had)
11. Don't ask him where he ..is.. living. (is/was).
12. You shouldn't pay the servant if she ..has.. not worked well. (has/had)
13. We ought not to have criticised him unless he ..had been.. wrong. (is/had been)
14. He can come with me if his mother ..permits..him. (permits/permitted)
15. My friend may not like your idea unless he ..is..in agreement with it. (is/was)

Locate the mistake and rewrite the concerned Complex sentence using the correct tense:

16. All of you ~~will go~~ *could* home only if the Coach gave you permission.
17. What does this child do when ~~it was~~ *he is* hungry?
18. Would any parents think that their children ~~will~~ not get promoted?
19. Won't your mother cry if you didn't reach home on time?
20. The parish priest told me that he ~~is~~ *was* present in the church from 10 a.m. onwards.
21. Make haste when the going was good.
22. My heart always jumped with joy whenever I ~~see~~ *saw* flowers.
23. Life is like a bubble because it blowed off with the wind.
24. My younger brother always gets nervous when he ~~had seen~~ *see* my father.
25. We have a stick in our hand when we saw a snake on our path.

Fill up the blank with a suitable auxiliary out of CAN, MAY, MIGHT, WOULD and COULD:

26. The HOD ..can.. be in the office by now.
27. Dennis the Menace ..can..pray to God daily for a small sister.
28. Shalini said that she ..may..take care of my children during my absence.
29. ..Could..you swim 100 meters without getting tired?
30. We ..can.. not get the correct answer yesterday for this equation.
31. ..Would..you kindly show me the way to the railway station please?
32. I ..could..have sent off this letter yesterday itself if you had told me so.
33. The rescuers ..could..not have located the victims if the police dog had not guided them to the spot.
34. This ointment ..could..cure your skin disease if you applied it regularly.
35. Unless I had ordered you, you ..would..not have set up your room., ..would.. you?

Rewrite the following sentences using any suitable auxiliary out of WOULD, SHOULD, COULD and MIGHT without significantly changing the meaning:

36. Does Ramu make speeches in Punjabi?
37. My neighbour's little son spends the whole morning in my house.

38. This vendor claims that his herbal medicines do cure AIDS.
39. Sundari was playing cards when her mother stepped into the room.
40. Do your children fight with each other?

Locate the mistake(s) and rewrite the sentences concerned without significantly changing the meaning:

41. Radhika cannot give ~~you~~ any kind of help if you asked her.
42. I ~~shall~~ have returned the money when you asked for ~~it~~ .
43. My Personal secretary ~~could not~~ have sent any money to his daughter when she ~~is in the~~ hostel.
44. My uncle should not misled you when he himself ~~isn't~~ well.
45. You ought to help this poor student if he ~~had~~ requested you.
46. You would be polite to him because he was small. (WOULD here is a Simple present auxiliary.)
47. I shall surely argue the case if he wanted it.
48. Nelson might not have taken part in the boxing bout if he knew Arthur well.
49. Shouldn't he have kept quiet unless the Staff had not punished him.
50. Mahima can row this boat unless the weather was bad.

Write the following sentences in as many ways as you can with different auxiliaries without changing the meaning significantly:

51. Meenakshi will write her First year exam in March next year.
52. Selvan is acting in my next film.
53. Sunny thrashed Babloo severely on his back.
54. Krishnan speaks Hindi equally fluently.
55. The TN express arrives at Central station in an hour's time.

Rewrite the following sentences using an auxiliary out of NEED and DARE:

56. Should I reply this letter today itself?
57. They should not go to the beach on any excuse.
58. The Superintendent can never employ this peon again in the college office.
59. Why did you buy so many table mats?
60. Can you go near a lion's cage?

Combine the following unconnected Simple sentences into a single meaningful sentence:

61. This is a nice building. My father designed it ten years back.
62. We were students of St James school earlier. We learnt the rules about Complex sentence there.
63. We heard the church bell. We ran fast.
64. We could not come for yesterday's match. There was no bus service in our area.
65. I always drink milk every morning? Today, I have a headache.

66.   The servant maid was absent for 5 days this month. Don't pay her full salary.
67.   You must agree with his idea. Isn't he our Captain?
68.   Would you call him a cheat? Samuel never tells lies.
69.   The clock struck one. The mouse came down.
70.   We had taken our evening tea at 3 p.m. We left the picnic spot immediately.
      (How many pairs could you connect through the Infinitive method?)

Split the following Complex sentences into two Simple sentences:

71.   Before we reach the college gate, we adjust our shirt and trousers.
72.   If you don't like omelette, eat *iddlis* then.
73.   You play table tennis while we read some magazines in the next room.
74.   If the Professor orders me, I shall conduct extra classes for you.
75.   When we were playing hockey till late evening, our parents became angry.

Contrast Clauses → although; though; even though; while.

Reason clauses → because, since, as

Place clauses → where, wherever, everywhere.

Purpose clauses → so that, so, because + want

Result clauses → so that, so...that, such.... that

Time clauses → when, before, after, since, while, as
          as soon as, by the time, until

Conditional clauses → if, unless, provided (that),
          as long as.

Chapter 28

CONDITIONAL STATEMENTS

Conditional statements are also Complex sentences.

Incidentally, what is a conditional statement? It is a statement or an undertaking wherein we agree to do a work on the fulfilment of certain condition(s) mentioned in the statement. There are three types of conditional statements.

Open conditional statement

We make the open conditional statements only in Present time. We use the Simple present auxiliaries CAN, MAY, SHALL, WILL, MUST or OUGHT TO in one part of the Complex sentence and any Present family tense in the other.

Q	:	Can I hold a discussion with you if I come to your office at 10 a.m.?
a1	:	You can hold the discussion if you come to my office sharp at 10 a.m.
a2	:	You cannot hold it if you come after 1030 hours.

Q	:	Will you help my son in his studies?
a1	:	I shall certainly help him if he approaches me for it.
a2	:	I cannot help him if he is not keen on studies.

a1	:	You may catch cold if you don't wear a sweater in this weather.
a2	:	You must not come to office if you have a temperature.

a2	:	Our team ought not to play the match if the ground is wet.
a1	:	You ought to accept the challenge if it is not a difficult one.

EQ	:	The new Asst.Lecturer must teach this subject if the HOD orders her, mustn't she?
EQ	:	If I finish my paper early, I can leave the exam hall early, can't I?
EQ	:	This student will fail if he doesn't work hard, won't he?
EQ	:	We ought to return home soon if we want to watch that T.V. serial, oughtn't we?
EQ	:	They can see me if I am in my office, can't they?

Past conditional statements

We make the Past conditional statements also for <u>Present time cases</u> only. In this variety, we use the auxiliaries WOULD, SHOULD, COULD or MIGHT (Past equivalent auxiliaries) in one part and any Past family tense in the other. You could look at this rule with a different eye as well. It is because we start a sentence with **would, should, could or might** that we are obliged to use Past auxiliaries in the second sentence to be in conformity with the tense rules. Though we use Past equivalent auxiliaries and Past family tenses, the time period of the whole statement will remain in **Present time** only. This is an important point to keep in mind. Study the following examples from the 'timing' point of view:

Q. Would you help me if I requested you?

Note:

"Would you help me if I request you" would be wrong.

The statement, "Would you help me if I requested you" is equal to, "Will you help me if I request you".

al : I would indeed help you if you requested me.
a2 : I wouldn't help you if you didn't request me.

Q : Could I see you if I came to your office at 9 a.m.?
al : You could see me if you came to my office at 9 a.m.
a2(a) : You couldn't see me if you came to my office at 9 a.m.
a2(b) : You can't see me if you come after 9.30 a.m.

Note:

Note the change in a2(b). If we write, "You couldn't see me if you came after 9 a.m." (Note that this sentence is grammatically correct), the sentence may give a wrong impression of the 'timing'. Thus, in order to stress that the timing of the sentence is in **Present time,** we switch over to the conventional present conditional statement with the auxiliary "cannot" and present family tense in the second part.

al : The doctor might oblige you if you approached him properly.
Q : Will you help my son in his studies?
al(a) : I shall certainly help him if he asks me for it.
al(b) : I should help your son if he asked me for it.
a2 : I cannot help him if he is casual on studies.

al(a) : You may catch cold if you don't wear a sweater in this weather.
al(b) : You might catch cold if you didn't wear a sweater in this weather.
a2 : You must not come to office if you have a temperature.

a2(a) : Our team ought not to play the match if the ground is wet.
a2(b) : Our team should not play the match if the ground was wet.
al : You ought to accept the challenge if it is not a difficult one.

EQ : The new Asst.Lecturer must give us a test if the HOD orders her, mustn't she?
EQ : The new Asst. Lecturer should give us a test if the HOD had ordered her, shouldn't she?
EQ : If I finish my paper early, I can leave the exam hall early, can't I?
EQ : If I finished my paper early, I could leave the exam hall early, couldn't I?
EQ : This student will fail if he doesn't work hard, won't he?
EQ : This student would fail if he didn't work hard, would he?
EQ : We ought to return home soon if we should watch a movie, oughtn't we?
EQ : We might return home soon if we wanted to watch a movie, mightn't we?
EQ : They can see me if I am in my office, can't they?

EQ :They could see me if I was in my office, couldn't they?

a2(a) : They couldn't see me if I wasn't in my office.

a2(b) : They cannot see me if I am not in my office.

Note:

Be cautious when you use COULD, especially in the a2 form. In the above examples, a2(b) is the correct form. "Past" -"Past" auxiliaries here would convey a wrong meaning.

To reiterate the rule, though we call these statements "Past conditional statements", the actions refer to the **present time** only. The use of past equivalent auxiliaries (WOULD, COULD, MIGHT, SHOULD) in one sentence compels us to use a Past family tense in the other part.

Past perfect conditional statements

We make the **Past perfect conditional statements** only for Past time cases. We use the FIP auxiliaries in one part and any Past perfect tense in the other. Here are the examples:

Q : Wouldn't I have gone to the station if you had told me earlier?

a2 : If the policeman had not guided me, I couldn't have reached your house on time at all.

a2 : The doctor might not have struck upon this new treatment method if the patients had not been complaining of ever-rising temperature.

a1 : The cricketers ought to have reported for the play if the Captain had informed them about it well in advance.

Q : Couldn't you have driven out the thieves if you had exercised some presence of mind.

a1 : I must have put very little salt if the guests had not relished my mutton curry.

a2 : You would not have wasted your time on this game if only you had consulted me earlier.

EQ : The invitees would have attended our college function if you had despatched the invitations a week in advance, wouldn't they?

The time - factor in all statements

We make all our statements, in any tense for that matter, only from two time periods - Present or Past. In the Present time period, we make statements of all Present family, all Past family and all Future family (including Future perfect). The only statement we make from a Past time period is the FIP kind statements.

Although some statements are known as "Past conditional statements", they too belong to the present time period only. For instance, "I would assist him if he requested me" is equal to "I will assist him if he requests me". The time-factor of the statement does not change all because we have used Past equivalent auxiliaries. Look again at all the Past conditional statements from this angle.

Whereas, we make all the FIP statements from the Past time period (imaginary past) only.

Incidentally, we can never make a conditional statement in the Future time period.

Use of UNLESS in conditional statements

UNLESS is equal to IF NOT. The conjunction **Unless** has a negative role in a sentence.

Rule to use UNLESS

The formula for using this conjunction in Complex and conditional statements is,

a1 - UNLESS - a2

or

a2 - UNLESS - a1

a2 may be with negative auxiliaries or negative in meaning.

Here are the examples:

a2.   You shouldn't play outside unless there was good sunshine.

Q.   Could you come with me in the bus unless you had some other programme?

a2.   You shouldn't use your cycle unless your mother had permitted you.

a1.   He shall become indifferent towards you unless you pamper him a little.

a1.   The audience ought to have remained silent unless they had disliked all the speakers.

a2.   Unless I permit you, you shall not attend my class.

a2.   Unless you behave well, I won't allow you anywhere inside the drawing room.

Q.   Wouldn't you do your homework unless I threatened you with punishment?

Q.   Why shall I take part in sports unless my House master orders me?

a1.   I shall come to college tomorrow unless I am sick.

a1.   I will spoil your birthday dress unless you give me some sweets.

Q.   Can't you be here on time unless I remind you?

Exercise

Locate the mistake(s) and rewrite the sentence:

1.   Could I discuss this problem with you if I come to your house before 8 p.m. tomorrow?

2.   The doctor will indeed get angry if you asked him any questions on anatomy.

3.   I will surely receive your son at the railway station if he had sent a telegram.

4.   I cannot help the needy persons unless they came to me personally.

5.   If I run fast could I catch that long distance bus?

6.   You must score over 90% if you wanted a seat in an engineering college.

7.   Your friend wouldn't have lost the fight if he has kept his cool in the boxing ring.

8.   I could have missed my flight if I had driven my car very fast.

9. You need not have come to my house if you considered my sense of judgement substandard.

10. Do you dare cross this line even after I will warn you.

Use the most suitable auxiliary in the blank in the following sentences:

11. We did not stop the car but, we _could_ have stopped and helped the poor travellers.

12. If you hadn't met my friend, you _would_ have told me about it.

13. We _cannot_ provoke him since he is only a child.

14. In future you _could_ be more punctual.

15. If you had helped your sister she _would_ not have failed in the finals.

Rewrite the following sentences using any suitable Past equivalent auxiliary:

16. Does your Hindi teacher make speeches in English? _could_

17. Your daughter spends most of her holidays in my house. _could_

18. The village medicine man often claims that his herbs _could_ cure cancer.

19. All of us were playing cards when Sebastian's parents entered the room.

20. Don't these small boys fight with each other often?

Write the following sentences in 4 different ways with four different auxiliaries without changing the meaning significantly:

21. Monica will write her final semester exams only in May this year.

22. Stephen acts in tomorrow's stage play.

23. Little Mona twisted the cat's tail severely.

24. Tina speaks good Tamil.

25. The Tamil Nadu express is arriving on platform 4 in half an hour's time.

Rewrite the following conditional statements using the conjunction UNLESS and yet without changing the meaning:

26. I shall board only this train _unless_ if you don't go with me.

27. I would have played the center half if you had told me before the start of the match.

28. If you had informed earlier I would not have sent my servant to the reservation office.

29. Couldn't you have written this letter since you hadn't been sick?

30. The crowd ought to have been patient if their favourite speaker was taking the dais next.

Chapter 29

PASSIVE VOICE
Passive forms of PRESENT FAMILY

Introduction

Whatever sentences we have written and spoken thus far in all the 16 tenses are said to be in **Active voice**. We can convert Active voice sentences into Passive voice. But, such conversion is possible only in 9 Active tenses. When so converted, there would be no change in the meaning between the two; in fact, there should be no change whatever in the meaning.

We will see the reasons later as to why we cannot convert the remaining 7 tenses.

For conversion into Passive form, it is essential that the Active sentence has one or more objects. When we did the sentence analysis in Chapter 2, we called the meaning part as "Object and / or Complement". You have also learnt how to identify an Object from a Complement. At that time you would have wondered why, since both O and C contribute to the meaning of a sentence. The distinction between O and C becomes useful in Passive voice. We can convert only a sentence that has an object or objects into Passive form. We can never convert a complement - based sentence into Passive form. Therefore, test an Active voice sentence for presence of object in the first instance, before you go in for conversion into Passive form.

This is how we obtain the passive form. Consider the sentences at (a) and (b) given below:

(a) Sekar eats   a mango. (Active)
       S (A) V   O
(aa) A mango is eaten   by   Sekar. (Passive)
         S   A V   Prep   O
(b)   Monica does not attend Practical classes at all.
(bb) Practical classes are not attended by Monica at all.
(c)   Could I meet you at 9 a.m. in your office?
(ac) Could you be met by me in your office at 9 a.m.?
(d)   Malathi danced nicely.
      Passive not possible.

There is no change in the meaning between (a) and (aa), (b) and (bb), (c) and (cc). We have followed 4 steps in converting an Active voice sentence into a Passive voice sentence:

4 Rules/steps for conversion

1.   We have interchanged the Subject and the Object.

2. There is a new auxiliary (known as the Passive auxiliary)
3. The new verb is in the PP form. (We always use the PP verb in Passive voice)
4. We have used the preposition "by" before the new object.

Follow the above 4 rules/steps for conversion from Active to Passive in all the 9 tenses.

<u>Points to note:</u>

If a sentence has only a complement(s), we cannot convert such a sentence into Passive form. See (d) above.

If a sentence has an object and also a complement, the complement will remain unaltered in the Passive form.

If there are two objects, use the more important one as the new Subject.

It is not possible to change both the objects into subjects. (A sentence can have only one Subject!)

Transitive and Intransitive verbs

If a sentence has an "object", we say that the verb has been used *transitively* in it or such a sentence has a *transitive verb*. If there is no object and only a "complement" we say that the verb has been used *intransitively* or the sentence has an *intransitive verb*. We can use several verbs both transitively or intransitively. Take the following sentences,

(e) Sekar eats nicely.
    S (A)V Adv

(f) Rajan does not write very well.
    S Neg A V C

(g) Sekar eats mangoes
    S (A)V O

(h) Rajan does not write short stories.
    S Neg A V O

Though the verbs are the same, we have used them intransitively in (e) and (f) and transitively in (g) and (h). Therefore, always use the expression "transitively used" or "intransitively used". However, there are some verbs which are basically intransitive - we can never use them transitively at all! They are GO and COME and their synonyms. These verbs will always lead to a complement and never an object. Thus, there exist only "intransitive verbs". There is nothing known as "transitive verbs".

Accordingly, before converting an Active sentence into a Passive one, apply the Noun test and ensure that it does have an Object.

Conversion of Present Family

The Present family has 5 tenses. Before conversion, you must know which auxiliary or auxiliaries are to be used for each tense besides the other three rules. Incidentally, we draw the Passive auxiliaries from the same list of 32. The major difference thus will be the verb form. In all Passive sentences we use the verb in its PP form. The Passive voice auxiliaries are shown alongside the Active voice auxiliaries for each tense.

	Tense	*Active aux.*	*Passive aux.*
1.	(a) Present	AM, IS, ARE	- - -
		am/is/are USED TO	- - -
	(b) Present (Possess.)	HAS, HAVE	IS/ARE HAD
	(c) Present Emphatics	AM, IS, ARE, HAS, HAVE,	Add BE
		DO HAVE, DOES HAVE	to each
2.	(a) Simple present	DO, DOES	AM, IS, ARE
	(b) Simple present	CAN, MAY, SHOULD,	Add
		WOULD, COULD, MUST,	BE to each
		NEED, OUGHT TO, WILL,	
		SHALL	
		Can/may/would/….will **get**	Add BE. Passive
		USED TO	possible only with 'got'
	(c) Simple present	KEEP, DARE	Any suitable aux.
3.	Present continuous	AM, IS, ARE	am/is/are/ BEING
		CAN BE, MAY BE …..	
		OUGHT TO BE, WILL BE	- - -
		Am/is/must be ….. **getting/ becoming** USED TO	- - -
		Can/may/should/……ought to KEEP	- - -
		GOING TO	Add BE
4.	Present perfect	HAS, HAVE, MAY	Add BEEN
		has/have got/become/been USED TO	Add BEEN only with 'got'.
5.	Present perfect cont.	HAS/HAVE BEEN	- - -
		MAY HAVE BEEN,…. KEPT,	
		Has been /have been/may have been getting/becoming USED TO	- - -

We cannot convert the Present tense (with AM, IS, ARE) and Present perfect continuous tense in this family. We shall see the reason why a little later.

Here are examples for each type wherein we follow the 4 steps:

Present

1. (a) (ACTIVE)   Mahadevan is a good student.
   (PASSIVE)   **Passive not possible** because A.V is present.
   (A) We are used to drinking milk.
   (P) **Passive not possible** since A.V is present.

   (b) (A) Paul has a good bicycle.
   (P) A good bicycle **is had** by Paul.
           S   A V   O

   (c) (A) I am not to watch some T.V serials from now on.
   (P) Some T.V serials are **not to be** watched by me from now on.

   (A) Philip is to teach me billiards.
   (P) Billiards **is to be** taught to me by Philip.
           S   A   V   O   O

   (A) My cousin sisters are to visit us today.
   (P) We **are to be/have to be** visited by my cousin sisters today.

   (A) Rohini has to pay for this notebook.
   (P) This notebook **has to be/is to be** paid for by Rohini.

   (A) All of us have to attend the students' meeting at 4 p.m. today.
   (P) The students' meeting **has to be/is to be** attended by us all at 4 p.m. today.

   (A) Sam and his sister have to practise the National anthem this evening.
   (P) The National anthem **has to be/is to be** practised by Sam and his sister this evening.

   (A) All students do have to contribute Rs ten each for the college sports.
   (P) Rs. Ten each **do have to be/have to be** contributed by all the students for the college sports.

   (A) Swaminathan does have to participate in the quiz competition.
   (P) The quiz competition **does have to be/has to be** participated by Swaminathan.
               S   A   A   V   O

Simple present

2. (A) My sister doesn't make good coffee.
   (P) Good coffee **is not** made by my sister.
           S   NegA V   O

   (A) We always give a good report about our friends.
   (P) A good report **is** always given about our friends by us.

Note:

Out of the two objects (i.e. **A report** and **our friends**), choose the more important one for conversion.

(A) Saroja does not like me at all.
(P) I **am not** liked by Saroja at all.

(A) Can Smitha throw this ball beyond 10 meters?
(P) **Can** this ball **be** thrown beyond 10 meters by Smitha?
    A   S   A   V   C   O

(A) May I borrow your bicycle for an hour?
(P) **May** your bicycle **be** borrowed for an hour by me?

(A) I would buy a ticket for you straightway.
(P) A ticket **would be** bought for you by me straightway.

(A) I couldn't contact your brother yesterday.
(P) Your brother **couldn't be** contacted by me yesterday.

(A) My brother should see you tomorrow morning.
(P) You **should be** seen by my brother tomorrow morning.

(A) All of you must avoid this particular student.
(P) This particular student **must be** avoided by all of you.

(A) The Lecturer need not meet our parents.
(P) Our parents **need not be** met by our Lecturer.

(A) This watchman can get used to our faces soon.
(P) Our faces **can be** got **used to** by the watchman.
          S   A   V   A   O

(A) We ought not to get used to bad habits ever.
(P) Bad habits **ought not to be** got **used to** by us.

(A) Some of us must get used to befriending the gate keeper.
(P) Befriending the gate keeper must be got used to by some of us.
          S   A   V   A   O

(A) Samson has become used to protecting bad students.
(P) **Passive not possible** because the verb used is "become".

(Although all sentences with "used to" are grammatically correct, we don't usually frame such Passive sentences. So, keep them in Active only)

(A) We ought to worship God daily.
(P) God **ought to be** worshipped by us daily.

(A) We shall eat our breakfast by 7.30 a.m.
(P) Breakfast **shall be** eaten by us by 7.30 a.m.

* (A) Mr.Thomas does keep coaching my brother in tennis.
(P) My brother is **being** coached by Mr.Thomas in tennis.
(A) I do keep visiting my grand parents once a month.
(P) My grand parents **are being** visited by me once a month.

(A) We dare not disobey the hostel rules.
(P) The hostel rules **are not to be** disobeyed by us.

Note:

*When KEEP and DARE are the auxiliaries in the Active, we have to use a totally unrelated auxiliary in the Passive as shown above in order to maintain the meaning.

Present continuous

3. (A) Rajan is not helping me in my studies.
    (P) I **am not being** helped by Rajan in my studies.
        S   Neg A   V   O   O

    (A) My friends are making a toy aeroplane.
    (P) A toy aeroplane **is being** made by my friends.

    (A) I am taking my sisters to the exhibition today?
    (P) My sisters **are being** taken to the exhibition today by me.

    (A) Some of us are going to stage a Shakespeare's play.
    (P) A Shakespeare's play **is going to be** staged by some of us.
                  S   A   V   O

Present perfect

4. (A) Someone has taken my lunch box from my bag.
    (P) My lunch box **has been** taken from my bag by someone.

    (A) We have not opened these windows.
    (P) These windows **have not been** opened by us.
            S   Neg A   V   O

    (A) We may have missed the bus.
    (P) The bus **may have been** missed by us.

Conversion of questions

Any question must sound like a question in the Passive form also. Here are some typical examples on all tenses:

(A) Sp Q : Has this animal any intelligence?
(P)   **Is** any intelligence **had** by this animal?

(A) Gen Q: **What** does John teach you?
(P)   **What is** taught to you by John?

(A) **How** has Philip hurt you?
(P) **How have** you been hurt by Philip?

(A) **When** do you do your revision assignments normally?
(P) **When are** your revision assignments done by you normally?

(A) **Who** buys the table tennis balls for you?
(P) The table tennis balls **are** bought for you by **who**?
    (**By whom** are the table tennis balls bought for you?)

(A) **When** could the local guardian meet their wards in this hostel?

(P) **When could** the wards **be** met by their local guardians in this hostel?

(A) **When** can you get used to writing better English?

(P) **When can** writing better English **be** got **used to** by you?

(The Passive with "used to" doesn't sound well, does it? Therefore, desist from framing Passives with this auxiliary in Answer form or Question form)

(A) **Where** must they keep their lunch pack?

(P) **Where must** their lunch pack **be** kept by them?

Conversion of EQs

(A) They cannot eat their tiffin before 11 a.m., can they?

(P) Their tiffin **cannot be** eaten before 11 a.m., **can it**?

(A) Some lady students of this group could score high marks in all exams, couldn't they?

(P) High marks **could be** scored by some lady students of this group, couldn't they?

(A) The college servants are cleaning up the sports ground, aren't they?

(P) The sports ground **is** being cleaned up by the college servants, **isn't it**?

1. The interrogative word remains as it is, in the Passive form. But when the interrogative is WHO, it comes at the end of the sentence or at the beginning with "By whom". When a question is converted, it must have the force of a question in the Passive form.

2. In EQs, use in the Q tag the auxiliary of the new Subject.

Conversion of Complex sentences

If both Simple sentences have an object each, convert both. If only one has an object and the other a complement, leave the latter sentence as it is. You cannot convert a Complex sentence if there is no object at least in one of the two Simple sentences.

(A) If you don't want this item, I could give it to someone else.

(P) If this item **is not** wanted by you, it **could be** given to someone else by me.

(A) While the men students wanted ice cream, the lady students stood silent.

(P) While ice cream **was** wanted by the men students, the lady students stood silent.

(A) We shall sit here until the Administrator gives us instructions.

(P) We shall sit here until the instructions **are** given to us by Administrator.

(A) The spectators shout compliments when the players do a good job, don't they?

(P) Compliments **are** shouted by the spectators when a good job **is** done by the players, aren't they?

Note:

1. In a Complex sentence, the conjunction remains the same.

2. In the EQs, use the more appropriate auxiliary of the two Simples, in the Q tag.

Conversion of sentences with two objects

Only one of the objects could be converted at a time and never both in the same sentence.

  (A) We should not have promised Monica so much money.
      S   01   02

  (P1) Monica should not have been promised so much money by us.
      S   02   01

  (P2) So much money should not have been promised to Monica by us.
      S   01   02

  (A) The committee asks the candidates some difficult questions.
        S   01   02

  (P1) The candidates are asked some difficult questions by the committee.
         S   02   01

  (P2) Some difficult questions are posed (asked) to the candidates by the committee.
         S   01   02

Conversion of Infinitive-verb based sentences

Conversion to Passive form will concern both the infinitive-verb and infinitive-noun. First, consider the infinitive-verb.

<u>Conversion of infinitive-verbs</u>

An infinitive-verb in a sentence would be either,

  (a)   a second verb
         or
  (b)   a connector (again in the capacity of a verb)

We can adopt any of the three methods described below to put the infinitive in the Passive form. But, whichever method you choose, do ensure that the meaning of the Passive is no different from the Active. The three conversion methods are,

  (i)   Through a Complex sentence using the conjunctions "so that" or "that".
  (ii)   By changing the infinitive-verb into a gerund.
  (iii)   By using the Passive infinitive like this,

Active	*Passive*
To write	To be written
To see	To be seen
To throw	To be thrown

Keeping the above guidelines in mind, shall we convert various types of infinitive based sentences into the Passive form? Rest assured that one of these methods will usually succeed in all the infinitive verb based sentences. Concentrate your attention on converting the infinitive part primarily.

Complex sentence method

1. (A) This social worker visits the patients in the hospital **to show** her concern for them.
    (P) The hospital patients **are** visited by this social worker <u>so that</u> her concern for them **is shown** to them by her.

2. (A) Mona is running fast **to catch** the last train.
    (P) Mona is running fast <u>so that</u> the last train **is caught** by her.

3. (A) The retailer is keen **to sell** all the new brand of soaps in his shop.
    (P) The retailer is keen <u>that</u> all the new brand of soaps in his shop **are sold** by him.

4. (A) Little Saroja does not want her sister **to accompany** her to the school.
    (P) Little Saroja does not want <u>that</u> she **is accompanied** by her sister to the school.

5. (A) Ram has declined admission in a college in order **to support** his sister in school.
    (P) Admission in a college **has been** declined by Ram <u>so that</u> his sister **is supported** in school by him.

6. (A) We haven't put aside any money **to send** the daughter for higher studies.
    (P) No money **has been** put aside by us <u>so that</u> the daughter **is (could be) sent** for higher studies.

Gerund method

1. (A) Sundaresan loves **to drop** his younger sister at school on his way to the college.
    (P) **Dropping** of his younger sister at school on his way to college, **is** loved by Sundaresan.

2. (A) The dog tries **to pick up** a bone from the drain.
    (P) **Picking up** a bone from the drain, **is** tried by the dog.

3. (A) Our Physics Demonstrator has refused **to take** any extra class for us.
    (P) **Taking** extra class for us, **has been** refused by our Demonstrator.

4. (A) Our servant maid hates **to gossip** with other servants in the area.
    (P) **Gossiping** with other servants in the area, **is** hated by our servant maid.

In all the sentences above, the entire infinitive part constitutes the object and passes the 'object test' as well. The *gerund* method therefore will be successful in such cases.

'Passive infinitive form' method

In cases, where the Complex sentence method and gerund method fail, consider the Passive infinitive method :

1. (A) The nurse has been keeping some tablets in her hand **to put** them in my mouth.
    (P1) The nurse has been keeping some tablets in her hand **to be put** into my mouth by her.
    (P2) Some tablets **are kept** by the nurse in her hand **to be put** into my mouth by her.
    S-A-V-O-C-Infin.verb-O/C

(P3)The nurse is keeping some tablets in her hand **so that** they are put into my mouth by her. (Complex sentence method also works here)

2. (A) Some visitors are waiting here to meet you.
    (P) Some visitors are waiting here **to be met** by you.
    S-A-V-C-Infin.verb-O/C

3. (A) Every examinee has **to write** his roll number on the top right corner of his answer paper.
    (P) The roll number has **to be written** on the top right corner of the answer paper by every examinee.
    S- A.V - Infin.verb-O/C

In examples 1-3, the infinitive appears in the middle of the sentence. But, study the following example and analyse it as well:

(A) This orphanage has many abandoned kids **to care**   for.
       S   A.V   O   Infin-verb   Adv

What is the identity of "to care for"? Is it an infinitive-verb or infinitive-noun? We noted in Chapter 24, that an infinitive-noun acting as *the object* will turn into an infinitive-verb if we add any words after it. Accordingly, we must view "for" as an adverb following an infinitive-noun object. Hence, "to care" must be treated as an infinitive-verb. For conversion of this infinitive-verb, we adopt the Passive infinitive form, i.e "to be cared". The adverb "for' will remain unaltered in the Passive sentence:

(P) This orphanage has many abandoned kids **to be cared** for.

We have to use the *Passive infinitive* method in all such cases where the infinitive-verb is followed by an adverb. Don't mistake these words for 'prepositions'. If preposition, it must show some relationship between two words. Does "for" show any such relationship? Whereas, 'for' passes the adverb test. Here are more examples of this variety:

4. (A) These are the clever people **to learn** from.
    (P) These are the clever people **to be learnt** from.

5. (A) Rangarajan is a nice boy **to watch** and **copy** at.
    (P) Rangarajan is a nice boy **to be watched** and **to be copied** at.

6. (A) We have no extra house **to let** out.
    (P) No extra houses **are** had by us **to be let** out.

Here are some examples wherein we follow a mix of the *Complex sentence* method and *Passive infinitive* method in the same sentence:

7. (A) The Drama director has told us **to allow** the latecomers into the auditorium only after 4.30 p.m.

(P) We have been told by the Drama director that the latecomers are **to be allowed** into the auditorium only after 4.30 p.m.

8.   (A) In an examination hall, the invigilators warn us **not to copy** someone else's answer.

     (P) In an examination hall, we are warned by the invigilators that someone else's answer is **not to be copied** by us.

So, what is the conclusion? If there is an infinitive-verb in a sentence, the infinitive part can be put in passive form in one of the 3 methods. In certain cases, more than one method may succeed.

Writing an Active sentence initially and converting it in Passive form may create some problem. Whereas, we can write a Passive sentence directly as well. In such a direct method, it will be easy to use the *Passive infinitives*. Here are the examples:

1.   Mohan wants **to be elected** leader of the trekking party by his classmates.

2.   The Chief minister likes **to be praised** frequently by the people.

3.   A candidate from a village school is eager **to be called** for the interview by the selection board.

4.   He has resented **to be hailed** by any nickname by his classmates.

5.   The urchins expect **to be allowed** to watch the match by the referee.

If you try to put the above in Active form, you may find the going difficult. Try. Accordingly, you could go in for a direct *Passive infinitive* sentence in all the three methods, more particularly the Passive infinitive type.

Conversion of sentences with infinitive-nouns as subjects/objects

Study the following sentences:

1.   (A) The King has fought several battles **to win**
                                                      O

     (P) **For winning**, several battles were fought by the King.
         S   O

2.   (A) We enter the library only **to read**.

     (P) **For reading only**, the library is entered by us.

3.   (A) Could you bring your bicycle **to verify?**

     (P) **For verifying**, could your bicycle be brought by you.

The above **Active examples** are of the pattern,

S- A -V-O- O(infin)

And, the infinitive-nouns here constitute the second object. In order to maintain the meaning, we find it necessary to change the infinitive-nouns into gerunds along with a preposition.

Let us see what happens when the infinitive-noun is the sole object:

7. (A) Santosh loves **to eat**.
          S   (A)V   O
    (P) **Eating** is loved by Santosh.
          S   O

8. (A) Martina loves **to dance.**
    (P) **Dancing** is loved by Martina.

9. (A) This brave soldier hates **to malinger.**
    (P) **Malingering** is hated by this soldier.
                S   A V   O

When an infinitive is the sole object, we have to convert it into a gerund. Only then the passive form would sound well.

Conversion of sentences with infinitive-nouns as subjects

Even when an infinitive-noun is the subject, we have to change it into equivalent gerund. Study the under mentioned examples:

10. (A) **To read** good books, enhances one's knowledge.
            S   (A)V   O
    (P) One's knowledge is enhanced by **reading** good books.
                                 O

You learnt in Chapter 24 (Infinitive) that we can use additional words as amplifying words when an infinitive appears as the Subject. "good books" in 10 (A) here, are those additional words. This privilege however, could be exercised only when an infinitive is the Subject.

You also learnt in Chapter 26 (Gerund) that one can use amplifying words to a gerund whether it is acting as the Subject or Object in a sentence. "good books" are the amplifying words for 'reading'.

Shall we examine more sentences?

11. (A) **To discuss** this matter, could we take some advisers?
    (P) Could some advisers be taken by us for **discussing** this matter.

12. (A) **To strike** a domestic animal needs no special courage.
    (P) No special courage is needed for **striking** a domestic animal.
            S   A   V   O1   O2

The conclusion is that we must change an infinitive-noun subject or object into gerund in the passive form, in order to maintain the meaning. According to the conversion rules, the Noun Subject and Noun Object merely change places without any modification. But if those nouns happen to be infinitive nouns, we have to change them into gerunds. This is an exception to the conversion rules.

Here are more examples:

13. (A) **To donate** money for a good cause will earn you **laurels**.
                S   A   V   O1   O2
     (P) **Laurels** will be earned by you **for donating money** for a good cause.
              S   A   V   O1   (new O2)

14. (A) This boy loves **to play**.
     (P) **Playing** is loved by **this boy**.

15. (A) **To live** well calls for **tremendous skill**.
                S   O
     (P) **Tremendous skill** is called for **for living** well.
              (new)S   (new) O

16. (A) **To find** fault in others creates **bad blood** .
                S   O1
     (P) **Bad blood** is created by **finding fault** in others.
              (new S)   (new) O

Don't think that every infinitive found at the end of a sentence would be object. Not necessary at all. If such infinitives don't pass the 'Noun test" they may turn out to be actually infinitive-verbs. Examine the following sentences:

(a) Nandlal loves **to sing**.

(b) Beant Singh joins the Army **to fight**.

(c) Shyam lal comes to my house daily **to play**.

Do the infinitives, shown in **bold**, pass the 'Noun test'? Are they really doing the job of nouns? No. (a) and (b) look to be incomplete sentences; some information needs to follow them but are missing. If we add that information, (which actually would become the object of the sentence) these infinitives seem to turn into verbs. (c) has an intransitive verb, hence, there is no question of passive form for this sentence.

For (a) and (b), we follow the Complex sentence method of conversion because these infinitives happen to be really verbs. For instance,

(A) Nandlal loves **to sing** classical songs.
(P) Classical songs are loved by Nandlal so that they are sung by him.
(A) Beant Singh joins the Army **to fight** for his country.
(P) Army is joined by Beant Singh so that he could fight for his country.

So, do ensure that the infinitive at the end of a sentence does pass the Noun-test before attempting conversion into passive form.

Infinitives where "to" is omitted

In Chapter 24 we noted that if any of the 9 special verbs is present in the S-A-V part, we have to omit the preposition "to" in the infinitive part. These special verbs are, LET, MAKE, HEAR, FEEL, DARE, SEE, BID, WATCH or HAVE. (Omission of the preposition with the verbs HELP and ENABLE is optional). But, when we convert sentences that have any of these special verbs, we restore the "to" in the infinitive part in the Passive form.

(A) The bully in our colony makes the small children run round him by way of punishment.

(P) The small children **are made** to run round him by the bully of our colony by way of punishment.

(A) The hostel warden lets the parents meet their wards only on Sundays.

(P) The parents **are let** by the warden to meet their wards only on Sundays.

(A) We hear your little sister sing daily.

(P) Your little sister **is heard** to sing daily by us.

(A) We feel the car vibrate heavily during starting.

(P) The car **is felt** to vibrate heavily by us during starting.

(A) You dare not touch a tiger with your hand.

@ (P) A tiger **cannot be touched** by you with your hand.

(A) We watch the tiger run into the cage.

* (P) The tiger **is watched to run** into the cage by us.

(A) Do you see me paint anything on this canvas?

* (P) **Am** I **seen** by you **to paint** anything on this canvas?

(A) The Vice Principal bids me walk into his office.

(P) I **am bid to walk** into his office by the Vice Principal.

(A) I can have you write this essay by tomorrow.

+ (P) I can have this essay written by you by tomorrow.

(A) The pedestrians usually help us push the car in a traffic jam.

(P) **We are** usually **helped** by the pedestrians **to push** the car in a traffic jam.

(A) My friends enable me solve some difficult integrals.

(P) I **am enabled** by my friends **to solve** some difficult integrals.

<u>Points to note:</u>

Though by rule we may convert any Active that contains an object, in certain cases the Passive may not sound well at all. See the sentences marked * for instance.

Next, with special verbs like, DARE, Passive will not be possible. Or, we may have to write them with different auxiliaries. See @.

With HAVE in the S-A-V Active, the Passive takes a different pattern and without "to" in the verb. Study + carefully.

Infinitives with interrogative word connectors

You know that with some special verbs in the S-A-V part, you have to use an interrogative word such as HOW, WHAT, WHEN, WHERE or WHICH in the infinitive part. (See Chapter 24) When such sentences are put in the Passive form, the interrogatives will continue to remain as shown in the following examples:

(A) The small kids soon find out a way how to outwit their mother.

(P) A way is found out soon by the small kids <u>how</u> their mother **can be** outwitted by them.

(A) Some voters always ask the Presiding officer <u>where</u> to press the switch on the EVM.

(P) The Presiding officer always is asked by some voters <u>where</u> the switch **is to be** pressed by them on the EVM.

All the sentences above have objects. Sometimes, the entire infinitive part may be acting as the object, (Apply the 'Object' test to be sure), in which case, convert that part as shown in the following examples:

(A) John invariably forgets <u>when to ask for his meals</u>.
           S   Adv   (A)V   O

(P) John invariably forgets <u>when</u> his meals **are to be** asked for by him.

(A) My older boys know clearly which serials to watch on the T.V.

(P) My older boys know clearly <u>which</u> serials **are to be** watched by them on the T.V.

(A) Only at the last moment I recollect what I have to emphasize in my speech.

(P) Only at the last moment I recollect <u>what</u> **has to be** emphasized by me in my speech.

Conversion of Commands/orders/suggestions in simple present

Conversion will be possible only if there is an object in the command/order/suggestion.

(A) (You do) blow the whistle now.
        S   A   V   O   Adv

(P) The whistle **is to be** blown by you now.

(A) Pay the servants today itself.

(P) The servants **are to be** paid today itself by you.

(A) Don't keep company with bad boys.

(P) Company with bad boys **is not to be** kept by you.

(A) Do not give false evidence ever at any time.

(P) False evidence **is never to be** given by you at any time.

Have you noticed in the Passive form, the 'power' of the command is missing? While in the Active, the command/order sounds direct and imposing, the same in the Passive sounds more like a request. Thus, to keep up the effectiveness and firmness inbuilt in the Active voice command/order, we use a different method like this,

(P) **Let** the whistle **be** blown now. (by you)
    V   S   A V Adv

(P) **Let** the servants **be** paid today itself.

(P) **Let** the company of bad boys **be** kept away/avoided.

(P) **Let not** false evidence **be** ever given any time. (by you).
    V   A   V

Here are more examples of this type:

(A) Don't insult the humble and poor.

(P) Let not the humble and poor be insulted. (by you)

(A) Don't encourage copying.

(P) Let not copying be encouraged. (by you)

(A) Don't take bribe.

(P) Let not bribe be taken. (by you)

You may have problem writing the remaining 6 categories when the given sentence starts with LET. However, let us try.

a2   : Let not bribe be taken by you

a1   : Let bribe be taken by you.

SpQ : Is bribe to be taken by you? (Or, should bribe taken by you?)

NegQ : Isn't bribe to be taken (rejected) by you?

EQ1 : Bribe is to be rejected by you, isn't it?

EQ2 : Bribe is not to be taken by you, is it?

Other than a1 and a2, we switch over to the emphatics for the remaining 4.

Do note however, that if the command has no object in it, conversion will not be possible. Take the following commands; they cannot be put in Passive form.

(A) Don't come inside.

(P) Not possible.

(A) Sit down.

(P) Not possible.

(A) Get out.

(P) Not possible.

Conversion of intransitive verbs

COME and GO and their synonyms are basically intransitive verbs. They will never lead to an object in a sentence. Analyse the following sentences:

(a)   Madhavi comes to my house every day.
      S   (A)V   C   C

(b)   All the school children   go   home by 4 p.m. in our school.
           S   (A)V   C

(c)   Padma rises from bed usually at 6 a.m.
      S   (A)V   C

None of the above has an object. However, suppose we put them in the passive form ignoring the "by" part, then the sentences will look like this,

(aa) Madhavi **is** come.

(ab) All the school children **are** gone.

(ac) Padma **is** risen from bed.

These are aberrations in terms of the Passive voice rules. But, the English world has accepted the above kind of grammatical distortions. Thus, "Madhavi is come" is considered equal to "Madhavi has come", "The school children are gone" as equivalent to "The school children have gone".

Here are some everyday expressions in this type,

"They are arrived."
"My father is gone." (meaning, "My father is dead")
"The match is gone." (meaning, "The match is lost")
"We are agreed."
"He is finished."
"We are finished."
"I am finished."
"Son of God is risen from the dead." (Mtt, 17:9 - Bible)
"The Lord is risen indeed." (Luke 24:34)

Exercise

Change the following sentences into Passive form:

1. I see a tall building over there.
2. Don't you know Hindi?
3. Which moped does Monica need?
4. Am I protecting you from any accusation?
5. Santosh is defending me in a theft case.
6. Aren't your friends accusing me of cheating?
7. Madhumati's sister is marrying your elder brother, isn't she?
8. Hasn't Bir Singh borrowed your cycle today?
9. Haven't your pet dogs dirtied our lawn this morning?
10. We are at the moment revising History of England.
11. Preeti has swallowed a 25 paise coin.

Convert from Active to Passive the following sentences with universal auxiliaries:

12. Can you speak German?
13. Venkat shouldn't have scolded you so harshly.
14. Would you give some money for this good cause?
15. All of you may take your seat now.
16. We might watch a video movie tomorrow.
17. A few students could not complete the First Aid course.
18. Visitors must not touch these flowers.
19. We need not meet the orphan children today.
20. I am going to give you a bad news.
21. You ought not to take weak players in your hockey team.
22. My youngest sister is going to receive the consolation prize for declamation.
23. The small kids in our colony do keep pestering us for a friendly table tennis match.
24. Doesn't your dog keep visiting our house every morning?
25. My pet cat dare not pounce on your little puppy dog.
26. Wouldn't you advise my brother on courtesy?
27. We should not ridicule the small children, should we?
28. Which gift would you choose for your friend?

Convert the following Complex sentences to Passive form:

29. His toes hurt him if he walks fast.
30. Can you tell me when I have to meet our leader?
31. The VC does not see students unless they secure a prior appointment with him.
32. Ramu does not breed coloured insects except when he has no other work.
33. Since he does not know any card game, he never enters the Card room in the club.
34. Can't you talk to your supervisor after he finishes his lunch?
35. Should you always place your hand on his shoulder whenever you talk with him?
36. Don't halt until I order you.
37. I take to my heels whenever I see a policeman.
38. You must not throw stones at a dog even if it happens to be a street animal.

Change into Passive form the following infinitive-based sentences:

39. The college rules do not permit us to take long leave of absence.
40. Haven't you requested the visitor to step in?
41. Dedicated medical staffs never refuse to treat any patient at any time.
42. Many prospective politicians take to social work only to throw dust on the eyes of the public.
43. Every candidate has to write his roll number on all pages of the answer book.
44. A head clerk has to guide all the other junior clerks working under him.

45. Small children will always ask for more toffees to satisfy their desire.
46. Do you let your son go for the college excursion every year?
47. This Eveninger makes you laugh even at silly and dry jokes.
48. When do you visit the library to update your current affairs knowledge?
49. We have been sitting here for hours to catch a glimpse of the visiting President.
50. He is not a leader to take up our cause with the hostel warden.
51. Don't you want to get admission in our social club?
52. You have to apply for admission, haven't you?
53. Isn't he our guardian to support us?
54. The nurse brought her tray to dress up my brother's leg wound.
55. I am trying hard to get into the merit list of our college.
56. Aren't we going to eat in this restaurant to assess its merit?
57. This boy has too many sisters to provide for.
58. I have too many children in the creche to look after.
59. The volley ball captain isn't too keen to retain you in the team.
60. Mala is sticking on to her job to earn.
61. You are not playing with her to lose, are you?
62. You cannot go to his house to retaliate.
63. I have managed to stay.

Convert the following commands/orders into Passive form in two different ways:

64. Don't make fun of lame people.
65. Stop pestering the people on the road.
66. Avoid gluttony.
67. Take these tablets thrice a day.
68. Eat your snacks now, boys.

Analyse the following sentences and justify the grammar used in them:

69. They are come.
70. My grandfather is gone.
71. Jesus is risen indeed from the dead.
72. I am finished.

Fill up the blank with a suitable Passive-infinitive:

73. Manoharan is willing ....to..be.. Captain of the University cricket team.
74. Everyone expects our last year's class prefect ....to..be.. prefect again for this year.
75. We cannot be such bad players .to..be..plessed by the other college.
76. Isn't Santosh going to..get..gift for your birthday party?
77. Vandana likes .to...visit in all the social parties.
78. These furniture are to.be..cleaned by the new servant.
79. Many voters cast their votes only to..be..fooled later by their candidate.
80. Many students copy .... in their exam.

should be collected

Write the remaining 6 categories of sentences for the following passive voice statements:

81. We have been deceived by many shop keepers.
82. This bill isn't to be paid by Ramanujam.
83. I could be met by you only during evening time.
84. Let this student be handled by you henceforth.
85. Mischievous students are made to run round the football ground by this person.
86. These are the children to be copied at.
87. He has refused to be called by his nickname by strangers.
88. Has taking extra classes been refused by the History lecturer?
89. Who is running fast so that the train is caught.
90. Beula Samuel is loved by all in her class.

Chapter 30

PASSIVE VOICE
Passive forms of PAST FAMILY

Can you list out all the tenses that belong to the Past family?

Here they are, along with their Active and Passive voice auxiliaries:

Tense	Active auxiliary	Passive auxiliary
1.(a) Past	WAS, WERE	- - -
"	was/were USED TO	- - -
(b) Past (Possess.)	HAD	WAS/WERE HAD
(c) Past Emphatics	WAS, WERE, HAD, DID HAVE	Add BE to the infinitive
2.(a) Simple past	DID	WAS, WERE
(b) Simple past	COULD, WOULD	Add BE to each
(c) "	did ... USE TO	WAS/WERE USED TO BE
3.(a) Past continuous	WAS, WERE	WAS/WERE BEING
(b) "	did KEEP	WAS/WERE BEING
(c) "	was/were getting/becoming USED TO	- - -
4.(a) Past perfect	HAD	HAD BEEN
(b) "	WOULD HAVE, COULD HAVE, SHOULD HAVE, MIGHT HAVE, MUST HAVE, NEED HAVE, OUGHT TO HAVE	Add BEEN
(c) "	had/would have/could have/ should have/must have/might have/need have/ought to HAVE **got/become** USED TO	HAVE BEEN **got/become** USED TO
5.(a) Past perfect cont.	HAD BEEN	- - -
(b) "	had/would....ought to have been getting/becoming USED TO	- - -

In this family too, we cannot convert Past tense, except the "Possessive case," and Past perfect continuous tenses into Passive form.

We follow the same 4 steps for conversion from Active to Passive. Here are the sample sentences.

1. Past tense

(a)   (A) Padmavathy was top student last year.

(P) **Passive not possible** due to presence of A.V.

(b)   (A) The children had a good time yesterday in the park.
      (P) A good time **was had** by the children in the park yesterday.

      (A) My brother and I had a nice cycle till last month.
      (P) A nice cycle **was had** by us till last month.

(c)   (A) A famous dance teacher was to teach Bharatanatyam to my sister.
      (P) Bharatanatyam **was to be** taught to my sister by a famous dance teacher.

      (A) Our footballers were to play a few friendly matches last month.
      (P) A few friendly matches **were to be** played by our footballers last month.

      (A) My father had to request the college for a scholarship for me.
      (P) The college **had to be** requested by my father for a scholarship for me.

      (A) This boy hadn't to hide the truth.
      (P) The truth **hadn't to** be hidden by him.

2.   *Simple past*

(a)   (A) We did not fool anybody during our play-time.
      (P) Nobody **was** fooled by us during our play-time.

      (A) A new Lecturer conducted our English periods today.
      (P) Our English periods **were** conducted by a new Lecturer today.

(b)   (A) Aspirin could cure light fever.
      (P) Light fever **could be** cured by aspirin.

      (A) Why couldn't you solve this problem?
      (P) Why **couldn't** this problem **be** solved by you?

      (A) Daniel would spend the week ends in my house.
      (P) The week ends **would be** spent by Daniel in my house.

(c)   (A) Our elder brother did use to collect the milk from the booth daily till last year.
      (P) Milk from the booth **was used to be** collected by our elder brother daily till last year.

      (A) My father did not use to read this newspaper in the mornings.
      (P) This daily newspaper **was not used to be** read by my father in the mornings.
      (This daily was not read by my father in the mornings)

      (A) Where did you use to take tuition in your previous year?
      (P) Where **was** the tuition **used to be** taken by you in your previous year?
      (Where was the tuition taken by you in your previous year?)

      (A) We never used to ask for help from others, did we?
      (P) Help **was never used to be** asked for by us from others, was it?
      (Help was never asked for by us from others, was it?)

      (A) My friend didn't use to collect shells from Marina beach.
      (P) Shells **weren't used to be** collected by my friend from Marina beach.

Note:

In a2, Q and EQ type sentences, always go in for the alternate forms with the auxiliaries WAS/ WERE along with PP verbs and omitting "used to".

3. Past continuous

(a) (A) Madan was helping my sister in Mathematics.
     (P) My sister **was being** helped by Madan in Mathematics.

     (A) Some of our colony children were selling fruits yesterday in the next colony.
     (P) Fruits **were being** sold by some of our colony children yesterday in the next colony.

     (A) Weren't you playing table tennis till late evening yesterday?
     (P) **Wasn't** table tennis **being** played by you till late evening yesterday?

     (A) Radha was looking after you during your illness.
     (P) You **were being** looked after by Radha during your illness?

(b) (A) Didn't the small child keep worrying your sister for more sweets?
     (P) **Wasn't** your sister **being** worried by the small child for more sweets?

     (A) Some spectators did keep looking at the sky for the arrival of the aeroplanes.
     (P) The sky **was being** looked at by some spectators for the arrival of the aeroplanes.

Note:

We don't normally use KEEP/KEPT in the Passives at all. When converting KEEP in passive form, we use "was/were BEING" treating it on par with the Past continuous tense.

(c) Some of my friends were getting used to copying during every examination.

Passive not possible.

4. Past perfect

(a) (A) The office had displayed the result on the college Notice board.
     (P) The result **had been** displayed by the office on the college Notice board.

     (A) This little girl had spoken to me about her leg pain.
     (P) I **had been** spoken to by this little about her leg pain.

     (A) What had you eaten for lunch today?
     (P) What **had been** eaten by you for lunch today?

     (A) Hadn't you tasted wood-apple before?
     (P) **Hadn't** wood-apple **been** tasted by you before?

(b) (A) We wouldn't have given you this loan without recommendation.
     (P) This loan **wouldn't have been** given to you by us without recommendation.

     (A) We must have taken a wrong step some days back, mustn't we?
     (P) A wrong step **must have been** taken by us some days back, mustn't it?

(A) Need you have committed yourself to this promise without consultation?

(P) **Need** this promise **have been** committed by yourself without consultation?

Note:

The auxiliaries under in 4 (b) are basically Future in the Past (FIP) auxiliaries. You should use these FIP auxiliaries in the Past perfect tense only in such cases whereof action had been completed.

(c)   (A) You had got used to driving the new car, hadn't you?

(P) Driving the new car **had been** got **used to** by you, hadn't it?

(A) You ought to have become used to your new house by now.

(B) Your new house **ought to have been** got **used to** by you by now.

5. Past perfect continuous

(P) **Passive not possible in this continuous tense.**

Conversion of questions

The interrogative remains unaffected in the Passive voice.

(A) From where could you have purchased this toy gun?

(P) From where **could** this toy gun **have been** purchased by you?

(A) Who gave you permission?

(P) By whom **was** permission given to you?

>   or

> You **were** given permission by who?

(A) In whose house did Samuel spend the holidays?

(P) In whose house the holidays **were** spent by Samuel?

(A) How did this snake bend the rods of the cage?

(P) How **were** the cage rods bent by this snake?

(A) Where had the culprits hidden the stolen goods?

(P) Where **had** the stolen goods **been** hidden by the culprits?

(A) Which door your sister could not open?

(P) Which door **could not be** opened by your sister?

(A) Who was doing Yoga in the sports ground last evening?

(P) Yoga **was being** done by who in the sports ground last evening?

Conversion of sentences with infinitives

The methodology is the same as for the Present family cases. Here are some examples; the method adopted is shown in brackets.

(A) The Basketball captain wanted **to choose** the team on his own.

(P) The Basketball captain wanted **that** the team **would be chosen** by him on his own. (Complex sentence method)

(A) The watch repairer could not keep my watch ready **to deliver** it on time.

(P) My watch **could not be** kept ready by the watch repairer **so that** it **was delivered** on time. (Complex)

(A) The cowherd had agreed **to look-after** my sheep as well.

(P) **Looking after** my sheep as well, had been agreed by the cowherd. (Gerund) (Here we have treated "look after" as a phrasal verb)

(A) The tuition master loved **to teach** a new lesson to me daily.

(P) **Teaching** a new lesson daily to me, was loved by my tuition master. (Gerund)

(A) That car was too fast **to chase** after.

(P) That car was too fast **to be chased** after. (Passive infinitive).

(A) This tree is too tall **to bring** down.

(P) This tree is too tall **to be brought** down. (Passive infinitive)

Active sentences with infinitive-nouns

(A) **To swim** across this fast river required strength and courage.
        S   (A)V   O

(P) Strength and courage was required **for swimming across a fast river**.
   (new) S   A   ·V   (new) O

(A) **To sing** melodiously needed a lot of practice and guidance.

(P) A lot of practice and guidance were needed **for singing melodiously**.

Direct Passive voice sentences

(P) The boys needed **to be taught** better English.

(P) Meena of the First year wanted **to be included** in the list of smart queens!

(P) Natarajan hadn't come to this college **to be treated** like a school boy.

Infinitives where "to" is omitted

(A) The traffic constable made the youngsters do 20 sit-ups before letting them off for the traffic offence.

(P) The youngsters **were made to do** 20 sit-ups by the traffic constable for the traffic offence.

(A) Why didn't you let the small children make their own sand models in the beach?

(P) Why **weren't** the small children **let** by you **to make** their own sand models in the beach?

(A) Surely we heard you sing a few songs in the concert, didn't we?

(P) Surely you **were heard to sing** a few songs in the concert by us, weren't you?

(A) The other day we saw you catch the intruding boys into your garden.

(P) The other day you **were seen** by us **to catch** the intruding boys into your garden.

Conversion of Complex sentences

(A) I accepted your advice because you gave it without any strings.

(P) Your advice **was** accepted by me because it **had been** given by you without any strings. (We have observed the 2-action rule, hence **had been** used instead of **was**.)

(A) The accused showed the exact place where he had buried the gold chain.

(P) The exact place where the gold chain **had been** buried **was** shown by the accused.

(A) I used to love cats when I was a small boy.

(P) Cats **were used to be** loved by me when I was young.

(A) When I am busy, don't disturb me.

(P1) When I am busy, I **am not to be** disturbed by anyone.

(P2) When I am busy, **let** me not be disturbed by anyone.

Sentences with two objects

(A) Didn't I give you a nice pen the other day?

 S V 01   02

(P1) Weren't you given a nice pen by me the other day.

 S V   01   02

(P2) Wasn't a nice pen given to you by me the other day.

 S   01   02

(A) After the accident, my friend conveyed to me a bad news.

 S   01   02

(P1) After the accident, I was conveyed by my friend a bad news.

 S   01   02

(P2) After the accident, a bad news was conveyed to me by my friend.

 S   01   02

Infinitives with interrogative word connectors

(A) These urchins soon found out a method how to sneak into the hall during a drama.

(P) A method **was** found out by these urchins <u>how</u> to sneak into the hall during a drama.

(A) The small kids always asked the bigger boys where to keep their shoes during play time.

(P) The bigger boys **were** always asked by the small kids <u>where</u> their shoes **were to be** kept by them during play time.

(A) Your son knew which books to take from the library, didn't he?

(P) Your son knew <u>which</u> books **were to be** taken by him from the library, didn't he?

(A) My small sister-patient always forgot when to ask for her meals.

(P) My small sister-patient always forgot <u>when</u> her meals **are to be** asked for by her.

(A) Did you remember what to say to the departing students?

(P) Did you remember <u>what</u> **was to be** said by you to the departing students?

Conversion of intransitive verbs

He was come.

She was gone.

All of them were gone.

They were arrived.

We were agreed.

Exercise

Change the following Actives into Passives:

1. All the Juniors spotted the Pole star last night.
2. The driver drove away the ambassador car quickly.
3. Did Neena hit you on your nose?
4. My close friend supported me in our verbal battle.
5. Weren't you and Sandra learning piano till 5 p.m. last evening?
6. Where had you picked up this little puppy from?
7. Didn't your Dad say that he would give one of your rooms on rent?
8. My aunt used to keep all our rooms clean always till last week.
9. You did keep promising me a good ride on your Moped, didn't you?
10. Three particular lady students were to sing the Opening song during the Convocation.

Change the following infinitive-based sentences into Passive form:

11. The protesting children raised slogans to attack the shop keepers in our campus.
12. The sales boy shouted protests to force the shopkeeper into taking him back.
13. The mason ordered the workers to put more cement into the grinder mixer.
14. Dennis refused to make any concession to Tina.
15. Mary had a little lamb to look after.
16. Madhuri was standing at the gate with a camera to take a picture of the crowd.
17. Our dance master refused to take more students for training.
18. Your brother walked into my house to speak with my sister.
19. Our servant maid made us go to bed without dinner.
20. The Matric students of a nearby school didn't know how to solve quadratic equations.
21. The sweeper women of our Municipality did not know where to deposit the garbage.
22. Weren't you waiting behind the door to catch the naughty boys?
23. This youngster was not strong enough to hold a cricket bat with his hands.
24. The cop caught two thieves to book on.
25. The key hole was too small to see through.
26. Mona would like to eat only cadbury chocolates.

27. My grandmother ate some *jilebis* quietly to satisfy her craze for sweets.
28. For acting in our annual drama, there were far too many eager students to choose from.
29. Didn't I let you off?
30. Surely Dorothy was very pretty to look at, wasn't she?

Convert the following Passives into Actives:

31. The accident was investigated by the police.
32. Astrology is believed in by some people.
33. This Govt was thought to be weak by many people.
34. This patient is going to be examined next by the doctor.
35. Dhanraj was elected Secretary by the members of the club.
36. The train accident was to be inquired into by a High court judge.
37. The cup of coffee was not touched by the visitor until he was told to do so by me.
38. Even a height of 2 meters could not be cleared by this pole vaulter because he was afraid of *height*.
39. Though the men did not react, a lot of noise was made by the women.
40. Wasn't the Lab assistant told by you that he should assist me in the Demonstration?
41. Samuel was a nice person to be emulated at.
42. Chasing any street dog is detested by my pet dog.
43. The students were let off with just a warning, weren't they?
44. They were good workers that they could be entrusted with any difficult jobs.
45. The right winger was ordered by the referee that playing be stopped by him immediately.

Analyse the following sentences:

46. We were never used to any kind of dressing down.
47. We wouldn't have got through the entrance examination if you had not helped us.
48. How were you being worried by your friend for some financial help?
49. Wasn't an essay to be submitted by you yesterday?
50. This equation surely could be solved by you without help, couldn't it?

Write the remaining 6 categories of sentences for the following statements:

51. You must not have written such a nasty letter to your friend.
52. Didn't you keep worrying your desk-mate to allow you to copy his notes?
53. Some SC students were being threatened with severe punishment, weren't they?
54. We ought not to have been criticised so badly by our seniors.
55. Your friend didn't have to see me earlier than the 14th of last month.

Write Passive voice sentences using the following infinitives:

(a) to see   (b) to watch   (c) to love

Chapter 31

PASSIVE VOICE

Passive forms of FUTURE FAMILY

Here is the list of tenses in the Future family along with the Active auxiliaries and Passive auxiliaries:

Tense	Active auxiliaries	Passive auxiliaries
1.(a) Future	WILL, SHALL	Add BE
(b) Future	COULD, WOULD, MIGHT,	Add BE
	will/shall/could/would/might/ **get** USED TO	BE **got** USED TO
	am/is/are GOING TO	Add BE
	WILL/SHALL KEEP	WILL/SHALL BE KEPT
(c) Future Emphatics	WILL/SHALL HAVE	Add BE
2. Future continuous	WILL BE, SHALL BE	- - -
	COULD BE/ WOULD BE	
	Getting/becoming USED TO	- - -
3. Future perfect	WILL/SHALL HAVE	Add BEEN
4. Future perfect continuous	WILL/SHALL HAVE BEEN, will/shall HAVE KEPT, will/shall HAVE BEEN **getting/ becoming** USED TO	- - -
5. Future in the past (FIP)	WOULD/COULD/SHOULD/ MIGHT/MUST/NEED/ OUGHT TO HAVE	Add BEEN
	Could/would/should/might/ must/need /ought to HAVE **got/ become** USED TO	Add BEEN
	WAS/WERE GOING TO	Add BE
6. FIP continuous	WOULD/COULD/SHOULD/ MIGHT/MUST/NEED/ OUGHT TO.... HAVE BEEN	- - -

In this family, we cannot convert 3 tenses into Passive, namely, Future continuous, Future perfect continuous and Future in the past continuous.

Here are the sample Passive sentences:

1. Future tense

(a) (A) The Boarders will / shall eat their dinner at 8 p.m.

     (P) Their dinner **will / shall be** eaten by the Boarders at 8 p.m.

(b) (A) The office manager could see our applications first.

(P) Our applications **could be** seen by the office manager first.

(A) Would we meet our Principal only on Monday?

(P) **Would** our Principal **be** met by us only on Monday?

(A) Roger might win a prize for High jump.

(P) A prize **might be** won by Roger for High jump.

(A) Couldn't we get used to night driving within a month?

(P) **Couldn't** night driving **be** got **used to** by us within a month?

(A) We shall get used to eating late very shortly, shan't we?

(P) Eating late **shall be** got **used to** by us shortly, shan't it?

(A) This man is going to finish the task by this evening.

(P) The task **is going to be** finished by this man by this evening.

(A) Won't you keep recording the results as the Sports events progress?

(P) **Won't** the results **be kept** recorded by you as the events progress?

(A) Will you keep forgetting all the Historical dates?

(P) **Will** all the Historical dates **be** forgotten by you?

(A passive with KEEP may not be always possible as we saw in the Present and Past families)

(c) (A) All parents will/shall have to attend the farewell function.

(P) The farewell function **will/shall have to be** attended by all the parents.

2. Future continuous

Passive not possible.

3. Future perfect

(A) My parents will have received my sister at Trichy station by now.

(P) My sister **will have been** received by my parents at Trichy station by now.

(A) My elder sister will have delivered her first baby by October this year.

(P) Her first baby **will have been** delivered by my elder sister by October this year.

4. Future perfect continuous

Passive not possible

5. Future in the past (FIP)

(A) You wouldn't have faced so many problems in my house?

(P) So many problems **wouldn't have been** faced by you in my house?

(A) You could have done something extraordinary about the incident.

(P) Something extraordinary **could have been** done by you about the incident.

(A) You should not have made such a bad remark about our Tamil pundit.

(P) Such a bad remark **shouldn't have been** made by you about our Tamil pundit.

(A) You might have lost your money purse in such a big crowd.

(P) Your money purse **might have been** lost by you in such a big crowd.

(A) You must have commented something derogatory during the argument.

(P) Something derogatory **must have been** commented by you during the argument.

(A) You need not have thanked me so much for such a small favour.

(P) I **need not have been** thanked so much by you for such a small favour.

(A) All of you ought to have submitted your application for leave a day earlier.

(P) Your application for leave **ought to have been** submitted by all of you a day earlier.

(A) You ought to have become used to writing high standard English by now.

(P) High standard English writing **ought to have been** become **used to** by you by now.

(A) You should have got used to this complex calculator by now?

(P) This complex calculator **should have been** got **used to** by you by now?

(A) My mother was going to see your mother yesterday evening.

(P) Your mother **was going to be** seen by my mother yesterday evening.

(A) I was going to collect these books by 8 a.m. itself but something happened.

(P) These books **were going to be** collected by me by 8 a.m. itself but something happened.

6. Future in the past continuous

Passive not possible.

Conversion of questions

(A) Will you postpone this work for tomorrow?

(P) **Will** this work **be** postponed by you for tomorrow?

(A) Won't you remove this employee from the staff roll?

(P) **Won't** this employee **be** removed from the staff roll by you?

(A) What will you eat for lunch today?

(P) What **will be** eaten by you for lunch today?

(A) Which audio cassette will you have purchased from this shop?

(P) Which audio cassette **will have been** purchased by you from this shop?

(A) Who will have to bring the juniors here?

(P) The juniors **will have to be** brought here by who?

> Or

By whom **will the** juniors **have to be** brought here?

(A) In whose house shall we hold our discussion?

(P) In whose house **shall** the discussion **be** held by us?

(A) Where will you record your speech?

(P) Where **will** your speech **be** recorded by you?

(A) How could we write an essay within such a short time?

(P) How **could** an essay **be** written by us within such a short time?

(A) When will we have achieved our college ambition?

(P) When **will** our college ambition **have been** achieved by us?

Conversion of infinitive - based sentences

(A) The lady students shall participate in the debate competition to uphold the image of our college, shan't they?

(P) The debate competition shall be participated by the lady students **so that** the image of our college **is upheld** by them, isn't it? (Complex sentence method)

(A) Your friends could contact our group to learn the new tactics in football.

(P) Our group could be contacted by your friends **so that** the new tactics in football **is learnt** by them. (Complex sentence method)

(A) We will try to win some prize.

(P) **Winning** some prize will be tried by us. (Gerund method)

(A) We might request the bus driver to stop at this point from tomorrow.

(P) **Stopping** the bus at this point from tomorrow, **would be** requested to the bus driver by us. (Gerund method)

(A) Shall we go to the toilet to freshen up?

(P) Shall we go to the toilet **to be freshened** up? (Passive infinitive method)

(A) Would you have received one more baby girl this evening to care for?

(P) Would one more baby girl have been received by us by this evening **to be cared** for? (Passive infinitive method)

(P) They would love **to be known** as 'angels from the blue' by the orphanage inmates.

(P) **We** won't allow the elderly people **to be ridiculed** by the children.

(P) **Was** the train **going to be stopped** by the demonstrators?

Infinitives with interrogative word connectors

(A) We would not have known how to invite the religious people for a social party.

(P) We would not have known <u>how</u> the religious people **are to be** invited for a social party.

(A) You must decide when to collect the car from the dealer.

(P) You must decide <u>when</u> the car **is to be** collected from the dealer by us.

(A) Shall we show where to keep your bicycles?

(P) Shall we show <u>where</u> your bicycles **are to be** kept by you?

(A) You will never know when to say 'no' to a request.

(P) You will never know <u>when</u> 'no' **is to be** said by you to a request.

(A) You will know what to say if you are knowledgeable.

(P) You will know <u>what</u> **is to be** said by you if you are knowledgeable.

(A) Will you please find out which pet to take out of this lot?

(P) Will you please find out <u>which</u> pet **is to be** taken out of this lot by us?

Infinitives where "to" is omitted

(A) Would you let me take my son home a few minutes before closing time?

(P) **Would** I **be** let by you **to take** my son home a few minutes before closing time?

(A) You should have heard him sing so marvellously in the birthday party.

(P) He **should have been** heard by you **to sing** so marvellously in the birthday party.

Conversion of Complex sentences

(A) We should not have spoken to him before he had received our request.

(P) He **should not have been** spoken to by us before our request **had been** received by him. (Objects in both Simple sentences, hence both converted)

(A) My uncle might see your friend if he is free.

(P) Your friend **might be** seen by my uncle only if he is free.

(A) You shall have to obtain an appointment in the first instance if you want to discuss anything with our Principal.

(P) An appointment **will have to be** obtained by you in the first instance if anything **is to be** discussed with our Principal.

Sentences with two objects

(A) Murali will receive money regularly from home for all his expenses.
      S   01   02

(P) Money will be received by Murali regularly from home for all his expenses.
      S   01   02

(A) Your mother will give you this medicine from tomorrow.
      S   01   02

(P1) You will be given this medicine by your mother from tomorrow.
      S   01   02

(P2) This medicine will be given by your mother to you from tomorrow.
      S   01 02

Reasons why certain tenses cannot be converted into Passive form

We cannot convert the following 7 tenses from Active to Passive form:

1. Present tense (with AM, IS, ARE)
2. Past tense (with WAS, WERE)
3. Present perfect continuous tense (HAS/HAVE BEEN)
4. Past perfect continuous tense (HAD BEEN)
5. Future continuous tense (WILL/SHALL BE)

6.   Future perfect continuous tense (WILL/SHALL HAVE BEEN)
7.   FIP continuous tense (COULD/WOULD/MUST ….. HAVE BEEN)

There are only 32 auxiliaries in the language to be used both for Active voice and Passive voice sentences. We are left with no spare auxiliaries for the 5 continuous tenses shown above after using AM/IS/ARE BEING and WAS/WERE BEING for Present continuous and Past continuous tenses respectively.

Similarly, we have used AM, IS, ARE for Simple present tense Actives and WAS, WERE for Simple past tense Actives. So, although sentences with the A.Vs (AM, IS, ARE, WAS, WERE) may contain objects, we cannot put them in Passive because of the shortage problem.

Do note that we identify the tense of a sentence by looking at the "Auxiliary and Verb" combination. Therefore the same A - V combination cannot be repeated in another tense.

With this lesson, we have covered 31 auxiliaries. The only auxiliary left now is BETTER. You would remember, this is an adverb and also a comparative adjective/adverb. And it happens to be an auxiliary as well. We shall learn its use in one of the advanced lessons later.

So, one could conclude that Passive forms are not as comprehensive as the Active forms. Yet, Passives have their own value in sentence-writing. We shall study that aspect in the next Chapter.

Exercise

Convert the following Actives into Passives:

1.   Won't you hand over your song book to me for a day?
2.   They shan't complete the construction work before 3 months.
3.   The spoilt-brats would know how to ask for forbidden things.
4.   The guests shall have finished their meals by now, shan't they?
5.   Where will you bury your dead pet cat?
6.   Who will have worn the black T shirt?
7.   How will small kids board the school bus on their own?
8.   When will your friends return home to catch with their sleep?
9.   Malathi will wear a Conjeevaram saree to impress the interviewers.
10.   Will you ask for more money even if I don't respond to your letters?
11.   When will your best friend meet us to discuss the details about the picnic trip?
12.   The boarders will have vacated their rooms by tomorrow morning, won't they?
13.   My servant maid would never steal a thing from the house.
14.   Weak students might not answer all the questions in this test paper.
15.   We could have carried out all the laboratory tests well before the laid down time.

16. You might have thought this incident funny but my view would be different.
17. The visitors need not have approached the Vice Chancellor for a small lapse like this?
18. Ought not they have consulted the HOD before they sought an interview with me?
19. We were going to speak to you about our son's performance but we could not get an appointment with you.
20. We certainly will not sell our house to pay off anybody's loan.
21. Won't you be my partner to run the three-legged race?
22. Krishnan might fight to keep this umbrella with himself.
23. Some actors will have stayed behind the curtain to give autographs to their fans.
24. You should have let them play tennis for some more time.
25. Surinder Mohan will not remember when to ask questions.
26. You must have wondered how to identify the chief guest at the reception gate.
27. Certainly I shall refuse to include Mahesh in my team.
28. You will have to include Mahesh in your team whether you like it or not.
29. You need not have come to the hall if you didn't want to listen to this lecture.
30. We were going to take part in the variety entertainment show but we lost interest in it at the last moment.

Convert the following Passives into Actives:

31. I won't have to be met by you.
32. Your purse could have been lost by you because you were careless with it.
33. The doctor should have been contacted if a medical certificate was needed by you.
34. Will your elder sister be kept informed by you about your mother's progress in the hospital?
35. The final examination shall have been finished by you well before end of March.
36. This puppy could not be kept in this house by you.
37. When would this house be taken on rent by your father?
38. What reason would be given by you for so many days of absence?
39. How could this accident have been caused except that you had been very careless.
40. This boy ought not to have been caught by you without sufficient evidence.
41. Raising any slogans would be disallowed by us during the play.
42. The little boy would have been made to go without dinner by the strict aunt.
43. The degree would have been completed by my elder brother last April.
44. Gossiping among themselves would have been loved by these girls.
45. We will never agree for this work to be completed before 20 minutes.
    (Hint: Use LET)
46. Wouldn't you be insistent that this student got punished?

47. When could this point have been taken up for discussion by the teaching staffs?
48. This talkative person will be sweet to be listened to.
49. You shall not be seen in this boy's company anymore.
50. A birthday present is going to be given to me by my little sister.

Analyse the following sentences:

51. You could have been punished by the police then and there.
52. The new boarders would have got used to the hostel routine by now.
53. Some nurses in the Govt hospitals could have kept grumbling about long working hours.
54. Aren't you going to use these new ball point pens?
55. We shan't keep using your microwave oven very frequently.

Write the remaining 6 categories of sentences for the following statements:

56. We couldn't have identified you in the crowd but for our friend's tip.
57. Won't you have to visit your mother in the hospital this evening?
58. Isn't Santosh Mukherjee going to attend your home function?
59. You ought to have said 'sorry' to him for your bad behaviour.
60. You need have become used to his new teaching methods in your college.

Chapter 32

WHEN TO USE WHICH VOICE?

Just to remind you, the English language uses 18 tenses. Of these we have covered 16 till now. We also noted that only 9 out of the 16 Active voice tenses, could be put in Passive form. Why then have the Passive form at all, especially when its usefulness is restricted to only 9 tenses?

The Passive voice has several advantages as we shall see in this Chapter. They are:

Variety

Since there is no change in the meaning between an Active and Passive, the Passive gives us another variety in writing a sentence. (We shall learn more about this advantage when we come to 'Paragraph writing'.)

Prominence

The choice of **voice** would depend upon to who we want to give the prominence - to the **doer** of an action or the person/thing **acted upon?**

If the **doer** is to be given prominence, we go in for the Active voice. If the prominence is for the **person/thing acted upon,** we opt for the Passive voice.

Silence

In the Passive form, it is quite permissible to omit the 'doer', i.e. "by … followed by a noun". Such a sentence would still be valid. Whether Active or Passive, the sentence structure formula remains the same. Thus, the Passive becomes valuable when we want to be silent deliberately about the doer. Sometimes we may not even know who the doer is. In such situations, the Passive form will prove very useful indeed. Here are some examples of exclusive Passive sentences where we remain silent about the doer of the action:

(a) My eraser has been stolen. (Here, you probably don't know who has stolen it.
        S   A   V   Thus, an Active form won't be possible here.)

(b) Hindi is not spoken all over India.
        S   Neg A   V   C

(c) All of us have been invited for the school function. (It is not important to know who the inviter is.)

(d) All applications will be examined. (We want to be silent on 'who will examine the applications'. The name of the person is possibly being withheld for security reasons.)

(e) Is cricket played in all the countries?

(f) These books   are not   to be taken   away. (The Active form - Don't take
　　　　　S　　　Neg A.V　Passive　　Adv　(these books - would sound like
　　　　　　　　　　　　　infinitive　　　　　(an order and impolite as well.)

(g) Smoking is prohibited. ("Don't smoke" is more of an order than a request.)

(h) Wasn't Pratap given an excellent present? (The sentence is silent on 'who the
　　　　　　　　　　　　　　　　　　　　　　giver is'.)

(i) The work must be completed today.

(j) Your bicycle is being washed now.

(k) The toy aeroplane was burnt/had been burnt.

(l) The young girl is hurt.

(m) All absentees will be punished.

(n) The erring students will not be spared.

(o) Let not this rule be forgotten.

(p) The culprit has been released on bail today.

(q) The prisoner has been placed in a special cell.

Hearsay type sentences

Sentences of the type, "Young parents think/consider/know/report/believe/say, that the disobedient children deserve punishment" have a slightly different kind of Passive form.

(A) "Some parents say that this college is very lenient towards the lady students."

The above sentence follows the same pattern mentioned earlier. This is a Complex sentence. In this, is "Parents think/say ...." or, "Some parents say ..." very important? Why not be silent about this part of the Complex sentence? Thus, the Passive form becomes advantageous here and we use a diplomatic phrase in the first part like, "It is said, It was considered" etc and followed by the second part in Active or Passive form.

(P) **It is said** that this college is very lenient towards the lady students.

Here are more such expressions:

(A) The audience considered that the last speaker's speech was quite poor.

(P) **It was thought** that the last speaker's speech was quite poor.

We use IT here as an 'impersonal subjective pronoun'.

The expression could be in the Present or Past families like, "It is...... or It was ...."

Here are more examples:

It is felt that ...
It is learnt that ....
It has been reported that ....
It is believed that ....

It has been decided that … (This is a Passive form)

It is known that ….

It is said that ….

It is considered that ….

It is desired that …..

It is understood that …..

It was thought that ….

It was considered …. etc etc etc

Theses kinds of Passive forms are used extensively in Official correspondences, Office circulars, Public notices, Gazette notifications and Govt orders and so on. Here are some typical sentences of this nature that are used frequently. See how polite but firm they are:

(a)   It is seen that many men students do not spend any time in the library.

(b)   It has been noticed that some members do not pay their club bill on time.

(c)   It has been decided that the teaching staffs of this institution shall not offer any private tuition to the students of this college.

(d)   It is hereby made clear to the citizens that ……..

(e)   The public are hereby notified that violation of traffic rules ……

(f)   It is requested that suitable instructions in this regard may please be issued by the Departments concerned.

(g)   It is understood that a few graduates from our college did not get admission for Post graduate courses.

Here are more examples of exclusive Passive voice sentences that we use daily and where we are silent about the **doer** of the action.

(h)   The rumour is believed to be wrong.

(i)   Your hostel warden is supposed to return from leave today.

(j)   This information may please be conveyed to the Minister.

(k)   The order has been cancelled.

(l)   You are mistaken.

(m) He is mistaken.

(n)   All are welcome to attend the meeting in the Auditorium.

(o)   Injustice has been done to us.

(p)   I have been deceived.

(q)   We had been cheated.

Politeness

Politeness is required not only in official correspondences but in normal life too. We are expected to be very polite in our dealings with others.

We use the Simple present for issuing a command/order. Commands/orders would sound direct and harsh. One might say that an order is an order and one need not be apologetic about it! True, but yet one could make them sound somewhat *polite* and make it look more like a *firm request* than an order. Passive voice would make this possible. Study the following orders:

Active	*Passive*
(a) (You do) Sit here.	(i) (You do) (Please) Be seated here.
	(ii) You are requested to sit here
(b) (You) Don't smoke.	You are requested not to smoke.
(c) Come to my office.	You are requested to come/go to my / his office.
(d) Report here.	You are requested to report here.
(e) Don't walk on the lawn.	You are requested not to walk on the lawn.

Points for and against Passive voice

A Passive voice sentence uses more words than the Active. Study the following examples:

(a) (A) One should always obey elderly people. (6 words)

    (P) Elderly people should always be obeyed by us. (8 words)

(b) (A) The Principal directed us not to allow any unauthorised persons into the auditorium. (13 words)

    (P) We have been directed by the Principal that unauthorised persons are not to be allowed into the auditorium. (18 words)

The points **against** Passive forms are,

(i) They are more expensive in words and long winded.

(ii) Some sentence constructions may sound odd and awkward. Go through such sentences in Chapters 29 - 31.

The points **in favour** are,

(i) Passives are extremely polite and persuasive.

(ii) We can be silent about the **doer** of an action.

So, choose whichever is appropriate. Just as 70% of our sentences will contain "infinitives", 30 % of our sentences would be in Passive voice. Apart from its advantages, certain sentences would sound effective only in the Passive form.

It is permissible to write one part of a Complex sentence in Active and the second in Passive.

Exercise

Write the following in Passive form:

1. Someone asked Raja his name.
2. The Management refused the new student any scholarship.
3. We bought a Moped for Meena.
4. One cannot pump out the sea water even in an age.
5. Don't stare at me like that.
6. Don't tell lies.
7. Could you lend me your bicycle?
8. Why have you done injustice to me?
9. What should you do when a stranger hails you?
10. You can achieve many things in life unless you like too much of leisure.
11. You will not see me again in that multi colour costume.
12. Did you use to live in this house before?
13. You could have done this job better, couldn't you?
14. We must answer all the questions in this test paper.
15. Don't keep smiling at me continuously.

Convert the following in Active form:

16. It is said that figs are better than apples.
17. It has been noticed that some senior students make the juniors complete their Lab reports.
18. We let ourselves be caught.
19. This task is to be completed within 10 minutes.
20. It has been rumoured that lady students will not be allowed in the next excursion

21. This girl allowed herself to be overtaken in the 200 meters race.
22. Fighting with the students of the next college is hated by our Principal.
23. We came here so that your 'on the spot drawings' could be seen by us.
24. Running on the lawn isn't permitted in this compound.
25. Copying will not be easy to be detected.
26. It has been announced that oranges will not be sold here henceforth.
27. Weren't we told by the Registrar that our term are to be paid before the tenth of next month?
28. So many poor students come here to be awarded some kind of scholarship.
29. The Bible is to be obeyed in all respects and not challenged.
30. Fishing is not to be allowed in this part of the river.

Each of the following Passive sentences has one error. Locate and rectify:

31. The table had broken.
32. The canteen contract had been awarding [*awarded*] by the Competent authority.
33. This girl was laughed at ~~with~~ [*by*] her friends.

34. Isn't this child happy to look after by her old aunt?
35. The gardeners would have handed over the seeds by next Sunday.
36. Let not be seen among you from tomorrow.
37. Madan has beaten by Sundar in the badminton match.
38. Promises be fulfilled without fail.
39. It is said frequently that violence will meet violence.
40. People sometimes believe that happiness bought by money.
41. The numbers were calling by Robert for the last round of Tambola.
42. They are came.
43. This month's Reader's digest been read to me by my sister.
44. He has gone.
45. Smoking is prohibit here.
46. We wouldn't allowed to sit here by the zoo authorities.
47. Will you have been reached London by tomorrow morning?
48. It is believed that you have failed in the finals.
49. People are believed to say that the petrol price will be increased from next April.
50. Some Finance companies cannot be trusted if a large sum promised as interest on deposits.

Chapter 33

THERE AND IT AS SUBJECT

Temporary subject

Often we use a particular **adverb** as Subject. This is against the rules you have learnt - A Noun or a Subjective pronoun alone will constitute the Subject. However, here is a violation of that rule and perhaps we could call it an 'exception'! THERE is that word and it is an adverb. But, we use it as a "temporary subject" as well in a sentence. This also means that the real subject will come later on.

Use of THERE as temporary subject.

If you see a small puppy dog at your gate, how will you convey this information to your parents? Normally you would shout, "Ma, there is a puppy dog at our gate," wouldn't you?

This is the correct way of conveying the information. If you say, "A puppy dog is at the gate, Ma," the sentence would be wrong although grammatically the sentence is correct.

Let's analyse such a sentence and see:

```
There    is    a puppy dog    at the gate.
 ?      A.V        S               C
```

"Puppy dog" is the real subject. What then is THERE? It is a "temporary subject" or we may even name it as "subject introducer."

In our daily conversations and also in written English, we use several sentences starting with THERE. This word, when it is doing the job of a temporary subject, cannot be anywhere in a sentence; it must be the starting word in a1 or a2 form; or after the Auxiliary in Q form; only then could we consider it as the temporary subject. If it appears anywhere else, it would turn out to be an adverb and would indeed pass the adverb-test.

Here are more examples of using THERE as temporary subject:

(a) **There** are some passengers already inside the bus. (Some passengers are
       TyS A.V   S   C   already inside the bus)
(b) **There** are several mistakes in your essay
       TyS   S
(c) **There** is no doubt about this man's guilt at all.
(d) **There** goes all your money.
(e) **There** you are mistaken.
(f) **There** you start all over again.
(g) **There** you are! You have done it again.
(h) Is **there** anybody at the counter?

(i) Is **there** anything to eat?

(j) Isn't **there** somebody here who could chase away those stray dogs?

(k) Is **there** a doctor among the passengers?

(l) **There** is nothing we could do in this situation.

(m) **There** are some people standing here who wouldn't taste death.

(n) **There** would be always some people among you who cannot read and write.

But, if you put THERE somewhere in the middle, see what happens?

(a) Some students   are   **there**   at the gate.
　　　　S　　　　A.V　 C1　　　C2

(b) **There**   are   plenty of thorns . in this area. (You) don't   go **there.**
　　 TyS　A.V　　　　S　　　　　C　　　　S Neg A V   C

(c) Don't roam about here and **there** .
　　　　　　　　　　　　　　　　　C

Use of IT as temporary subject

IT is a pronoun. We can use it as subject or object. IT is used primarily to refer to a noun going before. That being so, could we start a sentence with IT and in a new sentence? Which noun would it represent then? Yet, we do start many sentences with IT. In such cases, **it** will turn out to be a temporary subject and the real subject will appear later. Let us analyse some such sentences:

(a) **It**   was   a difficult paper.
　　 TyS A.V　　　S

(b) **It**   is not   easy to say 'no'   to a child's request.
　　 TyS NegA.V　 C　 S　　　　O

Here are more such sentences that we use on day to day basis. Analyse some of them and identify the real subject:

(c) **It**   is   a good habit to read books.
　　 TyS A.V　　S　　　　O

(d) **It**   was   correct to call him a thief.
　　 TyS A.V   C　　　S　　　　O   ("to call…" is infinitive noun)

(e) **It** is my privilege to give the vote of thanks.
　　　　　　　　S　　　　　　　　O

(f) **It** is John.

(g) **It** was a very nice party.

(h) Isn't **it** great to be with your parents during every holiday?
　　　　　　　　S　　　　　　　　　C

While indicating the 'time' also, we use IT as the temporary subject like this,

(i)   **It**   is   8 p.m.   now.   ("The time is 8 p.m" is bad English.)
    TyS   A.V   S   Adv

(j)   What time is **it** now? ("What is the time now? is bad English)

(k)   **It**   is   midnight.
    TyS   A.V   S

Use of IT as impersonal pronoun

Here is another use of this great pronoun. Without referring to any noun, it could be acting as the Subject. Examine these sentences:

(a)   **It** rains.
(b)   **It** snows.
(c)   **It** thunders.
(d)   Isn't **it** raining now?

Now, analyse some of them:

It   rains
S   (A)V

Isn't   **it** raining heavily outside?
Neg A S   V   C   C

The analysis shows that in all the cases, IT is doing the job of a Subject. IT refers to who, which noun going before? None at all. That's why we call it "an impersonal pronoun." (We used IT as impersonal pronoun cum Subject in Passive voice sentences. See Chapter 32.) We use IT as impersonal pronoun cum Subject also when a noun and a verb is the same word. Otherwise, we would have to say/write,

The rain rains.
The snow snows.
The thunder thunders.
The thunder is thundering.

Here are examples of day to day sentences whereof we use IT as "impersonal pronoun cum Subject" in that sentence:

(e)   It   is   all right with me.
    S   A.V   C   O

(f)   It is fine.

(g)   It is perfectly OK with me.

(h)   It is very bad indeed.

(i)   It is so sweet of you to visit us.

(j)   It is quite stupid of you to believe every Tom, Sam and Somu.

(k)   It is requested that you may sit as arbitrator. (Complex)

(l)   It   is   believed   that   the Principal's stand was   correct   in the matter.
    S A.V   Adv   Conj   S   A.V   Adv   O

Exercise

In the following sentences, state the role of IT:

1. We read a Harry Potter book. It was good indeed.
2. I need a favour from you. Will you do it for me, please?
3. It was a very good function.
4. Isn't it a sad occasion?
5. It is twilight already.
6. It is a bright day.
7. It is a poor consolation.
8. When does it rain in Cherrapunji?
9. I have committed a great blunder. Will it go against me?
10. Don't worry; it is all right.
11. Rangan is a smart person and he knows it.
12. It is understood that many students have failed in the Maths paper.
13. It is seen that you have been writing anonymous letters.
14. It has been noticed that many hostel students absent themselves without permission.
15. It is paining here.
16. It doesn't matter at all.
17. It was correct to call him a thief.
18. Where is it paining?
19. It is not always easy to stand first in the class.
20. It is hot here. How is it there?

The following sentences are incorrect. Rewrite them:

21. The time is 11 a.m. now.
22. We went out even when the rain was raining lightly.
23. What is the time now, please?
24. To call you the Principal, is it correct?
25. When is twilight?
26. Loud thunders thunder during every night in Monsoon time.
27. When the time is 8 a.m., come to me. OK?
28. Morning is here already.
29. When evening comes, all birds go to their nests.
30. Good, isn't it?

Chapter 34

THE EMPHATIC 'IT'

The pronoun IT

How many **personal pronouns** are there? There are in all 23. Go back to Chapter 1 and verify. You have used these pronouns in the SUBJECT and OBJECT parts of a sentence.

Just to remind you, we use only 4 personal pronouns for all the nouns in the world. They are, HE, SHE, IT and THEY.

We use IT to represent any common noun in the English language. We may use IT in the Subject part or Object part provided it is clear which particular noun it represents.

Further, we use IT for other purposes also as discussed in Chapter 33.

To recapitulate, we use IT:

(i) As Temporary subject, the real subject following it later.
(ii) As Subject in the capacity of "impersonal pronoun"

Emphatic expressions

In this Chapter we shall learn that IT could be used for making Emphatic expressions as well in the Present, Past and Future time periods. This is the most important use of IT.

Do recall that we could make emphatic expressions in the Infinitive method also. See Chapter 24; we called them "Emphatics" and Emphatics are Simple sentences.

Whereas, the Emphatic IT expressions are Complex sentences. Here also, we use IT as a temporary subject and the real subject follows thereafter. Examine the following sentences:

Present time (Present tense cases)

(a) **It is** Mano who is the trouble maker in our class.
   Ty S A.V S Conj/S A.V   O   C

(b) **It is** the men students who answer all the questions, don't they?

(c) **Is it** you students who made me volunteer for the trial demonstration?

(d) **It is** we who should say 'sorry' to the lady students in our class.

(e) **It is** she who is the leader for today's debate, isn't she?

(f) **Isn't** it you who is to blame for the mischief?

(g) **It is** certainly you who needs some hard punishment.

(h) **It is** I who seems to be the scapegoat every time, isn't it?

(i) **It is** I who is sending you on this evangelical mission.

(j) **Is** it I who comes late for all classes?
   A.V TyS S C/S (A)V   C

(k) **It is** always you who has to shoulder greater responsibilities here.

(l) **Isn't it** you who is the cleverest among these students?

Past time (Past tense cases)

(m) **It   was** you   who   was   totally ignorant about the State capitals.

Ty S A.V S   Conj/S A.V   C   O

(n) **It was** to Varanasi where my father went for making penance, didn't he?

(o) **It was** that silly remark on your part which ruined the child's mood.

(p) **Was it** you who was ignorant about every question?

(q) **Wasn't it** the Juniors who were to give all the performances in today's function?

(r) **It was** Pandian who sang well in today's function.

Future time (Future tense cases)

(s) **It   will be** Jane   who   will represent our University this year.

TyS   A   V   S   Conj/S   A   V   O   C

(t) **It will be** I who shall speak on behalf of this group, shan't I?

(u) **It won't be** you who will lead us in the debate, will you?

(v) **It will be** we who ought to guide the II and I year students.

(w) **Won't it be** the girls who will lead us in the singing of the Anthem?

(x) **It will be** they who will defend us in front of the Principal.

Shall we restate the rules we have followed in composing the above **powerful** sentences?

1. All the sentences, given for all the three time periods, are Complex sentences and they conform to the tense rules. In the first part, IT is the temporary subject and the real subject follows thereafter. Hence, if you are using a pronoun, it must be a 'subjective pronoun'. See (d), (e), (i) and (j).

2. The conjunctions used are only, THAT, WHO, WHAT, WHICH or WHERE.

3. These conjunctions also act as the subject for the second sentence. When a **conjunction** does the job of a subject, it virtually is a 'noun' and a 'Third person common noun' at that. Accordingly, we are concerned only with its *number* (singular or plural) in determining the verb form for the second part of the Complex sentence. The **number** of the conjunction-noun will be the number of the real SUBJECT of the first part and not its *person*.

(Consider the sentences, "Who **is** not going to school today?" and "Who **are** not going to school today?" How did we decide on **is** and **are**? In the first case, the subject is singular and in the second, the subject is plural. The *person* of the subject thus becomes irrelevant when a conjunction such as WHO is playing a dual role. Viewed in this light, the second sentences at (f), (g) - (m) and (p) are correct. The difficulty will arise only when YOU or I is the real subject in the first part. In such cases, use a singular verb for singular subjects and plural verb for plural subjects in the second sentences.)

4. Regardless of the number of the real subject in the first part, the first sentence always should starts with IT IS or IT WAS or IT WILL BE.

5. In this pattern, we cannot frame a General Q (starting with an interrogative). The Q can be in the remaining forms.

6. As regards the EQs, frame the Q tag with whichever subjective pronoun sounds appropriate.

Here are more sentences of this type that we use in our day to day life. You would also come across several similar sentences in newspapers, magazines and books. Watch out for them. Analyse and study the sentence patterns of every sentence in the following examples in the light of the rules enunciated above:

(a) It is you who is always late for any function.

(b) Isn't it you who has been complaining every time?

(c) It is I who is always blamed for everything. (Passive voice)
(Does the alternative, "It is I who am always blamed?" sound nice?)

(d) It has always been you who are to blame. ("You" here is plural)

(e) Aren't you the one who reads the prayer in the Assembly?

(f) It is you who has been carrying tales about everyone in our class.

(g) Aren't you a type who doesn't know A from B? (Here, since 'you' is singular, we use a singular verb in the second part.)

(h) You are the one who always grumbles about bad food.

(i) You are the God who does wonders. (Psalm 77:14)

(j) Aren't you the one who is being ignored by his colleagues?

(k) You are the only one who doesn't know all the persons here.

(l) I am the person who takes all decisions in this organisation.

(m) It is I and always I who acts as the usher in every function.

(n) Am I the one who is competing in the three-legged race?

(o) Am I the only one who has to compete in the 75 meters race?

Here are some more examples which we use every day wherein, the subject is IT and the sentences start with IT too, but as **impersonal pronoun**. They are very powerful (Emphatic) statements indeed:

(a) It is all right. Don't worry yourself about it.

(b) It is not quite proper to ignore old people.

(c) It was indeed an excellent show.

(d) Wasn't it a pleasure to meet the Chief guest this evening?

(e) It was very kind of you.

(f) It was indeed very thoughtful of you to invite us for this social party.

(g) It was a wonderful evening, wasn't it?

(h) Does it matter?

(i) It doesn't matter at all.

(j) It is important that you be here on time.

(k)   It will be nice if you could join us for lunch.

(l)   It won't be proper if you go away without informing the host.

The above are Simple sentences.

IT acting as impersonal pronoun cum subject, we can also write emphatic Complex sentences. Study the following examples:

(a)   It is then that I will step in to sort out the problem.

(b)   Isn't it then that you come into the picture?

(c)   It   is   then   that   I   shall   act.
      S A.V Adv Conjn S   A   V

(d)   Is it all right   if   we   leave   a little early?
      A.V S   Adv Conjn S (A)V   C

(e)   It was at that stage   that I walked into the examination hall.
      S A.V   C   Conjn S (A)V   C

(f)   It was then that we decided to function as an effective team.

(g)   It will be towards the evening   that   we shall lead the protest march.
      S   A   V   C   Conjn S   A   V   O

(h)   Won't it be then that you will be cutting the cake?

The adverb "then" refers to some previous situation - Adverb of place or time. Thus, these sentences will become meaningful only when we read them along with the foregoing sentence(s).

Usefulness of emphatic IT

Besides sounding powerful, we may make use of this method to connect two Simple sentences into a single one like we did in composing Complex sentences. In almost all the cases we would be successful in producing a meaningful Complex sentence even if the individual Simple sentences are totally unrelated to each other. Let us take Q No 61 - 70 from Chapter 27 (Complex sentence) and try connecting them by the emphatic IT method:

61. This is a nice building. My father designed it ten years back.
    It is my father who designed this nice building ten years back.
                                  or
    It is this nice building that my father designed ten years back.

62. We were students of St James school. We learnt the rules for Complex sentence there.
    It was during our student days in St James school that we learnt the rules for Complex sentence.

63. We heard the church bell. We ran fast.
    It was on hearing the church bell that we ran fast.

64. We could not come for yesterday's match. There was no bus service in our area.
    It was due to the absence of any bus service in our area that we could not come for yesterday's match.

65. I always drink milk every morning. Today, I have a headache.

It is because of my habit of drinking milk every morning that I have a headache today.

66. The servant maid was absent for 5 days last month. Don't pay her full salary.

It is because of the servant maid's absence for 5 days last month that you don't (shouldn't/needn't) pay her the full salary.

67. You must agree with his idea. Isn't he our Captain?

It is because of his captaincy that you must agree with his idea.

68. Would you call him a cheat? Samuel never tells lies.

Is it because of Samuel's honesty that you would call him a cheat?

69. The clock struck one. The mouse came down.

It was on the clock striking one that the mouse came down.

70. We had taken our evening tea at 3 p.m. We left the picnic spot immediately.

It was after our evening tea at 3 p.m. that we left the picnic spot immediately.

xx. The rehearsal will take place at 5 p.m. It is in my house.

It will be in my house where the rehearsal will take place at 5 p.m.

xx. I shall be very harsh with you. Don't be lazy.

It will be on account of your laziness that I shall be very harsh with you.

Instead of a noun after "It is/It was", you may use a phrase doing the job of a noun. (noun phrase) If you write a sentence such as, " Is it because Samuel doesn't tell lies that you would call him a cheat?" it will contain three Simple sentences. Although this pattern is quite in order but to conform to the rule of a Complex sentence, do not exceed two Simple sentences.

The Emphatic IT method is as effective as the Complex sentence method in connecting any two Simple sentences. But, do remember to follow the Tense rules.

Categories of sentences

It has been stated already that we cannot form 'General question' in Emphatic expressions. Therefore, you should be in a position to write 5 categories if one category is given. Here is an exercise on it:

*Given:*a1	:	It is my friend who has been acting foolishly during Students' meetings. The other 5 categories for the above a1 will be:
a2	:	It is not my friend who has been acting..........
Sp Q	:	Is it my friend who has been acting ....?
Neg Q	:	Isn't it my friend who has been acting ....?
EQ1	:	It is my friend who has been acting ......, isn't he?
EQ2	:	It is not my friend who has been acting ...., is he?
*Given:*a2	:	It was not I who was the culprit.
a1	:	It was I who was the culprit.
Sp Q	:	Was it you who was the culprit?

Neg Q	:	Wasn't it you who was the culprit?
EQ1	:	It was I who was he culprit, wasn't I?
EQ2	:	I wasn't I who was the culprit, was I?
Given:EQ2	:	It won't be these people who will work for me, will they?
a1	:	It will be these people who will work for you.
a2	:	It won't be these people who will work for you.
Sp Q	:	Will it be these people who will work for you?
Neg Q	:	Won't it be these people who will work for you?
EQ1	:	It will be these people who will work for me, won't they?

You may experience some problem in framing the 'Q tag' especially in Present time/ tense cases. Follow the same rule as applicable for Complex sentences. However, if you feel compelled to use the Subjective pronoun of the first sentence and the real subject happens to be "I" or "YOU", go in for the temporary subject "IT" in the Q tag. Some examples are shown below:

1. It is always you who are the leaders in any assignment, isn't it?
2. It is I who has been at fault, isn't it?
3. It isn't you who is the trouble maker, is it?

Exercise

Give emphatic affirmative or negative answers using IT IS/ IT WAS :

1. Where did they hold the prize-awarding function?
2. When did these students return to their room last night?
3. Which is the biggest State in India?
4. Aren't you the same guy who passed on a secret to the opposing team?
5. What did they want from us; sympathy or financial help?
6. On the basis of whose statement that the teacher took this decision.
7. Whose pen did you borrow to write your Practicals-report?
8. Why did you stay in the private ward during the night?
9. Were the boys or the girls the real culprits?
10. Who is responsible for this accident?
11. When did the fight between these two take place? Before or after the match?
12. Where was the Second Carnatic war fought?
13. Where did the German troops surrender during World War II?
14. When did the match referee blow the whistle?
15. When did I tell you not to play cricket?

Frame suitable Questions starting with IT IS or IT WAS or IT WILL BE as is necessary for the following answers: (Hint: Go in for EQs in most cases)

16. Today is a very warm day.
17. I got the appointment with the Minister with some difficulty.

18. Shalini is surely the beauty queen of BA First year.
19. The agent was unfair to give false hopes to the unemployed graduates.
20. We get rain in Chennai during October-December.
21. Of course, morning has arrived.
22. The time by my watch is 6.30 a.m.
23. Today's jam session was superb.
24. The college programme was an enjoyable one.
25. We felt great to talk to the visiting foreigners.
26. To fall in love with a puppy dog, is so easy.
27. What we have is a modern house.
28. Criticising is easier than praising.
29. To ask questions is easier than to answer.
30. I always take the blame for my brother and sister.

Locate the mistake(s) and rewrite the following defective sentences:

31. It is Ramanathan causing difficulties to all of us.
32. It is we who was sleeping in the afternoon.
33. Isn't evening already?
34. Isn't it you the youngest member in our group?
35. It was them that took away our seats in the front row.
36. Wasn't it me who told you so?
37. It will be always you to lead us all in our morning prayer.
38. Won't it be the poor people suffer when there is an earthquake?
39. It were they who spoilt all our fun during our excursion.
40. It is Ramanujam who was watching the T.V serial all by himself, didn't he?
41. It is I who have to cover the sports activities for our school magazine.
42. It is this which were a serious matter.
43. The snow is snowing now.
44. He always is the black sheep and he knows them.
45. When there is rain, don't go out.

Combine the following pairs of Simple sentences into a single Complex sentence using emphatic IT:

46. Go to the voting booth. You can cast your vote there.
47. Can the students choose any subject? They will be ready for the Declamation contest on time?
48. Ramani speaks Tamil very well. He scores high marks in that subject.
49. The teacher stepped into the room. All the pupils rushed to their seat.
50. It is raining heavily outside. Take your umbrella.
51. Meghna was a clever student. Johnny is her younger brother.
52. Godavari is one of the perennial rivers of India. It runs from West to East.
53. Cholas, Cheras and Pandyas ruled the Southern States. Their rule lasted nearly eight centuries.

54. Manickam was a great man. Many young maidens admired him.
55. Vaishali is a cheat. You should never trust her.

Split the following Complex sentences into individual Simple sentences:

56. It was the news of his examination result that made him sad.
57. It is by hard work that one succeeds in life.
58. It is the great city Chennai which is the State capital.
59. Isn't it the dirty walls that we shall paint today?
60. Won't it be in this college where you will admit your son?
61. When you come into the room, please wake me up.
62. If you are my real friend, you will complete this cleaning work, won't you?
63. It will be always my mother who will help you in times of trouble.
64. Isn't it you who betrayed my friend?
65. Because you were sick, we had to cancel our football match.

Write the remaining 5 categories of sentences for the following Emphatic statements:

66. It is your children who had caused this damage to my motorbike.
67. Wasn't it he who carried some tales about me?
68. It's not Ranjan who spoke against me, did he?
69. Is it you who is responsible for our losing the match?
70. It is always I who does not get involved in any kind of quarrels, isn't it?

Chapter 35

DIRECT SPEECH
and
DIALOGUE WRITING

Definition

When two persons face each other and talk between themselves, they would use the personal pronouns I, YOU or WE. Such a dialogue is referred as **Direct speech** because they will be addressing each other *directly*.

When we want to repeat the exact words used by somebody, we put such sentences between inverted commas ("....."). The contents inside the inverted commas are also known as **Direct speech**.

Thus far, you have been <u>writing</u> sentences in various tenses in **Indirect speech.**

In our day to day life, both in written and spoken forms, we use both the speeches. Hence, you must have knowledge of both and also know how to convert one into the other.

Direct speech

Here is a conversation between two persons, who are facing each other. Examine their words from the definition point of view.

Peter : Where are you going, Raju?
Raju : I am going to a medical shop to buy some medicines.
Peter : Medicines? Is anyone sick in your house?
Raju : Yes, my mother is ill with high temperature.
Peter : I am sorry to know that, my friend. Is she lying in bed?
Raju : Yes, she is. After I give these medicines, she ought to feel better.
Peter : Did a doctor see her?
Raju : Yes, he did this morning. This is his prescription.

Notice the following points:

(a) Both the young men are using the pure pronouns I or YOU. When they use the First person pronouns, we call their speech as Direct speech.

(b) When either of them refers to another being, they use the Third person i.e. HE, SHE, IT, THEY.

(c) All the sentences they use are grammatically correct. Some of them may look wrong but they are not. They are the short cuts in personal conversation, about which we shall learn more in the Chapters 52 - 55.

Now if a third person who has been overhearing this conversation reports it, it will be something like this:

> Peter asked Raju where he was going. Raju said that he was going to a medical shop to purchase medicines. A shocked Peter asked if anyone was sick in his house. Raju replied that his mother was ill with fever. A more worried Peter asked if she was in bed. Raju confirmed it. He also stated that according to the doctor, the mother would feel better after taking the prescribed medicines.

When Peter exclaimed, "Medicines?" his tone would have revealed some anxiety and concern, won't it? His feelings have been shown in the Indirect speech, "A shocked Peter asked." "I am sorry to know that" has been conveyed as, "A more worried Peter." It is relatively easy to express one's emotions in Direct speech, sometimes in single words. Expressing the emotions in Indirect speech would call for some skill. You must find suitable words/phrases to translate one's feelings and reactions. Otherwise, the Indirect speech would look reactionless and even jumpy.

What you must remember is, that *what each person has said* is the Direct speech. In the dialogue, we have indicated at the left PETER: and what he said, after his name. Similarly when it was Raju's turn we showed RAJU: and wrote after his name whatever he had said. The names on the left show, who is speaking. Another method of showing who spoke the Direct speech is like this,

> Peter asked Raju, "Where are you going?"
> Raju replied, "I am going to a medical shop to buy some medicines."

What is contained inside the inverted commas is the Direct speech - Where are you going? What about the other words i.e. Peter asked Raju? This is Indirect speech. So, when we have to show in writing a Direct speech, it will be a combination of Indirect and Direct speech; what one said will be Direct and will be inside inverted commas and the details of who said that, will be in Indirect speech.

Next, shall we study how to make Direct speech statements in various time periods and how to convert one into the other?

Present time period cases

Direct   :   Mother says, "I am going out for an hour."
Indirect :   Mother says that she is going out for an hour.

When we convert a Direct speech into Indirect, the sentence becomes a Complex sentence. (Strictly speaking, we must consider these as 'loose Complex sentences,' because the first part will in most cases have only S-A-V. Nevertheless you must observe the tense rules assuming them to be full fledged Complex sentences.)

Note the punctuations carefully - use a comma after the Indirect element (i.e. details of who makes the statement); then the inverted commas; the first letter of the first word in the Direct speech to be in capital; put a full stop to mark the end of the Direct statement; then, inverted commas. These punctuations are very important.

Here are more examples;

(a) D   : Babbly tells me, "I may not come for playing today."
   ID   : Babbly tells me that she may not come for playing today.

(b) D   : The watchman asks, "Are you coming with me to the shop?"
   ID   : The watchman asks if I am going with him to the shop?

(c) D   : The young lady informs, "My mother visited me in my college yesterday."
   ID   : The young lady informs that her mother visited her in her college yesterday.

(d) D   : The Delhi correspondent has reported, "Many newspaper employees are sitting near the front gate protesting against the wage cut."
   ID   : The Delhi correspondent has reported that many newspaper employees were sitting near the front gate protesting against the wage cut.

(e) D   : Tyagi responds, "I don't eat meat at all."
   ID   : Tyagi responds that he doesn't eat meat all.

(f) D   : The daughter replies, "I have finished my breakfast."
   ID   : The daughter replies that she had finished her breakfast.

(g) D   : Your friend conveys, "I have been waiting here for 15 minutes."
   ID   : Your friend conveys that he had been waiting here for 15 minutes.

Note:

1. When converted into Indirect speech, the sentence becomes a Complex sentence and accordingly you must observe the tense rules.

2. The first and second person pronouns inside the inverted commas are changed into third person pronouns. This may not be so in all cases; when the reference is to the writer/speaker, he/she must use I/We even in the Indirect speech. See (b).

3. The reference to the time and day and place to remain as 'today, tomorrow, yesterday, here, there'.

Past time period cases

(a) D   : Anuradha said, "I may not attend college tomorrow."
   ID   : Anuradha said that she might not attend college on the following day.

(b) D   : The Lecturer replied, "I have not corrected your test papers as yet."
   ID   : The Lecturer replied that he had not corrected our test papers till then.

(c) D   : Moses insisted, "I did not loan my fountain pen to Ahmed."
   ID   : Moses insisted that he had not loaned his fountain pen to Ahmed.

Note:

Although the Direct speech has used a Simple past auxiliary (did), we have used a past perfect auxiliary (had) in the Indirect. Why? We have followed the two action rule.

(d) D : Sheila said to me, "Shall we meet our friend this evening at her house?"
    ID : Sheila enquired if we should meet our friend that evening at her house?

(e) D : Manohar told me, "I won't be leaving for Lucknow till tomorrow."
    ID : Manohar told me that he wouldn't be leaving for Lucknow till the following day.

(f) D : The visitor asked, "Where is your father now?"
    ID : The visitor asked where my father was then.

(g) D : My father said, "Were you in your uncle's house last night?"
    ID : My father asked if I had been in my uncle's house the night before?

(h) D : The Principal was firm with my father, "I cannot give your son the Commerce group."
    ID : The Principal was firm with my father that he could not give me the Commerce group.

(i) D : Murugan said to me, "Do you understand clearly all the rules of Direct speech?"
    ID : Murugan asked me if I had understood clearly all the rules of Direct speech?

(j) D : Didn't he tell you, "You should have completed this task by yesterday?"
    ID : Didn't he tell you that you should have completed this task by the day before?

(k) D : The Professor reiterated, "You see the point now, don't you?"
    ID : The Professor reiterated whether I saw the point then or not?

(l) D : "I will come here again tomorrow," the Demonstrator conveyed.
    ID : The Demonstrator conveyed that he would go there again on the following day.

(m) D : He replied, "The milkman has been delivering the milk regularly, hasn't he?"
    ID : He replied that the milkman had been delivering the milk regularly, hadn't he?

(n) D : The bus driver confirmed, "I did give a leave application, didn't I"
    ID : The bus driver confirmed that he did give a leave application, didn't he?

(o) D : Couldn't he have said, "I will try."
    ID : Couldn't he have said that he would try?

(p) D : We should have told you, "We will try, shouldn't we?"
    ID : We should have told you that we would try, shouldn't we?

Note:

1. Since the Indirect element is in the Past family, the contents inside the inverted commas too must be in a suitable Past family and conforming to the tense rules.

2. If the speech is in Q form, use the verb "asked/enquired" in the first part.

3. Change the time and place inside the inverted commas when dealing with "Past time cases" as under:

Direct	Indirect
as yet	till than
now	then
today	that day
yesterday	the day before
tomorrow	the next day or the following day.
here	there
last night	the night before
this	that
these	those

4. As in the Present time case, change the First person into Third person pronouns. But, if the meaning demands it, keep the First person in First person only. See (g) and (h). As regards the second person pronouns, leave them unchanged.

5. The Direct speech part could be in any past family also as in (m) and (n). Convert such sentences in accordance with the tense rules.

6. The Direct speech part may be in EQ form. Convert it with an equivalent EQ form in the past family. Where an EQ does not sound well, use any alternate form to show the emphatic nature of the statement.

Future time cases

(a) D : Matthews will certainly say, "Come after two days."

ID : Matthews will certainly say that you may go to him after two days.

(b) D : The Administrator might remind you, "Don't forget to attend the sports committee meeting."

ID : The Administrator might remind you that you should not forget to attend the sports committee meeting.

(c) D : Madan will boast, "Wasn't I the class representative till last year?"

ID : Madan would boast that hadn't he been the class representative till last year?

(d) D : Sikandar would have said, "I am helping the weak students even now, amn't I?"

ID : Sikandar would have said that he had been helping the weak students even now, hadn't he?

(e) ID : He shall confirm to you, "I have been assisting the Lecturer till now."

ID : He shall confirm to you that he has been assisting the Lecturer till now.

(f) D : My uncle might ask you, "Didn't I send you to the library for a special purpose?"

ID : My uncle might ask you whether he hadn't sent you to the library for a special purpose?

Note:

1. If the tense of the contents inside the inverted commas is in a past family, modify the future auxiliary in the first part in tune with the tense rules. (Past equivalent - Past family) See (c).

2. If the first part has an FIP tense, use a Past family tense in the other part in the Indirect speech. See (d). In (d) we have also observed the 2 action rule.

3. As regards the 'adverbs of time' ('last year', 'now' 'today') keep them as they are in the Indirect like we did in the Present family case.

Use of infinitive-connectors

Instead of a Complex sentence Indirect speech, we could also write out an Infinitive-connector based Simple sentence. This would be possible if the first verb is a command/suggestion/order variety like, ORDER, DIRECT, INSTRUCT or their synonyms. Here are some examples :

(a) D : Rajan orders us, "Bring all your complaints to me first."
 ID : Rajan orders us **to bring** all our complaints to him first.

(b) D : The HOD shouted to me, "Hand over your class notes at once?"
 ID : The HOD shouted to me **to hand over** my class notes at once.

(c) D : Your friend will always direct you, "Don't come to me every time."
 ID : Your friend will always direct you **not to go** to him every time.

(d) D : You might have shouted at him, "Put on your socks right now."
 ID : You might have shouted at him **to put** on his socks right then.

(e) D : We could have told you, "Wait here till 5 p.m."
 ID : We could have told you **to wait** there till 5 p.m.

(f) D : The referee should have warned you, "Don't commit any more fouls during the play."
 ID : The referee should have warned you **not to commit** any more fouls during the play.

(g) D : John said, "Meet me at the theatre at 6 p.m."
 ID : John asked me **to meet** him at the theatre at 6 p.m.

(h) D : Talukdar said, "Don't drive this fast."
 ID : Talukdar advised me **not to drive** that fast.

(i) D : Mazumdar says, "Don't open the front door to everyone."
 ID : Mazumdar tells me **not to open** the front door to everyone.

When the order is in polite form, we follow the gerund or Complex sentence method as shown in the following examples:

(j) D : He said, "Let us leave the house at 9 a.m."
 ID : He suggested **leaving** the house at 9 a.m.
                    or
 He suggested **that** we might leave the house at 9 .a.m.

(k) D : Our leader says, "Let Krishnan not show his anger on them"
 ID : Our leader suggests **that** Krishnan may not show his anger on them.

(l) D   : The student leader suggests, "Let us stop here for a while."

  ID   : The student leader suggests **stopping** here for a while.

(m)D   : The Principal warned, "Let no one violate any rule."

  ID   : The Principal warned **that** no one should violate any rule.

(n) D   : My mother responded, "Let me do it myself."

  ID   : My mother responded **that** she would do it herself.

(o) D   : The Panchayat President said, "Let them come in person to me."

  ID   : The Panchayat President said **that** they could come to him in person.

Note that the gerund method would be suitable only when an objective pronoun "us" is present; if a subjective pronoun or a noun or other objective pronoun is present, adopt the Complex sentence method.

Conversion of Interrogatives into Indirect speech

The interrogative remains unchanged in the Indirect speech. Study the following examples:

(a) D   : Matthew said, "Where is she going?"

  ID   : Matthew asked **where** the other (or she) was going?

(b)D   : The visitor asked, "Where is the railway station?"

  ID   : The visitor asked **where** the railway station was?

(c) D   : The traveller enquired, "When is the next train to Hyderabad?"

  ID   : The traveller enquired **when** the next train to Hyderabad was?

(d)D   : The father asked, "How will you reach your destination?"

  ID   : The father asked **how** I would reach my destination?

  (The D sentence here is vague. It is not clear, who the father is addressing. If he had asked his son, then the correct ID is as given above. If he had referred to another person, the correct ID would be, "The father asked how he would reach his destination?")

Indirect to Direct speech

What we have learnt so far looks like an 'one way traffic', doesn't it? If we could convert a Direct speech into Indirect, so could we an Indirect into Direct. This would call for some skill. Study the following example of conversion from Indirect to Direct:

Ram gave some money to Abby and asked him to buy two shirts for him. Abby hesitated for a while and then agreed. He stepped into a ready made garment shop. The salesman welcomed him and asked what he would need. Abby explained. A little later, the salesman wanted to know what size of shirts the customer wanted. Abby couldn't tell because he had not enquired about it from Ram. The salesman asked next, about Ram's age and height. Abby gave the information. The salesman now guessed the correct size and showed the customer some half a dozen varieties. Two designs attracted Abby. So, he ordered two shirts of different colours, paid the money and returned home. Ram liked the shirts and thanked Abby profusely for the favour.

During the conversion, give the name of the speaker on the left and after a colon, indicate his words/sentences and so on. Here is a possible version:

Ram : Abby, kindly go to the market and buy me two shirts. Here is Rs 400.
Abby : Well … er … well. All right. Please hand over the money.
Ram : Here you are.
Salesman : Good afternoon, Sir. May I help you?
Abby : I need two Gents' shirts, please.
Salesman : What size, Sir?
Abby : I'm afraid, I don't know. These are for a friend of mine.
Salesman : Not to worry, Sir. What's his age and height?
Abby : 25. About my height.
Salesman : It's size 42, Sir.
Salesman : Here are six varieties; all of size 42.
Abby : I think I'll take this and that one. Please pack them up.
Ram : Abby, terrific. I like them very much. Thank you, Abby boy.

In the Direct speech, the greatest difficulty will arise while conveying one's reactions or emotions or in describing certain situations. For instance, Abby's hesitation to buy the shirts for his friend; this has been represented by "Well .. well.." which show his 'unreadiness'. If he was happy at that, we could have written something like, "Ah. Of course. Give me the money …" Next, how do we translate "A little later …" We really cannot. Thus we show *silence* and the Salesman continues with his action of displaying six shirts. Similarly, how do we describe Abby paying the bill and returning home? We can't. So the next piece of dialogue is by Ram, obviously at his home, which implies that he has paid the bill and left the shop.

These are the drawbacks of Direct speech. It would deal only with what one has said/ spoken. Incidentally, to write out a Direct speech two or more **human beings** must be involved. You cannot describe a scene or a building or a crowd etc by Direct speech. In such cases, we have to depend on Indirect.

When to use which Speech

Indirect speech

In our day to day conversations, when we refer to other people, we will be using the Indirect speech.

In written work also, we use mostly the Indirect speech, like writing out a report or an official letter, notices, etc. Indirect speech sentences are quite powerful if we use appropriate and dynamic verbs. In addition, we have the EQs to give greater strength in our sentences especially when we have to describe a situation or portray a weak or powerful personality and so on.

Direct speech

We use the Direct speech when we face a second person and talk to him/her directly. In which case, we will be using the pure pronouns I, WE or YOU. However, if the conversationalists refer to a third person, they would use HE, SHE, IT, THEY.

As regards the written work, we will use the Direct speech only when we want to reproduce verbatim what someone has said or when we quote a proverb or a quotation etc. Otherwise, our written work will be mostly in Indirect speech.

But, Direct speech is the exclusive domain of authors of novels and short stories. You could never find a novel or a short story without Direct speech in them and plenty of that too? They will always use the Direct speech for dialogues between two characters. Could they put such dialogues in Indirect speech as well? Of course, they could. Haven't we ourselves done some exercises on the art of conversion from Direct to Indirect and vice versa? But, it may not sound as powerful and realistic as Direct speech will. Further, Direct speech could never give any **colour** to any of your descriptions. However, Direct speech has its own attractions. Examine the following dialogue:

Selvi and Madhavi were walking along on their way to a nearby park. Suddenly stopping Selvi said, "Madhavi, I have a piece of good news for you…?" .

"You have? What's it? What's it?"

"My elder brother has agreed to give you tuition in Maths. Are you happy?"

"Oh! I am indeed happy, Selvi. How very nice of your brother. But, I wonder why he took so long to say it?"

"He is very busy in office, you see?"

"Yes, I understand. Did he say from when?"

"From next Wednesday, I think. Well. Why don't you come to my house this evening and talk to Anna *about it yourself?"*

Have you noticed, when we read the first sentence, they are just two girls walking. But when we put in Direct speech the words used by Selvi, she has become alive! Real life character! The remaining conversation has induced life into the piece, hasn't it? Authors use this technique to revive or sustain the interest in certain situations.

We may use the Direct speech also to express our own personal feelings and thoughts when writing an article or a description or a satire or some personal account etc. This would be like "talking to yourself!". Here, there is only one person. Examine the following expressions:

"Could this fellow be a cheat?" I debated in my mind.

" Go and drown yourself in the nearest lake!" I felt like telling him.

"Good," I reflected in my heart.

I thought silently about that grand man. "What an extraordinary human being he is? From rags to riches in total honesty?"

"He could have been more diplomatic about his statement," I thought to myself.

In writing some personal account, you must indicate to the reader whatever has been going on in your mind. In real life, before we answer anyone's question, don't we go through some kind of introspection or weigh the pros and cons or develop some good or bad feelings over the question and only thereafter we frame the answer? True or not? Your writing would be realistic only if you reveal those to the reader. Without these silent and 'off the record' reflections, what you write may look jumpy and out of context as well. Direct speech is useful in such writings.

Here is an example of a personal account or a Satire, in which the writer's personal feelings and reactions have been shown:

When I reached the Public library compound, I heard someone calling me. I turned around to see. Waving his hands at me, a middle aged man inched in my direction.

"Who could he be?" I wondered in my mind. "Could he be someone of my school days or a clever imposter ..? Eversince I was cheated to the tune of some Rs 200 by an innocent looking person some months back, I had become suspicious of any stranger."

"Hey, Jay, don't you recognise me? I am Samy, dammit. We met in London last June, remember?" the other said showing all his teeth.

A warning bell rang loudly in my ears instantly. *"Surely, this guy is a cheat, I had concluded and decided to be extremely cautious. You see, I had never visited London or for that matter any place outside India."*

In the above piece, the writer's own personal feelings, impressions and thoughts have been expressed in Direct speech.

Dialogue writing

A dialogue is nothing but Direct speech between 2 persons usually. One can write a dialogue straightway or convert an Indirect speech report or a description in Indirect speech into Direct speech. The participants usually would be 2 or never more than 3.

Here is a sample conversation between two persons given in Indirect speech. Convert the report into a dialogue form:

Venu greeted the Headmaster and expressed regret for disturbing him. The HM asked him what the matter was. Venu requested him to change him from the Maths-Physics-Chemistry group to the Commerce group. For a query, Venu replied that he found the MPC group very difficult.

The HM in turn demanded to know how he would manage the Commerce group since 5 weeks of teaching have already elapsed.

Venu said that his father would arrange private tuition for him. The HM asked him to bring his parents to his office on the following day. He also added that he would discuss the matter with his parents in the first instance and give his decision.

Here is the dialogue form of the above report. Study it carefully:

<u>Dialogue form</u>

Venu	:	Good morning. Excuse me, Sir. I have a request.
HM	:	Yes, what is it, Venu?
Venu	:	I request you to change my group from Maths-Physics-Chemistry to the Commerce group, Sir.
HM	:	Why?
Venu	:	I am finding these subjects very difficult, Sir.
HM	:	By now 5 weeks of teaching is over. How will you manage, Venu?
Venu	:	My father will arrange private tuition for me, Sir.
HM	:	All right. Please bring your parents to me tomorrow. I shall give my decision after discussing the matter with your parents. OK?

This is a straightforward conversion from Indirect to Direct. There is hardly any emotion in the situation. The only difficult part is the first sentence. "Greeted ..." translated as "Good morning"; "expressed regret ...." translated as , "excuse me, Sir". The next piece contains some emotions and personal feelings. See how these have been converted into Direct speech:

A gentleman, after some hesitation, asked a shopkeeper if he could give some smaller notes for a Hundred rupee note. The shopkeeper tightened his face initially, relented after a few seconds and gave him two Rs 50 notes He also added that he didn't have any ten rupee notes with him at that time. But, if the other bought any material from his shop he could manage to return some small change. It all depended for how much he would purchase things.

The gentleman purchased three chocolate bars, each costing Rs 13.

Feeling happy, the shopkeeper returned Rs 11 in smaller denominations against one fifty rupee note. The gentleman thanked him profusely, bid goodbye and went his way.

<u>Dialogue form:</u>

Gent	:	Er ... Excuse ... me. Could you give me some smaller notes for Hundred Rupees. Please?
S.Keeper	:	What ...? ..... All right. Here are two 50 rupee notes. I don't have any ten rupee notes, you see? But, if you buy any material from my shop I could manage the balance. It all depends on how much you would purchase for.
Gent	:	In that case, please give me three chocolate bars. How much do they cost? Oh, Rs 13 each? Take this 50 rupee note.

S.Keeper : That's good, Sir. Here is the balance of Rs 11.
Gent : Thank you very much. Good day.

We have translated the various emotions and other visible actions in the following ways:

"after some hesitation"- Er … Excuse … me.

"The shopkeeper tightened his face and relented .."- What ….? … All right.

"The gentleman purchased 3 chocolate bars …."- In that case, give me 3 chocolate bars …

"Feeling happy …"- That's good, Sir.

"Bid goodbye and went his way"- Good day.

You cannot ignore such feelings. While it may be easy to express them in Indirect speech, you have to think of suitable words/description while translating such actions/feelings in Direct speech.

2. Here is a dialogue between 3 persons given in Indirect speech. Convert the description into Direct speech.

Paul greeted Suresh heartily and he responded to it equally enthusiastically. When Paul asked Suresh about, what he proposed to do after XII standard, Mahesh joined them. Interrupting their conversation, Mahesh suggested that all of them may go for a matinee show; a great English film was running in Devi theatre. The other two looked at each other blankly murmuring. Suresh said that he would certainly join a Science college. An impatient Mahesh insisted on knowing whether they would see a movie that afternoon or not. Paul was agreeable. Suresh wasn't all that keen but when Mahesh pressed him, he agreed.

Dialogue form

Paul : Hi, Suresh. How are you Boy?
Suresh : Good morning, Paul. Nice to see you.
Paul : Suresh, what do you intend doing after XII standard?
Mahesh : Hi fellows! Sorry to butt in. How about going to a matinee show this afternoon? A nice English movie is running in Devi theatre?
Paul : Er …
Suresh : I … don't … know….. not sure …
Suresh : Ah! Yes, Paul. I certainly am going to join a Science college.
Mahesh : What the hell? Are we going for a movie or not?
Paul : Okay, I think.
Suresh : Well … actually ... possibly ….
Mahesh : Come, come, Suresh. Be a sport, man.
Suresh : All right. Agreed.

During a conversation, school and college young men use a lot of slangs. In the dialogue form, use such terms. Also note how certain feelings and reactions have been translated. They would also call each other by endearing names such as, "Boy", "fellows", "man", "yaar" etc. The dialogue form would be realistic only when you use such words and expressions. Don't stick to 'formal' language. One would normally use informal language in a dialogue.

Exercise

Change the following Direct speech statements of the speaker into Indirect speech:

1. "Give me a cup of tea," Rangan told his wife.
2. Mohana said, "How is your mother feeling today?
3. Our teacher always reminds us, "Haven't I told you several times not to copy any sentences from any book or magazines but write your own?"
4. Jaya wrote, "I am longing to receive your instant reply for this letter."
5. When I got up from my seat in the examination hall, the invigilator asked, "What is the matter?"
6. Sundaram will always complain, "The cook does not give me sufficient food."
7. Whenever I see the College Principal he says, "Your son is an excellent student in my college."
8. Petting my little cat I speak to her, "Be a good pet. Don't steal anything from the kitchen."
9. The History Lecturer explained, "Akbar won the respect of his subjects because of his justice and fairness to all."
10. The leader replied, "My classmates will reach here shortly."
11. The angry Professor remarked, "How dare you shout at me like this?"
12. Janakiraman said, "Don't worry, mother. I shall get better marks next time."
13. "Send the next candidate in," said the President of the selection committee.
14. "Hurry up," shouted the referee.
15. Mohan said to me, "Didn't you find out my marks from the office clerk?"
16. Shanti of course will talk to you sweetly and say, "Let me see."
17. Madam may say, "I didn't have time to look into your notes."
18. The office superintendent advises all students, "Pay your tuition fees on time."
19. Hannah always says, "I will join the best college in the city after my Plus 2."
20. Amirkhan must have told you, "I shall surely recommend your name to the Captain."

Write the following Indirect statements into Direct speech:

21. Sudha requested Monica to go with her to the saree shop.
22. Monica regretted that she couldn't go with Sudha to the saree shop that day.
23. Ashok says that he had already seen that tele-film.
24. Santanu wants to know whether his parents would listen to him.
25. My friend asked me if I would accompany him to the Principal's office.

26. Paul asserted that he wanted to be an IAS officer.
27. The hospital matron enquired whether the patient would like to get discharged that afternoon or on the following morning.
28. On Monday mornings I ask my students if they spent their week end usefully.
29. Whenever the mother is ill, the eldest daughter cooks all the meals.
30. Sunita demanded to know the name of the thief.

Write the following Indirect speech in a suitable Direct speech dialogue form:

31. When Enoch asked Manoharan if he would join his group, Mano could not reply immediately. He said he would think it over and reply on the following day. In the meantime, would Enoch please consider taking John also in the group.
32. Sandra did not listen to her mother's advice and volunteered to join the picnic group. Mohana and Vineeta consoled Sandra saying, that she should make up with the mother on return from the picnic trip.
33. The argument was between the History Lecturer and English Lecturer. The History Lecturer wanted to conduct the rehearsal only between 4 and 5 p.m. but the English Lecturer wanted that particular time for the extra classes since her daughter returned from school at 4.30 p.m. and the daughter expected to see the mother when she returned from school.
34. Menon insisted that Indirect speech was quite useless. But, Thangaraj did not agree. In his view, Indirect speech was more useful and powerful too than the Direct. Could Menon put the description of a long procession in Direct speech? Menon did not reply straightway. He promised to think about it and give a suitable reply next Monday. At this stage, Vinodhini joined them. She asked if she could be the umpire in their battle of words. The young men admitted that Vinodhini was excellent in English. Could she then express her views on Direct and Indirect speech? Clearing her throat Vinodhini said, both had their own good and bad points and the two males need not dispute over it. Menon and Thangaraj looked at each other clutching and unclutching their palms vigorously.
35. Three friends went to a Music shop. Chandra wanted to buy an audio cassette of the latest Tamil hits. When asked what she wanted, Ratna replied she needed a CD of Hindi songs. Neena had her own idea; she just wanted to listen to a few songs inside the music shop and come away without buying anything.

Chapter 36

PARTICIPLE

Definition

What is a Participle?

If we add the letters **ing** to a present form verb, it becomes a **participle; present participle,** to be precise.

Do you remember that we followed the same method for forming a gerund? So, how do we distinguish a participle from a gerund? Examine the following sentences:

(a) We didn't think **riding** difficult at all.

(b) My brother saw me **swimming** in the club pool.

In (a), **riding** is a gerund, because it passes the 'Noun test'. But in (b), **swimming** does not pass the 'Noun test'. So, we may say that 'swimming' here is not a noun. It is not a continuous verb either; if it is, it will have to its left an auxiliary. It is not an adjective, nor an adverb, nor a conjunction and not a preposition. What then is it?

Do you see some 'action' in the word? Yes, we do. You can imagine the action in your mental eyes. It seems to be an 'action oriented' word; for an ' on-going action' or an 'action in progress'. It looks to be the answer for a test question such as "doing what"? — My brother saw me ... **doing what** ...? My brother saw me ... **swimming** ....

Therefore, we may define a participle as a word of 'on going' action which will answer the test question "doing what?"

Study the following examples. The participles are shown in bold letters and you can see some 'on going action' in each.

(c) I see Daniel **playing** in front of his house every evening.

(d) I heard the Professor **scolding** you after the Maths class.

(e) During the earthquake, we felt our house **shaking**.

(f) Don't you smell something **burning** inside the kitchen?

(g) We watched the lady students **practising** a Shakespeare's play.

(h) My mother found the servant woman **stealing** some rice.

The verbs used in the above examples are: SEE, HEAR, FEEL, SMELL, WATCH and FIND. We may say that these six verbs, in any of their forms, will be always followed by a participle.

Can you cite any other rule?

Analyse the sentences and see. All of them have an object, haven't they? Can we cite this as a rule - A participle must be preceded by an object? What about a complement? Study the following sentences:

(i) Wasn't your Mother *busy* **cooking** our dinner when you came in.

(j) Shanti was *away* **playing** table tennis at 5 p.m.

(k) We still feel *depressed* **remembering** our defeat in the football match.

All these sentences too have a participle each and it is preceded by a complement.

Summarising all the rules, we may write a formula like this,

S - A - V - O or C – PARTICIPLE - O/C

In the absence of O or C after S-A-V, the word ending in **ing** will turn out to be a **gerund.** In the following sentences, the words in **bold** are doing the job of a gerund. Apply the Noun test and see:

(l) We intend **meeting** the Captain of the other team.
     S   (A)V   O   (amplifying words)

(m) Would you prefer **studying** or **playing** this evening?

(n) Doesn't your small brother love **cycling**?

(o) I prefer **riding** to **walking**.

The sentences from (l) to (o), follow the pattern,

S - A - V - O (in gerund form)

Thus, we pick out a participle in a Simple sentence by applying the following rules:

(i) The sentence must have O or C before a participle. (If there is no O or C, the word ending in **ing** after S-A-V will be a gerund)

(ii) The word concerned (i.e. the participle) must be the answer for the test question, "doing what"?

(iii) We must always use a participle after the verbs, SEE, HEAR, FEEL, SMELL, WATCH and FIND.

So far so good. You may ask, what good is a Participle to us in our day to day usage of the English language?

We use them as connectors in combining two Simple sentences. (Incidentally, what other methods have we learnt thus far, to connect two Simple sentences? Three methods - Complex sentence, Infinitive and Emphatic IT. Go through these Chapters once again to refresh your memory)

PARTICIPLES AS CONNECTORS

Broadly speaking, Participles fall under three varieties - Present, Past and Perfect Participles. All these are used to connect two Simple sentences

Present participle method

In this, we can follow any of the three different patterns:

(i) *Use of direct Present participle*

Take one of the verbs in its present form, convert it into a participle and use it in the sentence formula. Here are the examples:

(a)   I saw a pencil on the road. (b) I collected it.

Consider 'see' first. The present participle is, 'seeing'. The new sentence now is,

I   collected   a pencil   **seeing**   it   on the road.
S   (A) V   O   Parti   O   C

You may also start the sentence with the present participle like this,

Seeing   a pencil   on the road,   I   collected   it.
Parti   O   C   S   (A)V   O

(**Seeing** a pencil on the road, it was collected by me. (Passive voice)

There is no difference between the two sentences, which use **seeing**. But   suppose, we consider 'collect' for the connecting purpose. The present participle then will be, 'collecting'.

Collecting the pencil I saw it on the road.

or

I saw a pencil on the road collecting it.

In this example, the second sentence - I saw a pencil on the road collecting it - makes no sense at all. The first sentence sounds all right but the sequence of action has changed and as a result the new sentence doesn't reflect the meaning of the original sentences at all.

Now, we have two formulae for participle-based sentences:

1.   S- A- V- O or C - Participle - O/C
2.   Participle - O or C - S - A - V - O/C

Here are more examples:

(c) We heard the fire alarm at a distance. (d) We ran at top speed.

Hearing the fire alarm at a distance, we ran at top speed.

or,

We ran at top speed **hearing** the fire alarm at a distance.

(e) The student leader stood on the dais. (f) She displayed a beautiful painting.

Standing on the dais, the student leader displayed a beautiful painting.

The student leader displayed a beautiful painting **standing** on the dais.

In this case, the second participle also seems to work,

Displaying a colourful poster, the student leader stood on the dais.

The student leader stood on the dais **displaying** a colourful poster.

(g) I stopped suddenly. (h) I looked into the drain.

Stopping suddenly, I looked into the drain. I looked into the drain **stopping** suddenly.

The other participle fails when placed in the middle of the sentence, in that, the sequence of action has changed and as a result the overall meaning is not quite the same as in the original.

> **Looking** into the drain, I stopped suddenly.
>
> I stopped suddenly **looking** into the drain. ('Stopping' is the first action but the sentence gives the impression that 'looking' is the first action.)

In all the above examples, the doer of the action (Subject) is only one person. So, in most cases you can start the sentence with a suitable participle or put it in the middle so long as the sequence of the actions remains unaltered.

But if two different Subjects are in play you don't have the liberty of placing the participle where you like. Study the following examples:

(i) Moses stood under a tree. (j) I saw him.

Standing under a tree, I saw him.

This sentence creates a doubt about, who was standing under a tree, I or Moses? But if we put the participle in the center of the sentence, it makes the position clear.

I saw Moses **standing** under a tree.

If we make a participle out of the other verb (i.e. See), the sentence will convey no sensible meaning and the sequence will not be correct either.

Seeing Moses, I stood under a tree.
I stood under a tree seeing Moses.

So, what is the conclusion? When the doers of the action are two separate persons, use the selected participle in the center of the sentence. Here are more examples wherein the doers of the actions are two persons.

(k)   A woman was carrying her child in her arm. (l) I saw her.
      I saw a woman **carrying** her child in her arm.

(m)   Prasad was watching a strange sight. (n) A tree suddenly fell on a passerby.
      Prasad watched a tree **falling** on a passerby suddenly.

In the above 2 cases (k - n), if we start the sentence with the participle, the sentences will give no sensible meaning.

> Carrying her child in her arms I saw a woman.
> Falling on a passerby suddenly Prasad watched a tree.

When the doer of the actions is the same person, we can start the sentence with a present participle. (You could use the participle in the center also if the sequence of the actions do not get reversed). If you examine such sentences carefully, you will find the sentences following this pattern,

Pr Participle + Complement/Noun - S -A -V -O/C

In this kind of sentence structure we could make some modification.

Modified Direct present participle

(a) The principal took no notice of the complaint. (b) He didn't order any investigation.

Not taking any note of the complaint, the Principal didn't order any investigation.
     Parti   Noun

(c) He turned helpful all of a sudden. (d) The miser offered help to all and sundry.

Turning helpful all of a sudden, the miser offered help to all and sundry.
  Parti   Complement   S

(e)   The doctor became emotional suddenly. (f) He didn't charge that poor patient any fee at all.

Becoming emotional, the doctor didn't charge the poor patient any fee at all.
   Parti   adverb   S

Getting sorrowful, the young widow left the scene abruptly. [*suddenly*]
  Parti   Adv   S

Changing rational, the good old man gave donation for any cause.
   Parti   Adv

When an adverb (or complement) follows the participle, we can silence the participle and start the sentence with the adverb (complement) like this,

Helpful all of a sudden, the miser offered help to all and sundry.
adverb   C   S
(In the above sentence, we have silenced "Turning".)

Emotional, the doctor didn't charge any fee to the poor patient.
   adverb   S

Sorrowful, the young widow left the scene abruptly.
  adverb   S

Unmindful of her size,   she overate every day.
  adverb   compliment S

Beautiful, she would show a big nose to other maidens.
  adverb S

We could silence the participle only if it is followed by an adverb/complement. We cannot do so, if the participle is followed by a noun.

Next, you will notice that all the sentences in the above examples use normal verbs supported by appropriate auxiliaries. What will happen if one of them uses an A.V. Let us examine some cases:

(g) Peter is a good student. (h) All Lecturers love him.
(i) We are always available. (j) They should include us in the team.

The combined sentences will read like this,

All teachers **loving** him, Peter is a good student.
Including us in the team, we are always available.

The sentences make no sense whatever.

When there is an A.V in one sentence, we seem to run into difficulty because we see only one normal verb for conversion into a participle. And that verb has not proved a suitable connector at all.

If we could make a participle out of the A.V perhaps we may succeed. What is the participle form of "is" and "are"? It is BEING. (We know that AM, IS, ARE are equal to BE). But BEING cannot be used with similar ease. Accordingly we have to go in for the "Indirect present participle" method.

(ii) Use of Indirect present participle

In the Indirect present participle method, we start the combined sentence with BEING, followed by an <u>adverb</u> or <u>noun</u> like this:

(a) Sheila's performance has been disappointing. (b) The committee decided not to send her for the inter-college competition.

    Being disappointed with her performance, the committee decided not to
    Parti   adverb
send Sheila for the inter-college competition.

(c) The lady is childless. (d) She declines to attend any family function.

    Being childless, the lady declines to attend any family function.
          adverb

(e) We are Saroja's friends (f) Can't we talk to her any time?

    Being her friends, can't we talk to Saroja any time?
        Noun

(g) My friend and I are students of this college (h) We never talk against our teaching staffs.

    Being students (noun) of this college, we never ever talk against our teaching staffs.

(i) We are always available. (j) They should include us in the team.

Being always available (adverb), they should include us in the team.

(k) Peter is a good student. (l) All Lecturers love Peter.

Being a good student, all Lecturers love him.

It is permissible to start with a noun and put the participle plus adverb/noun after it like this:

(m) Roza is a fine actress (n) She accepts all kinds of roles.
Roza, **being a fine actress, (she)** accepts all kinds of roles.

(o) The sea is calm (p) Will you all come for a swim?
The sea **being calm** , will you all come for a swim?

(q) Pinky is not a bright student. (r) All staffs give special attention to her.
Not being a bright student, all staffs give Pinky special attention.
Pinky, **not being a bright student**, is given special attention by all the staffs.
(Passive voice)

(s) We are not always free. (t) The clients should not depend on us.
Not being free always, the clients should not depend on us.

(u) The old man is a furious person. (v) He won't tolerate evil people at all.
Being a furious person, the old man won't tolerate evil people at all.

We follow the "Being + Adverb/Noun" method only when one of the sentences has an Auxiliary cum verb (A.V) and the other sentence a normal verb. If both sentences have A.V, use BEING + Adverb/Noun in one and retain the other as it is. Study the following examples:

(i) Mohana is a naughty girl herself (ii) She has a naughty sister too.
Being naughty herself, Mohana has a naughty sister too.

(i) I am strict with my students. (ii) My students are very obedient.
Being strict with my students, they are obedient.

Note:

Connecting two sentences, that contain A.Vs may not be possible in every case.

(iii) *Participle with the preposition* ON

We can also use the **present participle** preceded by the preposition ON and followed by a *noun or noun of action* like this:

(a) **On seeing** a clearance sale advertisement, my mother rushed to the supermarket
      Parti   Noun   S
to buy as many things as possible.

(b) **On hearing** the sound of siren on the road, everybody made way for the VIP to pass.

(c) **On sighting** a strange object in the sky, everyone looked upwards to know what it was.

Thus, we can use the Present participle in three different ways.

Past participle method

One way of looking at the present participle method is, that we use it for 'on going action' or 'such actions that have not yet been completed'. (It does not matter in which time period that action is taking place; it could be in Past or Present time period)

What then about the activity that has been completed? This is where the **Past participle method** becomes useful. Study the following pair of sentences:

(a) The fabric and design charmed her. (b) My sister bought two sarees of the same variety. (Here, the actions refer to a past time period.)

Like before, we select the most suitable verb here also, convert it into its past participle form and use it as a connector:

Charmed by the fabric and design, my sister bought two sarees of the same variety.

We can put the past participle in the center also provided the sequence of action is not changed and the meaning of the sentences is maintained:

My sister bought two sarees of the same variety **charmed** by the fabric and design.

Here are the formulae for Past participle:

(i) **PP verb +** by **Noun** - S - A - V - O/C
(ii) S - A-V -O/C - **PP verb +** by Noun - O/C

(c) The intruder sat still. (d) He was taken by surprise.
Taken by surprise, the intruder sat still.
The intruder sat still <u>taken</u> by surprise.

(e) The police overpowered him. (f) The thief surrendered himself.
Overpowered by the police, the thief surrendered himself.

(g) A player kicked Surinder on his knee. (h) Surinder fell down with severe pain.
Kicked by a player, Surinder fell down with severe pain.
Surinder fell down with severe pain <u>kicked</u> by a player.

We need not start the sentence with a past participle. It could be some words away too as shown in the following examples:

(i) We completed the work quite fast. (j) We got ready to move.

The **work completed** quite fast by us, we got ready to move.
Noun   PP   C   S

(k)   We won the match. (l) We shook hands with the losing team.
The match **won**, we shook hands with the losing team.
        Noun   PP   S

Perfect participle method

(i) *Perfect participle method in Active voice form*

When two actions take place, we use one of the Present participle patterns to connect the two sentences. Sometimes this method may create some confusion, especially when one action finishes and the next follows. To make this situation very clear, we use the Perfect participle method.

Connect the following two sentences:

(a)   He read the instructions. (b) He broke open the emergency key box.
Reading the instructions, he broke open the emergency key box.

Doesn't the combined sentence give an impression that both actions are taking place simultaneously? Take the next example:

(c)   Robert removed his shirt. (d) He ran after the intruder.
Removing his shirt, Robert ran after the intruder.

Can't one think that Robert was running after the intruder and at the same time was in the process of removing his shirt? Therefore, shouldn't we indicate in the new sentence that the second action started only after the first one had ended? This would be possible when we use the Perfect participle method, like this:

Having read the instructions, he broke open the emergency key box.

Having removed his shirt, Robert ran after the intruder.

The formula for the use of Perfect participle is:

Having + PP verb - O - S - A -V - O/C

Here are more examples:
(e)   John finished eating his supper. (f) He drank 3 glasses of water.
Having finished his supper, John drank 3 glasses of water.

(g)   Mala had forgotten her friend's birthday. (h) She sent a greetings telegram to her.
Having forgotten her friend's birthday, Mala sent a greetings telegram to her.

(i)   Raman saw a snake on his path. (j) He took to his heels at once.
Having seen a snake on his path, Raman took to his heels at once.

(ii)   *Perfect participle method in Passive form*

(k)   He was not promoted. (l) Purushottam left the Company immediately.

Not having been promoted by the Company, Purushottam left the Company immediately.

(The organisation not having promoted him, Purushottam left the it immediately. - Active)

(m)   The selection committee rejected the Lecturer's case. (n) Mehta resolved to do better next time.

The Lecturer's case, **having been rejected** by the selection committee, Mehta resolved to do better next time.

(The selection committee having rejected the Lecturer's case, Mehta resolved to do better next time. - Active)

(o)   The aggrieved identified the culprit positively. (p) The culprit could not plead innocence.

Having been identified by the aggrieved positively, the culprit could not plead innocence.

(The aggrieved having identified the culprit positively, the culprit could not plead innocence. - Active)

Writing the 6 categories of sentences

*Given:*a1   :   Desiring a clarification, the journalist asked a difficult question.

a2   :   Desiring a clarification, the journalist didn't ask any questions. (Sounds meaningless !!)

Gen Q :   What did the journalist do desiring a clarification?

Sp Q   :   Desiring a clarification, did the journalist ask any questions?

Neg Q :   Desiring a clarification, didn't the journalist ask any questions?

EQ1   :   Desiring a clarification, the journalist asked a difficult question, didn't he?

EQ2   :   Desiring a clarification, the journalist didn't ask any questions, did he? (Sounds meaningless !!)

*Given:*EQ1 :   Caught at the neck, the poor kitten screamed like anything, didn't it?

a1   :   Caught at the neck, the poor kitten screamed like anything.

a2   :   Caught at the neck, the poor kitten didn't scream.

Gen Q :   Caught at the neck, what did the poor kitten do?

SpQ   :   Caught at the neck did the poor kitten do anything?

NegQ :   Caught at the neck, didn't the poor kitten scream like anything?

*Given:*NegQ: Having committed a great blunder, didn't your friend reform himself?

a1   :   Having committed a great blunder, my friend reformed himself.

a2   :   Having committed a great blunder, my friend refused to reform himself.

Gen Q :   Having committed a great blunder, what did your friend do?

SpQ   :   Having committed a great blunder, did your friend try to reform himself?

EQ1   :   Having committed a great blunder, your friend reformed himself, didn't he?

EQ2   :   Having committed a great blunder, your friend didn't reform himself, did he?

There should be no problem writing the various categories. As regards Gen Q, there may be some difficulty. At times it may turn out to be meaningless. And sometimes, a2 also may sound absurd.

Application of Participles in daily life

Any piece of writing such as, Articles, Reports, Essays, Stories etc, will usually have some 10 - 25 paragraphs; each paragraph may have 8 - 10 sentences. We have learnt so far only two types of sentences - Simple and Complex. If you write short and Simple sentences every time, they will look not only childish but also annoying to a reader. The participles enable you to convert two Simple sentences into one Simple sentence. You can look it from another angle: 2 Nos S-A-V would become 1 No S-A-V. Isn't this a miracle? (We saw earlier that an infinitive connector also produced a similar miracle.) Further, with a participle in your sentences, they would look stylish and sophisticated.

You have learnt in this Chapter, 5 different methods of using participles as connectors. When confronted with the task of combining any two Simple sentences (or any two Simple sentence **ideas**), see which participle method will be successful. In some cases, combining would be possible through more than one method. Another doubt you may develop is whether every pair of sentences in any tense combinations, could be combined through participles? Here is a practice exercise. Verify it yourself.

Practice cum Test exercise

1. Ravindran is a good student. He sits next to me in my class.
2. I am your Senior. Obey me always.
3. We are your students. We aren't that Department's students.
4. Isn't Shardha a clever engineering student? Isn't she studying well in the Third Semester?
5. We were nice to the primary class kids. They were scared of us, college students.
6. My performance was better than yours. The HOD said so.
7. Don't challenge any student in the next door Science college. They are rough with anyone.
8. Meena writes well. She hardly makes any grammatical mistakes in English.
9. You have been good in the Fourth Semester. Continue to do well in your next four also.
10. We are playing a match this evening. Call everyone to witness it.
11. Haven't we come a long way till now? Isn't it time to return to our base?
12. We have been working on these sums for a long time. Yet, we don't get them right at all.
13. You did not draw this painting. Your sister did it.
14. We worked very hard for our finals. But somehow we didn't do well.

15. Hadn't we seen this video CD before? Who then had brought it for a second time?

16. We had been practising table tennis for over 2 months. We might win this time.

17. Can you count the students in the hall? There are far too many.

18. I could not have attended class yesterday. I had a severe headache.

19. We would certainly have helped you. Why didn't you ask for our help?

20. We shall go on our picnic this Sunday. All of you will join us.

21. The lady students won't come on our picnic. Their parents wouldn't allow them.

22. We will have finished our exams by December. You may come after December.

23. Will you have been living with your grand parents? Your grandparents are fine people.

24. Wasn't he practising high jump till late evening? John is a keen sportsman.

25. Samuel has left this college. He hasn't felt sorry about it.

The above 25 sentences cover all the 16 tenses. Select a suitable participle to connect the pair of sentences so as to maintain the original meaning. After completing this trial exercise, you ought to come to some conclusions and inferences. What are they? Check your answers with the ones given at the end.

Conversion of Complex sentences

If a Complex sentence is given to you for conversion into a Simple sentence, initially break up the Complex into two Simple sentences and then proceed with the connecting.

Here are some examples:

(a) Before the football teams entered the field, they bowed down to say their prayers. (1. The teams bowed down to say their prayers. 2. They entered the field.)
   Having said their prayers, the football teams entered the field.

(b) The child is weeping because the mother has left it behind in the house. (1. The child is weeping. 2. The mother has left it behind in the house.)
   The mother has left the child behind in the house **letting** it weep.
   Or,
   Leaving the child behind to weep, the mother has left the house.

(c) Didn't the surgeon explain to you that the operation would take 2 hours? (Didn't the surgeon explain to you? The operation would take 2 hours?)
        ?   ?   ?   ?
   The operation time being 2 hours, didn't the surgeon explain that to you? (The sentence is grammatically correct, but meaningless, isn't it?)

Writing Participle based sentences directly

It is not necessary that you should initially think of 2 Simple sentences and then combine them into a single sentence in one of the participle methods. One could straightway write a participle-based sentence also. Here are some, taken from newspapers and magazines:.

(a)   Following the instructions of the PM, the Minister concerned issued suitable orders on the subject.

(b)   Admitting that the evidence could be correct, the magistrate proceeded with the case.

(c)   Citing six more witnesses in the report, the prosecution sought the court's permission to examine them.

(d)   Replying to his queries, the Special Public Prosecutor told the judge that the prosecution would clarify the same. (Complex sentence)

(e)   Having held discussion in-house, the Deputy Commissioner of police issued suitable instructions for protecting all the statues with cages.

(f)   Not satisfied with the Minister's reply, the members demanded an announcement of allocation of Rs 50 lakhs for each MLA. (PP verb + with)

(g)   Having inaugurated the function, the Minister proceeded with his speech.

(h)   Having been defeated twice in the Local elections, Vincent George hesitated to file his nomination again.

(i)   Having <u>been</u> his own boss for a long time, this politician found it hard to
                PP verb

take orders from others.

(j)   Woken by the sound of a heavy crash, he jumped to his feet.

Here is a variation. Examine the method carefully:

(k)   Convinced that his enemies were trying to poison him, the military dictator refused to eat anything on his own from his own dining table.

(l)   Expecting that someone would ring him up, he stayed on in the house till evening.

(m)   Believing that she is alone, the innocent girl talked loudly about her boyfriend.
        Pr parti conj S A.V adv   S (A)V   adv   O

(n)   Believing that he was a wizard, this student accepted any challenges thrown at him including physical bouts.

Sentences (k) to (n) are Complex sentences wherein one of the Simples starts with a present participle. The Noun or Adverb following the Present participle could be expanded into S-A-V-O/C form.

Starting a sentence with a Present participle appears to be the most popular method followed by the journalists. Look for such sentences in the newspapers.

Summary and Conclusion

Through participles, we can connect two Simple sentences in most cases. In some, we may fail because the meaning in the new sentence might look distorted or may not be the same as in the original.

The participle part has no tense (time element) of its own. The tense of the new sentence is derived from the S-A-V part.

For 'on going actions' or for 'actions not yet completed', use present participles. It doesn't matter if the action is taking place in the present time period or past time period.

For 'action completed' cases, use past participles.

When you want to stress that one action had finished before the next action started, go in for perfect participles. Use Active or Passive voice whichever is suitable in the new sentence.

Given one participle based sentence, you could write the remaining 6 categories; you my not be able to write the "General question" category in some cases.

With this Chapter, you have learnt 4 different methods of connecting any two Simple sentences, viz, Complex sentence, Infinitive connector, Emphatic IT and Participle methods. Of these, the versatile methods are two i.e. Complex and Emphatic IT.

Now that you have learnt Participle in full detail, the formula for a simple sentence stands updated as follows. And this is the final formula as well:

S-A-V-O/C - infinitive - O/C - Participle - O/C

or

Participle - S-A-V-O/C - infinitive - O/C

Thus, a Simple sentence (a1, a2, Specific Q, Negative Q) can have a maximum of 6 parts and a General Q, upto a maximum of 7 parts. O and C can appear in any combination but we count O and C as one part.

Answers for the Practice cum Test exercise:

1. Being a good student, Ravindran sits next to me in my class.
2. Being your senior, obey me always.
3. Not being that Department's students, we are your students.
   (Meaning distorted though the sentence is grammatically correct)
4. Being a clever engineering student, isn't Sharda studying well in 3rd Semester?
5. On being nice to the primary class kids, they were scared of us.
   (The new sentence is grammatically correct, but it does not reflect the original meanings)
6. My performance being better than yours, the HOD said so. (Meaning mutilated)
7. Students of the next Science college being rough with any one, don't challenge any of them.
8. Writing well, Meena hardly makes any grammatical mistakes in English.
9. Having been good in Semester 4, continue to do well in the next four also.
10. Call everyone to witness the match being played by us this evening.
11. Having come a long way till now, isn't it time to return to our base?

12. Working on these sums for a long time, we don't get them right at all.
    (Meaning distorted)
13. Not having drawn this painting yourself, your sister did it.
    (Meaning completely mutilated)
14. Having worked hard for our finals, we didn't do well in the exam.
15. This video CD having been seen by us before, it had been brought by who for a second time?
16. Having practised table tennis for over 2 months, we might win this time.
    ("Having been practising table .." doesn't sound well, hence changed over to the perfect participle method to indicate that one action follows another.)
17. The students being too many, can you count them in the hall?
18. Having had a severe headache, I could not have attended class yesterday.
    (or, Suffering from a severe headache, I couldn't have attended class yesterday)
19. Connection not possible.
20. Going on a picnic this Sunday, all of you will join us.
    (Meaning mutilated)
21. Not having been allowed by their parents, the girls won't come on our picnic.
22. Combining by participle method is not possible.
23. Your grandparents being fine people, will you have been living with them?
    (Sentence is meaningless)
24. Having practised high jump till late evening, John is a keen sportsman.
    (Past continuous tense is used for a completed activity. Hence, using perfect participle is in order.)
25. Having left this college, Samuel hasn't felt sorry about it.

Conclusions and inferences

(a) It is not possible to combine through participle methods every pair of sentences. The participle method has only a limited use.

(b) Participle methods are applicable only for present and past actions. Therefore, we cannot apply this for any type of Future tense sentences including FIPs. No.19 & 22 come under this rule. In the Future type cases, the combined sentences may not convey any sensible meaning.

(c) In certain cases of the Present and Past varieties too, though by rule we may combine the sentences, the meaning could get mutilated.

Exercise

Identify the participle in the following sentences and state what type it is:

1. I saw a pencil lying on the floor.
2. Hearing the college hooter, we rushed to reach the college gate.
3. A stranger rushed into my compound knocking on the front door.
4. Being beautiful, this girl thinks no end of herself in our class.
5. Attracted by the light, hundreds of insects fell inside the shade.

6. Impressed at the roadside paintings, the foreign tourist purchased a dozen of them.
7. Having rested for some ten minutes, the students resumed their trek.
8. Being motherless, the kind father gave his small son all kinds of privileges.
9. Curious, I opened the parcel with tremendous expectation.
10. Being a good singer, Malati sang dozens of songs.

Combine the following pairs of sentences using any suitable type of participle:

11. I listen to small complaints from my students. Sometime I feel tired of it all.
12. His father encouraged him. So, Samuel studied harder to come first in the class.
13. Little Dennis took out his catapult. He went on a hunting mission behind his house.
14. The Lecturer closed the book. He handed it over to the owner.
15. Mona helped me. I solved all the problems easily.
16. Sundar lost a lot of money in the exhibition. He stopped playing 'lucky dip'.
17. I don't eat chocolates. How can I tell which one is good?
18. The Professor had already entered the class. I sneaked in through the back door.
19. I did not know the location of the auditorium in our college. So, I sought someone's guidance.
20. Suresh completed his homework. Then he went out to play with his friends.
21. I am not a bad guy at all. Why do most of my classmates avoid me?
22. I felt sorry for the young lady student. I offered to carry her heavy bag.
23. I didn't hear the Lecturer's question. So, I gave a vague answer.
24. Mohammed is a good Muslim boy. I have a soft corner for him in my heart.
25. Shiva is a born leader. He is however, a lazy fellow.

Combine the following pairs in as many methods as feasible. (i.e, Complex, Infinitive, Emphatic IT and Participle)

26. Our class leader did not tell the real truth. He is a very protective person.
27. Ponraj doesn't drink milk. He always criticises the milk drinkers.
28. We were late for class that morning. The HOD summoned us into his office.
29. Some of us have been taking English seriously. It is not at all a difficult language.
30. Sunita is not feeling well today. She may not be able to go to college today.

Convert the following Complex sentences into one **Simple** sentence through any method and where possible:

31. When I leave college, the time is usually 4.30 p.m.
32. Martha isn't a clever student but she helps her mother in the kitchen routinely.
33. After my friend gave me her notebook, I copied the lesson notes.
34. Unless you score high marks, you will never get a seat in the B.Com course.
35. Though it is only 5.30 a.m. the sky is bright and shiny.

Convert the following Complex sentences into Participle based Simple sentences:

36. It is my friend who made these small cakes.
37. It was during the football match that I saw my village friend.
38. It is because of my habit of drinking coffee every morning that I have a bad stomach today.

39. Is it because of his poor marks, that he has been denied admission in this college?

40. Will it be on account of my lethargy that you shall punish me with imposition?

Convert the following infinitive connector based Simple sentences into Participle based Simple sentences: (Tip: First convert each into two Simple sentences)

41. He is slow to understand others.

42. My aged uncle has two young girls to provide for.

43. This old woman visits the sick people in the general hospital to show her love for them.

44. My small brother hates to get up from bed every morning.

45. I am not afraid to walk on dark roads at night.

Write the remaining 6 categories of sentences:

46. My name, having been struck out of the residential list, did not appear in any other.

47. Curious, I opened the registered letter with some misgivings.

48. Appreciating my efforts, the coach agreed to teach my method to all the players.

49. Angered by the statement, Robert pounced on a classmate.

50. Having seen better movies, I cannot appreciate this one.

Analyse the following sentences:

51. Having been disappointed by my marks, my father refused to allow me to join a self financing engineering college.

52. We see this little boy distributing the morning newspaper to the colony residents.

53. Disturbed by his son's low marks, the father took him to task.

54. He, being my student, seldom loses his temper.

55. Can we go home hauling this punctured cycle?

The following sentences have used gerunds. Identify the gerund in each sentence and use it as participle in your own sentences:

56. My jumping was terrible.

57. She does not see the writing on the wall.

58. I don't approve of your correcting my English.

59. Didn't I see his returning home late?

60. I could go jogging any time of the day.

Chapter 37

PERFECT INFINITIVES

Definition

What you had learnt in Chapter 24 could be called **Present infinitives.**

It is permissible to use the present infinitives in a modified form known as **Perfect infinitives**. We obtain a perfect infinitive by adding the auxiliary **have** and changing the verb into a **past participle** like this,

Present infinitive - to write, to run, to beat.
Perfect infinitive - to have written, to have run, to have beaten.

PAST IN THE PRESENT TENSE (Tense No. 17)

We can write *most* of the present infinitives in perfect infinitive form in any sentence without any change in its meaning. But when so done, something would seem to happen in that sentence. Study the following examples:

(a) Mona is very <u>happy</u> **to meet** my sister. (present infinitive)
(aa) Mona is very <u>happy</u> **to have met** my sister. (perfect infinitive)

(b) These students from the next class are very <u>nice</u> **to be** friendly with (present)
(bb) These students from the next class are very <u>nice</u> **to have been** friendly with.

(c) I am <u>proud</u> **to study** in this college.
(cc) I am <u>proud</u> **to have studied** in this college.

(d) The Director is <u>pleased</u> **to give** you a seat in this college.
(dd) The Director is <u>pleased</u> **to have given** you a seat in this class.

(e) My elder brother is <u>sorry</u> **to hear** about your mother's illness.
(ee) My elder brother is <u>sorry</u> **to have heard** about your mother's illness.

(f) We are <u>fortunate</u> **to win** yesterday's football match.
(ff) We are <u>fortunate</u> **to have won** yesterday's football match.

We can notice the following points in the above examples:

1. The meaning is not changed when converted into the perfect infinitive form but there is an **appearance** of a "tense" in the perfect infinitive part; this part looks like a past time case while the S-A-V part is in present time. Thus, two time periods seem to be in play in the sentence when put in the perfect infinitive form. Can't we then call it a **Past in the present tense**? This is our 17th tense.

2. The S-A-V part of all the sentences is in the Present tense and bears the pattern,

S - A.V - Adverb - Perfect infinitive - O/C

3. The auxiliary cum verbs (A.Vs) used are only AM, IS, ARE.

4. The adverbs used are, HAPPY, NICE, PROUD, PLEASED, SORRY, FORTUNATE. (Adverbs of **manner / quality**)

Can we use any other adverbs? Let us write and see:

(g)   Pratap is <u>mad</u> **to play** football in the rain.
(gg) Pratap is <u>mad</u> **to have played** football in the rain.

(hh) Mala isn't <u>delighted</u> **to have scolded** you.

(ii) Paul is <u>foolish</u> **to have said** such things about you.

(jj) We are <u>here</u> **to have rested** for an hour.

(kk) Midday is not the ideal <u>time</u> **to have eaten** one's breakfast.

(ll) I am <u>in the middle of a meeting</u> **to have met** any visitors.

Sentences from (gg) to (ii) sound meaningful all right. But the ones from (jj) to (ll) are meaningless. So, what is the conclusion?

It is this: If the adverb used before the infinitive is of MANNER/QUALITY, (the adverb that is the answer to the test question HOW) the perfect infinitive based sentences would be meaningful showing the action concerned in two time periods. If the word is adverb of time or place (TQ: WHEN and WHERE), the perfect infinitive based sentence will convey no sensible meaning.

The acceptable adverbs are, HAPPY, NICE, PROUD, PLEASED, SORRY, FORTUNATE or their synonyms like FOOLISH, BUSY, UNHAPPY, MAD etc. What is important is that the adverb must answer only the test question HOW and not WHEN, WHERE , WHY.

Other tenses in the Present family

Next, let us examine sentences with the S-A-V part in Simple present, Present emphatics and Present perfect tenses.

Simple present

(a)   Immanual *doesn't like* **to eat** bananas in the mornings. (Present infinitive)
(aa) Immanual *doesn't like* **to have eaten** bananas in the mornings. (Perfect infin)

(b)   Every student *cannot expect* **to stand** first in the class.
(bb) Every student *cannot expect* **to have stood** first in the class.

(c)   *Can* you *hope* **to run** 1KM in one minute?
(cc) *Can* you *hope* **to have run** 1KM in one minute?

(d)   Krishnan *hates* **to befriend** the young woman next door.
(dd) Krishnan *hates* **to have befriended** the young woman next door.

(e)   My HOD *would love* **to attend** everyone's birthday party.
(ee) My HOD *would love* **to have attended** everyone's birthday party.

Here, the perfect infinitive based sentences sound meaningful all right and also display the action in two time periods. Next, if you examine these Simple present sentences carefully, you will notice that the entire present infinitive part constitutes the object of the sentence. Apply the Noun test and verify. They are of the pattern,

S - A - V - O (infinitive part)

We can look at them in another way also: the present form verbs used are such that they would always lead to an object. Such Simple present sentences in the perfect infinitive form will show two time periods and will be meaningful too.

Let us see what happens if the *present infinitive part* is a **complement.** Study the following sentences:

1.   Meenakshi *comes* to my house **to check** her answers with me.
1a.   Meenakshi *comes* to my house **to have checked** her answers with me.
2.   The bully in my class *fights* with us **to extract out** some gift from us.
2a.   The bully in my class *fights* with us **to have extracted out** some gift from us.
3.   Sugirtha *goes* for music classes **to please** her mother.
3a.   Sugirtha *goes* for music classes **to have pleased** her mother.
4.   We *must keep thanking* God **to glorify** His name.
4a.   We *must keep thanking* God **to have glorified** His name.

Are 1a - 4a, which are in perfect infinitive form, meaningful? No. So, Perfect infinitive form is a failure here.

In the sentences from 1 to 4, the present infinitive part answers the test question WHY, hence, that part is a complement. But do you see that this part answers the test question FOR WHAT also in addition? So what exactly is it? Complement or Object? It could be either. So, we may classify this variety as 'doubtful cases'.

This leads us to the conclusion that if a Simple present, present infinitive based sentence answers the noun test and also the complement test, we cannot put them in the perfect infinitive form at all. But if the present infinitive part passes only the object test, we can convert such a sentence into perfect infinitive form.

It is the same as saying that if we can put the infinitive part into "Perfect infinitive form" that part will be the Object of the sentence.

Thus, the perfect infinitive-conversion method appears to be an useful tool to identify whether a group of words after the S-A-V part in a sentence is truly an object or complement. Some group of words would indeed respond to the object test and also complement test. If you put such sentences in the perfect infinitive form and they look meaningful, then that group is truly an object.

The present infinitive part will be an object when the verb used in the S-A-V part is one out of LIKE, EXPECT, HOPE, HATE or LOVE and their synonyms.

Present continuous tense

(a)   Sasi *is learning* cooking **to impress** the other girls.
(aa) Sasi *is learning* cooking **to have impressed** the other girls.
(b)   Moses *is studying* hard **to stand** first in the class.
(bb) Moses *is studying* hard **to have stood** first in the class.
(c)   Murugan *is selling* vegetables in his spare time **to augment** his family income.
(cc) Murugan *is selling* vegetables in his spare time **to have augmented** his family income.

Do the perfect infinitive based sentences convey any meaning? No. Therefore this tense is also unfit for conversion into the perfect infinitive form.

Present emphatics

(a)   I *am not* **to meet** you again.
(aa) I *am not* **to have met** you again.

(b)   The candidate *is* **to report** for duty today.
(ab) The candidate *is* **to have reported** for duty today.

(c)   Martina *has* **to complete** her Essay by 4 p.m.
(ac) Martina *has* **to have completed** her Essay by 4 p.m.

The perfect infinitive based sentences here are meaningful all right. The two -time period (Past in the present tense) concept also succeeds here.

Present perfect tense

Next, shall we see whether the "Past in the present tense" works with the Present perfect tense? Here are the sentences:

(a)   The First year Civil Engineering class *have postponed* the declamation contest just **to annoy** us.
(aa) The First year Civil Engineering class *have postponed* the declamation contest just **to have annoyed** us.
(b)   Daniel *has put* too much salt in all the dishes **to spoil** our mood.
(ab) Daniel *has put* too much of salt in all the dishes **to have spoilt** our mood.
(c)   The Second year lady students *have been learning* karate **to challenge** us men students one day.
(cc) The Second year lady students *have been learning* karate **to have challenged** us men students one day.

The above sentences in perfect infinitive form also don't give us any sensible meaning. Therefore, the present perfect tense including the continuous tense are unfit for the 'Past in the present tense.'

Rules for PAST IN THE PRESENT TENSE (Active voice)

Having examined all kinds of sentences in the present family, we can now summarise the rules. When the present infinitive form is converted into perfect infinitive form, sentences of the following tenses will turn into the **Past in the present tense**:

(i) Present tense sentences of the pattern,
S - A.V - Adverb - infinitive - O/C
The A.Vs to be only AM, IS, ARE. The adverb must be adverb of manner/quality only.

(ii) Simple present sentences.
The condition is that the entire present infinitive part must be the object and pass **only** the object test.

(iii) Any present emphatic sentences. (with AM, IS, ARE, HAS or HAVE)

PAST IN THE PRESENT CONTINUOUS TENSE (Tense No.18)

We can write all the sentences of the 'Past in the present tense' in the continuous form when we want to give importance for the duration of the action observing the following infinitive pattern:

Perfect infinitive	Perfect infinitive continuous
To have loved	To have been loving
To have written	To have been writing
To have taken	To have been taking

Here are the model sentences:

(a) I am proud **to have been studying** in this college.
(b) Some of us are fortunate **to have been receiving** concession in fee in this college.
(c) All students cannot hope **to have been playing** in the A team.
(d) Manian hates **to have been spending** his money on anything.
(e) Tony has **to have been completing** his B.Sc by now.
(f) Can you hope **to have been counting** the sand on a beach?

PAST IN THE PRESENT (Passive voice)

The passive form of the perfect infinitive will be:

Active	Passive
To have loved	To have been loved
To have sent	To have been sent
To have written	To have been written

We shall cover the Passive voice form in two stages. In the first, we put only the perfect infinitive part in passive voice and retain the S-A-V part untouched.

(i) *'Perfect infinitive part' only in Passive voice*

    (a)   Your customer is not **to have met** me at all. (Active)

    (aa)   Your customer is not **to have been met** by me at all. (Passive)

    (bb)   You are **to have been warned** by the Electronic Lab Demonstrator.

    (cc)   My small sister would love **to have been taught** dancing by this master.

    (dd)   Sriram does not need **to have been manhandled** by you.

    (ee)   It is nice **to have been met** by my stern uncle.

The sentences are meaningful all right. (A note of warning here: Don't write the perfect infinitive in Active form initially and then convert into Passive. You may not be successful in every case. However, you can write a passive-perfect infinitive form straightway.)

(ii) *The S-A-V part only in Passive voice*

Here, we keep the perfect infinitive part untouched.

    (aa)   The crowd is *reported* **to have gone** unruly after the leader's speech.

    (bb)   The English Lecturer is *said* **to have assessed** every student harshly.

    (cc)   All students are *expected* **to have come fully prepared** for a test.

    (dd)   Isn't the shopkeeper at the gate *known* **to have been fleecing** the students?

    (ee)   All the lady students of the Third semester *are believed* **to have passed** in 1st Division.

The first part of the sentence has been written in Passive voice directly, having omitted the "by" part. The verbs used in the S-A-V part are, REPORTED, SAID, EXPECTED, SUPPOSED, KNOWN and BELIEVED in their PP form. Although any suitable PP verbs could be used, the above are the commonly used verbs.

You will see many sentences of this variety in the Newspapers, for some special reasons. We shall see the reasons why for such sentences, a little later.

(iii) *Both parts in Passive voice*

Here are the examples:

    (aa)   Some spectators are *reported* **to have been beaten up** by rowdy elements.

    (bb)   The Question paper is *said* **to have been leaked out** by the office staff.

    (cc) Some students are *said* **to have been reprimanded** by the HOD.

The sentence patterns at (ii) and (iii) do reflect two-time periods, besides being completely meaningful. You can choose either of them for your sentence constructions.

PAST IN THE PAST TENSE

Study the following examples:

(a)   The burglars *were* **to attack** our house last night. (Pr. infi)

(aa) The burglars *were* **to have attacked** our house last night. (Pfct. infin)

(b)   My uncle *was* **to visit** me in the hostel yesterday. (Pr. infin)

(bb) My uncle *was* **to have visited** me in the hostel yesterday. (Pfct. Infin)

(c)   The relatives *had* **to obtain** permission for the visit. (Pr. infin)

(cc) The relatives *had* **to have obtained** permission for the visit. (Pfct infin).

The above sentences are in "Past emphatics". We could write meaningful perfect infinitive based sentences in Past tense and Simple past tense also. Here are some examples:

(d)   James *was* very happy **to meet** me last Sunday. (Pr. infin)

(dd) James *was* very happy **to have met me** last Sunday. (Pfct. infin)

(e)   Paul *didn't like* **to drink** milk at the dining table. (Pr. infin)

(ee) Paul *didn't like* **to have drunk** milk at the dining table. (Pfct. Infin)

"Past in the Past" perfect infinitive sentences could be written in (i) Past, (ii) Simple past and (iii) Past emphatics only, as in the case of "Past in the Present." All such sentences could be converted into Passive voice as well.

But, the time period involved here is only ONE - Past. Hence, we cannot treat this as a separate **tense** and club it with the Past family.

USES OF PERFECT INFINITIVE

There are two main advantages in the Perfect infinitive form.

1. The meaning of a sentence that contains a **present** infinitive, is not changed when converted into the **perfect** infinitive form. But, the perfect infinitive form sounds non-committal in essence. Take for instance the sentence,

(a)   The crowd is reported to have gone unruly after the leader's speech.

Compare this with the construction,

(b)   The crowd has gone unruly after the leader's speech.

Do you spot out an element of uncertainty in the sentence at (a)? Also, doesn't it sound as though the information was obtained from a third party and the writer himself has not witnessed the unruly behaviour?

Whereas in (b), the information sounds definite and authentic and also implies that the writer has witnessed the incident himself/herself.

The construction in (a) is essentially a journalist's language; he doesn't want to commit himself about the veracity of the news item. The journalist phrases the sentence as though it is a <u>hearsay</u> information in order to protect himself.

knp. hear but don't kno to be true.

Alternately, when **you** are not sure about a piece of information, you may resort to the perfect infinitive method because it is absolutely non-committal. You have made it clear that you are not sure whether the information so stated is correct or not. Next, we use the perfect infinitive form only for actions that took place in the past time period.

2. In Chapter 32 (Active or Passive?), we learnt that Active voice is direct, order-like and nearly rude. Whereas, Passive voice is polite. But here we note that one can be polite in Active voice also through the perfect infinitive form. Examine the following sentences:

(a)   I am not to keep company with you again.

(aa) I am not to have kept company with you again. (A)

(b)   Sundar is sure to apologise to you.

(ab) Sundar is sure to have apologised to you. (A)

(c)   Our Professor doesn't expect to see you in his house.

(cc) Our Professor doesn't expect to have seen you in his house. (A)

(d)   Never make false statements.

(dd) You are not to have made any false statements (A)

(e)   Walk in any time.

(ee) You are to have walked in any time. (A)

(f)   Many students grumble at the frequent examinations.

(ff) Many students are not to have grumbled at the frequent examinations. (A)

The perfect infinitive form, although in Active voice, does sound polite, doesn't it? Or, the same information has been conveyed in a round about and diplomatic way?

Writing the remaining 6 categories

Given a1: These students are to have submitted their assignments some days back.

a2   : These students are not to have submitted their assignments so late.

Gen Q   : When are these students to have submitted their assignments?

Sp Q   : Are these students to have submitted their assignments some days back?

Neg Q   : Aren't these students to have submitted their assignments some days back?

EQ1   : These students are to have submitted their assignments some days back, aren't they?

EQ2   : These students are not to have submitted their assignments so late, are they?

Given a2: James hates to have done any harm to others.

a1   : James loves to have done good to others.

Gen Q   : What does James love to have done?

Sp Q   : Does James love to have done harm to others?

Neg Q : Doesn't James love to have done good to others?
EQ 1   : James loves to have done good to others, doesn't he?
EQ 2   : James doesn't love to have done harm to others, does he?
Given
Neg Q : Aren't we to have reported for work by 9 a.m.?

Gen Q : When are we to have reported for work?
Sp Q   : Are we to have reported for work by 9 a.m.
a1   : We are to have reported for work by 9 a.m.
a2   : We are not to have reported for work after 9 a.m.
EQ 1   : We are to have reported for work by 9 a.m. aren't we?
EQ 2   : We are not to have reported for work after 9 a.m. are we?

Exercise

Write the following present-infinitive sentences into perfect-infinitive sentences in active voice:

1. Monica is sad to say good-bye to her lifelong friend.
2. Aren't you sorry to learn the truth?
3. Lawrence entertains his friends often to ensure their friendship.
4. Reena was to memorise Psalm 23 that Sunday.
5. Swarna has to hand over her essay by this evening.
6. The office clerks have to appear for an interview.
7. My uncle is here to talk with you.
8. Isn't Samuel a lucky guy to get your friendship?
9. Does he hope to meet you before departure?
10. My daughter expects me to give her more pocket money.

Convert the following into passive form:

11. All of us have to have written our entrance exam paper today.
12. I am to have coached you in Mathematics today.
13. The doctor is to have examined all the students on dental hygiene by 12 noon today.
14. You are to have purchased the new English text book this morning, aren't you?
15. The hostel students are to have vacated their dormitory by noon.
16. Sangita hasn't to have given a gift to every participant.
17. Your father was to have deposited your school fees by September.
18. Majority of our classmates hope to have secured more than 80% marks in all papers.
19. The boys from the next school had to have given their acceptance immediately.
20. The girl students were to have attended the rehearsal yesterday as well.

Write the following second hand information in a non-committal way:

21. Kathy has run away from home.
22. Krishnan has failed in Std XI.

23. The accident took place because the driver was sleepy at that moment.
24. The Correspondent had approved the appointment of two more teachers for our school.
25. We lost our football match because of our goalkeeper's carelessness.

The following infinitive-based sentences cannot be put in perfect infinitive form. Give the reason(s) why:

26. The teacher reaches my house to give me tuition in English.
27. Some boys fight with my group to score a point over us.
28. My servant maid's children work hard to increase the family's income.
29. Meenakshi learns violin to please her mother.
30. Go to the Headmaster to receive your report card.

The following sentences give vague and uncertain information. Modify them so as to convey a definite information.

31. Radha's pet cat is reported to have fallen into a well in her house.
32. This boy is said to have been roughed up by a bully in his area.
33. The girls in our class are expected to have not gone on the school picnic.
34. Aren't you known to have been copying in every examination?
35. This peon is believed to have pushed some students out of the classroom.

Convert the following sentence into Active voice:

36. You are not to have been taken out of the hospital by your parents.
37. This medicine hasn't to have been consumed by you.
38. The balance amount was to have been returned to you by the bus conductor.
39. The librarian is to have been met by you before the closing time.
40. Small children would love to have been invited by their grandparent for birthday parties.

Fill up the blanks with the correct form of infinitive:

41. We are bound *to reach* New Delhi by 7 a.m. tomorrow.
42. My uncle was . . . . met by me before he departed for Muscat.
43. I would love . . . . . *to be* . . . seen this movie before others.
44. The reporter is . . . . been scolded by the newspaper editor.
45. This girl is . . . . treated for cancer by a senior doctor.
46. We are . . . . taking part in the next field event.
47. You have . . . . looked after your small sister during your mother's absence, haven't you?
48 Wouldn't you like someone . . . . brought all your meals right to your bed when you were ill?
49 Isn't this information too good . . . . true?
50. I went to the station . . . . my father who was returning from Bangalore.

Modify the following statements as 'doubtful / uncertain' information:

51. We witnessed the accident ourselves.
52. You had stood in the sun for two hours, hadn't you?
53. My brother has never met you before anywhere.
54. All the Nuns in our college are not highly qualified teachers.
55. Very few nurses in this hospitals are impolite to patients.

Write the remaining 6 categories:

56. Can you hope to have run 100 meters in 7 seconds?
57. Lisa comes to my house to have learnt Mathematics.
58. We are not to have attended your coaching classes.
59. Rozario hates to have been spending his money on anything.
60. The English Lecturer is said to have corrected our papers rather harshly.

Chapter 38

MORE ABOUT ADJECTIVES

Introduction

In Chapter 7, you had learnt about Adjectives and their 3 degrees. When we have to compare two persons or more, we cannot do it without using the comparative and superlative degrees.

In this Chapter we shall see how adjectives are used in several other ways.

Emphatic comparatives

Ordinary comparison just brings out the difference between two qualities. We can highlight this difference in a very powerful way by using the words MORE, MUCH, LESS, ANY and NO as shown in the following examples. We call such statements that contain adjectives, **Emphatic comparatives:**

1. My daughter Martina is a more attractive girl than yours (is).
    (a) My daughter Martina is NO LESS an attractive girl than yours (is).
    (b) Your daughter is NO MORE an attractive girl than my Martina (is).

2. Your sister was a less prominent actress in yesterday's drama than my sister was.
    (a) Your sister was NO MORE a prominent actress in yesterday's drama than my sister (was).
    (b) My sister was NO LESS a prominent actress in yesterday's drama than your sister (was).

3. Did Arjun give a better performance than Govinda (gave) in that film?
    (a) Did Arjun give ANY LESS a performance than Govinda (gave) in that film?
    (b) Did Govinda give ANY BETTER (MORE) a performance than Arjun? (did)

4. Didn't Sudha write a better essay than Manohar? (did)
    (a) Did Manohar write ANY BETTER an essay than Sudha? (did)
    (b) Didn't Sudha write a MUCH BETTER essay than Manohar? (did)

5. Arun collected MUCH LESS money this time than last year, didn't he?
6. Isn't Manian a LESS wealthy man than Krishnan? (is)
7. Krishnan is NO MORE a wealthy man than Manian. (is)
8. Were the children ANY LESS happy boarders in the hostel this year than last year?
9. They were NO MORE happy boarders last year than this year.
10. This water melon is NO LESS a sweet fruit than yours. (is)
11. Isn't Mrs. Moses a LESS wealthy woman than we all thought her to be?

All the above are very powerful sentences (Emphatic comparatives), when used with ANY and NO in Questions and MORE and MUCH in Answers.

Examine the sentences in 10 and 11. The normal comparatives here are, "sweeter" and "wealthier". But when used in the form, NO LESS SWEET and LESS WEALTHY, the sentences do sound quite forceful.

Other forms of emphatic comparatives:

"The more the better."
"The bigger the better."
"The earlier the better."
"The less the better."

Have you noticed that the S-A-V part is absent in the above expressions? The reason is that they are not self contained Simple sentences. We use these as a follow-up of another sentence like this,

(a)   You should go in only for the big money; **the bigger, the better.**
(b)   Gather more volunteers; **the more, the better.**
(c)   Don't delay. Reach the station early; **the earlier, the better.**

The words become emphatic comparatives only when they are preceded by the definite article "the". Omission of "the" will be incorrect.

While in the above cases, "better" is the common word, we may also use other comparatives. When so used, the sentences will be Complex sentences with silent conjunctions and yet the sentence must comply with the tense rules.

By this method we can upgrade a low level adjective based sentence into high level English sentence. Study the following examples:

(a)   **The wealthier** a person you are, **the more selfish** (a person) you may become.
       (Low level English: If you are wealthy person, you may be selfish.)
(b)   **The sweeter** girl you are, **the more acceptable** (girl) you will be.
(c)   **The more hardworking** a student you are, **the more respect** you will earn from your colleagues.
(d)   **The poorer a student** you are, **the more scholarship** you will receive.
       (Low level: You will receive more scholarship if you are a poor student.)
(e)   **The earlier** a bird is, **the more worms** it will catch.
(f)   **The longer hours** the scientist worked in his laboratory, **the greater reward** he received.
(g)   **The kinder** a woman she was, **the larger** the circle of friends she had acquired.
       (Low level: She was a kind woman. She had acquired a large circle of friends)
(h)   **The more devoted** a worker- leader functioned, **the higher** the estimation he was placed at by his colleagues.

We may also use the comparatives in pairs like this,

(i)   **The farther** the distance he walked, **the farther** (the distance) he was away from the starting point.

(j)   **The larger** the products you sell, **the larger** the commission will be yours.

(k)   **The earlier** time you report for duty, **the earlier** (time) you may leave.

(l)   **The more** sweets you eat, **the more** blood sugar-count you will have.

Correct use of some special adjectives

Each, Every

Both the adjectives have similar meaning but **every** is a stronger word than **each**. We use **each** when we talk about a group of 'two or more persons or things' and it directs attention to <u>one person/thing</u> in the group. In other words, **each** refers to a person or thing considered separately/individually in the group.

(a)   **Each** student has a pen. (This would mean that in a class of 30 students, all of them possess a pen)

(b)   We **each** took a big step.

(c)   Samuel, Ebby and Sundar **each** put forward a different suggestion.

(d)   The chief guest gave the winners hundred rupees **each**.

(e)   The mangoes are five rupees **each**.

We use **every** when we talk about a group of two or more persons, but taken as a whole. Study the following examples:

(f)   **Every** seat in the hall has been taken. (All the 500 seats are occupied)

(g)   **Every** one of these houses requires heavy repair.

(h)   Does **every** student in your class score 100% marks in Mathematics?

(i)   On **every** attempt, this boy missed the target.

Few, a few, the few (= Little, a little, the little)

Few (Little) means, "nearly nothing." It is a negative adjective.

(j)   **Few** people speak English in any Indian village.

(k)   **Few** women can keep secrets.

A few means, "some, a small number." It is a positive word.

(l)   **A few** teachers did miss the Correspondent's lecture in the auditorium.

(m)   We are going on a holiday for **a few** days.

(n)   Have you **a little** milk to spare for me?

The few means, "not many" and also "the particular persons/things."

(o)   **The few** people who came, enjoyed the music concert.

(p)   **The few** persons I know are really great people in this colony.

(q)   **The little** knowledge I have about New Zealand is not worth mentioning at all.

Elder, Older

Elder is used for a senior in the same family. **Older** is used for seniors outside one's family.

(r) Thangaraj is my **elder** brother. (**elder** is adjective; same family)
(s) Thangaraj is **elder** to me. (**elder** here is an adverb; same family)
(t) Mike is **older** to me. (Different families. **Older** is an adverb here)
(u) Mike is an **older** person than I (am). (**older** is adjective. The sentence will be correct even if they belong to the same family.)

Exercise

Fill up the blank with a suitable adjective in positive, comparative or superlative degree as applicable:

1. This particular Tamil Daily has a *better* circulation than any other newspaper in TN state.
2. Australia is the .!...... Island in the world. *greater.*
3. Lead is a *better* Metal than any other.
4. Russia is a very .... country. *beautiful*
5. The pen is a ...... weapon than sword. *more sharp*
6. India is one of the .... democracies in the world.
7. Mount Everest is the ...... peak in the Himalayan range. *greater*
8. Isn't silver a ...... metal than gold? *less better*
9. Isn't Anuradha one of the .... students in your class? *most talen·*
10. My drawing is a *better* one than yours.

Locate the mistake if any and rewrite the sentence concerned:

11. Can't you keep less cheaper pens in your shop?
12. Surely your son has scored less marks this year than last year, hasn't he?
13. Between you two, who ran the farther distance?
14. Isn't Mala prettier than Sunitha?
15. She is a less affectionate child than him.
16. One of the most basic traffic rule is to drive always on the left side of a road.
17. Abraham is best footballer in the Fourth semester.
18. My brother James is elder than I am.
19. My older sister sings well.
20. James is the oldest child in our family.

Write the opposite word with reference to the adjective found in the following sentences:

21. Ashoka isn't any more costly a hotel than Pallava hotel.
22. Who is the worst dressed male student during this year so far?
23. Isn't this the least sensitive item on the agenda?
24. Venkat has been one of the most reasonable umpires we have seen.
25. I don't have much money with me at all.

Convert the following sentences into emphatic ones:

26. Your painting is not a nicer one than mine.

27. Ooty is a more picturesque hill station than Kodai.
28. Sanjana is a sweeter girl than Martha.
29. If you are wealthy you will become a more greedy person.
30. When a bird reaches the ground early, it could catch more worms.
31. If a student is very poor he would get more scholarship.
32. This student worked very hard and he scored high marks.
33. If you are a devoted worker you will receive more promotions in this Company.

Correct the mistake in the following sentences: (Every sentence has a mistake)

34. The strong you are, the more boastful you will become.
35. The less intelligent she is, no students will go to her for academic help.
36. The less productive you are in your work, the less you will take home.
37. Mala is more intelligent than you.
38. My friend is elder to me.
39. Loan to me little tea please.
40. The sooner, the earlier you could return home.
41. Elder persons should not go for a walk all by themselves.
42. My older brother dropped me in college this morning.
43. The more you eat the more fat you will become.

Write the remaining 6 categories of sentences for each of the following statement:

44. Is this young man any better a student than my son?
45. Janaki sang a much sweeter song than Sudha, didn't she?
46. Your daughter is no less a dream girl than Mrs. Manorama's.
47. Are my son and daughter-in-law any less a charming couple than yours?
48. You are no more a valuable helper than Chatterjee.

Analyse the following sentences:

49. The Brahmaputra is one of the longest rivers in Asia.
50. The wealthier a person you are, the less approachable a citizen you would turn out to be.
51. The less you speak, the more you could listen.
52. My elder brother was no less worthy a speaker than the others in the debate yesterday.
53. This rose plant is the best one in my garden.
54. Six large trees were felled down from this forest yesterday.
55. Neena and I had a more glorious time in the disco than anyone else.

Chapter 39

MORE ABOUT ADVERBS

Go through Chapter 8 before you study this Chapter.

You know how to identify adverbs in a sentence. They can appear anywhere in a sentence. There is no short-cut to identifying it except through the Test questions, HOW, WHEN, WHERE and also WHY.

Adverbs are of various types as shown below:

(i)	Adverb of time (TQ:WHEN)	- yesterday, today, morning, everyday, now, soon, then, yet, early,
(ii)	Adverb of place (TQ: WHERE)	- here, there, up, down, any noun such as town, city, market and also proper nouns like New Delhi, Madras etc,
(iii)	Adverb of manner/quality (TQ: HOW)	- quickly, valiantly, bravely, happily, fast, well, right, wrong, clearly, definitely, nice.
(iv)	Adverb of frequency (TQ: HOW many/often etc.	- often, never, twice, occasionally, sometime, always.
(v)	Adverb of degree/quantity (TQ: HOW many times/much - etc)	very, too, rather, quite, hardly.

You may call the above as COMPLEMENT also. The main word in a complement will be an adverb, supported by words of all parts of speech except Auxiliary and Verb. If there is only a single word and it passes the Adverb/Complement test, we call it, **adverb.** If an adverb is accompanied by other words, we call that group **Complement.**

(The test question WHY is used to identify an Adverb clause.)

Well

The word 'well' is an adverb of manner and it is a versatile adverb too. We use it in different ways in our day to day use of English. Here are the examples:

(a) Do well in your studies.
(b) Both the mother and the child are doing well.
(c) Isn't your daughter well-off in life?
(d) He did well to join this school at the right opportunity.
(e) You did well in seeking the teacher's advice.
(f) You may quite well give your sickness as the excuse for not taking the progress test.
(g) We may as well start the birthday party straightway.
(h) It is just as well that I didn't go with you for the movie.

(i)   It is all very well for you to suggest that we go on a holiday, but where is the money?

(j)   Very well then, shall we take leave now?

(k)   All is not well in our country, is it?

In every sentence the word **well** passes the adverb test. The sentences given above are of high level English. Learn and master the use of **well** in your spoken and written English.

But

But is a multipurpose word. We have used it as a simple conjunction in Complex sentences. It also happens to be an **adverb** with the meaning "only". We use **but** as adverb in the following ways:

(a)   He is **but** a boy. (He is only a boy)

(b)   They can **but** try.

(c)   This shirt was worn **but** once.

Since

Since is another multipurpose word and we have used it with the meaning "because" in Complex sentences. It is also an adverb with the meaning "from".

(a)   Our house was damaged heavily due to rain but it has **since** been repaired.
       (It is common to use it with another adverb 'ever', as **eversince.**)

(b)   **Eversince** your departure, your pet dog has been behaving strangely.

(c)   My uncle and aunt left for Kolkata in 1999 and they have been living there **eversince**.

Adverb pairs

In our daily conversation and writings, we often use adverb pairs. A pair cannot be split into individual words. We must use them as pairs only. Such pairs will display a lot of force in your sentences and your sentences would look rich and stylish as well. These pairs can be used in Q or A forms.

Now and then (= occasionally, not regularly). Used only in Simple present.

(a)   My Dad contributes short stories to some magazines now and then.

(b)   My parents visit their ward in the hostel now and then.

Off and on (= occasionally, not regularly) Used in Past and Future family.

(c)   My brother stayed in England off and on. ('now and then' here will be wrong.)

(d)   My old school friend wrote to me off and on for some 10 years.

(e)   This mechanic will accept the repair work only off and on.

Out and out (= *through and through* =definitely, beyond all comparison, completely)

We may use this pair in any tense. Don't use it with any normal verbs but only with A.Vs such as - **am, is, are, was, were**, and the auxiliaries, **will be, has been, had been.**

(a)   Niranjan was an out and out backbiter.

(b)   Our servant maid is an out and out cheat.

(c)   This man will be an out and out loyal worker.

(d)   This young maiden has been an out and out music lover.

(e)   He has been a reader of R.K.Narayan's books through and through.

(f)   Our master is through and through an expert in Mathematics.

Over and above (= in addition to, besides)

You may use this in any tense. It is normally placed in the middle of a sentence after the verb. A sentence could also start with this pair:

(a)   I purchased two pencils over and above a pair of fountain pens.

(b)   Over and above these points, I have to add one small one.

(c)   Shall I suggest one more name for the team over and above what I have already announced?

(d)   This student stands first in Mathematics over and above English.

Again and again (= repeatedly, several times)

You may use this pair in any tense.

(a)   Don't remind me again and again; I feel tired of it.

(b)   Didn't the Principal warn you again and again not to fight with the students of other colleges?

(c)   This street dog would come to my house again and again despite my chasing it everyday.

Time and again (= again and again)

This pair is normally used for past activities/events.

(a)   Haven't I told you time and again against driving beyond 40 kmph?

(b)   I had repeated the same warnings time and again.

Hardly ever

'Hardly' is negative in meaning. "I hardly meet him" = I meet him once in 5 years or so". Used normally in present and past family.

'Hardly ever' takes the frequency of meeting still less, possibly once in 20 years.

(a)   I hardly ever go out. (I, very very seldom go out)

(b)   We hardly ever visit a cinema theatre.

Far and near (= everywhere, in all directions). Used in any tense.

(a)   M.F Hussain's fame has spread far and near.

(b)   Mahatma Gandhi's name became known far and near within a few years.

Far and wide (= comprehensively). Used in any tense.

(a) The rescuers searched far and wide for the missing child.
(b) When a public meeting is held, people from far and wide come to hear the speakers.
(c) Don't worry. We shall keep an eye for him far and wide.

So far (= until now). To be used in present family only.

(a) The English course has been easy so far.
(c) So far, has anything happened?

So far, so good (= Upto now everything has gone on well). Use in present family *only*.

(a) So far, so good. Are you all keen to walk on further?
(This phrase is either to precede a sentence or follow it with the given meaning.)
(c) Most of you had done well in the preparatory examinations. So far, so good.

First and foremost (= *first things first* = first of all). Used in present family only.

(a) First and foremost, I wish to congratulate all the prize winners.

To and fro (= up and down, forwards and backwards). Can be used in any tense.

(a) The fare, to and fro, would be Rs.1300
(b) He walked to and fro until he memorised the poem.

First come, first served (= the service will be in the same order of arrival) Use in present time and Present family only.

(a) Those who come first will be served first. (= Those who come third will be served third in the order.)

Exercise

Identify the object and complement in the following sentences:

1. I heard his remark myself.
2. He left the class room dejectedly.
3. I did not see this boy in the super-market yesterday at all.
4. Someone has taken away my pen from my brief case.
5. He thinks he is wiser.
6. Don't think of him as an unworthy fellow.
7. Don't you think this student is always correct in his arguments?
8. The tasks the HOD gives us are usually very simple.
9. She is as shrewd as her twin brother.
10. We will be well prepared eventually.

State whether the words in *italics* have been used as adjectives or adverbs:

11. He is indeed a *clever* student.
12. Margaret is always a *cheerful* donor.

13. Margaret's face is always *cheerful*. Adj
14. *Yesterday* morning was very hot, wasn't it? Adj
15. My father returned from New Delhi *yesterday*. Adv
16. The *less* you talk the *more* work you shall perform.
17. Doesn't Suhasini speak English *fluently*? Adj
18. Of course, her English is *fluent*. Adv
19. *Occasionally* this student does fail in my subject. Adv
20. I waited for him but he *never* turned up. Adv
21. My small sister *hardly ever* fails in any subject. Adj
22. It is not a question of *now* but he does visit me *now and then*. Adv
23. Don't compel me to tell you *again and again*. Adv
24. He is *out and out* a stupid chap. Adv
25. Do *well* in your today's exam, OK? Adv

The following sentences are supposed to be of the <u>adverb-comparative</u> variety. Pick out the ones which are not:

26. Isn't Arumugam a better student than I?
27. He has been more hardworking than me.
28. Sugirtha is a more intelligent student that Amirtham.
29. I scored more than you in Physics, didn't I?
30. The Vice principal thinks you are a cleverer writer than Manoharan in BA II year.

In the low level sentences given below, replace the adverbs/complements with suitable adverb pairs to make them sound stylish.

31. This student reads any fiction several times.
32. He is a bright student. Sometime in the future his name will be known everywhere.
33. Although my father has paid the fee for private tuition I go to the master only occasionally.
34. I paid Rs 200 for both way journey.
35. My father did not visit New Delhi very frequently.
36. What we must do is, to thank God for our safe return from the boat ride.
37. He is honest and also hardworking. (Tip: Try, *Over and above*)
38. Hasn't the news of your brave act reached all parts of India?
39. I shall get to know about our servant thoroughly within weeks.
40. I used to see this vendor on my street a few times till last year.

Analyse the following sentences:

41. People know this actress far and wide within Andhra Pradesh.
42. Please refrain from coming every now and then.
43. How much taxi fare will you charge me to and fro to Trichy from here?
44. Didn't he do well by accepting the job immediately.
45. All but Ramanujam visited the Museum.

Chapter 40

MORE ABOUT PREPOSITIONS

Revise Chapter 9 before you proceed any further.

In a nutshell, what you learnt in Chapter 9 was that a preposition holds two words together and as a result the sentence will become really meaningful.

Yet, with certain verbs, the sentences will be meaningful even without a preposition. Study the following sentences that are in the Active voice:

(a) Please **give** Johny your notes.

(b) Will you please **show** the visitor his seat.

(c) Have you **told** Paul to wait for me?

(d) My father had **promised** me a bicycle if I passed with high marks.

(e) The football coach **advised** us against dribbling too much.

(f) My friend should not have **asked** you to go away.

(g) Our English teacher has **invited** us to her house this evening.

(h) Robin **reminded** me to take him on my moped to school.

(i) I **warned** you against borrowing money from anyone, didn't I?

(j) I **urge** you to revise your lessons again before you go for your examination.

(k) We **requested** the conductor for a front seat in the bus.

But, if we use the above in the Passive voice, prepositions may be necessary in certain cases to get a clear meaning. Study the following sentences:

(aa) Let your notes be given **to** Johny by you. (Or, Your notes are to be given **to** Johny by you).

(dd) A bicycle has been promised **to** me by my father if I passed with high marks.

There is an exception to this rule. When HOME is the complement in a sentence, no preposition is to be used between the verb and complement:

(l) Go **home** immediately after the match.

(m) After you return **home**, give me a ring.

But, if you use HOUSE in place of HOME, preposition would be necessary.

(n) All of you must come *to* my **house** this evening.

(o) We are coming *from* Esther's **house**.

(p) Aren't we going *to* your **house** after the movie?

Correct use of FROM, SINCE, FOR, DURING

One must be very careful while using the above words as prepositions. All these are used with reference to 'time and place'.

From is used normally with "to or till/until".

(a) Most of the colleges work **from** 10 a.m. **to (or, till)** 3.30 p.m.

Since is used for a 'point of time'. It has the meaning "from that time till now or till the time of speaking." It is wrong to use **since** for a place. (Incidentally, **since** is a multipurpose word; we have already used it as 'adverb'.) Next, we must use **since** as a preposition only along with Present perfect or Past perfect tense.

(b)   Rajan had not written to me **since** January last year. ('from' will be wrong)
(c)   Romila has been waiting for you **since** 4 p.m.   - do -
(d)   My sisters have been here **since** last week.   - do -

We cannot use **since** in 'non perfect tense' sentences. For example, the following sentences are wrong:

(cc)   Romila is waiting for you since 4 p.m.
(dd)   My brothers are here since last week.

When the time element is a 'period of time' (as opposed to 'point of time'), we use **for** and never 'since'. The correct use then will be for period of time:

(e)   Ram has worked in this school **for** 2 years. (correct)
(f)   Ram has worked in this school **since** 2 years. (wrong, because '2 years' is a period of time)
(g)   I was sick **for** one week.
(h)   I was sick since one week. (wrong)
(i)   I have been sick since one week. (correct)

During is used for a "known period of time" like this,

(j)   We worked only **during** daylight hours.
(k)   **During** the whole week, we did not touch our books at all.

Use of BUT

But is also a preposition. We have already used it as a simple conjunction and as adverb. When used as a preposition, it has the meaning "except". Here are some typical sentences with **but** as preposition:

(a)   All **but** Kandan took part in the school sports from our class.
(b)   **But** for your bad play, we would have won the match.
(c)   No one **but** me will reply the next question.

Preposition phrases

Instead of single worded prepositions, we may also **preposition phrases** in written English. All the Preposition phrases <u>must be followed by</u> a noun/pronoun or noun of action. These phrases cannot be split into individual words.

Because of (= for the reason of)

(a)   I couldn't attend office today because of sickness.
(b)   I was late for college because of a tyre puncture. ("tyre puncture" is a noun of action)

(c)   I couldn't reach here early because of heavy rain.
(d)   You are out of luck perhaps because of me.
(e)   I am not out of luck because of you/him/her.
(f)   Because of your unpunctuality, we never get the attendance prize.
(g)   Our families did not meet for 3 years because of some misunderstanding.
      between us.

For the sake of (= for the benefit of or advantage of)

(a)   For the sake of peace in our class, I maintain good friendship with all.
(b)   Won't you help my brother for my mother's sake?
      (Instead of a noun, we may also use a possessive noun/ pronoun)
(c)   We played this exhibition match for their sake. ("for the children's sake")
(d)   Please forgive this fellow for my sake.

On behalf of (= from his/her side, on his/her service)

(a)   I am attending this meeting on behalf of my class monitor.
(b)   On behalf of the English professor, may I congratulate you on your standing
      first in the subject.
(c)   On my mother's behalf (her behalf), I invite you for this home party.
(d)   My father is sleeping. On his behalf (my father's behalf), may I thank you for
      visiting him in this ward.

In case of (= in such a situation)

(a)   In case of fire, please dial 101 for help.
(b)   In case of any kind of emergency, please press this call bell.
(c)   In case of snake bite, break open the first aid kit box.

In lieu of /In place of

(a)   In lieu of coffee, you may take milk.
(b)   The librarian gave me a grammar book in lieu of a novel.
(c)   He accepted my friendship in lieu of money.
(d)   In place of Mahadevan, Shankar would play right half in today's match.
(e)   In place of the usual maid servant, a small girl came for work today.
(f)   In your place, I am going to send another student on the excursion.
(g)   Who will be then in my place?

Instead of (= in place of)

(a)   Instead of a card game, shall we play carrom?
(b)   Why did you go to a movie instead of the library?
(c)   Instead of gossiping, why don't you do something useful?
(d)   Our Group-leader took more lady students instead of men students for this debate.

Inspite of / Despite

This is a very important phrase with the meaning, "It may be so. Yet. Still. The condition may be so, but ...."

(a)   Inspite of my objections, your children went to the park this evening.
(b)   Despite stiff opposition, our son took part in the boxing competition.
(c)   Inspite of the heavy waves, this guard jumped into the sea to save a child.
(d)   Did you go into the water despite my warning?
(e)   You always make noise when I am at my study. Despite it, I shall stand first in the class.

On account of (= because of)

(a)   On account of a bad cold, I did not attend college yesterday.
(b)   On account of rough weather, the aircraft left Madras airport 2 hours behind schedule.
(c)   On account of a misunderstanding these two students are not on talking terms now.

Owing to/due to (= for the reason of)

(a)   Owing to heavy debt, my father is not sending me for higher studies.
(b)   Due to stomach trouble, I am not attending your birthday party.
(c)   I could not visit you due to a prior appointment with my HOD.

With a view to (= with a particular result in mind)

In most cases, we use a gerund after the phrase instead of a noun/noun of action.

(a)   With a view to playing in the national team, this student took to cricket very seriously from school days.
(b)   With a view to receiving allowance every month, I asked my father not to give me a lump sum.
(c)   With a view to standing first in the class, I studied upto 6 hours a day.
(d)   With a view to a permanent peace, I made up with my one time enemy.

With regard to (= in respect of)

This phrase is normally used in official and business correspondences.

(a)   With regard to your doubts on this proposal, we would like to assure you that we will never go back on our commitment.
(b)   With regard to the enquiries you had made on our letter, we propose to send our liaison officer to clarify all your doubts on the spot.

With reference to

This phrase is also used mostly in official and business correspondences especially while replying a letter.

(a)   With reference to your letter No. CSA/1/4321 dated 02 Jun 2002, we regret that we cannot accept your order.

(b)   With reference to the discussion we had last week on holding monthly friendly matches between our two colleges, we hereby agree to the arrangement.

By dint of (= with the help of, by means of)

(a)   He passed the entrance examination by dint of hard work.

(b)   It is only by dint of hard work could anyone succeed in life.

By virtue of (= by reason of)

(a)   By virtue of his age, Prasad has been appointed the Student-leader of our class.

(b)   He was let off lightly by virtue of his good conduct during the year.

In consequence of/consequent to/consequent upon (=as a result. A noun or noun of action to follow the phrase)

(a)   In consequence of our promotion, we moved to the class room in the next building.

(b)   Consequent to his transfer to another college, this Lecturer became more strict with his students.

(c)   Consequent upon his becoming a Vice Chancellor, Mr. Ramanan appointed ten more Lecturers/Associate Lecturers. ('becoming' is a gerund)

(d)   Consequent on his joining St Michael's college, Robert broke off all connections with our college.

In the event of (= if it happens …)

(a)   In the event of my admission to the hospital, Mr.T.Raghavendar would handle your class till my return.

(b)   In the event of my death in battle, the Second -in -command will assume command of this Regiment.

By reason of

This phrase is replaceable with "By virtue of"

(a)   By reason of low marks, he was denied a seat in the Science group.

By way of (= as a procedure)

(a)   By way of introduction, the new Lecturer made some good remarks about all the participants before he started off the debate on "Technical education".

(b)   By way of felicitations, the Chief guest gave a hearty hug to the Gold medalist.

In favour of (= for the benefit of)

(a)   In favour of his highly qualified son, the aged Professor resigned his post.

(b)   Are you in favour of promoting this student to the next class?

(c)   We are not in favour of going on a picnic this Sunday.

By means of (= with the help of)

(a)   By means of poles and sticks, they brought down the cloth from the tree.

In addition to (= over and above)

(a)   In addition to coffee, give the guest a glass of milk also.
(c)   In addition to hockey and football, Ranjan plays cricket also.

In order to (= so as to)

This phrase is quite different from the others. This is to be followed by a *verb*.

(a)   He walked into my office in order to <u>give</u> me a gift.
(b)   In order to <u>enjoy</u> the early morning breeze, some of us go to the beach.

Uses of Preposition phrases

It is difficult to write a sentence without a preposition unless it is of 3 or 4 words; sentences such as, "This is my pen", "You are correct" etc. You also know that simple prepositions may appear in the Subject part or Object part.

Preposition phrases perform the same function as simple prepositions but sentences with phrases would sound stylish and more effective in meaning. You would notice that these phrases also add some colour to a sentence.

The greater advantage is, that we can start a sentence with a preposition phrase. Framing every sentence on the pattern of S -A -V - O/C may look tiresome. Thus, preposition phrases give us another method of starting a sentence.

The greatest advantage however is, that they could convert a Complex sentence into a Simple sentence if a suitable preposition phrase is used. (Do recall that we performed such a miracle with "infinitive connectors" and "Participles" also.) Here are some examples:

(a)   If   I   fall   ill,   the Vice principal will take over my duties.
    Conj S   (A)V Adv   S   A   V   O
(aa) **In case of** my illness, the Vice principal will take over my duties.
    P.phrase   O   S   A   V   O
(b)   The father resigned his job in the factory, when his son applied for a post in the same factory.
(bb) The father resigned his job **in favour of** his son.
(c)   We wanted to enjoy the swimming pool facility, hence we joined this club.
(cc) **In order to** enjoy the swimming pool facility, we joined this club.
    (With a view to enjoying the swimming pool facility, we joined this club)

Preposition phrases do produce a miracle of converting a Complex sentence into a Simple sentence. (2 Nos S-A-V-O/C into 1 No. S-A-V-O/C). Such conversion would be possible with every Complex sentence. It is not necessary that you should use only the phrases covered in this Chapter. You could produce your own. What is a phrase after all? It is a group of words without A-V. Any group of words would give a meaning of sorts.

So, frame a suitable phrase of your own and you would be able to replace one of the two Simple sentences with that phrase.

Exercise

Fill up the blank with an appropriate simple preposition:

1. Isn't your small child hiding *behind* the door?
2. My deskmate quarrelled *with* me *on* a small point.
3. Dr.Sundar Raj is married *with* my elder sister.
4. We should be always loyal *to* our country.
5. Isn't there some exception *to* this rule?
6. A circle may not be equivalent *to* a rectangle; it all depends *on* the area.
7. A policeman saved my small brother *from* a possible traffic accident.
8. Isn't your report card different *from* mine as regards the examiner's remarks?
9. We discussed the details *of* our picnic *at* in a restaurant *with* a cup of tea.
10. May I go out *with* my rain coat since the rain has stopped.

Fill up the blank with a suitable phrase preposition:

11. My parents didn't want my elder brother to stay in uncle's house overnight. But *inspite of* the advice, my brother spent 2 nights in uncle's house.
12. Please buy three one rupee stamps *instead of* a single three rupee stamp.
13. Go over to your tutor's house and seek clarification *with a view to* figuring it out by yourself.
14. *With a view of* winning the first prize, he cunningly consulted the text book in the examination hall.
15. *........* the poor response from our sister colleges, the Management cancelled the competition.
16. May I submit this application *on the behalf of* my sister?
17. *Instead of* two shirts, my brother insisted on buying two vests as well.
18. Could Ravi attend the meeting *on behalf of* Murugan?
19. Kumaran isn't present here today *due to* stomach ailment.
20. *For the sake of* peace in our group, we allowed David to join it. You see, he is a trouble maker.

Wrong prepositions have been used in every sentence given below. Replace them with the correct ones:

21. Lalitha walks *to* (for) college every day.
22. Meet me *at* (over) the auditorium *at* (in) 3.30 p.m.
23. I was born *in* (on) Chennai but I now live with my sister.
24. Can you count one *to* (in) 100 within 10 seconds?
25. That shop is *on* (in) fire. Ring up the fire brigade.

Convert the following Complex sentences into Simple sentences by using suitable Preposition phrases :

26. If you have any problem on the way, apply your mind to solve it.
27. Several suggestions were made and yet the leader chose Vandaloor for our picnic.
28. After our Vandaloor picnic, we felt tired and we went to bed immediately.
29. I am attending this meeting because my brother is not feeling well.
30. As I am the senior student of this class, I have taken this decision.
31. He got through the entrance examination because he had studied very hard.
32. He took admission in a Govt college since he had been removed from our college.
33. His conduct had been good, therefore he was let off with a simple warning.
34. Please forgive him since I have apologised for him.
35. Since I had scored low marks in the selection test, I was not permitted to take part in the college debate competition.
36. Because my mother was running a high temperature we had to admit her in a nursing home.
37. My father tried his best but still he could not get admission for my sister in the nearby college.
38. My uncle resigned his job because he was not keeping good health.
39. My class friend and I had a quarrel the other day and now we are not on talking terms.
40. I told Venugopal not to fight with the boys of the next colony but he didn't listen.

Analyse the following sentences:

41. As a result of failing, my parents had stopped me from college.
42. We couldn't come here on time on account of bad weather.
43. By virtue of his promise, we took the step of coming here.
44. Without someone's help, we couldn't have reached your house at all.
45. Consequent to your refusal, we deferred our action plan.

Chapter 41

MORE ABOUT CONJUNCTIONS

Introduction

Conjunction is one of the parts of speech which we learnt in Chapter 1 itself. However, to recapitulate:

Conjunction is a word that joins two or more **Simple sentences**. "And" is the only conjunction which in addition, can connect any two words also, except two verbs.

A conjunction is a 'must' in Complex sentences and we have written many Complex sentences in Chapter 27, using simple (one worded) conjunctions. Some of the important ones are, BECAUSE, SINCE, THOUGH, IF, THAT, UNLESS, WHEN, WHILE, STILL, TILL, FOR, etc.

UNLESS is a tricky conjunction which means "if not". If you remember this formula you will not make a mistake while using it.

$$a1 - UNLESS - a2$$
or
$$a2 - UNLESS - a1.$$

Here are some sample sentences:

(a) I won't repair your bicycle unless you pay Rs 3 for it.
(a2 - unless - a1)

(b) We will be late unless we hurry.
(Here, the first sentence is equivalent to a2 in meaning)

(c) Unless you are sweet to her, the little girl will not go with you.
(Unless-a1-a2)

(d) Unless you work hard, you will not pass.
(Unless-a1-a2)

These 4 sentences could be written with **if not** also   like this,

(aa) I will not repair your bicycle **if** you **don't** pay Rs 3 for it.

(bb) We will be late **if** we **don't** hurry.

(cc) **If** you **are not** sweet with her, the little girl will not go with you.

(dd) **If** you **don't** work hard, you will not pass.

Lest

Lest is another tricky one but a very useful one at that. It has the meaning, 'In order that ... not' or ' for a fear that '. The word has a negative meaning. If you follow the given formula you won't make any mistake.

$$a2 - LEST - a1$$
or
$$a1 - LEST - a2$$

Here are some sample sentences:

(a) Don't oversleep in the train lest you miss your station.
(b) The culprit ran away fast lest he had got caught.
(c) I avoided their company lest my friends branded me an evil chap.
(d) Lest I lost my seat, I continued to sit there despite a lot of discomfort.
(e) Don't annoy this bully lest he beats you up.

Had

We can use the auxiliary HAD also as a conjunction. Study the following examples:

(a) **Had** I known this fact earlier, I would have come to your house earlier.
(b) **Had** I been in your place, I would not have taken such a step at all.

This conjunction is used only for Past - Past cases. The sentences sound like 'conditional statements', don't they? Do also notice that we have followed the 2-action rule in designing the sentences.

(a) It also seems equivalent to "If I had known this fact earlier, I would have...."
(b)   "   "If I had been in your place ....."
Accordingly, we may also look at these Complex sentences with "If" being silent.

Should

We can use **should** also as a conjunction. Study the following examples:

(a) **Should** anything happen to my son, I shall be forced to complain to the police.
(b) **Should** you repeat such a mistake once more, you shall be punished severely.

Should here looks to be equivalent to "If". It indeed is. We can use this conjunction only in Present - Present cases with the meaning IF.

CONJUNCTION PAIRS

Like Adverb pairs, there are conjunction pairs as well. They will perform the same function as simple conjunctions. The pair cannot be split up and must be used always as pairs.

Either ..... or ....

This pair is to be used in a1 only. We seldom use it in Q form.

(a) She will go either to New Delhi or to Kolkata.
   (Have you realised that this is a Complex sentence but a condensed one? The actual sentence would read - "She will go either to New Delhi or she will go to Kolkata." The S-A-V part being common, don't repeat it and show only the O/C part in the second sentence)
(b) Monica may like to buy either a green saree or a blue saree.
(c) At this time, Victor will be either playing football or watching T.V.

(Only S -A - C are common, hence not repeated; Vs and Os have been shown separately in each sentence)

(d)   Roshni has been either washing clothes or feeding the children the whole morning.

Neither .... nor ....

This pair is used in a2 only and seldom in Q. This pair is the negative of "either... or ..."

(a)   This wall clock is neither accurate nor very reliable.
       (Common A.V)
(b)   Yesterday's stage play was neither educative nor enjoyable.
(c)   He took neither lunch nor dinner in the hostel.
(d)   This boy neither stays with us nor spends his time with friends.
(e)   He has done well neither in English nor in Tamil.
       (S-A-V-C are common; only O is different.)

If we have to repeat the S- A-V in the second sentence, it should be in the sequence of A-S-V (like in a Q) though the sentence is an a2 type. *This is a rule!* (Incidentally, this rule is to be followed in respect of *neither, nor* and *seldom* also)

(ee) He has done well neither in English nor **has he done** well in Tamil.
       ("He has done well neither in English nor he has done well in Tamil" is not good English)
(dd) This boy neither stays with us nor **does he spend** his time with friends.
(cc) He took neither lunch nor **did he take** dinner in the hostel.
(bb) Yesterday's stage show was neither educative nor **was it** enjoyable.
(aa) This wall clock is neither accurate nor **is it** reliable.

Independent use of EITHER, NEITHER and NOR.

It is quite permissible to use **neither, either** and **nor** independently, in which case they will become pronouns, adverbs or adjectives.

(a)   **Either** of you only may go on out-pass today.
       (Use **either** like this when only two persons are under reference. And it is a pronoun here. If the number is three or more, we cannot use **either** in this way)
(b)   Do you know this person? I don't know him **either**.
       (We have used **either** here with the meaning 'also' and it is an adverb)
(c)   **Neither** do I condemn you.
       (Though this is an a2 type, the sentence is in the A-S-V pattern because of the rule. "Neither I (do) condemn you" will be bad English.)
(d)   **Neither** of them (of the two) drinks coffee. (**Neither** here is a singular subjective pronoun)
(e)   **Neither** book gives a good explanation.

(Only 2 books are under reference here. If there are more than 2, we use, "None of the books give a good explanation". Treat "none" as a plural pronoun.)

(e)   Do you know the answer? **Nor** *do I know* the answer.

(f)   Nobody wants to come with me. Can you? **Nor** *can I come* with you.

Though .... yet ...

(a)   Though he is a physically handicapped student, yet he is never late for class.

(b)   Though he is young, yet he competes with older boys.

(c)   Though he didn't open his mouth, yet he managed to convey the message to the visitors.

When this conjunction pair is used, you must start the sentence with **though**. You cannot use this pair in the middle of a sentence.

Whether .... or ....

Use this pair only when there is a choice between 'yes' or 'no'. If there is no choice involved and the answer is a simple 'yes' or' not yes', use the conjunction **if**.

(a)   Please tell me whether you are going to play with us today or not.

(b)   Whether you are accepting our invitation or not, we are going ahead with our plan.

(c)   My friend asked me whether I was going to help him or not in his studies.

One tends to use **whether** for 'yes' or 'no' answer as though **whether** is equal to **if**. This will be a wrong use of **whether**. The phrase **whether ... or ...** cannot be split.

(d)   I asked Rajendran whether he could lend his English notes for a day.
      (**Whether** has been misused here since no choice is involved here. The correct expression will be, "I asked Rajendran **if** he could lend his English notes for a day". Here, **if** has been used for confirmation of *one action* and not exercising an option between two actions)

(e)   My sister wants to know **if** you will accompany her to college tomorrow.

Not only... but also

We use this pair when we want to do two actions one after the other or at about the same time.

(a)   Ravi gave me not only good advice but (he) also (gave) financial help.

(b)   Minnie not only will dress you up but also accompany you upto the stage.

(c)   Selvan is not only a good hockey player but also an excellent chess player.

So ... that

(a)   I am **so** tired **that** I could sleep for the next 24 hours!

(b)   He is so thin that you could lift him with your smallest finger!

(c)   This small kid is so smart that he could outwit you in any game.

No sooner .... than

(a)   No sooner my father had left than my mother gave me some money.
(b)   No sooner you reach your destination than ring me up without any delay.
(c)   No sooner I receive a letter than I shall get in touch with you.

Both .... and

Use this pair only when there are two nouns, two adjectives or two adverbs in a sentence.

(a)   Both my father and uncle visited me in the hostel. (2 nouns)
(b)   He is both clever and crafty. (2 adverbs)
(c)   This fellow is both a mischievous guy and a cunning youngster. (2 adjectives).
(d)   He is both the Principal and Headmaster of St Peter's High school.

CONJUNCTION PHRASES

Then we have conjunction phrases i.e conjunction of more than one word. We use them as phrases and they cannot be split:

Even if

Use this phrase in conditional statements in a1 or a2 or Q forms.

(a)   I shall not play with them even if they force me to play.
(b)   He should have taken part in the competition even if he had no hope of winning a prize.
(c)   Would you leave this school even if your father's transfer is cancelled?
(d)   We shall surely play this match even if it rains cats and dogs.
(e)   Would you come with us even if your mother objects to it?

Even though

This phrase is similar to EVEN IF except that it is not conditional.

(a)   Even though she is not clever, she has never failed in any test.
(b)   Of course I shall meet him even though I don't know him well enough.

So that

(a)   The dwarf climbed up a tree so that he could see the roadside show.
(b)   Why don't you come closer to me so that I could see you better?
(c)   I shall be at your school before closing time so that we can catch your school bus together for home.
      (Do note the difference in the construction of the Complex sentence between **so that** and **so ..... that**)

Provided that (= if some conditions are fulfilled)

(a)   I shall lend you my Maths class work book provided that you return it by this evening.

(b)   Provided that you accompany me, I shall go to the hospital.

(c)   Didn't you promise me a birthday gift provided that I behaved myself?
(This phrase is usable in all the three tense families. Do not treat "provided" as a verb !)

As if / As though

We use this phrase to indicate an unreality or imagining something or pretending some situation:

(a)   Don't behave as if you are dog tired.

(b)   Don't you look as if you had seen a ghost in the graveyard?

(c)   You talked as if you are a Mister Know all.

(d)   The sky smelt as if it was going to pour down very heavily.

(e)   I shall cross examine you as though I am a lawyer.

As .... As

We have used this as adverb phrase in Simple sentences. This can be used as a conjunction phrase as well. Any suitable adjective/adverb can be inserted between **as ... as** except WELL. (See Chapter 8 for the reason why.)

(i)   **As soon as**

(a)   You may leave the class room as soon as I go out.

(b)   I shall announce your marks as soon as I correct your papers.

(ii)   **As good as**

(a)   This Newspaper is as good as the other one (is).

(b)   Satinder's play was as good as Mohinder's (was).

(iii)   **As close as**

(a)   I stood as close as it was possible to the stage.

(b)   I kept myself as close as it was necessary behind Gopalan.

(iv)   **As fast as**

(a)   Reach here as fast as you could.

(b)   Drive as fast as the roads permit you.

(v)   **As attractively as**

(a)   She dresses herself as attractively as a film actress. (does)

As far as ...... concerned

(a)   As far as this particular issue is concerned, I am not quite in agreement at all.

(b)   As far as I am concerned, please leave me out of the deal.

(c)   As far as my sister was concerned, she never showed any interest in your proposal.

In so far .... concerned

(a)   In so far as my college's interest is concerned, we would not join it at all.
(b)   In so far as our class performance is concerned, we are no less than any other.

In as much as (= since or because)

(a)   In as much as the class teacher demanded to see the top scorers, shall we see him at 3.30 p.m. today?
(b)   In as much as you have done it unto one of the least of these my brethren, you have done it unto me. (Bible. Mt 25:40)
(c)   I am doing this work in as much as that our Professor has ordered it.
(d)   In as much as the Principal has found no evidence about copying, our class has been absolved of the charge.

Conclusion

There are quite a few words in the English language which have multiple identities. Words like SINCE, BUT, BECAUSE and phrases like, AS ... AS can appear in a sentence in different part of speech. If these words have been used as conjunctions or conjunction pairs/phrases in a sentence, you should have no difficulty in differentiating them because they would be Complex sentences.

While writing a Complex sentence with the pairs and phrases covered in this Chapter, do observe the tense rules strictly.

Exercise

Fill up the blanks with suitable simple conjunctions:

1.   I came running .... so that I couldn't catch the last city bus for Tambaram.
2.   Unless. you work hard , you will not succeed in life.
3.   Take a lamp with you ..if.. it is dark outside.
4.   Some students had already left when we arrived at the gate.
5.   I am positive ..... he said so. weather
6.   I shall be angry because you don't ring me back.
7.   Please take down notes only when I dictate.
8.   My father tried several times still he couldn't get admission for my brother in this college.
9.   Uncle will surely help you because he is very fond of you.
10.   The baby was awake when the mother returned from the club.
11.   This is a glass vase. It will surely break .if. you drop it.
12.   Man proposes .... God disposes. while
13.   The train fell off the rail but no one was hurt.
14.   Hari would do well in life. as he persevered.
15.   Mummy told me that you had arrived an hour back.
16.   I wonder .if. he will come today.

17. I used to think that he was very clever ... ~~but~~ I was wrong.
18. The girls would have left their home .... you reach there. before
19. I promised him a place in the team ... he did not show any keenness on it. still
20. This mechanic completed the repair work .... you were waiting. that

Join each pair of sentences using a suitable **conjunction phrase** you have learnt in this Chapter:

21. This boy is poor. He has always been honest.
22. He may try his best. He will certainly not get any prize.
23. My cousin brother is tall. My cousin sister is also tall.
24. These pineapples are sweet. Buy some straightway.
25. His father stepped into the house. Suresh ran away.
26. Menon came last in this test. He acted like a first ranker.
27. One student enters the class. Another leaves about that time.
28. We shall go out. Let the rain stop.
29. My elder brother will help you on one condition. You come to him every day at 7 p.m sharp.
30. You may go where you like. I will not be bothered about it.

Identify the simple conjunction in each sentence and replace it with a suitable **conjunction pair** you have learnt in this Chapter:

31. Play football or sit in the library.
32. Sit inside the class room or sit outside.
33. You make up with him or not, but do let me know.
34. Your close friend is obstinate and he is also a foolish chap.
35. You go to the market or your sister may decide to go herself.
36. He does not stay in the house and he does not play outside either.
37. The train started at Tambaram quite late but it reached Egmore on time.
38. When we returned home quite famished after the match we ate our dinner immediately.
39. After we heard the footsteps of our Lecturer immediately we rushed to our seats.
40. You shall receive my class friend at the Park station and also you shall bring him to my house on your moped.

Identify the part of speech of the words in *italics* in the following sentences:

41. We have not met Jeyachandran *since* last Monday
42. My mother arrived soon *after*.
43. Raghavan came to the class *before* you had arrived.
44. The doctors did their best *but* they could not save him.
45. He is *but* a fool.
46. The long distance runners reached the finish line one *after* another.
47. *Since* the police has not come till now, shall we ring up for them again?

48. *Before* you turn the question paper over, put away all your books.
49. Isn't this student sitting right *behind* you?
50. *But* for you, he would have gone to the shop himself.
51. It is *but* right that everyone admits his fault.
52. Mohan has not been studying well *eversince* his illness.
53. Incidentally, have we met *before*?
54. There isn't *much* truth in what he says.
55. The Earth goes *round* the Sun once a year.
56. *Besides* his mother, he also took his younger sister to the hospital.
57. Must you always sit *beside* your brother?
58. *Once* he hesitates, we should send him away.
59. The girls slept *till* evening.
60. This will be your *last* chance.

Identify the type of phrase shown in *italics* in the following sentences:

61. Come to my office *as early* as possible.
62. *As soon as* I blow the whistle, you must stop playing.
63. Isn't your bicycle *as new as* mine?
64. Murali runs *as fast as* Joseph.
65. Radhika sings *as delightfully as* Monica.

Chapter 42

COMPOUND SENTENCE

Definition

The third and final type of sentence used in the English language, is the **Compound sentence.** (We have already covered Simple sentence and Complex sentence)

We may define a compound sentence as a single sentence that combines in it three or more Simple sentences. Its formula would be like this,

S - A- V - O/C - CONJN - S - A- V- O/C -CONJN - S - A- V- O/C

The above is the minimum length to qualify to be a compound sentence. It could have four or more Simple sentences also. But then, it will become a long and laborious sentence to read and understand. So, we normally restrict the length of a Compound sentence to 20 words or thereabouts. In other words, not more than 3 Simples connected by 2 conjunctions. In exceptional cases, if it exceeds 20 words, make sure that the reader will understand the meaning fully in one reading.

A Compound sentence may also contain one Complex sentence with one or two clauses.

Definition of a clause

A **clause** will be a Simple sentence with a difference, in that, it will be always attached to another sentence or to a part of another sentence. Here is how a sentence containing a clause is to be identified:

1. A clause will have S-A-V with or without O/C
2. Though it may have O/C, it will not convey a full meaning until it is read with some part or word or words in the main sentence, especially if it contains some pronoun.
3. The conjunction or the connecting word between the two parts will be part of the clause and play an important part in conveying the meaning of the clause. Often it may be acting also as the subject of the second half of the sentence.
4. The first half of the sentence may be in S-A-V or S-A-V-O/C form; whatever the form, the second half will answer the Noun test or Complement (Adverb) test.

Therefore, in order to distinguish a sentence having a clause from a regular Complex sentence, we may call it "**A sentence with a clause**". Do remember that a sentence with a clause will also have 2 Nos S-A-V but the meaning will be available only out of the entire sentence. Next, you cannot split a "sentence with a clause" into 2 Simple sentences as we could do in a regular and full-fledged Complex sentence.

Examine all the examples discussed hereafter from these angles.

Types of clauses

We use 3 types of clauses. They are, Adjective, Noun and Adverb clauses in their order of importance.

Adjective clause

An **adjective clause** is one that describes a noun. Alternatively, a group of words in the S-A-V-O/C form that does the job of an adjective can be named adjective clause. And, an adjective clause must be placed to the immediate right of the noun it is describing. An adje   ve clause may appear in the middle of a "sentence with a clause".

(a) The boy *who sits next to me* is from a village.

In the example at (a), the words in italics constitute an adjective clause because it describes the word "boy" and comes immediately to the right of that noun. And, though it is in S -A-V-O/C form, does it convey a proper meaning by itself? 'Who' here is a conjunction and also the subject for the clause. 'Who' refers to 'boy' in the other part. Thus we get the meaning of the clause only when it is read with 'boy' in the other part.

It looks like a Complex sentence, doesn't it? It has two S-A-V-O/C no doubt but one set of S-A-V-O/C belongs to the clause. But, we cannot split this sentence into two meaningful Simples after eliminating the conjunction.

Here are more examples of adjective clauses which are shown in italics:

(b) The tiger *which had got wounded earlier* was not brought out during this morning's circus show.

Analysis of the adjective clause:

 Which   had got   wounded   earlier.
Conjn/ S   A   V   C   C

(c)   My uncle visited the school *where I   had my primary education.*
          S   (A)V.   O   Conjn S A.V   O

(d) Madhu *who   wasn't   good in English* passed in English II comfortably.
          S   Conjn/S Neg A.V C   O   (A)V   O   C

(e) The schools *which   receive aid from the government* are known
             S   Conjn/S (A)V O   O   A   V
     as Government schools.
                O

Adjective phrases

Instead of the S-A-V-O/C form, we may cut out the A-V sections and use a group of words to convey the same meaning. Thus, we can achieve some economy. When so done, the group of words would be known as **adjective phrase**. An adjective phrase is also known as **adjunct. Adjunct** gives additional information about a noun and must appear to the immediate right of that noun. Here are the examples:

(bb) The tiger, *wounded earlier*, was not brought out during this morning's circus show.

(ac) My uncle visited the school *of my primary education.*

(ad) Madhu, *weak in English*, passed in English II very comfortably.

(ae) The schools, *receiving   aid from the government*, are known as the Govt.
      S   gerund   Amplifying words   A   V   O
     schools.
      O

Since an adjunct will always appear in the middle of a sentence, show the words between commas as done in (bb) (dd) and (ee).

Noun clause

A clause that does the job of a *noun* is known as **Noun clause**. Accordingly, a noun clause could appear as Subject or Object of a sentence. As the Object, that clause will answer the Object (Noun) test. Here are the examples:

(a)   *What the Principal had said about our son's conduct*   is   true.
       O   S   A   V   O   A.V Adv
      |—————————————————— S ——————————————————|

(b)   *The hand that rocks the cradle*   rules the world.
                        S   (A)V   O

(c)   The law will punish *whoever is guilty.*
       S   A   V   O

(d)   I do not believe *what he says.*

In (c) and (d), the words in italics answer the Noun test like this,

The law will punish WHO?
I do not believe WHAT?

Do notice that the conjunction plays an important part in conveying the meaning of the concerned clause. In (c) it (WHOEVER) is acting as the subject; same in (d). In (a) and (b), the words in italics are acting as the subject (Noun) but in the S-A-V-O/C form. In spite of having S-A-V-O/C, does the clause part (shown in *italics*) reveal a sensible meaning? Don't they sound incomplete, as though something is missing in them? But, the clauses sound meaningful when read with the other half of the sentence. That is the characteristics of a **clause.** A clause, although will have S-A-V-O/C, would give a complete meaning only when it is read with some other word(s) in the other part of the sentence.

Can you view the above as Complex sentences? Strictly speaking, No, though there are 2 Nos S-A-V in each. A Complex sentence must have two Simple sentences. A Simple sentence must be self contained in meaning. See (d) above. "I do not believe" is not a Simple sentence because it is not self contained in meaning; it has only S-A-V. Next, we can split a Complex sentence into two individual meaningful Simple sentences; the conjunction in a Complex sentence would merely help in giving a sensible joint meaning; a conjunction in a Complex sentence will play no other part.

Let us apply this test in these sentences:

(aa) What is   true. The Principal had said about our son's conduct.
     I/S A.V C   S   A   V   O

Although the first sentence has S-A.V-C, it does not convey a sensible meaning. We get a sensible meaning only when both sentences are read as a whole.

(bb) The hand rules the world.   That rocks the cradle.
      S   (A)V   O   S   (A)V   O

Though each sentence has S-A-V-O, no clear meaning is visible until we read both the individual sentences together.

So, it seems more reasonable to view all these sentences as **Sentence with a clause** rather than as Complex sentences. Each sentence becomes meaningful only when read as a whole and the conjunction here plays a vital part.

In Chapter 27, you learnt that any two Simple sentences could be combined into a single sentence with a sensible joint meaning if we use a suitable conjunction. It also means that a Complex sentence could be split into two Simple sentences, each with an independent meaning; one sentence will not depend on the other to reveal a meaning. Whereas, splitting a **sentence with a clause** into two individual meaningful sentence would not be possible although it too will have 2 Nos S-A-V or S-A-V-O/C.

Noun phrase

If we remove the A-V parts in the Noun clause (and modify the group if necessary to retain the meaning) we will get Noun phrase.

(aa) *The principal's report about our son's conduct* is true.
(ab) *The cradle rocking hand* rules the world.
(ac) The law will punish *the guilty persons.*
(ad) I do not believe *his statements.*

Adverb clause

A clause that passes the 'complement test' is the adverb clause. Or, a clause that acts as the complement of a sentence will be known as adverb clause. We may also define it as a clause that answers the test questions, WHEN, WHERE or HOW. (HOW many, HOW far, HOW long, HOW much, HOW often?) after S-A-V.

(a) Go home only *after you finish your assignment.* (Go home only WHEN?)
(b) We sing *when we are happy.* (We sing WHEN?)
(c) They go *where the crowd is less.* (They go WHERE?)
(d) Do this job *as I have explained.* (Do this job HOW?)
(e) Don't come to my house *when my parents are present.* (Don't come to my house WHEN?)

All the clauses shown in *italics* answer the test questions with the interrogative adverbs. Hence, they are adverb clauses.

Next, examine all the sentences with reference to the 4 identification rules cited under "Definition of a clause" Every rule has been fulfilled in all the examples from (a) to (e). Note particularly that the conjunction (or, sometimes referred as the 'introducing word') is a part of the clause in conveying the meaning.

Types of Adverb clauses

We could classify the Adverb clauses under 8 types. Each type will have its own test question listed above. But, basically there are only 4 - of Time, Place, Manner and Reason and the others are their extensions.

Adverb clause of Time (Test Q: WHEN)

(a)   (You)   Don't   get up   *until*   *the film*   *finishes.*
       S   Neg A   V   Conjn   S   (A)V

(b)   I came   *after*   *you had sent me an invitation.*
          Conjn

Adverb clause of Place (TQ : WHERE)

(c)   Can't I sit *where I like?*

(d)   We don't know *how we could proceed there.*

Adverb clause of Manner (TQ: HOW)

(e)   You may do *as you please.*

(f)   The story ended **as** *I had expected.*

Adverb clause of quantity/number (TQ: HOW many/much?)

(g)   *When* we stepped on the platform, *three delegates welcomed us.*

(h)   He doesn't pay *as much tax as we do.*

Adverb clause of distance (TQ: HOW far?)

(i)   The policeman said that *Martin's house was 3 KM away.*

(j)   We enquired whether *the next village was nearby or far off?*

Adverb clause of frequency (TQ: HOW often?)

(k)   He replied curtly that *he would teach any lesson only once.*

Adverb clause of reason (TQ: WHY?)

(l)   Do you know *why you had failed in Std X?*

(m)   The fuse blew *when we switched on the Microwave oven.*

(n)   I was glad *that my mother liked my gift.*

Adverb clause of result (TQ: WHY?)

(o) The picture frame dropped <u>because</u> *some visitor had touched it.*

(p) That alsatian dog would attack <u>if</u> *anyone teases it.*

<u>Note:</u>

To identify an adverb or a complement we don't use the test question WHY. This is used only for identifying a clause - an adverb clause for that matter.

Adverb phrase

In order to derive an Adverb phrase, remove the A-V elements in the clause but retain the meaning of the clause.

(aa) Don't go until *the completion of your assignment.*

(cc) Can't I sit *at a place of my liking?*

(ee) You may do *at your pleasure.*

(ii) The policemen indicated *the distance to Martin's house as 3 KM.*

(ll) Do you know *the reasons for your failure in Std X?*

(oo) The picture frame dropped *because of someone's touching.*

<u>Note:</u>

It may not be possible to convert every clause into a phrase. But, it would be possible to write a phrase directly; all you have to remember is, 'don't use A-V'.

Complex sentence or Adverb clause?

An Adverb clause is a tricky thing. It is quite possible to mistake a "sentence with an adverb clause" for a Complex sentence and vice versa. Of course, when you are writing a long sentence or a paragraph or an essay, it does not matter whether the sentence you have composed is a Complex one or a Simple with an adverb clause. But, you must be clear in your mind. Such distinction will be of academic interest only.

The key points of differences are, if you separate out the 2 Nos S-A-V-O/C and each reveals a self contained meaning, that sentence is a true and regular Complex type. But, if one part depends on the other for the meaning along with the conjunction/connecting word, then it is a "sentence with a clause" variety.

Structure of a Compound sentence

Now that you have learnt everything about the three types of clauses, let us write out some Compound sentences. Do remember that a Compound sentence is a single sentence which may contain three or more Simple sentences with conjunctions or a Complex sentence with one or more clauses.

Here are some Compound sentences with an analysis (or breakdown) of their structure:

1. The man who plays tennis constantly will become an ace player one day. (13 words)

   "The man will become an ace player one day" (1 Simple)
   " who plays tennis constantly" (1 adjective clause)

2. I knew an ambitious student who said that he wanted to become a writer. (14 words)

   "I knew an ambitious student" (1 Simple)
   "who said that he wanted to become a writer" (1 Complex in the form of
   an adjective clause)

3. Though a boy may hail from a rich family, he will flourish in life only if he studies well during his student days. (22 words) (3 Simples with 2 conjunctions)

4. A man who does not understand that every thing God created on the Earth is for his good, is a foolish person. (22 words)

   "A man is a foolish person" (1 Simple)
   "who does not understand" (1 adjective clause)
   "that every thing God created on the Earth ` (1 noun clause)
   "that everything God created on the Earth is for his good (1 Complex)
   overall: 1 Simple plus 2 clauses plus 1 Complex.

5. The village was asleep when the dacoits, who were armed with guns and iron rods, decided to rob all the rich men there. (23 words)

   "The village was asleep" (1 Simple)
   "when the dacoits decided to rob all the rich men there" (1 adverb clause)
   "who were armed with guns and iron rods" (1 adjective clause)
   The adjective clause could be reduced to a phrase like this,
   The village was asleep when the dacoits, armed with guns and iron rods, decided to rob all the rich men there. (21 words)

6. I have no sympathy for a boy who gambles almost daily and cheats his parents thus. (16 words)

   "I have no sympathy for a boy and cheats his parents thus" (1 Complex)
   "who gambles almost daily" (1 adjective clause)

7. This bicycle, bought 2 years back, has never let me down and can go on well for 2 more years possibly. (A Complex sentence with an adjunct) (21 words)

Length of a Compound sentence

According to modern practice, a sentence should not be of more than 16/20 words. This would mean that we restrict our sentences to the Complex variety or a Simple sentence variety with one clause.

What is wrong if a sentence is long? If it is so, one is likely to lose the meaning somewhere half way or so.

Therefore, we can score out combining 4 sentences. In combining 3 sentences also, the length should not go beyond 20. You may feel at times that writing a long sentence of more than 20 words may become unavoidable. True. In such cases, make sure that in one reading the reader is able to grasp the meaning without any kind of doubts. So long as you ensure this condition, there is no harm going in for a sentence say around 24 words. This would be possible only when you combine a maximum of 3 short Simple sentences.

The art of writing a Compound sentence

When you write anything such as, an essay/composition, an article, a report or a letter, don't transform your contents into Simple sentences only. It would then sound childish. After 2 /3 Simple sentences, write a Complex one. Make sure that every sentence doesn't start in the same way, viz, every sentence in the pattern of S-A-V-O/C. Go in for other patterns like, PARTI-S-A-V-O or PREPN PHRASE - S-A-V-O/C. Don't start every Complex sentence in the same way. Start some with the conjunction.

Another tip to observe is, convert your *ideas/thoughts* into Simple sentences initially and combine them into a Compound sentence like we have done in the exercise above.

Since a Compound sentence would certainly be longer than a Complex sentence, it would be good if you restrict it to One for every four paras.

Exercise

Pick out the Complex and Simple sentences and clauses in the following Compound sentences:

1. The cricket match which concluded this afternoon was criticised heavily by the spectators since not all the players played their best.
2. Having got hurt, the center forward stopped suddenly while the wingers waited for the ball to be passed to them.
3. The ship which was caught in a typhoon sailed into the harbour late last night when the Captain fainted due to exhaustion.
4. Food grain sell cheap when the grain output has been high and the rain had been plentiful in most parts of the country.
5. When the boy let go the stone from his catapult, the stone went straight into a bunch of mangoes out of which one fell down a few seconds later.

Pick out the clauses in the following sentences and state what type it is; later replace the clause by an appropriate phrase:

6. This is the house where my late uncle lived.
7. "Love your neighbour as yourself," is a great command of Lord Jesus Christ.

8. I hope that I shall teach you all English.
9. There shall be perfect discipline as long as I am the leader of this group.
10. That we should be present here 5 minutes before the laid down time, is the rule here.
11. We should not pay the maid the full month's wages since she had worked here only for 18 days during the whole month.
12. It is regretted that he retired from service so prematurely.
13. Will you please tell me why you stole this purse from my room?
14. This man does not know where I live.
15. We don't believe what he said in front of the Principal.
16. Shouldn't the police know where the liquor shop is?
17. Do you know the hospital where you were born?
18. He who climbs too high is sure to fall off.
19. Take a lamp because the night is dark.
20. I forgive you since you have repented.

Replace the adjective clauses by adjuncts in the following sentences:

21. Mohan's small kitten whose fur is white as wool, is only 2 months old.
22. My uncle's house which is a 2-floor bungalow was built within 11 months.
23. Our school won the finals which was held on the last day of March.
24. We could have easily caught the thief who was hiding in the bush to our left.
25. Suhasini, who is the tallest girl in our college, is actually only 16 years old.

Combine the following pairs of sentences in as many different ways as you can:

26. (a) We played a volley ball match against St John's school. (b) Unfortunately it was called off half way because of heavy rain.
27. (a) The seniors went on a picnic last Sunday. (b) Only 3 lady students and 10 men students participated.
28. (a) We shall surely submit our assignment tomorrow. (b) Please revise the lesson once again today.
29. (a) This small boy is my friend's brother. (b) He is in LKG class in the next school.
30. (a) It is raining heavily. (b) Shouldn't we take our umbrellas?

Combine the following groups of 3 sentences into 1 Compound sentence in as many ways as you can:

31. (a) Bharathiyar was a great poet. (b) He was born in Tamil Nadu. (c) Many do not know his date of death.
32. (a) Nehru devoted himself to public affairs. (b) He seldom took a holiday. (c) This went on for 40 years.
33. (a) He was a great writer. (b) He was an English man. (c) All his books are read even now by the students.

34. (a) The sun shone on the corn. (b) The corn ripened in due time. (c) The farmer was happy.

35. (a) The operation theatre was covered with blood. (b) Some parts of the wall got stained. (c) The floor was darkened too.

Break the following Compound sentences into their component Simple sentences/clauses:

36. You may or may not like this new magazine but nevertheless I am sending it to you since your father told me to do so.

37. Knowing that St Paul's is a stronger team, James refused to play against it on some excuse or the other because he didn't wish to be known as a losing Captain.

38. All hell broke lose when the RSS chief said that the Christian establishment members should become independent of foreign control (Indian Express, 21.10.2000)

39. While details of the fighting have been hushed up in Pakistan, reports say, in recent weeks, Kotli has witnessed gunfights between two factions and the security forces have just stood by and watched. (Indian Express, 21.10.2000)

40. India said it was keeping a close vigil along the international border with Pakistan following media reports from Islamabad that the latter was conducting a major military exercise near the Rann of Kutch (The Hindu, 22.10.2000)

41. We had a partial father, who gave me a better education than my two elder brothers because they could not go beyond the X standard.

42. Among the several reasons which make me happy to have been born in India, one of them is that I could learn and practise many languages here.

43. For many years this politician was marked for assassination but his spirits never failed, and he was never frightened about his future.

44. The physical stamina of the soldiers on both sides had become nearly exhausted, and on the part of the Indian troops there definitely was a determination to finish off the enemy and bring the matters to an end.

45. In a strict legal sense that is probably the domicile of a person, where he has his true fixed permanent home and principal establishment, and to which, after a long period of absence, he returns.

State whether the following sentences are true Complex sentences or sentences with clause. Justify your answer.

46. I will stay here till you return.

47. When Sam arrives he will tell us everything about the match.

48. They had such a fierce dog that no one dared touch it.

49. They had moved house three times since they got married.

50. After you have finished with this gadget, return it to me.

51. State the function of a conjunction in a Complex sentence and in a sentence with a clause. Justify your answer with examples.

Chapter 43

SYNTHESIS OF SENTENCES

Introduction

When you have to write a paragraph (incidentally, 'paragraph' is the basic unit of any piece of writing) if you write only Simple sentences and start each with the Subject, it will make an irritable reading.

In Chapter 27, we saw that 2 Simple sentences could be combined into a single Complex sentence.

In Chapter 42 we learnt that we could combine 3 or more Simple sentences into a single Compound sentence.

How many ways have we learnt so far of how to combine two Simple sentences into a single sentence? They are,

(a) Complex sentence method.
(b) Infinitive connector.
(c) By various participle methods.
(d) Through Emphatic IT method.
(e) By using clauses and phrases.

In this Chapter shall we employ all the above methods to combine Simple sentences? This is called, "Synthesis" of sentences.

Here is a trial exercise. In how many ways could you combine (synthesise) the following pairs of sentences into a **Single** sentence?

1. (a) Here is my college friend. (b) His name is John.

   : John is my college friend and he is here. (Complex sentence)
   : Infinitive connector method fails here.
   : Being my college friend, John is here. (Participle connector)
   : It is John, my college friend who is here. (Emph IT method)
   : Because of our college friendship, John is here. (Noun phrase)
   : Here is John, my college friend. (Adjective phrase - Adjunct.)

2. (a) The weather is pleasant today. (b) It is a little cold for me.

   : Though the weather is pleasant, it is a little cold for me. (Complex sentence)
   : It is a little cold to be pleasant today. (Infin. Connector)
   : The weather being pleasant, it is a little cold for me. (Participle)
   : It is because of the pleasant weather that it is cold for me. (Emph IT)
   : Due to the pleasant weather, it is cold for me. (Prep. Phrase)

3. (a) This piece of information is of no use to us. (b) It has come too late.

: Because this piece of information has come too late, it is of no use to us.
(Complex sentence)
: This piece of information has come too late <u>to be</u> of use to us.
(Infinitive connector)
: Coming too late, this piece of information is of no use to us.
(Participle)
: It is due to its late arrival that this piece of information is of no use to us.
(Emphatic IT)
: This piece of information is of no use to us because of its late coming.
(Adverb phrase)

4. (a) A little bird snatched away a samosa from the girl's tiffin box. (b) It then settled on a nearby tree to eat it.

: After it snatched a samosa from the girl's tiffin box, a little bird settled on a nearby tree to eat it. (Complex sentence)
: A little bird settled on a nearby tree to eat the samosa, snatched from a girl's tiffin box. (Infin connector with an Adjective phrase)
: Snatching a samosa from the girl's tiffin box, a little bird settled on a nearby tree to eat it. (Participle)
: It is because of its snatching a samosa from a girl's tiffin box that a little bird settled on a nearby tree to eat it. (Emph. IT)
: The little bird settled on a nearby tree to eat the samosa, snatched from the girl's tiffin box. (Adjective phrase)

5. (a) Menon ran at to speed. (b) At the bend he ran out of breath.

: Running at top speed, Menon ran out of breath at the bend.
(Simple with a participle)
: Since he ran at top speed, Menon ran out of breath at the bend.
(Complex)
: Menon ran out of breath at the bend because of his tremendous speed.
(Simple with Adverb/Noun phrase)

6. (a) This is Madurai city. (b) The Pandiyan king ruled it for long from here.

: This is Madurai city from where the Pandiyan king ruled for long.
(Complex sentence or a Simple with an adverb clause)
: Infinitive connector method fails here.
: It is from Madurai city that the Pandiyan king ruled for long.
(Emphatic IT)
: He, being the Pandiyan king, ruled for long from Madurai city.
(Participle)

Combining may be possible in more than one way in some of the methods.

Combining (synthesising) through Gerunds

A gerund would also look like a present participle and vice versa. When a sentence starts with a gerund, the word could be mistaken for a participle. But the noun test will show whether the words following the gerund are 'amplifying words' or part of the participle. Do remember that you would see some on going action in a present participle. Let us examine some sentences starting with a verb ending in ING:

(a) **Standing** near my scooter, I spotted my friend at a distance.
      ?   C

"Standing" is a present participle here because it shows an on-going-action. Can we consider "near my scooter" as amplifying words of 'standing'? No. These words merely show the place of that 'on going action'. Therefore 'standing' is a present participle.

(b) **Standing** for elections, is not everybody's cup of tea.
      ?   Noun

In this sentence, "for elections" certainly appear to be the amplifying words for the word "standing". Therefore 'standing' here is a gerund.

The question is, can we use a gerund in this way, to connect two Simple sentences. It may be possible in certain situations. Try to connect the pairs of sentences given below:

(i) Roshan demands his money. (ii) Kewal refused to give the money.

"Demanded by Roshan, Kewal refused to give the money." This is a participle method. (Past participle)

"**Returning** of his own money was refused by Kewal."

Gerund   Ampl. words

"Returning" here is certainly a gerund followed by the amplifying words.

Let us take the next pair of sentences:

(iii) Velan returned from leave. (iv) He called for a social get-together of all his colleagues immediately.

"Returning from leave, Velan called for a social get-together of all his colleagues immediately." (Participle method)

"**Holding** of a social get-together was ordered by Velan immediately

gerund   amplifying words

on his return from leave."

So, it is possible to synthesise two Simple sentences into one through gerunds also. But, it is a difficult exercise because one may have to use new words in order to retain the original meaning.

Compound sentence method

Combine the following groups of 3 sentences in as many ways as you can. Here we can include the Compound sentence method also in addition to the 4 given earlier:

7.   (a) I bought this bicycle 2 years back. (b) It has not let me down at all. (c) It can go on well for 2 more years possibly.

: Bought 2 years back, this cycle has never let me down and can go on well for 2 more years possibly. (Compound sentence with 1 Complex and 1 participle)

: Two years back I bought this cycle which has never let me down and can go on well for 2 more years possibly. (A Complex with one adjective clause.)

: Though 2 years old, it has never let me down and it can go on well for 2 more years possibly. (Complex with an adverb phrase)

: This bicycle, bought 2 years back, has never let me down and can go on well for 2 more years possibly. (A Complex sentence with an adjunct)

: It was because of its age of 2 years that this cycle never let me down and it can go on well for 2 more years possibly. (Emph. IT and a Compound sentence)

8.   (a) Our office superintendent opens all the letters himself. (b) He would read them all carefully. (c) He would reply each letter immediately.

: Opening all the letters himself and reading them carefully, our office supervisor would reply each letter immediately. (2 participles connected by 'and' in 1 Simple sentence)

: Having opened and read all the letters himself, our office supervisor would reply each letter immediately. (A Simple sentence with 2 participles)

: After the supervisor opens all the letters, which he shall read carefully, he would reply each letter immediately. (A Compound sentence with an adjective clause)

: Our supervisor would open all the letters himself and read them carefully in order to reply each letter immediately. (A Complex with an infinitive connector) (19 words)

: It is because of the habit of our supervisor of opening all the letters and reading them carefully that he would reply each immediately. (Emphatic IT)

9.   (a) This neighbour gave us a kitten. (b) The kitten looks lovely and pretty. (c) It drinks milk.

: This kitten, which was given to us by our neighbour, is lovely and pretty and it drinks milk. (A Compound sentence with an adjective clause)

: Having been given by our neighbour, this lovely and pretty kitten drinks milk. (A Simple sentence with a participle in passive voice)

: Given by our neighbour, this lovely and pretty kitten drinks milk. (A Simple sentence with a participle in active voice)

: Being lovely and pretty, this kitten, which was given to us by our neighbour, drinks milk. (A Simple sentence with one adjective clause and a participle)

: Because of its loveliness and prettiness, our neighbour gave us this kitten which drinks milk. (1 Simple sentence with an adjective clause and an adverb phrase)

10. (a) James took this medicine for headache. (b) He felt much better after 2 hours. (c) He went to school on the following day.

: Having taken this medicine for headache and feeling much better after 2 hours, James went to school on the following day. (A Simple sentence with two participles)

: After taking this medicine for headache, James, feeling much better, went to school on the following day. (A Complex sentence with 1 participle)

: Because of this medicine for his headache, James, feeling much better after 2 hours, went to school on the following day. (A Simple sentence with 1 participle and one adverb phrase)

: James, who took this medicine for headache, went to school on the following day because he felt better after 2 hours. (A Complex sentence with an adjective clause)

: It is because of taking medicine for headache that James felt much better after 1 hour and he went to school on the following day. (Emphatic IT and a Compound sentence)

11. (a) My friend went to Trichy last week. (b) He wrote a letter to me on arrival there. (c) He is likely to return to Chennai after 4 weeks.

: My friend wrote a letter to me on arrival at Trichy last week and he is likely to return to Chennai after 4 weeks. (Complex sentence)

: On reaching Trichy last week, my friend wrote a letter to me and he is likely to return to Chennai after 4 weeks. (Complex sentence with a participle)

: Because of his late arrival at Trichy last week, James wrote a letter to me saying that he is likely to return to Chennai after 4 weeks. (A Complex sentence with an adverb phrase; **saying** is a participle here)

: Announcing his arrival at Trichy, James wrote to say that he is likely to return to Chennai after 4 weeks. (A Complex sentence with a participle)

: James, after he arrived at Trichy, wrote to say that he would return to Chennai after 4 weeks. (A Complex sentence with an adverb clause)

Shall we now try combining 4 Simple sentences into a single sentence?

12. (a) Thambidurai is a careless student. (b) The other students in his class are not that careless. (c) The HOD's quarterly report said so. (d) Thambidurai's father read the report with sadness.

: The HOD in his quarterly report said that Thambidurai is very careless unlike the other students in the class and the father read it with sadness. (A Compound sentence with 2 conjunctions)

: The HOD's quarterly report, which was read by the father with sadness said that Thambidurai is a careless student unlike his classmates. (A Complex sentence with an adjective clause)

: Having read the HOD's quarterly report, the father felt sad to note that his son Thambidurai is a careless student unlike his other classmates. (A Complex sentence with an infinitive connector and a participle)

: Noting from the HOD's quarterly report that his son Thambidurai is a careless student unlike the others in his class, the father felt sad. (A Complex sentence with a participle)

13. (a) We could have won today's football match. (b) Mike failed twice in his attempt to score a goal. (c) The center-forward too didn't pass the ball to the correct player on many occasions (d) I noted down these lapses myself.

: According to my notings, if the center-forward had passed the ball to the correct player on every occasion and if Mike had not failed twice in his attempt at scoring goal, we could have won today's football match. (A Compound sentence with 2 conjunctions)

: But for the lapses, which were noted down by me, of the center-forward not passing the ball to the correct player on several occasions and Mike failing twice at scoring a goal, we could have won today's football match. (A Simple sentence with two noun phrases and one adjective clauses)

Summary

Going through all the combined sentences, you would note that it would be possible to combine 2 or 3 or 4 sentences into a single sentence by at least one method.

Keeping in mind that a Compound sentence should not normally exceed 20 words, we must desist from combining 4 Simples. Thus, restrict your synthesis to 3 Simples of average length and the combined sentence should not exceed 20 words.

In our daily life, we would be combining mostly 2 Simples. Here, in certain cases, certain methods may fail. But, two methods would succeed in combining any pair of sentences into a single meaningful joint sentence even if they are miles apart. They are: Complex and Emphatic IT.

Emphatic IT method may not be useful in every case in the 3 Simple combining.

The art of composing a paragraph

When you write anything such as, an essay/composition, an article, a report or a letter, go in for variations in your sentence structure. You know how to play round with a Simple sentence with infinitives, participles and phrases. To avoid any annoyance element, observe the rule of not starting every sentence in the same way and use of connectors.

Another tip to observe is, convert your *ideas/thoughts* into Simple sentences initially and combine them into a single Complex or Compound sentence like we have done in the exercise above.

It is a good practice to avoid compound sentences altogether. You may however use, possibly one or two in about 4 paragraphs! One could write a very effective para with Simple sentences alone, composed in various styles and combinations with connectors and one Complex sentence in every paragraph. Your aim should be to make your reader understand clearly and in one attempt what you have said and not show your ability of writing long and high sounding sentences!

Exercise

Combine the following pairs of sentences into one Simple sentence using infinitive connectors:

1. He paid off his debts. He sold away his second hand car.
2. The father went to the boarding. He met his daughter for ten minutes.
3. I hurried home. I talked to my father about my problem.
4. The doctor accelerated his car. He operated upon the patient in the operation theatre.
5. The servant maid lit the gas stove. She cooked the dinner within 45 minutes.

Combine the following pairs into one Simple sentence through any participle method:

6. She opened the letter. The girl fainted within minutes.
7. The MP was on his feet at the Speaker's ruling. He walked out in a huff.
8. A small school boy snatched the conductor's money bag. He jumped out of the bus thereafter.
9. I was very hungry. I swallowed the omelette in two gulps.
10. The lady doctor's mind went somewhere. She forgot to write out the prescription.
11. The bookseller telephoned to me. Then he sent a parcel of books.
12. I bought a remote-controlled car to my grandson. I remembered my promise to him.
13. We drove all day. We reached Chennai only towards the evening.
14. My friend promised to come to my house the next day. He did not however turn up.

15. The urchin climbed the mango tree. He pushed down to the ground dozens of mangoes.

Combine the following pairs of sentence into one Simple sentence using Gerunds:

16. The pawn broker wanted his capital back. Only then would he give the jewellery back.
17. My office colleague returned from his tour. He arranged a meeting of all members.
18. He violated the company rules. We protested.
19. I had promised to give my nephew a gift. He reminded me tactfully.
20. Rustom was disheartened. His friend had betrayed him.

Convert the following pairs into one Single sentence through any <u>one</u> method according to your preference:

21. Mani will surely come here. He will take back his books.
22. India is a big country. Here, the people speak 16 different languages.
23. This monument is very beautiful. It attracts every tourist's attention.
24. We wanted to sell off our house. We advertised about it.
25. Christ's Apostles sold away all their property. They wanted to lead a simple life.
26. This student was very careless. It was difficult to correct him.
27. Sheila had acted in many stage plays. She was a good actress.
28. Honesty is a great virtue. Sincerity is the next.
29. Cricket is an interesting game. People in India are lately losing interest in it.
30. Didn't you help me in my time of trouble? How could I ever forget it?

Combine the following pairs of sentences in as many different ways as you can:

31. (a) We played a volley ball match against St John's school. (b) Unfortunately it was called off half way because of heavy rain.
32. (a) B.Sc II year students went on a picnic last Sunday. (b) Only 3 lady students and 10 men students participated.
33. (a) We shall surely submit our assignment tomorrow. (b) Please revise the lesson once again today.
34. (a) This small boy is my friend's brother. (b) He is in LKG class in the next school.
35. (a) It is raining heavily. (b) Shouldn't we take our umbrellas?

Combine the following sentences (3 Simples in each question) into a single sentence using any suitable method:

36. (a) Sukdev knew Electronics very well. (b) He had a good mastery over the subject. (c) Soon he was able to assemble a television set on his own.
37. (a) It is bad to be selfish. (b) Many of us know it. (c) Yet, we continue with the habit.

38. (a) My elder brother bought a second hand car. (b) He knew driving earlier. (c) Now he uses it like an expert.

39. (a) A poet needs inspiration. (b) Many people can write some kind of verses. (c) Such pieces will not be accepted by the literary world.

40. (a) All the shops in the city were closed. (b) There were hardly any vehicles on the road. (c) The death of a leader caused all these.

41. (a) We had our annual day the other day. (b) The chief guest was the Vice Chancellor of our university. (c) He is an ex-student of our college.

42. (a) Many countries possess weapons of mass destruction. (b) All of them talk of peace. (c) They do not want any developing countries to join their club.

43. (a) One young scientist invented a machine. (b) He obtained a patent on it. (c) Some manufacturers are out to cheat him.

44. (a) I must work hard. (b) I shall be a failure in life otherwise. (c) No one will respect me for my inefficiency.

45. (a) Superstition is bad. (b) Some people associate this with religion. (c) True religion enables everyone to lead a good life.

Chapter 44

TRANSFORMATION OF SENTENCES

Introduction

How many categories of sentences have you learnt so far? List them out.

Question type (Interrogative types):

In this there are 5 varieties - General question, Specific questions, Negative questions, Emphatic question 1 and Emphatic question 2.

Answer type

In this there are 2 varieties: Affirmative answer and Negative answer.

Order/suggestion type (Imperative type)

Interjection (Exclamatory type)

It would be useful to know how to change one category into another without changing the meaning. You know, double 'negative' is equal to 'positive'. Keep this rule in mind while transforming sentences.

Interchange of Sentences

Assertive into equivalent Negative sentences without change in the meaning

1. (a) Students must respect their teachers.
    (b) Students must not disrespect their teachers.

2. (a) Susheela is more beautiful than Kamala.
    (b) Kamala is not so beautiful as Susheela.
    or
    Kamala is less beautiful than Susheela.

3. (a) Khan's actions are always foolish.
    (b) Khan's actions are never wise.

4. (a) There is a woman behind every man's success.
    (b) No man's success is without a woman behind him.

5. (a) Only the brave deserve praise.
    (b) None except the brave deserve praise.

Assertive order/suggestion into Negative

1. (a) (You do) Sit down.
    (b) (You) Don't stand up.

2. (a) (You do) Buy your train ticket today.
    (b) (You) Don't fail to buy your train ticket today.

3. (a) Smoking is prohibited here.
    (b) Smoking is not acceptable/entertained here.

4. (a) (You do) Show your ID card at the gate.
    (b) (You) Don't fail to show your ID card at the gate.

5. (a) (You do) Spare the rod and spoil the child.
    (b) If you spare the rod, the child will get spoiled.

Interrogative into assertive (or, double negative)

1. (a) Why should some people be rich?
    (b) All people shouldn't be poor. (or, why shouldn't some people be not poor?)

2. (a) Doesn't rose have thorns?
    (b) No rose is without thorns.

3. (a) Is every student intelligent?
    (b) No student is dull. (or, Is any student un-intelligent?)

4. (a) Some citizens are always helpful, aren't they?
    (b) No citizen is unhelpful, is he?

5. (a) Many young women don't like to wear sarees, do they?
    (b) Many young women refrain from wearing sarees, don't they?

Exclamatory to assertive

1. (a) What a splendid idea!
    (b) Indeed, your idea is splendid.

2. (a) If only all my troubles would end!
    (b) Wouldn't all my troubles come to an end sometime?

Active voice into Passive

1. (a) Thomas does not write good English.
    (b) Good English is not written by Thomas.

2. (a) Did we pay the shopkeeper the full amount?
    (b) Was the shopkeeper paid the full amount by us?

3. (a) Shakuntala is not keeping good health nowadays.
    (b) Good health is not being kept by Shakuntala nowadays.

4. (a) The Asst. Lecturer has kept all our classwork note books with himself.
    (b) All our classwork note books have been kept with himself by the Asst. Lecturer.

5. (a) Most of us had read this English novel in our previous year.
    (b) This English novel had been read by most of us in our previous year.

6. (a) Many of you ought to have taken the competitive exam.
    (b) The competitive exam ought to have been taken by many of you.

7. (a) One of you could have consulted me.
    (b) I could have been consulted by one of you.

8. (a) (You do) Hand over the students' answer sheets today.
    (b1) The students' answer sheets are to be handedover by you today.
    (b2) Let the students' answer sheets be handed over by you today.

9. (a) Where did you place my watch?
    (b) Where was my watch placed by you?

10. (a) Who is eating biscuits at this time of the night?
    (b) Biscuits are being eaten by whom at this time of the night?

Same word in different parts of speech

In the English language, some words could be used in more than one part of speech. Its meaning and role would become apparent only when we read the full sentence.

Take the word SINCE. We could use this as conjunction, preposition and also adverb of time.

LEAVE is a verb and also a noun.

BUT is a preposition, conjunction and also adverb.

We may use each of the above words as it is, in different parts of speech.

And there are some words, which with a slight modification, can be used in different parts of speech. Take the word WISE. As it is, it is an adjective cum adverb. With a slight modification i.e. WISDOM, we can use it as a noun.

Study the following examples and in particular the words in *italics*:

(a)   This silly joke doesn't *amuse* me at all. (verb)

(aa) *Amusement* does not arise out of silly jokes. (noun)

(b)   You have *priced* this book Rs 100. (verb)

(ab) The *price* of this book is Rs 100. (noun)

(c)   Isn't this chap a *disgrace* to the James family? (noun)

(cc) This chap has *disgraced* the James family quite a lot. (verb)

In all the examples above, we have not changed the overall meaning of the sentences though we have repeated a particular word in a different parts of speech. Here are more examples.

In the following sentences, replace the Nouns shown in italics by Verbs:

(d)   My daughter pays *attention* to her studies.

(dd) My daughter *attends* to her studies always.

(e)   Our garden is in a state of *neglect*.

(ee) We have *neglected* our garden for too long.

(f)   The *difference* between English and Greek is great.

(ff) English and Greek *differ* greatly.

Rewrite the following sentences so as to replace the Adverbs shown in italics by Verbs:

(g)   Our soldiers in Kargil *successfully* repelled the Pakistani attacks.

(gg)   Our Kargil soldiers *succeeded* in repelling the Pakistani attacks.

(h)   Field Marshal Manekshaw was *admittedly* the greatest General of the 20th century.

(hh)   We must *admit* that Field Marshal Manekshaw was the greatest General of the 20th century.

(i)   My students welcomed the news *joyfully.*

(ii)   My students were *overjoyed* at the news.

Rewrite the following sentences by replacing Verbs/Adjectives shown in italics by corresponding Nouns:

(j)   Though the ant is very small, it is as *intelligent* as a lion.

(jj)   Though the ant is very small its *intelligence* is equal to that of a lion.

(k)   He announced *regretfully* that he had *acted* foolishly.

(kk)   He announced with *regret* that his *action* was foolish.

Replace the Nouns shown in italics by Adjectives/Adverbs of similar meaning:

(l)   In all *probability* it is going to rain this evening.

(ll)   It is *probable* that it might rain this evening.

(m)   The Factory dismissed this sentry for *negligence.*

(mm) Being *negligent*, the factory dismissed this sentry

Conclusion

We can use several English words in different parts of speech; some of them with different meaning and some with the same meaning but in different part of speech.

So long as you understand the rules of sentence construction (i.e S-A-V-O/C) and the various words that go in the O and/or C parts, you can use any word correctly in a sentence.

Transformation of Complex into Simple sentence

Is it possible to transform a Complex sentence into a Simple sentence? Yes, it is possible. And it is quite easy as well. You have already learnt how to reduce a Simple sentence into phrases or group of words (without S-A-V) and still retain the meaning. Thus, in a Complex sentence, all we have to do is to reduce one of the Simples into equivalent phrase by removing the S-A-V part and the result would indeed be a Simple sentence. Do remember that the reduction into phrases would be confined only to the O/C part.

To achieve this feat, we would have to use several tools such as, infinitives, gerunds, nouns, participles or preposition phrases.

Transformation

What method could we follow for transforming the undermentioned Complex into a Simple sentence:

(a) I wanted to take this examination last year but I didn't have the courage.
Ans: I couldn't take this examination last year due to lack of courage.

Have you noticed that we have changed one Simple sentence into an equivalent adverb phrase. (TQ: WHY?) But the whole sentence had been put in negative form to retain the original meaning? This is one method.

(b) This was a light epidemic of chicken pox and hence there is no danger in it.
Ans: Being a light epidemic of chicken pox, there is no danger in it.

Here, we have used a 'present participle'.

(c) I don't know what I shall do in such a situation.
Ans: I do not know what to do in such a situation.

'Infinitive' has been used here.

(d) What does it matter whether you are a teenager or not?
Ans: Being a teenager or not, doesn't matter at all, is it?

'Participle' used along with EQ in order to maintain the power of the question. Do remember, the meaning and force of the original sentence should be maintained.

(e) Did you visit him even after he had asked you not to?
Ans: Did you visit him against his desire?
     Did you visit him even after his request not to?

'Noun phrase' has been used.

Preposition phrases will also enable us to transform a Complex into a Simple sentence. Please refer to Chapter 40 for the examples.

Let us do the transformation in the reverse order. Given below are some Simple sentences that use Preposition phrases. Convert them into Complex sentences:

(a) *In order to* catch the forest brigand, a special task force had been formed.
          O   S   A   V

(b) *Because of* the fear of arrest, the political leaders went underground.
          O   S   (A)V   C

(c) *In case of* fire in our premises, (You) break   open this key box.
          O   (A) V   C   O

Here are the answers:

(aa) A special task force had been formed so that the forest brigand was caught.
(bb) The political leaders went underground because they feared arrest.
(cc) If there is fire in our premises, break open this key box.

So, adopt any method found suitable for this transformation. Here is a sample exercise for you. Do it yourself in the first instance before you consult the correct answers.

Convert the following Complex sentences into Simple sentences through any suitable method:

1. He uttered only a few words and I recognised him immediately.
2. Before they flush out the water, I must jump out.
3. Whenever I look at this photo, old memories come rushing back to me.
4. Though we tried several times, we couldn't scale over this high wall.
5. As you work, you will be rewarded.
6. This student is less active than we had expected.
7. Unless you come on time, you will not be admitted into the hall.
8. (You do) Go where you like.
9. I give up my fight since you had admitted defeat without fighting.
10. If you want to get selected, you must work very hard.

Answers:

1. I recognised him immediately after hearing only a few words from him.
   ('gerund' method)
2. I must jump out before flushing out of the water. ('gerund' method)
3. Old memories come rushing back to me after looking at this photo. ('gerund' method)
4. In spite of several trials, we couldn't scale over this high wall ('preposition phrase' method)
5. You will be rewarded for your work. ('Noun phrase' method)
6. We had expected this student to be more active. ('infinitive' method)
7. In case of late arrival, you will not be admitted into the hall. ('preposition phrase' method)
8. (You do) go anywhere of your liking. ('noun' method)
9. I give up my fight on account of your admittance of defeat without fighting.
   ('preposition phrase' and 'noun' methods)
10. You must work very hard in order to get selected. ('preposition phrase' method)

So, it is not at all difficult to convert even a long Complex sentence into a Simple sentence in one of the several ways.

Exercise

Change the degree of comparison without any change in the meaning:

1. I am as strong as my brother.
2. This newspaper has a larger circulation than any other morning paper.
3. Isn't Australia the largest island in the world?
4. Isn't it better to starve than beg?

5. This father loves all his sons equally well.

Change the following into Negative sentences without any change in the meaning

6. Dushyant loved Shakuntala.
7. I became doubtful whether he was the same person.
8. Everyone in the hall clapped as soon as the top actor appeared on the stage.
9. We visit our old relatives quite often.
10. This fellow is always idle.

Change the following Negatives into Affirmatives without any change in the meaning

11. No one believes in this man's honesty.
12. This Missionary didn't live in India for many years.
13. Not many men of olden days are alive today.
14. Our Principal never fails to reward good students.
15. Kalpana is not as clever as you.

Change the following into interrogatives:

16. Every tourist to India visits the Taj Mahal.
17. We can do nothing more for your cause.
18. I cannot pardon your negligence.
19. You would have seen this serial already.
20. Surely we shall go to the beach today.

Change the following interrogatives into equivalent Affirmatives:

21. Can any man add one extra day by worrying himself daily?
22. Is that the way a venerable lady should behave?
23. Could I ever forget those golden days?
24. Why waste time in this useless hobby?
25. Can a Negro change his skin?

Change the following into Exclamatory sentences:

26. It was a terrible night for all of us.
27. It is hard to believe that Lionel got a seat in an Engineering college.
28. It is very stupid of me to forget your good deeds towards me.
29. It is a surprise that we meet after 20 long years.
30. The night is beautiful in the moonlight.

Change the following exclamatories into Assertives:

31. Oh, what a sight the sunset was!
32. What a great creature an elephant is!
33. How cold you are, my girl!
34. How thoughtful of you, Joyce!
35. Shame on you to rob a blind man!

Change the following Actives into Passive without any change in the meaning:

36. Summon the fire-service immediately.
37. I couldn't collect your suit from the dry cleaners.
38. I am opening the front door now.
39. Brutus accused Caesar of ambition.
40. Who has taught you such magic feats as these?
41. He could get used to your style of playing cricket quite fast.
42. Every hostelier should have brought his own bed.
43. We had a beautiful car last year.

Change the following Passives into Actives without change in the meaning:

44. This letter had been written by my clerk.
45. Without effort nothing can be gained.
46. Honey is made by bees.
47. We would be blamed by all our colleagues.
48. A little bird was killed by a playful boy.
49. Good food was used to by us.
50. Simple living ought to be got used to by us.

In the following sentences replace the words in *italics* in as many parts of speech as possible but without changing the meaning of the sentence:

51. You cannot get *admission* without a ticket.
52. I have a *disinclination* for work today.
53. The spectators welcome the good news most *joyfully*.
54. This boy has *disgraced* his family.
55. Didn't this boxer put up a brave *fight?*

Convert the following Complex sentences into Simple sentences (i.e each new sentence should have only one set of S-A-V-O/C through any method of your preference):

56. Ever since I took residence in Chennai, I have not been keeping well at all.
57. Though we adopted several measures, our paddy output from our fields have not increased at all.
58. I am sorry that I have made you the captain of our badminton team.
59. He is so sick that he cannot get up from bed.
60. I would have immediately accepted the job if I had been in your place.
61. Can you type this letter if I permit you to use my computer?
62. Will you attend my birthday party if I deliver my invitation to you personally?
63. The teaspoon is not on the table since my mother has cleaned up the dining table.
64. Haven't you been ill ever since you stepped into this house?
65. Must you decline every gift even when it is offered without any strings.
66. I said softly that he should withdraw from the contest.

67. We overlooked the boy's mischiefs because he is a playful fellow.
68. This isn't a wrong answer if you examine the question more minutely.
69. Which is the book that is torn and dirty?
70. She hasn't any marble left in her bag since I had snatched them away.
71. Doesn't the mother hope that her daughter would have boarded the plane by now?
72. Didn't the surgeon explain to you that he could start the operation an hour earlier than scheduled?
73. The Principal was firm that he would suspend the erring students.
74. The dance teacher would scold you if you reported late.
75. They must report to the office since they have not filled up the forms.

Fill up the blank with suitable preposition phrases:

76. ...After...... my advice, this student took part in the game.
77. Could you accept 3 stamps .with... three rupees?
78. Discuss your point personally with your teacher without wasting my time.
79. ......For...... the journalist's report, this man took a bribe of Rs one lakh.
80. Being low registrations, the tutorial college had cancelled this course.

Chapter 45

ONE WORD SUBSTITUTES

General

Improving your vocabulary, must be your constant and continuous effort. Often one tends to write long sentences especially when you have to describe a situation or a state of mind etc. This is dubbed as 'verbosity'. You cannot afford to be verbose in your writing. Always look around for **one word substitutes** to achieve economy of words in sentence construction.

In this Chapter, a list of one word substitutes has been given and how to use each in long descriptions. This is not the final list; you have to look for more.

Single words and their use

In the following sentences the **words shown in bold** could be replaced by the designated single word:

1. Assassinated

President Kennedy was **killed cruelly and wantonly** by a mad gunman.
(Assassinate = kill. We use this word instead of 'kill' when a VIP happens to be the victim. For ordinary people we use, "He was killed."

2. Ailing

Martha came all the way from New Delhi to see her mother, who was **very sick** and weakening day by day.
(Martha came all the way from New Delhi to see her mother who was *ailing*.)

3. Alien

Isn't a **person from some African nation** one of the students in our class?
(Isn't an *alien* one of the students in our class?)

4. Alcopop

These days many soft drinks **contain small amount of alcohol.**
(These days many soft drinks are *alcopops*)

In all the four examples given above, the designated words are NOUNS or VERBS or ADJECTIVES/ADVERBS and no other parts of speech. This is an important point to remember. Before using the one word substitute, study the part to be replaced - what role those words in it are playing? Accordingly, choose the correct part of speech of the substitute.

5. Bretharian

A serious Yoga practitioner is **a person who believes he can reach a high state** of consciousness.
(A serious Yoga practitioner is a *Bretharian*.)

6. Balm

Her words were **so consoling and so encouraging** to a bed patient like me.
(Her words were a *balm* to a bed patient like me.)

7. Confiscated

The CBI, after a raid, **took away** all his assets and currency notes.
(The CBI, after a raid, *confiscated* all his assets and currency notes.)

8. Clandestinely

In spite of prohibition, some people brew country liquor **secretly and illegally.**
(In spite of prohibition, some people brew country liquor *clandestinely.*)

9. Doff

It is customary for an Englishman **to take off** his hat when greeting a lady.
(It is customary for an Englishman to *doff* his hat when greeting a lady.)

10. Douse

When a person with clothing is on fire, **throw cold water on** him immediately.
(When a person with clothing is one fire, *douse* him immediately.)

11. Exile

Ex Prime minister of Pakistan, Nawaz Sharief, has been sent **away to live in** Saudi Arabia
(Ex Prime minister of Pakistan has been sent on *exile* to Saudi Arabia.)

12. e-tailer

One who sells goods on internet is known as *e-tailer.*

13. Flaunt

Modern girls love to **show off** their colourful costume wherever they wander.
(Modern girls love to *flaunt* their costume wherever they wander.)

14. Fissures

Lately many political parties are showing **splits and divisions** among themselves.
(Lately many political parties are showing *fissures* among themselves.)

15. Genius

Bethoven was a **music composer of great eminence.**
(Bethoven was a music *genius*)

16. Guru

Mahatma Gandhi was Jawaharlal Nehru's political **leader and mentor.**
(Mahatmas Gandhi was Jawaharlal Nehru's political *guru.*)

17. House-arrest

Apostle St Paul was **confined to his house** in Rome for over two years.
(Apostle St Paul was under *house-arrest* in Rome for over 2 years.)

18. Hail

I **shouted for an auto rickshaw** standing in the middle of a large crowd.
(I *hailed* an auto rickshaw standing in the middle of a large crowd.)

19. Inertia

All things **remain at rest** unless disturbed by some external force.
(All things are in a state of *inertia* unless disturbed by some external force.)

20. Imaginative

Nelson is a student **full of ideas and foresight**.
(Nelson is an *imaginative* student.)

21. Jay walker

Murali **would cross a busy road casually and carelessly**.
(Murali is a *jay walker.*)

22. Jingoist

Late Zulfikar Bhutto **loved his country but had contempt for India.**
(Late Zulfikar Bhutta was a *jingoist.*)

23. Kleptomaniac

Esther **loves to steal or just grab things that don't belong to her.**
(Esther is a *kleptomaniac.*)

24. Knapsack

When we go on a picnic we carry **our food items, clothes etc in a big bag**.
(When we go on a picnic we carry a full *knapsack.*)

25. Litter (verb)

Has your bitch **given any puppies** so far?
(Has your bitch *littered* so far?)
This word can also be used as a 'noun'. "Our bitch gave a *litter* of 7 puppies".

26. Lead

Will you please give **some clues and indications** about the thief?
(Will you please give us some *leads* about the thief?).

27. Miracle

It seems almost a **remarkable and rare thing** that you came back alive from the debris after the earthquake.
(It seems almost a *miracle* that you came back alive from the debris.)

28. Maverick

This politician has been a **dissenter and trouble shooter** in his political party.
(This politician has been a *maverick* in his political party.)

29. Motto

In this organisation we go by the **rule and practice** of 'selfless service'.
(In this organisation we go by the *motto* of 'selfless service'.)

30. Nanny

My mother has employed an old **lady to look after my little sister**.
(My mother has employed a *nanny* for my little sister.)

31. Nominal

The Indian President is only **the head of the nation without any powers**.
(The Indian President is a *nominal* head of the nation.)

32. Niche

He had **such achievements to his credit that will never be forgotten** in this city.
(He had a *niche* for himself in this city.)

33. Onus

The **responsibility and burden** to prove your brother's innocence lie with you.
(The *onus* to prove your brother's innocence lies with you.)

33. Oracle

This saffron monk **has the ability to give reliable guidance for your future**.
(This saffron monk is an *oracle*.)

34. Ombudsman

This official **receives complaints from citizens against the authorities** for suitable remedies.
(This official is an *ombudsman*.)

35. Panacea

The **universal and reliable remedy** to remove corruption is to remove the word from our dictionary !!
(The *panacea* for removing corruption is to remove the word from our dictionary !!)

36. Prerogative

Wherever this simple and ordinary lady went, she received such a welcome that is the **exclusive privilege and right** of Indian politicians.
(Wherever this simple and ordinary lady went, she received such a welcome that is the *prerogative* of Indian politicians.)

37. Questionnaire

During the interview, they gave me **a huge list of questions** to be answered within 20 minutes.
(During the interview, they gave me a *questionnaire* to be answered within 20 minutes.)

38. Quincentenary

This religious group celebrated their **500th anniversary** last March.
(This religious group celebrated their *quincentenary* last March.)

39. Resumé

He gave a **brief account** of his meeting with the Minister.
(He gave a *resumé* of his meeting with the Minister.)

40. Rejuvenate

This new leader has promised **to revive and make his party strong** once again.
(This leader has promised to *rejuvenate* his party once again.)

41. Snob

This rich person **looks down upon all ordinary persons**.
(This person is a *snob*)

42. Sweet vendor

This is the place **where a man makes sweets and sells them**.
(This is the place of a *sweet vendor.*)

43. Transparent

Her activities are **open secrets and she hides nothing from the public.**
(Her activities are *transparent*.)

44. Testimonials

When you come for admission, bring **all kinds of certificates that have** been given to you.
(When you come for admission, bring all your *testimonials*.)

45. Unwarranted

All your fears about the selection-interview are **unnecessary and unjustified.**
(All your fears about the selection-interview are *unwarranted*.)

46. Unique

He has an **exclusive Registration number** allotted to him.
(He has an *unique* registration number allotted to him.)

47. Valet

My mother has appointed **a man to look after my grandfather's personal belongings**.
(My mother has appointed a *valet* for my grandfather.)

48. Vanquished (noun)

Ranjan is **the loser in the small personal fight** with Sunny.
(Ranjan is the *vanquished* in the personal fight with Sunny.)

49. Wag

This boy in our class is **full of jokes and a practical joker.**
(This boy in our class is a *wag*.)

50. Warden

The History Lecturer is also **in charge of all the hostel students of the** college.
(The History Lecturer is also the hostel *warden* of our college.)

51. Yarn

Neela tells **a lot of imaginary personal stories.**
(Neela tells a lot of *yarns*.)
(Neela spins a lot of *yarns*.)

52. Yokel

Yadav is a **simple minded villager.**

(Yadav is an *yokel*.)

53. Zebra-crossing

Children ought to cross a busy city road only **where there are white lines**.

(Children ought to cross a busy city road only at the *zebra crossing*.)

54. Zigzag (verb)

The drunken man **walked very unsteadily on the road** that late night.

(The drunken man *zigzagged* on the road that late night.)

Exercise

Find the one word substitute for the phrases shown below. Don't consult the answer until you have found out the answer yourself:

1. The headman of the monks in a monastery. Abbot
2. The act of relinquishing a high office/kingdom. Abdication
3. An alternate word for stomach. Abdomen
4. Cancelling a legislation/law. Abrogation
5. An alternate word for a lawyer. Advocate
6. Close connection/resemblance between two things/persons. Affinity
7. A short wise saying/maxim. Aphorism
8. An animal that lives in water and land. Beaver
9. A person who brews liquor illegally. Bootlegger
10. Flashing about a large knife. Brandish
11. An armed robber. Bandit
12. A forceful person who brings about sudden changes in the society. Blockbuster
13. Political platform speech. Campaign
14. Items used to hide/cover persons and things from detection. Camouflage
15. A person who changes according to the situations. Chameleon
16. A person who pretends to have extraordinary skill and knowledge. Charlatan
17. An honorable name for a car driver. Chauffeur
18. Public merry making and procession. Carnival
19. The act of taking away the weapons from soldiers. disarm
20. A place where city youngsters go for dancing and fun. discotheque
21. To bring out some unknown/hidden information. Discover
22. A long discussion on a subject. Discourse
23. Giving evasive replies to questions. Dodge
24. Act of monopolising in a meeting. dominate
25. Unusual style, which is striking and pleasing. Exotic
26. All inhabitants vacating their present living area and moving over elsewhere. Exodus
27. Decoration with flowers, leaves, ribbons etc. Festoon
28. Total failure of any event. Fiasco

29. Talking quickly and indistinctly. Gabble
30. Extermination of a race or a community. Genocide
31. Taking a free ride in someone's vehicle. Hitch-Hike
32. To mix with all and sundry people. Hob-nob
33. An adult behaving childishly. Immature
34. A greedy person who cannot be satisfied. Isatiable
35. Celebration of a special event like an anniversary. Jubilee
36. A modern name for a road sweeper. Janitor
37. A small circular shop for selling coffee, newspaper, cigarettes etc. Kisok
38. A dishonest man; a man without any honour. Knave
39. Idlers roaming the streets aimlessly. Lounge
40. Don't return the money in instalments but make one full payment. Lump-sum
41. Wrong doing; misuse of one's official position. Malfeasance/Malpractice
42. To tear up and damage a living body. Mangle
43. A planned movement of army soldiers in an area. Manoeuvre
44. The lowest and weakest point in one's life. Nadir
45. The person who works out the direction/position in the air or sea. Navigator
46. This radio has finished its life. Outlived
47. Payment not made on due time. Overdue
48. Encouragement given by a well wisher. Protonage
49. Study of the development of a language. Philology/Philologist
50. The place where stones, slates are cut and collected. Quarry
51. Vagabonds and disreputable persons. Ragtag
52. An elevated place where cars are put for repairs or servicing. Ramp
53. A bad behaviour which causes indignation. Scandal
54. A person punished for someone else's wrong doing. Scapegoat.
55. Taking somebody's things through trickery. Scrounge
56. A deep feeling on a subject. Sentment/Sentimental.
57. The art of breeding silk worms. Sericulture
58. A long and winding queue. Serpentine queue
59. A table napkin used by the diners. serviette
60. To separate fine grain from a bag of grain. Seive
61. A person who escapes in a ship illegally without ticket or other documents. Stoaway.
62. Slow and untidy progress. Tardy.
63. A dress torn in pieces. Tatter
64. A permanent pattern drawn with indelible ink on some part of a human body. tattoos.
65. Transmission of an event through television. Telecast
66. Taking over power/authority wrongfully from someone. Usrop
67. A great and sudden change in the society. Upheaval
68. Keeping something in good shape and working condition. Upkeep
69. Healthy, sound and kicking. Vibrant
70. A person lacking in spirit or vigour; a sloppy person. Wishy/Washy

71. Whether wanted or unwanted; willingly or unwillingly. Willy-nilly
72. From where? Whence
73. A brute; a coarse person; inferior humans with the habits of animals. Yahoo
74. The Jewish language. Yiddish
75. A person who shows extraordinary enthusiasm on religion. Zealot

Answers

1. Abbot 2. Abdication 3. Abdomen 4. Abrogation 5. Advocate 6. Affinity
7. Aphorism 8. Beaver 9. Bootlegger 10. Brandish 11. Bandit 12. Blockbuster
13. Campaign/Campaigning 14. Camouflage 15. Chameleon 16. Charlatan
17. Chauffeur 18. Carnival 19. Disarm/disarming 20. Discotheque 21. Discover
22. Discourse 23. Dodge/dodging 24. Dominate/domination 25. Exotic 26. Exodus
27. Festoon 28. Fiasco 29. Gabble 30. Genocide 31. Hitch-hike 32. Hob-nob/
hob-nobbing 33. Immature/immaturity 34. Insatiable 35. Jubilee 36. Janitor
37. Kiosk 38. Knave 39. Lounge/loungers 40. Lump-sum 40. Malpractice/
malfeasance 42. Mangle 43. Manoeuvre 44. Nadir 45. Navigator 46. Outlived
47. Overdue 48. Patronage 49. Philology/philologist 50. Quarry 51. Ragtag
52. Ramp 53. Scandal 54. Scapegoat 55. Scrounge 56. Sentiment/sentimental
57. Sericulture 58. Serpentine queue 59. Serviette 60. Sieve 61. Stowaway
62. Tardy (adj/adv) 63. Tatter 64. Tattoo 65. Telecast 66. Usurp 67. Upheaval
68. Upkeep 69. Vibrant (adj/adv) 70. Wishy-washy (adj/adv) 71. Willy-nilly
72. Whence 73. Yahoo 74. Yiddish 75. Zealot

Chapter 46

RELATIVE PRONOUNS

Introduction

You know that the words WHO, WHAT, WHICH, WHOSE and WHOM are known as interrogative pronouns and WHEN, WHERE, HOW and WHY are interrogative adverbs. We use them in any General question and also for carrying out object and complement tests respectively in any type of sentence.

Adjective clause and its introduction

In Chapter 42 (Compound sentence), you learnt than an **adjective clause** is one that describes a noun and is placed after the noun while a simple adjective is placed to the left of a noun.

An adjective clause in a sentence is usually introduced by a **Relative pronoun.**

Examine the following sentences:

(a) He is the person **whom** *we all respect.*
(b) Please do come to the point **what** *matters most.*
(c) The animal **which** *broke its leg,* has been admitted in that ward over there.
(d) The house **whose** *terrace had been damaged,* is ours.
(e) This is that student **who** *won five prizes in yesterday's competition.*
(f) Read out the marks **that** *he had scored.*

In addition to the 5 interrogative pronouns, we may add the conjunction **that** also to the list of Relative pronouns. See (f).

Do notice the following points in the above sentences:

1. All the adjective clauses (shown in *italics)* are introduced by a Relative pronoun shown in **bold** letters in each sentence.
2. In every case, the adjective clause is related to a noun or it describes a noun in some way in the first half of the sentence.
3. These are not Complex sentences but "sentences with a clause". See Chapter 42 once again for explanation. (In every case, the Relative pronoun is part of the second half and we get a meaning only when the sentence is read as a whole)
4. The conjunctions are also acting as 'Subject' in (b), (c) and (e). This is a hallmark of a 'sentence with a clause'.

Adjunct

A clause is a sentence by itself in that, you will always find the S-A-V-O/C parts in it. But, you will get the true meaning of the clause only when it is viewed with respect to some word/part in the mother sentence. {A clause, though it will have S-A-V-O/C, by itself will not be self contained in meaning like a Simple sentence.}

Since an adjective clause will describe a noun, can we express that description in a phrase form? Yes, we can. All you have to do is to cut out the S- A-V parts. The O/C parts then will convey the meaning.

We may call an adjective phrase also as **adjunct**. If an adjunct appears in the middle of a sentence, it must be shown between two commas or, an adjunct must be separated by commas to make it clear that it is some information pertaining to a noun going before.

Read Chapter 42 for more details on Adjunct.

Compound relative pronouns

If you make the above relative pronouns as compound words like, WHOEVER, WHATEVER, WHICHEVER and WHOMEVER, they will turn into nouns or adjectives. You already know that the Subject and the Object in a sentence must have a noun. Therefore technically speaking, the **compound relative pronouns** can be used in the subject or object part. Study the following examples:

(a)   **Whoever** hides the truth, will be punished without mercy.
　　　 S　　　(A)V　　O
　　　————— Noun clause ———

(b)   **Whoever** failed to submit their homework, raise your hand.
　　　(Noun)

(c)   The Principal will accept **whatever** statement you may make.
　　　(**whatever** here is doing the job of an adjective and also conjunction)

(d)   I will not accept **whatever** you may say.
　　　(**whatever** here is a noun - object)

(e)   **Whichever** is your choice, will be ours too.
　　　(**whichever** is a noun and subject)

(f)   **Whichever** candidate you choose, will be selected by us.
　　　(adj)

(g)   To **whomever** this letter has been written, will reply it by this evening.
　　　(Noun & obj)

(h)   To **whomever** this condition applies, is eligible for admission in this college
　　　(Noun & obj)

Do notice that the above sentences are NOT Complex sentences but sentences with Noun clauses. (A noun clause does the job of a Noun)

Emphatic compound relative pronouns

If we add the letters SO in the middle of these relative pronouns, they become *emphatic compound relative pronouns*. Study the following examples:

(i)   **Whosoever** does this work, will receive a certificate.
　　　　S　　　 A.V　　O　　　 A　　V　　　O
　　　　　　　←—— Noun ——
　　　　　　　　　　clause

(j) **Whatsoever** is proper will be carried out by us without any reservation.

(k) **Whichsoever** is the right decision, will be accepted by the Management.

(l) To **whomsoever** my finger points, will come to the dais next.

The emphatic compound relative pronouns shown in bold letters are Nouns and are doing the job of Subject in every sentence.

Conclusion

Use of Compound relative pronouns and Emphatic relative pronouns in your sentences would add some sophistication to your language and the effect of a sentence would be greater.

Exercise

Combine the following sentences using a suitable Relative pronoun to produce an

Adjective clause:

1. We could hear a loud cry in your living room. Your daughter gave it possibly.
2. A mug is on the table. Please pass it.
3. Ravi's work is famous all over the country. He is a good writer.
4. Julie is my cousin. She is a good singer.
5. Tippu Sultan died in battle. The British respected him for his valour.
6. I had bought a pocket transistor radio. Where is it?
7. One of the kittens died this morning. It was sick.
8. Daddy wants you to do him a favour. You must do it at once.
9. You are looking for something. I know it.
10. This is Madhavan's house. He stays here during his vacation.

Convert the following statements into Simple sentences with Noun clause using suitable compound relative pronouns:

11. The maid chosen by you will be employed by us.
12. Which jeans do you like? I shall surely buy it for you.
13. Only a person fulfilling all the 3 conditions will be appointed for the job.
14. The measures suggested by you for improving our performance will be followed by us faithfully.
15. If any of you is guilty, I shall not spare him.

Make the following statements powerful by using suitable emphatic compound relative pronouns:

16. If you volunteer yourself for this work, you will be rewarded highly.
17. If your proposal is workable we shall surely follow it.
18. We shall send for this work only a person who is brave.
19. Isn't that action marvellous which people admire?
20. The person who is accosted by me will go to the field to play the game.

Replace the adjective clause by a suitable adjunct:

21.   This is the ground in which we played our finals.
22.   Martha is the woman who carries tales routinely.
23.   Here before us is a matter that deserves some consideration by us.
24.   My toe, which is unusually long but thin, has been giving me trouble often.
25.   A stylish and good looking calendar will always attract customers.

Analyse the following sentences:

26.   Whoever is guilty will be punished by the Court.
27.   I shall give this prize to whomsoever I like.
28.   Wherever one turned, one saw only water and water for miles and miles.
29.   Whatsoever is just, whatsoever is lawful, do them.
30.   Whichever flower you touch will be passed on to the guest as memento.

Chapter 47

RELATIVE ADVERBS

Introduction

In Chapter 42 we saw that a compound sentence may include an Adverb clause. We identify an adverb clause through the 'complement test', that is, by using test questions WHEN, WHERE or HOW after the S-A-V- part or after the S-A-V-C parts. There is no other way to spot out an Adverb or Complement or Adverb clause. We use WHY exclusively to pick out an adverb clause of "reason/result".

Adverb clause

Study the following sentences carefully:

(a)   Our dog didn't care **when** *we were going for a walk.*
(b)   Don't go **where** *I go.*
(c)   You know **how** *you should write an Essay*, don't you?
(d)   We camped there **since** it had become evening already.
(e)   My brother walked into the house **when** *we were watching T.V.*

Don't the foregoing sentences look like Complex sentences? But, strictly speaking, they are not Complex sentences though there are two S-A-V's in them! In a Complex sentence, each sentence must be a Simple sentence - a Simple sentence must be self contained in meaning; in other words, it must have 2 Nos S-A-V-O/C and not just S-A-V plus S-A-V-O/C. So, we could classify the sentences at (a) to (c) as "sentences with a clause." (See Chapter 42 in this regard)

Can we consider the words WHEN, WHERE, HOW and SINCE as conjunctions? Again No, because they are not connecting two Simple sentences. What are they then? They seem to introduce a clause. So we may call them as "introducing words" rather than conjunctions.

All the clauses in (a) to (e) pass the complement test, hence they are **adverb clauses.**

We may also say that a clause introduced by the interrogatives WHEN, WHERE HOW or WHY will always be an Adverb clause. (In addition, some other words may also introduce Adverb clauses. See (d) for example) The words WHEN, WHERE, HOW and WHY are called **Relative adverbs** because they will always introduce adverb clauses.

If these words appear in the middle of two sentences, they will be doing the job of conjunctions and the sentence would then be a regular Complex sentence. Study the following examples:

(f)   I shall go home   **when**   it is   evening
     S   A   V Adv   Conjn S A.V   Adv
(g)   Bomdilla is the place **where** Dalai Lama rested for a couple of days.

(h)   Do you know the method **how** you could reach the other side of the lake?

The above are regular Complex sentences and the words in **bold** are acting as conjunctions.

Be very clear at the distinction between a "sentence with a clause" and a "Complex sentence." The function and identity of the words WHEN, WHERE and HOW are different in each case.

Compound relative adverbs

Like in the case of Compound relative pronouns, we could convert the Relative adverbs also into **Compound relative adverbs** such as, WHEREVER, WHENEVER and HOWEVER. Study the sentences that contain the Compound relative adverbs:

(a)   After the flash floods, one saw only water and water **wherever** you turned.
(b)   Could I come to your house **whenever** I have some doubts in English?
(c)   This student will never stand first in class **however** hard he may try.

Do you see that they are all full fledged Complex sentences and the Compound relative adverbs are doing the job of regular conjunctions? Thus, the Relative adverbs turn into **conjunctions** when the adverb "ever" is added to them.

Instead of adding the suffix **ever,** if we add any other word, the compound relative adverbs may turn into some other part of speech as shown below:

Whereabouts

We don't know the **whereabouts** of my aged uncle. (= the place where he stays; Noun)

The absconder's **whereabouts** are not known to anyone in the family. (Noun)

Whereupon

We came to a war of words **whereupon** we had to terminate the meeting immediately. (Conjunction with a meaning, 'after which and then')

This student scored such low marks in every subject **whereupon** we felt compelled to withdraw him from the school. (Conjunction)

Emphatic Compound relative adverbs

Study the following sentences:

(o)   **Wheresoever** he may keep his cycle in this area, it is likely to be stolen.
(p)   My younger brother roams about **wheresoever** he sets his mind upon.
(q)   **Whensoever** it is convenient to you, you may drop in at my house for a chat.
(r)   **Howsoever** he might have tried, he could never catch me red-handed at the act.
(s)   **Howsoever** clever he may be, he cannot beat me in declamation.

All are emphatic **Complex sentences** and the compound relative adverbs are acting as regular conjunctions.

Use of WHY

WHY is not used in the Compound and Emphatic compound forms. WHY is an introducing word only to identify an Adverb clause of reason or result. We cannot use it in any other form.

Exercise

Combine the following sentences using Relative adverbs to produce Adverb clauses:

1. Don't walk over there. The place is full of filth. *where*
2. You complete your answer paper. You may leave the hall then. (When)
3. I am on my way to Trichy. Please tell me the routes to reach there. (When)
4. The clown entered the circus ring. The children clapped heartily. (When)
5. The chief guest started his high-flown speech. Some students fell asleep. (Where)
6. Keep the key somewhere. I must find it without difficulty. (Where)
7. I am getting ready. Please wait. (When)
8. Rome was burning. Nero was singing. (When)
9. I reached the football ground. The match had ended. When.
10. I do not sleep. I have no work. (Since)

Use compound relative adverbs in connecting the following pairs of sentences:

11. The girl cried nervously. She saw a big dog. (whenever)
12. Let the college hours be over. I shall coach you in tennis. (However)
13. My mother tidies up the kitchen. My father goes to the market for shopping. (Whenever)
14. The boy is ready to go with me. He is free from any work. whenever
15. Sam and Victor will play in the open. The sky is clear. whenever.

Make the following sentences emphatic by using emphatic compound relative adverbs:

16. Your money purse will be stolen no matter where you leave it unattended.
17. Once he makes up his mind, my small brother will do it.
18. Could I bank upon your company if I have nothing to do.
19. You cannot sit in any vacant chair.
20. The lights go out at the sound of a trumpet.

Pick out the Adverb clauses from the following sentences. If you feel that a particular clause is not an adverb clause, give your reasons for it:

21. This is the field where the thieves had hidden their booty.
22. When my friend entered my room this photo fell down with a crashing sound.
23. He rushed wherever he dared.
24. Shouldn't I stay wherever I halt?
25. Malini is not a girl who could be cowed down easily by anyone.
26. This is not the way I would have solved this problem.
27. Is this the sole reason why you came to rejoin work?

28. When I shall return from my tour will be conveyed to all by Secretary.
29. I could forgive you if you repent.
30. I hear the same complaints wherever I go in this factory.
31. We asked our teacher many questions when he returned from leave.
32. The troops march out whenever they hear the bugle sound.
33. The orphan children are grateful when the House superintendent gives them pocket money.
34. Mallika is a stupid girl if she seeks your help.
35. The boy ran away when he saw a snake.
36. Any student will do well if he understands the subject well.
37. Since I had no money with me I did not pay him immediately.
38. He rushed out to join the Queue when he felt hungry.
39. Wheresoever I turned I saw only snow.
40. Howsoever I might try I never succeed in life.

State if the following sentences are full fledged Complex sentences or are they sentences with a clause? Also give the reason for your answers:

41. I went straight home after I landed at Chennai airport.
42. I make friends quite fast wherever I am posted.
43. Since you make such a strong statement I must believe it.
44. My vacation was dull since I didn't have any company.
45. Radha said that she would not play with us.
46. Meenakshi was sad that we did not invite her for the party.
47. It was dark when the pot-carrying women reached home.
48. We were sorry because you had overlooked us.
49. He is that student who is good in sports and studies.
50. The rain was so heavy that our feet slipped at a number of places.

Chapter 48

EXPRESSING A WISH

We use the future tense for an action we propose to do in some future time. This would also mean that we have made the necessary preparations for that action and we have a clear picture of the action in mind and only its execution remains. The same reasoning holds good for 'implied future tense' as well, wherein we use the Simple present or Present continuous tense showing the action-time in some future time.

But, what tense or sentence pattern should we use in expressing a desire or a wish which would be mostly imaginary and one on which we have no clear idea possibly. All of us do entertain some such dreams in our heart and more often than not, wouldn't hope to realise any of them at all. But we do dwell on such happy thoughts with tremendous pleasure. Take the wishes like, "Will I win Rs one crore in the Crorepati programme? Would I be Prime Minister of India one day?" and so on. These are but desires, imagination and unclear visions.

The English language does give us a method to express such wishes of the future and articulated in present time.

I.   A future wish expressed in present time

Rule

All persons - **wish** or **wishes** - that - S - would/could -present form verb-O/C
(This is a Complex sentence with **that** as the conjunction)

Here are some examples:

(a)   I **wish** that you would do something about that noise from the next house.
(b)   We **wish** that you could be more polite to your elders.
(c)   Martin **wishes** that the weather would be fine tomorrow.
(d)   My parents **wish** it wouldn't rain today. (conjunction silenced)
(e)   **Does** your friend **wish** that the train would reach Chennai central not more than 45 minutes behind schedule?
(f)   How I **wish** I could be a center of attention in any social function?
(g)   My parents **wish** that I could speak one more foreign language besides English.
(h)   You **wish** that you could win a big lottery, don't you?
(i)   Don't you **wish** you could also go on this journey with your brother?

All are Complex sentences in Q, a1, a2 and EQ forms. Notice how we frame a2 as given in (d). (Incidentally, we can never start an a2 like "We **don't wish** …")

II.   Wish of the past expressed in present time

Don't we often think or talk about things/events that should have taken place but hadn't? Or, we regret some actions of the past and possibly wish that we hadn't done them. We express such *regrets* in the following way:

Rule

All persons - **wish/wishes** - **that** - S - Past tense verb (A.V) or Simple past or Past perfect auxiliary and verb - O/C

Examples:

(a) I **wish** that I knew Kumar's house address. (I don't know Kumar's house address as of now.)

(b) We **wish** Magda had accompanied you to town. (Magda didn't go with you. She could have gone with you)

(c) Do you **wish** you had taken an umbrella with you? (i.e You didn't have an umbrella with you at the time of the statement)

(d) We **wish** that we had gone to the beach instead of this useless movie.

(e) Samuel **wishes** that he hadn't eaten so much biryani.

(f) David **wishes** that he had done his post graduation before taking up a job.

(g) **Doesn't** Ranjan **wish** that he never gave a wrong statement.

(h) You **wish** you hadn't been that smart with the HOD, don't you?

(i) I **wish** I wasn't that unkind with a beggar this morning.

(j) All the staffs **wish** that you had taken part in the inter-college debate.

(k) I **wish** the match was yesterday.

Note

You may omit the conjunction **that** where considered redundant.

In the second part of the Complex sentence, use Simple past or Past perfect or Past tense (with A.V), whichever sounds appropriate. Do remember that the action hadn't taken place in some cases and in some the actions were wrong. It is only a corrective wish (thought) and the wish itself is expressed in present time like this,

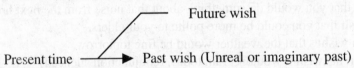

Future wish

Present time ———► Past wish (Unreal or imaginary past)

Examine the statements at (i) and (k). Here we have used the auxiliary cum verb - WAS. In such cases, it is normal to use WERE instead of WAS even for singular subjects like this,

(l) I **wish** I <u>were</u> present in yesterday's meeting.

(m) I **wish** my son <u>were</u> a little more intelligent.

(n) **Don't** you **wish** your daughter <u>were</u> present at this function.

(o) Do you **wish** that I <u>weren't</u> your friend?

(p) We really **wish** she <u>were</u> less beautiful.

On the same basis, we may express a wish in the unreal past (or, an impossible situation) using the conjunction IF like this,

(q) If I <u>were</u> you, I would solve this problem in a different way.

(r) If I <u>were</u> you, I wouldn't have bought this cassette.

(s) If a thief <u>were</u> to come into your house tonight, he would certainly steal your bicycle.

For all the unreal cases of **Present, Past** and **Future** times, we can also use the conjunction phrase AS IF or AS THOUGH. You will notice that these two phrases point towards imaginary happenings.

Rule 1

Imaginary past wishes (thoughts) expressed in <u>present time</u>:.

All persons - Simple present A & V - O/C - AS IF/AS THOUGH - S - A -V (of Past, Simple past or Past perfect tense) - O/C

(a)   Suresh talks **as if** his father owned this school.
(b)   You look **as though** you had been cheated.
(c)   He sings **as if** he were (was) a playback singer.
(d)   Don't talk **as though** you had known my mother for years.
(e)   You could treat me **as if** I <u>were</u> your relative, couldn't you?
(f)   This Asst.Lecturer ordered me about **as if** he <u>were</u> the Head of the Department.

In these examples, the first part of the Complex sentence is in Simple present and the second in a Past family. The second part deals with an imaginary event/situation of the past, whereof nothing really happened or no such action took place at all.

Rule 2

Imaginary past wishes (thoughts) expressed in real <u>past time</u>:

All persons - A- V (Simple past) - O/C - AS IF/ AS THOUGH - S - A- V (of any Past family)

(g)   Sundaram spoke **as if** he had broken his leg during the match.
(h)   It looked **as though** Matthew was going to walk away with the first prize.
(i)   The sky smelt **as if** it was going to rain.
(j)   Did she pretend **as if** she knew nothing about the theft.
(k)   The retiring Professor retraced his student days **as if** he were living those days.

In the second part of the Complex sentences we have dealt with the imaginary past wishes/thoughts whereof action did not really take place at all. And the first part could be in present or past family.

Rule 3

Imaginary <u>future wishes</u> (thoughts) expressed in present time.

All persons - A- V (Present or Simple present) - O/C - AS IF/ AS THOUGH - S - A - V (Future or Implied future) - O/C

Examples:

(l)   It looks **as though** Meena isn't coming for the party.
(m)   I am 16 years old. Don't talk to me **as if** I am a primary class kid.
(n)   You talk **as if** I won't bring my brother to witness the match.
(o)   It appears **as if** it is going to snow by this evening.
(p)   Doesn't he talk **as if** he would really go for a fight with the other?

III. Wish in real past for actions completed in the past.

Let us consider the actions that had taken place in the real past period. But, the results turned out to be wrong; things should have happened in a different way altogether.

Rule

All persons - **wished - that** - S - Past perfect A & V - O/C.

Here are the examples:

(a)   Your father and I **wished that** you hadn't gone on this pleasure tour.
(b)   Your friend **did wish that** he had abandoned the idea of retaliation.
(c)   **Did** you **wish that** we hadn't sent you to an Engineering college at such a heavy cost?
(d)   How I **wished that** I hadn't written that angry letter to your sister.
(e)   **Didn't** you ever **wish that** you would stand first in the State level list?

All are in Q, a1 and a2 forms. Notice the way how we have framed an a2 statement (see (c) and (d)). We could never start an a2 such as," I didn't wish that ...."

POLITENESS IN ISSUING ORDERS

Do recall that we use the Simple present for issuing an order. This method is direct and also blunt. We also saw that the bluntness could be made somewhat less offensive when the concerned order is put in Passive voice. There is one more method to make an order sound *persuasive* and *elegant* and yet firm in tone! This is where we make use of the 32nd auxiliary - BETTER.

Use of BETTER

Had better is the auxiliary set we use to make a command sound genteel. Its meaning is, "It is advisable; it not, there will be trouble." This set is used only in present time. (In a way we could consider this set as equal to *may, should, must* as well.)

Rule

All persons - **had better** - present form verb - O/C

Here are the examples:

(a)   You **had better** leave my office now.
(b)   Q. Shall I wear my canvas shoes for school today?
       A1. You **had better** wear them. It may rain.
(c)   You **had better** not leave the house the whole day today.
(d)   All of you **had better** come on time for my class.
(e)   We **had better** consult our Senior Lecturers about this programme. (suggestion)
(f)   You **had better** not keep any late nights till your exams are over.
(g)   You **had better** not tell your mother about this incident. OK?

All the above are in a1 and a2 forms only. We don't use this auxiliary set in Q, EQ1 or EQ2 forms. Next, this pattern will sound well only in the Second person and First person plural.

Exercise

Rewrite the following sentences/ideas in the form of a wish in the appropriate tense:

1. I want to spend a week end in a 5-star hotel; but, I want my parents to bear the hotel charges.
2. Could I watch the cricket match on T.V. today?
3. I hope my brother is on time for this evening's party at Subbu's house.
4. Once upon a time you wanted to learn piano, but you couldn't for some reason. You now regret it.
5. You would have taken a lot of snap shots on your previous visit to the Zoo. But you had forgotten to take the camera with you.
6. We should not have come to this church at all today.
7. You sent your mother to a wrong shop for buying your sarees. You are sorry now.
8. You hadn't given proper career guidance to your neighbour who had so much faith in you. You feel sorry about it now.
9. Your next door acquaintance is not doing well in college.
10. Your small sister has wasted all her pocket money on video games.
11. In the coming year, you want your elder brother to become an IAS officer.
12. After the late evening show, you don't find any taxi or auto to go home; the only way appears to be to walk home.
13. You have called your friend to go with you on your morning jogging; you are not very sure if he would join you.
14. The weather outside is very cloudy; there might be a drizzle.
15. Your father attended Swami Ayyappa's religious ceremony. You feel he should not have gone all the way to Sabarimalai for it.

Improve upon the following sentences so that they are more accurate:

16. I wish Swarna is here.
17. We wish the weather changed.
18. I wish that you wouldn't complain all the time about something or the other.
19. The picnickers wish that they didn't forget to bring a video camera.
20. Do you wish I am a clever student?
21. Did you ever wish that you could be the Captain of the Indian cricket team?
22. Don't talk like you are my tuition master.
23. Your mother wished that she hasn't given you too much of freedom.
24. Mona yelled like she had seen a ghost.
25. How I wish I am there during the prize awarding ceremony.

Make the following commands/suggestions sound somewhat polite and persuasive:

26. Go home immediately.
27. Be present in my office sharp at 9 a.m.
28. Don't come to me for help every week.
29. You are late. Dress up fast.
30. Shall we go in for dinner now?

Chapter 49

SUBJUNCTIVE

Definition

With certain Verbs, Nouns and Adverbs in one half of a Complex sentence, we are required to omit the auxiliary in the second half. This is the only occasion where we omit the auxiliary in an English sentence. Such words have been named : SUBJUNCTIVE verbs, SUBJUNCTIVE nouns and SUBJUNCTIVE adverbs.

There is also a lone "Subjunctive conjunction" - LEST. When 'lest' is the conjunction, we omit the auxiliary in the Simple sentence that follows it.

Subjunctive verbs

When any of the following verbs is present (in any of its form) in one half of a Complex sentence, omit the auxiliary in the other half of the sentence:

DEMAND, DESIRE, INSIST, PREFER, PROPOSE,
RECOMMEND, REQUEST, REQUIRE, SUGGEST
and URGE.

Examine the following sentences which contain the Subjunctive verbs:

(a) The professor DEMANDS that Miss Sunitha alone **act** as the spokesperson for the Post graduate class.

(b) Our parents DESIRE that your friend **come** to our house after 7.30 p.m.

(c) Will the Principal INSIST that his son alone **stand** for the election?
    A   S   V   Conjn   S   Adv   V   O

(d) The senior members PREFERRED that every new entrant to our group **sign** an undertaking instead of verbal assurances.

(e) The Management group had PROPOSED that the Personnel manager **reduce** the number of clerks in the main office by 10.

(f) Didn't you RECOMMEND that we **accept** candidate No 3 for the post?

(g) We REQUEST that the first prize winner **present** himself at the auditorium.

(h) We will REQUIRE an assurance that some of you **not attend** today's meeting. (" ….. do not attend …" will be wrong)

(i) Would you SUGGEST that we **not take** part in the next Assembly election?

(j) They URGED that every student **revise** their lessons more carefully.

(k) Mr.Rajesh Pilot DEMANDED that Mrs. Sonia Gandhi **take over** the party leadership of the Congress (Extract from a newspaper report in 1999 A.D)

(l) About 500 DK members DEMANDED in a procession that the Kanchi Acharya **withdraw** his disparaging reference to widows. (Extract from a newspaper in 1999 A.D.)

(m) The Minister DESIRED that his PA **be** present by his side during all meetings.

All the examples given above are grammatically correct and adhere to the following sentence structure:

S - A - V - O/C - THAT - S - V (present form verb only) - O/C

Any tense

No 's' sound and no
auxiliary DO or DOES

Whatever may be the tense of the first half of the Complex sentence, the verb used in the second half must be in *present form* only and without any supporting auxiliary. When the subject of the second part is singular, no 's' sound is to be given to the present form verb. If the second half is a negative (a2) type, omit the auxiliary and use NOT as shown in examples (h) and (i).

This is a violation of the rule you have learnt about Simple present tense, isn't it? This new rule is applicable when a SUBJUNCTIVE verb is present in the first half of a Complex sentence.

The next violation we have committed here is on 'the tense rules'. According to the Tense rules of Complex sentences, when the first half is in a Past family the second must be in a Past family or with past equivalent auxiliary or in Present family with Universal truths. But here, the Subjunctive rule is that even if the first half is in a Past family, the second must be in Simple Present tense only with a present form verb and without a supporting auxiliary.

And here is another surprise! See what happens if we use a Past family in the second half when the first half has a SUBJUNCTIVE. Study the following sentences:

(n)   The workers PROPOSED that their union leader **went** on a hunger strike as a mark of protest.

(o)   The Vice Chancellor had DESIRED that the suspended Lecturer **withdrew** his appeal from the High court.

Do the examples at (n) and (o), which conform to the tense rules, convey any sense/meaning? The sentences sound ridiculous, don't they?

Let us see what happens when the second half is in a Future family:

(p)   The professor DEMANDED that Miss Sunitha alone **shall act** as the spokesperson of the class.

(q)   You didn't RECOMMEND that my son **shall play** in 'A' team, did you?

(r)   You didn't say that the CBI **will investigate** this case, did you?

Future tense in the second half appears to match all right but use of an auxiliary seems compulsory. But then, it can be seen that the first verb need not be a Subjunctive at all and could be any normal verb too. See (r) So, this is no special case as such.

Subjunctive nouns

With the following SUBJUNCTIVE nouns in the first half (which may be in any tense) the second half must be in 'Simple present' only and with an unsupported verb. Future family will also match but with a supporting auxiliary:

DEMAND, INSISTENCE, PREFERENCE, PROPOSAL
RECOMMENDATION, REQUEST, REQUIREMENT and SUGGESTION

Accordingly, here is the sentence structure formula:

S - A - V -   O   - THAT - S -   V -   O/C

| - - - - - - - | | | - - - - - - - - - - -|

Any tense   SUBJUNCTIVE   Simple present

                   Noun   or

                                      Future with A-V

Here are the examples conforming to the above sentence structure rule:

(a)   The parents' firm DEMAND was that bride **not wear** a white saree for the wedding.

(b)   The Lecturer's INSISTENCE is that the students **submit** their project work by not later than 15th of that month.

(c)   Our PREFERENCE has been that every member **contribute** Rs 10 towards the Earthquake relief fund.

(d)   Wasn't it your RECOMMENDATION that the youngest student **shall garland** the Chief guest?

(e)   The magician ignored the SUGGESTION that he **reveal** the secret behind some of his magical feats.

(f)   The Headmaster of the nearby school had forwarded a REQUEST that our college 'B' team **play** a friendly match with his 'A' football team.

(g)   Our HOD complied with the REQUIREMENT that all his staffs **surrender** half their leave for the year.

(h)   My PROPOSAL is that you **shall stay** with your uncle instead of in the hostel.

Subjunctive Adverbs

Subjunctive adverbs in the first half too, places some restrictions in the composition of Complex sentences. They are:

ESSENTIAL, IMPERATIVE, IMPORTANT and NECESSARY

There are two rules with regard to the presence of Subjunctive adverbs in the first half -

Rule - 1

The first half is in Present tense and starts with "It is or What is…"

It is /What is -   C   -   THAT - S - V - O/C

                   | | - - - - - - - - - - -|

        SUBJUNCTIVE |- - - - - - - - - - -|

          Adverb   (Simple present
                                         verb without A)

Here are the examples:

(a)   It is IMPORTANT that he **attend** extra classes from today.

(b)   Isn't it ESSENTIAL that your brother **accompany** you to the movie?

(c)   It is quite IMPERATIVE that a Staff **lead** you all to the Zoo.

(d)   Is it NECESSARY that every new entrant **bring** a transfer certificate?

(e)   What is so IMPORTANT that your father **visit** you daily in the hostel?

According to the 'tense rules' when the first half is in a Present family the second could be in any tense according to the situation. But, the Subjunctive rule says that the second half must be in Simple present tense only. Shall we see what happens if the second is in a Past or Future family?

(aa) It is IMPORTANT that he **attended** extra classes from today.

(bb) Isn't it ESSENTIAL that your brother **accompanied** you to the movie?

(cc) It is quite IMPERATIVE that a Staff **led** you all to the Zoo.

(dd) Is it NECESSARY that every new entrant **brought** a transfer certificate?

(ee) What is so IMPORTANT that your father **will visit** you daily in the hostel? What is so IMPORTANT that your father **has been visiting** you daily in the hostel.

Do these sentences convey any sensible meaning? Do they sound correct in your ears? Only a Simple present verb without a supporting auxiliary in the second half, seems to give a meaningful sentence. Thus, here is another violation when a **Subjunctive adverb** is present in the first half.

A question would arise, could the second half have Present tense A.Vs?

The answer is No. Rule 1 stipulates that we should use only a Simple present tense verb without A. An auxiliary cum verb (A.V) doesn't fulfil this condition; it has an inbuilt A in it; next, AM, IS and ARE do not belong to Simple present tense. Whereas BE is a normal verb in present form and belongs to Simple present tense. Along with BE, you must not use any A although some universal auxiliaries (such as, Should, Would etc) may sound appropriate.

Let us examine some sentences with AM, IS and ARE in the second half:

(f)   Isn't it absolutely ESSENTIAL that every boarder **is** in bed by 9.30 p.m?

(g)   Isn't it IMPORTANT that I **am** on the Staff list to stand for election?

(h)   Why is it NECESSARY that they **are** present in the class room before time?

The second halves don't sound well, do they? Nor do they seem to give a sensible meaning. Replace them by BE and note that they sound not only nice but also meaningful:

(ff) Isn't it absolutely ESSENTIAL that every boarder **be** in bed by 9.30 p.m?

(gg) Isn't it IMPORTANT that I **be** on the Staff list to stand for election?

(hh) Why is it NECESSARY that they **be** present in the class room before time?

Rule - 2

The first half is in Past tense and starts with "It was .."

It was	-	C	-	that -	S	-	V	-	O/C

               | | Simple past

        SUBJUNCTIVE   or, Past perfect |

           Adverb   without A

If the first half is in Past tense with "It was ..", the second half must be in Simple past or Past perfect only. Rule - 2 is in contravention to Rule - 1 applicable for Subjunctive-verbs. But then, there it is. It would also appear that the normal tense rules hold good when a Complex sentence starts with "It was ...." and followed by a Subjunctive - adverb.

Here are the examples:

(i)   It was NECESSARY that the escort always **stood** behind the VIPs.

(j)   Wasn't it ESSENTIAL that he **went** for a morning walk daily?

(k)   Wasn't it IMPORTANT that your mother **had accompanied** you to your fiance's house?

(l)   Wasn't it IMPORTANT that your mother **accompanied** you to your fiance's house?

(m) It was IMPERATIVE that your son **met** me daily.

(n)   It was IMPERATIVE that your son **had met** me daily.

All the sentences sound correct when the second half is in Simple past and Past perfect tenses. It would appear that as far as Subjunctive **adverbs** are concerned, the normal 'Complex sentence tense rules' apply.

Subjunctive conjunction

Lest is a conjunction with the meaning, 'in order that ... not' or, 'for a fear that ...' It has a negative meaning. To avoid any error, observe this formula in composing a Complex sentence with LEST as the conjunction:

a1 - LEST - a2

a2 - LEST - a1

Rule- I

S - A - V - O/C -	**LEST** -	S -	V	- O/C

            | |

      Any tense   Present form

                                        verb without A

Here are the sample sentences:

(a) Don't oversleep **lest** you/he/she miss your/his/her detraining station.
(b) You must not annoy him **lest** he beat you to death.
(c) He has not come out of his house during day time **lest** someone spot him out.
(d) Isn't he keeping himself strong **lest** he experience defeat.
(e) Had not Moses stood before Him to turn away His wrath **lest** he destroy them? (Psalms 106:23, Bible)
(f) We never said anything **lest** he misunderstand us.
(g) I did not accept the new appointment **lest** I lose my seniority in the present job.

Often, to be on the safe side, many writers would use the auxiliary SHOULD before the verb. Thus, you would frequently find the expression, "Let him not oversleep lest he should miss his detraining station." Or, "You must not annoy him lest he should beat you to death." The above sentences are incorrect from grammar angle. The rule is very clear in that, there should be no auxiliary.

Summary

When a SUBJUNCTIVE Verb or Noun or Adverb is present in the first half of a Complex sentence, the second half must be in a tense without an Auxiliary and in conformity with the SUBJUNCTIVE TENSE rules, which are quite different from the conventional 'Complex sentence tense rules'.

The **Subjunctive tense** rules are applicable only to the Active voice sentences. They do NOT apply to Passive voice Complex sentences at all. In the Passive cases, we follow the conventional Complex sentence tense rules. Here are the examples:

Passive voice

(a) The doctor DEMANDS that all the female patients **are attended** to only by female nurses.
(b) The Management had PROPOSED that the number of clerks in the main office **should be reduced** by 10 by the Personnel manager.
(c) Wouldn't you INSIST that another attempt **is made** by the student concerned?
(d) The parents have made a REQUEST that a white saree **is not worn** by the bride for the wedding.
(e) Wasn't it your SUGGESTION that a thesis **was submitted** by every post-graduate student before the end of the semester?
(f) It is IMPORTANT that you **are accompanied** by your elder sister on every trip to the gymnasium.
(g) Wasn't it ESSENTIAL that the nursery class **was attended** by every child before admission to KG class?
(h) It is NECESSARY that a cadre course **is undergone** by every soldier before promotion.
(i) Didn't I caution you lest some mistake **was committed** by you unwittingly.

Summary of all 'Subjunctive tense rules'

First sentence		*Second sentence*
1.	Any tense with Subjunctive **verb** in Active voice	Simple present with unsupported present form verb
2.	Any tense with Subjunctive **noun** in Active voice	Simple present with unsupported present form verb
3.	It is ... Subjunctive Adverb in What is .. Active voice	Simple present only and without a supporting auxiliary
4.	It was Subjunctive Adverb in Active voice	Simple past or Past perfect

Exercise

Correct the mistake(s) if any, in the following sentences:

1. I suggested that your brother had joined the National Defence Academy next year.
2. Wasn't it essential that you participated in the tournament?
3. Would you insist that the hockey sticks were collected from the sports store by every player himself?
4. The Principal has proposed that the final year students not miss any classes during the last semester.
5. The Principal has opined that the final year students may not miss any classes during the final semester.
6. My father's insistence was that his daughter did well in studies.
7. Is it necessary that all college students underwent compulsory military training?
8. The Chief guest proceeded with the assumption that the student audience understand high level English.
9. The Lecturer would always insist that the Lab attendant was present in the Chemistry laboratory.
10. Didn't you prefer that the morning PT parade is held at 5.30 a.m. instead of 6 a.m.?

Make the necessary changes in the sentences if the words underlined are replaced by the words shown in brackets:

11. I would <u>recommend</u> that all the weak students attend the extra classes after college hours. (say)
12. Didn't the VC <u>urge</u> that we take more interest in the physical activities for our students? (spell-out)
13. The senior student of the first year class <u>requested</u> that he be permitted to lead the students in singing the National Anthem? (wanted)
14. The HOD's <u>desire</u> was that we did not miss any of his lectures. (insistence)
15. Would the lady students <u>prefer</u> that their leader act as their spokesperson? (like)
16. It is <u>vital</u> that the guilty person admitted his mistake voluntarily. (essential)

17. Isn't it <u>right</u> that the best student was appointed the leader of the class? (imperative)
18. It was <u>correct</u> that the car driver always remained inside the car. (important)
19. It is <u>important</u> that all students be present in the class 5 minutes before the starting time. (good)
20. Would you <u>say</u> that Ramanujam go out for 15 minutes? (suggest)
21. The doctor did not <u>desire</u> that the patient roam about inside the ward. (like)
22. We could have <u>demanded</u> that the culprit be punished for the offence. (asked)
23. It was <u>nice</u> that you got posted out of this place at last. (important)
24. Your <u>insistence</u> was that I don't miss any opportunity. (recommendation)
25. Didn't we <u>say</u> that your close friend ought not to see us at once. (insist)

Fill up the blank with the correct verb form : ·

26. It was exemplary that you .... in all competition.
27. It is essential that you .... present at the auditorium before 6 p.m.
28. We propose that your sister .... with you on your next visit.
29. Our requirement is that your ward .... all rules of the hostel.
30. The doctor has demanded that all the visitors ..... sent out of the hospital premises before 7 p.m.

The first part of the following Complex sentences contain a Subjunctive; use the correct auxiliaries or verbs in the second half:

31. It is essential that you accompanied by your elder brother during your shopping trip.
32. You could have given some excuse lest you had caught by the police.
33. You surely preferred that the Professor saw you directly.
34. It was indeed necessary that you see me during the lunch recess.
35. Our recommendation has been that Ibrahim took over the leadership of the training.

Write the remaining 6 categories of sentences:

36. The Lab Demonstrator proposed that the III Semester students repeat the previous week's experiments.
37. You didn't recommend that my brother play the goal keeper, did you?
38. Why is it important that this person be your local guardian year after year?
39. Wasn't it your proposal that everyone must be put through physical check?
40. Don't overwork yourself lest your mother worry herself to death about your health.

Analyse the following sentences:

41. Our HOD desired that Peter desist from teasing the lady students.
42. Did you say that the Police will enter our college campus to carry forward the investigation?
43. It is essential that my friend guide you in all your assignments, isn't it?
44. Isn't it imperative that you meet the Lecturer every day after college hours?
45. It is very important that you be present at the canteen during the lunch hour.

Chapter 50

IDIOMS

Introduction

Uptil now, we concentrated on how to write grammatically correct straightforward English sentences in various ways. In a straightforward sentence, we say or write what exactly we mean. And there is no question of a listener/reader misunderstanding our sentences; it will be bad writing if they do!

But, what if we don't mean what we say or write? Or, the same as "We say/write one thing and mean something else?" Could we call it straightforward English? Certainly not.

Yet, that is exactly what we do often in our English sentences. We don't use straightforward English sentences all the time. Sometime we drift into devious English; we use words with indirect meanings. Such use is accepted too. What's more, such use adds colour to the language. But if you don't recognise such words and their indirect meaning (or, hidden meaning) you are likely to misunderstand the sentence(s). Words with a hidden meaning are called IDIOMS. In idioms, the intended meaning is different from the dictionary meaning. How do we get a different meaning? This happens when we add selected prepositions to some special verbs.

Example of an idiom

Let us consider the verb, BREAK. Its dictionary meaning is, "a thing going into pieces or parts as a result of some force brought on it."

Now, if we add the preposition "down" to it, it becomes a compound verb, BREAK DOWN with a new meaning, "collapse."

If we add the preposition "off", the new compound word, BREAK OFF gets a new meaning, "suddenly withdraw."

With the preposition "into", the new compound word BREAK INTO derives the meaning, "forcing one's way."

Here are sentences that use this idiom:

(a) She **breaks down** every time she remembers her husband's death.
(b) Don't **break off** your connection with this college.
(c) Thieves will **break into** your house if you leave it unlocked.

We formed an idiom out of a verb and the new compound word thus will continue to be a verb. As a verb, it has three forms. They are,

Break down	Broke down	Broken down
Break off	Broke off	Broken off
Break into	Broke into	Broken into

Can we convert an adjective, adverb, a conjunction or a noun in this manner into an **idiom**? No. Can we add any word other than a preposition to derive an idiom? No, again.

We derive such idioms, not out of every verb, but only out of some selected present form verbs. Once formed, you must know the hidden meaning of that idiom. This meaning will be quite different from the dictionary meaning of the mother word. If the new meaning is the same as the original meaning, then it would not be an idiom. There is no shortcut to knowing the hidden meaning of an idiom. You have to learn and remember it. There are only a few of them. Here is a list of the commonly used idioms in our day to day sentences along with their true/hidden meaning. See how stylish a sentence sounds when an idiom is used. Idioms belong to high level English.

ACT

1. David, my classmate in BA I year, **acted upon** (followed) my suggestion.
2. Doesn't some lawyer **act for** (represent) your father in the court case?

BARK

1. The officer **barked out** (said in an angry tone) at his soldiers over their bad performance.
2. I would have **barked out** at my team if they had lost the match.

BEAR

1. P.T.Usha **bore away** (collected) several prizes in sports events.
2. Aurangzeb **bore down** (crushed) all oppositions when he came to power.
3. **Bear** yourselves **well** (behave well) during the school function.

BREAK

1. The young woman **broke down** (collapsed) on hearing the bad news.
2. You shouldn't have **broken off** (cut off/withdrawn) your talks in the middle of the negotiation.
3. Some students **broke into** (forced their way) the crowd to see what was happening.
4. After a kilometer or so we **broke into** (changed into) a sprint to reach the finish line.

BRING

1. His reckless spending **brought about** (caused) his downfall.
2. You should **bring in** (earn) some extra money to augment our family income.
3. That old lady **brought** me **up** (reared) to this status because I was an orphan.

CALL

1. We **called off** (cancelled) the match immediately after half time.
2. Shall I **call** you **up** (telephone you) this evening?

3.   We should not have **called off** (cancelled) the meeting without notice.
4.   We ought to **call on** (visit his house officially) our new HOD as soon as possible.

CAST

1.   The sailors were **cast away** (marooned as a result of a shipwreck) on the Eastern coast.
2.   We were **cast down** (shocked/disheartened) by our heavy loss in the business.

COME

1.   The patient **came round** (regained consciousness) in the late afternoon.
2.   How did such a situation **come about/off?** (take place)
3.   Our next door neighbour's daughter has **come of** age (has become a major).
4.   I think our Raju Pillai will **come round** (agree) to our point of view soon.
5.   Don't you worry; he will **come off** (fare brilliantly) the crisis hundred percent free.

CRY

1.   Many people **cry down** (depreciate/belittle) religion and God these days.
2.   Several male MPs **cried out** (protested) against the Women's reservation bill.
3.   My uncle did promise to help you but had to **cry off** (withdraw/back out) for some personal reasons.

CUT

1.   Our class mate, Sowmya, had been **cut down** (humbled) to size.
      (brought down to her natural self)
2.   Our car engine had suddenly **cut off** (suddenly stopped) while climbing a slope.
3.   Don't **cut into** (interrupt) our conversation, please?
4.   We were **cut up** (dejected) when the teacher cancelled the rehearsal.

DIE

1.   The excitement of the hostage's release **died down** (stopped) gradually after 3 days.
2.   The visitors waited till the noise of the airliner **died away.** (faded away from hearing)

DROP

1.   We **dropped out** (withdrew) of the contest due to ill health of some members.
2.   Sudarsan **dropped in** (paid an unannounced visit) at our house last evening.

DO

1.   We are **done for.** (ruined)
2.   Having wandered round the whole day, Abby was **done up. (exhausted)**

FALL

1.   When the riot police arrived, the crowd **fell back.** (retreated)

2. Immediately we **fell in** (attracted to) love with the white kitten.
3. Your proposal seems to have **fallen through** (failed/rejected) in the Staff meeting.
4. Many of our friends have **fallen out** (disagreed /quarrelled) on us.
5. The telephone maintenance efficiency has lately **fallen off**. (deteriorated)

GET

1. This student expected to **get off** (escape) with a warning but didn't.
2. How will you **get on** (live on/manage) with a deskmate like this young man?
3. The fish **got away** (escaped) all right.
4. How can I **get off** (get relieved) this tussle?
5. Though weak in Maths, our daughter managed to **get through** (pass) the final examination.
6. You will soon **get over** (clear away) the agony of this tragedy in your home.
7. We are **getting down** (alighting) at the next bus stop.

GIVE

1. The thief **gave** himself **up** (surrendered) when he was cornered by the police.
2. Our cricket team **gave up** (stopped) their fight when the opposite score was too high.
3. Mother told the father, 'If you persist, your son will **give in**.' (submit himself).
4. The father **gave away** (transferred) his daughter in marriage to the groom.
5. The chief guest **gave away** (distributed) the prizes at the end of the function.
6. The temporary bridge **gave away** (collapsed) when a heavy lorry passed over it.
7. I wish I could **give up** (stop/leave) the habit of eating chocolates.

GO

1. The drama did not **go off** (wasn't a success) well at all.
2. The lady has **gone through** hell (suffered tremendous difficulties) after her husband's death.
3. Are there any rules to **go by** (to be guided by)?
4. Ramanathan's name will **go down** (will be remembered) in the history of our school as a genius.

HANG

1. A small boy **hung about/hung around** (loitered/waited) the gate to make an entry into the theatre.
2. You **hang on** (continue/hold on) here until your brother arrives.

HOLD

1. A platoon of troops on a Kargil height **held out** (resisted) for over two weeks without giving in.
2. I **hold out** (give) no promise to include you in our trek party.

KEEP

1. My friend tried to **keep up** (maintain) with the others on a long distance run.

2. The guest speaker **kept on** (continued) talking for several minutes.
3. We had **kept up** (maintained) our pressure on our class teacher.
4. Shall I **keep back** (hide/conceal) this information from the girls in our class?
5. I was **kept in** (confined to the house) by high temperature yesterday.

KNOCK

1. Don't **knock down** (destroy) every tree in that compound.

LAY

1. The Pakistan troops had to **lay down** (stop fighting) their arms on instructions from their Government at the instance of USA.
2. He had **laid out** (invested) a lot of money in comics and toys.

LET

1. My elder sister wouldn't **let** me **into** (reveal) her secrets.
2. The Demonstrators were **let off** (set free) lightly with a few sit-ups.
3. Haven't you **let** me **down** (disappointed me) by not giving my friend some help?

LOOK

1. Who is **looking after** (caring for you) you in Chennai nowadays?
2. You should not **look down upon** (treat lightly) anyone around you.
3. We always **looked up** (waited upon) to you for guidance in our student life.
4. Will you please **look into** (examine) our cases before next January?
5. The prices of agriculture products are **looking up** (rising) lately.

MAKE

1. I cannot really **make out** (understand/comprehend) head or tail of what he is saying.
2. They were at loggerheads till yesterday, but now they have **made up.** (settled the quarrel)
3. That rich man **made over** (donated away) one of his houses to a poor widow.

PAY

1. We shall **pay** him **back** (retaliate) for the trouble he caused to our gang.

PICK

1. He lost his health after his last illness but he is **picking** it **up** (recovering from) in recent days.
2. Lakshman's new car **picked up** (gained speed) a speed of 80 kmph in 35 seconds.
3. Of all students, why did you **pick** me **on** (single out or select me) for this difficult job?

PULL

1. The doctor confirmed that our mother will **pull through** (recover from an illness) within a couple of days.
2. Isn't it easy to **pull down** (destroy) someone's chances of winning a prize?

PUT

1. The Senior Lecturer said, "I cannot **put up** (tolerate) with your casualness any longer."
2. When my younger brother said "No", I felt completely **put off.** (dejected disappointed)
3. He tried to **put** me **off** (discourage) by citing all the negative points.
4. As per the hostel rules the lights must be **put out** (extinguished) by 10 p.m.
5. Should we **put through** (float/pass) these measures in our college as well?
6. Joseph **put on** (displayed) an air of superiority in front of the lady students.

RUN

1. Purushottam has the habit of **running down** (condemning) whom he dislikes.
2. When we reached Tambaram, we **ran out** of petrol (no petrol left in the tank) in our motorbike.
3. If you **run through** your money (spend away all), ask my friend for help.
4. Our ration bill **ran up** (became high) to a large amount when we had too many guests in our house last month.
5. The water tank on the terrace is **running over** (overflowing).
6. My bicycle skidded and **ran into** (dashed/collided) the compound wall.

SEE

1. We went to the station to **see off** (bid goodbye) our friends.
2. Haven't you **seen through** (detected something bad) his plans?

SET

1. The Northeast monsoon **set in** (started) in Chennai on 2 November this year.
2. We **set out/set off** (started on) on a long journey on 21 December.
3. The High court **set aside** (annulled) the lower court's verdict.
4. Hasn't your ex-college friend **set up** (started) a shop in your area?
5. I was compelled to **set** this student **down.** (snub him)
6. In his valedictory speech, the Principal **set forth** (explained/made known) a number of new ideas about the pass-outs' future.

STAND

1. All of you must **stand up** (claim/fight) for your rights.
2. This leader always **stands up** (supports the cause) for his juniors.
3. We shall feel strong only if we **stand up** (give support) for one another.

STRIKE

1. My sister is **struck down** (attacked by) with jaundice.

2.   The college has **struck off** (removed) your name from the college register.

TAKE

1.   This little boy **takes after** (resembles) his elder brother.
2.   Recently he has **taken to** (got used to) tennis.
3.   My father **took** me **to** task (scolded/rebuked) when I had failed in 2 subjects.
4.   Don't be **taken in** (get attracted) by his clever arguments.

TELL

1.   The heavy assignments are **telling upon** (affecting) our health.

TURN

1.   My uncle promised to visit us last evening but he didn't **turn up** (appear/come) till 8 p.m.

WATER

1.   The other school tried to **water down** (reduce) our importance.

WASH

1.   When someone comes to you for help, don't **wash off** (close your eyes/refuse to involve yourself) your hands.

WEAR

1.   We couldn't read the inscription on the stone tablet since the writings have **worn away.** (faded/disappeared away)
2.   Your fear about the new teacher will **wear off.** (gradually disappear within a few days)

WORK

1.   Your suggestion will not **work out** (succeed) this time.
2.   This employee worked his **way up** (progressed in life) within 10 years.
3.   Politicians usually **work upon** (influence) the dreams of the voters.

WRITE OFF

1.   You should not **write off** (declare as useless) this boy ever.

A caution

It is quite possible to mistake a phrasal verb for an **idiom;** both will have a preposition to it. The meaning of a phrasal verb will be the same as the mother verb, i.e dictionary meaning. But the meaning of an idiom will be quite different from the dictionary meaning of the mother word.

Take the idiom "run over". This is also a phrasal verb and we use it this way: "This child was <u>run over (killed)</u> by a lorry."

But when used as an idiom, its hidden meaning is quite different. (See the examples on "Run")

Similarly, "cut up". As a phrasal verb, it has the meaning, 'cut into pieces/parts'. "We felled the rotten tree and <u>cut</u> it <u>up</u> for firewood."

"Wash off" is also a phrasal verb with the meaning, 'uprooted/ thrown out'. "During the heavy floods many trees were <u>washed off/away</u>."

Therefore, study the meaning of a compound word with reference to the context. If the meaning is literal, then it will be a phrasal verb and if it has a hidden meaning it will be an idiom.

Phrasal verbs

Here is a list of some phrasal verbs with their dictionary meaning; do not mistake them for idioms when you use them in sentences. At the same time, find out their meaning before you arrive at the conclusion that they are phrasal verbs:

Back out	-	withdraw from a promise or some undertaking
Break down	-	fail to work
Break up	-	disperse
Break out	-	start suddenly
Clear up	-	free from cloud, mist etc.
Get on	-	make progress/advance
Get up	-	rise from bed
Give up	-	abandon an attempt
Go off	-	explode
Go on	-	continue with what you are saying
Hold on	-	wait
Hold out	-	endure hardship or danger
Look out	-	be watchful/be careful
Make off	-	ruin away
Pull up	-	come to a stop
Set in	-	begin
Set off	-	start on a trip/journey
Set out	-	begin a journey
Stand out	-	easily identified over the others
Take off	-	leave the ground. (The Delhi flight <u>took off</u> a little while back.)

A miracle

A miracle seems to take place when we add a preposition to an intransitive verb. It then turns into a transitive verb.

You know that the verbs COME and GO (and their synonyms) are basically intransitive, in that, they will always lead to a complement and never an object. But when we use these verbs as phrasal verbs (along with a preposition), they will take on an object and stand the object test as well. Study the following examples:

(a)   My brother **comes** home at 3.30 p.m. (intransitive verb; <u>home</u> is complement.)

(aa) My brother **came to** his senses after his failure. (**came to** has turned transitive;
<u>his senses</u> is an object.)

(b)   We won't **come across** <u>any streams</u> on this highway.
                                              O

(c)   They **arrived at** <u>the correct conclusion</u>.
                                              O

(d)   We **went through** <u>hell</u> on our journey.
                                     O

(e)   Don't you **come to** <u>me</u> hereafter!
                                    O

Conclusion

When we add a suitable preposition to an intransitive verb, it turns into a transitive verb. We may treat this compound word as a **phrasal verb.**

Can we treat such verbs as idioms? No, because there is no hidden meaning when a preposition is added to an intransitive verb.

Exercise

1. In the passage given below, idioms could be used against the words underlined. In tune with the context, use the most appropriate idioms in those places:

During our trek to Vandaloor, four of us <u>were always lagging behind</u> the first group. Once or twice we tried to be with them but <u>had to retreat</u> by about 200 meters. After an hour or so, Muniam <u>collapsed</u> due to exhaustion. It was a very hot day as well. Muniam lay down for a while with his eyes closed. He <u>regained consciousness</u> only after we splashed some water on his face.

The leading group of 7 men students <u>terminated their leading spree</u> and came down to see what had happened. <u>Turning emotional,</u> Virendran gave Muniam a glass of cocacola to strengthen his spirit.

<u>Following my advice,</u> the group of 10 men students and one lady student decided to stick together and not split into two batches. When all our <u>anxiety about Muniam came to an end,</u> we resumed our trek.

When we were about 5 KM from our destination, Saraswati, the lone brave woman of the party, suddenly _retreated_ stating that her shoes were pinching her at the toes. Some men were angry that a female was decelerating their speed. "Don't _surrender_ like this," I advised Saraswati and simultaneously chided the males for taking a negative attitude towards a classmate. "How could we _tolerate_ a slow coach?" complained Suresh. "All right, all right, Saraswati will _overcome this crisis_ in no time and keep up with us," I said. And indeed, Saraswati was on her feet and _started off_ with us.

We reached Vandaloor around 12.15 p.m. The distance of 25 KM began _to affect_ our physical strength. So, we stretched ourselves and rested for half an hour under a tree.

2. Identify the idioms in the following passage and state the hidden meaning attached to each:

Our college bus stopped seeing a large crowd on our way. Someone said that a lorry had run over a school boy. While the victim was being taken to a nearby hospital, the crowd had surrounded the lorry and _barked out_ at the driver and _cried out_ against his callousness.

Though sad, we had to proceed on our way to our individual destinations. One of the lady students said that lorry drivers were very careless in the city and they must be _cut down_ to size. "What can we do as students?" she posed a question at the other travellers. All of us felt _tongue-tied_ for a while. Then Ravindran said, "Why can't we _drop in_ at the Chief Minister's office one day and submit a memorandum?" "What is a MEMORANDUM?" asked George, a First year student. "I can't _make out_ what it is?" Nobody answered him. _Cut up_, George murmured some unkind remarks about the seniors.

"I have a better idea," said Mohan, a final year student. "What? What?" everyone demanded in one voice. "The guideline to go by is," Mohan continued, "No lorry should be allowed to ply beyond 30 KMPH speed. The manufacturers should put a speed governor inside the engine."

"Governors live in Raj Bhavan" _barked out_ a First year student who was from a village school.

"Not that Governor, stupid," Mohan retorted.

In the meantime our own bus was picking up speed. And then .. then the bus suddenly ground to a halt. "Oh, oh," the driver whined. "I think I have _run_ out of diesel," he _lamented_.

grieved for.

Chapter 51

FIGURES OF SPEECH AND IDIOMATIC PHRASES

FIGURE OF SPEECH

'Figure of speech' is a method of describing persons and their qualities in a picturesque way. In such descriptions, we compare the person or his/her quality with something or someone famous for it. Use of figures of speech will enrich and liven up your language. There are quite a few types of figures of speech, but we shall restrict our learning to only two. ey are - SIMILÉS and METAPHORS. We use these two more often than others.

Similé

In a similé, we make a comparison between two persons/things of different kinds but with at least **one common point** between them. A similé is introduced by the adverbs, LIKE, AS, SO or AS…. AS.

How to make use of a similé in a sentence? Let us consider a hand to hand fight between two boys named Srinivasan and Norton. Srinivasan fought very bravely. So, we may say, "Srinivasan fought ferociously." We know that an animal such as a tiger or lion also 'fights ferociously'. Here are two different kinds - a boy and a lion. The common point between them is, 'fighting ferociously'. We can thus compare the fighting quality of Srinivasam with that of a lion and say, "Srinivasan fought <u>like</u> a lion."

Here are more examples:
- (a) The enemy tanks came <u>like</u> a herd of wild elephants.
- (b) The person in a saffron cloth often talks <u>like</u> a saint.
- (c) God-fearing people shall prosper <u>as</u> palm trees.
- (d) <u>As</u> you sow, <u>so</u> you reap.
- (e) The lake water was <u>as</u> clear <u>as</u> a blue sky.
- (f) Your compliments were <u>as</u> precious <u>as</u> gold.

Use of one of an adverb out of, LIKE, AS, SO, AS … AS, is a must. Otherwise, your sentences will be wrong.

Many Similés have become **Clichés** due to over-use. So, design your own instead of using the old ones. There should be no difficulty in this regard at all. Here are some possible ones:
- (a) Sachin Tendulkar often bats like Don Bradman.
- (b) This young boy of 14, ran like a cheetah in the track events today.
- (c) She glides on the dance floor as gracefully as a swan.

Metaphor

A **metaphor** is an indirect similé. This is another form of comparison wherein we proceed as if the two persons/things are one and the same.

Take the first example under similé - Srinivsan fought like a lion. Instead of making a comparison with a lion, why can't we say that Srinivasan and a lion were exactly alike or one and the same? i.e. "Srinivasan was a lion in the fight with Norton."

Thus we can write all the similé type sentences into metaphor types like this,

(a)   The enemy tanks were **a herd of elephants**.
(b)   The person in a saffron robe was **a saint** during his talk.
(c)   The God-fearing people are **palm trees**.
(d)   The lake water was **a blue sky**.
(e)   Your compliments were **gold**.
(f)   She was **a swan** on the dance floor.

The New Testament of the Holy Bible is full of metaphors as shown below:

(g)   I am the Way, the Truth and the Life.
(h)   I am the Bread of life.
(i)   I am the Door.
(j)   You are the Salt of the earth.
(k)   Out of his heart will flow Rivers of living water.
(l)   I am the True Shepherd.

Once again, work out your own metaphors and desist from using the worn out ones.

Other varieties

The other types are, Personification, Apostrophe, Hyperbole, Euphemism, Antithesis, Oxymoron, Epigram, Irony, Pun. These are of academic values only and you are likely to get confused by learning them. So long as you understand the mechanism behind **Similés** and **Metaphors** and are able to frame your own specials, your language will fly high!

Idiomatic phrases

We noted in Chapter 50 that **idioms** are of two words; are formed out of some selected present form verbs by adding suitable prepositions to them. These idioms are to be used as *verbs* only and in their hidden meaning.

Can idioms have more than 2 words? Yes, it can, in which case it is known as **idiomatic phrase**. All idiomatic phrases will have 3 or more words. They too will have a hidden meaning. We always use an idiomatic phrase in its hidden meaning and never in the literal meaning. They may appear in the forms of Verbs, Adjectives, Adverbs or Nouns. As verbs, they will have 3 forms. Using the phrases in your sentences should pose no problem so long as you spot out the 'part of speech' of a phrase.

Shall we study some examples?

To turn a deaf ear (verb = doesn't listen to a good advice, to disregard an advice) The literal meaning of this phrase is, to rotate your ears. The hidden meaning is given in brackets and it is a verb in the infinitive form. These are the ways how we could use this idiomatic phrase:

(i)   My classmate <u>turned a deaf ear</u> to all my suggestions. (Past form verb)

(ii)   Will you too <u>turn a deaf ear</u> to me like the other boy? (Present form verb)

Black sheep (Noun = a bad person, an undesirable company)

(i)   Please don't trust Shekar because he is a <u>black sheep</u> in our class.

(object)

(ii)   Any <u>black sheep</u> in our group is not to be tolerated. (subject)

Fit as a fiddle (Adverb = in perfect healthy condition)

(i)   My grandfather, though nearly 80, is <u>fit as a fiddle.</u> (complement).

Hard core (Adjective = uncompromising/determined)

(i)   Isn't this person a <u>hard core</u> tale bearer?

List of idiomatic phrases

A list of some idiomatic phrases in use as of now, is given at the end in alphabetical order. Learn as many as possible by heart. You could use these phrases in your written English and spoken English.

Quite a number of the existing phrases have become clichés. It is difficult to apprise you about which ones have become clichés (due to over-use) and which ones are not. What is a cliché in the English speaking western nations may not be so in India. However, to be on the safe side, do try to introduce some modification in a phrase, yet without changing the hidden meaning, so as to make it sound less offensive.

For example, a sentence such as, "This man <u>took the cake</u> (won the honour by eloquent presentation) when he said he was an ace athlete" can be modified to read as, "This man took <u>the jilebi</u> when he said he was an ace athlete." Similarly, "Martha set the Cauvery on fire" (caught everyone's attention/eye) for, "Martha set the Thames on fire." (Incidentally, an English man will tear off his hair if he hears a sentence like, "A Blonde set the Thames on fire by her mini dress" because he has heard the expression thousands of times!)

The best method will be to coin your own phrases. Design them in such a way that the reader understands the hidden meaning without scratching his head.

LIST OF SOME IDIOMATIC PHRASES IN USE NOW

- A -

1.   **Acid test** (Noun = a severe and conclusive test)
     The new job was an acid test for my elder brother.

2.   **An axe to grind** (Noun = a personal interest in the matter)
     Our political leader has no axe to grind in standing for election in this area.

3.   **At the heels of** (Complement = at a close distance)
     The police were at the heels of the fleeing robber.

4. **All out** (Complement = at full speed/effort)
   We went all out to catch the offender.

5. **Apple of one's eyes** (Noun = a great pet/a real loved one)
   Baby Pinky is the apple of her father's eyes.

6. **Above board** (Complement = without any blemish or suspicion or concealment)
   Our teaching staffs' conduct has been always above board.

- B -

1. **To burn one' fingers** (Verb = to get oneself into trouble)
   My father burnt his fingers by interfering in his neighbour's affairs.

2. **To burn the candle at both ends** (Verb = to overwork oneself /spending all one's energies on his work)
   Isn't our Prime Minister burning the candle at both ends?

3. **To bury the hatchet** (Verb = to stop the quarrels and forget the past)
   Why don't you bury the hatchet and work for your mutual friendship?

4. **To blow one's own trumpet** (Verb = praising oneself)
   After passing in the entrance test, this student is blowing his own trumpet.

5. **Bag and baggage** (Complement = with all one's belongings)
   After withdrawal from this boarding, this student had to go home bag and baggage.

6. **Broken-hearted** (Adverb =greatly oppressed)
   He was sad and totally broken-hearted when the bad news came.

7. **To burn one's boats** (Verb =to run into difficulties)
   We burnt our boats in a foolish adventure and lost all our money in the bargain.

8. **A blessing in disguise** (Noun = an apparent misfortune but ending in an unexpected good luck) The cancellation of our trip to Tripathi turned out to be a blessing in disguise because the van in which we were to travel, met with an accident en route.

9. **A bosom friend** (Noun = a very intimate friend)
   Nagarajan and Sudhir are bosom friends.

10. **To break the ice** (Verb = to break the silence in a group)
    Young Shalini broke the ice by commenting on the weather prevailing that day.

11. **To beat about the bush** (Verb = to approach the subject slowly / talking uselessly without coming to the point). The teacher beat about the bush and the students got bored.

12. **Between the devil and the deep sea** (Complement = to be in a totally helpless condition.) I found myself between the devil and the deep sea when I had to make a definite decision about going for higher studies.

13. **Birds of the same feather** (Noun = people with similar character)
    When this group met, the members found themselves to be birds of the same feather.

14. **By hook or crook** (Complement = by fair or foul mean; mostly by foul means)
    A few substandard students get their degree by hook or crook.

15. **In bad books** (Complement = out of favour with a superior)
    I feel I am in my boss's bad books.

16. **Once bitten twice shy** (Complement = one becoming cautious after an unhappy experience) Once bitten twice shy; that is the reason for his hesitation to accept additional responsibility.

17. **To the bitter end** (Complement = right to the end despite difficulties) The troops in Kargil fought to the bitter end.

18. **A black spot** (Noun = a poor point) Failing in one subject in the finals is a black spot in my student's career.

19. **A bird in hand** (Noun = what you already have/possess) A bird in hand is worth two in the bush. (= What you possess with yourself is far more valuable and assured than what is visible at a distance)

20. **A bolt from the blue** (Noun = a sudden and unexpected shock) The news of a clash in Kargil with Pakistan was a bolt from the blue for India.

21. **To burn the midnight oil** (Verb = to study till very late at night) During examination time, many students burn the midnight oil.

22. **To make one' blood boil** (Verb = to infuriate someone) My father's castigation made my blood boil.

23. **Bone of contention** (Noun = one's stand or argument) The HOD's bone of contention is that every student must score above 75%.

24. **To make one's blood run cold** (Verb = to horrify someone) His speech on 'Character' made my blood run cold.

25. **To make no bones about** (Verb = to make no fuss) This rich boy made no bones about losing his purse today.

26. **To make a clean breast of** (Verb = to admit/confess to the act) The lady student made a clean breast of her involvement in the theft.

27. **To be in one's good books** (Verb = to be in someone's favour) Some students are always in the good books of our class leader.

28. **To kill two birds with one stone** (Verb = to achieve two successes in one attempt) By attending the convocation, we killed two birds with one stone.

29. **To put all eggs in one basket** (Verb = to risk everything in one venture) He put all eggs in one basket when he deposited all his money in a new Company.

30. **To bend backwards** (Verb = to be humble and beg) You don't have to bend backwards to get what is your right.

31. **No one's business/None of your business** (Noun = not your concern at all) Please don't discuss our home matters; it is none of your business at all.

32. **The ball is in your court** (Complement = the next action is from your side) I have given my views and now the ball is in your court.

- C -

1. **In camera** (Complement = in private, without anyone being present) We held our group's meeting in camera right in my home.

2. **Castles in the air** (Noun = big things/dreams about the future) Many students build castle in the air after they write the Plus 2 exam.

3. **To build castles in the air** (Verb = to dream of big things about the future)
    Don't build castles in the air before you take your examinations.
4. **Cats and dogs** (Complement = heavily)
    It rained cats and dogs in my area last night.
5. **A cake walk** (Noun = a very easy matter)
    Getting through the entrance examination is a cake walk for my son.
6. **To put the cart before the horse** (Verb = to do things in the reverse/wrong order)
    Our English Lecturer put the cart before the horse when he called for a Departmental staff meeting without the HOD's permission.
7. **Chicken-hearted** (Complement = fearful, not courageous)
    If you are chicken-hearted, you cannot join the Army.
    Chicken-hearted men cannot join the Army. (phrase used as Adjective)
8. **Under a cloud** (Complement = under disfavour)
    Menon has been under a cloud because of some misdeeds on his part.
9. **In cold blood** (Complement = without any feelings/pity)
    The thieves killed an old woman in cold blood.
10. **To call it a day** (Verb = to end all activities)
    Shall we call it a day since it is 4 p.m. already?
11. **As the crow flies** (Complement = at the map distance/straight distance)
    As the crow flies, the distance from Tambaram to Chennai city is 8 KM.
12. **To cut a sorry figure** (Verb = to make a poor impression about oneself)
    This student cut a sorry figure in the eyes of the class by failing in all subjects.
13. **To call a spade a spade** (Verb = to speak bluntly and straightforward)
    People who call a spade a spade are not liked by some.
14. **To curry favour** (Verb =to use unfair methods for personal benefits)
    He is currying favour with his tuition master.
15. **Cat's whiskers** (Noun = geniuses/too clever for others)
    His daughters are claimed to be cat's whiskers, you see?
16. **To take the cake** (Verb = to win the honour by eloquent presentation of his theory)
    This boy took the cake by claiming to be an outstanding sprinter. (This phrase is always used in a negative way i.e. to ridicule a person on his personal claim)
17. **A cock and bull story** (Noun = an unbelievable statement)
    What he says is a cock and bull story.
18. **To have the cake and eat it too** (Verb = to enjoy a double benefit)
    This criminal had the cake and ate it too when he got himself released from the jail and appointed as a candidate for the local election.
19. **To count the chicks before they are hatched** (Verb = to make plans on imaginary hopes)
    As regards your admission to an engineering college, don't count your chicks before they are hatched.
20. **To shed crocodile tears** (Verb = hypocritical tears/tears without feelings)
    In every funeral in his constituency, this politician will shed crocodile tears.
21. **To let the cat out of the bag** (Verb = to reveal some personal secret)

This student let the cat out of the bag by pointing at a friend responsible for his success in the examination.

22. **To pay back in his own coin** (Verb = to retaliate using the other's personal method)
    When our turn came we paid him back in his own coin by charging him a hefty amount for the help rendered.

23. **Till the cows come home** (Complement = never)
    His father is not in the country; you can wait for him till the cows come home.

24. **The ball is in your court** (Complement = the next action is from your side)
    We have done our bit and the ball is now in your court.

25. **A cut and dried method** (Noun = a ready made solution)
    We should not expect a cut and dried result for everyone of our problems.

26. **A cold feet** (Noun = fear/scare)
    When little Ramani saw a huge five footer at the boxing ring, he developed a cold feet instantly.

27. **Cold shoulder** (Noun = a snub; distaste for someone's company)
    When I was introduced to Radha, she displayed a cold shoulder to me.

28. **To eat a crow** (Verb = to be humiliated)
    He had to eat a crow by saying that he would win the elections hands down

- D -

1. **To dance to one's tune** (Verb = to follow faithfully someone's advice)
   This great politician always dances to the tune of his wife.

2. **Demon for work/Workhorse** (Noun = working tirelessly for hours)
   Our colony supervisor is a workhorse. Our colony supervisor is a demon for work.

3. **Dead letter** (Noun = A rule/practice no more in force)
   The practice of Sati nowadays is a dead letter.

4. **To fall on deaf ears** (Verb = to listen and ignore completely)
   My statement that smoking is injurious to health fell on deaf ears.

5. **A dog in the manger** (Noun = preventing others to use what has become useless for himself/herself)
   Many people in our country follow a policy of dog in the manger in their daily life.

6. **To go to the dogs** (Verb = to go waste completely)
   All our labour to reform our mutual friend Radha, went to the dogs.

7. **A dark horse** (Noun = A person whose capabilities are not known and whose future cannot be guessed)
   In our batch of soft spoken maidens, the new entrant Monica looks to be a dark horse.

8. **To deliver the goods** (Verb = to do one's duty well)
   If we don't deliver the goods, nobody would invite us for any kind of odd jobs.

9. **To wash dirty linen in public** (Verb = to expose all home secrets)
   He washed the dirty linen in public when he revealed the reasons for the quarrels in the family.

10. **Over my dead body** (Complement = something could take place only after the person concerned is dead)
    You could go through this project only over my dead body.

11. **To give the devil its due** (Verb = to do justice regardless of any bias)
We must give the devil his due when it comes to judging a person on his performance.

12. **To let the sleeping dog lie** (Verb = not to disturb the progress lest such action produce trouble)
We should let the sleeping dog lie as far as the progress on fly over construction is concerned in Chennai.

13. **To dot the i's and cross the t's** (Verb = to be absolutely perfect in all details)
When calculating anyone's arrears of pay, one should dot the i's and cross the t's.

14. **To bite the dust** (Verb = to admit to a humiliating defeat)
We had to bite the dust when we could not qualify in the heats.

15. **Dog tired** (Complement = exhausted)
When I reached home after the long trek, I was dog tired.

- E -

1. **To end in smoke** (Verb = to come to nothing/not to bear any fruit)
The Minister's efforts and plans to eradicate corruption ended in smoke.

2. **To make both ends meet** (Verb = to live within one's means)
Heavy drinkers could never make both ends meet as regards the home-budget.

3. **To eat humble pie** (Verb = to face a humiliating defeat)
He had to eat humble pie when he discovered that his opponent was a crafty fellow.

4. **To eat one's words** (Verb = to retract your own statement)
You may have to eat your words if you don't argue your case carefully.

5. **To see eye to eye** (Verb = not to agree)
George and I don't see eye to eye when we discuss about colony functions.

6. **All eyes/All ears** (Complement = to watch intently or to hear intently)
When the Chief Minister came as the chief guest, we were all eyes and ears to him.

- F -

1. **To fall from favour/grace** (Verb = to find oneself away from favour/grace)
Madhavi fell from the Professor's grace after she was caught copying in an exam.

2. **To feel free to** (Verb = not to hesitate)
Do feel free to say 'no' if you don't like our proposal.

3. **To face the music** (Verb = to accept any criticism)
We should be ready to face the music if this method fails in our next match.

4. **A fish out of water** (Noun = a misfit in a particular environment)
I felt like a fish out of water when I attended a talk on Atomic physics.

5. **(To feel) fed up** (Complement = tired of something)
Are you fed up with the monitor's tantrums?

6. **At one's finger tips** (Complement = information ready on one's mind)
All the trigonometrical formulae are on my finger tips.

7. **In a fit of fury** (Complement = in a sudden wave of anger)
After the match, Somnath hit Banerjee in a fit of fury for not playing well.

8. **Out of the frying pan into the fire** (Complement = from a bad to a worse

condition) This young student found himself out of the frying pan into the fire when he joined another college close by.

9. **To put one's foot into the mouth** (Verb = to blunder/to get into scrap with someone) He is sure to put his foot into the mouth if he intervenes in this domestic problem.

10. **To fly in cloud nine** (Verb = to feel overly happy and joyful) He was flying in cloud nine when he heard of his winning the first prize.

11. **To come off with flying colours** (Verb =to emerge with honour and success) When he took part in the Declamation, he came off with flying colours.

12. **A feather in one's cap** (Noun = an honour / a compliment) The unexpected victory in the finals was a feather in our cap.

13. **A fly in the ointment** (Noun = a person who ruins a plan which otherwise would have been perfect) Don't accept him in our scheme because he is a fly in the ointment.

14. **To mend fences with ...**(Verb = to remove all obstacles between ..) We ought to mend fences with all our neighbours in a colony.

15. **To have a finger on every pie** (Verb = to involve oneself in many projects at the same time) This student has his fingers on many pies.

- G -

1. **Good for nothing** (Adjective - useless) Kandasamy is a good for nothing fellow as far as dependability is concerned.

2. **For good** (Complement = finally/for ever) Kamaleshwar left India for good.

3. **Go getter** (Noun = a real achiever) Being a go getter, Suresh could be given any job and he will come off with flying colours in it.

4. **Gift of the gab** (Noun = talent to speak well) Lawyers must possess the gift of the gab if they want to do well in their profession.

5. **To give a piece of one's mind** (Verb = to reproach some one) Our class HOD gave a piece of his mind when students came late for his class.

6. **To let the grass grow under one's feet** (Verb = not to remain idle in the job) Mallika never let the grass grow under her feet when she was learning computers.

7. **Going great guns** (Noun = faring excellently in some effort) Soman is going great guns in his job as the college football team captain.

8. **To kill the goose that lays golden eggs** (Verb = to destroy the source that gives great gains) When the college sacked the canteen contractor, it killed the goose that lays the golden eggs.

9. **Touch and go** (Adjective = a close thing/experience) We just reached the station at the last minute; it was a touch and go thing.

- H -

1. **Hard pressed** (Complement = under pressure/determined)
   I am very hard pressed for time these days since I am on an important assignment

2. **Heart of gold** (Noun = a generous heart)
   Our new Asst.Lecturer has a heart of gold; she would never scold any student.

3. **Heart to heart** (Adjective = intimate and personal)
   We should have a heart to talk with Sandy who has fallen out recently from our group.

4. **To make head or tail** (Verb = to understand/comprehend)
   We couldn't make head or tail of what the chief guest was talking about.

5. **Above one's head** (Complement = beyond one's understanding)
   This theory is above my head.

6. **To have it out** (Verb = to settle the issue)
   I certainly would like to have it out with that girl.

7. **To feel at home / At home** (Verb = to feel easy and comfortable)
   I never feel at home with Mathematics.
   This boy is never at home with English. (Used as a complement)

8. **Hand in glove** (Complement = together as partners)
   I was hand in glove with Madhuri on this teasing incident.

9. **A hard nut to crack** (Noun = a difficult person to deal with)
   This person is a hard nut to crack when it comes to arguing with him.

10. **Hue and cry** (Noun = a loud protest/noise)
    We made a hue and cry when our point was not accepted by the HOD.

11. **A Hobson's choice** (Noun = no alternative whatever)
    When the teacher announced that the list was closed we had only a Hobson's choice.

12. **Hall mark** (Noun = an important characteristic)
    The hall mark of this new student is his outright sincerity in whatever he does.

13. **To hit the nail on the head** (Verb = to say or do the right thing)
    He hit the nail on the head when he said that it was a very tough question paper.

14. **To hunt with the hound and run with the hare** (Verb = to have a double policy like for and against at the same time)
    Don't hunt with the hound and run with the hare on this situation; make up your mind.

15. **To get the hell out of here** (Verb = to leave the place at once/ to get lost)
    You have made some uncharitable remarks about us; get the hell out of here.

16. **To get into hot water** (Verb = to get into trouble)
    We understand that Samuel got into hot water even after he was let off by the Professor.

17. **To take one's hat off** (Verb = to compliment and praise someone)
    We should take our hat off to Sangeetha who stood by her statement.

18. **To make hay while the sun shines** (Verb = to seize a good opportunity)
Govardhan was lucky in every venture. So, he made hay while the sun shone.

19. **Nothing to write home about** (Noun = nothing worth mentioning about somebody) There is nothing to write home about the new benchmate I have in the new class.

20. **Seventh heaven** (Complement = A feeling of extreme joy)
I was in seventh heaven when the result of the declamation was announced. (Also, "I was in cloud 9 when the result was announced" "I was floating in cloud 9 when the result was announced.")

21. **In high spirits** (Complement = feeling extremely joyful/elated)
I was in high spirits when the exam results were announced.

- I -

1. **In the long run** (Complement = in the final analysis)
Honesty helps one in the long run.

2. **In the nick of time** (Complement = just at the last moment)
We reached the railway station in the nick of time.

3. **To strike when the iron is hot** (Verb = to strike when the situation is favourable)
In the battle field, you must strike when the iron is hot.

- K -

1. **To dress to kill** (Verb = to dress in an alluring way to attract others)
Sadhana of First year always dresses herself to kill the young men around her.

2. **To know one from Adam** (Verb = unable to recognise/identify someone)
I don't know this boy from Adam. (Use this only in the Negative form)

- L -

15. **To read between the lines** (Verb = to understand carefully including the hidden meanings) When this man makes any proposal, read between the lines; don't say 'yes' immediately.

16. **To lead by the nose** (verb = to make one obey him/her)
This lady always leads her husband by the nose.

17. **The lime light** (Noun = great publicity)
Modest people would always try to avoid the lime light.

18. **Let bygones be bygones** (Verb = to forgive and forget)
Being close friends, shall we let bygones be bygones?

19. **No love lost between them** (Noun = not on good terms with someone)
There is no love lost between the two brothers who have been at logger heads for years.

20. **A little bird told me** (A Simple sentence = a reliable information picked up from a reliable source)
A little bird told me that you have been engaged. Right or not?

21. **Lakshman rekha** (Noun = a restricting line and not to be crossed under any circumstances) Your Lakshman rekha is our front door. Don't you ever cross it. (This is a pure Indian idiom phrase)

- M -

1. **As a matter of fact** (Complement = truly; as it happens)
   As a matter of fact, my father is under transfer now.

2. **For that matter** (Complement = incidentally/accordingly) (This is a connector as well.) For that matter, may I also confirm to you my full co-operation in this case?

3. **To make a mountain out of a mole hill** (Verb = to exaggerate to a very high degree) It was such a small scratch on the little boy's knee and he made a mountain out of a mole hill.

4. **Music to the ears** (Noun = something very very joyful)
   The news of my father's promotion was music to our ears.

5. **To miss the boat/bus** (Verb = to miss an opportunity)
   You may miss the boat if you take your job interview lightly.

6. **To give one a piece of mind** (Verb = to scold someone for some lapse)
   I gave a piece of my mind to Saroja when she failed to return my class notes.

7. **Monkey business** (Noun = something totally foolish)
   If you ask me, selecting this place for an excursion is nothing but a monkey business.

8. **Once in a blue moon** (Complement = very rarely)
   Robert comes to my house once in a blue moon.

9. **To face the music** (Verb = to face some criticism)
   When I returned home late that evening, I had to face the music from my mummy.

10. **To hold on to/hang on to mother's apron** (Verb = to depend totally on someone)
    Though married, my elder brother hangs on to his mother's apron.

- N -

1. **Not worth his salt** (Noun = he is a worthless fellow)
   A boy who runs away from any problem is not worth his salt at all.

2. **Under one's nose** (Complement = within one's knowledge)
   Raju is so absent minded that he doesn't know what passes under his nose.

3. **A new broom** (Noun = a newly appointed person, hence works well)
   Our servant is a new broom as of now.

4. **To cut one's nose to spite one's face** (Verb = to do silly things and make his/her own personality worse)
   In order to become popular this boy cut his nose to spite his face.

5. **Neck deep** (Complement = to be in deep trouble) When I went to help my friend, more troubles came neck deep.

- O -

1. **Out of date** (Complement = something old fashioned)
   This kind of dress is out of date surely.

2. **Off their guard** (Complement = being careless)
   This boy attacked me from behind when I was off guard.

3. **Out of place** (Complement = not in the right order/sequence)
    This chair is out of place in this room, don't you think?

4. **Out of pocket** (Complement = without money after some loss)
    After my long leave I am out of pocket.

5. **With open arms** (Complement = being received very warmly)
    The host received us with open arms.

- P -

1. **To play with fire** (Verb = to engage oneself in dangerous activities)
    Those involved in gold-smuggling are playing with fire.

2. **To play upon words** (Verb = to use words with unusual meanings)
    Some authors play upon words in their writings.
    We can use this idiom as a noun also: There is **a play of words** in this line.

3. **To poke one's nose into** (Verb = to interfere)
    We should not poke our nose into someone's private affairs.

4. **To pay through one's nose** (Verb = to pay more than what is required)
    We had to pay through our nose for this CD player.

5. **To cast pearls before swine** (Verb = to describe a great information to a worthless person)
    To explain to this man about God is to cast pearls before a swine.

6. **To paint the town red** (Verb = to make everyone notice the doer)
    This girl painted the town red by walking in a mini skirt.

7. **To put the thinking cap on** (Verb = to examine an issue seriously)
    I had to put my thinking cap on when I was asked to teach a small poem to VIII standard children.

8. **To pick up the thread** (Verb = to restart from the previous closing point)
    Moses picked up the thread of the arguments where Manian had left.

9. **To put one's foot down** (Verb = to refuse to proceed further)
    I had to put my foot down when my small brother asked for Rs 50 pocket money.

10. **A pinch of salt** (Noun = not a serious information)
    I take every statement of this student with a pinch of salt.

11. **To run from pillar to post** (Verb = to run from one office to another)
    To get our visa on time, we had to run from pillar to post.

12. **To pull someone's legs** (Verb = to play a joke on someone)
    We pulled his legs by saying that he stood first in the class.

13. **To pull up someone** (Verb = to scold someone on his/her default)
    The teacher pulled up Shanti when she wasn't attentive in the class.

14. **Pull up your socks** (Verb = do your work with some seriousness) (A command)
    Your work is very casual and substandard. Pull up your socks, will you?

- R-

1. **Heart in the right place** (Complement = of a kind and sympathetic nature)
    Rajinder has his heart in the right place.

2. **Round the corner** (Complement = very near)
   My elder sister's marriage is round the corner.

3. **To take one for a ride** (Verb = to get fooled)
   You would be taken for a ride if you follow his ideas.

4. **Red tape** (Noun = Too many details asked for and too much of delay)
   There is too much of red tape when we want anything done from any Govt department.

5. **To ring a bell** (Verb = to remind one of something)
   Whenever I see you, a bell rings in my mind. Haven't we met before?

6. **A rainy day** (Noun = difficult circumstances/financially hard days)
   Everyone must save for a rainy day.

- S -

1. **To show one's true colours** (Verb = to reveal one's true nature)
   The young maiden showed her true colours only after marriage.

2. **To stick to one's guns** (Verb = to be firm in his/her stand)
   Sundaram stuck to his guns even when he was threatened with punishment.

3. **A storm in a tea cup** (Noun = a commotion over a small point)
   The quarrel between the brother and sister is only a storm in a tea cup.

4. **A shot in the arm** (Noun = a morale booster)
   The announcement of a scholarship was a shot in the arm for me.

5. **Spick and span** (Complement = neat and tidy)
   We must always keep our premises spick and span.

6. **To spill the beans** (Verb = to give away a secret)
   The child spilled the beans when she said that her father was a drunkard.

7. **At a stone's throw** (Complement = at a short distance)
   My house is only a stone's throw away from my school.

8. **For a song** (Noun = at a very low price)
   I got this famous book for a song.

9. **To smell a rat** (Verb = to suspect some foul play)
   When Samson made an unusual proposal we smelt a rat in it

10. **To leave no stone unturned** (Verb = to use all possible methods)
    The police left no stone unturned in locating the culprit.

11. **To talk shop** (Verb = to talk about office/workplace)
    You are not expected to talk shop during social gatherings.

12. **To sail in the same boat** (Verb = to suffer or enjoy equally)
    You and I are sailing in the same boat as far as this issue is concerned.

13. **To lose one's shirt** (Verb = to lose one's temper)
    Our football coach lost his shirt when the team lost to a weak team.

14. **To rub salt on one's wound** (Verb = to aggravate one's sorrow over some failure) Don't rub salt on a wound of failure.

15. **A snake in the grass** (Noun = one who attacks at an unexpected time)
    Don't trust this boy because he is a snake in the grass type.

16. **Skeletons in the cupboard** (Noun = has many misdeeds to his/her credit)
He is not a sincere politician at all because he has many skeletons in his cupboard.

17. **Spoilsport** (Noun = one who spoils the enjoyment/ruins others' prospects)
Whenever we plan a joint function with boys and girls, Ramanathan turns a spoilsport.
The weather played spoil sport when we went on a sightseeing trip the other day.

18. **To steal the lime light/thunder** (Verb = to snatch away a credit which naturally was somebody else's)
The small children stole our limelight / thunder in the entertainment show.

19. **A close shave** (Noun = a narrow escape)
In a car accident last week, we had a close shave.

20. **To go for a six** (Verb = to go out of control/to get destroyed)
Our picnic programme went for a six when it rained cats and dogs that morning.

21. **Saving grace** (Noun = a comforting factor)
The saving grace was that the chief guest shook hands with each one of us after we had lost the match to an unknown team.

- T -

1. **A tall order** (Noun = an aim which cannot be reached)
My beating this fat boy in a boxing bout is a tall order.

2. **To turn a blind eye** (Verb = to take no notice of some event)
This invigilator turned a blind eye to the copying going on in last year's exams.

3. **To turn a new leaf** (Verb = to change one's way for the better)
This lady student turned a new leaf when she entered the Fourth Semester.

4. **To throw/pour cold water on** (Verb = to discourage someone highly)
Every time I suggested something new, my uncle poured cold water on it.

5. **To take the word from someone's mouth** (Verb = to say exactly the same points which were somebody's ideas)
When he spoke, he took the words out of my mouth.

6. **To take one to task** (Verb = to rebuke someone for his/her faults)
Our Lecturer took me to task when I reported late for my English test.

7. **Thick skinned** (Complement = irresponsive)
This student is so thick-skinned that he won't accept any suggestions.

8. **Tooth and nail** (Complement = with all power and resources)
We shall fight our case with the teacher tooth and nail.

9. **On the tip of my tongue** (Complement = readily available in my memory)
His name is on the tip of my tongue but I can't get it out of my mouth.

11. **Tickled to death** (Complement = feeling extremely joyful)
He was tickled to death to meet me on a public road.

12. **To speak with the tongue in the cheek** (Verb = not to say anything sincerely and openly)
This boy always says things with his tongue in the cheek.

13. **Cup of tea** (Noun = a practice that pleases me) (to be used in the NEGATIVE.)
Attending everyone's birthday party is not my cup of tea.

14. **To throw in the towel** (Verb = to give up the play)
This champion threw in the towel when he sprained his ankle midway in the game.

- U -

1. **Under the carpet** (Complement = to hide something from public view)
He has the habit of sweeping all his misdeeds under the carpet.

2. **Under a cloud** (Complement = out of favour/under suspicion)
This leader is under cloud on account of some scandals doing the rounds.

3. **Underdog** (Noun = a person who submits himself/herself)
Ramanujam is the underdog in our group.

- W -

1. **To take the wind out of one's sail** (Verb = to frustrate someone's efforts)
He took the wind out of my sail by removing me from the basket ball team.

2. **To wash dirty linen in public** (Verb = to expose a personal matter in public)
You would be washing dirty linen in public if you say anything about the quarrel you had with your sister at home.

3. **A wolf in sheep's clothing** (Noun = a cheat posing to be a good fellow)
Don't depend on his promises at all; he is a wolf in sheep's clothing.

4. **A wild goose chase** (Noun = an useless search)
Finding honest and sincere persons these days is a wild goose chase.

5. **Writing on the wall** (Noun = a clear future possibility)
It is a writing on the wall that India will become a great power in the next decade.

6. **A windfall** (Noun = a sudden gain of wealth)
By getting this job, he will be experiencing a windfall.

7. **To walk an extra mile** (Verb = to help out someone more than what is minimum)
If you walk an extra mile with poor people, you would get great rewards from God.

8. **Much water has flowed under the bridge** (Past form verb = many things have happened since a particular time)
Much water has flowed under the bridge since we last met.

9. **To feel on top of the world** (Complement = a feeling of elation)
I felt on top of the world when the Professor gave me a remark "Very good" over my project assignments.

10. **A white elephant** (Noun = Something prohibitively costly)
This newly built house is a white elephant for us.

Chapter 52

CONVERSATION TECHNIQUE - I

Introduction

It is indeed certain that you would have been conversing with your friends, classmates and seniors in English over the past few years.

It is possible that when you wanted to put across a very complex thought or describe a tricky situation, you would have felt somewhat tongue-tied. In the process, you could have annoyed your superiors or some elders by using improper and impolite words.

English is known to be a very polite and polished language. It contains a lot of niceties and if you don't know them or don't know how to use them, your listeners may conclude that you haven't learnt the language thoroughly at all. Or, you may cut a sorry figure in front of them. Some people may even avoid your company on the impression that you are an ill-mannered person and it is not worth cultivating any friendship with you!

How to break the ice

Many English users at +1 or college levels would feel confident of talking in grammatically correct English. This would be the case when the conversation has picked up. But, the problem could be, how to start off a conversation especially with a stranger or even the opposite sex. As a matter of fact, you are absolutely sure that if someone could kick start it you could keep it going. It is that initial inertia that frightens you.

The English language has inbuilt in it so many phrases and simple rules on floating and keeping up a conversation with anyone including your next door neighbour who has moved in recently and whose name you have not found out !

The 'first step' is the real obstacle and tiding over it is known as "Breaking the ice". How to break the ice? It is not at all that difficult. Shall we take various situations and see how one could break this ice and feel free to talk?

Situation 1

You have just completed your Matric and are seeking admission in +1 in a nearby Higher Secondary school. You have gone to the school to collect your application form. There are quite a number of boys like you in the school premises. No face is familiar to you. You do feel lost and you notice that quite a number of the candidates too feel lost. You want to talk with someone but you don't know how to go about it.

Let us see how Thangaraj and Susheel manage to strike a conversation. You are a spectator. Note down carefully what each says. I have given at the right margin my comments on what each has said and why etc.

Conversation	Comments
Thangaraj: Excuse me ..?	
Susheel : Turns around and looks at the other with a surprised look.	
Thang : Good morning, I am Thangaraj. Sam Thangaraj (Extends his right hand ..)	*Shaking hands with the same sex is all right, but not with the opposite sex in our Society.*
Sush : Oh, hullo. I am Susheel. Arun Susheel (Extends his hand)	*When you reveal your own name, it is an invitation for the other to give out his. Never say, "What's your name?"*
Thang : I am new to this school. Are you an old student of this school?	*Having given some info about himself, Thangaraj has thrown a question at the other and Susheel has to answer it.*
Sush : Oh, no. I am new too. I have come for admission to + 1 class.	
Thang : Oh same here, Susheel. Which school are you from?	
Sush : St Thomas school, Bangalore ….	
Thang : Have you come all the way from Bangalore to Chennai? I am sure there are many Higher secondary schools in Bangalore, aren't there?	
Sush : Of course. But, my father has been transferred to Chennai, you see?	

Summary

Have you noticed how Thangaraj has broken the ice? Never feel shy. Just greet the other person warmly and with a big smile. If someone smiles at you, won't you feel honoured, smile back and talk to the other? "Excuse me" is the phrase to be used to attract the attention of a person who is not looking at you. If the other person is facing you, greet him warmly with a "Good morning or Good afternoon." Rest assured that the other would respond. Never hail a person with "Hullo?" This is considered impolite.

For any conversation to 'go on', always throw a question at the other. What kind of question? you would want to know. A question on something common between the two. Here, you have to be careful. Never ask any deep personal questions such as, "How many sisters have you or have you failed in any subject?" etc. Let your questions be innocuous and unoffending and such that would extract out an immediate response.

If there is no question from either, the conversation would come to an end.

Let us analyse some of their sentences. In a conversation, we make several shortcuts. A sentence need not have all the elements of S-A-V-O/C at all. Sometimes you may cut out S and sometime A and V as well. But, O/C must be there.

Take the phrase "same here"; this is only O/C. This means, "I have also come for the same purpose."

When Susheel answers, "St Thomas school, Bangalore", he has cut out completely the S-A-V part. This is not a grammatical mistake but an accepted shortcut.

Examine Thangaraj's sentence: I am sure there are many Higher secondary schools in Bangalore, aren't there? This is a Complex sentence and an EQ at that. You know that EQ is a powerful question.

And how does Susheel's answer? "Of course." It means "yes" but more assertive than "yes". The expanded or the long form of this answer is, "Yes, there are many Higher secondary schools in Bangalore." "Of course" is a powerful phrase. We use this as answer for many questions or when you agree with someone/s statement/view.

Susheel's next sentence, "But, my father has been transferred to Chennai, you see?" is a Complex sentence. 'But' here is a connector. After a connector, always use a comma in the written form; otherwise, it could be mistaken for a conjunction or a preposition. (Don't forget, this is a 'lose Complex sentence' or a 'sentence with a clause') The end sentence "you see", although has S- A-V, is more of an end phrase than a sentence. This means nothing at all. It is just a way of ending a sentence with a pleasant note in a conversation, and nothing else. One could also start a sentence with "You see?" or "You know?")

The conversationalists here could be Saroja and Bagyam as well. And they would talk in the same style and tenor.

Situation 2

Let us consider this time between a Male and a Female in the same school premises. See how Balan manages the situation. Incidentally, Balan is from a high profile English medium school.

Balan notices that there are quite a number of girls but all of them are in small groups. And one charming girl is standing all by herself and looking lost! Balan inches towards her and halts about 4 feet from her.

Balan   : Good morning. I am sure, you have come for admission, like me. Right?

Girl   : …. ….. Y - e- s

Balan   : You must be from a Convent school. Am I right or not?

Girl   : Indeed, I am. How did you guess?

Balan   : Well. First, you are very smart; standing upright and looking straight. And of course you have a charming face.

Girl   : What else?

Balan   : While all the other girls are in Salwar Kamiz suit, you are in a saree. A saree suits you very well.

Girl	: Well, I am Devyani. I am from St Philomena's convent.
Balan	: Isn't it wonderful? I am Balan, Balan Rajendran. I am from St Patrick's Matriculation school.
Devya	: Oh, St Patrick's in Madhavaram?
Balan	: Yes.

Summary

Devyani initially is a very shy and a cold girl. Most girls are, anyway. See, how she answered the first question - with a lot of hesitation and reticence.

What makes Devyani come out of her shell? A compliment from Balan. She has livened up all of a sudden. At this stage, words have begun to flow out of her mouth freely. Balan continues with his accolades. And Devyani is floating in cloud nine at Balan's observations and praises. This is the trick to make any person talk. But, be very cautious, especially with the fair sex. You could overstep and possibly invite the ire of the lady. Balan has made a very tactful and inoffensive entry into her mind and she is responding beautifully. So much so, she has revealed her name voluntarily and unasked.

And the conversation has picked up speed.

The 'compliment giving trick' would work with the same sex also. You could perhaps comment on the shirt or the school tie the other is wearing. Or, about his school and teachers etc.

Situation 3

This is your first day in a Self financing engineering college. You have got a Management seat here in the Civil engineering discipline. While you were looking at the notice board and the staff list board, a well dressed gentleman hails you. You turn around and note that the other doesn't look like a student; an elderly gentleman. You feel he is probably a Professor or a Senior Lecturer. Your name is Gunaseelan.

Prof	: Hullo there!
Guna	: Good morning. Good morning, Sir. Did you call me?
Prof	: Yes, I did. Are you sure you haven't lost anything?
Guna	: No, Sir. I don't think I have lost anything?
Prof	: Is this your pen?
Guna	: Yes, it is, Sir. I don't know how it had slipped out of my pocket. Thank you, Sir.
Prof	: You are welcome. What's your name young man?
Guna	: Gunaseelan, Sir.
Prof	: Good. I am Professor Natesan, Head of Department of Civil engineering.
Guna	: (Gulps) I am ... I am ... a Civil engineering student, Sir. I am ... I am ... a ... new student, Sir.
Prof	: Oh good. What a coincidence? So you will be coming to my department from next year, won't you?
Guna	: I suppose so, Sir.
Prof	: Well, see you, Gunaseelan.

Summary

The atmosphere here is quite different.

An elder or a senior teaching staff like a Professor or Principal could take the liberty of saying, "What's your name?" Similarly, you as an adult can ask a little child, "What's your name?" But, between persons of the same age or status, this practice is to be avoided.

When an elder is at conversation with an young man, the initiative to keep the conversation going will always be taken by the elder. So, there is no question of breaking the ice. You just answer all his questions correctly, accurately and respectfully. You don't have to ask any question from your side. An occasional one yes, and that too totally innocent and friendly.

Shall we analyse some of the sentences?

When someone has done some favour to you or done something in your favour, always thank the other. "Thank you or Thank you very much" is the right phrase. Avoid mentioning, "Thanks". "Thanks" is not considered quite polite enough. "Thank you" is the short form of "I do thank you". The acknowledgement for a 'Thank you' is, "You are welcome." Some persons have the habit of acknowledging it by, "No mention please or it is all right." These are wrong. Stick to "You are welcome."

"What a coincidence" looks like a phrase. It is equal to, "Isn't it a coincidence? or, It is a coincidence."

You must show the greatest respect to your teachers in a School or College.

What is the meaning of "see you" ? It is equal to, "Shall meet you sometime later." When you take leave, it is customary to use this sentence.

Be liberal with your "Thank you's". Here, Guna doesn't fail to thank the Professor for handing over his pen.

Situation 4

At a Bus stop, David, a first year student of a Science college meets his neighbour, Mr. Seshadri, a government official. Standing next to Seshadri is a girl of about 10 years, possibly his daughter. David knows that Seshadri is his neighbour and has bumped into him quite a number of times and sometimes along with his parents. Let's see how David manages the situation.

David : Good morning, Sir. Waiting for Bus 153?

Sesh : Good morning, young man. Yes. No 153 has come for more than 20 minutes. Unusual.   *Mr.Seshadri has used 4 sentences. Can you identify and analyse them? Three are shortcuts.*

David : It is unusual, uncle. I am also waiting for 153.

Sesh : How are you David? How far are you going?

David	:	Fine, thank you, uncle. Parry's uncle.
Sesh	:	How are your parents? Haven't seen them for quite sometime.
David	:	They are well, uncle. Dad is out of station. Will be back from Delhi next week, I think.

(Seshadri feels a tug at his waist and looks down at his daughter)

Sesh	:	Ah yes. David, meet my daughter, Selvi.
David	:	How do you do Selvi? Nice to meet you. Where have you been all these days?
Selvi	:	I just returned from Boarding last night.
David	:	Boarding? You studying outside Chennai?
Selvi	:	Yes, *Anna*. In Hyderabad. I am in the VI standard.
David	:	Isn't that wonderful? Well, hope to see you more often, Selvi.

Summary

When you sight someone known to you, even known casually, it is bad etiquette to ignore his/her presence. Here, David wishes Mr.Seshadri heartily with a warm "Good morning" as the first step in starting a conversation and also makes a small enquiry. Initially he addresses the other as Sir and later switches over to Uncle. An youngster addressing an elder "Uncle" or "Aunty" is accepted in our society and this, only in informal surroundings. If you happen to meet an elder outside, even an acquaintance, always stick to "Sir" or "Madam".

"How are you?" is an acceptable greeting when you meet someone known to you very well. "How do you do?" is the correct greeting cum response when you are introduced to someone. David does this to Selvi. Selvi here has no chance to say, "How do you do?" since David has thrown a question at her in the same breath. The acknowledgement for "How do you do" is again "How do you do?"

When you are introduced to someone, even if to a small boy or girl, don't stop after saying, "How do you do?"; always initiate some kind of a conversation appropriate to the situation and the person concerned.

Since the age difference between David an Selvi being about 8 years or so, David could have greeted her on introduction, "Hullo, Selvi or even Hai Selvi." But he chose to treat her as an young maiden.

Young girls calling an older boy as "Anna" or "Bhayya" is quite in order. "Brother" is an alternate form but it is not as respectful as "Anna" (elder brother).

Here are the various shortcuts used by the participants and their long form:

"Nice to meet you" = It is nice to meet you?
"Boarding?" = Are you studying in a Boarding?
"Yes, *Anna*" = Yes, *Anna*, I am studying in a boarding.
"Hope to see you more often" = I do hope to see you more often.

Situation 5

A blind man is standing at the edge of a busy road. He wants to cross over to the other side. He knows that the road is busy with high traffic that afternoon and it happens to be the rush hour too. Let's see what Shankar, a college student in his final year, does in this situation.

Shank : (*Gently touching the middle aged man*) May I help you, *ayya?*

Blindman : Yes. Could you help me get over to the other side, please?

Shank : Sure, *ayya.* (*When the red signal has come up, he tows the blind man carefully to the other side.*) Here you are, *ayya.* Can you manage from here?

B.man : Of course, son. Thank you. Thank you very much, sonny. May God bless you.

Shank : (*With tears nearly welling up in his eyes.*) Thank you, Sir. Go carefully.

Summary

Some people are born blind. Why, nobody knows. It is God's will, that's all. Perhaps, God wants to test us, the normal people! Hence, it is the responsibility of the society to help the handicapped people to the extent possible. Blind people can manage many things on their own without anyone's help. But, they wouldn't mind some help if offered voluntarily. Here, Shankar feels moved at the sight of a 'helpless' blind man.

"May I help you?" is the right sentence to use in such a situation. Don't ask, "Do you need any help?" This is not a correct etiquette.

Shankar addresses him as "Ayya" in Tamil. This is short of saying, "Sir". One could use similar term in other Indian language as well to probably uneducated people.

Had it been a woman, he would have said, "Amma".

See, how grateful the blind man is? He repeats "Thank you", calls him, " sonny" and also blesses the young man. The blind man must have recognised that the helper is an young man around 20 years of age.

Shankar suddenly turns emotional, possibly at "sonny" and shows his elation by addressing the other, "Sir".

You must give respect to elders even if they happen to be unfortunate people. Never treat them as 'dirt'.

Don't forget to say, "please" either when you ask for a help or offering a help to someone. "Please" is an adverb, which could be used at the end of a sentence or even as the starting word.

Here are the conversation-shortcuts and their long form:

"Sure" = I shall surely help you.

"Of course" = already explained.

"Go carefully" = You do go carefully.

Chapter 53

CONVERSATION TECHNIQUE - II

General

Our telephone network has grown phenomenally. Possession of a telephone at the residences has become a very common thing these days. But, it is a sad commentary that many do not know how to talk on the telephone. As a result, they make themselves sometime the laughing stalks or annoy a caller in no small measure.

Although as a college student you may not own a telephone yourself, it is very likely that your father or mother may have one, especially if either of them holds a senior position. In which case, sometime or the other you may have to attend an incoming call or make an out call on behalf of somebody in your home.

Shall we see how some selected college students conduct themselves over the network in various situations? What they say and how they react to certain questions, are absolutely correct in conformity with the Society's expectations and you need to copy their method.

Situation 1

Neena, a second year student, is in her house all by herself. Her parents, Mr. and Mrs. Satish Chandar are out on a social function. Mr. Satish Chandar is a Deputy Secretary in the Central Govt.

(The telephone rings)

Neena	:	Hullo.
Voice	:	Is it 2431678?
Neena	:	It is.
Voice	:	May I speak with Satish, please?
Neena	:	I'm afraid, Mummy and Daddy are out. May I take down a message?
Voice	:	May I know who is on the line? I am Tandon here, Satish's colleague.
Neena	:	Good evening, uncle. I am Neena, Satish Chandar's daughter.
Tandon	:	Oh, Hullo, Neena. Nice to hear you, my child. Any idea when your parents would be back?
Neena	:	No idea, uncle. They didn't tell me the time. They would have dinner and then return, I presume.
Tandon	:	Oh what a pity? Could you do me a favour, Neena?
Neena	:	Sure, uncle.
Tandon	:	Could you please tell Pappa to ring me back as early as possible? Even at dead of night? There is something urgent.
Neena	:	Of course, uncle. Does Pappa know your number?
Tandon	:	Yes, he does. Please leave a note to him in case you go off to sleep.
Neena	:	No uncle. I will be awake all right when they return. Am preparing myself for tomorrow's test, you see?
Tandon	:	Good. Wish you the best of luck. Good night Neena.

Summary

Over the residential telephone, it is good practice not to tell the caller who you are or even your own telephone number until you know who exactly is calling. So, to answer an incoming call with a "Hullo" is quite in order.

Once Neena knows that an elder is calling, she greets him and addresses him as "Uncle". This is correct etiquette. Neena could have addressed the caller as Mr.Tandon. But being young, she addresses him respectfully and this adds a little intimacy.

Mr.Tandon is quite impressed with the way Neena spoke on the line and the way she had composed her sentences. So, he addresses the young maiden as, "my child". This is a compliment for Neena.

Have you also noticed that Mr.Tandon doesn't order her about using Simple present sentences? He *requests* her every time and talks with her politely and sweetly.

The various shortcuts in the conversation are:

"I am afraid"	-	This is a phrase to precede any negative reply. ("I am afraid 'no' "is a very polite statement than saying bluntly "no".)
"Sure"	-	I shall surely do a favour to you.
"No idea, uncle"	-	I have no idea when they would return.
"Oh, what a pity?"	-	Isn't it a pity that you don't know the time of their return?
"He does"	-	Your father does know my telephone number.

Situation 2

Surinder Singh, a final year B.Sc student wants to talk with his classmate Darbara Singh. Copy his method.

(Telephone bell rings)

Voice   : Hullo. (*The voice is deep and powerful*)

Surinder : May I speak with Darbara, please?

Voice   : Sure. May I know who is calling?

Surinder : (Gulps) Surinder, his classmate, Sir. Good afternoon, Sir (*Surinder has* soon *realised that the person at the other end is probably Darbara's father. So, he changes tone and greets him*)

Voice   : Oh, I see. Please hold on, young man. Shall call him. (*Surinder could overhear a transmission, 'Darbara, call for you, son' and he also hears faintly Darbara's reply: Will be there in a minute. Tell the caller to hold on, Pappa'*)

Voice   : Darbara will be here in a minute. Would you like to hang on or call back?

Surinder : Thank you. Shall hang on, Sir.

Voice   : Good. Who is your father, Sonny?

Surinder : Dr.Santokh Singh, Sir.

Voice   : Is he Physician?

Surinder	:	No Sir. He is a Ph D.Professor in History in the Govt college.
Voice	:	That's nice. What games do you play Surinder?
Surinder	:	Hockey and Cricket and in that order, Sir
Voice	:	Ah, Darbara is here. (*Surinder for you, son*)
Darbara	:	Hi Surinder boy. How are you? How did you suddenly think of me?
Surinder	:	Hey, was it your father or someone else on the line?
Darbara	:	Of course, my Pappa. Why?
Surinder	:	His well modulated voice sent tremors in my veins for some seconds, *yaar*.
Darbara	:	I see ......

Summary

When you feel that an elder is attending to the call, give him full respect. Never ask, "Who are you ?" - This is considered most rude on the telephone network. If you do want to know who is at the other end, the most respectful way of asking is, "Am I speaking to Darbara's father? Or, I don't think I know you, Sir." Here, Surinder could have addressed Darbara's father as, Uncle. But, in his opinion 'Sir' was preferable. In case the other happened to be an elderly lady, Surinder could have addressed her as 'Aunty' or better still 'Madam'

It is because that Darbara's father was impressed with Surinder's telephone manners that he takes time to exchange some words with the caller. Surinder must take this as an honour and answer all questions courteously. If what you had said had annoyed the elder, he would have just put the handset down saying, "Wait".

Be liberal with your 'Thank you's and Please's". These are magical words and play wonders on the listener !

To ask, "How are you?" is all right between friends. Never use this phrase when introduced to a stranger.

Situation 3

Mira Chatterji has just completed her +2; has appeared for several competitive examinations. Her ambition is to join an IIT or some engineering college and go in for a Computer science degree. She had attended several coaching classes too and had prepared herself to face any kind of interview. See how she manages a conversation with a middle aged high society lady. Mira has rung up her friend (Nomita Roy) of hers for a chit chat.

(Mira hears the ring back tone)

Voice	:	Hullo?
Mira	:	Hey Nomita? Didn't you promise to ring me this morning to talk about the movie this evening? Forgot or what?
Voice	:	....
Mira	:	Why don't you say something, idiot?
Voice	:	Are you sure you are talking with Nomita?

Mira	: Come, come. Don't try to fool me. You are Nomita, aren't you? I know your voice well, idiot and a half. This isn't the first time I am talking, eh?
Voice	: This is Nomita's mother speaking. (*It is a commanding voice. Mira thinks the lady is sounding like her English teacher in Std XII of Lorretto school*)
Mira	: (*Gulps a few times*) I am .. er … I am sorry, Madam. Really .. sorry…. You sound so much like Nomita, Madam. Please forgive me.
Voice	: All right, my child. What's your name?
Mira	: I am Mira, Madam. Mira Chatterji from Salt Lake. Nomita and I are classmates.
Voice	: Good. I shall call her. Please wait.
Mira	: I am sorry, Madam. You sound so much like Nomita.
Voice	: What are you doing nowadays Mira?
Mira	: Nothing in particular, Madam. Just waiting for the results.
Voice	: Ah, here is Nomita for you. (*Passes over the handset to Nomita*)
Nomita	: Hi, Mira. How are you?
Mira	: Wait. Wait. Is your mother around or has she gone away?
Nomita	: She has gone. Why?
Mira	: I got frightened, stupid.
Nomita	: Why? Why?
Mira	: Because, she sounded so imposing and overpowering. I was scared to address her, "Aunty".
Nomita	: Oh, cut it out, yaar. Mom is a gentle lady. If you see her you would change your mind.
Mira	: Am not sure. Is she a teacher or something?
Nomita	: Didn't I tell you, she is an HOD in St Xavier's?
Mira	: No. Anyway, now I know. Which movie are we seeing today, my girl?

Summary

Mira has obviously picked up some choice 'homilies' and friendly invectives to be used with friends. What shock she would have felt on learning that she had been talking with Nomita's mother for a while. "Why did I use all those frightful phrases?" she would have regretted in her mind. Some young women may have put the phone down and run away at this point! But, Mira is a different kind of a person. She regains her composure and immediately apologises to the lady for her folly and addresses her reverentially as Madam.

What is "something" in the following sentence? "Am not sure. Is she a teacher or something?" "Something" here means nothing at all. It is a way of ending a sentence. You could take it as an end phrase also analogous to 'you see, you know'. But, use this only as an end phrase.

Situation 4

Sometimes, young people may get flabbergasted and blabber indistinguishable words and sentences if they encounter an opposite sex at the other end. No need at all. Keep your wits about. Let us see how Manoj manages such a situation.

Manoj had rung up 972 3456 to speak with his friend, Bhola. He is aware that Bhola has no sisters and only two brothers. But he encounters a female voice.

(*Manoj has dialled the number and waits*)

Voice	:	Hullo.
Manoj	:	(*Surprised at an young female voice*) Is it 972 3456?
Voice	:	Yes, it is.
Manoj	:	This is Manoj here. May I speak with Bhola, please?
Voice	:	I am afraid, Bhola isn't here. Has gone for some shopping. Could I take down a message or something?
Manoj	:	Thank you. But, I am eager to know who I am talking with? You have a wonderful voice.
Voice	:	Well, I am Bhola's cousin. A visitor to Lucknow.
Manoj	:	(*Deeply impressed with the lady's voice and mannerisms, he wants to float a conversation with her*) Welcome to Lucknow. You didn't tell me your name.
Voice	:	I am Nandini.
Manoj	:	Welcome to Lucknow, Miss. Nandini. Will you be staying in Lucknow for long?
Nandini	:	Just a couple of days, I think.
Manoj	:	What a pity? I would love to meet you, you know? You have such a lovely voice, you see?
Nandini	:	Thank you. Isn't it just an ordinary female voice?
Manoj	:	No, I think it is an extraordinary voice.
Nandini	:	Thank you. Shall I tell Bhola that you rang up.
Manoj	:	Please do.

Summary

Do note that Manoj had kept his cool all the while. The dialogue is highly dignified; no irrelevant and silly questions. It is of a high level English as well.

See the sophistication in the sentence, "I am eager to know who I am talking with?"

Some young men may ask, "What are you, what is your name etc?" Similarly, mark the diplomacy in the sentence, "You didn't tell me your name?" He is entitled to frame the question this way because he had mentioned his own name earlier.

Manoj has followed the trick of 'giving a compliment' to make the other talk and keep the conversation alive. He had picked on her 'wonderful voice'. Nandini has been only modest by saying, "isn't it jut an ordinary female voice?"

When you have to give out your name, say, "I am …. so and so." Never use the phrase, "My name is … so and so."

The various shortcuts used here are:

"I am afraid … Bhola isn't here"	-	"I am afraid" is a prelude to a negative statement that has followed.

| "Just a couple of days" | - | I shall be staying in Lucknow for a couple of days. |
| "Please do" | - | Please tell Bhola that I rang him up. |

The correct acknowledgement for "Thank you" is, "You are welcome." Here, Manoj had no opportunity at all to use this phrase.

Situation 5

Another occasion people use strong words or lose their temper is when they receive a wrong number. It is not a caller's fault at all if he gets a wrong number, is it? He/she didn't mean to inconvenience you at all. Yet, the caller in such situation is expected to be nice and console the 'telephone-disturbed subscriber'.

Let us see how Norton behaved in one such situation. The time now is 1030 p.m. and Norton is the only member awake in the house; he has been revising his lessons. Norton is a First year engineering student.

(Telephone bell rings)

Norton : Hullo?
Voice   : Is it 627 4317?
Norton : I am afraid, No. I think you have got a wrong number.
Voice   : But, I dialled the number correctly, you know?
Norton : Well, sometimes one may get a wrong number, you see?
Voice   : I am very sorry. So sorry to have disturbed you at this hour. My apologies.
Norton : You are welcome.

Summary

When you encounter a wrong number, don't shout at the caller. It is not his/her fault at all. Just say politely, "Sorry, wrong number." And don't curse the caller either.

The caller at this stage is duty bound to apologise because she/he had certainly caused some inconvenience to the other. Copy the method used by Norton.

Chapter 54

CONVERSATION TECHNIQUE - III

Introduction

If you happen to be a college student, the Society expects some norms in your day to day behaviour. What are the reasons? That you are moving about in an educated environment hobnobbing with cultured people; read books of higher learning and accordingly acquire greater knowledge on how to carry yourself among people.

So much so, you are expected to stand out in a group proclaiming yourself silently that you are a role model to be copied by others.

You are likely to find yourself at maximum exposure in a social party of some sorts. So, this is the occasion to watch your own conduct and demeanour.

Situation 1

It is Pradhan's birthday party. Pradhan has invited a number of friends; some from his college and some from his own colony. Both young men and women are present. Among the invitees are two Lecturers from other colleges - Miss. Shanti Menon and Mr. A. Kaul.

The time now is 4.30 p.m. The invitees have started arriving. Pradhan, as the chief host, is at the entrance door, greeting everyone and showing them in. Except three from your own college you don't know anyone.

By 4.40 p.m., all invitees have arrived.

Pradhan now joins the crowd of 20 odd persons and welcomes everyone for the birthday party. A number of invitees seem to know quite a few in the group. But you seem to be the only one who is new to many.

Let us now watch the proceedings as silent spectators. Note the way every guest goes about in Pradhan's living room.

Pradhan: Good evening everyone. A hearty welcome to you all. Over the next 15 minutes or so, kindly find out everybody's name because you would be partnering them in some games. OK?

(*There is a lot of buzz and noise and giggles as everyone is moving freely greeting and shaking hands. Pradhan tows a close friend of his, Peter, to one corner and introduces him to an young lady, who looks to be around 21 years of age.*)

Pradh : Peter, meet my cousin sister, PINKY RAJESHWAR. She has come all the way from Ambala to attend my party. (*Turning to Pinky, he says,*) "Pinky, meet my close college friend and a classmate, Peter, Peter Samuel".

Pinky : Hullo Peter, how do you do?

Peter	:	How do you do Miss. Rajeshwar? I recollect Pradhan telling me about you. You are undergoing 'air hostess training'. Am I right?
Pinky	:	Yes, indeed. You have a good memory.
Peter	:	Thank you, Miss.Rajeshwar. I am honoured.
Pinky	:	Call me Pinky, young man. I am not all that senior to be addressed as Miss. Rajeshwar.
Peter	:	Thank you. Thank you, Pinky.

(Pinky, being senior in age, Peter initially addressed her formally. Since she has allowed him to use her first name, Peter must thank her for the privilege)

Pinky	:	What is your stream in the engineering college, Peter?
Peter	:	Beg your pardon?
Pinky	:	I said, "Which is your discipline in the engineering college?"

(When you haven't caught someone's question, you must say, "(I do) beg your pardon", which means in low level English, "Please repeat your question or please say again". See how Pinky has responded to "Beg your pardon")

| Peter | : | Electronics and Communication engineering. Same as Pradhan's. |

(In a social party, you are expected to move around, meet and talk to as many as possible. At this stage, Peter detaches himself from Pinky saying, "Excuse me" and goes near another young lady.)

| Peter | : | Hullo. Good afternoon. I am Peter. Peter Samuel. |
| Lady | : | Oh Hi. I am Suguna. Pradhan's neighbour. My house is just over there. |

(Suguna is a high-profile girl; daring and no-bar type young maiden. Says "Hi" even though she is meeting Peter for the first time. Doesn't give out her own surname or any other name for that matter. She is around 16 or 16+. Nevertheless, Peter prefers to address her formally.)

Peter	:	I am happy at meeting you Miss.Suguna .....
Suguna	:	(Interrupting him, says) Oh cut out that Miss and all that yaar and call me, Sukki, OK? What you propose to do after your college, Peter boy?
Peter	:	(Somewhat stunned at Suguna's free-speech) Nice knowing you, Sukki. See you later. (Earlier, Peter said to Pinky, "Excuse me ..." and here he says to Suguna, "See you later". Another phrase to be used when you take leave of a person in a social party is, "Nice meeting you". Without some kind of apology, to leave one guest and moving over to another abruptly will be considered bad manners. Nor are you expected to stick to one person the whole time.)
Young man	:	May I introduce myself? I am Chakraborty. Pradhan's friend. (Extends his right hand towards Peter)
Peter	:	How do you do Chakraborty? It's a nice gathering, isn't it?

(Chakraborty looks to be of the same age. So, Peter addresses him by the same name. This is quite in order. But, don't take such liberties with the opposite sex. Address the lady formally even if she looks equal to your age. You could however address by the first name if the person concerned is a small girl. Peter doesn't stop after the formal greeting. He throws a question at the other in order to keep the conversation going.)

(At this juncture, Pradhan comes near Peter, taps him and says, "Peter I would like you to meet someone special. Peter excuses himself from Chakraborty and follows Pradhan)

Pradhan : Madam, may I introduce to you a good friend of mine, Peter Samuel? *(Turning to Peter,)* Peter, she is Miss.Shanti Menon, Assistant Lecturer in St.Stephen's college, Delhi. She was my mother's student years back.

Peter : How do you do, Madam? Nice meeting you, Madam. *(Peter raises his pressed palms in the true Indian style to greet her. Peter prefers to address her "Madam" and not by her formal name. This is one way of showing extraordinary respect to the teaching community who hold a special place of honour in our society)*

Shanti : Nice meeting you Peter. *(A senior person my not return the greeting in the formal way but could say something nice instead like, "Nice to know you, It is nice to meet you" etc.) Where you studying, Peter? (Short form of "Where are you studying?")*

Peter : I am in a self financing engineering college, Madam, near Meerut.

Shanti : Oh, excellent. You know Peter, I too wanted to be an engineer but luck didn't play favourable at all.

Peter : Is it, Madam? What a pity? And I suppose you landed at BA (Literature)? *(Laughs lightly)*

Shanti : Well, I did enjoy English literature. See, that's why I am a teacher in a leading college.
(Pradhan barges in again. "Excuse me. Sorry to cut into your conversation" and pulls away Peter. In a social party, such interruptions do take place. When you want to break in like this, use any of the phrases given here: "Sorry to butt in. May I interrupt your interesting conversation for a moment?" "Sorry to interrupt you, but this is something urgent." Sorry to interrupt you, may I join you or may I join your group?")

Pradhan : Peter, I want you to meet another important person. *(Tows him to a senior gentleman)* Sir, I would like to introduce my good friend , Peter Samuel, my classmate. *(Turning to Peter)* Peter, he is Mr. Anand Kaul, Senior Lecturer in Mechanical engineering from a Chennai college, on vacation now in Delhi.

Peter : How do you do, Sir? Welcome to Delhi.

Kaul : Thank you, Peter. Pradhan tells me, you 're a good cricket player. Is it right?

Peter : Yes, Sir. But I couldn't get into the Delhi State team at all. If I had, I would have made cricket my career.

Kaul : Isn't that wonderful?
(Another interruption. Pradhan raises his hands and announces in a high pitch)

Ladies and gentlemen, sorry to terminate all your discussions and pow-wow's. We are going to have some party games for the next 30 minutes or so ...

Summary

In a social party, you need to observe excellent etiquette. You must keep up with the tempo of the party as well. Mingle with others and don't keep yourself isolated. You can talk to anyone whether you know that person or not. Don't expect the host to introduce you to everyone. Self introduction is to be observed here. See, how Chakraborty does this.

Sometimes, you may have to play the host yourself. See how Pradhan went about his job as the chief host. Follow his method.

Situation 2

Madan is a final year undergraduate student. His parents, Mr. and Mrs. Surinder, are on a social call to a friend of theirs - Mr. and Mrs. Santokh singh. This young couple have a small daughter, Mona , aged 4 years. Earlier Surinder has given telephonic information to Santokh about their social call that evening.

(Knock on the door.   Mr.Santokh singh opens the front door ..)

Santokh	:	Welcome. Good evening. Do come in.
Surinder	:	Well Santokh, you have met my wife earlier, haven't you?
Sant	:	Of course. Welcome, Mrs. Surinder.
		(In the living room)
Suri	:	Mr. and Mrs. Santokh, do meet our son, Madan.
Madan	:	Good evening, Sir. Good evening, Madam.
Sant	:	Good evening, young man. You still studying?
Madan	:	Yes, Sir. I am in B.Sc final, Sir.
Sant	:	Oh good. Do sit down Madan.
Mrs.Surinder	:	You have a nice house Mrs. Santokh. Is it your own or on rent?
Mrs.Santokh	:	Our own. Grandpa's property, you know?
Surinder	:	Punjabi Bagh, is a posh area, isn't it?
Sant	:	It sure is. The land cost has gone up sky-high, you see?
Suri	:	Indeed, it has. In fact, Delhi has become a very costly place.
Sant	:	Ah, here is our daughter, Mona. *(Turning to Mona)*
		Say 'good evening' to all, *beti*.
Mona	:	GOOD EVENING, everybody.
Mrs.Surinder	:	Isn't she a charming young thing? Come here, my child.
		(Now seated comfortably on Mrs.Surinder's lap) In which class are you in now, Mona?
Mona	:	LKG 'A', Aunty.
Suri	:	Wonderful. What is the name of your school, baby?
Mona	:	Saint John's Matriculation school, Uncle.
Sant	:	Is this your first visit to Punjabi Bagh, Mrs. Surinder?
Mrs.Surinder	:	Oh, no. We have been here before.
Mrs.Santokh	:	Ah Madan? What you intend doing after graduation?
Madan	:	Will be trying for MBA, Mrs.Santokh?

Mrs.Santokh	:	Going to attend any coaching classes?
Madan	:	Yes, positively, Madam. It is a tough exam. Can't get through without full preparation.
Sant	:	Yes, you should go all out for it.
Madan	:	(*Turning towards Mona*) Mona baby, you like your teachers?
Mona	:	Yes, 'chotta uncle.'
Madan	:	My, my, you are a smart girl, aren't you? Why don't you call me bhaiyya?
Mona	:	You too small for a bhaiyya. Why? You don't like 'chotta uncle'?
Madan	:	Of course, I do, Mona.
Mona	:	You see, my teacher says, "call big people 'uncle' and small people bhaiyaa or didi" (*She laughs lightly*)
Madan	:	Your teacher is correct, Mona.

(*Mrs. Santokh invites everyone into the dining room for some snacks and tea*)

Suri	:	How is life treating you, Santokh?
Sant	:	Nothing to complain, Surinder. God has been very kind to us. A lovely house, a lovely wife and a lovely child. What else does one want?
Suri	:	Well said, Santokh. I wish everyone would feel the same way.
Sant	:	Thank you. By the way, how is your work in the Department?
Suri	:	Fine. No problems whatever. I have a very understanding Joint Secretary, you know? And he takes work out of you without your knowledge!
Sant	:	Isn't it great?
Suri	:	Mrs. Santokh, I must say these gulab jamans are delicious. Did you make them yourself?
Mrs.Santokh	:	Thank you. Yes. I am glad you like it.
Mrs.Surinder	:	I must say, you are an excellent cook.
Mrs.Santokh	:	Thank you.

Summary

During a social call, don't be too formal; but, not too informal either. When introduced, they don't use the phrase, "how do you do?" The Surinders and Santokhs do not know each other very well. So, they address each other by their surnames. Madan prefers to address the hosts as Sir and Madam. He could have used Uncle and Aunty but this only after he comes to know them more intimately. Have you noticed that even Surinder and Santokh use their formal names?

If there is a little child in the host's home, one must talk to him/her also. Don't ignore the children whatever may be their age.

The topic of conversation is innocuous. Never get into any kind of serious discussion. Avoid talking 'shop'. Choose always such topic or ideas of mutual interest.

It is nice to give some compliment to the hostess about any food items. And such praises must be acknowledged by a "Thank you. Am glad you are relishing it .."

Chapter 55

POLITENESS AND DIPLOMACY

Introduction

We learnt that Passive form is inherently polite and we may use it when we want to make a request. An Active form in this regard may sound more like an order ! You could make your order sound like a request if you put the adverb 'please' somewhere in your sentence.

There are other methods of being extremely polite as well. During any social occasions and when you move about in aristocratic circles, you are expected to use the most polite phrases and your language itself must be dignified, honourable, praiseworthy and most diplomatic.

In this Chapter, we are going to learn how to say 'yes' and 'no' in a polished and oblique way; .how to express your dissatisfaction over something in an unoffending language; how to show preference for something - 'Preference' is a subtle word and is virtually equivalent 'yes'. And how to give an order in an elegant way without using 'Please' or, 'Let ...' .

Use of WOULD RATHER for showing Preference

Rule

All persons - WOULD RATHER - present form verb - O/C
(WOULD RATHER is a phrase consisting of an Auxiliary and an Adverb)

Here are the examples:

(a) I **would rather** drive the car myself. (This type of sentence is considered more polite/subtle than saying, "May I drive the car myself?")

(b) **Would** you **rather** drive the car yourself?
    A   S   Adv   V   O

(c) **Wouldn't** you **rather** supervise this job yourself?
  Neg A   S   Adv   V   O

(d) My son **would rather** not go for the picnic. ("My son would not go for the picnic" is blunt and impolite, isn't it?)

(e) Peter **would rather** join a reputed college.

(f) We **would rather not** meet the Principal today.

(g) **Wouldn't** you **rather** spend 2 more days in our house?

(h) **Wouldn't** your daughter **rather** go in for an MCA course?

(i) **Wouldn't** you **rather** say 'sorry' to your brother?

(j) I **would rather** not go to bed so early.

(k) My parents **would rather** stay at home today.

Showing Preference along with a comparison

Rule

All persons - **would rather** - present form verb - O/C -**than** - (Subject) - present form verb - O/C   (Complex sentence form)

Here are the examples:

(a) My brother **would rather** watch a Hindi movie **than** see an English serial.
     S   A   Adv   V   O   Con (A)V   O
(The 'subject' in the second sentence can be silenced if the subjective noun is common for both the Simple sentences)

(b) **Wouldn't** you **rather** stay in our house **than** in a hotel? ('stay' is a common verb)

(c) I **would rather** join this Institute for computer training **than** the one in the next street.

(d) She **would rather** marry her uncle's son **than** an unknown person.

(e) We **would rather** get on with our work **than** spend time in gossip.

(f) **Wouldn't** you **rather** fight it out **than** running away like a coward?

Note:

The sentences would have to be in the 'Specific/Negative question' form or a1 form. It is not common to frame an a2 sentence in this pattern.

Use of WOULD RATHER THAT

Rule

All persons - **would rather** - (present form verb but silenced) - **that** - S - past form verb - O/C

This is a Complex sentence form whereof the tense rules are required to be observed. Though past auxiliary and past form verb are used in the second sentence, the overall tense of the sentence is 'present time'. (See Chapter 28)

Here are the examples:

(a) I **would rather** (like) **that** you didn't go out today.
    S   A   Adv   Con S NegA V   C

(b) The Vice Chancellor **would rather** (appreciate) **that** the Principals made prior appointment instead of freely walking into his office.

(c) The Queen and I **would rather that** you didn't marry that girl.

(d) We **would rather that** you spend your week-ends more profitably.

(e) I **would rather that** you didn't tell anyone about my visit to your house this evening.

(f) Q : Do you mind if I smoke?
a : I **would rather** that you didn't. (This is much more diplomatic than saying, "Please don't")

(g) **Would** you **rather that** I cooked the dinner myself?

(h) I **would rather that** you didn't miss any of my Lectures during this Semester.

(i) This is a personal letter addressed to me. I **would rather that** you didn't read it.

(j) Q : Shall I stay back home and not accompany you?
a2 : We **would rather that** you didn't.
a1 : We **would rather that** you came with us.

All are Complex sentences and the time period is 'present time'; we can't use this pattern for any kind of past time periods.

All are polite expressions whether in a1 or a2 form.

Written in the conventional way, the sentences would read as follows:

(aa) You may not go out today.

(bb) The VC desires that all Principals make prior appointment before seeing him.

(cc) The Queen and I don't like your marrying that girl.

(dd) You may spend your week-ends more profitably.

(ae) Don't tell anyone about my visit to your house this evening.

(af) I do mind.

(ag) Should I cook the dinner myself?

(ah) I don't want you to miss any of my Lectures during this Semester.

(ai) Don't read my personal letters, please.

(aj) Don't stay back. Come with us.

The phrases WOULD RATHER, WOULD RATHER ... THAN and WOULD RATHER THAT are used to show Preference for some action without using the verb 'prefer' in the sentence. This is a sophisticated way which sounds grand and royal.

The other common method of conveying a 'no' is through, "I am afraid no/not". We have covered this phrase in the Conversation technique Chapters. Though this is high level English, we now see that one could use a still more superior method to say 'no'.

Use of IT IS TIME ...

This is another polite phrase used in *present time only* as a suggestion. It may also be used for expressing some dissatisfaction over someone's behaviour/conduct in an indirect way. (Remember, we used MIGHT also for this purpose?) The meaning of this phrase is: "It is already late; don't delay your action any longer." "It" here is an impersonal pronoun and the Temporary Subject as well. Use this phrase only for preset time cases.

Rule

It   is   time - O1 - infinitive - O/C.

TyS A.V   S

Examples:

(a) **It is time** to go to college. ('O1' is absent here)

(b) **It is time** to return home. (- do -   )

(c) **Isn't it time** for you to pack up   your box?

              O1   infin   O2

(d) **It is not yet time** to ring up for the priest, is it? (O1 is absent)

(e) **Isn't it time** for all of us to get going?

The sentence could be in Q, (except Gen Q) a1, a2 or EQ forms.

Rule

It is time - that - S-A-V-O/C. (The A-V sections could be in any past family)

Examples are:

(a) **It is time** that you spoke to Sharmila about her callous ways with boys.
TyS A.V S Conj S (A)V O O

(b) **Isn't it time** that the children got up from bed?

(c) **It is** indeed **time** that they came out of bed.

(d) **It is time** that you did something about your life.
(You should have done something about your life already)

Though we use past auxiliary and past form of verb in the second sentence, the full Complex sentence deals with present or future actions only and never past actions.

(e) **It's time** that the boarders were in bed.

(f) **It's time** that we elected a new party to run the country.

We can make some minor modification in the sentence structure like this,

(g) **It is about time** that he acted and not merely talked.

(h) **It is high time** that we stopped harassing this student.

(i) **Isn't it high time** that you revised your lesson for tomorrow's test?

(j) **It is time** that we ate our lunch, isn't it?

(k) **Isn't it about time** that you got married?

a2 is not common in this structure and wouldn't sound well either.

Writing the categories of sentences

It will not be possible to write the General Question in all the methods. You could write the remaining 6 without any difficulty.

Exercise

Rewrite the following sentences in a high profile polite way:

1. I don't like seeing this boy in my house so often.
2. I would like to see an English movie.
3. My father wouldn't like us to go on a picnic on a working day.
4. The nurse refuses to go near this patient.
5. Wouldn't you prefer to accept the Science group instead of the History group?
6. I think you should take some interest in games.
7. We would prefer to play billiards than cards.
8. Shouldn't we spend our spare time in the Electronics laboratory than slouch around?
9. I would like to be friendly with my next door neighbour than fight with him.
10. Robert likes to play around with his Keyboard than with the violin.

Answer the following questions in a high degree polite way in a1 or a2 form:

11. Wouldn't you prefer Rajdhani express to an ordinary Express train?
12. Would you like coffee or tea?
13. Could you wait here till 4.30 p.m.?
14. Between CDs and video cassettes, which one would you prefer?
15. Do you want me to go with you during your golf practice?

16. Would you need some additional money for your travel expenses?
17. Would you prefer to walk or hitch-hike for office?
18. Should I give this money as a loan or gift?
19. Would you like to watch the match on the T.V or go to the stadium?
20. Would you want to swim in the sea?

Make the following commands sound polite: (Use 'had better' where appropriate. See Chapter 48)

21. Don't go to his house so very frequently.
22. Take your seat in the second row, please.
23. Don't issue any warning to any student without proper approval.
24. Talk to your HOD about this issue?
25. You' re already late. Dress up fast.
26. Shouldn't you take this subject more seriously?
27. You must submit your Lab reports on time and get them signed by the Asst.Lecturer.
28. You must be more orderly in your daily routine.
29. Report this matter to your hostel warden straightway.
30. Don't ask me for money every other day.

Give the following advices in a polished way:

31. Get lost from here at once.
32. Get your tyre repaired in this shop.
33. You must come to church on time always.
34. Apologise to your mother for your rude words.
35. Won't you say 'sorry' to your brother?
36. Don't waste money on ice-cream.
37. Be nice to everyone.
38. Give a warm smile to all your colleagues.
39. It is not good to make enemies of every neighbour.
40. Go to bed always before 10.30 p.m..

Analyse the following sentences:

41. Isn't it high time that you corrected our attitude towards poor people?
42. We would rather that you abandoned this person's friendship.
43. Philip would rather spend some time reading the Bible than play cards on a Sunday.
44. My son would rather not go with you all for the 'day out'.
45. You had better go home right away.

Write the remaining 6 categories of sentences, where possible, for the following statements:

46. Wouldn't you rather spend some time with your children at home than go to the club for bridge?
47. We would rather not meet the Labour union leader this morning.
48. My uncle would rather that you completed your studies in the first instance.
49. Isn't it time that you pulled up your sock about your life in general?
50. It is about time that he got married.

Part - II

COMPOSITION

Chapter 56

HOW TO WRITE A PARAGRAPH

Introduction

Till now you have learnt the technique of composing a Simple, Complex or Compound sentence. Next, you have been writing a single sentence at a time. A sentence is the basic unit of a paragraph and a paragraph may contain usually between 2 and 10 sentences. (It is not good to write a paragraph of more than 10 sentences). These sentences may be a mix of Simple, Complex and Compound sentences.

Can we take about 8 excellently well written sentences, package them and call it a paragraph? No.8 well written sentences packaged together may turn out to be an awful paragraph. The paragraph may not read well at all. So, it is not enough to have just well written individual sentences but each should be connected to the next in such a way that the reading is smooth, understandable and enjoyable.

To produce such an effect, a writer has to observe what is known as "Paragraph writing rules". As otherwise, your para may sound insipid and boring as well! And, do remember that a Para is the basic unit of any piece of writing, be it an essay or article or letter or short story. Accordingly, you must become an expert initially in "Para writing" before you attempt any kind of writing.

Once you master the art of writing a single para, it is relatively easy to link one para to another and next and next and so on. Any writing may contain say, 5 -100 paras.

What is a paragraph?

We may define a para as a group of sentences that talk about one idea or one point of argument or one situation, unitedly. Shall we call this henceforth, "Para theme"? All the sentences in a para must point towards the "Para theme." Only then will the para be readable, understandable and enjoyable.

Para writing rules

While composing a para, do keep in mind the following rules:

(a) Let the first sentence be a **catchy** one. (More about this later)

(b) Don't start every sentence the same way. For example, if a para contains only Simple sentences, start the first in the pattern S-A-V-O/C, the next as C-S-A-V-O, and the next O-S-A-V, Participle -S-A-V-O/C, Infinitive -A-V (A.V) - O/C and so on.

(c) It is good to have a combination of all three types of sentences. Something like, Simple, Simple, Complex, Complex starting with the conjunction, Simple, Compound and in some such sequence. (It is however, good to write a Compound sentence only once in 2 or 3 paragraphs.)

(d) Do not repeat the same words, especially verbs or common nouns or adjectives; use their synonyms. Nor should you repeat the same sentence idea/thought even if they are in different sentence patterns.

(e)   Let one sentence lead to the other smoothly in thought and continuity like climbing a staircase. For some reason if this is not possible, use a "connector" which should act as a bridge between the two sentences.

(f)   Restrict the length of your Simple sentences to 16 words and Complex / Compound to a maximum of 20 words. If for some reasons you have to write a sentence of 24 words or thereabouts, make sure that the reader understands the contents in one go. Otherwise, go back to the 16/20 words rule.

One could list out more guidelines. But, the above are enough for the present. As you keep writing more and more paras, you would evolve your own formulae as well. At this stage, shall we attempt writing a couple of paragraphs keeping in mind the above rules? Here is a poorly written para of 10 sentences. Read it and write down all the defects noticed by you:

> Everyone develops headache. Headache causes a lot of inconvenience. Some people may see a doctor with the complaint of headache. Some people may apply a balm of sorts on the forehead to remove the headache. Some may take some kind of tablets to eliminate the headache. Some brave people may ignore it completely. Everyone develops headache some time or the other. We must do something about it. We may carry a pocket calculator or some gadget like that. Calculators are easily available everywhere. Calculators don't cost much.

Observation

As you could see, all sentences are grammatically correct. Each sentence is good by itself and conveys a complete meaning. Yet, the para doesn't read well at all. Some readers may feel that it makes a painful reading. Why? Here is my list of defects. Compare it with yours:

Defects

1.   All are Simple sentences of the pattern, S-A-V-O/C
2.   Many sentences start with "Some people".
3.   The common noun "Headache" has been repeated several times.
4.   The adjective "some" appears too many times.
5.   "Everyone develops .." repeated twice.
6.   Para theme rule not adhered to.

While the theme is about "headaches", why bring in a new topic "calculator". What has calculator to do with headache? Assuming that this writer insists on starting every sentence with S, shall we see how the para could be improved upon with the help of **connectors** to make it more readable?

> Everyone develops headache. <u>Thereupon,</u> it causes much inconvenience to them. <u>As a result,</u> some people may see a doctor about it. <u>And</u> a few may apply a balm of sort on the forehead to remove it. <u>Whereas,</u> tablets may be the preference of a small number. <u>Yet,</u> somebody could be ignoring it completely as well. Most of us seem to suffer from this ailment. <u>Accordingly,</u> we need to do something about it.

You would agree that there is a slight improvement in the readability now. What ingredients have made the para more acceptable? Use of **connectors**. (shown underlined) Next, any repetition of verbs and common nouns has been avoided. The information on calculators has been deleted since the para theme is on "headache".

Connectors provide a smooth bridge of change over from one sentence to another especially when not connected logically. But for these connectors, the sentences would sound jumpy. ➜ tense state

Let us improve upon the para further by using a mix of Complex/Compound sentences and starting every sentence in a different way.

> Everyone developes headache sometime or the other causing much inconvenience to them. While some may see a doctor about it, a few may apply a balm of sorts to remove the pain. Taking medicine may be someone's preference. A brave group may love to ignore it completely. Since most of us seem to suffer from it often, shouldn't we do something about it?

This version sounds better, doesn't it. Why? Instead of using Simple sentences we have used Complex sentences to merge 2 or 3 thoughts into one sentence. As a result, the level of English has shot up. Too many Simple sentences will not only sound childish but annoying as well.

Use of connectors

Connectors produce two effects - if two sentences start with S, the annoyance part is removed; if the second sentence is not a logical development of the first or if there is a shift in thought, it provides a smooth change over (bridge).

Here is another poorly written para, which is in low level English as well. Firstly, point out the defects and then improve upon it by using connectors:

> T.V is one of the most modern inventions. The majority of households have T.V sets nowadays. Many villagers also own T.V set. Schools use T.V. for teaching lessons. Several subjects are taught through T.V. We can see film shows also on it. Some people like to see serials. A number of teachers do not know how to use T.V. for teaching. They will keep the T.V untouched and use the blackboard. Children love the T.V cartoons. T.V stations conduct education classes before the examination season. I like to watch only the sports events like tennis, cricket on T.V. It saves us the trouble of going to the stadium to witness a match. T.V. is a desirable gadget in every home.

Observation

The para contains 14 sentences which are grammatically correct; each sentence does convey a clear meaning. However, the para theme is not clear at all.

jumble → in utter disorder.

disorderly pile of clothes

Defects

1. All sentences start the same way.
2. The sentence ideas/thoughts are conflicting. Does the description belong to "T.V as a teaching medium" or "T.V as an entertainment medium"?
3. As a result, the sentence ideas have become jumbled and not logically built up at all.
4. One good point is that nouns and verbs haven't been repeated but pronouns/synonyms could have been used for the noun "T.V"

without - logical and meaningful conn

However, notwithstanding the fact that this para is incoherent containing clash of thoughts, let us improve upon it using suitable **connectors** to make it sound less offensive!

> T.V is one of the most modern inventions. The majority of households have a T.V set nowadays. Even many villagers own a T.V. In addition, schools also use them for teaching lessons. Several subjects are taught through it. Further, one could also see film shows. Some people like serials. As a matter of fact, a number of teachers do not know how to use the small screen for teaching. They will keep the T.V. untouched and impart all their instructions through the blackboard only. Incidentally, children love the T.V cartoons. T.V stations conduct education classes before the examination season. But, I like to watch only the sports events like tennis and cricket on the box. Accordingly, it saves us the trouble of going to the stadium to witness a match. Undoubtedly, T.V is a desirable gadget in every home.

The para could be made far better if we rearrange the Simple sentences under entertainment and education separately instead of mixing them.

Do you see that **connectors** make all the difference between poor English and good English? They are like magic wands and useful tools at that. Here is a list of connectors that can be used for different situations. They are to be used in between two sentences:

Connectors of Time and Sequence

Immediately, thereafter, thereupon, next, soon, then, even then, after, later, finally, in the meantime, meanwhile, afterwards, now, while, a little later, since, at least, of late.

In due time, Henceforth,

Connectors to link up contrasts

But, however, nevertheless, on the other hand, otherwise, yet, and yet at the same time, despite it, instead, still, on the contrary, in contrast, even so, for all that, while, nonetheless, *Notwithstanding, All the Same*

Connectors to show additional information

In addition, also, moreover, further more, likewise, similarly, finally, besides, again and then, too, equally important, and, further, last, added to all these.

Connectors for results/conclusions

Therefore, hence, thus, consequently, as a result, for, accordingly, thereupon, then, truly, finally, in conclusion. *corollary,*

(blind jealousy is a frequent corollary of passionate love)

Connectors for examples

For instance, as an example of this, for example, take the case of, in other words, that is, as noted earlier, as noted already, in fact, specifically, in particular, indeed, incidentally. To illustrate, To demonstrate.

Connectors for emphasis

Even, actually, as a matter of fact, as a matter of truth, surely, in fact, in actual fact, certainly, undoubtedly, indeed, true, for sure, come to think of it, that being so.

Connectors indeed liven up a paragraph. Use a suitable connector whenever you find a **gap** or **a break of thought** between any two sentences. You would come across many such occasions. It is then that you use a connector to bridge the two sentence-ideas. Connectors should be the starting words of the new sentence.

Connectors alone are not the only aid to convert a bad para into a good one. There is one more method called, "the Curiosity Question (CQ) method".

The CQ method

Rule (e) says that "Let one sentence lead to the next smoothly in thought and continuity like climbing a staircase." How is this to be achieved? It is by forcing the reader "to look forward to something" after digesting the first sentence. That 'looking forward to' will come into play if you frame a sentence to arouse a curiosity question or curiosity questions. In order to find the answer(s) for those CQs, the reader will feel compelled to read the next sentence. The possible CQs are, IS IT, HOW, WHAT ARE THEY, WHAT HAPPENS NEXT, WHAT ELSE etc. But, do make sure you answer the CQ satisfactorily in the subsequent sentence.

If a sentence does not arouse a CQ, it will become a 'dead end sentence' and the reader would not proceed further. It is not difficult to frame and reframe any sentence so as to produce a CQ of some kind in it. You must be conscious of that, that's all.

Read the following passage written according to this approach. Notice how every sentence drives you to the next. The kind of CQs a sentence has induced is shown inside brackets.

"It is comparatively easy to improve the <u>coherence</u> of your writing. (CQ: HOW?) All you have to do is to observe two simple rules. (CQ: IS IT? WHAT ARE THEY?) The first is, use suitable connectors. (CQ: OK. WHAT NEXT?) The next is, let every sentence arouse a curiosity question. (CQ: OK. WHY?) That will compel the reader to read the next sentence to find the answer. (CQ: ALL RIGHT, THEN?) You continue this process. (OK. THEN?) By the time the reader comes to the last line, he would have discovered the full theme of your para."

Have you understood the trick contained in the CQ method? Your aim is to drive the reader to the last line of the para. You may ask, wouldn't the last sentence look like a 'dead end sentence' since it would have answered the CQ? It would. This is the place where your sentence not only should answer the CQ but also generate another CQ. The reader then would naturally go to the next para.

At times you may find that your sentence has answered the CQ of the previous all right but does not create another CQ; such a sentence might look like a dead-end sentence too. In such an event, use a connector.

A sentence in the middle of a para need not fully answer the CQ. It could answer the CQ partly and yet leave the reader somewhat thirsty and unsatisfied. He would then read the next sentence which will quench his thirst completely. Even at this place, you may have to go over to the connector method.

Such writing does not call for any special expertise as such. Once you are fully aware of this necessity, you would automatically frame your sentences to arouse CQs.

So, you have now two methods to write an effective para - use of connectors and the CQ method. Use both of them judiciously and your para is guaranteed to be interesting.

Catchy sentence

Rule (a) tells you to make your first sentence **catchy** What is **catchy?** It is the same as framing the sentence to arouse a CQ(s). But this CQ must be quite loud, that's all. On reading the first sentence, the reader should jump up or raise his eye brows and yell, "REALLY? IS THAT SO, WHAT HAPPENS NEXT? IS IT? TELL ME MORE ABOUT IT and so on."

Unless your first sentence is catchy, a reader may not read your piece at all. Why should he/she? The readers are busy people. They have many better things to read and do. So, you have to literally "pull them by the ears and command them to read what you have written." That's what your first sentence is supposed to do. If you have designed it in such a way, the reader will put aside whatever he was doing and apply his attention on your writing. This is the trick followed in all the articles in the "Reader's Digest" magazine. Read all the first sentences in any article/story in any issue. You'd feel compelled to read through it right down to the end.

In this requirement, you need some practice. While it may be easy to compose a sentence with CQs, to write one which would raise a LOUD CQ would need some skill. You will have to develop it on your own. Ask your own self initially, show it to your friends, consult some more, until your method clicks.

Here are some opening lines collected from magazines and newspapers. Don't they raise your hair or your eye brows?

(a)   Is life worth living? That depends on the Liver!

(b)   Has a cobra, with a wide open hood, ever greeted you with a good morning smile on opening your front door?

(c)   The best way to get praises about yourself is, to die.

(d)   There is no money in poetry, but then there is no poetry in money either.

(e)   When the teacher asked Tina, "One and one make what?" she replied, "Love".

(f)   That particular night was so still and icy that you could hear the stars twinkle.

If you follow this rule in every para, but not to the same degree as in the opening para, your writing will earn a lot of fans.

There is one more small tip which you could employ at times. If you open a para with IF or WHEN, the reader will certainly read the first sentence because the curiosity element would be inbuilt in the sentence. Even then the sentence must contain some CQ in it and only then the reader would go to the second sentence.

Exercise

For each sentence given below, choose the most suitable subsequent sentence out of the given alternatives:

1. I love reading science fiction stories.
    (a) The book S for "Science" by Dr.Premila is very interesting.
    (b) For instance, I found Subash Roy's book on "Satellites" very impressive
    (c) So, I read science fictions regularly.

2. Daniel likes to travel a lot.
    (a) Daniel likes to travel because his father travels a lot.
    (b) As a result, he is always travelling.
    (c) He likes it because his father is in the railways.

3. It is quite easy to be the "life of a social party". One method is to be up on all the latest gossips in your area.
    (a) It is always handy to keep ready a lot of funny jokes.
    (b) Another is, to help keep the conversation lively and of interest to everyone.
    (c) In particular, I like any gossip connected with film actresses and young college maidens.

4. The Plus 2 pass outs are invariably counselled to keep their aim clear before joining a college.
    (a) But, some of them ignore any kind of counselling.
    (b) However, some listen and ignore them.
    (c) Despite it, some would join any type of college where they get admission.

Without using any connector, improve the dull passages in Q 5 & 6 by remodelling the same sentences :

5. A professional cricketer becomes the crowd's darling during one or two seasons. The fans may take a fancy over the way he played. The bowlers may get tired of him. Stylish batting also sometimes <u>endear</u> him to the spectators especially if he reaches a century. If he could take a few catches, he would become the man of the series.

6. T.V watching is good. Listening to radio could be entertaining. Sometimes video could be more interesting. Comics are interesting too. They are as educative and enthralling as T.V.

Sentences in Q 7 and 8 look jumpy and with gaps in thoughts and continuity. Improve the para by using suitable connectors or introducing additional sentences or by the CQ method to make the para readable:

endear → make attractive and loveable

7.   Our friendly football match was to be on the coming Sunday. That was the only convenient day for all members in our group. It rained early morning. Monday was out of question, being a school day. Tuesday was not a holiday. The match was finally fixed for the following Saturday. We had a good time.

8.   A hobby can often pay rich dividends if you devote some of your time in it. For one thing, it can make boredom a thing of the past. It also would make you feel great. Third, a hobby can bring one into contact with new and interesting people. Perhaps the greatest payoff is, that sometimes a hobby can be financially profitable.

Identify the **connectors** in the following passage:

9.   It is difficult to give up smoking. For one thing, a smoker gets used to not only the nicotine but also to a series of behavioural habits. For instance, the smoker becomes accustomed to lighting a cigarette when he finds himself under stress. A telephone call or a letter or a visitor - all these could be the occasion of some kind of stress and hence a cigarette. In addition, the smoker has possibly got into the habit of associating a cup of tea or coffee with each cigarette. Or, the other way round. Accordingly, coffee break turns into a cigarette break. Further, he also concludes each meal with a cigarette. And, if he or she happens to drink, would reach out for a cigarette to accompany each glass of liquor. Matter of factly, such habits are hard to break. That being so, these habits cannot be discontinued so easily.

In the following passage, some sentences arouse CQ and some do not. Identify the dead end sentences and also write the types of CQ(s) some sentences have generated.

10.   All animals preserve their health far better than the human beings. They know what type of food to eat and which would be useful to their body system. They would find a quiet place and go to sleep almost instantly there. Animals do not push themselves into such a level of activity that would exhaust them and threaten their health. Instinctively they could recognise any impending danger and get ready to flee the place as fast as possible. Do they dream during their sleep like us? Perhaps yes. Their dreams would be either about a new grazing area or about predators.

11.   Having located the deficiencies in Q 10, rewrite it to make it an interesting para.

12.   Here is a poorly written para and it is in low level English as well. Improve upon it following all the guidelines covered in this Chapter. (Use Direct speech, Infinitives, Participles and Passive sentences where considered necessary)

I went to St paul's school. My son studies there in Std X. Mathematics class was in progress at that time. I sensed he had sighted me. He waved to me quietly. I ignored it. Went near the door. Caught the teacher's attention. "Yes?" He looked up. May I see Devraj for a minute? I am his father. The period will finish after ten minutes. Then there is a break. You could see him then. I thanked and waited. Ten minutes looked like ten years. What to do? I moved over to the next class. It was a girls' section. They were giggling and making noise. There was no teacher there. They saw my face. Everyone rushed to their seat. The talking stopped. They probably thought I was their new teacher. Luckily the bell rang. Devraj rushed out to meet me.

Chapter 57

WRITING MORE THAN ONE PARAGRAPH

We have spent quite some time on writing a Single para. The next problem is, how to write more than one para? Are there any rules for it? Yes, there are.

One para deals with one **idea** or one **point of argument** or one **situation**. We named this, **theme**. Thus, every para must have a theme and every sentence in it must point towards that theme so that the whole para gives a coherent meaning.

Admittedly, any written piece will have several "themes", won't it? Then, each theme cannot go in any direction, can it? Each theme cannot be an independent unit. All the themes therefore must point towards the Subject heading. In other words, if any piece of writing should convey any sense, all the paragraphs in it must be "connected" logically and point towards the "Subject theme."

The rules for achieving 'connectedness' (or coherence) between paragraphs are similar to linking/connecting two sentences. The two methods we finalised in this regard are, the CQ and CONNECTOR approach.

If the last sentence of your first para arouses a curiosity question or questions, the reader will feel impelled to read the next para, won't he/she? Here, besides answering the CQ, try to make the first sentences of the second para catchy, possibly not as catchy as the first but all the same catchy enough to sustain the interest.

If the last sentence happens to be a **dead** one, and indeed it sometimes could be so, then use an appropriate connector as the first word(s) of the next para.

Shall we study some examples so that the rule gets home? Are the following two paras coherent?

(A) In Indian joint families, quarrels do take place because of communication failures between the members. One would suspect the other's motives for no rhyme or reason and work out plans of their own to outwit one another. When they thus drift apart, quarrels would be the result over a period of time.

(B) When members work at cross purposes, no one knows what the others are thinking. Misunderstanding might arise then. And a little spark from someone might cause a tremendous explosion one day in the family.

What are the defects in the above paragraphs? It is obvious that they are not 'connected' and are indeed incoherent. Don't both paras talk about the same situation, same circumstance albeit in different words!

The last sentence of (A) appears to be a dead-end one because it is a repetition of the first sentence, in **thought**. It does not arouse any CQ either.

The first sentence of (B) is a repetition of the sentence, "One would suspect ... one another" of para (A). Nor is it a build-up over the last sentence of (A)

Coherent → capable of thinking and expressing yourself in a clear manner.

In order to make the two paras coherent, we need to modify the last sentence of (A) in such a way as to arouse some curiosity questions and lead to the next para. Possibly something like this,

> "If only they could talk their mind out openly, a lot of imaginary misunderstandings would stand removed." (CQ: IS IT? HOW?)

Won't such a sentence lead to a new sentence in para (B) like this?

> "No longer would they then work at cross purposes. Harmony would prevail among them. Even a wrong statement on someone's part would be taken lightly or completely overlooked thus avoiding any possibility of a quarrel."

Now, read both the paras together. They do make full sense, don't they? While completing a para, make sure that the last sentence does throw up some curiosity question. And also make sure that the first sentence of the next para does answer those CQ(s).

Here is another pair of paras. They are certainly not coherent. How will you improve upon them?

(C) When Saroja asked me to play a game of chess with her, I couldn't agree readily. Mother had given me some urgent work to be completed before noon. "Very sorry. Could you wait for some 30 minutes?" I had requested. She thought over it and scratched her head for a few seconds.

(D) "You could join me for a second game," Saroja said, bent her head down and continued her play with Mohini. Mohini, just to spite me, must have come out of her room to oblige Saroja. You see, Mohini and I had a quarrel the previous evening.

You would notice that there is a big gap between C and D. The last sentence of C does not initiate any CQ. Nor does it tell why Saroja was scratching her head, what she was thinking etc.

Para D says that Saroja was playing a game with Mohini. So, there must be a couple of sentences to clarify how and why Mohini came into the scene. We can connect both the pars in the following way:

(CC) ... scratched her head for a few seconds. About that time, Mohini peeped out of her room and asked if she could be of any help. Saroja was only too happy to play a game with her and invited her into her room.

(AD) When Mohini sat in front of the chess board, Saroja transmitted a message to me that I could join her for a second game. Mohini, just to spite me had come out of her room to oblige Saroja. You see, Mohini and I had a quarrel the previous evening.

In certain cases, a connector or a connector phrase could bring about coherence. Take the next set of paragraphs, for instance:

(E) A computer doesn't have the human brain's complex structure. While the human brain consists of billions upon billions nerve cells, a computer contains only about ten million electronic components to do the given job. It is obvious that it cannot do all the jobs a human could, going by the sheer volume of the operating devices available in each.

(F) A human has the ability to create, to exercise initiative, to deduce and to reach conclusions logically. His reasoning power is amazing indeed and varies immensely from ordinary to the genius. No task is beyond his competence.

(G) A computer can only compute, multiply, add, subtract, divide and find out roots. It cannot provide answers for every problem flashed at it unless it has been programmed to do so. A computer cannot **think** for itself, for example.

Para F is not a logical build-up of para E as the sentences go. But, if you put the connector "Furthermore" before the first sentence of F, a miracle seems to take place and para F sounds quite logical. Similarly for para G, add the connector phrase "in contrast".

Thus, to achieve coherence between paragraphs, follow the CQ method or Connector method, whichever appears suitable.

Exercise

1. The last sentence of a para is shown. Choose the most coherent sentence for the next para out of the given alternatives:

(a) Sanjay enjoyed reading the Phantom comic series.
    (i) Comics in general always appealed to Sanjay even from his boyhood days.
    (ii) For instance, "The Cave man's trials" was his favourite book.

(b) Tina likes to travel a lot.
    (i) Perhaps Tina likes to travel because her father gets many free rail passes.
    (ii) Why not, when free rail passes are available through her father
    (iii) Tina loved travelling even when she was a child.

(c) Solomon forgot to bring sufficient money to buy my ticket.
    (i) Consequently, I couldn't accompany the group in the train.
    (ii) He said, he remembered it till last evening but forgot when he left the house this morning.

(d) Breeding prawns near a sea shore is becoming a profitable hobby.
    (i) It is liked by all types of people because there is a lot of money in it.
    (ii) This is one way of earning a livelihood.

(e) My mother preferred to punish me by making me stand in a corner on one leg.
    (i) I was afraid of corners in an empty room from childhood.
    (ii) Mother never condoned any offence of her children.

(f) A simple misunderstanding sometimes can become a stumbling block in communication between husband and wife.
    (i) They will avoid each other for a couple of hours and then make up after saying 'sorry'.

(ii) Misunderstandings could often occur between husband and wife; it is not unusual.

(g)   All materials were ready and I was about to start the assembling work.
   (i) There was a last minute hitch; I had left my spectacles at home.
   (ii) I started counting the materials along with the blue - print.

2.   In the following pairs of paras, write the last sentence of the first para on the dotted lines so that it leads smoothly to the second para.

(a)   (i) The chief asset of an Indian woman is her hair. A long and thick tress gives her beauty. If you happen to pass by a semi-bald woman, you wouldn't take second look at her even if she has a shapely body and charming face. *Even some modern women like to keep short hair*

   (ii) But then, women don't allow themselves to become bald like men, not in modern times anyway. A variety of wigs is available in the market nowadays.

(b)   (i) The first question one usually asks on meeting a newly married couple is, "Arranged or Love marriage?" This perhaps is an exclusive Indian habit. But, *there is not much different between in love and arranged in Indian culture,*

   (ii) In my opinion, both are the same. While 'Love at first sight' is the triggering point in Love marriages, it is similar in pattern in the 'Bride seeing' ceremony of arranged marriage as well; the prospective bride appears before the P.Goom only for a couple of seconds!

(c)   (i) The convocation over, we went in different directions doing several career courses and hunting for a better job after each additional qualification. It was during this phase of our lives that Rahul seemed to have completed his M.Phil and had secured a Lecturer's post in a city college. And I had become a bank officer with an MBA diploma. *Hence, we were to busy to get along with eachother,*

   (ii) The irony was, we were never able to meet face to face after our post graduation although we kept in touch through our monthly newsletters.

Chapter 58

PUNCTUATIONS

Introduction

We learnt the art of writing a Paragraph in Chapters 56 and 57. It is important to use proper punctuations when you write a paragraph. For instance, when a sentence had ended, you put a full stop. "Full stop" is a punctuation which marks the end of a sentence and allows you to start the subsequent sentence. In addition, there are many other punctuations which are required to be used while writing a paragraph. But for the use of accurate punctuations, a sentence may not give the right meaning or may even give a wrong meaning.

When we talk, don't we give a short or long pause in between words and sentences? Such pauses represent different type of **breaks** and **rhythms** in the spoken sentences. And while writing too, we have to follow the same kinds of pauses and rhythms and this is done through Punctuations.

In this Chapter we shall cover the following punctuations which you must use in your written English and for that matter, in any language. They are - Full stop (.) Comma (,) Semicolon (;) Colon (:) Dash (-) Question mark (?) Brackets ( ) Quotation marks (" ...") Exclamation (!) and Apostrophe (').

WHEN AND WHERE TO USE PUNCTUATIONS

Full stop (.)

We use this to represent the longest pause,

(a) to mark the end of a complete sentence, be it a Simple or Complex or Compound sentence.

James came home by seven thirty last night.

(b) after all abbreviations and initials,

Dr.   M.L.A.   Co.   Mr.T.Anandan   Dr. D.G. Sundaram

Note:

We can mark the end of a sentence also by a Question mark or Exclamation. In such cases, we don't use a Full stop in addition.

Comma (,)

A Comma represents a short pause and it is used,

(a) to separate a series of words in a sentence.

(i) *England, India, New Zealand, Australia and Sri Lanka took part in the Cocacola cup cricket match.*

(ii) *This man lost lands, vehicles, houses and friends.*

Note:

In such series, we don't use a comma before the conjunction 'and' since this conjunction marks the last word in the series.

(b) To separate an adjunct. (Adjunct is:extra/additional information or phrases added to qualify a word in a sentence such as an Adjective clause without the S-A-V elements in it)

   (i)*Sir.C.V.Raman, a Nobel prize winner, was a great Indian scientist.*

   (ii)*My brother, the Captain of our District football team, is studying in XII standard in this school.*

   (iii)*Milton, the great English poet, became a blind man.*

(c) to separate any pairs of words connected by **and.**

   High and low, rich and poor, wise and foolish, will be always among us.

(d) before and after Direct speech.

   (i)*He said, "I must leave immediately."*

   (ii)*"All my students are good," announced the class teacher.*

Semicolon (;)

We use a **semicolon,**

(a) to show a pause whose duration will fall roughly between a comma and a full stop.

(b) To break up two or more closely allied ideas in the form of Simple sentences.

   (i)*This crocodile is a friendly type; it will not charge at you ever* . (allied idea)

   (ii)*This boy crossed my path at the beach; we became friends at once.* (allied idea)

   (iii)*Reading makes a full man; speaking a ready man; writing an exact man.*

   (Here, the semicolon saves A-V. This is the most important use of semicolon.)

Colon (:)

Colon also is used for a pause which will be slightly longer than a semicolon. We use it,

(a) when we give out a list of names or articles one by one.

   (i) *The big rivers in India are: The Ganges, the Brahmaputra, the Narmada and the Cauvery.*

   (ii) *Three kinds of fuels are now in use in India: coal, oil and electricity.*

(b) for a follow up information.

   (i) *To summarise: Adjectives are simple words; they must describe a noun; so, place an adjective to the left of a noun.*

   (ii) *Many students secured first division. They are: Mohan, Sugirtha, Christian, Sundari ...*

(c) though not necessary, we may use it along with a dash.

   (i) *For example:- steel, coal, electricity etc.*

   (ii) *Examine the following sentences:-*

   (1) *Didn't you ever touch a cigarette?*

   (2) *Sam shall never commit a mistake like that?*

Dash (-)

A **dash** also represents a pause but in a different way. We use it to,

(a) indicate a sudden stop or a change of thought but somewhat allied with a foregoing sentence.

   (i)*If my father were alive - but, why go into the past? - he would have attended this function today.*

(ii)Some of my relatives and friends - they no longer live here - never identified themselves with me.

(iii)When the Chairman began his speech - the hum and chatters had died down by then - the microphone went dead!

Question mark (?)

We use this symbol at the end of a question.

(i)Where are you going?

(ii)You went to market on your own, didn't you?

(iii)Isn't Chennai the capital of Tamil Nadu?

Note:

When we use a Question mark at the end of a sentence, **don't** use a Full stop to mark the end of that sentence.

Brackets (   )

We use the **brackets,**

(a)   to mark of the words used in any explanation.

(i) My son will return from England (He is abroad for higher studies) by the end of this year.

(ii) We depart on 26th January (Our Republic day) at 6 a.m.

(b)   to separate from the main part of a sentence a phrase or a clause.

(i) Saravanan gained from his investment (Which was out of his savings) made with a known Finance company.

(ii) No trespassers (Men or women or children) will be spared from prosecution.

Quotation marks (" ....")

We use these marks,

(a)   to reproduce the exact words used by a person.

(i)The Minister said, "I shall get a legislation passed about this."

(ii) "I would rather die," the accused conveyed, "than give false evidence."

(b)   to mark off a familiar quotation.

(i) Didn't your mother ever remind you, "Waste not, want not?"

(c)   if a quotation occurs within a quotation, it is to be marked by single inverted commas.

(i) "If you say, 'I get what I like', I would say, 'I like what I get'."

(d)   in Direct speech.

(i) My mother said, "Your father will take you to school today."

Note

Note the following points while writing a Direct speech:

(i) Use a comma before writing the Direct speech.

(ii) Put the Direct speech sentence(s) inside inverted commas.

(iii) The first word inside the inverted commas must be in capital letter.

(iv) Before the closing inverted commas, use a full stop/question mark to show the end of the sentence or a comma if the Direct speech projects into Indirect speech as shown below:

"Don't compel me to guide you every time," warned our brother.

Exclamation (!)

This is a 'part of speech' as well. Read Chapter 1. We use this symbol (!) to show a sudden joy or surprise or shock through a particular word or a whole sentence in the written form. (In the spoken form, we will be using the body language or audible sounds of some kind to show joy, surprise, shock etc)

> *(i)Alas!*
> *(ii)The patient is dead!*
> *(iii)Oh my God!*
> *(iv)Ah! How terrible?*

Note:

When we use the exclamation mark at the end of a sentence (like in (ii) and (iii)), there would be no need for a full stop.

Apostrophe (')

We use this sign,

(a)   to show possessive nouns.

> *(i)This is Mohana's note book.* (This is her note book)
> *(ii)The children's bed room is over there.*
> *(iii)The boys' homework books are here.*
> *(iv) The Inspector's jeep met with an accident.*
> *(v) The VIP's escort is way ahead in the convoy.*

(b)   to show an abbreviated word.

> *(i)Don't* (do not)
> *(ii)I've* (I have)
> *(iii)Won't* (will not)

Note:

Here, if we remove the apostrophe sign, the word (wont) will have a different meaning altogether - what someone is fond of doing usually.

> *(iv) Isn't* (is not)
> *(v) Shan't* (shall not)
> *(vi) We're* (We are or we were); *they're* (they are or they were)
> *(vii) He's, She's, It's* (He is/has, She is/has, It is/has)
> *(viii) Wouldn't, couldn't, shouldn't* (Would not, could not, should not)
> *(ix) Musn't* (Must not)

(c)   to show the plural of Figures and Letters.
> *(i) Add two 5's with two 7's.*
> *(ii) Don't put too many e's or t's in your spelling.*

(d)   to show the plural of some nouns and proper nouns especially those ending with an 's' sound or in such cases where the apostrophe will not be mistaken for possessive cases or where addition of the letter 's' is likely to cause confusion.
> *(i)Thermos's* (Thermos flasks - plural)

(ii)The Thomas's (Mr. and Mrs. Thomas)

(iii)Up's and Down's

(iv) In's and Out's

Use of Capitals in sentences

Use the **Capital letter,**

(a) for the first letter in the first word while starting a new sentence after a full stop.

(i) The boy was bad. He had joined a new school.

(b) for all proper nouns even if they are in the middle of a sentence.

(i) When we reached New Delhi, it was raining. Madhavan and Raghuvaran were at the station to receive us.

(c) for all adjectives derived from a proper noun.

(i) Several Indian scholars and British poets were present at the meeting.

(ii) We don't sell Kashmiri dresses in our shop.

(d) for all nouns and pronouns referring to God wherever they may appear in a sentence.

(i)God is our creator. In His name we always pray.

(ii)It is always He (God) who meets all our needs. We must thank Him always.

(iii)When you pray, say, Lord our Father...

(e) for all titles of honour, office, salutations in official letters and all initials wherever they may appear in a sentence.

(i)My dear Sir. Dear Madam. My dear Professor.

(ii)Mr.Vishwanathan, Padma Sri.

(iii)Dr. S.Ratnasamy, M.B.B.S.

(iv) Miss. Leela John, M.Tech.

(f) for all months, days of week, seasons and festivals wherever they may appear in a sentence.

(i)It rains in October in Chennai.

(ii)See me next Tuesday.

(iii)Deepavali and Dussera fall in October this year.

(iv) 25th December is the Christmas day all over the world.

(g) for the first person singular pronoun and interjections wherever they may occur in a sentence.

(i)I didn't take your cycle nor did I see it near my house.

(ii)Sue and I are good friends.

(iii)Oh! he is out.

(iv) Oh dear! Oh dear!.

(h) for the first word in a sentence inside the inverted commas. (Quotation marks)

(i) Rajinder shouted, "Catch that thief."

(ii) We all agreed, "Wednesdays would be observed as half working days."

(i) for all abbreviated titles, captions and words.

(i) UN, UNESCO, AIR, SIDCO.

(ii) OK

Exercise

Use **commas** in the following sentences so as to change the meaning :

1. (a) They are good friends.   (b) They are good friends.
    (c) There you are,come over. (d) There you come over.

Punctuate the following sentences:

2. come along,young chap said the drill master loudly you are malingering aren't you next you are habitually lazy I notice"

3. i am sorry i interrupted you you said stop me if you don't understand

4. people say subash chandra bose is dead or he would have come to india,which is waiting for years to give him a grand reception.

5. after lunch we resumed our trek and reached a village named hastinapurandar what a tongue twister I couldnt help saying. Oh we call it hasti usually said , the village headman."

6. who is the girl sitting cross-legged on the bench i asked i am tired, sir she answered with impunity.

7. give me the instruments box father he said i will set it right

8. that was how matters stood,when on that monday morning of august 8 a little boy called abraham was brought to me he was our ayahs youngest son only 9 years old 3 days earlier he had been bitten by a snake small and not poisonous.

Punctuate the following dialogue between two friends:

9. are you coming no why should i it is because the dr ordered you to come doesn't matter i mustnt disturb him at this hour you go don't forget today is sunday ah yes i forgot *yaar* shall we then go after eleven ok i think hes a kind fellow you know

10. when krishnan called me i wasn't ready at all hey krish wait 5 minutes all right make it snappy will you he shouted back cant wait beyond 5 minutes ok don't be all that fussy my dear fellow he added all right i shall give you 2 more minutes

11. one day walking together along the beach i said to yashwant do you not wish yourself in your own village again now that you have finished your studies in the city yes he replied what would you do there said i would you turn back to farming and eat your own vegetables he looked amazed and shaking head said no I will put my knowledge to good use in my own village you should not look down upon farming he told me sternly.

Insert comma, where necessary in the following sentences:

12. History it has been said is the essence of any human record.

13. Nothing probably has contributed more to perpetuate poverty and backwardness in India than the want of selfless leadership.

14. Most of us or nearly all of us fail to live upto our full length of time owing to accidents and heart burns and avoidable illnesses.

15. At midnight however the senior politician was awakened by the sound of heavy boots of some dozen men in uniform.

Chapter 59

ESSAY PLANNING AND WRITING

Introduction

An Essay is a piece of writing on a particular subject. It may have 20 to 30 paragraphs.

Every para must have a Para theme. All the sentences in it must point towards or talk only about that para theme. Any sentence not connected with the theme should be discarded as such sentences would make a para incoherent.

Since two consecutive paras would have different themes, how do we produce coherence between them? In Chapter 57, we saw that the last sentence in a para must not only answer the CQ of the previous sentence but at the same time create such a CQ that would drive the reader to the next para. Where the CQ method fails, use a suitable connector which would lead the reader to the next para. This method of connectedness would be easier if the "para themes themselves are connected in logic."

Types of Essays

Incidentally, the titles like **Essay, Composition** or **Article** mean the same thing - a piece of writing on any subject.

Other than official correspondences and stories, all other writings and in particular Essays/Compositions/Articles will fall under 4 categories as follows:

1. Expository — A piece of writing on the rules and regulations of games like football, cricket etc. Explanation and interpretation of some theory.

2. Descriptive — Description of any event in great details such as a picnic or sports item or Republic day parade or some personal experience. Description of a historical building or monument or a city etc.

3. Narrative — One that deals with the details of an event such as a long train journey or a holiday or an excursion or the complete proceedings of a meeting of any kind. The details must be covered in the same sequence as they occurred without any frills or imaginary additions to it. The difference between a Descriptive essay and a Narrative essay is in its presentation. In the former the writer has the privilege of highlighting certain occurrences and even omitting some, all according to the preferences of the writer. Whereas in the Narrative type, the description must cover all occurrences and events in the same sequence from A to Z without any additions. Further, there is to be no "Conclusion" in the Narrative while this is permissible in the Descriptive.

4. Argumentative — Many subjects have two sides to them - for and against. The writer gives equal importance to both. He is expected to give a verdict in favour of one of them but supported by strong arguments.

Some subjects could be presented in all the 4 types. Some may be suitable for a particular type only. No matter which type you write on, every essay must be organised in 3 major parts as follows:

INTRODUCTION   -   Here, give a very short description of what the reader is going to read about. This will be usually of a single and short para. The first sentence must be a catchy one.

MAIN BODY   -   All the supporting points/arguments come next. The body will have as many paras as the elaborating points but each with a para theme.

CONCLUSION   -   This again will be a single and small para summing up all the important points and linking up with the Introductory para in some way. So much so, if a person reads the Introduction and Conclusion, he must be able to guess the contents of the Main body.

While actually writing the Essay, you don't write out a heading such as Introduction, Main and Conclusion but the contents must be so presented that your INTRO and CONCLUSION para stand out prominently proclaiming themselves to be what actually they are.

Planning an Essay

Often students scratch their head when asked to write an essay on a given subject with reflections such as, "I don't know anything or don't know much about this subject. How could I write some 500 words about it? How do I begin and fill up …?" etc. Wrong. You know quite a lot about the subject. During your previous 16 or so years of your life, you have seen many things with your own eyes or have personal experiences connected with the subject. And they are all logged in your memory. Human brain is like a computer. You can 'open up any file' from your memory store even after years and examine the contents.

Let us say, you have to write an essay on an <u>unearthly</u> subject like, GRASS. May I say that you have sufficient material in your memory store to write a booklet on it? Surprised? All right, take a piece of paper and write everything that comes to your mind about GRASS. Don't forget you have been seeing grass almost every week of your life in various places like, villages, along roadside, inside house compounds, parks and in fact everywhere where there is no cement or concrete portions! The earth is full of various types of grasses. And your eyes have seen it all during every season. All what you had seen had been recorded in your memory store. All you are required to do now is to extract out the contents. Go ahead. Write whatever comes in your mind about GRASS in any order. But, write your impressions/ideas in sentence form or in broken sentence form and NOT as 'cryptic points'. This method is called the "Mind exploring method." And here we go on the **'Mind exploring** list':

1. Grass is seen everywhere.
2. You could see them like they are green carpets in some areas.
3. Grass grows immediately after rain.

4. As far as I remember, they grow on their own like God had planted the seeds on the ground some time back.
5. Once it sprouts out, it grows up.
6. Sometimes I have seen the grass being mowed with a machine or sickle or long sword like gadgets.
7. Lawns look lovely if it is well maintained.
8. Some grasses are not fit for developing a lawn.
9. Can we call such grass, wild grass? Wild grass have long blades.
10. Animals eat grass; animals like cows, goats, deer etc.
11. Do elephants eat grass? I am not sure. Oh yes, they too eat grass, long grass. Have heard something like 'elephant grass'.
12. Horses are fond of grass; the horse owners tie a bag full of grass round its neck and it will keep munching it.
13. I think cows too love grass.
14. Village women cut the grass from the field and sell them to animal owners - such as dairy farms and horse farms.
15. In villages, cowherds take the cows and bulls and buffalos for grazing in the fields beyond the habitation area and they would bring the cattle back home at sunset time.
16. Same way, the shepherds also take their goats and sheep outside for grazing.
17. Grazing the animals is a profession among the villagers. Perhaps this is the lowest kind of profession. You don't need any qualification.
18. In village schools, if nothing gets into the head of a boy or girl, the teacher would usually say, "You are fit only to graze goats and cows ..."
19. However, a job is a job. Cowherds and Shepherds earn a living this way.
20. Grass grows even in a cricket pitch. Before the toss, you could see the respective Captains go and examine the pitch; if they see any grass on the pitch, they know how the pitch would behave during the play.
21. Have never seen a cricket field without grass. I think the cricket ground Management ensure that there is grass around the pitch.
22. Come to think of it, even football and hockey fields also would be green and grassy. One cannot play the game well on a brown or sandy field well.
23. Some grasses grow to a height of just a couple of inches.
24. Some grasses grow quite tall upto 3 meters or so in height. Even elephants could hide themselves inside a field of such tall grass. That's why perhaps they have been named 'elephant grass'.
25. The colour of grass is always green; animals like to eat only green grass; when does grass turn dry and brown? Yes, during summer season.
26. That is the time the ground also shows cracks and become barren until the next rain. Once the rain comes, the grass sprouts out as if they had been hiding inside the ground.
27. Nobody wants dry grass.

28.   But hay is dry and yellowish and I think cows and horses eat them. This hay is produced out of paddy crops and after removing the paddy grains what is left over is called 'hay.'

29.   Is there any grass in a desert? No. I don't think so. For instance there is no grass on Marina beach or any beach.

30.   Oh yes, I have heard of 'prairie' - a kind of plain and open stretch of land which is full of grass only; no trees at all; I have seen such scenes on T.V. We don't have prairies in India.

31.   Some mountain tops look green, something like an undulated prairie.

32.   Three types of grass could be seen - the ones that don' grow beyond a height of say 6 inches (the lawn type); ones with wide blades growing upto a height of 1 foot. These may be called the 'weeds' or unwanted growth in a vegetable field; the tall elephant grass which could hide an elephant from view.

33.   Grass, like trees, absorb carbon dioxide and convert it into oxygen.

See how many ideas/thoughts/impressions on grass we have listed out? The list probably could be further expanded. Now, what you have to remember is the above are your *ideas*, *thoughts* and *impressions* on the subject; they are NOT your sentences for your paragraphs. These ideas have to be converted into sentences in conformity with the para writing rules.

Therefore, shall we have an exercise on "how to convert an idea or a thought or an impression into a proper sentence and in several ways.?" Your ideas etc may have been expressed in the S-A-V-O/C form or with silent S-A-V. But that doesn't mean that they are fit enough to enter into a paragraph; you have to match them into it keeping in mind the para writing rules.

How to write sentences out of an idea/thought/impression

Idea

Flowers are found on trees, ground and in water.

Sentences

1.   You don't have to hunt for a flower; they can be located on trees or ground or water.

2.   Whether the place is ground or water or trees, you could find some kind of flowers there.

3.   God has created different kinds of flowers that grow on trees, ground and water.

Idea

We use flowers in places of worship like temples and churches.

Sentences

1.   Have you seen any place of worship like temples and churches without flowers of some kind?

2.   Flowers remind us of God and that's why we use them in temples and churches.

3.   It is not uncommon to see worshippers carrying flowers with them when they visit a temple or church.

Idea

Rich people's houses will have a garden (small or big depending on the land available) *in the front part of their compound; they would invariably have one or two gardeners to look after the home garden. Middle class people would look after it themselves; people living in flats will grow flowers in flower pots. Most people are flower lovers.*

Sentences

1. Someone is required to look after home gardens; it may be the house owner himself or hired gardeners.
2. People living in multi storey flats usually don't employ gardeners to look after their balcony flower potted garden; the household members do it themselves.
3. A home garden, be it in front of a house or in the balcony, adds charm and colour to the living place.

Have you now seen the difference between a sentence that contains an idea/though/ impression and the actual sentence converted out of it? Do recall that you cannot take any odd sentence and insert it into a paragraph. It has to be fitted into a paragraph from the angles of logical development and CQ method.

Para planning out of the ideas/thoughts/impressions

Now look through your list and pick out the serial Nos that would contribute to the Intro para.

Take Points 1, 4, 10, 13, 15 and 16. Don't they suggest to you an opening para of say 2 or 3 sentences? Something like, "Grass is vital both for animals and human beings. Nobody has to plant grass; they grow on their own perhaps on God's command. Except in the desert and sea shores, one could see grass everywhere on the Earth."-

The introduction para sounds all right. Perhaps we could add a little more frill and also make the first sentence more catchy? How about a sentence like, "Have you seen any place on the Earth, other than a desert and sea shore, without some kind of grass?" Sounds all right. Now the subsequent sentences in the Intro para should read like this:

Nobody plants grass. It is at God's command that grass grow. Grass is vital for animals and human beings.

You can add sentences of your own like the last one - Without grass, any land would look barren and dry. This sentence looks out of place in terms of para writing rules and also does not arouse a CQ to push the reader to the next para. So, shift it to the 4th place. Now, the full Intro para will be like this:

Have you seen any place on the Earth, other than a desert and sea shore, without some kind of grass? Nobody plants grass. It is at God' command that grass grow on land. Without grass, any land would look barren and dry. Grass is vital both for animals and human beings.

Please note that the listing of your ideas, thoughts and impressions are only to get you started. Don't view the list as "sentence providers" for your paras. They are only "idea providers". If you develop new ideas at this stage, put that also in sentence form so long as it fits into the para logic. Read the para once again. If it could be improved further, go ahead.

Now the Main body. Here we have to determine the "para themes" based on your list. At the same time, your first para must link up with the Intro para as well.

Since we have said in the Intro para that grass is vital for human beings and animals, why not pick out the ideas on these two headings? First, animals.

Consider the Points 11, 12, 13, 15, 16. They seem to suggest a para theme such as "Grass is the main food for cows, buffalos and horses."

Note:

Don't think that only the points out of your mind exploring list alone will provide the contents for your para. At this stage also you may add some more thoughts. What is important is, all your new/additional thoughts must point towards your para theme.

And the first para may go something like this:

The main food for cows, buffalos and horses, is grass. One could see cowherds and shepherds take these animals for grazing near mountains or such fields where grass is available. They would return home only at evening time. Elephants normally don't live on grass. They would need something bigger like tree branches. Could grass be useful for human beings in some way?

Points 14, 15, 17 and 18 seem to suggest another para theme - profession/job for some people especially in villages.

Grass also provide job to people, especially in villages. Women cut the grass and sell it in bundles to the animal owners in the cities and towns. Young boys from villages, who leave school for various reasons, take to grazing the animals. This is a kind of job for them to earn a livelihood. They might become professional cowherds and shepherds in course of time. One does not need any qualification for the grazing job. So much so, some teachers may dub a dull student as one fit only for grazing cattle!

Points 21 and 22 stress the necessity of grass in playing fields. So, here is another para theme.

Next, most of the cricket fields, football and hockey play grounds would have green grass. Such growth protect the players from getting hurt during the play. As regards tennis courts, there are equal number of hard courts and green courts. "Lawn tennis" is a popular phrase. All the courts in Wimbledon are the lawn types.

In tune with the last line of the above para, it is good to put a para theme on the 'types of grass.' Points 23, 24, 25 and 32 provide sufficient ideas for such a para.

The grass on tennis lawns and in home lawns belong to a special type. It doesn't grow very high. Mowers are used to trim the grass height to about 2 cms. So that the ground looks neat and levelled. The grass that grow to heights about 3 feet are the useless variety which even the animals may refuse to eat. They have only nuisance value and possibly stifle the growth of vegetables and other crops. They are periodically cut off by the farmers. The third variety is tall ones growing up to a height of 3 meters or so. They are known as "Elephant grass" The word derives its name possibly because elephants go inside such area to hide themselves from poachers!

Points 25, 26 and 28 lead towards a para theme, "dry grass".

Is every type of grass green in colour? All grass change colour during summer time; they become dry and yellowish. Cows and buffalos would refuse to eat the dry grass. However, cows and bulls do eat hay (paddy extracted plants) which is yellow. They must be tasty to their tongue.

Points 30 and 31 suggest a para on 'prairie'. And a contrast of that - desert In Point No 29 could also go in the same para.

Vast plain lands full of green grass is known as Prairies. These are found in Northern America. The grass found here are of the lawn type and the area too would like huge lawns. The important feature of a prairie is that one cannot find any trees on a prairie. Some mountains, especially in Srinagar area, also look like prairies of a different kind. Total absence of grass would mean that the land is a desert or sea shore.

Point 20 looks like another para of 'sportsmen's interest'.

A cricket pitch is supposed to be plain and hard but grass seems to grow here also. Before the match begins you could see the respective Captains examining the pitch for grass. If they do find signs of grass, it means something to them and about the way the ball would behave on such a pitch.

Points 26 and 33 have the ideal contents for the concluding para. Don't forget that the conclusion para must summarise the main body and also must link up with the Introduction paragraph.

If green grass is absent, we know the summer season has started and there is no water or moisture below the surface. The ground then will turn brown and will show cracks. Would such a sight be pleasing to your eyes? We should thank God for raising and looking after the grass for our benefit. Grass besides trees convert carbon dioxide into oxygen which is so vital for our life.

The list of points is only an exploration of your own mind on the subject. The ideas buried in that list will have to be converted by you into proper sentences to fit into your para.

You may consider the above as your first draft. Now, go on with rewriting the essay in polished English according to your personal formulae. You may not introduce any new ideas at this stage. Since you have adhered to the para writing rules, what you need to do now is only to upgrade your English in your subsequent draft.

The above is a **Descriptive type** essay.

Narrative Essay

If you have to write a Narrative type, your approach could be slightly different. Here, you may opt for the next method known as, "Para theme" method. In that, you first determine the para themes and write the sentence ideas against each. In a narrative type of essay, you know the exact details of every stage and at the sequence each event occurred. (You don't have to explore your mind over these) and it is only a question of recollecting them from your memory. Let us say you want to write a Narrative essay on a 2 day trek you had undertaken along with your friend Robert. This is how your para planning would go:

Para theme		Sentence ideas, thoughts and impressions
Introduction	-	During teen age years, it is essential to exercise your body regularly to keep it in good shape. Added to that, you must try to do certain things on your own without depending much upon your parents. A trek seems to be an ideal thing which could achieve both the aims.
Preparation	-	Robert and I decided on a trek to a nearby mountain fort. It is about 15 km from our town. We collected a map of the area and chalked out our route. Bought a haversack each to carry our food articles, coffee, sugar etc, air pillow, shawl, one change of dress etc.. We had no Army type boots but the thick soled jungle shoes we already had seemed all right. I had a tent, which I had bought in a jumble sale. Fathers gave us each Rs 50. This for any emergency purchases on the way.
Stage 1	-	Trek started at 5 a.m. on a Wednesday. Till 7 a.m. nobody sighted on the way through the town. At the road end, a wayside tea shop. Had tea and breakfast here. Hot *iddlies* and *vada*. Felt energetic. Rested for 15 mins and resumed our real outdoor walk.
Stage 2	-	The pucca road stopped. There was only a track. Map showed a village after 5 km. Name Sendharpuri. Map also showed Sendharpuri at a height of 1000 ft above sea level. It turned out to be a mountain village. Reached there at 11 a.m. Kuccha road. Walking was not difficult. Finished up all our stock of water. Filled up the water bottles at Sendharpuri. Met some elderly people. Talked nicely. They asked, where we were going. Arcot fort. Oh, that, it is over there, they said. Any school boys in this village. No. But only young men; they spend time hunting animals for food.
Stage 3	-	Reached Arcot fort. Height 1500 feet. Contained only ruins. Long wall of about 2 KM circumference. In the center, about 8 buildings, built in stones. Perimeter walls had gaps at intervals of 30 feet, possibly for observation. No plaque stone to know the history behind the fort. Nawab of Arcot built this fort to resist the British troops. A battle took place here sometime in 17th century. All this from History book.
Stage 4	-	Found a tree, a large one. Pitched the tent here and spent the night. Ate our pack dinner consisting of parotas , boiled eggs, pickles and sweets. Went to sleep around 8 p.m. Place was noiseless. No barking dogs or jackals. Not even mosquitoes. Had a sound sleep. Woke up at 5.30 a.m.

It was dark. Twilight came around 5.50. And then the sunrise. There was a huge well in the center. Peeped into it. Water was full almost at arm's depth. Collected some water to wash our face. Breakfast finished. Started our trek back home. We hit a proper road after 8 KM or so and halted near a tea shop. Time then was 12 noon. It was nice to eat something hot - *dosai* and *vadais* followed by a couple of bananas. The time was 4 p.m. when we reached home.

Stage 5   -   Some 30 KM of cross country walk in 2 days. Didn't feel much tired at all. Something to boast with friends in school when the school reopened after summer vacation. Robert asked, what would you have done if we had come face to face with a tiger or a cheetah? He said bravely, I would have fought with this knife and he showed me a pen knife used for sharpening pencils. But thank God, we did not encounter any wild animals, not even thieves. Nobody visited Arcot fort, we heard. There was nothing but ruins there. Even snakes refused to live there!

Sounds like a diary, doesn't it? It truly is. As you would notice that the events have been recorded in a progressive order of time and place. Put here as many details as possible. But, all factuals. No imaginary thoughts and reflections should be recorded here.

In a Narrative essay, there is no Conclusion para. But, the essay could be ended in a pleasant note. In order that your essay is readable, follow the CQ method of presentation and of course with connectors where necessary.

The Essay will contain seven paras including the introduction. Convert all the ideas into proper sentences. A para should not contain more than 10 sentences. So, it is entirely up to you; what details are to be left out. If some sentences sound odd and misfits, omit them.

Argumentative Essay

If you have to write an Argumentative type, you have to pick up the points for and against the title. Let the topic be "Should college students or even Plus two students be given unlimited freedom?"

Which method would be appropriate here: the Mind exploring or Para theme?

Certainly, Mind exploring, wouldn't it?

So, write down all your thoughts and ideas as they occur in your mind giving each a serial number. Don't worry at this stage, whether your ideas are 'for' or 'against':

1.   The Modern time is an era of IT (Information Technology). Information about every subject is available at the press of a button-history, geography, social life, art, beauty, sex, drug and what not. You can become highly knowledgeable very fast.

2.   Are all the above required and suitable for teen agers? Aren't some harmful at that age? Like drugs and sex? But then, we are on the verge of adulthood. Further, aren't we responsible persons when we are in XI standard and beyond? At this young age one needs some fun and frolic also.

3.   Perhaps. But then it is up to the teenager to select what is useful and reject others. They must be strong willed in such selections and rejections.

4. Should we quell inquisitiveness and the curiosity element at the initial stage? Won't these lead to discoveries and inventions? Why not permit the youngsters to go into details and discover for themselves whether pursuance would be desirable or not. Drugs, particularly. Also possibly, sex. Isn't freedom the right of every individual. Freedom of choice?

5. For instance, why should my parents tell me which movies I must see and which not?

6. Studies could get affected if you see too many movies or read too many magazines and books not connected with your school curriculum.

7. We know certain things are taboos for girls, especially in Indian society. Take late night movies and social parties. Parents tell the daughters to return home before a particular time. Whereas for young men there is no such restriction. Is this fair?

8. Who says, male students could enjoy unrestricted freedom on seeing movies and attending late night dances etc. They too need to be restricted but perhaps not as much as young maidens. Young men should not think they are above parental control all because they are masculines. But we know that parents observe different rules for sons and daughters in the same family.

9. Too much of anything is bad whether young men or women.

10. Our attention must be on 'studies' and 'improvement of knowledge' about life around us. We should groom ourselves to become useful citizens. Learn more about your own country and countries similar to ours.

11. The world consists of good things and bad things. If you don't know what is good and what is bad for your future, ask parents. And go strictly what the parents or teachers say. Don't be dictated by your own thoughts and preferences.

12. Is it bad for males and females to mix, especially when they study in the same class? "I am a girl and my mother tells me not to speak with boys." Is this correct? Well, some old fashioned mothers may say so. But, why don't you assure them that you would never go on the wrong path and hence you be allowed to consult boys about studies or on such subjects some boys may have better knowledge. Agreed.

13. Let us say, you are in First year B.A. and your sister is in Matric. Would you personally allow her all the freedom she wants? No, certainly not. I would certainly like her to grow up to be a pure girl and get married and so on. So, is there anything wrong if your mother toes a similar line? You shouldn't have different standards for your own sister and other maidens. Right or not? Right and agreed.

14. As lady students shouldn't we be allowed to mix with others of our kind? I agree that my mixing with boys may be restricted but why any such restrictions in mixing with other young females? Like "all girls" dance parties or "gossip sessions?" Any guarantee you girls won't talk about drugs or pornography etc? You could you know if you know that no one is listening? So, some restrictions or some kind of supervision is necessary even in men groups and solely female groups.

15. A via media appears to be, "This far and no farther" kind of restriction. We shouldn't think that our parents are killjoys; they do want their teen age sons and daughters to enjoy life but within the limits laid down by them. This approach is good for both parties.

Now, decide upon your Intro para initially after an overview of your Mind exploring list. It could be something like this:

Teenage proclaims near adulthood. Shouldn't he or she be allowed to probe the mysteries of the world all on his/her own? The modern environment and educational facilities enable that?

<u>Main body.</u>

Points 1, 2 and 3 suggest a para theme such as "Modern world offers many information on many subjects and opportunities of learning for all age groups." Against this theme, write the sentences "for" and "against" pattern.

It is true that the modern world offers varieties of opportunities for all age groups almost in any field of knowledge. At the touch of a button you can get any information you want and become knowledgeable very soon. But, it is also possible by touching a wrong button you could get access to wrong and harmful knowledge. While strong willed young persons could keep away from such evils, the weaklings could become prey to Drugs and Pornography. Sex and pornography would be interesting initially but in course of time would divert all your attention away from studies.

Point 4, 5, 6, 9 and 11 would lead to a theme, "Inquisitiveness leading to inventions and discoveries …"

One should be inquisitive about everything in life. You could develop a scientific mind. Our country would progress only if youngsters get into this kind of thinking. Knowledge from the prescribed books could be further enhanced by information available outside it. Further, aren't teenagers equally responsible, being on the verge of adulthood?

Here again, too much of inquisitiveness could lead to a downhill path. If not checked in time, the youngsters could get ruined permanently. Some kind of parental control on what books to read, which movies to see, which serials to watch and so on, is necessary.

Points 9, 10 and 11 talk about "freedom".

Some of us may think, "Why can't I enjoy life with my friends such as going to movies of our choice, dance parties and so on? Why should the elders restrict my freedom?"

The world consists of good things and bad things. At the tender age of 16/17, a girl or a boy wouldn't be in a position to distinguish good from evil. Some guidance from parents or other elders in the family is therefore good in this regard. At this age, the first priority must be for studies and more time must be spent on it.

Points 12, 13 and 14 give enough tips for a theme like, "Should young men and women in our society mix freely?"

Girls would love to mix with boys freely especially if they study in co-ed schools. Mothers seem to be against this. Won't the girls pick up many good things or principles from others since we come from different social and academic levels?

It is true indeed. But what if girls go astray or if unlimited freedom leads to sexual liberties? Once the reputation of a girl becomes bad, her chances of marriage are slim. In our society, the grooms want virgins and maidens of purity in mind and habits. It is because of this condition that the parents abhor the idea of much socialising between males and females. Even a teenage elder brother would not allow his sister to ruin her image by free-mixing. Admittedly, boys enjoy relatively greater freedom.

Conclusion

While on the one hand, the creative urge and inquisitiveness on the goings on in the world, should not be suppressed, some measure of parental supervisory control and guidance is considered a must. Teenage children on their part should not insist on too much of freedom of action as this would not be in their long term interest in the Indian society. Parents should not treat the children as some kind of prisoners. They must lay down a rule of "this much and no farther" both for boys and girls.

If you have very clear ideas on a subject, you may write it following the **Para theme** method, which will go something like this:.

First, determine your para theme headings and against each, write down the sentence ideas. These ideas/thoughts should then be converted into proper sentences conforming to the para writing rules. The approach is same as what we did under the "Narrative type" composition.

Once you become an expert, you need not follow the Mind exploring method at all and go straight for the Para theme method.

Expository type

Let's say you want to write an Expository type essay on "Cricket". In this type, whatever you write must deal only with the rules of the game. Your "Mind exploring list of Points" may therefore be something like this:

1. Two teams participate, each of 11 players.
2. While one team bats the other will field.
3. From the batting team, only 2 players will be at the wickets.
4. The bowler of the fielding team will throw the ball to the batsman at the striking end. If he hits the ball away, both of them will exchange places. One such exchange will constitute a 'run' and will go in favour of the batsman who hit the ball and thereof to the team.
5. If the fielding team hits the wicket with the ball and drops the bails while the batsmen are running between the wickets, the batsman who has not reached the wicket line, will be considered 'out'.

6. The full fielding team (of 11 players) will be spread out in the entire field while one player called the 'wicket keeper' would stand behind the wicket; their aim is not to give away runs to the batsmen.

7. When the whole team is 'dismissed', the other team will start with the batting. Method of declaring the winner.

8. Two types of matches are played - Test cricket and One day internationals. The duration and rules thereof. Definition of one "over" and the number of overs to be bowled in each type.

9. Types of bowlers - fast, medium fast, slow, spinners.

10. Two umpires needed, one at each wicket-end.

11. The length of the pitch is 66 feet and is prepared specially for every game.

The points have been written down at random. While planning the paras, they must be logically developed with clear-cut themes, something like this:

Intro

As in 2001 A.D, only 15 countries of the world play serious cricket. It is a very popular game from viewers'/spectators' angle. National and International matches among the 15 Nations are invariably telecast live or given running commentary over the Radio. If you live in a cricket playing country and do not know the basic information and rules about this game, you are likely to be branded as a cricket recluse!

Main body

A. Types	-	Test matches; last 5 days and two innings. One day International match, usually of 50 overs each side.
B. Cricket field	-	Size, boundary, wicket to wicket length, fielders' positions in the field.
C. Team strength	-	11 players in each team. The fielding team will have bowlers, wicket keeper and fieldsmen. The batting team will have two players at any time at the crease.
D. Aim of the game	-	To score runs; definition of a 'run'; to whose credit every run goes; definition of 'no ball', 'wide', 'leg by'. Team's collective score. How winners declared in test matches and in One dayers. Aim of the fielding team is, to get every batsman out by 'catch' 'stump' 'bowled', 'lbw' and 'run out'. Game ends when 10 batsmen are dismissed.
E. Types of bowling	-	Fast, medium fast, slow, spin, leg break , off break.
F.Prize money	-	All players get it. Winning team and runner-up get more money. Special prizes such as Man of the match, Man of the series, best catch, highest wicket taker etc, are awarded by the sponsors.

Conclusion

Since the game is played for some 7 hours including 'breaks', one should be physically fit with good stamina. It has become so popular and profitable that many young men have taken to cricket as a profession.

When a subject is given to you or you yourself have decided to write an essay on a subject, be clear in your mind in which category you are going to present it. Some subjects could lend themselves to all the four types and some only to one or two. But, don't write a mix of all types; the reader is likely to get confused.

The **Para theme** method is marginally superior and less time consuming as well. But, you should have thorough knowledge on the subject, only then could you attempt the para theme method.

If you are not absolutely clear, go to the **'Mind exploring'** method to get you started and to enable you to determine the para themes.

Let the essay be your own effort. Don't copy from any tutorial books or someone's essays. Once you have trained your mind on the methods recommended in this Chapter, you would have prepared yourself fully to writing any piece on any subject on your own when you get into some professional life in later years.

Exercise

1. Write a composition of 500 - 600 words each on the following subjects adopting the "Mind exploring" method. Show clearly your 'para plan' and the para themes. Your composition may belong to the Descriptive, Narrative or Argumentative type depending on the nature of the points listed out by you.

(a) Hair (b) Dust   (c) Mango   (d) A Football match

2. Write a Narrative cum Descriptive type Composition of about 500 words on the following topics:

(a)   Summer holidays
(b)   My hobby
(c)   The monsoon season in my city
(d)   A government hospital
(e)   Street beggars in a city
(f)   Friendship with the same sex
(g)   Friendship with the opposite sex
(h)   Life in a multi storey flat

3.   Write an argumentative type Composition of about 500 words on the following

(a)   Horse race
(b)   Three language formula at High school level

Chapter 60

CREATIVE WRITING

Introduction

We could say that there is a fifth type of Essay/Composition. This is known as "Creative writing". And, we call this by a different name as well - ARTICLE. A college student is eligible to write "Articles" because of his/her exposure to the intricacies of daily life and better command over the English language.

Why call such writing, **Creative** or **Imaginative?** Because this piece of writing would not relate fully to any actual happening at all. It would deal with imaginary situations, imaginary encounters/characters or one's own suggestions/thoughts and recommendations on particular issues. Sometimes it could deal with make-believe situations that could take place in real life. Sometimes, one could develop a make-believe situation based on some true story or a part of a true life incident. Sometimes, such writings could also deal with factuals.

The creative writing may be of the following types:

(a) Light humour pieces (Satires, Middles or Human interest stories)
(b) Informative articles on health, about life in other countries and their people
(c) Political articles.

The approach to writing (b) and (c) is the same as for Essay/Composition but would be of higher level of thinking and language, meant for adult groups. These writings would follow the pattern: INTRODUCTION - MAIN BODY - CONCLUSION. The writing technique could be through the **Para theme** method or **Mind exploring list** method.

As regards (a), which most college students could attempt, the approach is slightly different. You would be writing such pieces as your contribution to newspapers or magazines for publication. If they are of acceptable quality and standard, they would publish your contributions.

The introductory para must introduce the subject or of what will follow in a very attractive way. You may choose a catchy sentence or an anecdote or a famous saying/proverb or even a joke. Whatever you write in this part, must be thought provoking or so tempting that the reader would feel compelled to read through. If your intro para is dull and insipid, be assured that the reader will certainly toss it out or go over to the next item.

Instead of adopting the para theme/mind exploring method, you could work out the "outline" of the situation(s) you wish to write about. Here is a sample outline of an imaginary article:

Many lottery winners happen to be those who bought their tickets from Madurai in Tamil Nadu. While asking for direction to a particular seller, you bump into a pensioner who gets wild and chases you back. You return to Chennai without the lottery tickets and tell a lie to your friend. Your friend also is a pensioner like you.

The above is the outline to develop your article. The para theme may not work out here because some para may be of a single line especially when you write in 'Direct speech'. Hence, the suggestion to adopt the outline approach.

You have to pad up the broad outline with relevant situations and information so that every thing looks real or such that could take place in one's real life. During this process, do observe all the rules of para-writing. Use dialogue because Direct speech will make your characters come alive.

The above outline could lead to a Satire. A Satire is one wherein we highlight some of our superstitions and blind beliefs and silly actions to laugh at ourselves. It is to be written in lighter vein as a humorous piece. Satires are normally written in First person as a personal experience.

Here is the first draft of the Satire whose tittle is, THE FORBIDDEN FRUIT.

THE FORBIDDEN FRUIT

(a) The moment Ceekay came to know that I was visiting Madurai for a day, he asked if I could do him a favour. "Sure," I assured him. He wanted me to buy for him 6 lottery tickets for any six bumpers. He gave the name of a particular agent known as KSK on some small lane around the bus terminus. Ceekay is my college day friend. "I say, you could buy those darned tickets right in Chennai. Why in Madurai ....?"

(b) He believed that the temple city is a very lucky place. According to his statistics, half the winners of any bumper, purchased their tickets in Madurai. KSK was supposed to be the luckiest agent.

(c) My personal work finished, I went on the hunt for the KSK shop. Being new, I had to ask for direction from the passers-by.

(d) "Oh, a Kiosk? There's one down there," an aristocrat looking man pointed at a sign board.

(e) He had vanished before I spelt out KAY YESS KAY.

(f) The next citizen shrugged and continued his quick pace.

(g) Every person around the bus stand that afternoon seemed to be in a hurry. No one had any time for me. At this juncture when an old man tapped my shoulder and asked, "Could I be of any help to you?" I felt like hugging him.

(h) "I am looking for a shop called KSK, Sir, " I said reverentially. He looked very senior.

(i) "I see ...." he hummed and scratched his head. I wondered if he would direct me to some restaurant or a hotel. Oh no. He knew the difference between KSK and KIOSK.

(j) "What's KSK's business, brother?" he inquired benignly. "What a helpful attitude!" I reflected and said, "He is a lottery agent, Sir."

(k) Alas! Tongues of flame leapt out of his aged mouth. "Lottery agent you said?" he screamed out. Then breathing hard he studied me from head to toe with his hands on his hips. "You a pensioner?" he demanded. I nodded. Couldn't hide my age.

(l) "I am a pensioner too. A couple of years older to you ..." He was a tall man with scorpion moustaches. I found myself like a small chap caught for some wrong doing and too frightened to open the mouth in front of a ferocious elder brother.

(m) His voice had sparks of fire in it "Why do you want to waste your precious pension on lottery tickets, eh?"

(n) This indeed was a shock to me. Me, a lottery addict? "Excuse me … Excu … It's … it's …. Ceekay …" Words failed to emerge out of my shaking lips. He stared at me bending forward a little with coals burning on his eyes. "Get lost !" he ordered me in blunt words as if I were his immediate subordinate. When I tried to escape from him, he blocked my way and commanded me to go back to wherever I came from.

(o) I had no alternative but to retreat to the station because I had only some 45 minutes to catch my train.

(p) On the following morning, Ceekay rang me up and asked when he could collect his *Prize winning* tickets. "I just returned Ceekay," I told him. "Shall get in touch a little later."

(q) I needed time to think. How to tell him that an Angel of Light had forbidden me from buying the deadly piece of paper. An hour later, I rang him up. "Ceekay, I seem to have left the tickets at the KSK counter itself, *yaar*. Can't locate them in my bag, you see? " I thought it was better to tell a lie than to make Ceekay poorer by 60 rupees.

After all, he too is a pensioner, isn't he?

In a Composition or Essay, one is expected to be very particular about grammar and that your sentences have been constructed according to the grammar rules. An examiner may not worry much about the specific meaning or meat in your sentences so long as your paras are somewhat coherent.

But, a Satire is written with a different set of guidelines like, (i) Have you used the most appropriate word(s) (ii) Does it make an easy - to - read material (iii) Is there a natural flow in the language (iv) Have you kept the interest alive from beginning to the end (v) Have you observed economy of words in your sentence constructions.

When a publisher pays you on the number of words used, he would be fussy about the length. If you have used 6 words where 3 would have been sufficient, he is going to edit your sentences heavily. If you have been verbose everywhere, he is likely to reject your contribution outright.

So, revise your article meticulously on the five points. If you feel there is something wrong in a sentence or word, put an underline against it for a relook. If you find a 'dead end' sentence, mark it and reframe it so that it contains CQ(s).

After my first draft, I have underlined a number of sentences and groups of words for a second look. The revised version is given below. Compare it with the first draft and note the logic behind the corrections. I have given my reasons for the revision of the underlined parts on the right hand half of the page.

THE FORBIDDEN FRUIT

On learning about my visit to Madurai for a day, my college day friend Ceekay, asked me if I could do him him a favour. "Sure." I assured him. He wanted me to buy for him 6 lottery tickets for any six bumpers. He gave the name of a particular agent by just 3 letters -

The first sentence of (a) modified. Yet, it raises a CQ

KSK, on a small lane around the bus terminus. "I say, you could buy those darned tickets right here in Chennai. Why Madurai ...."

"Ceekay .... college friend" seem out of place hence shifted to the first para.

Cutting me short, he added that the temple City is a very lucky place. According to his statistics, half the winners of any bumper had purchased their tickets in Madurai. KSK was supposed to be the luckiest agent.

"Cutting short ..". Participle used instead of a Complex sentence.

My work over, I went on the hunt for the KSK shop. Being new there, I had to ask for direction from the passers by. "Oh, a Kiosk? There's one right down there", an aristocrat looking man pointed at a signboard.

"My personal work finished" (c) shortened - economy of words." There's one right down there" sounds more effective

He had vanished before I spelt out KAY ESS KAY. The next person shrugged and continued his quick pace. Every person around the bus terminus that evening seemed to be in a hurry. No one had time for me. At that juncture, when an old man tapped my shoulder and asked, "Could I be of any help to you?" I felt like hugging him.

No change.

"I am looking for a shop named KSK, Sir," I said reverentially. He looked very senior and imposing"

"called" changed to "named". "...and imposing" added to show the man's personality.

"I see ..." he hummed and scratched his head. I wondered if he would direct me to some hotel or a restaurant. Oh no!. He knew the difference between KSK and KIOSK.

No change

"What's KSK's business, brother?" he inquired beningly. I was impressed by his good manners and helpful attitude. "He is a lottery agent, Sir" I replied brightening up.
Alas! Tongues of flame leapt out of his aged mouth immediately. "Lottery agent, you said?" he screamed out. Then breathing hard he studied me from head to toe with his hands on his hips. "You a pensioner?" he demanded.

"I replied brightening up" added to show my own enthusiasm and satisfaction.

"immediately" added in sentence 1 of (k)

I nodded. Couldn't hide my age. "I am a pensioner too. A couple of years older to you ..." He was tall with scorpion moustaches. I felt like a small chap caught for some wrong doing and too frightened to open the mouth in front of a ferocious elder brother.

No change
Economy of words in "He was a tall man" and in the sentence, "I found myself ..."

His voice had sparks of fire in it. "You want to waste your precious pension on lottery tickets, eh?"

"Why do" removed to make the sentence more effective and commanding.

This indeed was a shock to me. Me, a lottery addict? "Excuse me ... exc... it is.... Ceekay..." Words failed to emerge out of my shaking lips. He stared at me bending forward a little with coals burning on his eyes.

"Me a lottery addict?" is a self reflection, hence the inverted commas removed.

"Get lost!" he ordered me angrily as if I were his immediate subordinate. When I tried to forge ahead, he blocked my way and commanded me to go back to wherever I came from.

No change

I had no alternative but to retreat to the station because I had only some 45 minutes on hand to catch my train back to Chennai.

"45 minutes on hand" sound better.

On the following morning, Ceekay asked on telephone when he could collect his *Prize winning tickets*. "I just returned Ceekay," I answered. "Shall get in touch a little later."

No change

I needed time to think. How to tell him that an Angel of Light had forbidden me from buying the deadly fruits!

"deadly fruits" is more idiomatic and ties up with the caption.

An hour later I contacted him. "Ceekay, I seem to have left the tickets at the KSK counter itself, *yaar*. Can't locate them in my bag, you see?"

"rang him up" changed to "contacted him." Economy of words.

I thought it was better to tell a lie than to make Ceekay poorer by sixty rupees. After all, he is a pensioner too, isn't he?

No change

Since we are not following the "para theme method" as recommended for Essay writing, the situations described or information conveyed must include *inter alia* the writer's own reactions, reflections. Only then the writing would be realistic. If you don't record your own feelings at a certain statement, what you write next would look jumpy. So, in order to take the reader with you and with your mind, show your responses. Check Chapter 35 (Direct speech) in this regard.

Shall we attempt another satire?

We know that there is heavy security right from the airport to Raj Bhawan or wherever the VIP like a Minister of the Central Govt would be staying on his visit to the city. Ordinary people like you and me just cannot get to talk with these VIPs. Often people would pine to give him memorandum or application for some kind of help. Alas, no! They are unapproachable.

Based on this scenario or true to life scenario, one could develop a Satire of an ordinary citizen getting the best out of a VIP's visit. He is a heart patient and needs an open heart surgery which he could not afford even in decades. So, he thinks of a plan and avails the free treatment. We also know that those who are remanded for judicial or police custody (especially politicians) are attended to promptly if they complain of any physical problem. This could happen also to a key witness/key accused, couldn't it? The following article is based on these perceptions.

Here is the final draft of a Satire titled, "Shortcut to expert treatment".

SHORTCUT TO EXPERT TREATMENT

Are you suffering from any high class ailment like kidney failure or heart problem? You know, such types that are not terminal but curable and unfortunately at a very high cost? And you don't have the necessary finances to get yourself treated? Life is very precious to you and you don't want to lose it at the young age of 25. So what do you do in such a situation?

The country has a solution for it. After all, ours is a democratic country and the government does look after every citizen. But, don't interpret the word 'every citizen' in its literal meaning. Not quite. You have to be a "particular citizen" to attract the hospitality of our democratic government.

Muthu, an ordinary unknown citizen of 24 years, had a modest daily income at doing odd jobs now and then. A doctor told him one day that he had a hole in his heart and only a bypass surgery could save him. The cost? Rupees one lakh only. He felt totally shattered. He shed liberal tears right in front of the doctor expressing his helplessness.

The doctor was moved. He could have operated upon Muthu himself but he was in no mood to do it free of charge. He remembered how much money he had to shell out to join a medical college. Nevertheless, developing a soft corner for this poor patient, he cupped his mouth and whispered privately into Muthu's ears a novel plan to become that 'particular citizen' and get the operation done by a team of experts. On hearing it, Muthu jumped with joy. "Great, Sir, I'll get down to it straightway," he cried out.

The morning newspaper announced the arrival of a Cabinet Minister from New Delhi. So, Muthu reached the airport well before the touchdown time of the special aircraft. Then he saw the Minister step out of the escalator with pressed palms surrounded by black cats holding AK 47's. While the onlookers shouted slogans of praises, Muthu managed to break through the cordon and charged at the Minister's throat flourishing a pen knife.

Even before the black cats reacted, the alert policemen of the State of Tamil Nadu, grabbed him by the neck and bound him well and proper. The assailant was whisked off immediately to the police station. After the preliminary investigation, Muthu was produced before the magistrate who placed him under police custody for 14 days. "So far, so good" Muthu reviewed gratefully inside the Central jail.

The following day's news papers carried all kinds of headlines, part of which were supplied by the police themselves such as, "This is an Opposition plan to destabilise the government." "CIA and possibly ISI's joint effort to create chaos in India." "A fallout of India's refusal to sign the CTBT." "A deep rooted sabotage to sink India into the Bay of Bengal." "Assassination averted by a watchful policemen."

Muthu waited for the fourth day. When the prison staff served him breakfast that morning, he suddenly fainted and crouched clutching his chest. Soon there was a flurry of activities. Guards hurried hither and thither. Telephones rang everywhere. Shortly the prison doctor accompanied by the jail superintendent arrived at the cell. After examining the prisoner patient the Doctor yelled out , "Emergency! Quick. Summon the ambulance. Send advance information to the General hospital. "Within half an hour, Muthu found himself inside the operation theatre for an open heart surgery by the specialists.

After some four hours, the team of doctors received congratulatory messages from the Prime Minister, other senior Central Ministers and Chief minister over the success of the operation. But for this, the country would have missed a great opportunity of unearthing a great plot. "Thank God, the accused is alive. Now we can screw him to reveal the truth behind the assassination."

When Muthu was arraigned before the Magistrate two months later, he was a hale and hearty young man fit for any manual work. He didn't care about the punishment he would receive for the offence. "They can't hang me for brandishing a plastic knife, can they?" he mused and wished the Magistrate a very good morning.

A Satire is written to expose and highlight the ridiculous side of our daily life.

One has to develop it based on some real life incidents or possibly some blind practices and beliefs. The reader must agree that such a thing could happen after reading your piece. But, don't make it sound most unbelievable and foolish.

Here, the article has been written in Third person. Write it in First person if it happens to be a personal experience.

A Satire must be in a humorous language and in a lighter vein.

Informative article

Para theme method is to be followed in writing any informative articles on subjects like, Health, Sports, Character, Festivals etc. Here, you have to collect a lot of information through books and magazines. You cannot depend on your Mind exploring list because what you know may not be much at all. There is no question of using your imagination. Everything stated must be factual and absolutely true.

Let's say you want to write an article on "Valentine's day" After you have collected all the information about it, your para theme may be something like this:

Para theme		Sentence ideas
A. What is LOVE	-	Many kinds - between parents and children, between husband and wife and between two young persons. This is inevitable in modern times. However, love is giving, sharing, forgiving and sacrificing.
B.Valentine's day	-	Definition - a saga of sacrifice, commemorated in

honour of St Valentine and given the meaning lover's day.

C, D & E. What did Valentine do?- 3rd century B.C. King Claudius forced all able bodied bachelors to join the Roman Army. Priest Valentine secretly conducted marriage of several young men to escape Claudius's conscription plan. This having come to his knowledge, Claudius had Valentine executed. In his death Valentine had immortalised 'love'. So, year after year, 14 Feb is celebrated as Valentine's day. The new meaning of Valentine is "lover". On this day, young lovers exchange greetings and good wishes, especially the unmarried ones, just married couples and those betrothed lovers. "Valentine" has now become a figure of speech; it is synonymous with 'lover'.

F. Echoes in India   -   Essentially a western practice. In the last few years, lovers in India have started observing the day. Newspapers provide separate columns for the Valentine day msgs on 14 Feb. Greeting card manufacturers have also introduced special cards.

G. Conclusion   -   Some politicians are against the practice of aping the West and abhor the idea. Lovers are everywhere. We have Father's Day, Mother's day. And why not Lovers' day? Valentine is a secret code as well.

Such informative articles must invariably be written in Third person.

VALENTINE'S DAY

"Love" is as old as Adam and Eve, the first married couple. They loved each other immensely. So, do every husband and wife in present time. Then there is love between father and son, mother and daughter, brother and sister. Love between two young minds has now been accepted as something normal and inevitable and could be openly displayed as well. This adult-love is greater than the others because it is one of giving, sharing, forgiving and sacrificing. In modern times, there is one more method of giving expression for the mutual love.

Valentine's day is a saga of sacrifice commemorated in honour of a priest named Valentine. So much so, the name Valentine has become a figure of speech with the meaning "lover".

Sometime during the 3rd century A.D., King Claudius forced all able bodied bachelors to join the mighty Roman Army. Since bachelorhood was the criterion, a priest named Valentine secretly got several young men married to escape conscription. The King became wild at this and had Valentine executed before he caused further damage to the image of the Army.

In his death, St Valentine had immortalised 'love' between young people. So, the day of his death, 14 February is being observed as Valentine's day year after year. On this day, young lovers, especially the betrothed ones, just married couple and young persons in love, send messages of reassurance through various methods. As a result, Valentine has become a Metaphor and a Synonym for 'lover'.

The celebration of Valentine's day was essentially a western practice. In the last few years however, the Indian lovers too have come to accept it as a day worth rejoicing. On 14 February, the newspapers provide exclusive columns for the Valentine day messages. Greeting card manufacturers have also introduced special cards with touches of admiration and affections for the other. If the lovers reside in the same city or town, flowers or some gift would be sent. In doing so, they ensure that the memory of the man who died to bring two hearts and souls together, would live on through these acts love and gestures. After all,

> "The mind has a thousand eyes
> And the heart but one,
> Yet the light of a whole life dies
> When love is done."

Some Indian politicians have criticised the idea of aping the West and abhor the very idea. Don't we have lovers in India? Lovers are everywhere. We observe Father's day, Mother's day and why exclude Lovers' day? Valentine's day also offers an oblique way to express one's mind! If you are hesitant to ask the other in plain English, "Do you love me?" or tell "I love you", one could say boldly, "Will you be my Valentine?"

Political article

This is not an easy subject for every college student. Students of Political science could have a go at it with some confidence. Others, with a political bent, could dare if they have sufficient information and knowledge on politically linked subject. A note of warning - do not enter into a highly controversial arena.

Here, the "outline approach" would work better. But, your mind must be very clear about your arguments.

Let us take a thought provoking subject. Are we fully satisfied at our present Democracy or at the way the country is being administered through the Democratic path? Do we need a different system or does the present system need some modification?

Here is an outline of a proposed article title, "A new democracy for India".

> *Our democracy now is over 50 years old. The land hasn't made much progress. Why? Could it be that our democracy is not working well in its present form, although the Democratic system itself seems to have taken deep roots in our thinking? Possibly the "Party type of democracy" has failed to take off. The details of the proposed new system and how it would work. Various rules and guidelines on how to elect our representatives, their obligations to the people etc, how to make laws and how they are to be implemented.*

Unlike in the other two models, here we may show the "para heading". This will make the reading easier. A political article would indeed be longer, going to around 2000 words and such para titles would make the reader tune his mind to the subject matter.

Here is the fully edited article:

A NEW DEMOCRACY FOR INDIA

Review

In our multi-party political system, a citizen has no option but to vote for ONE of the candidates standing for election regardless of the personal merits of that candidate. No political party would guarantee about his/her credentials and whether he/she has any shady past. On the contrary, most of those nominated would not even make the average grade in terms of integrity and competence of any kind. The electorate is aware of it all too, but as stated already, finds itself totally helpless when it comes to casting the vote. But then, in our election system, we vote for the Party and not pointedly for the candidates representing it. We also know that citizens of high morals and excellence do not become members of the political parties.

It is every political party's ambition to get a majority so that it could form the Government. And once successful and in order to maintain its majority on the floor of the House, a party- whip is issued to bring compulsion on an MP/MLA. Thus, the elected MP/MLA too has no option but to cast his/her vote as directed by the party whip regardless of his/her personal views and convictions on the issues under consideration in the House.

We hear of collective responsibility of the Cabinet in the Center. That is, all decisions of the Cabinet are arrived at on consensus or unanimity basis. One would wonder if this is truly so. It is a known fact, strange as it may sound, that a minister holds office at the 'pleasure' of the Prime Minister/Chief Minister. The fear of being 'dropped' lurks constantly on the mind of every Minister especially if he/she happens to be a sort of rebel holding independent and radical views. Because of this fear, a Minister has no option but to toe the line of the Prime Minister/Chief Minister in the collective responsibility game.

So, it would appear that we have an unique gathering of sycophants in the Lok Sabha and the country is run, euphemistically speaking, according to the whim and fancy of one person, viz, the Prime Minister. And we unashamedly call our Government in the Indian capital as "one of the people, by the people and for the people."

Why can't we have a system that depends on the individual judgement of every elected member through free voting without a whip? Let's say, that we put the best brains available in the country in the Lok Sabha and if every decision is taken on the strength of the uninfluenced majority voice, that indeed would be collective wisdom, wouldn't it?

Next, why can't the citizens or their direct representatives have a say in the identification and nomination of a candidate to stand for election? This may amount to giving up the "Party type nomination and Election" and "Party type Lok Sabha/Government" and going over to a different type of system - a Partyless system. Why not? Where is it laid down that a Democracy should be practised only through political parties? It might have succeeded in other countries, but in our own land, the system seems to have failed. Hence, this appeal to try out an alternative system yet within the framework of the conventional democracy.

General Elections

It is the "Citizens Council", instead of the political party bosses, who will pick out and nominate the candidates to stand for the General Elections at the rate of three or four candidates per constituency. No other candidates will be permitted to stand for the General Elections.

The candidates so nominated by the CC will be 52 years of age or above. They will be the highly qualified and experienced citizens of India with significant achievements and excellence to their credit in their field; those who have climbed up to high positions by dint of hard work and devotion; very competent in their profession and well known for their honesty, integrity, nationalism and a clean life. They will be spotted out wherever they may be. They may be serving Government employees or ordinary citizens, self employees or retired persons.

The Election Commission will conduct the general elections, for the Lok Sabha and State Legislative Assemblies simultaneously once in five years. It will not be upto the Cabinets to order midterm elections. In fact, there will be nothing known as mid term elections at all. The date of General Elections will be determined by the EC about the time of the expiry of five years. The elected candidates will then get baptized as MP/MLA. It is only at this stage that they will be required to relinquish or resign whatever job/post they might have been holding till then.

Central and State Governments

The MPs of the Lok Sabha will elect the Prime Minister by a simple majority vote. The PM will constitute the Central cabinet out of the MPs ensuring that every State is properly and adequately represented in it.

The Cabinet will appoint the State Governors, Ambassadors, High Commissioners, Consuls etc out of the MPs.

The President and Vice President will also be elected out of the MPs only, but by the majority votes of all MPs and MLA put together.

The MLAs likewise will elect the Chief Minister for the State and the CM will constitute the State cabinet out of the MLAs.

All Ministers, Ministers of State and Junior Ministers of the National and State Cabinets will hold the same portfolio for full five years. A Cabinet reshuffle would become necessary only if a Minister dies in harness or resigns. Resignation will become mandatory in case of any strictures on them by a High court or Supreme court.

The Central and State Cabinet will introduce the various bills/legislations during the different sessions of LS and LAs. The bills/legislations will be thoroughly discussed in the respective houses and a decision taken on them by a simple majority vote; two thirds voting will be essential for constitutional amendments. "Voting down of a bill/legislation or suggestions for severe modifications" will not be a reflection on the Cabinet or Government. The majority decisions of LS and LAs by the elected wise men is bound to be far wiser than the opinions/ views of the few in the Cabinet. "Voting" in the LS and LAs will be totally voluntary and according to the dictates of the conscience of the individual MP/MLA. "National interests" will be the sole guide star for the politicians to exercise their vote in the House. There will be no kind of official or unofficial whip or coercion or canvassing. However, there could be 'meeting of minds' through mutual and group discussions prior to voting.

The Cabinet and more particularly the Minister concerned will be responsible and accountable to the electorate for implementation of the legislations and decisions of the LS and LAs and the laws of the land within the stipulated time frame.

In all other respects of Government functioning, the existing laws, rules, practices and procedures of the Constitution will hold good.

Every elected MP or MLA is required to serve the Nation for a period of five years only. In exceptional cases and if the performance of a politician especially in the capacity of a Minister, has been publicly recognised and hailed as outstanding, that politician may be nominated by the CC for a second Election. A third tenure is not permissible no matter how good his/her performance may have been.

An unselected candidate in the first round may be re-nominated to stand for a second or third General Election. A fourth or subsequent nomination is not permissible.

In the new set up, the Rajya Sabha and State Legislative Councils will stand abolished.

Citizens Council

There will be a Citizens Council at State level and National level with headquarters at the respective capitals.

The State Council will have two members representing each District plus 10 to 20 members, (depending on the size of the State) at the State headquarters level. A Chairman and Vice Chairman will be elected out of and by the State Council members.

The National CC will be have 20 members out of whom a Chairman and Vice Chairman will be elected. The Chairman and Vice Chairman of the State CC will be the ex-officio members of the National CC. In addition, one member will represent each Union territory at the National CC.

The CC members for both levels will be nominated by the Central Government. As regards the State Council members, nominations will be made after consultation with the State governments concerned.

The CC members nominated will be out of : all types of National awardees, Defence and Civil gallantry awardees, Government or Public sector or Private sector or Defence services officials with a good track record, lawyers, judges, social workers of repute, philanthropists, teachers and such private sector employers who have provided employment for 25 persons or more. The minimum age for nomination as CC members will be 55 years.

The primary responsibility of the CC will be to identify and nominate candidate for General Elections for the Centre and States.

After the Governments are formed, the CC will revert to the role of a "watchdog" over the performance of the governments concerned.

The National CC and State CC may resort to suing the Governments or the Ministers concerned, in the High courts and Supreme court, for non implementation or half hearted implementation of any legislation and non performance and also corruption if any.

The CC will remain in constant touch with the people, their ideas, aspirations and also their reactions and attitudes towards the Governments. Any citizen or Association will have free access to a CC member to project his/her/its views and suggestions for improving the quality of life and also bring to the CC's notice any serious public grievances for immediate redressal.

The CC will be the body for eliciting, sensing and projecting public opinions on various issue. The voice of the CC will be the voice the people of India truly.

The State CCs and National CC will meet periodically and their deliberations and recommendations that would be of interest to the citizens will be published through notices and newspapers. The Governments will give very careful consideration to the recommendations made by the CC and honour them to the extent feasible.

The CCs will be funded entirely by the Central and State Governments for its accommodation, office establishments, secretariat and other day to day administrative expenditure.

The Chairman and Vice Chairman at all levels will be regular full time members and will receive regular salary accordingly. The other members will be part time workers and will receive nominal honorarium for attending meetings, carrying out investigative tasks and reimbursement of travel and allied expenses.

Every CC member including the Chairman and Vice Chairman will hold office for five years and only once in their life time. CC members will not be eligible for nomination as candidates for General Elections.

Poll campaigns

The outgoing Central and State Governments will conduct the "poll campaigns" for the candidates. This may be done in the form of informing the electorate about the candidates' complete bio-data, his/her present standing and how he/she had climbed up to that status, his/her contributions to the society and the Nation and so on, through distribution of pamphlets and announcements through the mass media. The candidates are prohibited from doing any kind of publicity for themselves. Nor will they be permitted to make any kind of 'election promises'. From the Nation's point of view, election of any of the candidates put up by the CC will be acceptable since they all will be nearly equal in eminence and stature.

Code of conduct of MP/MLA/CC members

MPs, MLAs and CC members will not in any way interfere with the administrative machinery of the State or Center at any level either directly or indirectly or remotely. This restriction is to ensure that the officials are responsible and accountable only to their superiors in their chain of command and ultimately to the Minister concerned and not to the MP, MLA or CC member of the constituency. If however, they do find or come to know of any malfeasance, inefficiency, misconduct or corrupt practices on the part of government servants and feel strongly that positive action is necessary in particular cases, they should lodge formal complaints with the concerned Ministry. Towards this, every Ministry will set up a "public grievance cell" headed by a senior official upto District level. This cell will entertain complaints only from the MPs, MLAs and CC members.

Retirement benefits

The retired MPs and MLAs will draw 80% of their last salary as 'political pension' for life over and above the other benefits they may have been enjoying prior to their election. They will not be allowed to accept or hold any job with salary or honorarium or function as consultant or adviser or agent to any organisations after their retirement. The concerned Government will ensure that the retired politicians lead a life of comfort and are free from any kind of wants for himself/herself and the spouse. The Nation will look towards them as 'think tanks' and reservoirs of ideas.

The retired CC members will also receive a nominal CC pension for life. In addition, they will be allowed to pursue any profession or hold any office in any capacity during the retired period.

Conclusion

The highlights of the proposed new Indian Democracy described in this article are: That there is no permanency in Indian politics. Indian politics is not a profession for earning a livelihood. It is a 'National Service', a Service of great honour, to be rendered by highly mature and competent persons who have already realised all their life-ambitions in their professional life and are in position to **give away** their knowledge and experience. Being the cream of the society, they will be role models and mentors for the new generation.

In order to catch the eye of the CC, every Indian will try to work hard and achieve excellence in their performance. As a result, one would notice a significant improvement in our work - efficiency and productivity.

Money will play no part whatever in Indian life and General Elections.

The CC will be the *de facto* opposition party but functioning from outside the Government. It will have all the time in the world to feel the pulse of the people and project their expectations to the Governments from time to time on important issues. Thus the electorate will have a voice through the CC and make its presence felt in the day to day running and will indirectly but effectively participate in Governmental affairs.

The CC will closely observe and monitor the government's performance. It will have the authority to sue the concerned Minister for any kind of lapses or laxity or slackness as regards himself and his Ministry. Accordingly, the Ministers will be always on their toes and ensure that his/her Ministry discharges its functions properly and efficiently. The Minister concerned would have to resign over any strictures by a High court or Supreme court on the Ministry's performance or on the Minister himself. Such forced resignation will be a national disgrace on him and he/she shall lose all the priviligers of an MP/MLA.

The CC would resort to this type of court action also against individual MPs and MLAs for interfering with the bureaucracy, indulging in any malpractices or corrupt practices and any irresponsible behaviour unbecoming of a politician. The concerned politician would then have to resign his post and suffer national disgrace.

The change over to the new system may be effected in the following manner: The Central Government in power at that time, will nominate the members for the first Citizens Councils in such a way that they get approximately two year's time to identify the politician-candidates for the oncoming General Elections.

Chapter 61

COMPREHENSION

Definition

"Comprehend" is a verb which means, "understand fully." 'Comprehension' is a noun. When you read any para or a passage containing a few paras, you are expected to digest the contents and register all the details in your memory. Don't forget, a human brain can store a lot of information provided you 'save' it. **Saving,** a computer term, amounts to comprehension. Once you understand fully the material you have read, it will get automatically stored in your brain memory.

How to comprehend

Read a given passage *seriously* with total *concentration* in order to remember the essentials in it. At the end, you must be in a position to answer a set of questions on the passage. The questions themselves may be straightforward and without any catches in them.

Here is an example:

Read the following passage and pick out the correct answer out of the given alternatives for the questions:

A. *If you believe you can, you can. If you believe you cannot, you cannot. Think negatively and you will get a negative result because by your thoughts you create a negative atmosphere which is hospitable to negative results. On the contrary, think positively and you create a positive atmosphere which makes positive result a certainty.*

To cultivate positive thinking, speak hopefully about everything. Then feed your mind with good, nourishing and wholesome thoughts. Keep good company of friends who are optimistic. Read scriptures which will cast away your negative thoughts. Lastly, pray a great deal and count the blessings that God has given you. Thus you can overcome negative thoughts of failure and cultivate positive thoughts of success.
(Mar 1997 Std XII examination)

Questions:

1. This passage is on ——————
   (a) pessimism (b) optimism   (c) tourism   (d) naturalism
2. Think negatively and you will get ————— result.
   (a) negative   (b) positive   (c) immediate   (d) bad
3. If you want to cultivate positive thinking, you ——
   (a) think and speak hopefully   (b) speak boldly (c) speak softly (d) speak loudly
4. ——— will cast away your negative thoughts.
   (a) reading newspapers (b) reading magazines (c) reading books (d) reading scriptures
5. Which of the following statement is not true?
   (a) Good friends elevate our thoughts (b) Prayer helps us to keep our minds clean
   (c) It is not possible to change a pessimist into an optimist. (d) For cultivating optimism, we should speak hopefully always.

Correct answers are :

1. (b) optimism
2. (a) negative
3. (a) think and speak hopefully
4. (d) Reading scriptures/holy books
5. (c) It is not possible to change a pessimist into an optimist.

Method

This is a different variety of Comprehension. It is not quite like the Comprehension at Matriculation level.

Here, you are required to pick out the right word/phrase from the given text and to make sure that answer fits into the text as well. Don't use your own words anywhere except modifying if necessary in order to fit the answer into the text from grammar angle.

Before picking out the correct answer out of the given alternatives, read the relevant portion again and again.

Here are a few more examples. Write your own answer first before you refer to the official answers given at the end.

B. *When we got down from the Everest, there was much talk about who got there first. Some said it was I and some others said it was Hillary. Some said that only one of us reached the summit; or, neither. To put an end to such talk, Hillary and I signed a statement in which we said, "We reached the summit almost together." Mountaineers can understand that when two men are on the same rope they are together. This other people could not understand and kept on asking questions. It is not for my own sake I give it. Nor is it for Hillary's. It is for the sake of Everest - the prestige of Everest and for the generations who will come after us. "Why", they will say, "should there be a mystery to this thing? Is there something to be ashamed of? Or, to be hidden? Very well. Now they will know the truth. Everest is too great, too precious for anything but truth."*

A little below the summit, Hillary and I stopped. We looked up. Then we went on. The rope that joined us was thirty feet long, but I held most of it. I was not thinking of 'first' and 'second'. We went on slowly and steadily. And then we were there. Hillary stepped on first. And I stepped up after him.

- **Tensingh**

Questions

1. The word 'I' in the passage refers to who?
   (a) Hillary   (b) Military   (c) Tensingh   (d) Mt Everest

2. The joint statement of Hillary and Tensingh ——————
   (a) brought an end to the talk (b) proved the fact as to who got on the summit first
   (c) encouraged the other mountaineers to have further talk   (d) showed how difficult it was to climb the Everest.

3. The public talked so ——————
   (a) as they were innocent (b) as there was a lack of understanding
   (c) as they were foolish   (d) as they wanted to support either one of the two.

4. Climbing the Everest was ——————

    (a) an impossible task (b) a greedy task (c) a prestigious talk (d) a mysterious task.

5. The conquest of Everest was ———

    (a) an individual effort (b) a joint effort (c) an useless effort (d) a childish effort.

C.   *Our Defence service consists of 3 wings - Army, Navy and Airforce. As a matter of fact, the Navy and Airforce happen to support the Army in any operation. It is only the Army that can capture and hold the enemy land. Navy and Airforce can bombard the enemy areas and bring about destructions and damages to their war materials or industries. The Airforce can destroy bunkers and enemy tanks in the battle area, thus help the army to advance, neutralise the enemy's firepower and occupy ground.*

The Navy controls our waters and the coasts. They ensure that no enemy forces enter our land through the seas. Navy does not have the capability to capture land except for the immediate area around a harbour. Like the Airforce, Navy also has fighter, bomber and reconnaissance aircrafts besides powerful guns that can fire upto 30 miles or so. This is a common factor between the Army and Navy.

Airforce can drop bombs at long distances but the air crafts have to physically fly closer to the concerned area. Not so with the Army and Navy; without even seeing the enemy target their guns could fire at them.

In modern times, instead of guns all the three services use Missiles. Missiles have long ranges - some upto thousands of kilometers. Without seeing the target, missiles could be fired from our own area into enemy land very accurately.

Questions:

1.   Who could capture and occupy large areas of enemy land?

    (a) Army (b) Navy (c) Airforce (d) Navy and Airforce together.

2.   What is the common factor between Navy and Army?

    (a) Long range guns (b) fighter air crafts (c) ships (d) none

3.   Who can fire their guns at the enemy land without seeing the target?

    (a) Navy alone (b) Airforce alone (c) Navy and Army (d) Army and Airforce

4.   Which wing supports which?

    (a) Army supports the Navy   (b) Airforce supports the Navy

    (c) Army supports the Navy and Airforce (d) Navy and Airforce support the Army.

5.   Who has fighter, bomber and reconnaissance aircrafts?

    (a) The Army (b) Airforce only (c) Army and Navy together (d) Airforce and Navy.

Answers for **B** and **C:**

B. 1. (c)   2. (b)   3. (b)   4. (c)   5. (b)

C. 1. (a)   2. (a)   3. (c)   4. (d)   5. (d)

Exercise

Read the passages carefully and answer the questions:

(I)   Mark Twain was a great American writer. One day he met a friend at a race course. The friend said, "I've lost all my money betting on losing horses. Can you buy

ticket for me to our place?" Mark Twin told his friend that he had not enough money to buy two tickets and asked him to hide himself under a seat. The friend agreed as he had no other go. Mark Twain went to the booking office and bought two tickets. After some time the train had started and a ticket examiner came around. Mark Twain showed him both the tickets. When the surprised ticket examiner asked Twain where the other passenger was he said, "He is travelling under the seat. He likes to do strange things."

Questions:

1. The race referred to here is ————
   (a) Horse race (b) a motor race (c) running race (d) none of these

2. The friend agreed ————
   (a) to travel without a ticket (b) to buy a ticket for Mark Twain
   (d) to travel hiding himself under a seat (d) to cheat the ticket examiner.

3. The friend had no money on him ————
   (a) to pay the ticket examiner (b) to buy a ticket for the race
   (c) to help his friend Mark Twain (d) to buy a train ticket for himself.

4. This incident reveals that Mark Twin ————
   (a) loves to cheat others (b) enjoys to see his friends travelling under a seat
   (c) likes to make fun of others (d) loves to do strange things.

5. The reply of Mark Twain should have ————
   (a) surprised the ticket examiner (b) shocked the ticket examiner
   (c) hurt the feelings of the ticket examiner (d) made the ticket examiner angry.

(II) Many young women are planning careers which they hope will make them financially independent. They are averse to be wholly dependent on their husbands. They wish to make their own mark in the world while at the same time making a marriage which will be emotionally fulfilling. They seem confident that they can handle these dual roles with ease. Many of them would like to have children, but they realise there are other options. They no longer see child bearing as their obligatory function. They seem unaware that their plans might be somewhat threatening to the kind of young man they hope to marry. They do not seem to know that some young men are fearful of liberated women and hope to marry a girl who will be content to look up to them and be happy caring for their meals, laundry and children.

Questions:

1. Many young women are planning their own careers because ————
   (a) they want to earn money (b) they want to be financially independent (c) they want to feel satisfied earning a lot of money (d) they want to enjoy their profession.

2. Many modern women consider that child bearing ————
   (a) is bothersome (b) is not their obligatory function (c) is one of their duties.
   (d) is their true function.

3. Some young men are rather fearful of ————
   (a) beautiful young women (b) liberated women (c) career women
   (d) nonworking women

4. The modern women are confident of handling the dual role of,

(a) child bearing and earning through their profession (b) child bearing and caring for their husbands (c) making their own mark and making the marriage emotionally fulfilling (d) a wife without children.

5. Do the modern young men look forward to having a wife who is,
    (a) wholly independent (b) partially dependent on him (c) a liberated woman (d) caring for their meals, laundry and children

(III) *Every student should learn to type because of the many advantages typing has over script. First, typing is much less fatiguing than writing; more so, when one uses a computer key board or a portable electric typewriter. One can type for hours without fatigue, while steady writing for a time will soon tire one's hand. Second, no matter how tired a person becomes, the character of typed letters never changes. On the other hand, script will tend to become sloppy after long periods of writing. Next, typing is always legible with a minimum of effort. At times personal script is so poor that it is difficult, if not impossible, to read. Legibility can contribute to an improved grade since a teacher is more likely to give a low grade to a sloppily written paper than to a neat, typewritten one.*

But, all this is only a dream. You cannot expect the Indian authorities to let you carry a mini typewriter with you to a classroom and carrying a computer is out of the question. Nor, could you submit your home assignments in type written form. So, we have to choose one of the following options: 'improve your handwriting' so that your teachers fall in love with it or train the teachers on deciphering bad handwriting!

Questions:

1. Give a caption for the above passage.
    (a) Fatigued by long writing? (b) Legibility or illegibility?
    (c) Scripting versus typewriting (d) Is your handwriting poor?
2. Scripting will tend to become sloppy after,
    (a) a few minutes (b) you develop some sleepiness
    (c) your pen becomes defective (d) long periods of writing.
3. What does 'dream' refer to in the passage?
    (a) Presenting all written work in type written form (b) Carrying a mini typewriter to your class room. (c) authorities allowing you to do all your class work inside your own home (d) None of these.
4. Why is learning typing considered desirable?
    (a) It is much less fatiguing than writing (b) at present time all information is given in printed form. (c) one would make less spelling mistakes (d) it is more easily readable than scripting.

(IV) *One of the amazing things about 'ants' is that it can eat living things. This is a special kind seen in Africa. This species is called the 'driver ant'. They always go out in 'armies' and not even in groups. On their way whatever they see they would kill and eat. You might wonder how a little insect like an ant can kill and eat. The reason is they attack as an army, each individual ant covering only a small area of the body of the victim. Even the largest animals would run away when they see the ant-army approaching them. If that creature does not run away, then it is goodbye to it. The ant-army could kill a fly or a crocodile or a wounded lion.*

Such ant-armies are also seen in the southern and central parts of United States, and South America. In Mexico, people would move out of their houses at the very sight of the deadly invaders.

Questions:

1. Ant-armies are found in,
   (a) Australia (b) India (c) Mexico (d) Mangolia
2. They are known as 'driver ants' because they move,
   (a) in groups (b) as an army (c) in pairs (d) singly
3. "If that creature does not run away, then it is goodbye". This means,
   (a) the animal concerned will say goodbye to the ants (b) the creature will invite sympathy from the ant army (c) that the creature will move to a safe place and bid goodbye to the ant army (d) the creature will get killed by the ant army.
4. Can an ant-army eat a dead elephant?
   (a) yes (b) no (c) difficult to say (d) possibly.
5. What do the Mexicans do when see an ant- army approaching?
   (a) they will take up arms to meet the challenge (b) they will move out of their houses (c) they will hide themselves inside the house (d) they will wave their hands to the army.

(V) *In our Electoral roll there is wrong inclusion of names. Ineligible voters are permitted to include their names. True, the eligible voters, except a very few, do not take any interest to get their names included. Only the political parties take steps to enrol voters. In which case, fictitious names could enter into it. For instance, how did Veerapan's (the forest brigand) name get into the list voters of T.Nagar, Chennai? Whereas, names of genuine voters do not find a place at all in the roll. In some cases even after repeated reminders, the Election commission has failed to add their names, obviously due to clerical inefficiency.*

To correct all the anomalies, the Election commission should understand first that it had failed in its primary duty of preparing the electoral roll. It must first devote its attention on the preparation of the electoral roll and updating it by door to door enumeration without leaving an opportunity to any political party to enrol only persons who would vote for it. It is always the voluntary enrolment that creates problems. All the eligible voters should be included based on door to door enumeration and verification by the Election commission.

Questions:

1. The passage refers to,
   (a) Election commission (b) Electoral roll (c) General elections (d) Political parties
2. Who is the authority to include a name in the electoral roll?
   (a) Political parties (b) Every individual voter (c) The Central government
   (d) The Election commission
3. Fictitious names will get into the electoral roll when,
   (a) We allow political parties to prepare the electoral roll of certain wards.

(b) When the election commission is careless (c) Impersonation is permitted (d) People take interest in elections.

4.   The primary duty of the Election commission is,

(a) To educate the citizens about democracy (b) To tell people how to cast votes (c) To prepare the electoral roll with accuracy (d) To advertise about the date of elections.

5. In order to have an upto date electoral roll one must,

(a) leave the matter to the political parties. (b) Ask every voter to vote

(c) Ask every voter to go and meet the Election commissioner (d) Resort to door-to-door verification of the voters.

Chapter 62

NOTE MAKING AND
SUMMARISING/PARAPHRASING

What is note making?

It may not be possible for you to write every word a person speaks unless one takes it down through 'short hand'. But, those of us who are not familiar with shorthand, could note down the vital/crucial guideline points of the speech or talk and expand them into a prose form. Such expansion may not be in the same words of what the speaker had said but would cover the essential elements in *one's own words*.

During note making one could use symbols such as > (greater than), < (less than), ∴ (therefore), μ (because), abbreviations and so on. In other words, use any thing that would remind you and lead you to the main substance(s) of the speech.

With the help of your "notes", you must be able to produce *in your own words* a summary containing the essential features of the original passage/speech. Such transformation can also be called "paraphrasing". In doing so, omit all the rhetorics, explanations (including adjectives) and references. Condense the details where necessary by using a single word equivalent by phrases. The summary should be in readable English without grammatical errors and in a logical sequence as well.

Example - 1

Task: Summarise/Paraphrase the following passage. Notes have been given to enable you write out the passage in condensed form (Summary) without losing the essential features.

> *The President of Mauritius, as well as a group of ministers and officials, arrives at Madras air port at 12 noon on October 5. He takes rest at Raj Bhawan till 1 p.m. The visiting group have lunch with VIPs at 1.30 p.m. The Governor of Tamil Nadu and Chief Minister pay a courtesy call to the President at 2.30 p.m. The President and his party meet a trade delegation of Tamil Nadu in Raj Bhawan to discuss at 2.45 p.m, various proposals for setting up a few industries in Maldives. The Minister for Foreign trade of Mauritius explains the different incentive schemes his Govt has designed for the prospective industrialists and interacts with the Indian delegation. The meeting will conclude at 5.30 p.m with tea. At 6 p.m. the President will grant an audience to the Vice Chancellor of Madras University. The President and his party leave for Meenambakkam air port at 6.30 p.m. for departure to Mauritius.*

Notes:

1. President of Mauritius and party arrive at Madras 12 noon, 5 Oct.
2. Rest at Raj Bhawan till 1 p.m.
3. Lunch with VIPs at 1.30 p.m.
4. Courtesy call by Governor and CM at 2.30.
5. The visiting party meet trade delegation between 2.45 p.m and 5.30 p.m. along with tea.

6.   VC's audience with the President at 6 p.m..
7.   Leaves for Meenambakkam airport at 6.30 p.m.

Summary:

The President of Mauritius and his party arrive at Madras at 12 noon on 5 Oct. The visitors, after some rest, have lunch at 1.30 p.m. with VIPs. The Governor and CM will pay a courtesy call to the President. At 2.45 p.m. the party meets a trade delegation to discuss various proposals for setting up industries in Mauritius. Tea will be served during discussions. At 5.30 p.m. the meeting concludes. The President has an audience with VC, Madras university. The President's group leave for airport at 6.30 p.m.

Example - 2

Task: Summarise/Paraphrase the following passage. Notes have been given at the end to enable you build up the summary.

> In the beginning, the earth was without form, void and was covered with darkness and waters. God created light to separate it from darkness. It is not known what kind of light this was. The light was called Day and darkness Night. Then, God separated the heavens from the Earth. There was water above the heavens and below the heavens. He gathered all the waters on the Earth together in one place and called it Seas and the dry land Earth. He commanded grass, herb and various kinds of fruit trees to grow on the land. Then He created the Sun to rule the day and Moon to rule the night. God made the stars also. He created all kinds of living creatures to inhabit the seas and the birds to fly in the sky. At His command, the Earth also brought forth living creatures, cattle, creeping things and beasts of different types. God did all these in six days.

Notes:

1.   In the beginning Earth void, no form, all darkness and waters.
2.   God created light, called light Day and darkness Night.
3.   The earth was separated from the heavens with waters in both parts.
4.   He gathered all the waters on the Earth in one place and called it Seas and the dry land Earth.
5.   Grass, herbs and all kinds of fruit trees grew on the land.
6.   God created the Sun to rule the day and Moon along with stars the night.
7.   He created living creatures to inhabit the sea and earth.

Summary

In the beginning the Earth was void, formless and full of darkness and waters. Separating the darkness from light, he called the light Day and darkness Night. The waters were separated between the Heaven and Earth. The Earth waters were gathered in one place and was called Seas and the dry land Earth with grass, herbs and fruit trees. He created the Sun to rule the day and Moon along with stars the night. He created all kinds of water creatures to inhabit the seas, birds to fly across the sky and other creatures to live on the dry land.

Example - 3

The Chinese claim to be the first to make the gun powder, invent the magnetic compass and give to the world the art of making paper. About 2000 years ago the Chinese made gun powder by mixing sulphur and saltpetre. The mixture exploded when set on fire. The Chinese were the first to find out the fact that a narrow magnet floating in a bowl of water would always point to the North. This discovery led to the invention of the magnetic compass. This device helped the sailors find out the direction when they were out of sight of land. Soon the device reached the Arabs and the Europeans. Using this compass, great explorers like Columbus, Magellan and Vasco da Gama made their historic discoveries. The Chinese invented the art of making paper during the second century. Soon the art of making paper using vegetable pulp reached Arabia, Spain and Europe. In course of time paper factories came into existence. The fourth invention of the Chinese was the art of printing; before this invention, books were written by hand. The Chinese invented the art of printing with movable types. With this invention, reading and learning became open to ordinary people as they were able to print the books in large numbers.

Note making:

1. The Chinese inventions were,
    (a) gun powder (b) magnetic compass (c) paper (d) printing.
2. (a) Gun powder from sulphur and saltpetre - explosive.
    (b) Magnetic power - finding direction -great explorers discovered new lands.
    (c) Paper from vegetable pulp - paper industries
    (d) Art of printing - books, learning

Summary

The Chinese were the first to make the gun powder by mixing sulphur and saltpetre and setting fire to the mixture. They were also the first to design the magnetic compass which became valuable to sailors. Columbus, Magelian and Vasco da Gama used the compass to discover new lands separated by the seas. Their third invention was the art of making paper out of vegetable pulp giving birth to a number of paper industries in Arabia and Europe. The fourth invention was printing. Reading and learning became easy and accessible to ordinary people as they were able to print books in large numbers.

Example - 4

It would be possible to produce a summary solely with the help of the Notes if the notes are fairly comprehensive and in proper sequence.

Task: Expand the given Notes into a readable passage.

Notes:

1. Third century B.C. - Asoka, a power hungry king invaded Kalinga.
2. Heavy casualties. He walked through the silent battle field with the pride of victory.
3. Suddenly he was moved by the sight of thousands of dead soldiers - lost his peace of mind.

4.   He met a Buddhist monk named Upagupta, embraced Buddhism.
5.   He gave up war - spent life spreading the principles of Buddhism the world over.

Passage

In the third century B.C., Asoka, a great king and warrior, invaded Kalinga region and captured it. The battle was severe. There were heavy casualties on both sides. The victorious king walked through the now silent battle field with pride of victory. The sight of dead soldiers pleased him initially but when he saw only dead bodies for miles and miles, he was overcome by a sudden feeling of guilt and remorse. At the end of the day, king Asoka had lost his peace of mind. Guilty conscience began to prick him. He went over and fell at the feet of Upagupta, a great Buddhist monk. Then he felt a sudden joy and change of heart. Renouncing war completely, he embraced Buddhism and spent the rest of his life spreading the principles of Buddhism the world over.

In such an exercise, you need to pad up the feelings/emotions/ given hints with suitable details or rhetorics and make such descriptions sound logical as well. Use your imagination in painting the situation(s).

Example - 5

In the same manner, it would be possible to produce a summary without the "note making" also. But then, it would call for considerable experience and excellent concentration.

Task: Write a short summary of the following passage.

The last five decades in the independent India, have been the years of hope and aspiration as also of frustrations and desperation. Independence led to great expectations in terms of raising the standards of living and upgrading the quality of life of our people. Equity, equality and social justice were assured even prior to Independence. The Constitution fully reflects this societal ambition and mandates of equality of opportunity for every citizen irrespective of social, economic, cultural or religious diversities and stations in life. It was also very aptly reflected in the Report of the Education Commission (1964-66):

"The destiny of India is now being shaped in her classrooms. This, we believe, is no more a rhetoric. In a world based on science and technology, it is education that determines the level of prosperity, welfare and security of people."

The Commission further elaborates that it is the quality of human beings coming out of the learning centres which would determine the success or failure of national efforts for reconstruction and development. For a prosperous nation, however, the foundation stone is its sound educational system. Such a system can no longer be an alien, borrowed or transplanted one. It must be rooted deep in the indigenous soil and must remain alert and open to the changes taking place all around and the need to progress ahead.

But, alas! All the above have truly turned into rhetorics and our progress towards better quality of life still remains a dream.

Summary

Independence raised several hopes in the minds of people of India. The Constitution also promised equality of opportunities regardless of caste, social and cultural diversities. The Education Commission of 1964-66 stressed that the destiny of India should be shaped in classrooms. The persons coming out of the learning centres would determine the success or failures of national reconstruction. Alas! Nothing much has happened in fifty years and we still remain backward without much progress in our quality of life.

Exercise

1. Paraphrase the following passage. Note making has been given at the end:

It is not difficult to pick up bad habits such as smoking, over eating, eating chocolates, chewing gum or even drinking too many cups of coffee and tea. The more we resort to these the more we want to go on with them all. And if we don't continue with the same quota of each, we feel unhappy and some people could even turn violent and depressed. One of the most widely known habits is drinking cheap liquor - arrack, by the labour class and villagers all over India. Even women consume liquor. Similarly, tobacco. Smoking is a habit difficult to give up. They say, once a smoker always a smoker till the age of 50.

The best way to lead a healthier life is not to get into any of the above bad habits. Think before you adopt any of them. It is easier to desist from taking the first step than to retreat from a habit that has taken deep roots into your system.

Note making:
1. Easy to form bad habits.
2. Examples in cities and villages.
3. Once addicted difficult to give up.
4. How to keep away from bad habits.

2. Summarise the following passage with the help of the notes given at the end.

Much importance is being given to Education in present time. Millions of children attend school now while it was not so some 50 years back. In ancient times, children went to a guru and learnt moral science orally from him. But, today they learn many subjects in school under a set of teachers. Teachers would use Maps for learning History and Geography; diagrams are a must for learning Science; figures for Mathematics. School teachers use more effective methods to impart training. This type of teaching is called "Visual education". Films/video clips appeal to the mind and the students not only become more attentive but also pick up the lessons easily. Films are useful in educating the villagers as well. Films on "small pox and polio" make a deep impression on them and they take the necessary precautions against them voluntarily. Verbal teaching may become tiresome boring and if they are supplemented with films, slides and other visual aids, the listeners take a greater interest in the subject. Similarly in schools. Films and videos have become aids of great value in the field of education.

Notes:
1. Education and its importance and its impact on children.
2. Improvement in the system of education - maps, diagram, figures and visual aids.
3. How films have influenced learning and understanding - effect on villagers.
4. Difference in impact between oral teaching and other visual aids.

3.   Paraphrase the following passage with the help of the notes given at the end:

Medicos advise that we should include more and more fruits in our daily diet to ensure sound health. It is true that some of the fruits are beyond the pocket of common people. But, there are many varieties of fruits which are available at reasonable and affordable prices. So, it is for us to go in for such fruits and consume them liberally. One of them is grapes. The origin of the fruit is a matter of debate. Some botanists believe that it was first found in Armenia; from there it went to West Asia, Europe, North Africa, India and other countries. Then, each country developed its own method of cultivating grapes in their vineyards. As a result, grapes from different countries have different tastes. There are others who believe that Central Asia was the first home of grapes. In India, grapes are grown in Kashmir and northern Uttar Pradesh. In the South, Pune, Coorg, Aurangabad and Hyderabad are well known for their grapes. In some districts in Tamil Nadu also, grapes are grown. Some Indian varieties are seedless. There are big and small varieties also. One could get grapes almost round the year. The production may be very high in some months.

Notes:

1.   Why fruits in our daily diet?
2.   Origin of grapes - two beliefs: Armenia and Central Asia.
3.   Different countries provide different tastes.
4.   Where grown in India - Kashmir, UP, Pune, Coorg, Aurangabad, Hyderabad and Tamil Nadu districts.
5.   Seedless varieties.
6.   When available; some lean seasons and some plentiful.

4.   Paraphrase the following passage:

One usually tends to judge the quality of a book by its cover. Sometimes a good preface or a reviewer's short report at the back may influence a buyer. But, what really matters is the inside contents of a book. So it is with any product and more so if it is a consumer item. The manufacturers spend a lot of money and time in designing the outer look of a product, such as a powder tin, a toothpaste tube, cooking oil and so on to make a buyer fall in love at first sight. The way a consumer product has been packed, the uniqueness of its shape, the choice of its colours, all have a remarkable influence on the consumer. In fact, spending lakhs of rupees on advertisements would fail to make the necessary impact if the product is not attractively packaged. Even for the products that have become popular and enjoy a stable and sustained market, their manufacturers will periodically go in for a new look from time to time. When you walk into a shop and if you see an attractively packed item, looking colourful and glossy with all the essential details about the item shown on the packet, won't you feel tempted to buy it?

Now, for the other side of the picture, if the manufacturer had shown no interest in the mode of packaging used for his product, the product would surely fail to impress and he would have to bite the dust even if he had spent a fortune for advertisement purposes through several media. But if his product is good, he will pick up sales in course of time. In the long run, such a manufacturer will not be a loser.

The outer look may backfire if the contents inside are of low quality or rotten. Consumers have become wise and alert. A manufacturer cannot sell any longer a bad product with attractive covers. All the advertisements would prove wasteful if the product itself is unacceptable to a consumer. Same way a person who is charmed by the attractive presentation will not buy the product a second time if the quality is substandard.

Note making:

1. Cover of a book; contents of a book
2. Consumer items - packing, colour of outer cover, will attract a customer.
3. If the contents bad, good packing will backfire. Manufacturer will suffer loss.
4. Good product, badly packed, will also pick up in course of time. Consumers are wise and alert.
5. Consumers cannot be fooled if the quality of the product is good.

5. Summarise the following passage without any note making:

Home-makers who diet usually are conscious about food and food preparations without their own knowledge. They cannot open any magazine without seeing page after page of advertisement of food products, usually pictured in luscious colours. If they turn to an article on homemaking, they will undoubtedly be attracted to the long passages on creative cooking and table presentation of delicious meals. No matter how determined they are, dieters can hardly avoid being shaken by the delightful descriptions and illustrations. If they avoid such obvious traps and turn to the newspaper, even there they will find a thick food section with enticing recipes and picture of the final products. Perhaps dieters need the help of a family censor who could go through all the reading matters and remove the temping allusions on food. Or, the researchers might produce some kind of gadget either to flip over the pages on food at great speed or demagnetise the mind of the dieting readers in such a way as to make the printed lines on food look blurred and distorted. Then they might find their dieting much easier.

6. Paraphrase without any kind of notes:

Many upper middle class Indian families would have one of the four categories of pets in their home. The first choice is for some kind of dog. The next preference is for cats. Dog lovers sometime are amazed that anyone could even touch an animal like a cat. The third category of pets is birds. They include the large and impressive birds who reside alone in a big cage with some freedom. The last choice is fish, colourful fishes inside a water tank. Almost all high class and upper middle class householders would invariably keep one of these pets regardless of whether they have children or not. Any pet in a home moulds the character of children into loving and kind human beings as they grow along. The relationship they could develop with a pet dog is amazing indeed. As days pass by the children would get so attached to a dog that they cannot live without seeing the dog first thing in the morning or the first to be greeted when they return from school. And if by some chance the dog gets lost, they would be devastated and refuse to eat or do any homework until the father runs out, trace the dear fellow and bring him back. Why did the dog run away? Well, he would like to have a look at the world around him. All pet dogs love to roam about once in a while.

7. Summarise the following passage without notes:

Why would anyone enter politics? Why would anyone give up the ease of private life to struggle with the obligations of public life? Even politicians find it difficult to answer these questions. But whatever the answer of each individual politician, the struggle - and the obligations - are real. Politicians, once elected, are thereafter obliged to consider the moral and social standards of those who elected them, and their behaviour must reflect those standards. In fact ,one veteran old time politician has said, there are cardinal rules of behaviour to observe if one wishes to succeed in politics. Politicians should marry young and stay married ,upholding the sanctity of the home by spending as much time as possible in the bosom of the family. They should retain strong and active ties with the religion into which they were born or inducted in, and, most helpful of all, politicians should spend as much as possible associating with those who voted for them and demonstrating their appreciation of the roots from which their lives have grown.

8. Develop a brief, readable and logical summary out of the notes give below:

    (a) Low percentage of attendance in village classes - a big problem.
    (b) Absenteeism and its causes in village environment.
    (c) How to overcome these; how to attract village students to the school.
    (d) How should teachers motivate them and also their parents.
    (e) Shouldn't the style of teaching be different in village schools? How and what are they?
    (f) How to reduce school drop outs.

9. Develop a readable and logical summary out of the following hints:

    (a) Salary drawn must be high- buying and enjoying better things in life.
    (b) Credit cards, hire purchase systems to be promoted. How they will help individuals to improve their quality of life.
    (c) Incentives for enhanced income. Extra work during off time and holidays. Part time work.
    (d) Happy homes make a happy nation.
    (e) But, any extra income should come out of productive work. Only then the nation will benefit.

10. Develop a readable summary or paragraph out of the following hints:

    (a) Two student friends; one dull and the other very bright.
    (b) The dull is from a rich family and the other poor family.
    (c) Their parents become friends.
    (d) Regardless of status, they visit each other's house.
    (e) Poor father picks up many good things.
    (f) Both fathers stand for election.
    (g) The poor father gets elected by a large margin.

Chapter 63

LETTER WRITING

Introduction

Broadly speaking, there are 3 types of letters as follows:

(a) Informal letters

(b) (i) Formal letters   -   Official letters

     (ii) Formal letters   -   Commercial/Business letters

(c) Demi official letters

Formal letters will fall under two categories – Official and Business.

No matter which type of letter you would be writing, each should have 5 parts. They are,

(a)	The heading (The letter head)	:	to contain the writer's address, date and file reference.
(b)	Salutation	:	this will usually start with "Dear…."
(c)	The body	:	to contain the main message/contents.
(d)	Leave taking	:	this will be in the form of, "Yours faithfully/ sincerely/truly" preceded by some kind of personal greetings.
(e)	Signature	:	All letters must be signed (show the name of the writer or his/her designation if necessary only)

INFORMAL LETTERS

Any letter written to a friend or a member of the family will fall under this category. We may also name it, "Private letter". Three model letters, along with foot notes, are shown below:

A private letter

(to a close friend)

T.R. Balachandran

560 Kendriya vihar
Velappan chavadi
Chennai. 600 077
15 Aug 2001

My dear Muthu,

How are you old chap? Why no letter from you for ages? Surely you haven't forgotten how to write letters, have you? Ha! Ha!

All is well with me and my parents.

Sugu is appearing for an interview for 'air hostess' training. She is fascinated with airliners and flying. Hope she gets through although Dad was against the idea.

Remember good old Chetan, who was in the Commerce group in college, I bumped into him the other day. He was on a day's visit to Chennai; at present he is an accounts manager with some firm in Mumbai. He remembered you with his good wishes.

Am planning a holiday in Kodaikanal next summer. Why don't you join me? Write to me immediately if you want to know further details about the Kodaikanal trip. OK?

With regards,

Yours truly,

Bala

Notes:

1. Give your own address on the top right and also the date.

2. On the left top, you may write your name. If your friend could recognise your handwriting, you may omit this.

3. Start the letter always, "My dear ..." followed by the name you call him by. Here Balachandran has addressed the friend as 'Muthu' though his full name is Muthusamy.

4. The body contents need not follow any sequence; write as thoughts come to your mind.

5. The letter is always ended with, "Yours truly" or "Yours affectionately" or "Your loving friend". Being a private a letter, it may show some intimacy as well. Accordingly, you may close the body of the letter with, "With regards or kind regards" or if you are very intimate with the other as, "With love/ with lots of love/affections" and so on..

6. Sign the letter by the pet name by which the addressee has been calling you.

7. The full name and address of your friend are not shown on the letter. These details will go on the envelope for the benefit of the post office. You may also give your own name and address on the backside of the postal envelope, if necessary.

A private letter

(An invitation to a friend)

T.Samuel Raj

22 Bethlehem
Colony,
Ambur. 635 802
01 Oct 2001

My dear Sri,

I am celebrating my 17ᵗʰ birthday on 5 Oct 01. I shall be happy if you could attend it. A number of our mutual friends are attending it. The party is at 5 p.m.

With affections,

Your loving friend,

Sd/- Sam

Notes:

1. You sign the letter by the name (pet name, nick name) known to the addressee.
2. The address of the addressee will be written on the envelope.
3. The leave taking here is a little intimate – With affections.

A private letter

(To the father)

A.Sugirtha

134 Mehta Nagar
Madhavaram
Chennai. 600 051
18 April 2001

My dear Pappa,

I just finished my last paper.

The school is having its annual day on 22 April. Would you and Mamma be able to attend it at 4 p.m? Thereafter you could take me home for the summer vacation.

Uncle and aunty are fine here and they have looked after me very well.

With love,

Yours lovingly,

Sd/ Sugi

Notes:

1. When you write a letter to a member in the family and a senior person, you address the other as, "My dear Appa/Daddy/Mummy/Uncle/Brother" or by whatever title you call them with. You could also modify the salutation like, "My dearest Amma or Dearest Appa". Never address a family senior by his/her formal or informal name.
2. The leave taking should be somewhat intimate. Since Sugirtha is writing to her father, she ends it with, "With love" and not with, "With regards/ kind regard"
3. Sign the letter by the pet name used by the parents; even names like Candy, Bubbles etc.

A private letter

(A thanking letter to an uncle)

21 Mahatma Gandhi Road,
Bangalore. 560 001
15 September 2001

My dear Uncle,

Thank you for your beautiful birthday gift sent through your friend. It was very kind of you indeed.

I had been planning to buy a good dictionary myself and your gift came just on time. In order to improve my written English I was on the lookout for a dictionary that gave not only meanings but also sample sentences. And yours is the best choice to meet my requirement. Thank you very much once again.

With love,

Yours affectionately,

Prasant.

Address on the envelope

Mr. G.Swaminathan
3 CIT colony
Chennai. 600 035

A private letter

(A condolence letter to a teacher)

Shilpa Reddy

15 Ganga Reddy Street
Egmore
Chennai. 600 008
6 October 2001

My dear Lecturer,

I write this letter to express my deep condolence at the passing away of your dear father. It would indeed be a blow to yourself and other members in the family.

I pray to God that He would give you the needed consolation and comfort to put up with this great personal loss.

But, I am sure you would overcome this tragedy very fast because you are a strong willed person. And, I am proud of you on account of this disposition.

With respects,

Yours truly,
Shilpa

Notes:

1. One could write this letter as a "Demi official letter" as well. But since it is from a student to her favourite lecturer and with a view to showing some intimacy, it has been written as a private letter.

2. Just because it is a private letter and to a senior person outside the family, don't take any undue liberties. You should be restrained in your emotions and still respectful. "Dear Lecturer" sounds better than "Madam or Dear Madam."

3. This is a special kind of occasion. So, follow the format shown in this model letter including for any congratulatory variety.

FORMAL LETTERS - Official

A formal letter is written between two organisations or between an individual and an organisation.

A formal letter

(From one department to another in the Government)

GOVERNMENT OF INDIA

CABINET SECRETARIAT

DIRECTORATE OF PUBLIC GRIEVANCES

SARDAR PATEL BHAWAN

NEW DELHI. 110 001

Tele: 3363733, FAX 91-011-3345637

DPG/I/1999/0068(4A)   2-6-2000

New India Insurance Co
Poonamalle branch
661, Trunk Road
Chennai. 600 056

Dear Sir,

Refund of excess amount

Further to our letter under reference dated 30-5-2000

You are hereby directed to refund an amount of Rs 53 (Rupees Fifty three only) to Mr. A.Mazumdar. It has been finally proved that your calculation of the insurance amount due from Mr.A.Mazumdar has not been found to be correct. In the circumstances, the insurer is entitled to a refund.

A copy of your letter addressed to Mr.Mazumdar may please be endorsed to this department for information.

Thanking you,

Yours faithfully,

Sd/ B.C.D

(Y.P.Yadav)

Under Secretary

Notes:

1. Some orgnisations may give their own address on top and in the middle of the page. Most Govt departments follow this style.

2. The designation of the officer signing the letter must be given. In this case, the addressee could send his reply to the Under Secretary, Y.P.Yadav. Accordingly, the reply letter will reach the Under Secretary promptly.

3. In certain cases, other than the government circles, the name and designation of the signatory may not be stated at all and someone might sign "for Managing Director/ General Manager" etc. What is important is, that the letter must bear some signature; only then it would be a valid correspondence.

4. The format will be the same if a Govt department sends a letter to an individual.

A formal letter

(From an individual to an organisation)

S.S. Adhikari

D 30 , Sector 32

NOIDA. 201 303

UP

15 April 2001

Principal

H.I.E.T

16 St Thomas Mount

Chennai. 600 016

Sir,

Admission in Aircraft maintenance course

I wish to seek admission for my son, Mahesh Chaturvedi, in your "Aircraft maintenance course". Mahesh has passed his 12th Standard from an English medium school in New Delhi with 78 % marks.

Kindly forward your prospectus along with a copy of the application. I have enclosed herewith a bank draft for Rs 250.

Thanking you,

Yours faithfully,

Sd/ S.S.Adhikari

A formal letter

(A formal application for a job)

From

     Mr.Matthew John
     235 G.S.T. Road
     Chennai. 600 032

To

     M/s Kothari Bros Ltd
     23 Sowcarpet
     Chennai. 600 001

Sir,

Post of accountant

This is with reference to your advertisement in THE HINDU dated 13 Sep 2001.

I wish to apply for the post of an Accountant in your esteemed Company.

I am 25 years of age and a B Com graduate from Loyola college, Chennai. I have 2 years' work-experience as an Assistant Accountant in a medium Company. I am fairly well versed in all branches of Finance. Better prospects, is the purpose of this application in your Company. My application therefore may please be evaluated from that angle.

If I am appointed for the post in your organisation, I assure you of my best performance to your entire satisfaction.

     Thanking you,

                                       Yours faithfully,

Chennai - 32

14 Sep 2001   Sd/ M.John

Notes:

1. The layout is different here since such applications will be usually written on plain paper. The salutation is usually, "Sir". Avoid "Dear Sir".

2. Write the application in First person and in Direct speech. Don't brag about your experience, abilities, sincerity etc. And don't humble yourself much either. Be modest about all these. Many employers would be able to judge you by the way you had drafted your application. Don't go in for ready made application nor one written by someone else. The contents should be your own and of your own style.

3. Here, the place and date are given at the bottom left end.

A formal letter

(A complaint)

From

Kendriya Vihar Residents' Association
Velappan chavadi
Chennai. 600 077

To

The Officer-in-charge
Thiruverkadu Police station
Thiruverkadu
Chennai. 600 077

Sir,

Theft

A resident occupying Flat No 529 in this colony has complained of theft of his Hero Honda motor cycle, black colour, Regn No TN 20 A 0375 on the night of 20/21 Aug 2001. The vehicle had been parked in front of his flat and locked.

You are requested to take suitable action to trace the lost vehicle.

The owner is Mr. M.Thandavan. He is unable to give any clue on the theft nor was he in the habit of lending his vehicle to anyone.

Thanking you,

Yours faithfully,
Sd/ XYZ

Chennai - 77
21 Sep 2001

Secretary

Notes:

1. Although a formal letter, the layout is different because it has been written on plain paper instead of the letter head of the Association.
2. The complaint has been written in Third person because it is the Secretary who has lodged the complaint.

Formal letters from Students

Students may need to write a letter to their class teacher/Head of Department/ Principal about some personal matter, especially leave. They too must write only formal letters. Here are two model letters.

From

    A. Madhavan

    Std XI

    2 Maharani colony,

    Chennai – 7

To

    Class teacher, Std XI

    St Peter's Higher secondary school

    Perambur

    Chennai – 7

Sir,

Leave of absence

I am required to be present at my elder sister's wedding at Trichinopoly for 2 days excluding Sunday.

Therefore I request you to grant me 2 days leave of absence from 15 Oct to 16 Oct 2001.

    Thanking you,

                                 Yours faithfully

Chennai - 7

15 Oct 2001   Sd/ A.Madhavan

Notes:

1. Students should not take leave unnecessarily unless there are good reasons.

2. Though they are not entitled for leave like other employees in a Govt office or Private sector industry etc, still they must apply for leave of absence. As otherwise they would be marked "absent". A student is required to have a specific percentage of attendance before they are permitted to take the examination. "Leave of absence" for legitimate reasons is better than "absence without leave".

3. The letter may be addressed to the Principal also.

4. Even if you are sick at home or are admitted in a hospital, you must apply for leave. This is a normal courtesy on the part of students.

Letters to Editor

A citizen is entitled to address a letter to the Editor of a Newspaper to bring to the notice of other readers or the concerned authorities, of a matter of common interest.

One cannot write such letters about personal complaint/personal problem. If the contents come within the purview/ policy of the newspaper, the Editor will publish it.

Here are two model letters from students. Note the format and language to be followed.

A. Saravanan

5 High tower colony,
Neelankarai
Chennai. 600 041
15 December 2001

The Editor
THE NEW INDIAN EXPRESS
Chennai. 600 002

Sir,

Frequent power failures

Lately there have been frequent power failure in Neelankarai area especially during night time. The duration has been sometimes as long as 4 hours. Lest the student community is affected in their preparation for their half-yearly examinations during this period, the Electricity Board authorities are requested to be good enough to maintain continuous power supply in our area.

Thanking you,

Yours faithfully,
Sd/- A.Saravanan

Notes:

1. Letters to the Editor must be crisp and to the point. Don't beat about the bush. If you do, the Editor would mercilessly cut out all the irrelevant stuff.

2. Newspaper is a good medium to bring certain points of common interest to the notice of many people in 'one go'. But this privilege should not be misused by frivolous complaints. In any case, the Editors wouldn't pass such letters for publication.

3. Use Passive voice only; Active voice may sound offensive.

From

    Soundari Pandiyan
    C/o G.S.Pandian
    Staff Quarters
    Karthikeyan College, Poonamalle
    Chennai. 600 054

To

    Editor
    The Hindu
    Chennai. 600 002

Sir,

<u>Clash of Examination dates</u>

The Entrance examination for IIT and TNPCEE have been scheduled for 29 and 30th of April this year. Since many students would like to appear for both the examinations, it is requested that the dates may please be shifted suitably. It should not be difficult for the TN Govt to stagger its dates.

    Thanking you,

Yours faithfully,

Chennai. 54
30 Mar 2001

Sd/- Soundari Pandiyan

- - - - -

FORMAL LETTERS – Commercial/Business

Introduction

Business letters fall under the category of "Formal letters". While the official formal letters are written using a formal language and always to the point without being verbose, the Business letters could be long-winded with warm phrases and compliments.

In Business matters, it is essential to keep your customers in good humour and towards this goal, one could adopt any tactics.

Business letters, written in good and perfect style will not only enhance the image of the Company/Industry but also fetch more business.

Strangely, nearly 98% of the Business letters/correspondences in India are written in English. Even small traders adopt English. E-mail has become the order of the day in present time, especially with regard to trade overseas. All e-mails are sent only in English.

ESSENTIALS OF A BUSINESS LETTER

General

Business letters are written to industrial houses, commercial organisations, departmental stores, shop keepers and so on. They may be in the form of "Quotations, sales letters, insurance letters, memoranda, import/export letters" etc.

Business letters are mini ambassadors that establish a pleasant rapport between the writer and recipient. A good ambassador brings two parties together and to a closer understanding as well.

Every business letter should furnish all important information to a client and also be designed in such a language which would influence his/her whole attitude. If they fail to make an impression on the recipient, they could no longer be considered business letters.

It should be positive in content. Even if you have to convey a negative information, it could be done in a **positive** way, something like this,

> Thank you for your valuable order. The merchandise you had ordered will be despatched to you positively before July. We sincerely hope this little delay would not disturb your time frame in any serious way.

Compare the above "positive type" with the one given below, which is utterly negative:

> Thank you for your valuable order but we are unable to send the merchandise till some later date.

Don't you think the customer will be put off by the second letter? Is there any positive indication that the merchandise will go out by any particular date?

The YOU rule

Use more YOUs and I's and WE's. You would charm the reader. Take the following sentence,

> "Thank you for your letter. We now know what exactly you need ..."

The reader would feel elated and elevated at such wordings, won't he?

Cheerful tone

A business letter ought to leave a pleasant feeling in the recipient's mind. A dull and insipid letter will not only annoy a customer but also that he/she may never turn to you ever again. Use warm phrases like these,

    (a)   It is/was a pleasure
    (b)   You will be happy to know that ....
    (c)   We appreciate very much your ....

Courtesy

Not simple courtesies but double-decked courtesies are to be used in business correspondences. Courtesy pays high dividends. In fact, it is an absolute must. But it should not amount to flattery or servility. It means, a dignified approach to a customer. You must buy or win over your customer through pleasant compliments; even if you have to say an unpleasant thing, it must be conveyed in a roundabout and unoffending way.

For instance, if your customer has made a mistake, don't tell him so directly, but in indirect words such as, "omission" or "oversight" and never by the words "error" or "mistake".

If some information is 'wrong', say it as, "this doesn't seem to correspond to the facts ..."

The punch line of courtesy is, "never be offensive, be nice about it yet not making an enemy of your client."

Style

Be natural in your English. Let the language have a smooth and natural flow in it along with music if possible. But while you are dealing with a high profile client, do use high standard and sophisticated English to impress upon him/them that you are no less in fluency and style.

Clarity

Whatever you have to say, even if you say it in an indirect and roundabout way, be clear, very clear actually, lest your client misunderstand or misinterpret your sentences. Nothing ever should be vague.

GUIDELINES TO WRITE EFFECTIVE BUSINESS LETTERS

1. In the first instance, be clear about the contents/main body of the letter. This would call for, collection of all relevant materials/data and arranging them in some logical order.

2. Until you are fully experienced, always go in for a 'draft' initially. Correct the draft and then ask for the fair copy (copies) for signature. The draft may be produced through dictation to your steno or in your own handwriting. A draft letter means, it is put up to you in typed form – the contents only without the address and on a plain paper. (It should not be typed on your Company's letter head. Typists and Stenos know how to type and put up draft letters for 'approval'.)

3. All letters should be in 3 distinct compartments like in a composition. They are – INTRODUCTION, MAIN BODY and CONCLUSION.

4. If the letter is of more than one paragraph, number the paragraphs serially from the second one onwards. The first para is not to be numbered.

5. While the CONCLUSION para in a Composition will sum up in a nutshell, the contents of the main body, in Business letters it would be in the form of "What is required from the addressee."

6. Just as there is a leave taking in official/personal letters, there is also a special type of leave taking in Business letters. They will be something like these,

      (a)   Awaiting your order/reply.

      (b)   Looking forward to hearing from you soon.

      (c)   We shall be glad to hear from you soon.

      (d)   Assuring you of our prompt action.

Shall we now study one specimen Business letter, analyse it, compare it with Official letters in terms of the Format and note the differences?

@ **MODERN HITECH EQUIPMENTS**

Tele: 265 9219. Fax:265 4848

* 90 Leo Estate
Pallikarni
Chennai. 601 302

Our ref: MHE/Q-1/L-S-3/625/01

$ (Date)

M/s J.S.L. Towers
M.G.Road
Bangalore. 560 001

+

Dear Sirs,

% **Aluminium ladders - Catalogue**

We understand that you are a leading manufacturer of Aluminium ladders.

2. Kindly send a copy of your latest catalogue of Domestic and Industrial aluminium ladders along with your price list for whole sale purchase.

3. As we have not done any business with you previously, be good enough to tell us about your supply terms such as whether you require advance payment or you would send the 'despatch documents' through the Bank etc.

4. Incidentally, we deal with Laboratory instruments, Laboratory glasswares etc of high quality. If we could be of any service to you, we shall welcome your enquiries.

&

5. Assuring you of our best attention on all matters.

Yours faithfully,
Sd/-
Manager (Mktg)
for Modern Hitech

Notes:

@   Every Business organisation must have its own printed letter head. (If you write a letter on ordinary plain paper, you would paint a very poor image of your Company) Along with the name of your organisation/company, give the telephone numbers, FAX No, e-mail address as shown above.

*   At the right hand side, give your own address along with the date of signature which may be typed or written by hand.

$ On the same line as the date, give on the left hand side your file reference and letter reference number.

+   The salutation to be always, "Dear Sirs" or "Sirs". The letter S must be in capital.

%   It would be useful if you give the subject matter and underlined before you start the main body. This will help the Receipt Desk at the receiving end to send the letter to the correct department concerned. As otherwise, he/she would have to read the whole letter to identify the dealing Dept.

Main body

Number all the paragraphs in the main body from the second one onwards as shown. Observe all points under the "Essentials of a Business letter" in designing your paras.

&.For leave taking, some organization may use "Thanking you" in addition to the usual business phrases." To close the letter without 'leave taking' is not good business ethics.

#. Every letter should be signed by some official on behalf of the organization/company. It is a good practice to show the designation of the signatory so that the reply could be addressed to his department.

Here are some typical Business letters and replies thereof. Note how polite and pleasant the contents are in tone.

New Delhi
20 December 2001

Ref: PG/10/2001/105

M/s Games & Toys
Chandni Chowk
Delhi

Dear Sirs,

<u>Supply of plastic toys</u>

You would be glad to know that we have lately received a large stock of plastic toys from different manufacturers. All of them are of excellent quality and are guaranteed to last for a long time despite rough uses.

2. Please find enclosed the price list of the items we are to ready to offer.

3. It will be good if you could send your representative for direct examination of our goods and placement of an order as well. (This suggestion, since we both are at Delhi). We shall arrange to deliver the goods ordered at your shop/godown or wherever, in our own transport.

4. We offer a special discount of 10% if the order exceeds Rs 2000 in a single consignment.

5. We look forward to hearing from you.

Yours faithfully,
Sd/-
Managing partner

COLOURFUL PLASTICS LTD
6 Covent Garden, Safdarjang, New Delhi
Tele : ………. Fax: …….. E-mail: …….

- - - - - - -

Note:

In the above case, the name of the Company, address etc appear at the bottom. This is also an accepted practice.

FREEDOM SOFTWARE CO., LTD
17, G.Menon Road, Kodambakkam
Chennai. 600 024. Tele: 4838390, 4818328

Our Ref: FS-1/Cust/ SW-1/ 231   12 Sep 2001

Intel. System
23 Ritherdon Road
Chennai. 600 007

Dear Sir,

Special software for "Intel system"

Please refer to your IS/SW/P-II/124 dated 9 Sep 2001.

2. We are happy to inform you that the Software you had ordered is ready for your examination. Kindly send your expert to test it at our premises before we finalise the project.

3. Assuring you of our co-operation at all times.

Thanking you,

Yours faithfully,
Sd/ A.B.C
for Freedom software Co Ltd

Notes:

1. Every organisation will have its own "Letter head" which will show in print, the name of the organisation, its address, telephone Nos, FAX, E-mail address etc. These details may be on top, or on the right hand side or even at the bottom of the sheet.

2. Only the date of signature/despatch is typed on the right hand side as shown.

3. The salutation is always as, "Dear Sir," or "Sir,"

4. In official letters, always mention the File reference No. so that the letter could be connected up at both ends. This necessity, since hundreds of letters will be received by every organisation and are required to be sent to the relevant dealing file.

5. The leave taking in a formal letter is always with, "Thanking you." Some organisations may omit this or add along with it, one of the pleasant business phrases as shown in this letter.

6. The language is formal and to the point.

7. The signatory hasn't mentioned his name nor the designation. In such cases, the reply is to be addressed to the organisation i.e. Freedom Software Co Ltd

8. In all formal letters, it would be helpful to mention the 'subject' before the main body.

Don't expect every transaction in business would be smooth and dinky-dory. There will be problems with some customers and there would be problematic customers too. Develop the art of dealing with complaints from your customers in a very nice and diplomatic way. Here are some specimens – the main body only.

A complaint from a private citizen about the goods supplied
Complaint

Two days back, I visited your grand shop and ordered 5 Conjeevaram silk sarees. You were kind enough to pack them and deposit the package in my car parked outside your shop.

2. On reaching home, I found that there were only 4 silk sarees and one cotton saree of low quality. You would recall that I had paid for 5 silk sarees at the rate of Rs 4500 each. One cotton saree seems to have been packed probably by mistake by your salesman.

3. I request you to replace the wrong saree immediately. Kindly indicate the method how this could be done.

4. I would appreciate an early response.

Yours faithfully,

Sd/- Mrs. Shakuntala

Reply

We have your letter dated ... and sincerely regret our grave error in the packing of your Conjeevaram sarees.

2. As a matter of fact, our salesman did realise the mistake immediately but before we could do anything you had driven away. And, we didn't have your address.

3. It is agreed that such lapses should never have taken place with esteemed customers like your good self. We are really sorry for the mishap.

4. To set the matter right and not to inconvenience you any further, we are sending our salesman to your house along with 5 Conjeevaram sarees from which you may kindly select one. In case you do not like any out of the lot, we shall send another batch of 10 sarees. The cotton saree may please be handed over to the salesman.

5. With deep regrets and also with an assurance of better service when you visit our emporium again.

Yours faithfully,
Sd/-
Sales Manager
Golden saree emporium

Notes:

1. In business matters, one must readily accept the errors/lapses without giving any kind of excuses or explanations. Here, Golden emporium has done it so gracefully.
2. Besides tendering apologies, the emporium has gone out of the way to retrieve the situation instead of asking the lady customer to visit the shop once again. As a result, Mrs. Shakuntala would never step into any shop other than Golden emporium for her future shopping.
3. In business matters, customers are your life-source; never antagonise them; win them over and keep them within your closed palm, as it were, by good etiquette and personal relationship.

- - - -

Here is another specimen wherein the customer is surely at fault but see how the seller manages the situation and wins over the customer.

Complaint

I purchased a high priced camera from your shop vide your receipt No.... dated ....

2. But, I was horrified to see blurred pictures out of the very first film roll. Surely there is something terribly wrong with the camera you had supplied to me. I never expected this. Will you please exchange it and at the earliest?

Notes:

1. The customer has every right to show his annoyance openly; he doesn't have to couch them in sweet words! After paying Rs 5000 for it, who wouldn't feel worked up at seeing awful pictures?
2. See how the Camera firm deals with this customer.

Reply

Thank you for your letter dated ....

2. We can understand how disappointed you must have felt when you saw bad fruits of your first effort with your first film roll with our camera. It is a real let down when some good shots go to garbage.

3. To get a clear idea, we consulted our technical department along with some of your photos and the negatives. They examined your exposures carefully and felt that the actual trouble lies in your lens adjustment.

4. Rather than ask you to return the camera to us for replacement, the technical department has suggested that you take it to our 'Service center' in your city at ...(address given) for adjustment of the lens, if required. They would also give you the necessary technical advice on using the complex camera. We are writing to the service center separately about your complaint and would request them to forward the Bill to us.

5. We are sure that your camera would surely function perfectly after the adjustment and your shots would come out superb by following the Center's technical guidelines. Do not hesitate to approach us if you experience any further problems with the camera.

Notes:

1. The supplier knows that there is nothing wrong with the camera and the trouble lay with the 'photographer'. It is a sophisticated camera (not the pre-focussed or with fixed focus type) wherein one has to set up a number of controls precisely. If not done properly, the pictures would surely come out wonky. This is exactly what had happened at the customer's end. But how to tell the customer that he hadn't handled the camera properly.
2. The 'lens adjustment' is jut a cover plan. It didn't need any. This is for the customer's consumption. Have you noticed that the supplier has not endorsed a copy of the letter to the service center? Why did they write to the center separately? Probably in that letter, they had asked the center to give a few lessons to the customer on how to use the camera and   set up its numerous controls.
3. This is a very tactful action. The shop has not closed its doors from replacing the camera, quoting all kinds of terms and conditions. They would have replaced it willingly if the complaint made was genuine. But the shop knew that the customer would be happy after his visit to the center. Win over a customer and make sure that he is satisfied with your product. Do remember that a satisfied customer is your PRO without salary!

DEMI OFFICIAL LETTERS

A DO letter is half official and half personal. Note, it is 'personal' and not 'private'.

A DO letter is like an express train and will reach the table of the person concerned directly and without delay. Since a DO letter will be addressed by name, no one else is permitted to open it, such as the Office superintendent or the Receipt clerk. (Incidentally, a formal letter is always to be addressed by Appointment/Designation of an officer or to a particular department). The letter in unopened form is to be handed over to the addressee. A DO letter would normally bring in a prompt reply because it has in it a personal rapport.

2 Model letters have been given below:

A DO letter
(Between two officials)

STUART CONSTRUCTIONS
301 Chengalrayan street
Chennai. 600 099
Tele: 439 1204. E-mail: stuart@usa.net

K.Sandeep
Chief Engineer

DO/SC/Cont -5 / 201   10 Oct 2001

My dear Steve,

We submitted our quotation for construction of an 8 storey residential cum commercial complex in Chennai vide our letter Con-5/VII/Quo/ 39 dated 12 Aug 2001.

We do not seem to have received any response from your end. For that matter, we have not even received a formal acknowledgement of our quotation. We are a little anxious about this.

According to our knowledge, you have not sought quotations from any other builders. In the circumstances, I wonder why there is total silence from your end. I am sure the reason is that someone is sitting on the file.

For our old time's sake, could you involve yourself in this case and chase it up? We have spent a few lakhs on the survey and preparation of the quotations. This cost is quite a bit for us, you see? Please do keep this in mind.

With kind regards,

   * *How are Nalini and the baby girl?. Is Candy keeping you occupied when you go home?*

Yours sincerely,
Sd/ Sandy

Mr.Steve Norton
Manager, Sales
Electronics Home Appliances
Anna Salai
Chennai. 600 002

Notes:

1. On the Company's letter head, type your own name and designation. Some organisations may have letter heads with printed names for DO letters.

2. Sandeep and Norton have been college mates and know each other well, hence Sandeep salutes the other as "My dear ....." and uses his pet name and also ends the letter with the name used by Norton for him. You can take such liberty only when you know the other intimately.

3. See the wording of the main body and the personal touch Sandeep throws in it. You can use such a language only on person-to-person basis and never on official basis at all.

4. After leave taking (With kind regards), Sandeep adds a little personal note about the family. This part* must be written by hand only and will not appear on the file copy at all. This is optional but see the dividend such scribbling would bring - Steve would feel elated, wouldn't he? And would ensure that the quotation is accepted and replied thereon.

5. The letter is always ended with, "Yours sincerely". In certain organisations, the custom may be to write "Yours sincerely" by hand.

6. The addressee's details are given at the bottom left. This is one major difference between a DO letter and a formal letter.

- - - -

A DO letter
(From an individual to an officer)

S.Arun Menon

363 Kendriya vihar
Velappan chavadi
Chennai. 600 077
11 Sep 2001

Dear Mr. Elangovan,

I am writing this letter for a personal favour. We have not met personally at all but I have heard quite a lot about you.

My servant maid, Lakshmi, says that she had lent Rs 500 to one Swaminathan, a security guard working in your factory, some 3 months bank. Both of them live in the same area. But Swaminathan has been avoiding her for some days now. Nor has he returned the loan amount even in part. In fact, he hasn't said a word about it to Lakshmi.

I wonder if you can do something about it. Lakshmi is a very sincere worker and very honest too. I am sure she is telling the truth.

With kind regards,

Yours sincerely,
Sd/-S.A.Menon

Mr.V.Elangovan
Personnel Manager
Modern Motor Industries
Poonamalle
Chennai. 600 056

Notes:

1. This DO letter is to an unknown person. One could write a DO letter to anyone. Here the issue is such, one could sort it out only by involving the employers at the demi official level. Hence one employer takes the case up with another employer at the officer level.

2. Since Menon doesn't know Elangovan at all, salutes him as Mr.Elangovan. He cannot do this in any other way.

3. Accordingly the language has to be somewhat formal and to the point.

4. Leave taking is in the conventional way. There's no question of Menon adding any personal note.

5. The other methods of salutations, between two unknown persons, are, "My dear Professor/Principal/Bishop/Father Rector/General/Brigadier" or "Dear Professor John, Dear Dr Raju, Dear Colonel Swamy" and so on. The latter salutations are to be preferred.

Reports

It is the duty of every citizen to bring to the notice of the Police any occurrence you have witnessed personally so as to enable the Police carry out the investigation in the matter. This is called, "First information report" (FIR) Here is a specimen FIR:

I was standing at the KMC bus stop at 10 a.m. on 10 December 2001. I saw a Hero Honda motor cycle speed by and knock down a small girl just opposite the Canara bank. The Regn No is TN 30 D 0375. The rider did not stop at all although he was aware that he had hurt the child.

Suddenly a lady charged to the spot, picked the girl who was about 4-5 years of age and rushed her into the hospital.

I am an eye witness to the above accident.

Sd/-
Name: in Capital letters
Address:
Date and time

Submitted to:

G3 Police station
Poonamalle High Road
Chennai – 10

Note:

There is no regular format for lodging an FIR. What is important is, as an eye witness, you must give all the details you had personally witnessed. Make 2 copies of the report and keep one copy with you. This, in case you are asked to appear in a court so that you could recall to your memory the contents of the FIR

Short messages

In a neighbourhood, we often have to depend on others for some help or the other. We want our next door friend to do some work for us such as paying some bill or giving the postman some information etc. At such times, you may leave a small 'Note' or a 'Short message' to the concerned person and paste it on his/her door if necessary.

Such Notes must be crisp, short and may be telegraphic. But the meaning must be clear and should not cause any confusion in the other's mind.

There is no particular format. So, follow the specimens given herein:

Message No. 1

To Santosh

I shall be out of town for a day. Could you please collect my personal letters, if any from the common letter box and keep them with you?

Thanks.

Sd/- Mohan
15 Dec, 8 a.m.

Message No. 2

Suresh

Do me a favour, pal. If the postman comes with a registered letter for me, please direct him to the Association office. I shall be there till 1.30 p.m.

Sorry for the trouble.

Sd/- Gobind
12.30 p.m.

Message No. 3

Dear Nandini (Flat 362)

Please see me in my flat anytime after 6.30 p.m. today. Important.

Sd/- Pratiba
22 Dec

Exercise

Write letters in the proper format on the subjects shown below:

1. To your Uncle thanking him for all his efforts in getting a seat for you in a Self financing engineering college.

2. To the Inspector of Police of your area Police station about a theft of 4 cycles in your compound. You have no security guard in your compound which houses 15 quarters. You may suggest posting a policeman on 'beat' during night time.

3. To the Captain of the hockey team in your nearby college for a friendly match on Republic day. Request him to bring the maximum number of spectators from the residential areas of his college students. You have arranged some refreshments for both the teams. Your own college Principal along with some staffs would also be present. It would be good if he could persuade some staffs from his college to attend the match.

4. Write a DO letter to your HOD suggesting an educational trip to Mumbai. To detail a senior Lecturer to accompany your group, which will consist of 15 students of the final year BA/B.Sc. Suggest the places to be visited in Mumbai and the lessons proposed to be learnt.

5. (a) Write a letter to a book-shop complaining about the badly damaged notebooks you had received. You had ordered 100 x 400 pages notebooks. Of the 100, at least 20 require replacement while the others could be acceptable for use. Also express your disappointment/anger about such poor service from a reputed Stationery manufacturer; you have developed second thoughts on placement of further orders on this shop.

   (b) As Manager of the above book-shop, send a suitable 'Business reply'.

6. As the Business manager of a certain manufacturing industry, write a letter to another industry placing a demand for steel sheets (measuring 5' x 3' and thickness 3 mm) of 10 tonnes. You would like to send your own representative for inspection of the item before despatch. You would withhold 10% payment until the final inspection at your factory premises.

7. Write a letter to the Editor of your city newspaper complaining about the frequent power shut down in your locality. You and some persons had personally approached the Asst. Engineer in the EB office who promised to do something but has not responded thereafter at all. In a subsequent meeting, he expressed his inability to do anything about it since the shut-down has been ordered by the State Govt in order to favour some farmers. As a college student, you feel that the public must raise its voice against such treatment to the public.

8. You were a witness to a street quarrel between two women in a slum area behind your house. What started as a light quarrel turned into something big because the men concerned from both the parties joined the fray with home-weapons and in the battle that followed, two men were seriously injured and had to be hospitalised. (You may make any suitable assumption about the identities of the key persons; make your report as informative as possible so that it helps the Police carry out detailed investigation and bring to book the guilty persons)

9. You have just completed your degree and are on the lookout for a job. You have no other qualification except your degree in History. But, you are in a position to learn anything and satisfy your employers. Your *forte* is 'managing people'; you could sway a crowd of even 500 people. Write an attractive application to the General Manager of a medium scale industry. The GM must be so highly impressed with the contents of your application and ability that he offers you a job straightway (of course, after a formal interview)

10. Write three short messages to some persons in your colony on some imaginary situations. (You may make any suitable assumptions)

Chapter 64

RECORDING OF MINUTES

Introduction

When any meeting is held at any level, a record of the Minutes of that meeting should be prepared and circulated to the members who attended the meeting. The Minutes may also lay down who would be responsible for pursuing action on the various decisions taken/arrived at in the meeting.

It is usually the Secretary who will record the Minutes. But, any person could be asked to record the Minutes. An under graduate should be competent in such a task.

During such meetings the members may tend to be longwinded and verbose and would try to impress others by their rhetorics of the points they would want to put across. This is where the "note making and summarising" aspect covered in Chapter 62 will become useful in recording the Minutes.- cut out all the inessentials and write down only the 'meat' of the argument.

Having jotted the **notes** of the arguments/statements made by a member against each point on the agenda, the notes could be expanded into a proper **summary** which will constitute the Minutes.

Note taking in a meeting

As an example, study how the Secretary of a residential colony takes down notes at a meeting. What each member spoke verbatim is given at the left and the corresponding 'note making' is given at the right:

Actual statements	Note making
Present : President,	WHO PRESENT
Jt sec - Pandian	
" Ray	
" Krishnamurthy	
Sec - (self)	
Members - Radhakrishnan	
" Menon	
" Janaki	
" Paul James	
" Jessie Daniel	

President: May God bless us all and guide us in our deliberation during the 6th meeting today.

Pres:
god's blessings
6th meeting.

President: Ladies and gentlemen, I have something sad to announce to you. Far too many students have come into our colony. This is a family colony and all the flats are meant for married people only and of course their children. The flat owners in their enthusiasm to recover their investment, have

Pres:
too many
bachelor
students.
privacy lost.

been renting out their flat for all and sundry. Students studying in the colleges adjoining our colony are easy tenants and without weighing the pros and cons, they have been letting out their flat to the student community. The result is, our families have lost their privacy since most of the students are bachelors. Next, there is a danger that these single students may tease our grown up girls; there is a possibility too of some of them molesting our girls. Our own permanent residents don't feel very comfortable with bachelors roaming our area. We need to take a policy decision on this matter. I invite the views of the members present

Pandian: Sir, if we prohibit students, the absentee landlords may feel the pinch. After all they have invested a lot of money for buying the flat and they can't afford to keep their flat vacant and a monthly income is essential for them to offset their loan payment.

Janaki Ramdoss: While agreeing with Mr.Pandian, I wish to state that the safety and well being of our family members are more important than collecting monthly rent from tenants. What if one of our girls is raped by some fellow. Are we going to feel sorry then? What control do we have over the behaviour of these young men? Some of them may become adventurous and foolhardy and do something rash. I am of the view that students should not be allowed to hire any of our flats. They are meant only for families. Of course, married students could be allowed. There are quite a few such as MDS and MCA students, you know?

President: Anymore views? How about you Mr. Ray?

Ray: I agree, Sir. We should not permit students. Some of them make a lot of noise and play their music system very loud. Our own families should live in total comfort and freedom.

President: Anyone in favour?

Menon: I think we should refer this point to the GB meeting. Many members may not like the idea of prohibiting the students.

President: I don't think we need to go to the GB for this. A decision is within the power of the Association committee. Further, this is a policy matter and we have to view it from this angle. Do remember that we have all given a certificate that the flat is for own use or for use by our family members. We haven't said that we would like to rent out the flat nor has the Govt given us the freedom to rent out our flats.

Teasing, Molesting feared. Members' views

Pandian: Regular income for loan return

Janaki: Same fears as President. Students not to be allowed.

Ray: No Students

Menon: Must refer to Gen Body Meeting.

Pres: Renting not permissible as per agreement given.

So, it is decided that henceforth no member shall rent out the flat to 'single students'. No harm if the tenants happen to be families. The present lot of students must be asked to vacate by some cut off date. Any ideas on that?	No more students.
Self: May I propose, April next year as the cut off date? All the present students would have finished their academic year by then?	Cut off, next April
President: The decision is: With immediate effect, no flat will be rented out to single students. The present students will be allowed to stay on till April next year.	Decision: no student wef Apr next year
Secretary: The next point on the agenda is about "Cable T.V.. operation". The present operator has not provided 40 channels as promised by him. We have given him 6 months' time and yet he has not kept up his commitment.	Sec: Cable T.V.
Radhakrishnan: Even the 32 channels he has provided are not of good quality at all. Several members from my own block have come out with the same complaint. Some of the channels he has given on his own and in lieu, are the unwanted types like Bengali, Chinese, Spanish etc. Who understands Spanish in this colony?	Radhakrishnan: Poor service; unwanted channels given.
Paul James: The operator must provide some channels of Educational value for our children like, "Discovery", "National Geography", "Animal planet".	Paul: Need channels of edn value.
Jessie Daniel: They are all 'pay channels', I think.	
Pandian: So what? The 40 channels include some pay channels also, don't they?	
Secretary: The 40 channel contract include only 3 pay channels which we already have. Three more would mean that he would demand more money.	Sec: Contract for 3 pay Ch. for additional channels we have to pay
Menon: How much have we to pay for 3 more pay channels Mr.Samuel?	
Secretary: Rs 4 per channel. Against the present payment of Rs 100 per member, we may have to pay Rs 112 for 3 additional channels.	Sec: New Subs.Rs 112 for 43 Ch.
President: I think it is worth it.	
Janaki: Some members may oppose this increase.	Janaki: Opposition expected fm members.
President: Could we negotiate with the cable operator to reduce the 'per channel' cost? What do you say Mr. Mohan?	

Secretary: We can try, Sir. In fact we should pressurise him. If he wants the contract renewed year after year, he must oblige us. Shall we say that we would pay just Rs 10 extra for 3 additional 'pay channels'?	Sec: New Subsc. 110 for 43 Ch.
President: The Secretary may kindly negotiate with the operator and put up a note for my formal approval before implementation. Incidentally, will there be any protest from the members?	Pres: Sec to discuss and put note.
Jessie Daniel: I don't think so, Mr. President. However, the Committee members must convince them privately. In the meantime, the negotiation may be started with the operator.	Jessie: We must convince. Start negotiation.
President: OK. What is the next point on the agenda?	
Secretary: There is a proposal to observe a 'social day' once a week in the community hall. The aim is, this will be a meeting occasion. We could also have some entertainment programmes such as Tambola and some cultural activities. Saturday evening is an ideal day.	Sec: Social get together every Sat.
Ray: I agree with the proposal. But we need to lay down the timing. The programmes shouldn't go on indefinitely. I suggest a duration of 90 minutes.	Ray: Time limit of of 90 mins.
Janaki: I suggest the timing of six thirty to eight p.m. People then could get home for dinner.	Janaki: 6.30 - 8 p.m.
President: Any opposition to the proposal? If none, are we agreed over the day and time?	
Secretary: The day and timing seem acceptable to all.	Sec: Sat and 6.30 - 8 p.m. Acceptable to all.
President: The decision is, there will be a social get together on all Saturdays between 6.30 and 8 p.m. I propose that Mrs.Janaki take care of this and organise the function effectively. We must popularise it. Shall we have the initial ceremony on the second Saturday next month?	Pres:Proposal agreed. Janaki the organiser. Notice to all residents.
Secretary: We have covered all the points on the Agenda Does any member want to raise any other point?	Any other point?
Krishnamurthy: The vegetable shop is not at all providing good service, Sir. Either we change him or give him a stern warning to stock all vegetables and sell them at reasonable price.	Krish: Veg shop. Poor service. Change him or warn him.
President: Has he been overcharging or what?	
Radhakrishnan: His rates are 50% over the market rate. This is too much of a profit, I think.	Radha Krish: Rate 50% more.

Secretary: Well, we can't lay down at what rate he will sell his vegetables. The contract does not state it. If a member does not like his rate, they are at liberty to buy the stuff from outside.

Sec: Can't force him, contract doesn't lay down any rate.

Jessie Daniel: I am afraid, I am not in agreement with the Secretary on this point. He is here to serve the members and not to fleece us. Some of us depend only on him, the old people especially. Shouldn't we keep the old people's interest in mind?

Jessie: He is fleecing us. Old people depend on him solely.

Menon: I understand Mrs.Jessie Daniel's sentiment on the issue. But, what can we do about it? We can only say that he must reduce his rate. A better approach perhaps would be that all of us don't buy from him as a protest and compel him to reduce. Within two days he would come to his senses.

Menon: Protest, don't buy for two days. He would then reduce.

Krishnamurthy: I think it is an excellent idea. But then, we can't advise the residents in writing, can we? Why not pass a word around in each block and fix two particular days for abstaining?

Krish: Pass verbal instr.To abstain for 2 days.

President: All right, shall we agree on 27th and 28th of this month? Nothing is to be put in writing. Even this discussion is not to be recorded in the Minutes.

Pres: Nothing in writing.

President: Thank you Ladies and Gentlemen. The meeting is hereby closed.

Pres: Meeting closed.

The Minutes must sound like a Summary. It is not at all necessary to record everything that has been said or talked about in the meeting. Similarly, it is quite unnecessary to record every argument a member has cited; record only the salient points. There is no need to mention the name of the member unless it is absolutely vital for any future reference. What is important is the decision arrived at or conveyed by the President and not the supporting arguments for such decision.

Based on the 'Note making', here is the Minutes produced by the Secretary.

MINUTES OF THE 6TH MEETING OF MAHARANI COLONY ASSOCIATION HELD ON 5 NOVEMBER 2001 FOR THE YEAR 2001 - 2002

The following officials were present in the meeting:

President:	Mr. M.Govindasamy
Joint Secretary:	Mr. Pandian Ramesh
"	Mr. Ray Satyan
"	Mr. J.Krishnamurthy
Secretary	Mr. D.Samuel
Members	Mr. L.Radhakrishnan
"	Mr. Rajeev Menon
"	Mrs. Janaki Ramdoss
"	Mr. Paul James
"	Mrs. Jessie Daniel

The monthly meeting was presided over by the President after a short opening prayer invoking God's blessings.

After detailed discussions on the various agenda points, the following decisions were arrived at.

Decision	Action by
1. Henceforth the flats in this colony will not be rented out to any Bachelor students. The present lot will be asked to vacate by April next year.	Secretary. All flat owners
2. The cable operator to provide 43 channels in all including 6 pay channels at a monthly rental of Rs 110 per member per month. The secretary to negotiate with the operator to provide 3 additional pay channels for an extra subscription of Rs 10.	Secretary
3. The colony will observe a social get-together every Saturday between 6.30 and 8 p.m. beginning from second Saturday Jan 2002. Mrs. Janaki Ramdoss will be the co-ordinator and ensure that the get together goes smoothly and to everyone's satisfaction.	Mrs. Janaki Ramdoss. All members of the colony.
4. The vegetable vendor must be persuaded to reduce his rate for all the items sold by him.	

Sd/ D.Samuel
Secretary

7 Nov 01

Distr:

All committee members.
Colony Notice boards - to show only the points of interest for the flat owners/ residents.

Chapter 65

SHORT STORY WRITING

Definition

Many persons write a narrative essay and think they have penned a short story. A short story is not a condensed long story either. For instance, everyone's life from birth till some date, will constitute a long story. We may also call it a novel.

A long story/novel will cover every bit of one's life history or life's happenings. But a short story, should not cover every detail.

So, what then is a short story?

A short story is one that gives a fleeting glimpse of a part of one's life or experience. A fleeting glimpse is something equivalent to a view you will get of the goings-on inside a railway compartment when it runs past you at 60 kmph. How much can you see? A little only. But that's what a short story is all about. A mere glance on a particular aspect of one's life. Any details you may write should focus on that aspect only.

Next, short story must be about people. You can't write short story on a building or an animal or about space!

So, the elements of a short story could be summarised as follows: 1. About people 2. About a particular aspect or incident of their life.

Here is an example of "particular aspect."

Let's say, you lost your money purse while travelling in a bus. Here, you give the details concerning the circumstances such as, what dress you wore, where you had kept your purse, in which bus you travelled, how many people travelled with you, when you noticed the loss and what you did about it. The particular aspect should cover only the happenings pertaining to the loss and the circumstances. There is no need for you to say anything about your family, whether you own a car or a 2 wheeler, the reason why you had to travel by bus on that day, your own qualifications, where you studied, how many friends you had then and how many you have now, whether you had a hearty breakfast before leaving your home etc.

Restrict your writing only to such details that concern the purse and its loss and any relevant information connected with the incident and nothing else. These would amount to "fleeting glimpse."

Plot

This is another misunderstood term and many aspiring writers use it in a loose way. When someone says, "The plot of this story is good," they refer to the "general set up or the story line." That's not plot at all.

Let us take an example and get a clear idea of what PLOT is.

You are going on a train journey say from New Delhi to Kolkata by the Kalka mail. If you describe the details of the journey such as, in which class you travelled, how many were your co-travellers, in which station or stations you had got down and for what purpose, whether you carried your own meals or ordered it from the dining car, how many beggars you came across etc, these will amount to a Narrative essay because you have described the events as they occurred and in the same sequence. It will NOT be a short story at all even if you had struck a durable friendship with a co-passenger.

But, imagine you had alighted at Allahabad to buy some magazines, oranges and also to have a soft drink during that time and the train started moving all of a sudden; your compartment was 4 carriages away; the train had picked up speed; you sighted the guard van; you shouted and waved your hands frantically at the guard who understood the situation, applied the emergency brakes and brought the train to a stop. The inclusion of such details and happenings would constitute a **short story**. Why?

During your train journey, you had a PROBLEM (CRISIS/CONFLICT) and the train guard solved that problem. The "**Problem - Solution**" syndrome form the Plot. So, a **plot** comprises of **problem and a solution for it.** The train journey is the story line. The training-missing part is the plot because the problem arose there and a solution came about for it. The description of the train missing part must be given as a fleeting glimpse without any unnecessary and irrelevant details. Write only the essentials of the missing drama. Of course you may do that in an emotional way.

A story line can have more than one plot but they must be inter-related. A story line with one plot is an ideal short story. Here, use the maximum number of words over the plot and the remaining details just about one third length.

The whole business of SS writing is "Problem and Problem-solving". If you don't give a solution to the problem, it will not be a full-fledged plot at all.

Earlier we noted that an SS deals with people. So, there would be only human players (characters) in your story line. You must portray your players in such a way that they become live.

The next ingredient of an SS is **characterisation -** characterisation of all your players in the story line.

There are two types of characterisation; (i) DIRECT by the author;
(ii) DIRECT by a player and (iii) INDIRECT.

"Direct by the author" is, the author himself/herself describing a situation in the Third person, something like, "Leela is a good teacher". However, the same description about Leela could come out of the mouth of another player like, "Mona said that Leela was a good teacher." This is, "Direct by a player" kind of description.

It is good technique that the author keeps himself/herself in the background and let the players take over the description part. In other words, let one player portray another or others in his/her own words. The "direct by the author" kind of description must be kept to the minimum.

Whether Direct by the author or Direct by the players, the characterisation itself must be INDIRECT for greater effectiveness. Confusing? Let me clarify it through an example: Sheila, a teenager, is one of your players in your story. She is a tomboy kind of girl.

It will be poor story writing if the author describes her as, "Radha is a tomboy kind of teenage girl." It will be equally poor if one of the players said the same thing. (Direct by the player). It would be excellent story writing if Radha's tomboyishness is explained through a series of realistic incidents and behaviour so that the reader concludes that Radha is a tomboy kind of teenager. Such portrayal could be done by the author or one/two of the players.

A short story should never be of more than 3000 words. Ideally it should be around 1500 or thereabouts. Therefore, every word used must be informative and exact to the point. You can't be very generous with words much less being verbose.

Next, every line must take the story forward and at a fast pace. There should be no dull moments nor words wasted in any kind of picturesque description.

To summarise all the points on short story writing,

(a) It deals with people.
(b) Gives a fleeting glimpse on a particular aspect of life.
(c) Should have one or more plots in the story line.
(c) Characterisation of the players/participants to be 80% indirect.
(d) Speed

Planning a short story

Once you have a story line, you must be absolutely clear in your mind about the age, qualifications, status, nature, life style, any special or peculiar behavioural pattern etc. of every player in the story.

Every player must behave and talk conforming to the Indian society's norms. (You can't make your hero run away with a friend's wife. This certainly will not be acceptable to an Indian reader while a western reader may not bat an eye over such a development at all). Any unusual/abnormal behaviour must be explained and fully justified. For instance, a tramp must talk a tramp's style of language; he should not use a high flown language; if he does, the reason must be explained to the satisfaction of the reader.

With the above guidelines, shall we attempt a short story?

The story line is like this:

Sebastian's family consists of a daughter, Mona, son Alex and younger daughter, Vineeta. Mona dropped out of school after her 6th standard while Alex and Vineeta became engineers. Mona became an excellent cook and house keeper. She literally ran the household while the mother Milli Sebastian took rest most of the time. However, to keep herself occupied, entered into evangelical work. Mona declined marriage because of her poor academic performance in comparison to others. The other two got married in course of time and had two children each.

One day Mona, 31 years, fell ill. Was admitted to a private hospital. After comprehensive tests, doctors diagnosed her disease as cancer - blood cancer. She was a terminal case as well. She was given just about a month's life. She overheard this conversation between two senior doctors from her bed. The family too came to know about it but the doctors advised the members not to tell Mona about her impending death.

One day, Mona asks a doctor what her problem was; why was she not getting healed. The senior doctor pacified her saying it is a rather long treatment and she would become hale and hearty very shortly; she shouldn't worry about her future at all. Mona shocks the doctor by saying that she knows she is suffering from blood cancer and had just about a month to live. She requests the doctor (Dr.Srinivasan) not to tell this news to any of her family members. She makes him promise her. The trouble is, he promised the same commitment to the family members also.

The D day comes and the family collects Mona's body for the funeral. As they were on their way out, the son walks up to the doctor and thanks him for not telling Mona about her ailment. The doctor, a custodian of two secrets, couldn't even acknowledge it. As he enters his chamber, he sees a vision of Mona seated on his chair, smiling. "Thank you doctor for not telling the family members about my terminal illness," she said.

You can see two plots in the story. Of course these have to be developed properly. Next, note down clearly the personal particulars and the characteristics of all the participants.

Sebastian	-	A devout Christian; has brought up his children in the Christian faith. A professor of distinction with a Ph D degree in Ancient and modern History. Has a two storey house of his own and financially well off.
Milli Sebastian	-	A graduate in Home science. A good housekeeper and a strong Christian. An active person. When the elder daughter Mona takes over the household duties, she takes to Christian evangelism through social contacts in and around her house.
Mona	-	Weak in studies; low IQ. Good with her hands. Very loving with parents and brother, sister. Prepared to sacrifice anything for the family. She prefers to remain single and look after the family.
Alex	-	A clever young man with a degree in Computer science; gets married at the age of 22.
Vineeta	-	A dutiful married daughter with total attachment to the family. Moves out after marriage.

While developing the story observe economy of words and let the story keep advancing. Use Direct speech for maximum effect. Initially, make a draft, revise and re-revise it before finalising it. Here is my final draft.

TWO SECRETS

When the mother noticed Mona losing her health and weight, she decided to consult the family doctor, Dr.Srinivasan. He was a family friend as well for years. The father, Sebastian agreed. Mona protested saying she was feeling fine. "I may have lost some weight but so what? I do all the housework without help, don't I?" Mother would have nothing of it. "If she had a husband …?" Milli Sebastian began to reminisce.

Mother knew the reason why Mona had refused marriage. She considered herself next to an illiterate, having dropped out of school after the VI standard. "An unmarried daughter would be a great liability on the parents," Milli would reflect often. But she could do nothing about it. As a compensation, she resolved to show Mona some extraordinary concern and love.

In her turn, Mona offered to take over the full house-running responsibility. Wouldn't mother like to relax? Mona loved to cook and keep the house spick and span. She became such an expert she felt that she could teach 'Home science' in a college!

Milli made full use of her respite from kitchen duties. She took to Christian evangelism, home evangelism to people around her house. After all, "Preaching the gospel" is a command to every Christian and she couldn't back out of it. And now Mona had given her an excellent opportunity as well.

Her son and the second daughter were contrasts. Both of them had secured competitive seats in Govt engineering colleges and obtained their degrees; Alex in Computer science and Vineeta in Electronics and Communication. Vineeta opted for marriage and hoped that her husband would allow her to work as an engineer somewhere within the city. Alex preferred to go for Post graduation and was trying for a chance to study abroad.

Dr.Srinivasan suggested that they admit Mona in his hospital for a thorough check-up. Some fear was visible on the doctor's face after he perused the result of some initial tests. "Not to worry," he assured the Sebastians. "She would be all right .." Srinivasan was well aware that he was telling a lie. But then, such was the duty of a doctor.

Milli suddenly realised that she was walking into her kitchen after some 2 years. But she picked up the thread pretty fast and within 48 hours. She carried all the meals herself to Mona. Dr. Srinivasan's nursing home happened to be within walking distance. "Would you like anything special, my child? Remember, you have to regain your old weight?"

Mona would smile. "I am getting bored here without any work, mummy," she would complain. "How long have I to be here? What's wrong with me, mummy?"

Mummy gave evasive but encouraging replies.

It was after a week that shrapnels pierced into their soul. The report from the Cancer institute confirmed Srinivasan's worst fears. "I can't hide it from the parents any longer," he reflected. "What a pity? A maximum of 30 days from today?"

The Sebastians felt totally shattered at the news. Within hours Alex and Vineeta too had come to know about the diagnosis. Their visits to the hospital became twice daily. They had to keep encouraging the elder sister; give her all possible comforts and worldly joys and to some extent 'hope' as well.

The father requested Srinivsan and also the junior doctors and nurses not to say a word about the terminal disease in any manner to Mona. "Promise, doctor?" Sebastian stretched out an open palm. Srinivasan slapped the palm with tears nearly welling up in his eyes. "Another thing doctor?" Sebastian requested. "Keep her in the hospital until .. until … We want Mona to know that everything is being done for her. She would become suspicious if you discharge her all of a sudden and prematurely …" Srinivasan agreed, again with a slap of hand.

"Why isn't anyone telling me what's wrong with me?" Mona demanded one day. "Mummy, you please tell, how long more before I come?" "You would be all right soon, my child. Dr. Srinivasan has also said so. So, be brave and take rest. You have been working very hard in the house ..."

One evening Mona asked the mother, "Mummy, what is 'lucky me'?" Milli missed a few heartbeats. It took her several seconds to recover from the blow. "Well, it's a kind of .... a kind of... itching disease, Mona. You do feel itchy at your back, don't you?" By then, Mona was developing bedsores. Mona felt satisfied at mother's diagnosis.

Vineeta and husband visited her sharp at 6 p.m. and used to bring her fruits and other eatables. "*Akka*, you will be all right shortly. In fact the doctor has recommended a week's holiday in Ooty immediately after you come out. You would return then a changed human being from Ooty," Vineeta said one day.

"Oh, really? I glad. But what I need a holiday for?" Mona asked.

One afternoon, after the duty nurse had administered the usual dose of medicines, Mona closed her eyes trying to sleep. But sleep wouldn't come. Then she heard soft whispers in the corridor. The senior nurse was explaining to a newcomer. "All these are eye wash; the injection is only distilled water. Poor thing, seven more days and she would be gone. Don't give any inkling of this to her. Okay?"

That evening, Mona cornered Dr.Srinivasan. "Doctor, I have 'lucky me'. No?" Srinivasan raised a small hand. "I know it doctor. I know, I am going to die in 6 or 7 days time. No?" Don't tell anything opposite, Doctor." Dr.Srinivasan stood dumbfounded.

"Doctor?" Mona hailed him, "Promise me, you won't tell Mummy and Daddy that I ... I .. die. They trembling at death news .... See? They think I go on a holiday to Ooty. Promise me doctor." Her shaking open palm pulled a corner of his white coat. "Promise me Uncle?" Srinivasan had to bite his lips hard. He had nearly burst into a howl. "Pro.....mise .." he mumbled with difficulty.

When Mona breathed her last on the fourth day, the usual howls and breast-beating were absent. The entire family was present at her bedside. When Dr. Srinivasan walked in, he couldn't even say the customary words, "Sorry, we tried our best."

"But then doctor, did you notice she died with a smile on her face and she was so fearless?" Sebastian observed. "Probably she was thinking of her train journey to Mettupalayam. Thank you doctor for not telling her about her end. Thank you."

After the hearse moved away, Dr.Srinivasan walked towards his chamber. Death was not something unusual for him, for any doctor. He had witnessed quite a few in his own nursing home. But, Mona's case was different and special. He had seen Mona grow up from day 1. How long would he take to forget Mona's innocent face?

The party having departed, he stepped into his chamber and even while one leg of his hung in the air, he felt a sudden thump at what he saw inside. And for an instant he was totally stunned. Mona was sitting on his chair with the same smile. "Thank you doctor. Thank you. Thank you for not telling my parents that I go away," she said briefly. When Srinivasan wiped his eyes, he saw only an empty chair.

Story analysis

What are the plots? Milli Sebastian noticing Mona's falling health is the first problem. Solution: She is taken to the hospital. Next problem, the diagnosis of blood cancer. Solution: Family members informed and the news is not to be conveyed to the patient. A promise extracted out from the doctor. Next problem, her impending death within days. Solution: more encouragement and consolation from family members; news of a holiday in Ooty. Next problem, Mona getting to know about her ailment and that she would live for 6 or 7 days only. Solution: Mona takes out a promise from the doctor not to tell the parents about her final departure.

Characterisation

This is not much in the story. Milli behaved like any loving mother. She spent all her time with Mona. Surely she would have given up her evangelical work. This is to be understood.

Mona is not well educated. Somewhere she heard the word "leukaemia". Nor would she have understood the expression "blood cancer". Her behaviour and talks certainly revealed that she is not an educated woman and weak at general knowledge.

"Characterisation by the author" is dominant in this story; about one third. But it cannot be helped. It is the author who is telling the story. So he has to resort to 'direct characterisation by the author'. That's the trouble when a story is written in Third person. If one of the players tells the story, the author would certainly be completely in the background and in fact he wouldn't be visible at all.

Have we wasted any words? Is any description not connected with the story line? The speed is there. Perhaps the language could be improved in terms of economy.

Do remember to use 'simple to read sentences'. And also observe the para writing rules and follow the CQ method. In revising your first draft, frame and reframe your sentences so as to arouse CQs.

Here is another short story, written in third person and told by the author. Look at it from the angle of all the rules. We shall have a post-mortem on the story at the end.

THE REFORMATION

Along with some 20 candidates, Chandran, a part time worker, too applied for the permanent post of a conductor in the City bus service. He was aware that others had paid a bribe on the quiet to get this job. But, Chandran did not believe in it. "If I am good enough, I'd get the job," he told himself bravely. And Hurrah! One day he did receive the appointment letter. He was overjoyed, prostrated himself before his favourite deity, thanked her profusely and vowed that he would perform his duty most sincerely and honestly with the fear of God in mind.

He was a married man with a small child. He had done his S.S.L.C in a Tamil medium school with just pass marks. His wife, Lakshmi was only a VI standard qualified woman. Chandran didn't much bother about her educational qualification; she was an excellent cook and a good housekeeper; fed him well and kept him happy and contented. She was a typical Indian wife - soft spoken, no arguments and all obedience, perfect obedience to the husband. And more than all these, she was a God fearing woman. What else would a breadwinner need from his better half? He was more than satisfied with Lakshmi in every respect.

After his probationary period, he was allotted a house in the city transport colony at a nominal rent. He left his parents' house and walked into his official house immediately.

Chandran was very particular about returning the correct change to the passengers. If he had to give back 25 p, he returned a 25 p coin and not a 20 p coin like many conductors did. If someone had given him a ten rupee note, he made sure that the balance was handed back before the passenger alighted. Yet, one day he found himself with an extra three rupees in his money bag after he had handed over the collection for the day. "How come?" he wondered. Nevertheless, he transferred it to his personal money purse. Strangely, he was richer by 2 to 3 rupees daily though he knew that he hadn't cheated any passenger.

Some two weeks later, he too began to toe the line of other conductors. Often he told some commuters that he would return the change a little later and never did. On receiving a ten rupee or fifty rupee note, he invariably held back some small amount. The extra income, though small, now began to swell in his purse. When it could contain no more coins, he decided to put the bonus money in a piggy bank and placed it alongside the dozens of idols in the 'puja corner' of his house.

"What is this?" Lakshmi asked him one day with her index finger pointing at the large clay piggy bank.

When he replied, "It's none of your business" she kept quiet. A little later she reflected benignly, "He must be saving money for some happy occasion, probably our 6th wedding anniversary!"

In course of time, Chandran adopted some novel measures to fleece the passengers. He issued tickets of lower denomination. Many passengers never bothered to cross-check the ticket value against the money collected. Chandran adored such travellers. Then, he became bold and stole a Rs.3.50 ticket bunch from the cashier's table. He made a quick calculation; this would give him about Rs 160 extra over the next 3 days.

After some 6 months, Chandran found himself with an additional income of over Rs 750. He went on a spending spree; took his wife and child to restaurants, beach, horse riding, VGP sight seeing and what not. Lakshmi wanted to ask where he got all that extra money from, especially after admitting their son in an English medium school at a heavy cost. But she daren't.

"It's a fine life," Chandran told himself. He was certain that he could not be caught easily. After all he was only a 'small time thief'. He wasn't like the hundreds of politicians and high officials who minted money in lakhs and crores.

That evening, little Chinnu, now a 4 year old LKG going son, returned from school with high fever. Lakshmi was alarmed. She took him to a doctor on the following day. The fever did not subside even after 4 days of treatment. "Why? Could God be punishing them for some lapse on their part?" she debated. A pricking thought punched at her. That piggy bank? Could it … could it …?

On a Sunday morning Lakshmi cornered her husband. "I have been watching you putting some currency notes in it every day. How and Why?" she demanded.

Chandran couldn't give a satisfactory answer and yet he was afraid of accusing her of much curiosity.

"I had a bad dream last night. Someone was saying constantly, 'you are going on a wrong path, you on a wrong path'." Just now she bubbled with an extraordinary courage. Turning towards Chandran she demanded point blank, "You haven't been looting the passengers, have you?"

Chandran's heart raced wildly. He gasped for breath. In a moment of extreme stress, he blurted out, "I .. er … I … did, Lakshmi. I cheated, Lakshmi. I … did …" Chandran cried. Recollecting his promise made on the day he received the appointment order, he cried loudly like an errant school boy.

"My God, my God .." she beat her breasts violently and howled. Then inhaling the morning air deeply she commanded Chandran, "Go. Go at this moment and return all that extra money you had robbed, to the cashier with an apology. OK?"

The conductor hesitated. "What would his colleagues think of him?" he thought. He was known as an honest worker. The office staff had a great regard for his integrity.

All that apart, he couldn't take his wife's reprimand lightly. Something told him that he must do what she had directed. When he entered the cashier's office with his confession, the cashier too was astonished. "It is true, Sir," Chandran said with tears welling up in his eyes. Mustering all his courage, he placed the piggy bank right on the other's table and made a hasty exit.

By evening, that day, little Chinnu sat up like a normal child and was talking away merrily.

----x----

Now, write down the characteristics of every player in the story, viz, Chandran, Lakshmi and Chinnu.

Name the plots; write down the problem and solution(s) for each.

How much of the characterisation belong to the author? Quite a lot, about 40%. This cannot be helped when the story teller is the author and the whole story is written in the Third person.

If the story is told by one of the players, then you may not find the author anywhere at all. Let us verify it in a First person story, which is given below.

The story line:

Vanitha is the only daughter of her parents, The Sudharsans. She grows into a teenager, as the lone child, always pining for an elder brother. She developed a great admiration for an imaginary elder brother - tall, handsome, dynamic, protective etc. In course of time her pining for an elder brother turned into a boy friend who would be older to her by some 5 years. This new thought enveloped her when she entered college as a 17 year old young and pretty maiden.

In the college canteen she sights a dashing young man, a man of her dreams. "He is it, he is it" she tells herself. The young man is Sunil, an MA final year student. They meet as acquaintances initially. Their friendship grows. Sunil lost his small sister when she was about 17 in a road accident. Her death devastated Sunil's life. He was highly attached to Madhavi. Sunil notices a resemblance, why a replica of Madhavi in Vanitha. This is what brings him and Vanitha together. One day Sunil becomes courageous enough to ask Vanitha to visit his house on the following day immediately after college. "Oh he wants mother's approval before hand" she ruminates. She was dressed to kill the next day. Though the time was 4 p.m. she looked as fresh as in the morning in a dashing conjeevaram saree. "I hope Sunil's parents like me, his mother in particular" she kept thinking as she sat on the pillion seat of Sunil's motor bike.

Sunil summons his mother, points at Vanitha and asks, "Isn't she exactly like our Madhavi?" Sunil brings out a large picture frame and shows it to Vanitha. "See? See yourself in this photo?" Vanitha is astonished at the resemblance. "She was your own sister, was she ?"Vanith asks.

"Yes, my little sis" Sunil answers. "Sis? … Nothing else?" Vanitha asks anxiously.

"Nothing else, my little sis. You will be always my little sis, Madhavi" he replies.

It took Vanitha minutes to say, "Sure, Anna" and she charged into his open arms.

Caption: **A DEAD SISTER CAME ALIVE**

The story is narrated by Vanitha in the First person.

The players are only two actually - Vanitha and Sunil. Others have only a minor part. As a writer, be absolutely clear in your mind about their characteristics.

Here they are:

Vanitha - As a little girl when she goes to school, a girls' school, she always missed a chaperon; say an elder brother, like some of her classmates. Yearns for an elder brother. So, she creates for herself an imaginary elder brother whom she adores. An average student in school. But, when she joins a co-ed college, the elder brother picture turns into a boy friend of same qualities.

Sudharsans - Vanitha's parents. Unable to have any more issues, they bring up Vanitha with all love and care.

Sunil - A loving elder brother. Cares for his sister Madhavi much more than his parents. Very very fond of and highly attached to Madhavi. An age difference of 6 years. When Madhavi meets with an accident and dies, he is a devastated man. Thereafter, views every young girl as his sister. From a well to do family. Has been given a motor bike when he joined college. A keen student; wants to touch the pinnacle of education. Nothing else would distract him from this goal.

Ashok &	-	Sunil's parents with their own house. Ashok is a Vice president in a
Mrs. Anita		multinational company. Though left with only one child now, they expect
Ashok		Sunil to go higher and higher in academics and not settle for marriage

after post graduation. Loss of Madhavi was a severe blow to them and they couldn't get over it at all.

Here is the final draft of the story.

A DEAD SISTER CAME ALIVE

It was only after a week that I came to know about the existence of a canteen in the college premises. We were allowed to eat the home lunch there. Most of us brought our own luncheon box while a few purchased their meal from the canteen.

Sight of men inside the class room and in the canteen, was something totally new to me, having spent over 12 years in a Girls' school. One afternoon, I suddenly realised that I was on the lookout for a life time partner. "Perhaps this was the result of studying in a co-ed institution," I guessed. An inner voice told me, "Why not Vanitha? In another 6 months or so you would be a major and …." I couldn't put aside the thought from my mind. I was here to get a degree in English literature and not spot out my future husband. But my mind seemed pinned on it. I started dreaming about my dream man. "How would he be?" I speculated that Monday lunch hour. "Naturally, tall, handsome, dynamic, protective etc. "A distant voice said to me at once, "Hey, that were the very qualities of your imaginary elder brother, remember?" My thoughts went back to my LKG days recollecting ….

My mother stopped accompanying me to school after I was promoted to the LKG class. "Your school is just 50 meters away; you could walk there all by yourself, can't you? You are a big girl now, aren't you?" she had said. I felt puffed up all right. But, when I saw three of my friends come to school towed by their big brothers, I felt that I too must be taken by someone, preferably by an elder brother.

When I reached Standard IV, an elder brother became more real and urgent. How wonderful it would be to stay in one room, study in the same room, ask him for any doubts in the text book and .. and … hug him tight when lightnings and thunders came. But that was not to be. It also dawned on me that I could never have an elder brother; only a small brother or sister. But I didn't care for a small brother or a small sister. I was not interested in being the senior child but a junior one looking up to someone bigger than me.

When I got promoted to the VII standard, I configured in my mental eyes an imaginary elder brother, all for myself - tall, handsome, dynamic, protective etc.

I felt some consolation to think that my *Anna* was always by my side. Often I would consult him for some thing or the other and he would help me. Sometimes I used to summon him even in the examination hall when I was stuck with some questions. *Anna* always came and whispered the correct answers. While walking home after the school hours, he was always beside me. Often, I would hear a voice say, "Hey Sis, I am here. Walk on… When we reached our compound gate, I would say, "You first," and then follow him majestically into our two storey house.

Life went on marvellously for me.

When I announced to him one fine morning that I had passed my +2 with distinction, he clapped hands mightily and showed a pair of open arms. Then I rushed with a loud hail and surrendered myself into those inviting arms.

My whole outlook on life seemed to have changed when I stepped into a men dominated college campus. "Why can't one of these men be my future husband?" I began to think one day. There were several senior men studying in the final year or in post graduation; they were of the right age to be my partner. "What would he be like?" I queried that Wednesday lunch hour closing my lunch box.

And suddenly ... suddenly, I noticed a pair of eager eyes, some 3 tables away, staring at me. He wouldn't take off his eyes. And I found my heart gallopping. He was my dream man. It was love at first sight. I had read such things in magazines or in some film stories but here it was actually happening to me - love at first sight, at the tall, handsome, dynamic and protective young man.

Two days later he walked right up, stood next to me and said, "Hi?" I didn't know how to reply. Had it been a girl I too would have said "Hi". So, I did the next best thing returned his Hi with a light smile. Whether he was surprised at my smile or not, I couldn't tell but he proved to be a braver man than I had thought. "Nice seeing you," he said as his acknowledgement. For quite some minutes I didn't understand his words. One would use such a phrase only on meeting a friend after a long gap. Whereas, we were seeing each other at close quarters for the first time. It was only some two months later that I was able to decipher the "Nice seeing you" greeting.

Our first face to face encounter inside the canteen blossomed into a great friendship. We sat at the same table much to the chagrin of my class friends. But I couldn't care less. I preferred a male company more than the female company.

He was a final year MA student named, Sunil.

The lunch break was glorious. I looked forward to it and so did he. What did we talk? you ask. Well nothing but sweet nothings. I had fallen in love with him deeply within a week and I was sure, so had he. And did I float in cloud 9 when he asked me, "Could you come to my house tomorrow after college?" Good progress, I had thought, very fast progress indeed. "He wants to show me to his parents first, his mother in particular" I imagined. The right step, in my opinion. But then, why hadn't he proposed to me formally? Perhaps he wanted to do that after securing his mother's approval. "A real mother's apron boy" I dubbed him with some disappointment.

On the following day some of my friends observed, "Eh, you are dressed to kill, Vanitha. What's going on?" I ignored it all. "When a bride goes for groom- seeing and in his own house, you don't tom tom about it!" I was dressed in an attractive Conjeevaram saree with a face as fresh as on any morning. Sunil turned my face towards his and chuckled briefly, "A'hm". I felt pulses of electricity pass through my veins when he touched me for the first time. He took me on his Hero Honda bike.

As soon as he stepped inside the house, me in tow, he hailed his mother shouting, "Mamma, see who has come?" And the mother sprinted out of the kitchen holding a long spoon in hand. The moment she saw me, her mouth shaped into a tiny cave. "Ah ...! " she cried; words, wouldn't come out of her mouth.

Sunil, leaving me completely unattended, dashed into a room and brought a big photo frame. "Here, look at yourseif," he said and held the photo right before me. I couldn't believe it. I wiped my eyes twice at the figure. It was me; 100% me.

"It's my sister. Madhavi." Sunil said breaking into my thoughts.

"Really? Where is she, Sunil?"

"She died 6 months back. A city bus overran her. She was 17 then."

"Oh! And she was your real sister, was she?" I asked just to make sure.

"Yes, my little SIS" he replied.

"My little Sis?" I was both alarmed and tickled. I looked up at him questioningly.

"Yes, my little Sis" he repeated.

"And I am nothing else to you?" I asked displaying my heart's anxiety.

"No. What else do I want? You will always be my little Sis, Madhavi. I lost my precious little Madhavi and she has come back to me. Nothing else matters."

My school day craze cut through me. It took me quite some minutes to say it and I said it very clearly. "Sure, *Anna*. My Anna ..." I felt a big lump in my throat.

Sunil who was some 6 feet away, stretched out a pair of open arms and without any hesitation, I charged into them.

Regaining her composure, Anita Ashok inched towards me, examined my face more closely and enveloped me in her arms. Still stunned and speechless, she planted a tender kiss on my forehead.

When Sunil's father walked in at 5 p.m. he stood spellbound at the sight of what he saw.

While two streams of warm tears flowed down my cheeks, I thought silently and most pleasurably, "Not only have I got an elder brother for real but two sets of parents as well !"

Post-mortem

How many plots have you detected? The major plot is, Vanitha pining for an elder brother and she found him at the end. (Solution).

Minor plots are: Sunil staring at Vanitha and approaching her boldly. Solution: Brings her to his house and reveals that she is literally his sister.

Sunil, very attached to Madhavi, finds her in Vanitha.

Have all the players lived upto the characteristics assigned to them? Yes, they have. Vanitha's parents don't appear anywhere at all. No need either. It would have looked irrelevant.

Where is the author? He is nowhere in the story at all. Everything is told to us by Vanitha.

Characterisation becomes easier when the story is written in First person. But, the story teller has to be one of the players and he/she cannot be an outsider.

Exercise

Develop short stories out of the story line/outline/hints given below. Each story must have a minimum of 3 plots including the main one.

1. Two parents-dominated high school friends in the Plus one class. They decide to run away from the house for a couple of days so that they could taste what total freedom was like. Weren't they big boys then having finished their Matriculation? They manage to collect Rs 200 each, put a few clothes in a carry-bag and walk out saying that they are going for a swim in the Corporation pool. They do what they like in the next town like visiting all the cinema theatres, eating where they liked and slouching about. They spend the two nights under a bus shelter. Commotion in the homes. Police complaint lodged. Parents worried. Commotion in the school circles too. On the fourth day both the boys walk in with smiles on their face. When asked, each explained to the respective parents that he wanted to experience what real 'freedom' was like.. Parents realise their folly and allow them some kind of freedom of action.

2. Two men sitting on a bridge and talking. The time was about 11 p.m. The road looks lonely at that hour. An occasional vehicle passes by. Suddenly two policemen on 'beat' appear there and ask them to go the police station. The men protest. One of them talks in chaste English. What crime had we committed? Policemen say, they are drunks. We haven't taken any liquor, they say. In any case, how is drinking a crime in a State where there is no prohibition? You had brought a woman, the policemen accuse. "Show us the woman" the men demand. She must be hiding behind you. The men, who are actually business men now get brave and threaten the policemen. "If you don't get lost, we shall inform the Police Commissioner" one of them threatens pulling out his cell phone. The policemen vanish out of sight. The two business men could not find a suitable place to discuss some new business ventures. They didn't want anyone to overhear their proposals. Hence they chose a lonely spot in the outskirts of the city.

3. Two kids around 6 or 7 are playing in front of their house. A man in tattered clothes appears at the scene, talks the boys into following him. And they do so innocently. He takes them to an abandoned house. You are following the threesome. You feel that the man is a kidnapper. You don't know what he wants to do with the kids. The time now is about 11 a.m. Develop a short story out of these hints.

4.   A fond mother chooses a nice young man for her daughter. And the father is in agreement. The girl, a graduate, though believes in arranged marriage (She has had one bad experience; one day her lover boy walked out on her because he spotted a more beautiful girl) does not like the parents' choice. The parents are adamant since the boy is from a wealthy family and the lone son. Develop the story with a happy ending or sad ending.

5.   A lady college lecturer, about 35 years old, is very popular among the under graduates. She is a single lady, living all by herself. Her parents have died, leaving behind a small house .in which she lives alone. She is very much a homely type of woman, wants a husband and a family. But she had been ditched by an young business man when she was 22 years. Thereafter she begins to hate men and decides to remain single. One day, a girl from BA second year named Leela comes to her for advice. She has set her eyes on a male classmate of hers and is madly in love with him. She is bent upon marrying him only and otherwise she would commit suicide. But the young man does not reciprocate. Not that he was in love with anyone else. He just doesn't like Leela, that's all. How does the middle age lady lecturer solve the problem? Develop a suitable short story.

◆◆◆◆